Fleeting Cities

Fleeting Cities

Imperial Expositions in *Fin-de-Siècle* Europe

Alexander C. T. Geppert
Emmy Noether Research Group Director
Freie Universität Berlin

First published 2010
First published in paperback 2013 by
PALGRAVE MACMILLAN

Palgrave Macmillan in the UK is an imprint of Macmillan Publishers Limited, registered in England, company number 785998, of Houndmills, Basingstoke, Hampshire RG21 6XS.

Palgrave Macmillan in the US is a division of St Martin's Press LLC, 175 Fifth Avenue, New York, NY 10010.

Palgrave Macmillan is the global academic imprint of the above companies and has companies and representatives throughout the world.

Palgrave® and Macmillan® are registered trademarks in the United States, the United Kingdom, Europe and other countries.

ISBN 978–0–230–22164–2   hardback
ISBN 978–1–137–35832–5   paperback

This book is printed on paper suitable for recycling and made from fully managed and sustained forest sources. Logging, pulping and manufacturing processes are expected to conform to the environmental regulations of the country of origin.

A catalogue record for this book is available from the British Library.

A catalog record for this book is available from the Library of Congress.

Typeset by MPS Limited, Chennai, India.

Meinen Eltern

Time here becomes space.

Richard Wagner, *Parsifal*

Contents

Figures and Plates

Figures

Plates

Acknowledgments

Conceptualizing, researching and writing this book has taken more time and effort than I had ever dreamt. Although composed during numerous hours of 'Einsamkeit und Freiheit' (Helmut Schelsky) in varying places, no academic product is ever the sole achievement of its lonesome author. That such solitude and freedom, clearly indispensable as they are, never developed into isolation and despair is to be credited to numerous friends and colleagues who helped in ways big or small during the years of work. Without them, it would have been a truly dreary time.

This book is based on my PhD thesis entitled 'London vs. Paris: Imperial Exhibitions, Transitory Spaces, and Metropolitan Networks, 1880–1930', submitted to and defended in the Department of History and Civilization of the European University Institute (EUI) in Florence, Italy. First and foremost, I would like to express heartfelt gratitude to my trinity of dissertation advisors, John Brewer, Luisa Passerini and Bernd Weisbrod, as well as to Peter Becker and Jürgen Osterhammel, the two additional committee members. At the project's initial stages, when I was still in Göttingen, Bernd Weisbrod's generous help and critical encouragement were indispensable; fortunately, he has never ceased offering it ever since. John Brewer persuaded me to join the EUI, supervised my work especially intensely during my first two years there, and continued to do so after his return to the United States. Peter Becker and then Luisa Passerini stepped in, bid me welcome amongst 'their' students and made me their Research Associate in Florence and Essen, respectively. Finally, Jürgen Osterhammel maintained a continual interest in my work and readily agreed to serve as a fifth committee member. Having profited tremendously from their enduring patience, never-ending generosity and, above all, benevolent criticism, I am deeply obliged to this admirable quintet of world-class historians.

Florence – as Georg Simmel, the chief witness of this book, argued in a 1906 essay – constitutes a city in which mind and nature complement each other more effectively than in any other European conurbation, thus creating in visitors the impression of forming part of one coherent and grand work of art. This book, too, can be regarded as an immediate product of the institutional setting in which substantial parts of it were conceived, planned and produced: the European University Institute. This magic mountain and *locus amoenus* proved a congenial site, and afforded a permanent learning experience, as Olwen Hufton once put it, of a kind that I have never known anywhere else. Florence, this book and the grand institution where much of it was realized, share a second structural feature: they entail and provide an enormous amount of physical, psychic, social and cultural mobility. Thus, this book reflects the circumstances of its many different origins of production: Germany, Italy, the United States, Great Britain, France and Austria. That I was given the indispensable opportunity to study, work and research in numerous archives and libraries in more than half a dozen national settings – and to give papers and lectures in even more – was a direct, demanding, but enriching consequence of an attempt to not only conceptualize, but also to write a genuinely trans- and international, though distinctly European piece of historiography. The question of whether this approximates a miniature history of Europe, however partial, specific and incomplete, is one of the preoccupations of this book.

The technical possibility of so doing has been cause and effect alike of a type of academic nomadism that would have been impossible without the encouragement and constant support of numerous friends, family and colleagues in all these locations. They include, in chrono-chorological order, Judy Walkowitz in Baltimore; Sergio Amadei, Massimo Baioni, Martin Kohlrausch, Matthias Leonhard Maier, Serge Noiret and Anna Pellegrino in Florence; Gail Cameron in London; Tom Laqueur and Carla Hesse in Berkeley; Muriel Rouyer, Imke Nienaber and Sophie Maisonneuve in Paris; Raimund Magis and Alexander Mejstrik in Vienna; Jürgen Arimond, Jochen Hartz, Friedrich Jaeger, Jan Christoph Steines and Jörn Rüsen in Essen and the Ruhr; David Blackbourn, Jim Cronin, Charles Maier and Bruce Mazlish in Cambridge, Massachusetts; and, last but not least, Jürgen Ast, Boris Barth, Tobias Becker, Wolther von Kieseritzky, Valentina Leonhard, Claudia Schmölders, Nina Verheyen, Christiane Wirtz, Paul Nolte and his entire *Lehrstuhl* at Freie Universität in Berlin. Thanks are also due to Dorothee Dehnicke, Friederike Mehl, Tom Reichard and Sarah Molinoff, my superb research assistants in Berlin and Cambridge, respectively. Uffa Jensen, Till Kössler, Jörn Weinhold and Hanns Wershoven bore with this project from its very inception and yet remain my friends. At Harvard, I met picture-loving Anna Kathryn Kendrick; fortunately, she has stayed with me ever since.

Numerous archives and libraries were so kind as to supply documents, images and source material of often obscure provenance, all meticulously listed in the Appendix. One, however, deserves a special mention: The Special Collections Research Center at California State University, Fresno, where Tammy Lau, Jean Coffey and photographer Randy Vaughn-Dotta reign over the Donald G. Larson Collection on International Expositions and Fairs, a veritable goldmine of material and arguably the best collection in this specific field worldwide, a true haven for historical exhibitionists. I would recommend any devoted aficionado not to miss this wonderful research library, geographically remote as it may seem from a European perspective. Special credit goes to Randy for being the pictorial perfectionist that he is.

Writing in a foreign language is a tricky business and a risky enterprise. Not only does it take much longer but it also makes one's own rhetoric more stilted, less elegant and at times blunter than usual. Although as work obviously exclusively authored by myself, both the thesis and later this book were read, corrected, reread and then corrected again by various native speakers in order to compensate for most of my linguistic deficits as a non-native-speaker. Thanks are due to Nicki Hargreaves, Nicky Owtram and, most notably, Rita Hortmann. When I was attempting to transform the various fragments into a coherent whole, she proved a fantastic editor and indispensable critic, indeed a much more congenial one than I could have ever hoped to find. She, her daughter Barbara, and Susan

Emanuel also provided translations from German and French sources. At Harvard, Bronwyn Roantree helped me transform the thesis into a book proper, patiently reading revision after revision and commenting with her characteristic spark and wit.

The research undertaken for this book was made possible through various generous scholarships, grants and fellowships provided, at different stages, by the Studienstiftung des deutschen Volkes, the Deutscher Akademischer Austauschdienst, the EUI, the University of California at Berkeley, the Ecoles des Hautes Etudes en Sciences Sociales in Paris, the German Historical Institute in London, the Gerda Henkel Stiftung, the IFK Internationales Forschungszentrum Kulturwissenschaften in Vienna, the Kulturwissenschaftliches Institut (KWI) in Essen, the Alexander von Humboldt-Stiftung, and the Minda de Gunzburg Center for European Studies at Harvard University. The dissertation on which this book is based was awarded the Austrian Theodor-Körner-Preis zur Förderung von Kunst und Wissenschaft. At Palgrave, Michael Strang and Ruth Ireland guided me with great elegance, patience and much appreciated professionalism through a complex publication process that proved very different from anything I knew from a German context. During the final production stages, Penny Simmons was as congenial and meticulous as any queenly copy-editor should be.

Last but not least, it is my parents, Adelheid and Christian Geppert, to whom I dedicate this book. I owe so much more to them than they can possibly know.

The usual disclaimers apply.

Abbreviations

AA	Abendausgabe
ANOM	Archives nationales d'outre-mer, Aix-en-Provence
AUMA	Ausstellungs- und Messeausschuss der Deutschen Wirtschaft
BA	Brent Archive, London
BArch	Bundesarchiv Berlin
BDI	Bundesverband der Deutschen Industrie, Berlin
BEE	British Empire Exhibition
BGA	Berliner Gewerbeausstellung
BHVP	Bibliothèque historique de la Ville de Paris, Paris
BIE	Bureau International des Expositions, Paris
BL	British Library, London
BPL	Boston Public Library
BrPL	Bromley Public Libraries, London
CARAN	Centre d'accueil et de recherche des Archives Nationales, Paris
CFEE	Comité français des expositions à l'étranger
CSU	California State University, Fresno
CUL	Cambridge University Library
ECI	Exposition Coloniale Internationale
FBE	Franco-British Exhibition
GL	Guildhall Library, London
GMCH	Grange Museum of Community History, London
GStA PK	Geheimes Staatsarchiv Preußischer Kulturbesitz, Berlin
HCL	Widener Library, Harvard College Library, Cambridge, MA
HFALHC	Hammersmith and Fulham Archives and Local History Centre, London
IKC	Imre Kiralfy Collection, Museum of London
KB-SMB	Kunstbibliothek Berlin – Staatliche Museen zu Berlin
LAB	Landesarchiv Berlin
LCC	London County Council
LMA	London Metropolitan Archives
LtE	Letter to the Editor

LTM	London Transport Museum
MA	Morgenausgabe
ML	Museum of London
n.d.	No date
N.F.	Neue Folge
n.p.	No publisher/no pagination
N.S.	New series
NAL	National Art Library, London
NARA	United States National Archives and Records Administration, College Park, MD
OED	*Oxford English Dictionary*
PCF	Parti Communiste Français
RCSAC	Royal Commonwealth Society Archives and Collections, Cambridge
RIBA	Royal Institute of British Architects, London
SBB-PK	Staatsbibliothek zu Berlin – Preußischer Kulturbesitz
TNA	The National Archives, Kew, London
TUB	Technische Universität Berlin
USL	University of Sussex Library, Special Collections, Brighton
V&A/AAD	Victoria and Albert Museum, Archive of Art and Design, London

1
Introduction: How to Read an Exposition

[handwritten margin note: Fin-de-siècle but covering a much larger period]

EXPOSITION: *Sujet de délire du XIXe siècle.*
(Gustave Flaubert)[1]

On 25 July 1896, the Viennese weekly *Die Zeit* published an elegant and remarkably brief review of the Berliner Gewerbeausstellung, the grand trade show that had opened in the south-east of the German capital a few weeks earlier. Little known today and only one and a half single-spaced newspaper columns in length, this short essay arguably proved one of the most perspicacious and powerful anatomies ever published of the most spectacular mass medium of the urban imagination in *fin-de-siècle* Europe: the imperial exposition. This astute observer understood that the national trade exhibition, temporarily staged in Berlin's Treptower Park on the banks of the River Spree, had exceeded its relatively limited scope and, as such, could only be comprehended in the context of much larger international expositions previously held elsewhere, particularly France. Indeed, the author argued that these 'momentary centers of world civilization', which assembled 'the products of the entire world in a confined space as if in a single picture', were nothing less than a defining feature of modernity. In hosting this trade exhibition, the German capital had managed to transform itself into a 'single city to which the whole world sends its products and where all the important styles of the present cultural world are put on display'. Berlin had thus transcended the status of a mere *Großstadt* or ordinary *Hauptstadt* and, 'despite everything', had at last been elevated to a genuine *Weltstadt*, a world city.[2]

This brief essay stood in marked contrast to the usual array of celebratory and effusive accounts that normally appeared at the opening of similar expositions in London, Paris or other European cities. Its author had clearly paid an extensive visit to the site and carefully studied its numerous attractions *in situ*, yet did not indulge in the florid descriptions which had become almost *de rigueur*. Unlike other contemporaneous observers, who tended to be entranced by the heterogeneity of the spectacle temporarily staged, this critic made his and other visitors' 'paralysis of the senses' (*Paralyse des Wahrnehmungsvermögens*) the cornerstone of his analysis, arguing that the exposition was unified by a prevailing sense of amusement. He realized that no other medium of modern life succeeded so

1

Simmel

Exp. of mass culture & reflection of capitalism(?)

spectacularly in presenting a no longer given vision of unity: 'Nowhere else [than in the great exhibition] is such a richness of different impressions brought together so that overall there seems to be outward unity, whereas underneath a vigorous interaction produces mutual contrasts, intensification and lack of relatedness.' The author demonstrated that the Berlin trade exhibition could be read as a site for an investigation into the visualized consumer culture and condensed urban spaces that he considered at once condition and consequence of current globalizing processes as well as pivotal to the very modernity that global capitalism depended upon for its universalizing effects. 'Perhaps', he wrote, 'it has never been so apparent before how much the form of modern culture has permitted a concentration in one place, not in the mere collection of exhibits as in a world fair, but how through its own production a city can represent itself as a copy and a sample of the manufacturing forces of world culture.'

The author of this remarkable account was none other than →Georg Simmel, the German sociologist and cultural philosopher, at this time *Privatdozent* at Friedrich-Wilhelms-Universität in Berlin. While this unassuming newspaper article might prima facie resemble his other much-praised analytical deciphering of cultural artifacts and social minutiae running the gamut from bridges, ruins, coins to plagiarism and clocks, Simmel here first presented some of the key ideas on commodity culture and urbanism that were later developed in his *Philosophy of Money* and, above all, in his seminal 1903 treatise on the 'metropolis and mental life'. The central topos in this essay, the dweller's constant 'stimulation of the nerves' in the big city, is a direct evocation of the 'paralysis of the senses' and the 'veritable hypnosis' that Georg Simmel experienced when strolling through Treptower Park as an exposition critic in the summer of 1896.[3]

Simmel interpreted the Berliner Gewerbeausstellung as an emblem of modernity and a testing ground for Berlin's new role as an internationally established and globally recognized world city, on par with world-class cities such as London and Paris, already centers of vast colonial Empires when Berlin was still merely the residence of Prussian monarchs. Since the mid-nineteenth century, the very act of mounting large-scale exhibitions had been considered a de facto manifestation of the modern. 'The utility of exhibitions has been so universally recognised that they have become an institution in every country that pretends to a fair share of civilisation', a contemporary observer noted in 1883.[4] Thus, the Gewerbeausstellung confirmed Berlin's new status as a world city. Yet, as a by then widespread medium, the exhibition's significance far exceeded any local context. Not only was the exposition modern, but modernity itself was on display: the continuous attempts to create an illusionary unity, a fictitious, transitory and largely self-contained realm in which the audience could immerse itself on each such occasion, was reflexively considered 'modern'.

In its attempt to assemble and concentrate 'the world' in one place, the Berlin trade exhibition served as a laboratory for scrutinizing the fundamental characteristics and contradictions inherent in modern culture. Just as Simmel had, in another famous dictum, described the boundary not as a 'spatial entity with sociological consequences, but a sociological entity that is formed spatially', the physical layout and spatial boundaries of the exposition were crucial to its functioning as they provided the only means to limit – and thus to establish uniformity – from a heterogeneous assembly of exhibits.[5] This understanding of expositions as not only catalysts and agents, but also as indicators of modernity, was not ahistorical. Quite to the contrary: investigating how a particular style for such exhibitions had developed over time was, as Simmel deduced, 'of great cultural historical interest'. Thus, Georg Simmel figures not only as the conceptual inspiration, but also as the chief witness to the present study.[6]

Spaces of modernity

In this book, five imperial expositions – the Berliner Gewerbeausstellung of 1896, the Exposition Universelle of 1900, the Franco-British Exhibition of 1908, the British Empire Exhibition of 1924–25 and the Exposition Coloniale Internationale of 1931 – held in Berlin, Paris and London over the course of 35 years and with a world war in between, serve as interconnected exemplars of urban modernity. Following Charles Baudelaire's classic definition, the latter is understood as a set of representational practices that embraces 'the ephemeral, the fugitive, the contingent' and characterizes the present in general, and the world of the *fin-de-siècle* metropolis in particular.[7] At the same time, expositions are treated not as symptoms or expressions of some other concrete historical phenomenon, but rather as a particular medium with its own special problems and internal dynamics. *meta -* Conceptualizing exhibitions as 'meta-media', as specific means of communication *media* that encompass and incorporate other communicative technologies, particular attention is paid to questions of medialization, visualization and virtualization. Taken as dense textures stretched over time, expositions require both a close hermeneutical reading and also a broad spatial analysis. Only then is it possible to scrutinize their internal functioning while simultaneously analyzing interactions with the surrounding cityscape and their effects on the urban fabric.

Imperial expositions held in *fin-de-siècle* London, Paris and Berlin were knots in what together constituted a worldwide web; contemporary observers already termed them 'nodes in the course of history' (*Knotenpunkte des Geschichtslaufes*).[8] A 'Crystal Palace' could be found not only in London but also in New York, Munich and Paris; a so-called White City not only in Chicago but also in London; the notorious 'Rue du Caire' not only several times in Paris, but also in Chicago, London, St Louis and Berlin. This book offers several distinct perspectives within which to locate, read and explain five carefully selected nodes in both space and time, woven into a delicate but resilient web of national and international networks. Through a detailed analysis of each of the five cases, the book examines their specific aims and aspirations, their changing form and execution, and the public debates they engendered. Who was responsible for collecting items, assembling displays and orchestrating vistas? How were exhibits perceived and consumed by various audiences, communities and individuals on the local, national and global levels? What legacies did these expositions bequeath? And how did they position themselves vis-à-vis the medium's own tradition and the surrounding metropolis?

Each chapter emphasizes three underlying issues: space, time and the *personae*. The first of these three categories, space, fulfills a double function. Borrowing and operationalizing the terms 'spaces of representation' and 'representation of space' from Henri Lefebvre allows access to the expositions' external spatial repercussion and their modes of internal operation. Understanding space as a built, material environment, the former notion establishes references to a more conventional metropolitan history. Both the layout and the location of the exhibition sites within the respective metropolis must be described. The book also analyzes the architecture and overall consequences for the surrounding environment and subsequent local development. In this respect, the problematic of how the city's expansion correlated to the expanding exhibitions and their resulting move to the outskirts of the city is another central issue of concern – particularly if one takes seriously the plea, justly asserted by historical geographers in recent years, that history should be written 'as a series of spaces, rather than a single, seamless narrative', a move that developed into the now much-discussed and widely accepted 'spatial turn' within historiography and cultural studies.[9]

'Representation of space', on the other hand, concerns the various forms of space as embodied in the exhibitions themselves and their respective taxonomies. As complex constructs, the majority of expositions seem to have experimented with all conceivable possible forms of space. Frequently, for instance, the host city was represented in a special metropolitan section that formed part of the 'exhibition city' within the 'real' exhibiting city, with the same principle applying to the representation of different colonies, countries or nations. Strategies of representation and layers of meaning overlapped with one another and formed spaces of modernity that, though radically condensed, were never 'annihilated'. Articulating how these compressed spaces were fabricated and what kind of itineraries they stipulated for visitors-cum-consumers yields important insights into the ways in which modernity was created and displayed, consumed and disputed at these protean sites within the European metropolis around 1900.

By the late nineteenth century, the central conundrum of the so-called exhibitionary complex was no longer why international expositions of ever greater scope were repeatedly held in almost all European metropolises, but rather what made them so similar. Why were these ephemeral urban spaces furnished with analogues, intertextual *accessoires*? A glacial pace of change and striking resemblances between different exhibitionary sites seem the most marked feature of the entire medium, which was, from the beginning, dominated by far-reaching internal references and formative transnational and inter-urban connections. As a consequence, the – historical – notion of an 'exhibitionary system' (*Weltausstellungssystem*) or the – contemporaneous – concept of an 'exhibitionary complex' should be replaced with that of 'exhibitionary networks' in order to allow for adequate historicization. Though the exhibitionary complex was undeniably complex, it is more accurately described as an overlapping series of networks that evolved over time.[10] Uncovering why expositions were sustained even after their capacity to express the latest version of 'the modern' had waned requires an analysis of that peculiarly Victorian emotion: 'exhibition fatigue'.

International expositions of the nineteenth and twentieth centuries were characterized by their fleeting nature. The vast majority of all material structures, including buildings and pavilions, were usually planned with a view to immediate demolition after the event's closure and were, in Simmel's words, 'intended for temporary purposes only'.[11] This temporality did not hinder them, however, either individually or collectively, from acquiring meaning, founding traditions and creating legacies in architecture, urban development and media history that far outlived the expositions themselves. Composed of similar and/or closely related elements arranged in analogous ways, exhibitions can be considered 'isomorphous'. Such a family resemblance can only be excavated by careful chrono-chorological contextualization. To this end, expositions must be conceptualized as transitory yet recurrent meta-media that, despite their transitional character, established both internal and external traditions, not only with regard to the specific composition of the medium itself, but also to the numerous urban legacies and metropolitan residuals they bequeathed. Such a development is not metaphysical in its origins, but rather is the result of multifarious inter-urban competition and the widespread, transnational entanglements among the main protagonists in this extensively internationalized field.

For this reason, the book introduces individual agency into the historiography by describing the expositions not merely as hyper-representations of overarching cultural constellations, but also as the result of the personal strategies of planning, building and financing by the particular individuals responsible for their organization.[12] Both the medium's longevity and expositions' increasing resemblance to one another must be explained by the impact of a well-organized and very mobile class of cultural bureaucrats, exhibition experts, and entertainment entrepreneurs. Their intermingling led to transnational adjustments in consecutive expositions. Once successfully introduced, new elements and novel features were quickly transferred across borders and integrated into later exhibitions, largely regardless of their respective national contexts. Thus, ephemeral exposition spaces were usually furnished with analogues – ethnographic ensembles, so-called native villages, or exclusively domestic assemblages like *Old London, Vieux Paris* and *Alt-Berlin*, for example – precisely because originators, commissioners and organizers copied from each other, transferring not only specific features, but at times even entire sections, from one national and socio-cultural context to another.

Because of general similarities in the organization processes, five groups of actors can generally be distinguished for each exposition. First and foremost are the exhibition's initiators, sometimes acting as private individuals, though more often as representatives of groups, associations or even by governmental fiat. Second, the official organizers, commissioners and representatives of the participating nations, regions, cities and colonies, charged with the exhibition's actual realization *in situ*. While 'curator' commonly refers to a person responsible for the conceptual work and the subsequent management of ongoing expositions, 'exhibitors' are the individuals, institutions and organizations providing the actual exhibits. Third, there are the domestic and foreign active participants, including numerous employees working at the site and so-called natives, human beings of 'exotic' origins put on display. Fourth are the reviewers, critics, mediators and professional observers who reported on the respective mega-event in different forms and formats, to various kinds of audiences and publics. And, fifth, the local, regional, national and international audiences and visitors themselves, composed of both actual fair-goers and sightseers, and including those who participated in the events via the mass media. 'The public – the exhibiting and the visiting public – are the real actors in the Exhibitions', British commissioner John Forbes Watson (1827–1892) stated as early as 1872: 'The whole thing is done by and for them.'[13] These categories are neither mutually exclusive nor all-inclusive. While, given the available sources, not all the groups of actors can be treated systematically at all times, such a typology proves useful in analyzing the different ways in and various levels on which meanings were ascribed, negotiated and contested. What makes these groups of men – there are, unsurprisingly, almost no women to be found in groups I (initiators), II (organizers, curators, exhibitors) and IV (reviewers and critics) – appear particularly heterogeneous is that they all assumed various and occasionally overlapping functions at different stages of the organization processes.

Based on the respective definitions in the *Oxford English Dictionary*, throughout this book the terms 'exhibition' and 'exposition' are used interchangeably to refer to a coherent complement of goods that was, for a limited time, publicly displayed at a spatially confined location in a big city, usually the capital. An 'exhibit' is understood as one object or a set of objects composing such an exhibition. While the British 'exhibition' and the French 'exposition' are used interchangeably, 'world's fair' always refers to an exposition held in the United States. Also used is the German *Weltausstellung*, translated as 'world exhibition' or 'world exposition', as this best conveys the notion of a world on display for the world.[14]

Thus, the present book constitutes a transnational and transdisciplinary investigation into how urban modernity was displayed, formed and disputed at and through one of the most momentous and powerful media in *fin-de-siècle* Europe. These events exposed divergent notions of modernity, from the machinery and huge blocks of cast steel characteristic of the mid-century, to the electricity and colored illuminations introduced in 1900, to the grand sports arenas made of reinforced concrete prominent in the 1920s. In each of the five closely 'read' cases, numerous debates about the medium's modernity in different national contexts are reconstructed in order to chart changing sites of representation and forms of performance, as well as to analyze the competitive, mutually conditioned components of transnational controversies.

1851 ff.

'As a cultural phenomenon', sociologist and economist →Werner Sombart agreed with Simmel in 1908, 'the exhibition is exceptionally interesting, for it appears in entirely different meanings, can be judged by very different criteria and classified in quite different contexts.'[15] Taken as a means of studying the way societies represent themselves, the numerous urban, regional, national and international expositions held in nineteenth- and twentieth-century Europe as well as the United States and Australia have attracted considerable scholarly interest for more than a century. With their rotating venues, great number of participating nations, and role in developing both a standardized exhibition language and a community of exhibition professionals, as well as their massive international audience, exhibitions have often been considered among the most characteristic inventions of the nineteenth century and one of its few genuinely international cultural institutions.

After the immense and largely unexpected success of the epoch-making Great Exhibition of the Works of Industry of All Nations held in London in 1851 – described by Prussian ambassador Christian Karl Josias Freiherr von Bunsen (1791– 1860) as 'the most poetic and world-historic event of the time' – international expositions quickly became a recurrent feature of public life in western Europe and the United States. 'Exhibitions have come to be a regular part of the bill of fare annually served up for the enjoyment of society during the London season', a British guidebook commented some 37 years later, 'and when that fashionable period is at an end, they remain open for the pleasure of that far larger and more important section of humanity – the general public.'[16] In its after-effects, the signifi- cance of the Great Exhibition as the first decidedly international exposition with its 19,000 exhibits on display and a prevailing 'spirit of encyclopaedism' cannot be overstated. It defined mid-century Britain. Establishing an unsurpassed founding myth and profoundly shaping the new medium, the syntax inaugurated in the Great Exhibition remained the standard for decades to come.[17]

In France, where the first international exposition was organized only four years later, in 1855, the degree of institutionalization was especially high. Unlike those in Great Britain or the United States, French expositions were inevita- bly official, state-sanctioned affairs. Over the course of the second half of the nineteenth and the beginning of the twentieth century, numerous grand-scale exhibitions were held not only in London and Paris, but also in Vienna, Turin, Antwerp, Barcelona, Berlin, Stockholm, Brussels, Milan and Liège. Outside Europe, cities such as New York, Philadelphia, Chicago, St Louis, San Francisco, Sydney and Melbourne hosted well-regarded international expositions, most of them several times.[18] All were complex and well organized, composed of numerous sections and subsections devoted to diverse themes including indus- trial, artistic, geographical, ethnographic and historical topoi. Despite differ- ences between individual 'cases' with regards to their respective use of forms and representation, these expositions aimed at replicating a European version of 'the world' in the metropolis' center. While the objects displayed were ordered in ever-varying and increasingly complex systems of classification, each was allocated a specific spot in an ideally ordered world.[19]

Available numeric data support Simmel's argument of the expositions' absolute socio-cultural centrality to the late nineteenth and early twentieth centuries. Both their frequency and popularity was immense: 210 international large-scale exhibi- tions were held worldwide between 1851 and 2010, more than half of them (112) in Europe (Figure 1.1). Three quarters (161) of these 210 expositions took place between the 1880s and the Second World War, with a similar majority held in Europe (86). There was a considerable increase in frequency at the beginning of the

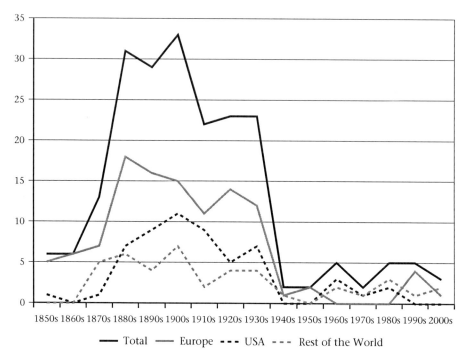

Figure 1.1   Number of international expositions held in Europe, the USA and the rest of the world per decade between 1851 and 2010[20]

1880s: no fewer than 18 expositions were organized in various parts of the Western world and Australia between 1880 and 1885.[21]

The emerging picture is further complicated if the number of expositions is correlated with their respective attendance figures, though the latter should generally be treated with considerable caution since the statistics were neither always reliable nor was the data collected based on common criteria. According to conservative estimates, European expositions attracted approximately 415 million visitors between 1851 and 1958, three-quarters of whom (320 million) attended expositions held between 1885 and the Second World War (Figure 1.2). Almost 110 million consumers saw the five Parisian Expositions Universelles held in the French capital over the course of the second half of the nineteenth century at regular 11-year intervals, the so-called *règle des onze années*.[22] The last in this line of spectacular mega-events, officially named the 'Exposition Universelle Internationale de 1900 à Paris', attracted over 50 million sightseers alone – a number greater than the population of France at the time and roughly equal to the population of the German *Kaiserreich*. It was 'by far the vastest [...] gathering of men and of things, of all kindreds, kingdoms, nations and languages in the entire course of history', a contemporaneous critic observed.[23] Indeed, the 1900 exposition set a record that would only be broken in Montreal 67 years later. Before the advent of television, no other mass media reached so many individuals. Figure 1.2 reveals three other noteworthy trends: consistently

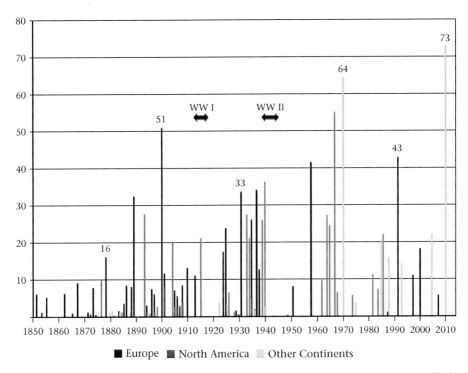

Figure 1.2   Attendance in millions at international expositions held between 1851 and 2010

high attendance despite far fewer expositions after the Second World War; the rapid rise in significance of American world's fairs over the course of the twentieth century; and the success of non-Western expositions in the last 40 years, with the Japanese Expo '70 in Osaka being the second best attended exhibition ever. With altogether 73 million visitors, Expo 2010 in Shanghai set a new world record.

The rise of exposition studies

Hailed by contemporaries as the 'age of expositions', the late nineteenth and early twentieth centuries inspired so-called 'exposition hysteria', 'mania' or 'circus', which is reflected in the flood of scholarly attention they continue to inspire over a century later. Academic interest is not, however, a recent phenomenon, but rather dates to the turn of the century when the first historical overviews and specialized monographs on single aspects of the history of large-scale expositions began to appear. Among them, →Adolphe Démy's 1100-page 'Essai historique sur les Expositions universelles de Paris' published in 1907 can, despite a number of inaccuracies and careless mistakes *en détail*, still be considered one of the most comprehensive historical accounts available, especially on the medium in France.[24] Since then, international exhibitions and world's fairs have attracted considerable scholarly attention precisely because in them societies claim to represent and thematize themselves in a highly condensed and aesthetically fascinating manner.

Academic interest increased steadily over the course of the twentieth century, rising most notably in the mid to late 1980s. American historian and aspiring doyen of international exposition studies Robert W. Rydell's first book, *All the World's a Fair*, was published in 1984, art historian Paul Greenhalgh's broad synopsis *Ephemeral Vistas* followed four years later and, in 1989, political theorist Timothy Mitchell's groundbreaking article 'The World as Exhibition' appeared. At the same time, French historian Madeleine Rebérioux could still diagnose a 'relative rarity of contemporary books devoted to universal expositions, particularly to those that took place in Paris between 1855 and 1900', while museum curator Robert Brain expressed his annoyance that, 'until quite recently, exhibitions have remained largely neglected by historians.'[25] A year earlier, in 1988, sociologist and cultural analyst Tony Bennett had brought a Foucauldian perspective to bear in coining the expression 'exhibitionary complex', a term that proved as influential as it was misleading since it assumed a type of consolidation that was, historically, not given but rather evolved over time.[26] Summarizing extant scholarship in the early 1990s, Rydell noted that 'comparative studies of expositions have been few. Systematic inquiries into colonial expositions can be counted on one hand. Though important work has been published about international exhibitions, much of the literature is tentative, eclectic, and far from complete.' He concluded:

> Some of the most influential fairs – including most of the Paris expositions – have not received the kind of attention to archaeological detail that they deserve. Above all, there is an acute need and golden opportunity for comparative work on exhibitions. Even if such comparative studies were limited to the great exhibitions, it would advance our understanding of the way human beings in the modern world came to see – or were encouraged to see – themselves and others.[27]

In the interim, the situation has dramatically improved, both quantitatively and qualitatively. Figure 1.3 charts the number of scholarly publications on national

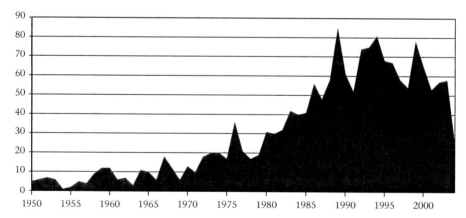

Figure 1.3 Number of scholarly publications on national and international expositions printed between 1950 and 2004

Must of the research is scholarly new

and international expositions annually printed between 1950 and 2004. The overall trend is immediately apparent: though perhaps not quite an explosion, the field has grown considerably in the last two decades. While in the 1970s an average of 17 titles was published per year, numbers climbed to 47 over the course of the 1980s, with a preliminary climax in 1989 with 85 publications. Two further peaks occurred in 1994 and 1999, with 81 and 78 publications, respectively. Ever since, an average of 63 scholarly publications tackling the 'exhibition complex' have been issued each year. As a consequence, 40 percent of the entire body of literature currently in existence is less than ten years old, and more than 60 percent is under 15 years old. Although there is still neither an academic journal nor a professionally monitored electronic discussion network exclusively dedicated to the historical analysis of expositions worldwide, it is clear that a new field of 'exposition studies' was created, with substantial contributions stemming from a wide variety of disciplines including history, art history, history of architecture and design, museology, urban anthropology, geography, sociology, political science, economics and others.[28]

Why has research in this area flourished in the last two decades? The ongoing popularity of exhibitions as an object of study must be attributed to the polysemantic and protean character of the subject matter itself. Scholars approaching the material from different directions collectively realized the analytical potential of expositions. An insight initially formulated by Georg Simmel gradually prevailed: exhibitions, with their complex interplay between nationalism and internationalism in a concrete urban locality, constituted direct precursors of, and early testing grounds for, a rapidly globalizing society as well as for the creation of spectacular visual-virtual ersatz realities – two traits frequently regarded as characterizing the present age. From a historiographical perspective, the study of exhibitions provides an almost ideal occasion to connect a historiography of structures with one of events. Historians eager to translate the various theoretical 'turns' into scholarly practice that followed the groundbreaking 'linguistic turn', especially the 'pictorial'/'iconic' and the 'spatial turn', have found appealing material here. As a direct consequence of these three forces at play – political, cultural and historiographical – national and international expositions are now widely regarded as a central feature of Western cultural history whose popular impact was anything but ephemeral.[29]

signs of the present age

ripe ground for cultural history

Such intense research interest from various disciplines has led to an ever-increasing number of studies, several of which have proved invaluable.[30] It is unsurprising that the three arguably most significant international exhibitions of the nineteenth century – the previously mentioned Great Exhibition of 1851, the Parisian Exposition Universelle of 1889, and the Chicago World's Columbian Exposition of 1893 – have attracted the greatest scholarly attention.[31] Imperial exhibitions in particular have been used as socio-cultural gauges to measure attitudes toward empire and imperialism, their meaning, role and perception in the motherland throughout the period. They provide, as historian John M. MacKenzie has argued, 'the best insights into national obsessions, character, and morale'.[32] At times imperial exhibitions have been treated as static propaganda exercises, selling colonial exoticism to domestic audiences in an effort to persuade them of the political necessity of continued imperial expansion, while, in turn, allegedly offering far-reaching possibilities for developing so-called national identities that were in sharp distinction to an exoticized and eroticized colonial 'other'.

Frequently, however, their synchronic embedding in different temporal and spatial contexts remains unsatisfactory. Few studies have focused on the ways in which modes of self-representation functioned, internal dynamics operated, and media-related rules were followed. Rather, exhibitions are considered historical gadgets, fleeting magnifying glasses, under which it is possible to gain immediate insights into societies as they represent and regard themselves. Expositions are taken at their word: detached from their immediate historical surrounding and urban environment, they are too often superficially read according to the wishes of their originators and 'authors'. Such approaches do not allow a proper analysis of the manifestations of progress and modernity materialized in the exhibitions. 'We have moved from issues of consensus to those of contest', historian Peter H. Hoffenberg aptly summarized the state of the art in international exposition scholarship a few years ago: 'Questions of hybridity, audience participation, and shifting identities inform current exhibition studies.'[33] Thus, a small but growing number of works argue for a greater distance between the medium of exposition and its self-implemented rhetoric. These new studies suggest that scholarly attention first be turned to medial conditions and contexts, to the rules and principles of staging, displaying and representing as well as forms of receiving, consuming and appropriating, before analyzing a society's self-thematization via the exposition medium. The operative metaphor is not that of a magnifying glass but that of a prism.[34]

Moreover, many existing studies suffer from an overly narrow approach to the traditions established by the exposition medium itself. Particularly if only a single exposition is analyzed, the central significance of transnational and transatlantic entanglements and far-reaching inter-urban competition is necessarily disregarded. Certain qualities and characteristics are attributed to one particular exhibition when they are, effectively, less a consequence of the local text than a part of the larger rules and grammar governing the whole medium. Though largely unacknowledged, references between different nationally organized exhibitionary networks proved determinative both in terms of internal organization (design, layout and size of location, for instance) and external organization (sequence, timing, participation). That this is less true with regard to reception and consumption is a further argument of the present study, already *in nuce* in Simmel.

In order, first, to avoid such a diachronic deficiency, second, to analyze the emergent language that these expositions shared, and, third, to read the subject matter back into the transnational context from which it stems, a concentration on one or two cases within the boundaries of a particular nation-state cannot do justice to the phenomenon. Only by reading a carefully selected sample of different types of expositions as embodiments of a much larger medium is it possible to comprehend their public impact and popular meaning. In the end, far-reaching international similarities and increasing codification must be explained by the widespread networks and personal connections between the internationalized and exceedingly mobile actors in the field. The present study endeavors to analyze these interrelations as not only representational and semiotic, but also personal and professional.

Modus procedendi

By the late nineteenth century, exhibitions were a well-established feature of public life in the Western world. By 1931, they had lost much of their original luster and were no longer considered the *dernier cri* in displaying urban modernity in Europe, though they continued to be held, largely thanks to a variety of vested interests and institutions who had a stake in their continuing, even in the face of criticism and hostility. This study, based on extensive archival research, offers a rethinking of international expositions in their heyday, analyzing a heterogeneous sample of five rather 'late' exhibitions of various type, scope and character, including a trade fair, a bi-national exposition, two colonial exhibitions and one genuine Exposition Universelle, that took place in three different European metropolises in order to demonstrate their deep interrelatedness. To decipher their protean character in detail, these five cases are carefully placed in their respective contexts, both geographically and chronologically. Parallel to such a diachronic and synchronic embedding, each exhibition undergoes both a horizontal and vertical analysis of its reception, based on autobiographical accounts including personal correspondence, postcards, letters to the editor, as well as a number of oral history interviews.[35] However, as anthropologist Penelope Harvey has convincingly argued, insisting on too clear a distinction between a representational and a practice-oriented approach is problematic, as such artificial dichotomies are almost always disfiguring. Knowledge and meaning are negotiated and generated in the space between representation and consumption.[36]

At the same time, the book is comparative, arguing that expositions can only be properly analyzed in relation to one another. Their structural similarity is emphasized: In all these cases, the 'arts of display' functioned according to comparable, if not analogous, sets of discursive rules and equivalent principles of visual-spatial composition, despite profound national, social and cultural differences.[37] Though perhaps less perceptible to contemporaneous participants and observers, such 'quotations' ran through the entire medium. Hence, the book gives due weight to the medium's transnational and transcultural character, either implicitly, by studying the historical displaying and staging of cultural differences, or explicitly, by analyzing particular references, interrelations and transfers. Thus, the book combines empirical research with an underlying interest in larger theoretical issues in order to explore the possibilities of a relational historiography that is simultaneously open to multiple perspectives and considers mutual influences, perceptual interdependencies and transnational interrelations in a new form of network analysis.

Arguably the biggest drawback of endeavoring to treat all expositions in the sample with the same empirical rigor while also reading them as exemplars is the need to be strictly selective in choosing cases. In theory, numerous other European expositions could have been added: in Great Britain, the Franco-British Exhibition and the British Empire Exhibition receive full treatment, while the earlier Crystal Palace exhibitions such as the Festival of Empire, held in Sydenham in 1911, is only mentioned in passing. The study ends with the most momentous Parisian colonial exhibition, the Exposition Coloniale of 1931, but neither the earlier Marseilles expositions of 1906 and 1922 nor the Parisian Exposition Internationale des Arts Décoratifs of 1925 or the 1937 Exposition Internationale des Arts et Techniques dans la Vie Moderne, also held in the Champ de Mars and best remembered for its juxtaposition of the giant Nazi and Soviet pavilions on the banks of the Seine, receive in-depth attention. Moreover, with international exhibitions held in 1897, 1910 and 1935, a third European capital, Brussels, was transformed at the beginning of the twentieth century into an important and dramatically under-researched exhibition hub, with a Paris–Brussels axis largely responsible for popularizing Art Nouveau on the continent.[38] But even if these nine momentous expositions had been included, other, hardly less important European exhibitions held, for instance, in Barcelona in 1888 (Exposición Universal) and in 1929–30 (Exposición Internacional), in Milan in 1906 (Esposizione Internazionale del Sempione) or five years later in Turin (Esposizione Internazionale delle Industrie e del Lavoro) would still have been left out, not to mention the numerous American world's fairs. This is a simple consequence of the exhibitionary complex being such a vast network spread over time and space.[39] Such selective decisions are always easily impugnable yet indispensable. Therefore, the choice was made to cast a wide but still manageable net and gather a representative European sample. As the host capital of the first international exhibition, London could not be done without, and it was also necessary to include Paris, the oft-quoted 'Queen City of Expositions'. Third, and perhaps somewhat unexpectedly, the Gewerbeausstellung of 1896 was chosen as a counter-case: Berlin's reluctant and eventually frustrated aspirations for status as both a world city and a capital city where large-scale exhibitions would be held were never realized. Indeed, the medium gained significantly less of a foothold in Berlin than elsewhere, such that the Gewerbeausstellung stands as a remarkable and counter-intuitive, albeit under-researched, case.

There is a further consequence of comprehending these five examples in three European metropolises as specific nodes within a worldwide web. Despite the primary expectation that expositions operated within a metropolitan framework and were thus expected to stimulate national unity and local self-confidence, they were also widely regarded as important arenas for international competition and alignment. While these repercussions are hardly disputable, it has nonetheless caused a historiographical shift, with the notion of 'identity' having become one of the cornerstones of analysis within the ever-expanding literature. Expositions, or so the standard argument goes, were central instruments in the making of 'national identities', not the least because they commonly featured displays of an exoticized colonial 'other'. Such an 'identity through non-identity' (that is 'otherness') argument, or juxtaposing 'l'autre et nous' might be politically correct, yet it often proves simplistic and an impediment to challenging and opening the exposition medium's self-implemented rhetoric. Insisting on a simple metropole/colony opposition may have been heuristically necessary in the early stages of historicizing exposition practices, but it is now insufficient.[40] From the outset the evolving exhibitionary networks were characterized by multipolarities including overlapping dimensions of intra-metropolitan, trans-European and even global competition.

Moreover, 'identity' is a conceptually vague, highly charged and worn buzzword that is unsuitable for stringent historiographical analysis, and does not possess sufficient heuristic potential for describing and analyzing the complex repercussions and processes of consumption and appropriation. It is the very existence of the exhibition medium's worldwide web that renders all arguments about national characteristics and the forming of collective 'identities' unsatisfactory, as it calls for a new form of relational network analysis. By responding and reacting to each other through various types of networks – personal, professional, institutional – these representational spaces developed a specific use of forms, thus giving further shape to the medium and codifying a standard repertoire, while continuing to differentiate the specific language of the exhibition. Although a central interpretative element in many other studies, 'identity' is, therefore, a notion that is peripheral to this book.[41]

Finally, the *modus procedendi* within each of the following five chapters is largely identical and is inspired by the conceptual triad of 'presentation', 'representation' and 'perception' advanced by French cultural historian Roger Chartier. In an attempt to render the superordinate of these terms, 'representation', the cornerstone of conceptualizing cultural history, Chartier has described three modes of relations toward the social world which the notion helps elucidate: first, the construction processes of distinct, possibly competing, realities by different individuals, social groups and powers through classification and delineation; second, their respective organizational practices that aim at exhibiting a specific way of being in the world and through which groups, communities and powers propose an image of themselves, including the sharing of signs and symbols; and third, complex processes of perception and reception, consumption and appropriation which lead to quite different results in the making of meaning. Understood along these lines, the concept of representation, Chartier has argued, 'leads to thinking of the social world and the exercise of power according to a relational model'.[42]

In the following, these three facets of the superordinate notion – presentation, representation and perception – serve as underlying guiding principles but also return more concretely as subsections on the construction/politics, the site/sights, and the reading/meaning of each individual exposition visited and read in each of the subsequent chapters. Such a procedure can be understood as a specifically historiographical variant of field reconnaissance, an operation developed by urban ethnographers and town planners such as Kevin Lynch in the 1960s to cover and map urban spaces. By querying ceremony, ritual and representation – and, likewise, participation, reaction and reception – it is, finally, the interplay of imperial, spatial and spectacular elements within European *fin-de-siècle* urban modernity that this book examines. Over the course of five virtual visits to five different expositions, it fashions an analysis of the complementary imaginative geographies of the metropolis London; the classic nineteenth century capital, Paris; and the would-be global city, Berlin.[43]

These guys love following terms:
- spatial
- spectacular

2

Berlin 1896: Wilhelm II, Georg Simmel and the Berliner Gewerbeausstellung

Ausstellung is nich, wie meine Herren Berliner sagen.
(Wilhelm II to Chancellor Leo Graf von Caprivi)

1896 wurde Berlin zur Weltstadt. Bis dahin war es nur eine europäische Provinzstadt. Die Markscheide bildet die Gewerbeausstellung im Treptower Park.

(Eduard Spranger)[1]

For a long time, Germany's role in the global exhibition networks was extraordinarily complex. Until the opening of EXPO 2000 in Hanover on 1 June 2000, it was largely overlooked that no universal or international exhibition comparable to those in London, Paris and most other West European capital cities had ever been held in Germany. Over the course of the nineteenth century, Germany participated with its own sections in exhibitions held in London (1851, 1862), Paris (1855, 1867), Vienna (1873), Melbourne (1888–89), Philadelphia (1876) and Chicago (1893), but did not take part in the two Paris expositions of 1878 and 1889. Moreover, with the exception of the Viennese Weltausstellung of 1873, no world exhibition proper ever took place in Germany or a German-speaking country. Thus, with the arrival of EXPO 2000, the only event of a similar scale, the long unnoticed and for the most part ignored Berliner Gewerbeausstellung (trade exhibition) of 1896, held on the occasion of the twenty-fifth anniversary of the German Reich, aroused new public and academic interest, with its status suddenly upgraded from a 'would-be world exposition' to a direct precursor of the mega-event in Hanover.[2] Yet the Berlin trade exhibition can only be understood properly if situated in the context of the so-called *Ausstellungs-* or *Weltausstellungsfrage,* the German exhibition question. Under this heading, politicians, businessmen and self-proclaimed experts debated fiercely for over 35 years, from the late 1870s to the early 1910s, whether an international exposition should be organized in Germany, preferably in the capital, thus following the example set not only by Great Britain and France but also other great powers such as the United States. In the course of this debate, not only did they make (and dismiss) one proposal after another; they also scrutinized the medium's possibilities and limitations, its role and function in public life, its direct and indirect results and benefits as well as its general future development. Why did this much-desired international exhibition never materialize? And was this debate as pointless, ineffective and inconclusive as it prima facie seems?[3]   *Germans downplay the media's possibilities*

Why never in Germany?

Undoubtedly, numerous trade fairs, national, regional and municipal exhibitions of different sizes, scales and lengths were held in nineteenth-century Germany, both in Berlin, Munich, Düsseldorf, Hanover and elsewhere; for instance, an *Allgemeine Deutsche Gewerbe-Ausstellung zu Berlin* on the occasion of the *Zollverein*'s tenth anniversary in 1844, and a second, much bigger and more successful trade fair in Berlin-Moabit in 1879. While the former was held in the rooms of the armory, featuring more than 3000 exhibitors and attracting 270,000 visitors between August and October 1844, the latter took place in an area situated between the Lehrter Bahnhof, Alt-Moabit and Invalidenstraße, and would afterwards be called an exhibition, 'so fresh, sweet, charming as a young bride'.[4] Open from May to October 1879, this 'young bride' attracted fewer exhibitors but had more than 2 million visitors. Yielding considerable profit, it proved exceedingly successful in boosting local merchants' and industrialists' self-confidence and gave rise to the *Stiftung der Berliner Gewerbe-Ausstellung im Jahre 1879*, referred to as *Vereinigung von 1879* (Association of 1879), a non-profit union of exhibitors formed in its immediate aftermath. 'It is, in the history of exhibitions, possibly a unique phenomenon', a contemporary critic noted in retrospect, 'that the Berlin exhibitors of 1879, even today, after 12 years, are unanimous in their grateful recognition of this epoch-making success for Berlin as an industrial city.' In addition, there were also regional exhibitions in Germany. Some of the wealthier southwestern regions such as Württemberg or Baden, but also Saxony in the east, had introduced industrial fairs early in the nineteenth century. With the first general industrial exhibition held in Württemberg in 1812 and a *Zentralstelle für Gewerbe und Handel* founded in 1848, exhibitions here were subject to a level of centralized coordination unthinkable in a national context.[5]

Yet, although a national exhibition tradition had been tentatively established, international expositions were a different matter. Sources disagree as to when the question of whether such a grand-scale event could be organized in the German capital was first posed, and when it developed into a full-fledged public debate. Arising in the aftermath of the Parisian Exposition Universelle of 1855 and taken up again on the occasion of the next French exposition in 1867, the *Ausstellungsfrage* became increasingly acute after Germany's national unification in 1870–71 and its subsequent attempts at great-power politics. Controversies about the Viennese Weltausstellung of 1873, especially the German self-representation at the American Centennial International Exhibition held in Philadelphia three years later, and its non-participation at the 1878 Exposition Universelle in Paris, intensified the debate towards the end of the decade. In the following years, the *Ausstellungsfrage* reappeared almost as a matter of course with each such subsequent event, and remained a controversial issue well into the twentieth century.[6]

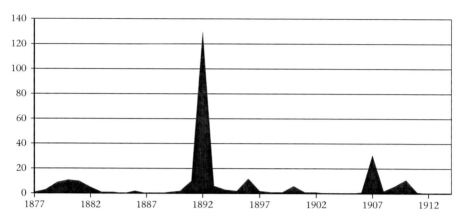

Figure 2.1   Three phases of debate: number of publications on the German *Ausstellungsfrage* (exhibition question) between 1877 and 1914

A simple tabulation of the number of newspaper and journal articles published on this question between 1877 and 1914 reveals three particular phases of this debate. As Figure 2.1 shows, the *Ausstellungsfrage* was discussed intensively from July 1878 through to April 1882, with 41 articles; in 1891 and 1892, especially from June through to December of the latter year, with more than 140; and, third, from the second half of 1907 together with a brief reappearance in April 1909, leading to a final controversy in 1910 and encompassing 52 articles altogether.[7] Over the course of these 35 years the question was discussed most extensively in 1892, with the Gewerbeausstellung of 1896 as its indirect consequence. In time the overall tone became far less sharp, and the opinions expressed more uniform. The arguments of both advocates and opponents grew increasingly codified, morphing eventually into an ever-wider, yet largely repetitive, debate.

In all of these three phases, several Berlin-based associations of businessmen and industrialists were major driving forces: the already mentioned *Vereinigung von 1879* under the chairmanship of →Fritz Kühnemann; the *Verein zur Beförderung des Gewerbefleißes für Deutschland* (Association for the Promotion of Trade Activities in Germany); and, more prominent, the *Verein Berliner Kaufleute und Industrieller* (Association of Berlin Merchants and Industrialists), also founded in 1879 and presided over by the Jewish banker and economist *Geheimer Kommerzienrat* →Ludwig Max Goldberger (Figure 2.2), one of the leading protagonists of the German exhibition movement. Having sold the bank that he had inherited from his father to devote himself exclusively to charitable and non-profit making work, Goldberger had been elected president in 1891 and was to remain in office for the next ten years. He soon began to advise high government officials such as Chancellor Leo Graf von Caprivi (1831–1899). While the *Stiftung der Berliner Gewerbe-Ausstellung im Jahre 1879* had been founded with precisely the purpose of organizing an international exposition in Berlin, the *Verein Berliner Kaufleute und Industrieller* already

Figure 2.2 Ludwig Max Goldberger (1848–1913), long-time president of the *Verein Berliner Kaufleute und Industrieller*
Source: Courtesy of Verein Berliner Kaufleute und Industrieller, Berlin.

established in the winter of 1879–80, the first year of its existence, a commission intended to campaign and prepare for an international exposition in Berlin.[8]

As shown in the following section, while the first attempt failed in 1882 because of Chancellor Otto Fürst von Bismarck's (1815–1898) personal objections as well as a general lack of support on part of the government, a second attempt, ten years later, was abandoned due to Kaiser Wilhelm II's brusque intervention, after the entire planning process had been postponed several times, and in order to avoid jeopardizing German industry's participation in the World's Columbian Exposition 1893 in Chicago. What remained possible was the Gewerbeausstellung, held in Treptower Park in 1896 and the focus of the later sections of this chapter, reduced to an 'extended Berlin trade exhibition' and often considered only a remnant of the original, more comprehensive, but finally abandoned exposition project. It is against this background that the exposition's status as a 'would-be world's fair' must be discussed. The central question is whether the Berliner Gewerbeausstellung was actually a success (since it did eventually take place, despite various setbacks), or, instead, a failure (because, technically speaking, it was in the end simply a trade fair assembled by some local businessmen). Any answer depends on the perspective and context in which the exhibition is discussed, that is, either bottom-up, seen as a privately organized fair and the largest ever held in Germany, versus top-down, as an imperfectly realized, largely downgraded version of what had been intended as a much grander international mega-event.[9]

The first phase of failure: 1878–82

Why did all projects fail? Before turning to the Gewerbeausstellung itself, the aforementioned three phases of the debate (1878–82, 1891–92, 1907–10) must be addressed, including an analysis of the numerous elaborate, though never realized, architectural proposals advanced throughout. The first stage lasted for almost four years, from July 1878 to April 1882. Identifying its precise origin proves difficult, but it was clearly triggered by both the so-called *billig und schlecht* (cheap and nasty) scandal caused by German products' putatively poor quality at the Philadelphia exhibition of 1876 and the government's controversial decision not to take part in the Parisian Exposition Universelle two years later.

The scandal was caused by Professor →Franz Reuleaux, an engineering expert and exposition veteran, who had been appointed official German commissioner for the Philadelphia 1876 world's fair. Reuleaux stirred up huge public controversy when he reported that Germany had suffered a severe blow at the American exposition. According to him, the fundamental principle of Germany's industrial production was *billig und schlecht* – cheap and nasty. Much to his own surprise, Reuleaux's report sparked a storm of outrage in the German press, reflecting deep unease and widespread embarrassment, and prompting accusations of having insulted the entire nation. What proved decisive, however, was not so much his diagnosis per se (the justification for and relevance of which is difficult to ascertain anyway), but rather the ensuing debate itself. Reuleaux's formulation of 'cheap and nasty' not only dominated and polarized the entire controversy, it also became a catchphrase remembered for decades after the scandal itself, synonymous with the severe 'moral' international defeat of the 'young' Germany, afterwards to be avoided by any means necessary. This expression colored exhibition standards for years to come. Minister of Commerce Ludwig Brefeld (1837–1907) would still evoke this *alte, harte Wort* (old harsh comment) 20 years later in a speech delivered on the occasion of the closing ceremony of the Berliner Gewerbeausstellung on 15 October 1896, contrasting it with the 'Made in Germany' label, the mark which, though introduced by the British parliament in 1887 in an effort to protect its domestic market against foreign goods (Merchandise Marks Act), had yielded counterproductive results.[10] The second factor, Germany's non-participation in the Paris exposition two years later, was politically motivated. Enemies in the recent Franco-Prussian War (1870–71), Germany and France were divided by nationalist ideologies and conflicts between their respective political systems, monarchism and republicanism. Historians have taken this as a sign of how extreme ideologically determined elements of foreign policy had become by the late nineteenth century: close collaboration in the field of culture and public representation seemed out of the question. Yet German visitors to the Paris site felt that a German section was obviously lacking and

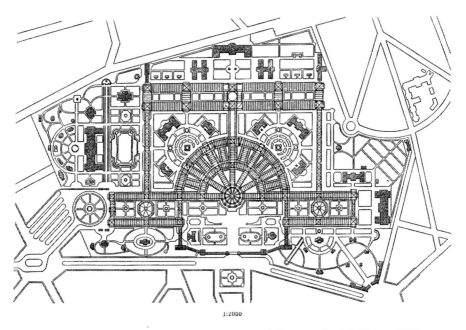

1:2000

Figure 2.3 Plan for a *Weltausstellungspalast* (world exhibition palace) in Berlin, 1879
Source: Messel, 'Ausstellungsbauten', 508.

wondered what it would take to create an exposition that could compete with the French achievement. The plan of holding an international exhibition in Berlin almost seemed to suggest itself.[11]

The first concrete proposals to organize such a Berlin exposition were made in the fall of 1879, when two architects, Walter Kyllmann (1837–1913) and Adolf Heyden (1838–1902), presented their study for a semi-permanent exhibition building in Berlin as part of the annual exhibition of the Academy of Arts (Figure 2.3). The proposal was based on, and attempted to synthesize, exhibition models first developed in Paris 1867 (an ellipse with concentric and radial streets) and Vienna 1873 (a fishbone system with a central rotunda) in a new, semi-circular layout with 'national streets' and a monumental cupola building. Even if details remained to be discussed, the issue was clearly established as a matter for public debate. 'It was the intention of the artists to simply propagate the idea', the *Deutsche Bauzeitung* commented, 'in this they have been singularly successful and should be given great praise.' Understood as a reaction to Reuleaux's severe condemnation, however, the attempt at international rehabilitation was widely criticized as too little too late.[12]

The issue achieved official status when the *Deutscher Handelstag*, the union of chambers of commerce and trade associations, raised the question of holding an exposition in Berlin during its general assembly on 21 November 1879. An inquiry among its industrial and corporative members yielded ambiguous and paradoxical results, revealing just how divided opinions were. On the one hand, the inquiry showed a largely critical and reserved attitude toward the entire medium. 'The initially wide-spread enthusiasm for exhibitions has died down in the meantime', the *Handelstag* stated, 'so that one thought one could abstain from participating in the last Paris exposition.' On the other hand, no willingness was expressed to give precedence to any other nation as possible host for the next universal exhibition. Eventually, the *Handelstag* passed an agreement to approach the government officially in order to ensure that the necessary political pressure was exerted. They would support the project only on the condition that a German exposition project be linked to an international agreement on the future regulation and organization of universal exhibitions. Furthermore, the *Handelstag*'s overall position remained somewhat reserved, as the discussion itself was the result of pressure created from without, in response to the fear that other governments might soon announce their respective exhibition plans for the coming years and thus render a German project impossible. In the end, however, it left no doubt that if such a mega-event was to be held in Germany, Berlin would be the only suitable venue because it 'offers all these qualities and conditions which are essential for an exhibition city, and even if there are other more suitable places in Germany they would gladly give pride of place to our imperial capital'.[13]

An unexpectedly fierce national debate flared up, its precise subject matter at times unclear. There were a number of issues at stake: Should an exposition be organized in Germany at all? If so, where? In the capital or in one of the competing big cities, such as Hamburg or Munich? If such an exhibition were to be held, should it be international or national? Positions varied enormously. Fritz Kühnemann, the aforementioned organizer of the 1879 Berlin trade fair and another prominent member of the German *Ausstellungsbewegung* (exhibition movement) until his death in 1917, did not rule out an international exhibition, but he campaigned aggressively from 1886 onward for repeating a similar, exclusively national event, though on a much grander scale. Others, including Reuleaux, argued just as intensely for an international exposition. Describing the importance of such enterprises in international economic competition, Reuleaux demanded that a German universal exhibition be organized as soon as possible. According to him, expositions formed a central feature of modernity and were likely to continue to do so, such that the organization of an international exhibition was in the national interest. If Germany decided not to proceed, others would step in: 'Our time is the time of world exhibitions, they will not soon disappear. If we do not take the initiative, other nations will do so, in fact they are doing so without asking us and will, in an unexpected fashion, sharpen their knives in order to compete with Berlin.'[14] Yet a third faction focused on more pragmatic aspects, including the exposition's potential venue and its possible repercussions on the capital: Could such an event give proof of Berlin's status as a world city? Would the capital profit from it – or was it all made utterly impossible by Berlin's provinciality, its innate lack of attractiveness and its remote geographical position? Could an international exposition finally promote the new German capital – 'a settlement advanced to a city of millions and imperial capital of formerly Germanic farmers and Wendish fishermen', to quote Karl Scheffler's famous 1910 dictum – to the status of a genuine and globally recognized metropolis?[15]

It was on this *Hauptstadtfrage*, the capital question, that critics denounced the *Ausstellungsfrage*, together with the entire plan. Henceforth, these two questions would always be closely connected; one could not be solved without the other. Among the numerous opponents was the ethnographer and Hamburg-based museum director →Karl Lüders, who published a number of articles vehemently denying the question's presuppositions. He feared the incalculable expenses implied in such a risky enterprise. According to Lüders, Berlin lacked the necessary flair to attract foreign visitors, and any exposition could not compensate for its absence. Generally, his criticism was perceived as being so harsh and unjustified that it at once provoked a number of indignant reactions. It was instantly rejected by Albert Brockhoff, for instance, who replied to Lüders' pamphlets in great detail, arguing that a process of national concentration as well as cooperation was urgently needed in the German exhibition system. When no agreement could be reached on whether the planned exposition should be national or international, a joint meeting of all interested parties including the *Verein Berliner Kaufleute und Industrieller*, the *Verein zur Beförderung des Gewerbefleißes*, the *Architekten-Verein* and many others met on 17 June 1881 at the City-Hôtel in Berlin. A vote was taken after a fierce and heated debate with a majority of delegates declaring that the exhibition should be international rather than merely national.[16]

In January 1882, the question was debated in parliament. Asked to take an official stand, Secretary of State Karl Heinrich von Bötticher (1833–1907) cited a certain 'overproduction in this field' and explained that the government had come to the conclusion 'that one should not insist on new exhibitions' because 'the advantages of a country, in which the international exhibition is to be held, would not stand in a reasonable relation to the great expenses incurred.' In the end, Bismarck intervened personally, ensuring that the question was not further discussed. Thus, the first phase of debate came to a sudden halt, due to an official decision by the authorities taken mainly in view of the precarious economic nature of an enterprise with seemingly incalculable expenses. Needless to say, the private businessmen and merchants involved were deeply disappointed, disagreeing strongly with the government's half-hearted reasons.[17]

Although still officially unsolicited, there were, even at this early stage, a number of fairly detailed projects in the works for a German world exhibition. One of them proposed that a huge artificial mountain should be constructed as the exhibition's general leitmotiv and 'great attraction' in an otherwise excessively flat landscape (Figure 2.4). Surrounded by a ring of exhibition buildings and a circular railroad line, the building of such a mountain was to be combined with the development of an entire new civic area, including artificial lakes and railroads. Thus, the project's realization was not only seen as promoting general development to the great advantage of Berlin, but also as constituting a major challenge to German engineers and architects. Since the mountain, together with a lookout tower to be erected on its summit, was to be higher than the Eiffel Tower, it was also meant as a step towards further inter-urban, inner-European and inter-exhibitionary competitiveness. 'At the end of the nineteenth century nobody would dare to suggest that the realization of this plan was impossible', the *Deutsche Bauzeitung* commented benevolently, 'especially since those costs would hardly exceed those incurred by the Eiffel Tower and the Grand Machine Hall seen in last year's exhibition.' Yet the project was indeed never realized: the

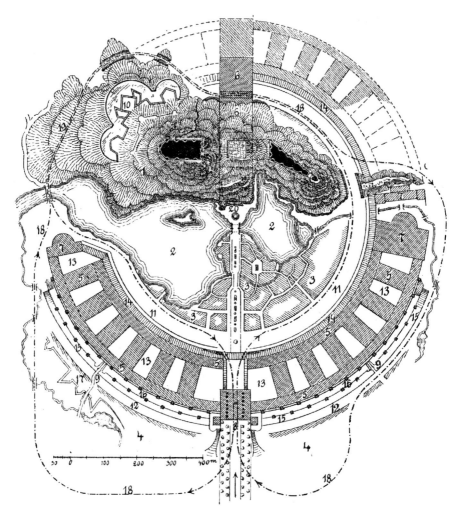

Skizze für die Anordnung einer Weltausstellung in Berlin.

1. Berg. 2. See. 3. Stadt. 4. Vorstadt. 5. Haupt-Ausstellungs-Gebäude. 6. Maschinen-halle. 7. Wirthschaften usw. 8. Hauptthor. 9. Nebenthore. 10. Alte Befestigung. 11. Innere Ringstrafse. 12. Aeufsere Ringstrafse. 13. Höfe. 14. Wandelgang. 15. Stadt-graben. 16. Zwinger. 17. Schanze. 18. Endlose Eisenbahn. 19. Tunnel. 20. Haupt-eingang der Maschinenhalle.

Figure 2.4   Sketch for the arrangement of a world exhibition in Berlin, including an artificial mountain, various lakes and a 'never-ending railroad'
Source: Deutsche Bauzeitung 24 (4 October 1890), 481.

entire plan was abandoned, along with that for the projected national trade fair, the Deutsch-nationale Gewerbeausstellung zu Berlin im Jahre 1888, to be held in Treptow. Anticipated competition with the upcoming Paris exposition of 1889, the fourth to be held there, dissipated any existing support for the endeavor.[18]

The second phase of failure: 1891–92

The second phase of the debate, from 1891 to 1892, proved the most heated and controversial of the entire *Ausstellungsfrage*, eventually but indirectly leading to the Berliner Gewerbeausstellung. After long and complex internal discussions, the Prussian *Verein zur Beförderung des Gewerbefleißes* issued a new resolution in April 1891 for a universal exhibition to be held in Berlin before the end of the century, and sent an official declaration to the chancellor to that effect, supported in its efforts by the *Verein Berliner Kaufleute und Industrieller* and the *Vereinigung von 1879*. This time, ten years later, the previously aloof *Handelstag* also voted in favor after a survey of all German chambers of commerce yielded an overwhelmingly positive result. On 15 January 1892, it issued an official resolution that the next world exhibition should be held in Berlin to ensure that German industry would profit from the attendant advantages in trade and business. Aiming to draw the government's attention to the matter, they hoped to win its indispensable political, financial and organizational support for the project.[19]

However, in addition to public disputes and a dizzying number of pamphlets, declarations and resolutions issued by the different bodies involved, at this stage there were also a number of concrete projects and partially developed schemes. In May 1892, approximately one year after the second phase of debate had begun, a competition organized by the *Architekten-Verein zu Berlin*, a dignified association of Berlin-based architects founded in 1824, invited proposals for a universal exhibition to be held in Berlin in 1896 or 1897. This competition had two tasks: to find a suitable location for a possible universal exhibition, ideally located not too far from the city center, and to develop provisional outlines for the layout of the potential site. Given Berlin's specific urban situation, the former of the two tasks, the so-called *Platzfrage*, presented an enormous challenge to the participating architects. As the British *Builder* commented from abroad, 'the Prussian capital has no natural site for an exhibition within its area such as Paris can boast of. [...] A conveniently situated site will be most difficult to find, and when found the monotony of Brandenburg's dusty plain will have to be diversified by artificial means.' Aware of this difficulty, the official project description did not indicate any further specifications and requested proposals to be submitted by 5 September 1892.[20]

The competition aroused much interest. Twelve complete proposals were received by the deadline, only two of which were within a 3.5 kilometer radius from the Royal Palace, taken as the city's center, and indicated on the specially issued map by a circle (Figure 2.5). Seven selected various sites between the historical Grunewald and the Anhalter Bahnhof to the west, one proposed using a part of the Tempelhofer Feld, a huge drill ground in south Berlin, and two selected different areas of Treptower Park in the city's south-east. As was to be expected, some architectural journals complained that the *Platzfrage* had generally proved insoluble.

The two award-winning designs by architects Thomas Köhn, Cremer and Wolffenstein, and by Paul Hentschel were characterized by detailed proposals, carefully adapted to the city's potential. The first project (Figure 2.6), entitled *Verlorene Liebesmüh* (Love's Labors Lost), proposed a combination of two different venues – one a larger, more urban and better developed site at Witzleben around the

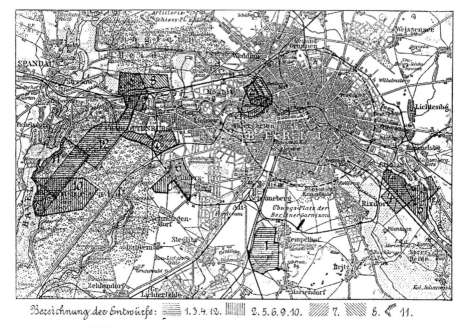

Bezeichnung der Entwürfe: ≡ 1.3.4.12. ▓▓ 2.5.6.9.10. ▓▓ 7. ▓▓ 8. ◁ 11.

Bei Ueberschneidungen verschiedener Entw. sind die entsprech. Schraffirungen durchgeführt.

Figure 2.5   Map indicating the 12 submitted proposals for a world exhibition to be held in Berlin, 1892. The circle indicates a 3.5 kilometer radius around the Royal Palace in Berlin's center
Source: 'Die Preisbewerbung um den Lageplan einer in Berlin zu veranstaltenden Weltausstellung', 549.

Lietzensee in west Berlin's Charlottenburg, and an additional smaller, more rural site only four kilometers away. The main venue was to feature a machinery hall, somewhat reminiscent of the British Crystal Palace, together with a huge dome, and was planned as a permanent exhibition building; the smaller site was to include several stretches of water that the architects considered essential. The two areas were to be connected by a small railroad especially built for this purpose. Although it suggested a less clearly defined structure in Berlin-Moabit on the banks of the river Spree, the second project (Figure 2.7), called *Fromme Wünsche* (Pious Hopes), won the competition mainly because its architect, Paul Hentschel, had found a site in the city's center, which the *Centralblatt der Bauverwaltung* immediately acclaimed as not only 'one of the most beautiful exhibition facilities imaginable in Berlin' but also its particular version of the Parisian Champ de Mars. Yet, whether the required area would actually be available for such use remained uncertain.[21]

In the interim, however, the Kaiser's final negative verdict, made public three months after the bidding but only five weeks before the deadline, had disposed of the entire controversy. Some participating architects hence chose ironic, melancholy titles such as *Verlorene Liebesmüh*, *Fromme Wünsche* or *Behüt Dich Gott, es hat nicht sollen sein* (It was Not To Be, oh Lord) for their suddenly superfluous and now almost certainly never-to-be-realized projects. Others tried to conceal

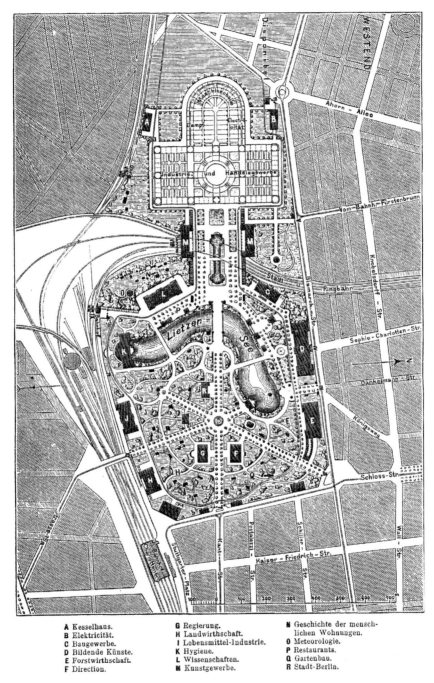

A Kesselhaus.
B Elektricität.
C Baugewerbe.
D Bildende Künste.
E Forstwirthschaft.
F Direction.

G Regierung.
H Landwirthschaft.
I Lebensmittel-Industrie.
K Hygiene.
L Wissenschaften.
M Kunstgewerbe.

N Geschichte der mensch-
lichen Wohnungen.
O Meteorologie.
P Restaurants.
Q Gartenbau.
R Stadt-Berlin.

Figure 2.6 Competition for a world exhibition to be held in Berlin: proposal *Verlorene Liebesmüh* (Love's Labors Lost)
Source: 'Preisbewerbung um den Entwurf des Lageplans für eine Weltausstellung in Berlin', 485.

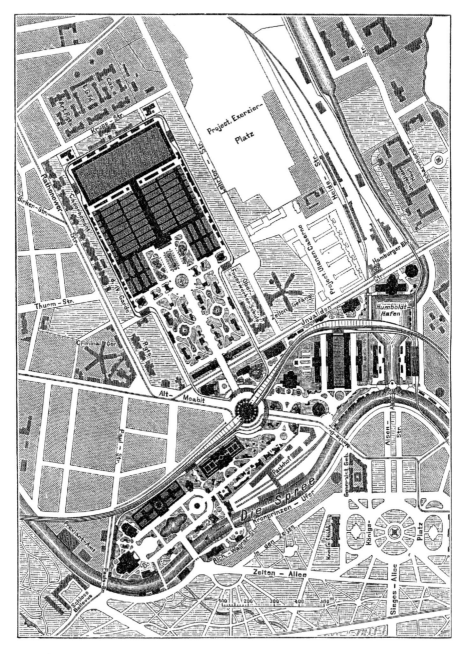

Figure 2.7 Competition for a world exhibition to be held in Berlin: proposal *Fromme Wünsche* (Pious Hopes)
Source: 'Preisbewerbung um den Entwurf des Lageplans für eine Weltausstellung in Berlin', 502.

their disappointment by creating overtly nationalistic names such as *Deutschland, Deutschland über alles* or *All-Deutschland*. Although there was no hope of realization, the organizers were still not entirely satisfied with the competition's results and considered the *Platzfrage* unresolved. As Berlin's urban growth continued, they warned, finding a suitable site for a German international exhibition would become even more difficult, even in the near future.[22]

Around the same time, in early 1892, a self-proclaimed *Comité für das Weltausstellungs-Terrain im Norden Berlins* (Committee for an Exposition Site in the North of Berlin) had commissioned yet another, never-to-be-implemented, scenario for a Berlin world exhibition. Historiographically, such unrealized projects and exposition plans are of interest precisely for their 'pre-factual' character. It is revealing which components and ensembles were considered so obligatory and constitutive for an international exposition that their inclusion was thought a must, regardless of possible restrictions, special local conditions or specific problems of realization. Thus, the historian gains insight into conceptions of how the exposition medium was supposed to function, for elements included in such proposals were obviously considered indispensable.

For the project proposed by the *Comité*, a vast area of 340 hectares adjacent to the Plötzensee in the city's northwest had been selected, far larger not only than the later chosen venue in Treptow (120 hectares) but also more spacious than any previous European exposition, and, supposedly within walking distance of both Tiergarten and Wedding, much closer to the city center.[23] A panoramic view, originally published in a propaganda booklet, conveys an impression of the projected venue's enormous dimensions, with its dominating, 500-meter tower whose artistic debts to the French original were more than obvious (Figure 2.8). Only three years after the erection of the *Tour Eiffel,* the incorporation of such a tower was already considered an obligatory component of each exposition, determined by the international competitors' previous success and largely dictated by the latest fashion in exhibition design. Even an otherwise skeptical supporter such as Stefan Reiländer insisted on the construction of such a monument, if only to outshine the Eiffel Tower. 'Such towers are certainly becoming fashionable', he declared, 'and will be the hallmark of every world city.'[24]

A second, more detailed map of the same scenario (Figure 2.9) illustrates the planned spatial arrangement of pavilions, ensembles and various 'attractions'. Along a double axis, crossed only by the still existent Seestraße, were lined additional constructions. At an estimated cost of 40 million marks (Berliner Gewerbeausstellung: *c*.16) they included a Palace of Industry and Applied Arts, a Pavilion of Electricity, a Machinery Hall as well as an illuminated fountain containing an aquarium and surrounded by gardens and lakes. Neither could a 20-meter high statue of the Kaiser nor a Women's Palace possibly be omitted. Roughly a fifth of the entire area had been reserved for pavilions to be built by the participating foreign nations at their own expense. Since their design and implementation could not be anticipated in detail, the authors declared, these foreign sections had been sketched in only roughly. From a bird's-eye view they, in fact, seemed to disappear entirely in the panorama's upper-left corner, melting into the horizon.[25]

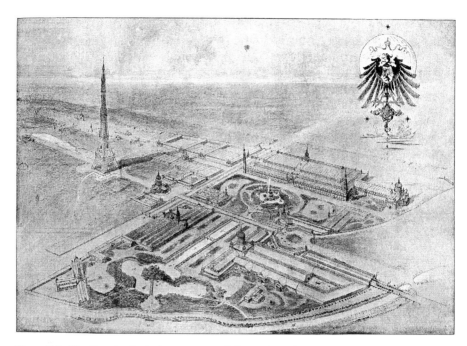

Figure 2.8   Northeast-oriented panorama of the projected exposition site in north Berlin, with the Spree at the bottom, 1892
Source: Courtesy of Geheimes Staatsarchiv Preußischer Kulturbesitz, Berlin, I. HA Rep. 120 MfHuG, E XVI 2 Nr. 13 F, vol. 2, 150.

Although their precise societal impact is difficult to ascertain, concrete and detailed scenarios such as these played a central role in the increasingly widespread public debates that marked the second half of 1892. Seven patterns of argumentation, three in favor and four against a German exposition, can be isolated from the extensive press coverage. While not specifically limited to this phase of the overall debate, they were articulated most vehemently during the second half of 1892.

1. A vast majority of partisans and protagonists argued that Berlin's turn to invite the world had arrived. Having been welcomed as a guest at numerous expositions before, it seemed high time for the 'great German nation' to return the invitation and act as host itself, Franz Reuleaux, →Hermann Grothe and others agreed. 'We have long enough been guests at foreign expositions that we are now obliged to play host', a member of the *Verein zur Beförderung des Gewerbefleißes* succinctly summarized the argument: 'To constantly sponge on others is unworthy of the German nation' (*Being a Host Argument*).[26]

2. This line of reasoning was further extended in 1891–92. Now the gesture of playing host was frequently described as a 'national duty', a 'matter of decency' (*Anstandspflicht*) or an 'international obligation'. Soon, however, it became unclear whether one felt beholden to the world or to one's own position in it as an imperial

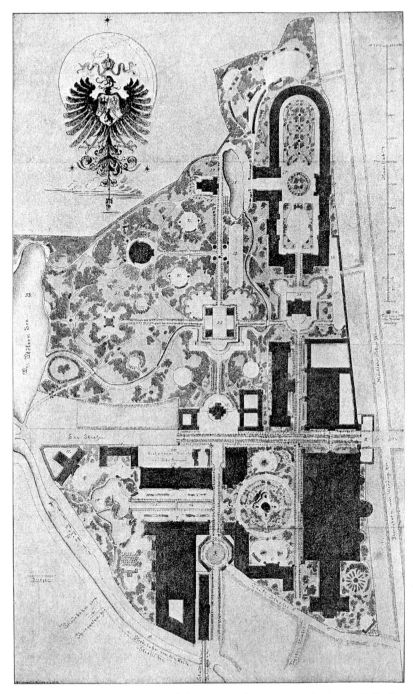

Figure 2.9 Northwest-oriented map of the projected exposition site in north Berlin, with the Plötzensee on the left, 1892

Source: Courtesy of Geheimes Staatsarchiv Preußischer Kulturbesitz, Berlin, I. HA Rep. 120 MfHuG, E XVI 2 Nr. 13 F, vol. 2, 137.

power striving for international recognition. →Julius Lessing, director of the Berliner Kunstgewerbemuseum, summarized this argument, adding an imperial slant, when he stated that a world exhibition formed a part of Germany's recently gained world stature, and another sympathizer proclaimed that a German exposition constituted 'both a just demand and right of the German Nation'. Here, the standard metaphor of expositions as an arena for peaceful competition among the nations was taken literally. The hosting of an international exhibition was considered a matter of national prestige, a status symbol, and a welcome means to reinforce the nation's place in the international hierarchy. Thus, it became more a matter of enhancing one's own image than of returning hospitality – and the organization of an international exposition the perfect instrument for its implementation (*National Duty Argument*).[27]

3. Executing such a plan, its supporters assumed, would unleash centripetal forces and directly affect the German capital by elevating Berlin to the much-desired status of a genuine metropole. Resolving the pressing *Ausstellungsfrage*, they argued, would be tantamount to putting an end to the equally troublesome *Hauptstadtfrage*. Berlin would finally have the long-awaited opportunity to prove 'on the spot' and demonstrate vis-à-vis the world its newly gained status as a world city, especially in comparison with Vienna, London and Paris. 'We can [...] now boldly vary the former phrase "Berlin will soon become a world city!"', exclaimed one commentator, expressing a new urban self-confidence that still required public, and especially international, backing, 'and instead proudly state "Berlin is a world city!"'. Another expressed the hope that only by 'holding international *cercle*' would Berlin be able to 'dismiss old prejudices against the former Wendish fishing village', 'discard the remnants of its former *petit-bourgeois* past' and at last begin to 'feel itself as a world city'. The organization of such an exposition would bring nothing less than the process of national unification to its symbolic conclusion, confirming Berlin's position as Germany's capital (*Learning to Feel Like a World City Argument*).[28]

Such self-positioning and self-assurance in the context of the competing West European capitals seemed unavoidable, yet public confidence remained tenuous. On the one hand, the World's Columbian Exposition in Chicago planned for 1893 and the 1900 Parisian Exposition Universelle proved two of the most significant points of reference. While the former was in a state of preparation, the latter was publicly announced on 13 July 1892, during the most heated phase of the German debate. Having organized an exhibition in Paris every 11 years since 1867, France assumed its natural right and legitimate claim to hold another in 1900, and so asserted that the German initiative was meant simply as an insult. German propaganda, in turn, betrayed some strong anti-French and, in particular, anti-Parisian sentiment. It accused the French faction of a fait accompli, fearing that they would strive to make world's fairs an exclusively French institution and thus Paris the 'permanent center of the economic world'. Suspecting political calculation to be the main objective, some newspapers even spoke of a concerted *Überrumpelung* (surprise attack), going as far as to declare this the first clash between the two nations since 1871 with serious political consequences.[29]

The importance of these points of reference during the whole lengthy decision-making process shows how significant other, more established focal points in the global exhibitionary network had become by the end of the nineteenth century, and the pivotal role played by inter-urban competition.

The opponents argued structurally in very similar ways: *con*

4.   The first and foremost argument, presented with ever-increasing frequency from the 1880s onwards, was that the entire medium had become out-dated and a particular type of 'exhibition fatigue' had set in (*Ausstellungsmüdigkeit*).[30]

5.   As expositions became both more frequent and less useful, opponents argued, more and more efforts had to be taken to guarantee their effectiveness. As expenses increased, more and more visitors would have to be attracted in order to cover all the additional costs. One critic went so far as to call expositions an altogether exorbitant and excessive luxury. 'Their present day form', he wrote, 'makes them seem as a superfluous luxurious passion, which only an industrial and strongly trade-oriented community, accustomed to fluctuations and equipped with the necessary mental elasticity, can put into practice with real conviction.' Thus, one major argument against such an exhibition was, time and again, that the expense was far too great for the participating nations and exhibiting industries (*Expenses versus Effects Argument*).[31]   *Costs > Benefits*

6.   Critics not only feared inflationary effects on the local economy of Berlin, but they also argued that the new German capital was simply not ready to be a world city and could not compete with its international counterparts. The *Reichshauptstadt* would not attract sufficient numbers of foreigners, thus increasing *Berlin* the danger of suffering financial deficit even further. In 1879, Karl Lüders, one of *really not* the most outspoken opponents, had already expressed such objections very clearly. *? analy* 'We believe', he wrote, 'that Berlin is less attractive to the foreign visitor than Paris, *or* London and Vienna, and that it is probably the first industrial, commercial and *can't* political capital of a not particularly wealthy Empire yet not a comparable center *compete* of world traffic [*Weltverkehr*].' Opponents often pointed to the Viennese exhibition of 1873 and the disastrous effects it had had on both local hotel prices and the real estate market, giving this as a warning example (*Inferiority Argument*).[32]

7.   Last but not least, opposition against a centrally organized German world exhibition invoked a familiar theme within the tradition of German federalism: provincial fear. The idea of a German universal exhibition held in Berlin was deeply troubling to the provinces, whose criticisms →Georg Bobertag, a former mayor, in turn ridiculed as 'petty jealousy and the unfortunate [and] still influential prejudice against the "hydrocephalic" city of Berlin [*Wasserkopf Berlin*].'[33] Supporters of this argument attempted to turn the tables by describing the frequently held provincial and regional fairs as being one virtual, but already existing and highly successful 'decentralized national exposition'. In addition to a universal central and international exhibition in Berlin, they suggested, various specialized fairs should be held in Hamburg, Berlin, Munich, Leipzig and Mainz. Thus, they

anticipated one of the major planning elements of Hanover's EXPO 2000, namely decentralization and conceptual inclusion of the entire national territory. 'Therefore we intend', one advocate affirmed as early as 1892, 'to turn the *whole* of Germany into an exhibition terrain with Berlin as its focal point.' Reminiscent of a short story by Jorge Luis Borges in which a map on a scale of 1:1 is drawn, the medium and its subject matter would have conflated and become identical (*German Federalism Argument*).[34]

All of a sudden, and much to the surprise of all parties involved, the heated and emotionally laden debate came to a second, if temporary halt in the fall of 1892. A laconic note published in the official *Reichs-Anzeiger* of 13 August 1892 meant an abandonment of the *Ausstellungsfrage* and all connected plans and projects. The Kaiser had decided, the note read, that the plan for an international exposition in Berlin was not to be pursued any further, at least not on the Empire's part. A notorious personal letter written on 20 July 1892 and sent to Graf von Caprivi, Bismarck's successor as Chancellor, gives further details of why Wilhelm II was so strongly opposed. 'The glory of the Parisians robs the Berliners of their sleep', the Kaiser wrote, 'Berlin is a great city, a world city (perhaps?), consequently, it must have its exhibition. [...] However, Berlin is not Paris. Paris is the great whorehouse of the world; therein lies its attraction independent of any exhibition. There is nothing in Berlin that can captivate the foreigner, except a few museums, castles and soldiers.' Excluding any possible contradiction, Wilhelm II's arguments culminated in the apodictic statement: 'I am against this exhibition because it will bring very serious trouble to my fatherland and also to the city itself! [...] There ain't going to be no exhibition, as my Berlin friends would put it.'[35] Further personal correspondence between Wilhelm II and Caprivi shows that the Chancellor himself was, at this point, no longer as firmly opposed to an exhibition project as he had been previously; yet his attempts to convince Wilhelm II failed. As a consequence, the final decision *not* to hold a German international exhibition must be attributed exclusively to the Kaiser.[36] The various partisans and advocates, including the architects and engineers engaged in the 1892 architectural competition, could not conceal their great disappointment at what they considered a mistaken decision that spelled both professional defeat and, indeed, national misfortune, even if they did not dare to contradict the Kaiser openly. 'Vain hopes, vain efforts!', they mourned: 'The plan for a German world exhibition now rests in its own coffin, and considering the opposition it has aroused it is hardly likely that present-day citizens will ever experience its resurrection.'[37]

The third phase of failure: 1907–10

For better or worse, the architects erred. Shortly after, new plans were made, and the Berliner Gewerbeausstellung of 1896 was their direct outcome. Yet, as Figure 2.1 above shows, the *Ausstellungsfrage* never vanished completely from public print discourse. A decade later it became once again a subject of controversy – and remained so, intermittently, for a number of years, re-emerging from March to early May 1907, with a brief resurgence in April 1909, and a final flare-up in 1910. Although this latest round of initiatives provoked yet another round of reactions, rekindling the old controversy, both the protagonists involved and the arguments exchanged remained very much the same as before, as did the results.[38]

There was no lack of prominent supporters. As in 1879 and 1892, one of the most outspoken remained Ludwig Max Goldberger, now president of the newly founded *Ständige Ausstellungskommission für die deutsche Industrie*, and joined by many influential writers and politicians such as →Hermann Hillger, Martin Kirschner (1842–1912), then mayor of Berlin and later foreign minister, and Chancellor Gustav Stresemann (1878–1929) who publicly expressed his support for the lingering project in a parliamentary debate.[39] The dispute gained momentum, reaching its climax in the summer and fall of 1910 when Germany's successful performance at the Brussels Exposition Universelle et Internationale of the same year inevitably revived the question of organizing a similar event in Berlin.

The Kaiser's negative verdict and explicit unwillingness eventually put an end to the entire, seemingly intractable, controversy. After a long silence, Wilhelm II expressed his views on this matter anew, ironically enough during an official visit to the Brussels exposition. His opinion had hardly changed since 1892. According to the Kaiser, Berlin lacked three essential requirements: a suitable site, the necessary financial resources for such a risky and cost-intensive enterprise, and the general attractiveness for potential visitors and foreign tourists. One of the newspapers quoted one of Wilhelm II's statements verbatim:

> The average Berliner, the Kaiser explained, works overmuch and thus has no time to visit exhibitions. He might possibly sacrifice his Sunday for such a dubious pleasure. But also fewer visitors would come to Berlin as they did to Paris and Brussels. Berlin lies outside the usual route for world tourists, and all attempts to turn Berlin into a city of foreigners [*Fremdenstadt*] such as Paris will fail, simply due to its geographical position.[40]

Like the architects and engineers in 1892, writers and journalists such as Siegfried Lilienthal – publishing under the pen name →Fritz Stahl – could hardly conceal their disappointment and interpreted the Kaiser's second denial as a rejection of the entire exhibition medium. Wilhelm II seemed to endorse, and even prefer, German provincialism to cosmopolitan localism.[41] Although the issue was subsequently raised several times, including by Adolf Hitler in the late 1930s after the successful 1936 Berlin Olympic Games, never again in the course of the twentieth century was the German *Weltausstellungsfrage* so widely and controversially discussed.[42]

In the end, how does one explain Germany's domestic absence from the nineteenth-century *Ausstellungszirkus* (exposition circus)? On the one hand, this absence is surprising and counter-intuitive. Numerous examples show that Berlin's newly gained status as capital was directly reflected in both representative architecture and the visual arts soon after the national unification of 1870–71, for instance with the construction of the new government quarter along the Wilhelmstraße on one side of the Brandenburg Gate, the nucleus Königsplatz on its other side, and the Reichstag and Siegesallee inaugurated in 1894.[43] On the other hand, the very existence of such initiatives proves that the seemingly obvious reference to Germany's federal structure or, in a global context, its comparatively marginal position as an imperial power, by no means suffices to explain its remarkable absence from international expositions. Though numerous attempts were made, none succeeded, a phenomenon that can be explained by varying configurations of four different factors.

Initially there was, first, a certain disinterest and indecision on the part of the government, and later among industrialists who became increasingly skeptical and hesitant as well. The economist, journalist and prolific world's fairs critic →Alfons Paquet, for instance, laid the blame exclusively on industry for the failure of the plan in its second and third phases, and other observers, such as the physicist and writer Emil Arnold Budde (1842–1921) agreed. 'The Berlin world exhibition', he wrote in 1908, 'has been shelved for the time being, because the great majority of German industrialists do not wish to become involved.'[44]

Second, the unresolved and highly controversial problem of financing such an enterprise could not be settled, together with the largely unanswered question of liability in case of financial loss. The exhibitions held in Vienna 1873 and Paris 1889 had suffered considerable financial deficits and were taken as severe warnings.

Third, there was not only fierce international competition with other potential host cities and their respective exposition projects, but also questions of how to strategically anticipate their respective claims. In 1882, for example, a similar, yet never realized Italian exhibition project had been announced for Rome for 1885–86 to which the German government wished to give priority. Ten years later, in 1892, with Germany's participation in the World's Columbian Exposition in Chicago the following year already decided upon, the probable competition with Paris for a *fin-de-siècle* exposition was another much-debated topic.[45]

Last but not least, Wilhelm II's personal aversion and scornful attitude, coming into play after his accession to the throne in 1888, is the single factor which not only proved decisive but is also the most difficult to explain. As a young successor to the throne, Wilhelm II had visited the expositions in Paris in 1867 and in Vienna in 1873 with his parents. As to his personal motives for rejecting all proposals for a comparable project to be organized in Berlin approximately a quarter of a century later, only vague – and not entirely satisfactory – speculation is possible. While both a mutual disinclination and a certain amount of tension between him and the capital itself have long been recognized by historians, Wilhelm II may have feared intuitively that a successful international exhibition in Germany would represent and celebrate the civic achievements of the *Bürgertum* and the German Empire rather than himself – and would, therefore, redirect public attention away from him and empower his 'enemies'. Yet, once the realization of the Berliner Gewerbeausstellung as an alternative privately organized event had been decided upon, he found no difficulty in taking over official representative functions, for instance during the opening ceremony, thus instrumentalizing the spectacle in order to promote his own grandeur.[46]

this inability to decide/downgrading shows Berlin's insecurity

Labor, water and the site

Seen in this light, the official guide's brief remark, 'the strong desire to host a major exhibition in Berlin was not at all new', seemed something of a euphemism. Due to a constant downgrading of size and scope – from an international to a national, from a national to a local, from a universal to an industrial exhibition – the Berliner Gewerbeausstellung of 1896 had 'one of the most remarkable pre-histories which had ever preceded such an enterprise', as the *Deutsche Bauzeitung* aptly commented.[47] Many of the project's supporters were dissatisfied with this development. In the eyes of the world, they feared, Germany had suffered yet another self-inflicted defeat. A national exposition would share all the shortcomings of an international one, but feature none of its advantages, Prussian historian →Hans Delbrück worried. 'The national exhibition shares in common with other world exhibitions the danger of becoming overloaded and may succumb to the temptation to dazzle the visitor, in fact, even to mislead him', he wrote: 'On the other hand it also lacks the merits of preceding world exhibitions: their impressive size, their glamour, the strong contrasts, their informative scope, their attraction for the foreign visitor, who should, in fact, also get to know and admire Germany.' Such a striking discrepancy between ambitious plans and actual events was gleefully registered abroad, for instance in the French press. 'The Exposition currently open in Berlin', noted the *Revue de Paris* with a certain condescension, 'is neither universal nor even national but purely local. Berlin had dreamed of something else', and the *Figaro* proved even more forthright when calling its planning nothing less than a 'gigantic fiasco'.[48]

When the German government publicly declared its definitive withdrawal from all exhibition proposals, thus expressing the Kaiser's final verdict, the *Verein zur Beförderung des Gewerbefleißes*, the *Vereinigung von 1879* and, above all, the *Verein Berliner Kaufleute und Industrieller* intervened, declaring the organization and realization of the Berlin trade exhibition as the only feasible alternative. At a public meeting in April 1891, its members had already passed an official resolution for an exposition to be held either in 1895 or 1896, which was to be as international as possible. A year later, on 6 April 1892, a further, more detailed resolution openly demanded that there should be a 'discussion about the exhibition question in Berlin and in the whole Empire without further delay, and a guarantee issued and signed in due time'. A letter to this effect was sent to Chancellor Graf von Caprivi. In his somewhat reserved reply, dated 3 June 1892, Caprivi avoided giving a definite statement by referring the *Verein* to the forthcoming Chicago exhibition, and asked its members for their support, 'so that the dignified and successful representation of Germany on American soil should not be impaired by the new project in Berlin'.[49]

However, with the government's negative decision taken and made public in August 1892, such a move had suddenly become inappropriate. Holding a universal exhibition was now completely out of the question. A turning point was reached at a public meeting on 10 November 1892, in the course of which Goldberger gave an impassioned speech restating the *Verein*'s arguments for the vital importance of such an enterprise. Goldberger made it clear that a more extensive, Berlin-based trade fair now remained the only solution and feasible alternative. His arguments emphasized the mutual benefits for the projected exhibition and for Berlin, giving the city the chance to demonstrate its newly won position to a global audience: 'Berlin has much to show to the world and that is precisely what we are aiming at!', he proclaimed.[50] In a circular letter and a pamphlet following the assembly, members of the *Verein* left no doubts as to their motives and objectives. Openly criticizing the government but not mentioning the Kaiser, they explained their reasons for supporting a reduced version of the original project while still striving for something grander:

> Since the Reich's Government had refused to proclaim and de facto to ensure a world exhibition in Berlin in this century, we have now set ourselves a more modest aim. We had to admit that to achieve this we would have to limit ourselves to a project that could be realized without government support. And this is: a major trade exhibition in Berlin. [...] We are all of the opinion that we would prefer a German to a Berlin exhibition. Therefore we have made it clear, for both the experts and also for those who will be affected practically, that we are expressing our support not for a Berlin exhibition, but for an exhibition in Berlin.

Thus, they did not conceal their disappointment, and even invoked an unusual legal construction which would allow national and international exhibitors to participate with their own exhibits if they operated a local branch in Berlin, no matter how small or insignificant.[51]

Even after the decision for a local, privately organized trade exhibition was made, public controversy did not end. The planning stages continued to be beset by problems of logistics and location. Again, it was the *Platzfrage* that was most vehemently discussed in the immediate run-up to the exposition. 'The choice of location for the Exposition was difficult', the *Revue de Paris* observed, downplaying the affair.[52] The search for a venue had been narrowed to two sites, one to the west around the Lietzensee lake in Witzleben, and the other to the southeast in Treptower Park. While the western area was identical with the site chosen for the *Verlorene Liebesmüh* project, Treptower Park had also been under discussion for some time, though it was situated outside Berlin's municipal area proper and was distant from its center.

Given Berlin's continual westward expansion and the attendant construction, the *Centralblatt der Bauverwaltung* predicted that a site in the east would have to be selected out of sheer necessity, despite its obvious practical disadvantages. In the end, the journal was convinced, it would only be possible to use public or state-owned property. This ultimately proved correct, although at first the better developed Witzleben site was selected. In the late 1920s, a permanent exhibition center would later be erected there, with the Berlin radio tower, the *Funkturm*, as its central landmark. Yet at this point the terrain was still under private Jewish ownership. A self-proclaimed *Komitee der Aussteller und Interessenten der Berliner Gewerbe-Ausstellung 1896* (Committee of the Exhibitors and Other Interested Parties in the Berlin Trade Exhibition of 1896) quickly formed, objected to this decision, organized a fund-raising campaign with anti-Semitic undertones, and succeeded, with support from the press, in having the decision reversed in favor of the Treptower Park site, despite evident disadvantages, including its 'considerable distance from the centre of the capital', as even *The Times* observed.[53]

On 26 April 1894, the Berlin municipality finally decided to make Treptower Park available at no additional cost, but on the guarantee that it be completely restored to its original condition after the exhibition's closure. While the state confined itself to building a new railroad station close to the exhibition venue, the City of Berlin allocated a guarantee fund and contributed a subsidy of 300,000 marks to cover general costs. Infrastructural changes undertaken for the

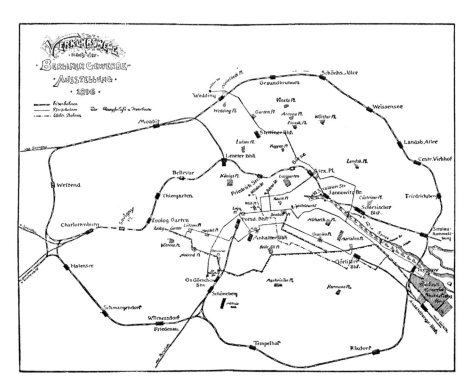

Figure 2.10 The site of the Berliner Gewerbeausstellung in relation to the metropolis. The exposition is located in the bottom right-hand corner of the map, in the southeast of the city, just beyond the Ringbahn
Source: *Illustrierter Amtlicher Führer*, 2–3.

Gewerbeausstellung thus included the new Ausstellungs-Bahnhof (Figure 2.10), which contributed to the extension of Berlin's so-called *Ringbahn*, a tram route surrounding the entire city that first opened in 1872, as well as the widening of pre-existing streets, the creation of six new landing places on the banks of the Spree and a circular electric tram for transport within the venue. Traversing the entire site in only 24 minutes, this direct precursor to the moving sidewalks or *trottoir roulant* featured in the Paris exposition of 1900 would prove especially popular with the exhibition-going public. A so-called *Stufenbahn* was built to transport visitors from one part of the venue to another. In this and other, particularly organizational, aspects, this entirely privately sponsored exposition constituted an exact counter-model to the state-financed Parisian Expositions Universelles – something French commentators could scarcely believe.[54]

Already in the first half of the nineteenth century, Treptower Park, situated on the banks of the Spree, was a popular place for weekend excursions. Between 1876 and 1888 it was redeveloped in the style of an English landscaped garden to become a so-called *Volkspark*, a public municipal park, with numerous trees. Its enormous size, approximately 120 hectares (1.5 × 0.8 km), made it the largest exhibition venue to date, barring the 1893 exposition in Chicago. Since the organizers were contractually obliged to restore the park later to its *status quo ante*, all buildings and pavilions were to be removed and the especially built *Neuer See* (New Lake), a former playground, filled in once the fair had closed. Thus, except for a huge telescope, the Berliner Gewerbeausstellung was restricted from leaving any urban legacy, another indication of its uncertain position within the global exhibitionary network. Nor did it establish a specific Berlin exhibition tradition or generate a *lieu de mémoire* comparable to the London Crystal Palace (1851; 1852–54 re-erected in Sydenham, 1936 burned down), the Viennese Rotunda (1873–1937), the Parisian Champ de Mars with the Eiffel Tower (1889–), the Empire Stadium in Wembley (1923–2000), or the Brussels Atomium (1958–). In fact, if the present-day site has lost little of its symbolic character, this must not be attributed to the trade exhibition but rather to the site's subsequent fate: Here, at exactly the same location, after 1946 one of the largest Soviet war memorials in Germany was constructed for 13,000 fallen soldiers. Its shape follows the former lake's contours, with the central mausoleum-hill of the memorial area, marking the burial place of 200 Red Army soldiers and complete with quotations from Stalin, located where the main restaurant of the trade exhibition had been. Thus, as a site Treptower Park is firmly established as highly symbolic of various – and differently connoted – phases of Berlin's urban history. Just like the exposition itself, it must be read as yet another symbol not only of the 'haunted city' of Berlin but also of its own contested identity, rife with inner conflicts, and as a gesture towards the city's attempts at modernity, in competition with its European counterparts, as well as Berlin's highly politicized urban landscape.[55]

Although construction was not yet complete, the exhibition opened, with the Kaiser and his wife in attendance, on 1 May 1896 with a grand ceremony, another recurrent ritual of all exhibitions. Even the French press could not but express a certain admiration, calling it a 'splendid visual': 'Berlin has maintained its pride', the commentary continued, 'there could be no greater pomp on display to open a universal exposition.' Thereafter, it was to remain open for 165 days, until 15 October 1896, featuring the displays of almost 4000 exhibitors and attracting almost seven and a half million visitors, at a general admission price of 50 pfennige. On average, this translated into 41,000 visitors per day instead of the expected 55,000. Such comparatively meager figures were largely attributed to unfavorable weather conditions as it rained on 120 of these 165 summer days. Nevertheless, a visit soon became a social obligation and the exhibition *the* event of the season, as numerous observers, critics and journalists agreed. Active interest on the part of the Berlin public was evident. Already after the first week, the *Vossische Zeitung* reported that everybody 'simply has to visit the exposition; whoever has not been there, will be regarded as hardly entitled to exist; he cannot join into the conversation at his usual seat in the pub, and he will be looked at critically by his sons and daughters whom he has not yet given the opportunity to see the spectacle in Treptow.'[56]

For mundane organizational matters, a responsible *Arbeitsausschuss* was created, chaired by Fritz Kühnemann with Ludwig Max Goldberger and Bernhard Felisch as vice-chairmen. Together they formed the exhibition's central controlling body – 'a kind of triumvirate', as the *Revue de Paris* commented – supported by a large *Geschäftsführender Ausschuss* (executive committee) consisting of numerous local dignitaries. With the Kaiser's consent, Prinz Friedrich Leopold von Preußen took over the general patronage, while the politician Hans Hermann Freiherr von Berlepsch (1843–1926), at that time Prussian minister of commerce, became the exhibition's honorary president. The predominant architects were →Karl Hoffacker, →Hans Grisebach and →Bruno Schmitz. Both Hoffacker and Grisebach had designed parts of the German section at the world's fair held in Chicago three years earlier, and were thus considered experienced experts for this particular type of ephemeral architecture.[57]

The *status quo ante* clause in the contract constituted a major difficulty for landscape architects and garden designers. 'Although the site is highly attractive because of its proximity to the Spree and its fine park, considerable difficulties concerning the buildings necessary for the exhibition have arisen', the official *Centralblatt der Bauverwaltung* stated. For this reason, the proposed schedule had to be altered several times. A planned north–south axis was never realized. Eventually, the site's geographical limitations came to dominate its architectural development, rather than vice versa. 'So, here, the basic plan was based on the park's design, quite in contrast to the usual procedure of initially developing the architectural project, which in this case had to be adapted to a massive, yet flowing intake of visitors, and thus giving a first idea of the general effect, and then adding the garden grounds to round off and enhance the created image', commented the *Berliner Tageblatt* with apparent astonishment.[58]

In the end, the most important buildings and sections were lined up along a west–east axis, leading from the main building to the *Neuer See* as the site's central pivotal point, and the main restaurant together with a water tower on its other side, and continuing to the 'Theater Alt-Berlin' (Old Berlin Theater) and the retrospective section *Alt-Berlin* (see Plate 1). Some additional buildings, such as a palace for chemistry and optics and another for fishery and foodstuffs were located further north. The City of Berlin occupied its own pavilion, located beyond Treptower Chaussee, just behind the chemistry building, with recently opened public buildings such as swimming pools and hospitals, as well as school programs and a wide array of administrative activities presented to the interested public in the form of models, diagrams, photographs, maps and illustrations. All told, some 300 smaller structures and pavilions were erected on the site (Figure 2.11).[59] There were, additionally, three feature sections which did not form part of the main grounds but were each set apart by a street: a huge colonial exhibition in the east (10 ha), an adjacent amusement park featuring an automatically functioning restaurant, and a privately run *Sonderausstellung Kairo* (Special Exhibition Cairo; 3.4 ha). Thus, further to the east and the south, the educational mission gave way to entertainment and exoticism. The entire site was enclosed by a tall wooden fence, separating it visibly and unmistakably from the surrounding city.[60]

The so-called *Hauptgebäude* (Main Building) formed the nucleus of the architectural composition and housed the main exhibits. In this respect, the Gewerbeausstellung was clearly not in accordance with the latest developments in international exhibition design. While all early expositions, starting in 1851, had been characterized by the attempt to present all exhibits in one building – thus subjecting them to a single unifying scheme of classification – by the mid-1870s, this encyclopedic mode of representation had been replaced by a national principle. After similar experiments at the Parisian Exposition Universelle of 1867, with national pavilions serving as the headquarters of the foreign participants, and at the London International Exhibition five years later, it was decided for the first time at the Philadelphia exhibition of 1876 to allow participating nations to each erect their own separate pavilion in lieu of a huge, common palace. Two years later, in 1878, this 'pavilion principle' or 'pavilion system' was successfully adopted in Paris, resulting in the construction of the so-called *Rue des Nations*, which, by 1900, not only formed an integral part of subsequent expositions, but was also one of their main attractions. This characteristic feature could not be implemented in Berlin for the simple reason that no foreign nation participated.

Although the criticism was often made that the huge *Hauptgebäude* (400 × 200 m) had its back turned to the city center and opened up towards the east rather than the west, local conditions did not allow for any other solution, with this the only site within Treptower Park both spacious enough and free of trees. There was also much consternation that no such grand effect, comparable to the Champ de Mars in Paris, had been achieved. Professional journals, however, considered its unifying purpose and centripetal function fulfilled, lauding it as the fair's *pièce de résistance* and focal point of the entire Berlin exposition, producing 'a unanimous voice of great and unlimited praise'. The *Deutsche Bauzeitung* seemed likewise content with the site's general layout. 'We may consider the exposition with justifiable pride. It has become a shining example of excellent planning and considerable persistence', one of the critics noted laudatorily a few days before the actual opening. If the Berliner

Figure 2.11 Panorama of the Berliner Gewerbeausstellung from a bird's-eye view
Source: Lindenberg, *Pracht-Album*, 8–9.

Gewerbeausstellung did have a feature which could be considered its *clou*, it was undoubtedly this *Hauptgebäude*, 'the focal point of the whole', as the official guide put it – which itself could also be seen as another attempt on the part of the organizers to engage in an international and inter-urban competition by engaging self-ascribed forms of modernity, which had long found other forms of expression elsewhere.[61]

Tellingly, however, there were still a number of literally inbuilt references to previously held international expositions. The semicircular shape of the building's main entrance, for instance, reminded numerous visitors and foreign observers of the Parisian Trocadéro Palace, erected for the 1878 Exposition Universelle, while in other parts of the building large structural elements of one of the halls built for the Exposition International d'Anvers of 1894 had been recycled. Transnational imports and direct references were not limited to the physical components of buildings: entire sections were modeled after successful foreign examples, such as the *Sonderausstellung Kairo*.[62]

Two additional themes were featured in the exposition's general conception: 'labor' and 'water'. Since the first constituted one of the central notions of any *bürgerlich* sense of self-understanding, the entrance to the main building was decorated with a verse from Friedrich Schiller's ballad *Die Glocke*, 'Arbeit ist des Bürgers Zierde/Segen ist der Mühe Preis!' (Labour is the citizen's adornment/blessings are the reward for all his efforts). Critics found apt architectural expression of the celebration of labor in the main building, deeming its cupola hall so impressive that it could even compete with the Parisian *Dôme central* built for the Exposition Universelle of 1889. Similarly, on the occasion of the exhibition's extravagant opening ceremony, the *Vossische Zeitung* predicted its success by calling it one of the finest results of German labor and diligence: 'The trade exhibition in Berlin will win a place of honor in the history of German labor, German diligence.'[63]

'Water', the second theme, was expressed not only in the inclusion of the Spree, the construction of various ponds and artificial lakes, the incorporation of the pre-existing *Karpfenteich* (carp pond), a pavilion exclusively devoted to fishing, but above all in naval shows. A gigantic, 88-meter long replica of an imperial steamship reaching into the Spree, the *Kaiserschiff Bremen*, which also contained the Kaiser's private room for when he visited the exhibition. 'One of the special features of our Berlin exhibition', one commentator noted, 'is that it has such an outstandingly maritime character.' In a similar vein, the *Karpfenteich* was used for spectacular performances by the exhibited colonial 'natives'. Yet again, behind this special and intentional emphasis on water there was also a reference to another earlier international exposition, the World's Columbian Exposition of 1893, where Chicago's Lake Michigan had been incorporated into the exposition venue in a comparable manner.[64]

Pleasures of the metropolis

All three feature sections – the colonial exhibition, *Kairo*, and *Alt-Berlin* – were concentrated in the southeastern part of the Treptower Park venue, with the first two spatially secluded from the exposition's main venue by pre-existing streets.

All three, including the amusement park and the *Alpen-Panorama*, were privately organized enterprises and constituted almost self-contained smaller exhibitions in themselves. Yet, while each functioned according to its own principles and stood in its own specific trans- and international exposition tradition, they also formed part of the main exhibition complex, and were hence all perceived and discussed in the same context.

If the trade exhibition as a whole was a privately organized enterprise, realized without official state support, the *Kolonialausstellung* was again independent.[65] Originally suggested by a number of export companies, its prehistory was equally complex and characterized by various, largely organizational, conflicts including financial difficulties. The composition of the organizing body changed several times. Semi-official representative institutions such as the *Deutsche Kolonialgesellschaft*, an influential lobby group founded in 1887, remained reluctant in their support at first until eventually deciding to endorse the project.[66] However, and somewhat ironically, the government eventually chose to play a more active role only in the colonial section, with the Foreign Office defraying at least a part of the expense, because of the obvious possibility to instrumentalize the section for political and propagandistic purposes. The *Kolonialausstellung*'s special status was further underlined by the fact that it formed its own section in the otherwise rigid classification system of 23 groups and numerous subgroups, strictly applied to all other exhibits on display in the entire exposition. As a consequence, an *Arbeitsausschuss* had been formed in February 1895 with →Hans Hermann Graf von Schweinitz as chairman, and industrialist Karl Friedrich Emil von Beck and lawyer Franz Imberg as vice-chairmen to serve as the section's own organizing committee and central controlling body. The noted German imperialist and long-term editor of the *Deutsche Kolonialzeitung*, →Gustav Meinecke, was persuaded to author a popular guide to this particular section and afterwards to edit the voluminous official report. Additionally, the colonial exhibition allowed companies *not* based in Berlin to participate, and had its own patron, Herzog Johann Albrecht zu Mecklenburg-Schwerin (1859–1920), one of the presidents of the *Kolonialgesellschaft*.

In order to gain public support and to achieve as wide a participation as possible, the committee made an appeal in May 1895 in a number of different newspapers, hoping to stimulate participation by colonial departments, interested industrial circles, the authorities, representatives of the sciences and the large number of experts on Africa and thus 'to awaken interest even in the most remote circles of society'.[67] Given that Germany had acquired its first colony only 12 years earlier, the *Kolonialausstellung*'s official aims were threefold: first, to reduce public ignorance about the colonial cause; second, to appease and convince its political critics; and third, to document Germany's imperial efforts and global ambitions. Colonization was legitimized not as a *mission civilisatrice*, but rather as a domestic, national and cultural duty of considerable significance for the future of the home country and its position in the global order. 'The nations in Europe who are major powers [...] are also colonial powers' served as the legitimizing slogan.[68]

The colonial exhibition was divided into two separate sections: an ethnological section, located south of the carp pond and *Alt-Berlin* that included a number of

Figure 2.12 Layout of the colonial exhibition that formed part of the Berliner Gewerbeausstellung. Situated at the southeastern ends of the exposition grounds, it adjoined *Alt-Berlin* and the amusement park
Source: Arbeitsausschuss der Deutschen Kolonial-Ausstellung, *Deutschland und seine Kolonien*, 369.

so-called native villages representing the diverse German overseas possessions, and, further east, beyond Parkstraße, a second, more science- and commerce-oriented section featuring more than 300 different companies and associations (Figure 2.12). The latter – the more 'serious' but 'actually less interesting' section, as one observer commented – contained six huge halls, including the so-called *Kolonialhalle*, a machinery hall, as well as a two-storied, wooden *Tropenhaus*, in which the Foreign Ministry's colonial department displayed its various activities at home and abroad through diagrams, photographs and numerous sample products from the colonies. At its center stood an enormous globe, two meters in diameter, representing all the widely distributed German possessions. After the exhibition's closure, the entire pavilion was to be re-erected in Togo, a German colony since 1884.[69]

Thus, the section's overall structure was literally a dichotomy: on the western side displays of the timeless, 'original' state of the colonies; on the eastern side, exhibits of the various instruments and institutions founded and maintained by western powers, in particular Germany, with the aim of intervening, altering and eventually 'improving' the colonies' 'untouched' nature. 'It should not be overlooked that the natives still live in the Stone Age', the official report reminded its readers. While the more serious section was, ironically, located next to the amusement park, the 'native houses' bordered directly on *Alt-Berlin*. Contemporaries noted this physical proximity and instantly recognized an imagined historical connection. 'It is a very strange coincidence that the colonial exhibition is located in the immediate neighborhood of "Old Berlin", considering that the Grand Prince-elector had already created a significant Brandenburg colonial possession in Africa', a critic noted.[70]

With a total of more than two million visitors, each of whom paid an additional admission fee of 50 pfennige (later reduced to 30), including 26,587 schoolchildren who entered for free, the *Kolonialausstellung* proved one of the most popular sections of the exposition. On 13 September 1896, for instance, this part of the

Gewerbeausstellung was seen by 120,362 visitors alone; only 9000 of the total number of visitors on that particular day decided *not* to include it in their grand tour of the exhibition grounds. Such overwhelming interest on the part of the fair-going public was directly attributed to the numerous 'natives' on display. For many, it was their first chance ever to encounter non-Europeans. 'The natives themselves awakened, of course, the greatest interest among the visitors', the official report noted retrospectively with a certain satisfaction about an initially contested decision, 'for the "savage" had never before been so tangibly brought to the public's attention.'[71]

Sources disagree as to the exact number of indigenous people imported from locales ranging from Cameroon (a German possession since 1884), to Togo (since 1884), to New Guinea and East Africa (since 1885). Between 60 and 100 persons were put on display over the course of the five and a half months.[72] While all were required to live and work on the premises, often in self-built huts, some of them also found accommodation in a reproduction of the *Quikuru*, an East African fortress modeled after the *Quikuru qua Sike*, which German colonial troops had conquered during an uprising in June and August 1892 under the command of Graf von Schweinitz, now chairing the organizing committee. Their exhibitionary function was obvious: to provide the ensemble with a degree of authenticity otherwise unattainable. 'It was the intention', a journalist explained, 'to present the visitor of the colonial exhibition with a number of settlements *in natura*, which are characteristic of our main colonial territories, and to inhabit these settlements with human material from the colonies themselves.'[73] Even Wilhelm II appeared impressed by the special performances with which the exhibited indigenous people welcomed him and his wife on the opening day, and they spent considerable time in the colonial exhibition during their visit. 'In the "Quikuru" East Africans performed war dances, which the spectators watched with interest for quite a long time', a report described the scene: 'Then followed the rowing contests on the carp pond. Togo negroes were also given the opportunity to show their war dance, while the Cameroonians welcomed their Emperor with a loud threefold "Hip, hip, hip, Hurrah!".' Curiously, despite his continuous opposition to any kind of German international exposition, Wilhelm II did not have any difficulty in officially participating in this and other events organized as part of the Gewerbeausstellung, presumably because it augmented his own visibility and contributed to his public image.[74]

While a considerable number of smaller colonial exhibitions had been held in Germany before, none was as large and comprehensive as this, the officially entitled *1. Deutsche Kolonialausstellung.* 'With this image of the tropical colonies', it was noted, evoking a clear contrast between the savage purity on display and the surrounding metropolis with its modern civilized life, 'the natives infused this picture with a vivid colorful life. They transferred an element of natural wildness and simple culture to the heart of the world city with its refined manners, fashionable people and proud splendor. Precisely such contrasts, for the first time presented so clearly in such a relatively small framework, made the exhibition so fascinating and attractive for everybody.'[75] While such inanimate exotic exhibits had been a main characteristic of all European expositions since 1851, a decisive shift in both quantity and quality could be observed in the 1880s. Before the first distinct 'native villages' (*village indigène*) were annexed to the Parisian exposition of 1878 and the 1886 Colonial and Indian Exhibition in London, these *Völkerschauen*, that is short-lived, commercially oriented and privately organized touring exhibitions featuring 'exotic human beings', had been held on a regular basis in almost all European countries from the 1860s onwards. The first German *Völkerschau* took place in 1874. Soon, the displaying of 'natives' from a wide range of colonized cultures became a standard feature of the evolving exhibitionary networks.[76] 'I wish to emphasize especially', a German journalist wrote in 1896, reminding his readers of the existence of similar ensembles staged elsewhere across the world, 'that such exhibitions have often been held in such an exemplary way and have thus lost their novelty. This includes the world exhibition in Antwerp in the year 1885, the colonial exhibition in London [1886], the world's fairs in Chicago [1893] and Melbourne [1888–89] and various other exhibitions', thus highlighting the clear, if somewhat obscure situatedness of the *Kolonialausstellung* in the international exhibitionary network and its inherent reference system, of which average German consumers were largely ignorant. From a contemporary functionalist perspective, exhibited 'natives' were put on par with visiting royals, as both attracted the desired throngs of spectators. 'This type of attraction has long been an essential element of modern exhibitions', another commentator noted laconically, 'crowned heads or distinguished foreigners from exotic and fabulous countries attract the masses.'[77]

For more than half a century both *Völkerschauen* and ethnographic ensembles as part of international expositions were inextricably linked to the career of the Hamburg-based animal trader, entrepreneur, impresario and zoo founder →Carl Hagenbeck.[78] From the early 1870s onwards his company gradually established itself as the uncontested market leader in the trading of exotic animals, remaining so for some decades. This position allowed Hagenbeck to develop a plethora of other activities meant to complete the range of products his firm offered and which included importing 'exotic' people from overseas for exhibition purposes. While *Völkerschauen* were periodically held in all big cities in Germany up to 1932, similar events were found elsewhere – in France, for example – until the early 1940s.[79] Often, entire ensembles of exotic representatives were put together, sometimes even several times a year, and sent on carefully organized tours throughout Europe and even beyond. Thus, in one of the earliest of these groups, organized by Hagenbeck himself, 15 Nubians from Egyptian Sudan performed in 1877–78 in Hamburg, Berlin, Frankfurt, Dresden and London. Later tours would include both more participants and more diverse countries of origin. Although such a statement cannot be verified, the organizers of the 1896 trade fair repeatedly congratulated themselves for having assembled the largest and most comprehensive German colonial exhibition to date. According to them, never before had so many 'natives' of so many different origins lived for such a long time together in Europe. However, a lengthy medical report listing numerous cases of illness gives a bleak impression of how difficult the actual adaptation process was. Two of the exhibited Swahilis died of pneumonia and meningitis respectively, and were buried in a Berlin cemetery.[80]

The organizers considered the inclusion of a colonial section a functional necessity for the entire exposition. The *Kolonialausstellung* was intended to provide the event with a veneer not only of authenticity, but also internationality and cosmopolitanism that would otherwise have been lacking. For that reason, A. Haarmann, president of the chamber of commerce in Osnabrück, had suggested incorporating a colonial ensemble into the as yet unplanned German world exhibition as early as 1892. Given his amalgamation of cultural and political arguments operating on national, international and colonial levels, Haarmann is worth quoting at length:

> What gave the Paris expositions an international and in a sense an exotic flair, were mainly the ethnographic and colonial sections, which afforded an almost unlimited display of exotic sites and pompous processions. If we consider such ingredients an absolute necessity, nothing prevents us from vividly presenting the life, the conditions and the products of the German protectorates, together with the necessary help of our colonialists in foreign countries to give the German national exhibition a touch of internationality. All this should satisfy the public's need for sensation. The inclusion of the German protectorates would additionally afford welcome possibilities to awaken general public interest in our colonial ventures within all levels of our society.[81]

Thus, while the desire to imitate, compete with and outdo Paris was the external incentive for incorporating the colonies, political and propagandistic reasons provided the internal incentive. Moreover, an exclusively colonial section was considered essential if the exposition's merely national scope was to be transcended. The final report fully adopted this argument when stating *ex post*, and not without considerable pride, that 'by including the colonial exhibition the usual framework of a *Berlin* exhibition was considerably exceeded.' Even if the original aim of organizing a German Exposition Universelle had not been achieved, the incorporation of a colonial section ensured that the fair's local and national limitations were transcended.[82]

One of the most unmistakable references the Berliner Gewerbeausstellung made to other nodes within the western exhibitionary networks was the 'Egyptian special exhibition' *Kairo*, modeled directly on the successful Parisian structure, the notorious *Rue du Caire*, an integral and exceedingly popular section of the Parisian Exposition Universelle of 1889 that had claimed to reproduce authentically an entire street of medieval Cairo in the midst of modern Paris. The 1896 Berlin version took the form of a comparable, commercially oriented 'best of' selection of the Egyptian capital's oldest sections, temporarily inhabited by some '500 Egyptians of the various races', and including a 38-meter high replica of the Cheops pyramid (Figure 2.13) as its supreme feature. Although enlarged, diversified and conceptually altered in comparison with the French original, 'Kairo in Berlin' derived its basic forms and representational principles from the Parisian prototype.[83]

Kairo, 'this magical creation from the Orient', as it was hailed in the official guide, consisted of four distinct sections devoted to Old Egypt, modern Cairo, a

Figure 2.13 The special exhibition *Kairo* with its towering pyramid from a bird's-eye view and with Berlin just visible in the background. The elongated building on the left is the railroad station built for the exposition
Source: Courtesy of Landesarchiv Berlin, F Rep. 290-09-01, Nr. 61/5348.

town square, and a huge arena for enacting scenic spectacles such as camel and horse shows, in addition to a number of 'native villages' and settlements inhabited by several hundred indigenous Arabs and Bedouins complete with a harem, a hotel, two restaurants and various souvenir shops. The putative authenticity of such vistas was reinforced by the numerous dioramas incorporated into *Kairo*. The organizers sought not only to recreate the essential features of the entire cityscape, but also to 'transplant the pulsating life of Cairo' into imperial Berlin. While the first three sections adopted a topographical approach, the last was ethnographic in character. Thus, though its representations were based on the same kind of domesticated alterity and exoticism as in the colonial sections, here this was accomplished in a much more contextualized and historicized manner. The basic question of whether such a genuinely French import could make sense in a German national environment remained, yet the conceptual *mélange* went still further. As a French journalist discovered when investigating the personal background of *Kairo*'s Arabic inhabitants, they were far less 'authentic' than assumed, coming from Damascus and speaking, to his astonishment, the 'purest French' which they had studied in Beirut, and were now learning English.[84]

Quite aptly, the section's special feature, the pyramid, was only half erected, allowing the visual illusion of its wholeness to be solely perceived from the perspective of the exhibition grounds, a veritable *trompe l'œil*. Functioning only from within the venue, it was essential that the visitor-cum-viewer adopt the correct position if this vista was to be perceived at all and the illusion maintained. Made entirely of painted cement rather than solid rock and held together by an iron framework, the pyramid was hollow, containing a burial chamber complete with two mummies. This Potemkin village fulfilled four distinct functions: First, the pyramid contributed to the entire section's overall 'reality effect' (Roland Barthes), burnishing its veneer of authenticity. Second, it offered a background illustration for the spectacles enacted daily in the arena directly in front. Third, it served as an unusual – though functional – exposition building, providing space to display some of the items most commonly associated with ancient Egypt. Finally, since its visitors could use an electric elevator in order to reach the top, the pyramid offered an unusually spectacular, panoramic view over site and city alike, thus offering a literal overview of both. 'The Pyramid', the official guidebook described, 'can be climbed by an electric lift, and seen from its height one has an fascinating overview of Berlin as well as the entire Treptower Park with its exhibitions halls.'[85]

Although a private enterprise, the assembling of *Kairo* was actively supported by the Egyptian government, both materially and financially. The official guide vacillated between describing the section and Egypt itself, effectively blurring the boundaries between the two. It suggested following a fixed itinerary through the grounds, using replicas of various historic gates, temples, graves and sculptures all reproduced at half their actual size as an opportunity for learning about Egyptian history and geography. The program offered both a virtual tour down the Nile, 'with all its remarkable features and splendid remnants of a remote past', as well as a written introduction to contemporaneous Arabic society and culture. This little guidebook, an amalgamation of distinct topics, historical and present, domestic and distant, culminated in the inclusion of a German–Arabic dictionary at its end, thus completing the blend of subject matter and *in situ* tourism. *Nolens volens*, the guide transformed the more than two million visitors into potential travelers in both space and time. In order to survive, visitors were encouraged to acquire at least a basic knowledge of Arabic.[86]

Professional critics were only too aware that sections of this kind had formed integral parts of previous expositions, and they mockingly criticized such *Ideenarmuth* (lack of originality). Yet, when limited to a German context, *Kairo's* openly orientalist style and its contribution to the exposition seemed both original and appropriate, eliciting, therefore, much praise from other critics: '[Bruno] Schmitz has [...] produced the tone of the foreign, fairy-tale elements typical of such short-lived phenomena and which, in its singularity, has an exceptional impact on our senses; it is not by chance that "Kairo" is an essential accessory of our exhibitions.'[87] Prominent visitors such as the liberal politician →Friedrich Naumann agreed. He deemed *Kairo* especially successful, describing the escapist experience of entering into an utterly different culture and remote world in itself. 'Under the pyramids, in the shadow of palm trees and minarets and the Arabian cry: "Baba, Baksheesh!" ("Sir, please give me a tip!"), we feel we have completely left our familiar cultivated Europe', he wrote after a visit. Likewise, the German engineer and writer →Max Eyth seemed pleased by what he saw. Reflecting his divergent impressions after a visit to Treptow, Eyth noted in his diary on 10 July

1896: 'Exhibition. Alpine meadow. Colonial exhibition. Sea battle. – "Kairo" quite good, as a picture. Somewhat overloaded, of course, but in many ways perfectly "true to style".'[88]

The fact that this particular means of expression originated elsewhere by no means hindered the section's success in a different national, cultural and social context in which it appeared new and innovative. Despite its success, however, behind the scenes not all ran smoothly, thus disrupting the colonial order so carefully staged and enacted. In fact, none of the professional observers even hinted at the massive problems that arose with the indigenous population and allegedly 'refractory staff', resulting in a number of fistfights and leading to violent conflicts, in which the excessive consumption of alcohol seems to have played a decisive role. Having become homeless after their dismissal, these 'brown sons of the desert' applied for temporary political asylum, intending nevertheless to return to their home countries as soon as possible.[89]

'Reminiscent not of foreign countries, but of foreign times', *Alt-Berlin*, the third feature section, marked a dramatic contrast by evoking a domestic past.[90] To integrate retrospective ensembles and to juxtapose them with the slightly older colonial ensembles, was, in 1896, a comparatively recent development. First introduced in London in 1886 and repeated at an exposition held in Manchester the following year, so-called old villages such as *Old London*, *Vieux Paris*, *Vieil Anvers* or *Alt-Berlin* had, by the turn of the century, become a standard inter-exhibitionary feature and an indispensable element. Although politically controversial, the practice enjoyed a certain degree of familiarity and widespread acceptance in the second half of the 1880s: In 1884, the Esposizione Generale Italiana held in Turin included a replica of an entire medieval castle, in 1886 the Colonial and Indian Exhibition in London featured a so-called *Old London Street*, and for the 1889 Parisian Exposition Universelle, a symbolic replica of the entire Bastille was constructed. In the aftermath of these three exhibitions, the 'retrospective principle' was developed and popularized at expositions in Bremen (1890), Antwerp (1894), Amsterdam (1895) and here in Berlin (1896), and subsequently in Brussels (1897), Paris (1900), Liège (1905) as well as London (1908, 1911). While the concept of enticing visitors into a virtual journey in space had been present, implicitly or explicitly, since the mid-nineteenth century beginnings of the exhibition medium, 'traveling in time' as a complementary feature was added only later.[91] Such a development must be seen as further evidence of the increasing process of differentiation of the entire medium and its specific language, in which self-reference became more important than adapting to the particular socio-political context.

In 1896, the ensemble no longer consisted of a small subsection or merely a single street as in Turin or London, but comprised an entire, self-contained small city on an area of approximately 4.5 hectares, erected on the eastern banks of the carp pond and designed by the renowned architect Karl Hoffacker (Figure 2.14). Unlike the colonial section and *Kairo*, 'Old Berlin' formed part of the exhibition's main venue. Its central importance within the overall conceptual framework can also be deduced from the fact that *Alt-Berlin*'s site, including the 'Theater Alt-Berlin', was situated along a direct prolongation of the exposition's central west–east axis and

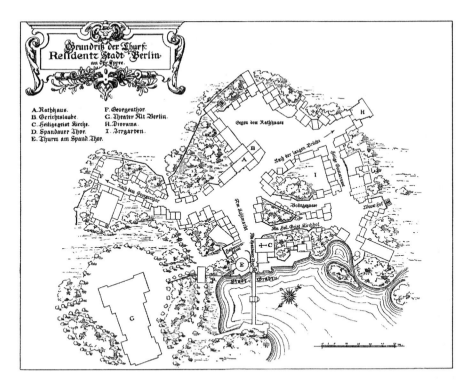

Figure 2.14 Southeast-oriented ground plan of *Alt-Berlin*, located along the exposition's central west–east axis and adjacent to the colonial exhibition
Source: Rapsilber, *Offizieller Führer durch die Spezial-Ausstellung Alt-Berlin*, 88–9.

was, thus, in line with the main building and the new lake. Its function as a contrast was reinforced by its placement directly bordering the colonial exhibition. A retrospective section of this size had not been foreseen in the exhibition's original concept, and was added only later when the fair's overall layout had to be altered because of the limitations placed on the site. When the non-profit making *Verein für die Geschichte Berlins* (Society for the History of Berlin) found it impossible to finance the creation of *Alt-Berlin*, a commercially oriented syndicate was formed, with the Society remaining responsible for the section's 'artistic' management. Additionally, it also provided many of the exhibits and, with the help of its members and their personal collections, organized a historical section of its own.[92]

Alt-Berlin was entirely surrounded by high merlon walls, with only two entrances, and featured numerous historic structures such as two gates, the 'Spandauer Thor' [letter D in Figure 2.14] and the 'Georgenthor' [F], a museum, a chapel 'Zum Heiligen Geiste' [C] containing a special exhibition of more than 200 pieces of Berlin memorabilia, a town hall [A], a massive round tower as its 'true symbol' [E], and a number of restaurants which soon proved both popular and lucrative. The structures, especially the monumental 'Spandauer Thor', were meant to be a historical counterpoint to the fair's modern main building. In addition, there was a huge diorama [H], a historical maze of Dutch origin where 'spectators could turn into actors' [I] as well as the already mentioned theater [G], where scenes from Berlin's urban past were reenacted by more than 500 participants. Altogether, *Alt-Berlin* comprised some 120 structures. According to official numbers, almost 1.8 million tickets for *Alt-Berlin* alone were sold in the course of the six months during which the exhibition was open, making it and the colonial sections the most profitable of the entire exposition.[93]

Despite being an overall success, *Alt-Berlin* was not untouched by conflict. Already in the run-up to the exposition, the *Verein für die Geschichte Berlins* had complained bitterly that commercial interests were taking precedence over accuracy in some of the historical reproductions staged. It was widely criticized that some of the lease-holders had disfigured the historical house-façades with huge 'modern' advertisement posters to increase profits.[94] Although the entire exhibition tried all possible ways of convincingly demonstrating Berlin's self-perceived modernity as a newly established world city and to position itself in a Europe-wide framework, such modernity swiftly proved very unwelcome when it appeared in unsuitable places and without the approval of the authorities. *Alt-Berlin* functioned on a time- rather than a space-related mode of representation. The second half of the seventeenth century, roughly from the 1650s onwards, had been selected as the broad historical reference point to which, in one way or another, all historical reproductions and re-enactments had to relate – the time of the end of the Thirty Years' War and the legendary *Großer Kurfürst* (Grand Prince-elector) of Prussia, and before Berlin's transformation into a fortress. In flowery language that echoed the section's historicity, an architectural journal explained why this period in particular had been chosen:

> Gates, circular walls and fortified towers, winding streets and lanes, the market with the town hall and courthouse, the Dutch windmill, all the cozy picturesque houses and cottages of the Berlin patricians and farmers, with their oriel windows and little towers, weather vanes, their flights of steps and little, almost hidden summerhouses, all these have reappeared, leading us back to times when the life of our ancestors passed tranquilly. Yet, the same times contained the seeds of the great prosperity which this modest, medieval little town was to achieve in the course of the centuries.[95]

Perceived as a historical watershed, the mid-seventeenth century allowed for sufficient distance in time to evoke a sense of unfamiliarity, yet was not too remote to have no direct historical connection and hence relevance.

Alt-Berlin's concept was for visitors to enter a time warp from the moment they set foot on the site, and from there to undertake a journey through time (Figure 2.15). For this reason, its over 500 employees were obliged to wear historical costumes. 'Every day', an announcement read, 'between 1 and 11 o'clock, there will alternately be choirs and music, parades and tournaments to entertain the spectators so that they really feel transported back into the seventeenth century', and the official guide

Figure 2.15   View of the 'Spandauer Thor', the architectural *clou* of *Alt-Berlin*
Source: Courtesy of Landesarchiv Berlin, F Rep. 290-09-01, Nr. 61/5325.

spoke likewise of 'an utterly different world' and 'times long past' into which one would feel transported.[96] Professional observers agreed, going so far as to call this multiple contrast (past vs. present/here vs. there) the central aim of the entire section: 'Artistically and artificially, its main effect is to take the visitor back in time, in which in contrast to today, the life of the individual flowed like a tranquil stream whose murmuring was hardly audible to the neighbors and seldom broke its banks. Today, all this is quite different, and Old Berlin will make its visitors aware of such contrasts.'[97] The explicit and deliberately chronotopic character was more than evident. Yet there was an additional, escapist motive besides the intrinsic lure of the past: *Alt-Berlin* seemed to allow the visitor to flee from the 'sober realism of today' (*das Nüchterne der Jetztzeit*) into a more glamorous and less troubled past.[98]

The reception was mixed, and the opinions expressed by no means homogenous. A number of German observers lauded *Alt-Berlin* precisely for this past-oriented, chronotopic character and extolled its authenticity. 'It is very satisfying', the architect and expositionist →Franz Jaffé commented in the *Berliner Neueste Nachrichten*, 'to meet a more or less exact description of Berlin at that time [...]. Living in this modern monster, Berliners rarely find occasion to think back to their forebears', thus evoking a contrast to the surrounding metropolis and its garish modernity. Another observer also noted with appreciation, that 'when strolling through these very dignified streets, one is forced into a historical

[handwritten: German critics generally positive. Foreign critics w/ more perspective more negative]

frame of mind', almost literally echoing the official guide's instructions.[99] Other, mostly foreign, critics however, better informed about recent developments in international expositions, proved less benevolent and altogether more disapproving. Referencing similar retrospective ensembles in different European cities and thus accentuating *Alt-Berlin*'s lack of conceptual originality, a French journal, for example, showed little enthusiasm. It also criticized the apparently arbitrary way in which the organizers had chosen objects and exhibits for the different displays:

> Since the success a few years ago in Turin of a Middle Ages village, and in Paris in 1889 of the 'Bastille and Rue Saint-Antoine', every exposition thinks it should offer its visitors something analogous. 'Old Anvers' provided the charm of the Belgian exposition in 1894; Prague in 1895, and Cardiff and Rouen right now are endeavoring in their local exhibitions to flatter the public taste for this kind of resurrection of the past – and Berlin has followed these examples. But 'Old Berlin' is much less successful. [...] The reconstructions of 'Old Berlin' and of 'Cairo' are adaptations or imitations of what has been done elsewhere.[100]

What seemed innovative and effective within a local or national setting, proved much less so when seen in a larger, transnational context, even if this particular feature had been further developed in Berlin. Thus, *Alt-Berlin* contributed, though unintentionally, to the medium's historical process of differentiation in general.

Wilhelm II versus Georg Simmel

As is the case with every exposition, the Berliner Gewerbeausstellung's reception, or rather its consumption, is difficult to ascertain. There were (and still are) as many ways of reading an exhibition, both historically and today, as were presented in its numerous sections and subsections, buildings and exhibits, both official and unofficial. There can be no doubt, however, that it left a deep and lasting impression on the Berlin public which had never experienced anything so spectacular. The number of letters and postcards – themselves 'tangible reflections of an ephemeral past' – sent from the venue may serve as a valuable indicator of the mega-event's popularity: According to official calculations, almost one-quarter of the 7.4 million visitors wrote altogether more than two million letters and, most often, sent picture postcards directly from the venue itself, for the purpose of which 200 different varieties were issued and 20 special letter boxes installed in the grounds.[101] The historian can only speculate about the innumerable messages and greetings, opinions, observations and comments originating from, expressed about and communicated through the Berliner Gewerbeausstellung.

But there is further evidence for its absolute, if transitory, socio-cultural centrality during the summer of 1896. The influential journalist, drama critic and raconteur →Alfred Kerr, for instance, reported extensively on the Gewerbeausstellung in his letters regularly published in the *Breslauer Zeitung*.[102] Apart from numerous acute observations, his letters convey a sense of the enormous excitement the exposition caused within Berlin upper-class circles well before, throughout, and even after the grand event. In the summer of 1896, the Gewerbeausstellung was clearly *the* talk of the town: 'At present, everything seems to revolve around the exhibition', Kerr diagnosed, 'all Berlin is under the spell of one idea and one destination: Treptow. The exhibition attracts visitors [...] as if by magic. With every visit, one discovers new sections where one is quite content to linger.' Public opinion seems to have overlapped to a considerable degree. It is remarkable, though, the extent to which all this was carefully orchestrated and arranged by the Ausstellung's official Pressbureau and Propaganda-Bureau, created exclusively for the purpose of orchestrating public opinion. 'There has never been so large a local exhibition nor, in its contents, one so significant as the Berlin Trade Exhibition of 1896', Goldberger himself concluded after the fair's closure in October 1896, and continued: 'It is indeed considered one of the major world exhibitions and really deserves this somewhat extravagant claim. The world press has reported enthusiastically on the marvels to be seen in Treptower Park, and even less enthusiastic critics had to admit that here one encountered a place of great import.' A collection of official press releases, now housed in the Staatsbibliothek zu Berlin and consisting of pre-written articles, ready for print, which the Pressbureau placed at the disposal of various newspapers, raises far-reaching questions about the authorship of the material traditionally used to analyze patterns and processes of reception and appropriation. The widespread usage of such pre-formulated material by editors and journalists may help to explain the significant overlap of 'official' and publicized opinions, and the relative absence of critical coverage in the media.[103]

Yet, even if criticism was thus muted, some critical analysis did emerge. Given the enormous repercussions of this local mega-event, it is unsurprising that sociologist Georg Simmel published his seminal article on the Berlin trade exhibition in *Die Zeit*, a weekly Viennese newspaper. This brief and little-known essay represents, in its lucidity and conciseness, one of the best analyses of any exposition. Whereas the text's theoretical qualities and conceptual statements relevant to other exhibitions were discussed in the introduction, here Simmel's argument about the Berliner Gewerbeausstellung, and the specific role he ascribed to its host city, is relevant.[104]

In Simmel's complex analysis, the Berliner Gewerbeausstellung served as a prototype laboratory of modernity, an experimental theater and testing-ground for Berlin's new position as a world city, a genuine metropolis. Among the seven theoretical and one historical argument Simmel advanced concerning the role, function and importance of expositions in modernity, two specifically apply to the Berlin fair. Though Simmel's other six arguments relate to different expositions, it is noteworthy that he developed these generic arguments in response to the Gewerbeausstellung, a largely national trade exhibition, which he nevertheless discussed as if it were a world exhibition proper, without differentiating between a universal and a purely local exposition.[105] In Simmel's analysis, the inherently paradoxical character of the Berlin event is revealed only in his conclusion. Having argued that each world exhibition created a 'momentary center of world civilization' where the intrinsic 'shop-window quality of things' is exposed – and which thus *nolens volens* elevates the surrounding city to an actual world city – Simmel raised doubts as to Berlin's status vis-à-vis other West European capitals. Could the *Reichshauptstadt* really compete with metropolises such as Vienna, London and, above all, Paris? Simmel categorically rejected such a possibility. In spite of its unprecedented urban growth and the promise of the exposition itself, Berlin could never equal Paris, nor keep pace with the international standards set there. The German capital had undoubtedly been transformed into a world city, yet not on the Parisian scale. Simmel did not resolve the question of the exposition's complex success or failure so doggedly discussed by most other observers. Rather, he projected the problem into the future when the exhibition's aesthetic impulses would, hopefully, have had sustained effects on the exhibiting city. In quite an unexpected way then, Wilhelm II's and Georg Simmel's respective assessments were similar. Both ascribed a largely uncontrollable but fundamentally globalizing potential to the exposition medium. However, while Wilhelm II feared the globalization of vice, Simmel cordially welcomed the arrival and spread of that type of visualized consumer culture, cosmopolitanism and condensed urban spaces that were, for him, linked inextricably with modernity.[106]

Simmel's powerful interpretation and brilliant analysis was confirmed by other less eloquent but equally prominent critics who argued along similar lines, using city and nation, consumption and cosmopolitanism as interpretative tools and argumentative elements to contextualize and thus to make sense of what they perceived at the Treptow site. One observer, for example, felt overwhelmed by his sublime experience, describing an imaginary sun rising from the Treptow venue, stretching its beneficial rays all over both Berlin and his beloved German *Heimat*. 'I saw', he commemorated raptly, 'all these proud buildings, with thousands and thousands of visitors from every corner of the world, I saw how they were all filled with admiration and quite happy to take out their purses to buy as many of the splendid treasures on offer as possible, and I had the feeling that this exhibition radiated a glow that warmed all Berlin, and in fact, spread over all our German fatherland.'[107]

Other prominent critics – all of whom have already appeared in the course of this chapter – included Julius Lessing, Franz Jaffé, Friedrich Naumann, and Franz Reuleaux. The first, museum director Julius Lessing, for instance, drew a careful distinction between the huge success of the exhibition in the eyes of the normal fair-going public, and the doubts he, as a serious critic, expressed, especially concerning the seemingly haphazard and unrepresentative choice of exhibits. Mediocrity was the inevitable consequence: 'Everywhere mediocrity abounds, [...] pettiness dominates', Lessing lamented. That the Gewerbeausstellung had achieved the popular success it clearly did, could not, he felt, be attributed to its creative, conceptual originality or the superior quality of its displays, but rather reflected the overwhelming demand for spectacle on the part of the Berlin public. The exposition succeeded to such an extent because the metropolis had for many years been longing for this type of event.[108]

Another prominent commentator, Friedrich Naumann, regularly reported from the exhibition venue for a self-edited journal entitled *Die Hilfe*, just as Franz Reuleaux had done for the *National-Zeitung* 30 years earlier. Fully aware of the exhibition's representational significance, he did not deem it trifling or ineffectual, in fact quite the reverse. Rather than 'the world itself', Naumann pleaded for the Gewerbeausstellung to be read as a 'shop-window of the industrial world' – thus choosing the same terminology as Simmel – where nothing less than a substantial 'part of the future' would be decided. Since 'all historical times, landscapes and types of business' had been assembled and condensed here in a clearly delimited and well-defined site, nowhere else could one gain such profound insights into 'modern labor'. The role of the visitors and spectators grew from the encompassing and comprehensive character of this carefully staged and consciously enacted scenario, he suggested, proclaiming: 'The prime task of the visitor is to see! Here you have to drink with your eyes.' While many of his unsystematic and often detail-oriented observations remained impressionistic, Naumann still aimed to comprehend the exposition in its totality and to analyze its meaning for and within a wider social context. Asked whether the Berlin trade exhibition had appealed to him, Naumann pithily responded, 'generally speaking, yes', but then continued more critically, challenging the question's legitimacy, and highlighting instead the exhibition's character as both commerce- and consumption-oriented:

> Basically, the question whether the exhibition has given pleasure either to me or anybody else, is quite insignificant. What does it matter whether I enjoyed it or not? An exhibition is not like a Sunday boat trip which has no other aim than simply to entertain. The exhibition intends to be business on a grand scale and must be judged as such.

Consequently, Naumann made it clear that he wanted the exhibition to be understood principally in its effects on the world economy and hence in a global, capitalistic context, declaring it a 'parade of capitalistic production'.[109]

Considering the event from a broader, albeit somewhat condescending perspective, foreign correspondents generally remained more reserved. Having covered the various turns of the *Weltausstellungsfrage* in great detail, *The Times* of London limited its reporting to two largely favorable articles, while the *New York Times* deemed the Gewerbeausstellung 'not an impressive fair'. According to the already mentioned anonymous and surprisingly well-informed French critic, the exposition could have succeeded as it did only within a German environment; in an international context it had little unusual to offer. It was only because the inhabitants of Berlin were not used to better projects – more elaborate, far grander – that they could enjoy themselves here so well. Thus, a critical view of the general provinciality of the German metropolis was transferred to the subjective realm of its visitors' experience. Cut off from the outside world, their pleasure and amusement was seen as final proof of the city's insurmountable belatedness and lack of sophistication. 'In truth, Berlin has a certain prestige in the rest of Germany', the critic explained. 'So possibly the Industrial Exhibition of Berlin is drawing Germans, but this is not absolutely certain. It is unlikely to attract foreigners. Berlin is not a city of pleasure.' 'Berlin is a large, populous and thriving city, and, if not beautiful, at any rate massive enough to deserve the name of a *Großstadt*', *The Times* agreed, 'but it still lacks that indescribable something which would entitle it, in company with London, Paris, and some other capitals, to recognition as a *Weltstadt*.'[110] If international expositions derived a large part of their representational quality and appeal not only from the intrinsic temporal tension between transience and permanence, but also from the constantly varying interplay between different spatial-geographical – global, national and local – constituents, the decision for an exhibition limited to Berlin, rather than the world, resulted in a clear shift towards the latter of these three elements – a characteristic feature which Simmel, accordingly, chose as the central point of departure for his entire analysis.

In the end, is the Berliner Gewerbeausstellung accurately described as a national success but an international failure? This much is certain: The exhibition was subject to – and, in fact, accurately mirrored – Berlin's insecure status as a would-be global city. 'It is difficult for the Berliner Gewerbe-Ausstellung 1896 to find the right measure', conceded the official catalogue with regards to the difficulty of placing the fair in its appropriate context, with Wilhelm II betraying the same lack of confidence when he added the tentative '(perhaps?)' to his 'Berlin is a great city, a world city' in the afore-quoted letter. In retrospect, the organizing *Verein Berliner Kaufleute und Industrieller* showed itself far more satisfied with what had been achieved, calling the exhibition a 'commercial and moral success of which we have every reason to be proud'. 'We may say […] that the Berlin trade exhibition of 1896, despite its limitations as a local event mainly aimed at German industry, achieved in terms of effect and importance the status of a world exhibition that does not fear comparison with many of the previous expositions, as regards the scope and value of its display.' The organizers' endeavor to make the Gewerbeausstellung appear as a somewhat reduced world exhibition was shared by consumers and critics alike. Some even considered it superior to *any* universal exposition previously held, since it had 'exceeded almost everything hitherto […] displayed at world exhibitions', as an important German architectural journal concluded. Given the initial discursive context of the *Weltausstellungsfrage*, from which the project originated, such an argumentative rhetorical maneuver was unsurprising and is perhaps best understood as a self-fulfilling prophecy.[111]

Yet the organizers' official position remained unavoidably contradictory. Although they never tired of repeating that the Gewerbeausstellung could count – possibly not *de jure*, but certainly *de facto* – as a world exhibition, they nevertheless labeled it a 'trial run', a 'final rehearsal' or a 'test case' that was necessary before the next 'logical' step, the organization of a German universal exposition, could be taken. Berlin had just 'passed the final test' which would justify a later world exhibition, the argument went. Again, there was significant agreement between the organizing bodies and the public. Press and critics alike agreed on the exposition's precursory character: greater things were yet to come. On the occasion of the exhibition's closure in October 1896, the *Vossische Zeitung* drew a historical parallel to the 1879 exposition, declaring that 'the exhibition of 1879 was a preparation for that of 1896. The trade exhibition of 1896 is a forerunner of the international exhibition which Berlin will and must hold in the near future.' Strategically downplaying the exhibition's financial deficit, writer Alfred Kerr concluded his final letter on the trade exhibition by anticipating a future German world exhibition: 'And yet: what does a paltry million matter?', he wrote: 'It has been found from other sources, and we have in turn been afforded quite remarkable sights. The trade exhibition is dead: long live the coming world exhibition!'[112]

Judged by the standards set by international expositions held in London, Paris, Vienna and elsewhere, the Berliner Gewerbeausstellung was unquestionably a minor event, even if it tried very hard to position itself within various trans-European networks. Yet, in a national and specifically local context, its central importance and long-lasting psychic effects can hardly be overestimated. Its role and function in what historian Heinz Reif calls the process of 'innere Reichshauptstadtbildung' (creating a capital city considered worthy of the German Empire) were of great significance. The same holds true of the entire debate surrounding the *Weltausstellungsfrage*. 'At this point, Berlin consciously became aware of itself', a souvenir volume reflected. Soon, this was taken as the final proof that Berlin had, at long last, achieved a genuine *Weltstadtphysiognomie* (physiognomy of a world city), putting it on a par with global cities such as London or Paris. However, the moment proved fleeting, giving rise neither to a Berlin exhibition tradition nor leaving any direct legacy. Just a few days after the Gewerbeausstellung's official closure on 15 October 1896, a newspaper marked its demise with a melancholy air, hailing 'the enterprise that, in the course of the whole summer, had become the hallmark of Berlin'. Soon after, its structures were completely dismantled, leaving far fewer material traces on the urban fabric than other expositions. Indeed, it was precisely this fleeting dimension, oscillating between permanence and transience, which Georg Simmel considered central to the so-called *Ausstellungsprincip*.[113]

3
Paris 1900: The Exposition Universelle as a Century's Protean Synthesis

L'Exposition constituera la synthèse, déterminera la philosophie du dix-neuvième siècle.

(Jules Roche)

Vielleicht ist das Wesentlichste getroffen, wenn ich sage, dass diese Weltausstellung von grossartigster Einheit in ihren Grundgedanken, von verwirrendster Vielheit in ihrer Durchführung und äusseren Erscheinung ist.

(Alexander Poppović)[1]

In the wake of →Walter Benjamin and numerous other cultural critics, it has become an oft-repeated, though equally disputed, cliché to characterize Paris as the capital not only of the nineteenth century, but also of modernity itself.[2] Another less well known but more tangible metaphor is that of Paris as the 'Queen City of Expositions' or the 'Fairie City of the World'. In the course of the second half of the nineteenth century, the French capital hosted five of the most important Expositions Universelles, held at regular 11-year intervals in 1855, 1867, 1878, 1889 and 1900, whose impact on the capital's urban fabric and cosmopolitan image of itself cannot be overestimated.[3] 'Paris is par excellence the city of expositions', an Austrian visitor avowed in the spring of 1900: 'If it has not invented the techniques of the art of exhibiting, it has at least pushed them to their most refined development. When Paris undertakes an exposition, it puts itself on the stage.'[4] Since the city's fame as 'a center for great exhibitions' was globally acknowledged and never seriously challenged abroad, it seemed only appropriate that the finale of the nineteenth century should be enacted there. Not only did the 1900 exposition prove to be synonymous with the end of the French 'monopoly of the international exhibitions of the Old World', as →Pierre Baron de Coubertin put it, but it also proved to be the conclusion of the era of great universal expositions as such (Plate 2 and Figure 3.1).[5]

At the Exposition Universelle Internationale de 1900 à Paris, 'the world' was to be put on display to an extent hitherto unknown. One foreign observer considered such an attempt at global comprehensiveness to be the exhibition's central attraction, applauding 'the infinite variety of its details and the multitudinous array

Figure 3.1 Panoramic view of the Exposition Universelle Internationale de 1900 à Paris, taken from the Trocadéro Palace on the northern banks of the River Seine
Source: Campbell, *Illustrated History, 179.*

of the productions of the earth and of its inhabitants, which picture the world at the close of its most wonderful century as no attempt was ever made to picture it before.'[6] Moreover, in comparison with its spectacular 1889 predecessor, the exposition's area was considerably enlarged to 108 hectares, 13 hectares more than 11 years before. Altogether attracting more than 50 million spectators over the course of seven months, it set a record that was broken only at Expo 67 in Montreal.[7] The 1900 exposition, protean and polymorphous, was impossible to grasp *in toto*, and remains so today. After closing on 12 November 1900, only three large-scale international expositions would be held in Paris in the twentieth century, all before the Second World War and within little more than 12 years: in 1925 the Exposition Internationale des Arts Décoratifs et Industriels Modernes, in 1931 the grand Exposition Coloniale Internationale, and again six years later the Exposition Internationale des Arts et Techniques dans la Vie Moderne, the latter memorable for its menacing, face-to-face juxtaposition of the Nazi and Soviet pavilions on the banks of the Seine, each attempting to outdo the other in daunting monumentality. However, in all three cases the term 'universal', with the attendant aspirations, was absent from the titles.

Due to its unprecedented size and inclusiveness it is only possible to analyze the 1900 Paris exposition in several carefully selected instances. Though this treatment focuses more narrowly on a handful of representative elements, it draws on a wide range of sources, stemming from different national contexts, not only French, but also German, Austrian, Czech, British and American. Indeed, almost thirty visitors' accounts and personal reports could be identified – far more than in any other case – evincing the exhibition's unparalleled scope and momentousness.

The role of the 1900 Exposition Universelle is, in this context, threefold: First, it embodies the specifically Parisian exposition tradition without which no other European exhibition of the late nineteenth and early twentieth centuries can be fully comprehended or historicized.[8] Second, although 'Paris 1900' is the only 'official' universal and international exhibition included in the sample of five European ones treated here, qualitative differences in modes of representation and appropriation to other, smaller fairs were less significant than one might presume. It is only against the backdrop of such a genuinely international – and standard-setting – French exposition tradition that the more limited European fairs were perceived. Third, both contemporaneous observers and present-day historians have frequently argued that the Exposition Universelle of 1900 marked a decisive turning-point after which the entire medium became irreversibly spectacularized and commercialized, losing much of its former seriousness.[9] However, the standard argument that a fundamental break took place in 1900 requires closer examination. The medium's apparent decline in importance may instead be due to a shift in its function, which in turn shifted the overall meanings ascribed to it.

Queen city of expositions

The Parisian bourgeoisie of the Third Republic knew that their capital's position as an internationally acknowledged world city was inextricably linked with its role as the leading exposition venue, the 'Queen City of Expositions'. By 1900, Paris was also widely regarded as having held the 'exalted position of Queen of Municipalities' in Europe for a considerable time, so that it seemed only appropriate to hold a grand exposition as the culmination of a 45 year tradition. According to the unofficial dictum issued by →Jules Roche, French minister of commerce and industry, in a report presented to the French president on 13 July 1892, this mega-event aimed, on an unprecedented scale, to present a synthesis of the entire nineteenth century while inaugurating the twentieth. Not only was the '11-year principle' formally adopted on this occasion, but Roche also positioned this latest enterprise as the logical continuation of the previous expositions' successes. 'At the very moment the Universal Exposition of 1889 in its full apotheosis was closing its doors, exhibitors and visitors instinctively made a rendezvous for Paris in 1900', the minister wrote, locating the medium's position in the inexorable 'march towards contemporary civilization':

> Still under the impression of the imposing spectacle in which they [exhibitors and visitors] had just been actors or witnesses, they were already wondering by what marvels the genius of France and of its guests might, if not outdo the éclat of the great celebrations of the Centenary, then at least worthily inaugurate the twentieth century and thus mark a new stage in the forward march of contemporary civilization.[10]

Paris must become, once again, 'for a few weeks, the focus of the civilized world' and 'draw the attention of the entire civilized world to a particular point, at a particular time', as museum director Julius Lessing similarly defined the centrifugal forces of the exposition. By transporting the whole world into its European center (Figure 3.2), the Paris exposition of 1900 aimed to present a 'picture of the world at the close of the nineteenth century with a minuteness and vividness never approached before', bringing the 'charms of life in other lands within reach of the bourgeois'. 'All the world will go to Paris', one of the numerous journalists enthused: 'the exhibitors to show and sell their wares and win prizes, the general public to be amused.'[11] This particular notion of a complete 'synthesis of the nineteenth century' to be staged in the metropolis already signaled *in nuce* the largely retrospective character of the entire enterprise. The 1900 Exposition Universelle certainly did 'close history', as one observer described it, but whether it also 'opened the future' is a different matter. Given its essentially backward orientation, it is appropriate that the exposition's *clou* should be a remnant from an earlier exposition, however rehashed and recycled it may have been.[12]

Tabula rasa

Probably nowhere else is the overwrought metaphor of space – urban in general, and exhibitionary in particular – as a 'texture' or as a 'palimpsest', to be inscribed and re-inscribed with meaning, more appropriate than here. With the exception of the first French Exposition Universelle, held along the Champs-Elysées in 1855, and the huge 1931 colonial exhibition in the Bois de Vincennes, on the southeastern outskirts of the city, all Parisian expositions were assembled in or around the huge, centrally located Champ de Mars on the *rive gauche*, the Seine's left bank. Almost all of them added new structures to the urban landscape and left something of 'substantial beauty and value to the city', as a report had it.[13] These legacies included, for instance, in 1878 the *Palais du Trocadéro* planned by the renowned architect Gabriel Jean Antoine Davioud (1824–1881), only dismantled in 1934 for the 1937 fair, in 1889 the Eiffel Tower, and in 1900 a representative triple ensemble consisting of the *Grand* and *Petit Palais* as well as the Pont Alexandre III, all still in use. Thus, the expositions contributed to the successive furnishing and symbolic enrichment of an already momentous *lieu de mémoire*.[14]

Paris' global fame as the leading exposition city was reflected in the significance of its major exhibition site, the Champ de Mars (Figure 3.3), a 49-hectare park that stretched along the south bank of the Seine, with the Ecole militaire at its end. Bounded on the east by the Avenue de la Bourdonnais, and on the west by the Avenue de Suffren, the Champ de Mars developed, over the nineteenth century, into *the* prototypical exhibitionary space. A local historian conveyed the site's undisputed status – despite its obscure origins as a former swamp – on the occasion of the Exposition Universelle of 1889: 'Of all Parisian sites', he stated, 'the Champ de Mars is probably the one that enjoys the most fame in the world. One could say that [...] its name has toured the world, and yet there is no place

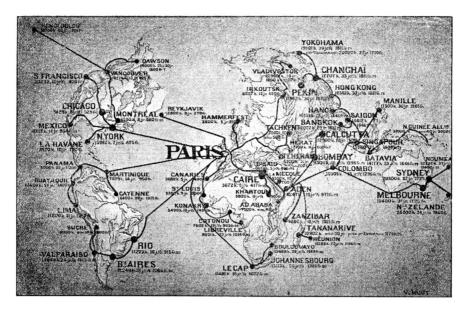

Figure 3.2 Paris as world center and global nexus in 1900. The number below each city indicates its distance from Paris, the length of traveling time required, and the cost of such a journey in francs
Source: Exhibition Paris 1900, viii–ix.

in the capital whose origins are less precisely known.'[15] Another commentator agreed, describing how the Parisian population had slowly grown aware of the site through its importance to the international fair-going public: 'Since the Exposition Universelle of 1867', he wrote, 'the Parisians, until then more or less

Figure 3.3 The Champ de Mars and neighboring sections on a crowded day in 1900, with the *Château d'Eau*, the *Palais d'Electricité* and the *Salle des Fêtes* in the background
Source: Paris Exposition Reproduced From the Official Photographs, n.p.

confined to the center of the city, have become familiar with what used to be distant. It appeared to them as a remote Sahara, no doubt, but still worthy of their benevolent and dutiful attention.'[16]   ⌐ Connection to revolution

Yet, as an urban location, the Champ de Mars' history was older and more complex. The site had played a significant role in the late eighteenth century. Named after the Roman Campo di Marte, its construction dated back to 1765 when the newly founded Ecole militaire required a training ground for the drilling and parades of 10,000 soldiers. The Champ de Mars was the scene of a number of key events during the French Revolution, among them the celebration of the fall of the Bastille and *La Fête de l'Etre suprême* (Festival of the Supreme Being) on 10 May 1794. It was here that many national celebrations had been held since the beginning of the Revolution, such as the *Fête de la Fédération* (Festival of the Federation) on 14 July 1790, over which Louis XVI presided, or the *Fête de l'Unité et de l'Indivisibilité de la République ou de la Réunion républicaine ou de la Fraternité* (Festival of the Unity and Indivisibility of the Republic or of the Republican Reunion or of Fraternity) on 10 August 1793. More gruesomely, on 17 July 1791 – during the post-revolutionary instabilities – the signing of a petition demanding the abolition of the monarchy resulted in an uprising, as a consequence of which approximately 500 persons were executed on the site.[17] Hence, it was not without good reason that half a century later, in 1847, historian Jules Michelet (1798–1874) declared the Champ de Mars, in a later oft-repeated dictum, to be 'the only monument left behind by the Revolution – albeit an empty one': 'The Empire has its column, and it has claimed the Arc de Triomphe virtually for itself; the Monarchy has its Louvre and its Invalides; the feudal church of 1200 still reigns at Notre Dame; even the Romans have their Thermes of Caesar. But the Revolution has [...] the void.'[18]

Contrary to Michelet's reading, however, such a 'void' was by no means without significance. This 'virtual emptiness' can also be seen in the maps of nineteenth-century Paris: while the city grew ever more compact, and the maps, color coded for population density, became dominated by dark grays, the Champ de Mars remained white, recalling a *terra incognita*. Yet, if other 'unknown' territory had to be 'discovered' and 'scrutinized' only once for a cartographical lacuna to be filled, here the blank space on the map was a result of the site being superscribed time and again and at regular intervals. Its unusual character was clear to foreign visitors. After visiting Paris in 1900, one young American tourist noted with admiring nostalgia:

Behind was the vast, open, desert space of the Champ de Mars, silent and empty as so much land in the Sahara, and yet which has been the theatre of so many historical spectacles. There is no place in the world where the contrast between past and present – between many different pasts and the one monotonous present – is so striking and decided. No place in the world presents such a *tabula rasa*.[19]

Thus, in the nineteenth century the Champ de Mars' symbolic quality and spatial legacy were of a latently revolutionary character. This, however, only surfaced when the Exposition Universelle of 1889 was organized for the centenary of the Revolution. During its run-up, no question occupied so much of the official commission's time and aroused such public interest as the choice of an appropriate site.[20] Several major European nation-states declined to participate in the exposition with some, such as Austria-Hungary and Italy, citing the prohibitive cost and others, such as Great Britain, Russia and Germany, objecting to the fair's connection with the Revolution.[21] Writing in the year of the exhibition, Ernest Maindron (1838–1908) of the Institut de France hinted at the highly politicized heritage of the site, linking its very existence to that of the nation itself:

This immense area where the whole world meets; this empty plain where yesterday, amidst total calm, our dear infantrymen and our brilliant cavaliers were again exercising, inspires a certain respect composed of hopes and memories.

The reverberations of the many events in the history of civilization that took place in the Champ de Mars indissolubly link it with the nation.[22]

Yet the Revolution had a further, more immediate effect on the continuous reshaping of the Champ de Mars and its festive character, which would, eventually, contribute directly to the square's development into the exhibitionary site *par example*. When Nicolas Comte François de Neufchâteau (1750–1828), minister of the interior, organized, on behalf of the government and for the very first time, in *l'an VI* (1798), a trade exposition of manufactured goods in order to demonstrate France's commercial prosperity and technological progress, the Champ de Mars was chosen as the venue. With such fairs repeated in 1801, 1802 and 1806 either here or in the Louvre, a specifically French tradition of national trade expositions was soon established, even if the original intention to hold these exhibitions on an annual basis was thwarted by the outbreak of war and consequently held on a modified five-year schedule. Thus, the tradition of national exhibitions taking place at the site existed well before the international expositions were initiated in 1851. Following 1855, each consecutive event strove to be more comprehensive and more spectacular than its predecessors, in part in an effort to reap various political benefits, including the legitimization of a new regime and the recruitment of supporters for its policies.[23] When reviewing the past half-century of expositions in 1900, Julius Lessing reminded his readers that 'in 1798 a shopping area was set up on the Champs de Mars that has ever since seen an infinite number of expositions, with a few rows of little booths. 110 exhibitors were represented: This whole enterprise was only on show for three days, yet it was crowned with success.'[24] Another visitor, writing in the same year, depicted the reputation the site had gained over time both vividly and enthusiastically, summarizing the reasons why the Champ de Mars had come to constitute *the* classic venue of all nineteenth-century expositions held in Europe – or simply 'le centre principal des Expositions', as the *Larousse* expressed it laconically in 1929:[25]

> Paris is certainly the exhibition city par excellence! One could not imagine a more attractive location for the rendezvous of the world than on the broad expanse of the Champs de Mars, extending down to the Seine, and on the other bank of the river adjacent to one of the most attractive areas of Paris and extending to the highly impressive Champs-Elysées. All this is enriched by the fast-moving, vivid life of this especial world. In fact, it presents, as it were, a memorable orgy of all human emotions; and the influx of cultured people to this 'Babel' on the Seine turns it into a playground for all mankind.[26]

Thus, with scenes of military, revolutionary, imperial, republican, national and international displays and performances following one after the other, the Champ de Mars had, by 1900, come to epitomize, in one place and in a most complex manner, distinct and contradictory phases of French history. Numerous foreign visitors looked at this 'playground of humankind' with a particular mixture of admiration, envy and respect, thus contributing to its global reputation as an unparalleled exhibitionary model-site. Yet, their praise should not obscure the fact that the Champ's revolutionary associations remained a source of unease that found expression in various increasingly ferocious disputes about the suitability of the site for future mega-events.

Fitting as it may seem in retrospect, in the fall of 1894 the selection of the site for the forthcoming exposition proved indeed more controversial than ever before. 'There was no other choice than the Champ de Mars', the writer and former consul →Adolphe Démy reminded his readers in 1907, continuing: 'This is because Paris, in prodigiously extending the centuries, has kept – perhaps uniquely in the history of European capitals – the character of its earliest constitution; this free space from the center would constantly be enlarged from the same side towards its circumference.' Yet, Démy overlooked the fact that there had already been a number of disputes about the question of the exposition's *emplacement*, not only in 1867, but again in 1878 and 1889.[27] Due to the expositions' continual growth, it was clear from the outset that the Champ de Mars would either have to be enlarged considerably or entirely abandoned. 'A new exhibition with the Champs de Mars as its center point would not offer its visitors much innovation unless completely new urban areas were included', the *Deutsche Bauzeitung* pronounced in 1893.[28] From among the more than 100 proposals submitted to the official competition for finding a suitable site, the *sous-commission* charged by the *Conseil municipal* selected only three schemes. Among the rejected proposals were a variety of different locations in and around the Parisian municipal area – including Versailles, the plateau of Courbevoie, the Bois de Boulogne together with parts of Auteil, and the Parc de Saint Cloud on the western outskirts, or the Bois de Vincennes on the city's eastern fringes (Figure 3.4).[29]

The numerous proposals submitted to the commission were certainly imaginative. Various architects envisaged, for instance, the building of entire temporary towns, vast terraces bridging the Seine, four towers together with a huge *Tour Ville* with 45 floors and more than 2000 apartments, a theater, gardens and restaurants, or a novel palace of electricity, to be built completely of steel and dwarfing the Eiffel Tower. Yet, these projects shared two central problems: they neither clarified a feasible means of mass transportation to and from the site, nor did they satisfactorily specify how to design the new exposition grounds in such a way that they would prove attractive for a sufficiently large number of tourists and visitors at such a considerable distance from the city center.[30]

Eventually, however, the competition's results were determined by the municipality of Paris. For commerce-oriented reasons it refused to contribute to the exposition funds unless the fair was held in the very heart of the capital. While public opinion generally favored transferring the venue to the Parisian *banlieue*, the municipality stipulated that the Champ de Mars was once again to be the exposition's pivot, as it was the only venue large enough in the densely populated urban conglomeration, with the *Palais du Trocadéro* (1878) and the Esplanade des Invalides (1889) as additions to the core site.[31] Emphasizing the significance of the future site's proximity to the city center, the reputable *Construction Moderne*

Suburb

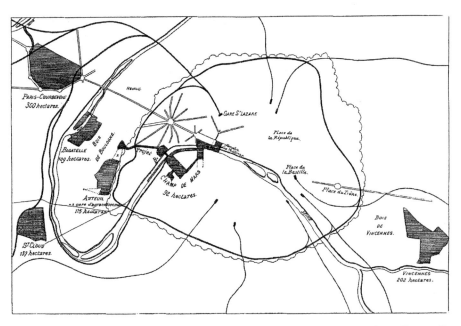

Figure 3.4   Six of the numerous venues proposed for the 1900 exposition in Paris. Eventually the smallest location centering around the Champ de Mars was chosen, with the site in Vincennes as an annexe
Source: 'Emplacements divers proposés pour la prochaine Exposition', *Construction Moderne* 8 (8 April 1893), 314.

rushed to the commission's assistance, stating that holding the exhibition at the Champs was 'quite necessary to enable people to come and go the exposition on foot'.[32] Similarly, *Le Temps* could not envisage any other possible venue: 'The somewhat providential destiny [of the Champ de Mars] is to offer in Paris a blank slate where everything can be exhibited', going on to pronounce vigorously: 'Down with the Bois de Boulogne, long live the Champ de Mars!'[33]

What at first had seemed a largely technical debate of limited scope developed into a fiercely contested matter of fundamental significance. For the first time ever, not only the venue itself, but also the general necessity of holding yet another international exposition in the French capital was seriously debated in public. →H. Georges Berger, son of the 1889 *Directeur général* of the same name, commented with a certain bewilderment on this development, noting that the 'project of the Exposition of 1900 has raised objections that previous Exposition projects did not'. The French debates of the mid-1890s recall German anxieties over the *Weltausstellungsfrage* and the *Hauptstadtfrage* a decade before. The question of the exposition's adequate *emplacement* became inextricably intertwined with a debate about the medium's modernity.[34]

Serious doubts and fundamental objections were voiced by a variety of parties. The *Figaro*, for instance, questioned a number of prominent citizens about the benefits of expositions in general and the one to be held in 1900 in particular.

Many of the answers were unfavorable, arguing that the enormous sums necessary could and should be better spent, to much greater advantage, on direct infrastructural measures such as streets and railroads, or on educational and social institutions such as schools and hospitals.[35] The recently founded *Ligue Lorraine de Décentralisation* (Lorraine League of Decentralization) under the chairmanship of →Maurice Barrès, a conservative writer and regionalist politician from Nancy, was especially vehement, campaigning against the planned exhibition by publishing brochures, holding conferences and launching critical, often polemic, articles in the national press. In an important and later oft-quoted pamphlet published on 24 August 1895, the *Ligue* bluntly demanded 'Pas d'Exposition en 1900!' (No Exposition in 1900!). The *Ligue* considered the repeated holding of one Parisian exposition after the other not only economically disastrous for the rest of France, but they also feared an increasing moral depravation of the people. Its criticism of a far-reaching concentration of all national efforts on the capital was accompanied by numerous alternative proposals, all suggesting non-central locations outside the center. One could diagnose the same, anti-centralistic basis of disapproval, but from two different perspectives – one metropolitan, the other provincial.[36]

The fiercest debate took place between early August 1895 and February 1896, with the opponents being politicians, journalists and lobbyists, who, as veritable *hommes de lettres*, were all accustomed to arguing in the public arena with the necessary *effet*. With articles mainly appearing in the *Figaro* and the *Matin*, the debate was opened on 2 August 1895 when Barrès published a leader in the *Figaro*, entitled 'On peut éviter l'Exposition de 1900' (We Can Avoid the Exposition of 1900), in which he first presented his anti-centralist, anti-exhibitionary arguments to a wider national public.[37] Later that month, Emile Beer reacted to Barrès' polemics by defending the forthcoming exposition as a necessary boost to the economy and in turn attacked Barrès in a leader, published on the front page of the *Figaro* under the heading 'Contre 1900!', in which he emphasized the economic benefit of the project for the entire nation.[38] On 24 August 1895 Jules Méline (1838–1925), *député* and one of the editors of *La République française*, penned an article entitled 'Faut-il faire l'Exposition de 1900?' (Must We Have the Exposition of 1900?) in which he criticized the government's handling of the project.[39] The very same day, Barrès intervened yet again, defending his original arguments and publishing the aforementioned pamphlet.[40] At the end of that month, →Paul Planat, commissioning editor of *Construction Moderne* and later one of the most prolific and astute reporters on the 1900 exposition, summarized the entire debate.[41] Little more than three weeks later, Barrès himself intervened for the third time, arguing that the question of holding the 'disastrous exposition' (l'Exposition funeste) was not to be confused with that of national decentralization, and that it was appropriate to give preference to international competitors such as Germany. In the end, yet another exposition would merely amount to 'Limonade et Prostitution', thus mobilizing both anti-commercial and pro-moral reasons for rejecting the projected enterprise.[42] In early December, the well-known economist and convinced nationalist Paul Leroy-Beaulieu (1843–1916) broadened the debate by vigorously attacking the very fundamentals of the exposition medium and challenging its general legitimacy, though

Leroy-Beaulieu ultimately moderated his position, suggesting instead a smaller, more specialized exhibition.[43] In mid-December Octave Mirbeau (1848–1917), nationalist and well-known author, followed Leroy-Beaulieu in questioning and condemning the entire 'exposition principle' in a thoughtful piece, suitably entitled 'Pourquoi des Expositions?'.[44] Later that month, a lengthy article by art critic Camille Mauclair (1872–1945) summarized the debate for the second time.[45] Last but not least, on 1 February 1896, with considerable delay, →Henri Chardon, the exposition's designated *Secrétaire général*, tried to refute Mirbeau's polemic, once again emphasizing the medium's general utility for modern society and its central significance for the international exchange of goods and ideas.[46] Similar to some of the German disputes, the debate gradually petered out in March 1896. No particular action was taken after the opponents' arguments had been rebuffed in the national press. At last, the *Figaro* expressed a certain sense of fatigue with and disinclination toward the prevailing opinion of the press, stating: 'Don't you find that this debate on the big fair is starting to become tedious? Since the thing is in the bag, what is the purpose of this tiresome controversy?' This statement effectively brought the debate to a close.[47]

Even if the dispute did not produce immediate consequences, institutional or otherwise, it nonetheless indicated and in turn contributed to a decisive discursive shift in the French context. In its course, the debate's focus had gradually grown from a specific, largely polemic quarrel about the holding of a future exhibition on an unspecified site into a general argument, questioning – and eventually undermining – the medium's theoretical basis. Méline attentively observed this momentary shift when noting that 'until now the principle of the exposition [...] seemed to have been consecrated'.[48] By the turn of the century not only in Germany, but also in France and Great Britain, the general vocabulary and theoretical premises of the medium of expositions had changed fundamentally. The results of this particular debate were twofold: On the one hand, questioning its expediency was, in the long run, tantamount to undermining the medium's credibility and therewith its legitimization. On the other hand, during the immediate pre- and interwar periods, this discursive shift was to result in a certain Europe-wide rapprochement, at least on an institutional level. While the practical, largely organizational problems would be clarified on an international basis through a number of conferences in the 1910s and late 1920s only – notably in Berlin in 1912 and in Paris in 1928, leading directly to the creation of the *Bureau International des Expositions* (BIE) – the more fundamental theoretical issues remained unresolved – and contributed to the medium's loss of importance over the course of the twentieth century.

The *Ligue*'s intervention had come 'a bit late' in any case if it sought to effectively influence the preparations for the 1900 exposition, as a critic remarked.[49] With the decision taken to hold the exposition within the Parisian municipal area rather than *extra muros*, the problem shifted in an unexpected direction. The new task now consisted in finding adequate space within the city center and defining the site's exact shape and size. Both the long- and short-term effects of this new dilemma proved paradoxical and unpredictable. The self-imposed directive to continuously enlarge all subsequent Parisian expositions had multidimensional infrastructural effects. Although the Champ de Mars remained their pivot, through the additions and repeated inclusion of new sites such as the extension across the Seine in 1878 or the newly opened Esplanade des Invalides 11 years later – all of which largely occurred in a northeastern direction – the expositions eventually moved closer and closer to the city's actual hub, roughly defined as centering around the Ile de la Cité with Notre Dame. 'It is essential to remember that the size of the various world exhibitions has been enlarged and that they have continuously approached closer to the very center of Paris', a German guidebook observed: 'In this way a new part of the city has been opened up so that the exposition has now truly become an integral part of Paris.'[50]

In the end, the area occupied by the exposition buildings and grounds included not only the Champ de Mars, the Esplanade des Invalides, and the Trocadéro, but also a large part of the Seine's north bank, reaching as far as the Champ Elysées and the Place de la Concorde. Thus, the exhibition became an increasingly integral part of the urban fabric into which it was inscribed and re-inscribed on a previously unheard of scale. Although entirely surrounded by a green stockade demarcating the exposition grounds from the actual city area and interrupted only by 43 gates, visitors found it difficult to distinguish between 'inside' and 'outside' or, as it were, 'in-site' and 'out-site'. 'The Exhibition', Henry Heathcote Statham (1839–1924), editor of the *Builder*, observed, 'is indeed so mixed up with the city that it is difficult sometimes to be quite sure when you are in it and when you are not.'[51] Looking at a contemporaneous photograph showing a panorama of Paris and the exposition grounds, the beholder could hardly tell them apart (Figure 3.5; see also Figure 3.7). Similar photographs showed the *trottoir roulant* (moving sidewalk), the exposition's internal means of transport, as disappearing in between blocks of bourgeois, multistoried apartment buildings typical for this part of Paris, rather than among the multiple pavilions and sections.

The paradoxical effects of the exposition's emplacement were manifold. Because the free space in the city center was not large enough to hold the entire exhibition, the Exposition Universelle of 1900 was the first of the numerous Parisian fairs to extend beyond the city limits. Parts of the Bois de Vincennes were selected as an auxiliary venue where, on an additional 112 hectares, not only various means of transport – such as railroads, automobiles and balloons –, agricultural exhibits as well as some of the bigger machines were displayed, but where also, between 14 and 16 July, the second modern Olympic Games were held. At this time still varyingly known as the 'Concours internationaux d'exercices physiques et de sports', the 'Paris Championships' or the 'Olympian Games', they attracted so little public attention, were so poorly organized, and proved such a complete failure that sports historians have questioned whether these Games were Olympic at all and should be reclassified accordingly.[52]

The second paradoxical effect was due to the vastness and fragmentation of the inner-urban venue. How was a cohesive whole to be made of the many heterogeneous parts? The problem was provisionally solved by simply declaring the river, the Seine, the 'controlling idea' and 'missing link' meant to connect all the numerous sections of the vast grounds. More consistently integrated into the

Figure 3.5 Panorama of Paris inside and outside the exposition grounds. The retrospective section *Vieux Paris* can be seen on the left, along the banks of the River Seine; the huge grey building in the background is the *Grand Palais des Beaux Arts*. The apartment buildings in the foreground lay between Avenue de la Bourdonnais and Avenue Bosquet
Source: Olivares, *The Parisian Dream City* (16 August 1900), n.p.

exposition's layout than 11 years before, experts considered such a conceptual incorporation of a natural feature a major innovation in urban development. Buildings and pavilions were adjusted accordingly. For instance, the various national edifices composing the *Rue des Nations* were aligned in such a way that they could only be perceived *in toto* from the waterside itself, the opposite banks or one of the five connecting bridges.[53] Many souvenir photographs featured views taken from this perspective (see also Figure 3.9). Deploring the venue's general inner disintegration, international experts such as the already quoted Julius Lessing astutely recognized this particular deficit-turned-asset of the 1900 exposition, noting that the 'only unifying connection' among the host of grand buildings at various points was the course of the Seine itself.[54]

Intended legacies and unintended remnants from previous expositions posed a third grave problem. How, for example, were relics such as the famous *Palais de l'Industrie*, situated on *rive droite* (the right bank) between the Champs-Elysées and the Cours la Reine and remaining from the first French international exhibition in 1855, or the notorious Eiffel Tower, that 'symbole gigantesque' dating back to

1889, to be dealt with? In what way could they be incorporated into the venue's new spatial layout and the exposition's overall plan?[55]

Two different decisions were taken, one negative, the other positive: With regard to the spacious *Palais de l'Industrie* located on the Grand Carré Marigny, an elegant promenade along the Champs-Elysées, a public debate took place in *Le Temps* and *La Construction Moderne*. Explicitly decreed by Napoléon III to be 'similar to the Crystal Palace in London' and to house all future Paris expositions, the *Palais de l'Industrie* had opened in 1855, only four years after the Great Exhibition. In the interim it had become a much-celebrated and lucrative national monument and urban landmark, indeed the Parisian pendant to the Crystal Palace, although it was smaller and less iconic than its London counterpart. Despite protests against the transformation of the Champs-Elysées for the exposition, it was nonetheless decided to pull the *Palais* down to make room for the *Grand Palais des Beaux Arts* and the *Petit Palais des Beaux Arts*, two of the new permanent edifices subsequently to be used for the annual *Salon* and as an archeological museum, respectively. Thus, the demolition of the *Palais de l'Industrie* in 1897 could be read as a signal that the nineteenth-century exhibition tradition had come to an irrevocable end.[56] Independent of the circumstances, however, this incident serves as a reminder that expositions also entail destruction. Planned permanence and 'intentional monumentality' can change suddenly, as can initially unintended transience. A journalist concluded his personal 'obituary' for the 'condemned' *Palais de l'Industrie* by stating and bemoaning 'the irony of fate in this country, where what is provisional easily becomes definitive, that this palace, constructed to be definitive, was only provisional'.[57]

The famous Eiffel Tower stands for the opposite: with attendance dramatically declining as soon as the exposition of 1889 had closed, and in 1900 by no means regarded as a popular tourist attraction [cf. also Figure 7.2], the Tower was far more controversial than the *Palais de l'Industrie*. Even in foreign architectural circles, it was vehemently rejected, despite the fact that it was the tallest man-made structure in the world. The British *Builder*, for instance, could not conceal its strong disapproval by insisting time and again upon 'the general ugliness and the outrageous scale of this too-celebrated structure', suggesting a speedy removal or, at least, an 'embellishment' by cutting the Tower off at the point where the four pillars meet. Yet, despite several times being on the verge of immediate demolition, *la Tour de 300 mètres* was eventually saved by the proposals' mediocrity, existing contracts, and budgetary restrictions. With the addition of electric lighting, the Eiffel Tower was eventually integrated into the new scheme, though it was no longer the exposition's principal attraction. Thus, the exposition's most outstanding monument was a relic of the past, 'nothing more than a worn-out tourist attraction for visiting provincials and a laughably oversized scaffolding for a few scientific experiments', in the words of its biographer Henri Loyrette.[58]

Polynuclear or *clou*-less?

Unlike in Great Britain, the United States or Germany, French expositions were inevitably state affairs, and hence always legally sanctioned. On 2 July 1892, the leftist *député* François Deloncle (1856–1922), supported by his colleagues in the Chamber of Deputies, asked the French government to decree that an international exposition should be held in 1900. With the government acceding, president Sadi Carnot (1837–1894, assassinated at an exposition held in Lyon) passed a decree on 13 July 1892 – just one month to the day before Wilhelm II's final verdict against a rival German event, and on the eve of 14 July, the momentous French national holiday – that 'a universal exposition of works of art, of industrial and agricultural production' (Exposition universelle des œuvres d'art, des productions industrielles et agricoles) under the auspices of the Ministry of Commerce and Industry should open in Paris on 5 May and close on 31 October 1900. Later, these dates were changed to 15 April and 12 November, so that the projected exposition would last 212 days in all. 47 nations, including all the great powers and, notably, Germany, accepted the invitation by the French government and participated with exhibits and pavilions of their own.[59]

On 9 September 1893 →Alfred Picard, engineer by training but civil servant by profession, was appointed to the prestigious position of *Commissaire général*, and given far-reaching competences, although by no means the 'almost complete autonomy' that some historians have claimed.[60] Theoretically, Picard still required the approval of the, Ministry of Commerce and Industry, though cabinet instability resulted in numerous changes in this position during the preparatory years. Critical judgments of his suitability for this post differed considerably. While some imputed 'a high level of competence, sure judgment, prompt decision-making, and an extraordinary clearness of sight' to him, others described Picard as 'anything but practical'.[61] As in earlier cases, the extent of continuity in personnel matters is noteworthy. Not only had Picard been president of the Parisian urban departments of public works, agriculture and commerce since 1885, but he had also served, together with →Jean-Charles-Adolphe Alphand and →Georges Berger, as one of the three *Directeurs générals* at the Paris exhibition of 1889. As its official historian, Picard had won great merit by writing a history of international exhibitions as part of the multi-volume report which is still today considered by some as one of the best works in the historiography on nineteenth-century Expositions Universelles through 1889.[62]

With the respective laws passed on 27 July 1894 and 13 June 1896, the amount of credit necessary for such a mega-event could be provided. Because of the enterprise's public character – and unlike in Great Britain – soon after the issuing of the decree, three governmental committees were set up to study the exposition's future location and means of transport, construction, organization and finance. In most instances public competitions were held. An official main commission was established together with 500 [*sic*] specialized sub-committees to begin preparatory work. Never before had a consecutive exposition been decided upon so shortly after its predecessor, and neither had preparations ever begun so early – indeed, possibly even too early, as de Coubertin conjectured.[63]

One motive for so doing was the coinciding of various exposition projects and the international competition this brought, especially with the German *Kaiserreich*, between 1892 and 1893. A comparatively neutral observer, *The Times* of London, reported in July 1892 a 'strong feeling in Germany in favour of holding an international exhibition at Berlin towards the end of the century', which it predicted would grow even stronger in reaction to the French announcement. Comparing the two competing projects during their respective run-up, *The Times* even spoke of 'Rival Exhibitions', with the Germans appearing particularly 'heated' on the subject.[64] With French preparations set to begin, the German debate came to a sudden, if temporary, end after Wilhelm II intervened in the debate on 13 August 1892. But soon after, in the winter of the same year, it flared up again in response to the decision to organize the Berliner Gewerbeausstellung as an independent and self-contained German rival enterprise, even if on a much smaller scale. While the early beginning of the French preparations can be read as a reaction to the German debate and, at the same time, as an attempt to create faits accomplis, a third simultaneous event, the epoch-making World's Columbian Exposition, held in Chicago from May through October 1893, exerted considerable influence on both European exhibitions, especially in terms of conception, design and layout. Likewise planned as a reaction to the Parisian expositions of 1876 and 1889, the Chicago fair had reached its final phase of preparation during the summer and fall of 1892. The German Reich had already accepted the American invitation and committed to contributing a pavilion of its own, another incentive to abandon the various projects to hold an exposition in Berlin, whereas Parisian proposals to transplant the entire 1900 fair outside the city center – and to connect their various areas with the latest mass-transport technology – were, in turn, clearly stimulated by analogous considerations for the Chicago world's fair of 1893.

The exposition's grounds consisted of five distinct parts (Figure 3.6) plus an *addendum extra muros*: first, the entire Champ de Mars with the Eiffel Tower on one end, and the *Château d'Eau*, the *Palais d'Electricité* and the *Salle des Fêtes* on the other, with numerous additional pavilions and palaces in between; second, on the Seine's northern banks, the Trocadéro with the various colonial sections, both French and foreign; third, further up the river, the *Rue des Nations* on the *rive gauche*; fourth, the *Rue de Paris* and *Vieux Paris* on the Seine's opposite side; and, fifth, another large complex consisting of the Esplanade des Invalides on the left bank together with, across the Seine and connected by the Pont Alexandre III, the eastern part of the Champs-Elysées featuring the *Grand* and the *Petit Palais* where the fine arts were exhibited. Anything not considered suitable for the city center was put on display in the annexe at Vincennes, in particular automobiles, machinery and agricultural exhibits. With the exception of he two new art palaces, all other buildings were temporary constructions with an enormous amount of surface modeling and plaster sculpture following the – unlike in 1889 – then current architectural axiom of *cachez le fer* (hide the iron). Reactions to the complex setting were far from favorable: One German visitor classified the entire arrangement as nothing but a vast *Stuckorgie* (overabundance of stucco-work), while the British *Builder*, in complete agreement, denounced the buildings as 'palpable shams'.[65]

Next to the first, pre-existing main vista – reaching from the Trocadéro over the Pont d'Iéna to the Eiffel Tower, across the entire Champ de Mars and leading to the

Château d'Eau, the *Palais d'Electricité* and the *Salle des Fêtes* in the south – an equally spectacular second axis was created further east. Here, a broad avenue called Nicolas II was built, leading from the Avenue des Champs-Elysées between the two new palaces across the new bridge to the Esplanade des Invalides, thus opening another grand vista and new thoroughfare through the urban fabric. As would become common practice on later occasions, these two infrastructural measures were given explicitly political meanings through their names. Inaugurated by the Russian Emperor Nicholas II (1868–1918) during a state visit to Paris in October 1896 – who, on this occasion, also laid the foundation stone of the Alexander III Bridge, named after his father, the late Russian Czar (1845–1894) – both structures were intended to celebrate the Franco-Russian *entente*. The simple act of naming was perhaps, as a French architect stated in a lecture delivered to the Royal Institute of British Architects in London on 19 February 1900, 'the most original and durable work' of the entire exposition and would undoubtedly remain 'irrefutable testimony of the need for an alliance between architects and engineers in works of public utility'.[66]

Since the entire venue had grown by an additional 13 hectares in comparison with 1889, an internal means of transport became crucial for visitors to move about the exhibition grounds without much delay in order to make a visit feasible. In particular the two distant centers of the exposition on the left bank, the Champ de Mars in the west and the Esplanade des Invalides in the east, had to be connected. The resulting *trottoir roulant* was featured in many of the itineraries published in numerous languages and suggested by travel guides. Although the Gewerbeausstellung in Berlin had included a similar, if much smaller system of internal, circular transport, this 'most marked characteristic feature' constituted yet another direct transatlantic transfer from the Chicago 1893 world's fair.[67]

This *trottoir roulant* or 'moving sidewalk', as the English-language guidebooks called it, consisted of three parallel platforms, two movable and one fixed, on which passengers could travel at two speeds (Figure 3.7). It formed a complete circuit of almost four kilometers in the shape of an irregular quadrilateral along Quai d'Orsay, Rue Fabert, Avenue de la Motte-Picquet – where it continued outside the actual exposition grounds – and then back to the Avenue de la Bourdonnais before adjourning to the Champ de Mars. In addition, a specially built electric railroad followed the same path, but in the opposite direction. As a system of 'automatic' transport, the *trottoir* offered visitors the possibility of an easy passage in either a half hour or a full hour through the entire grounds, presenting – as they stood on the platform, gazing at the spectacular attractions passing by – in a film-like manner one 'interesting view' after another.[68]

Such an unusual way of traveling fascinated many visitors-cum-spectators. In the first month alone, it was used by 799,479 paying passengers. 'The effect, from the street below, was an extraordinary one', one of them retrospectively described his impressions, 'endless crowds of people were seen being swiftly carried along, a few who were walking had the effect of skaters rapidly and easily skimming past the rest. All seemed to be travelling in a manner which the tired pedestrian looked upon with envy.'[69] In a state of almost sublime contemplation, another observer

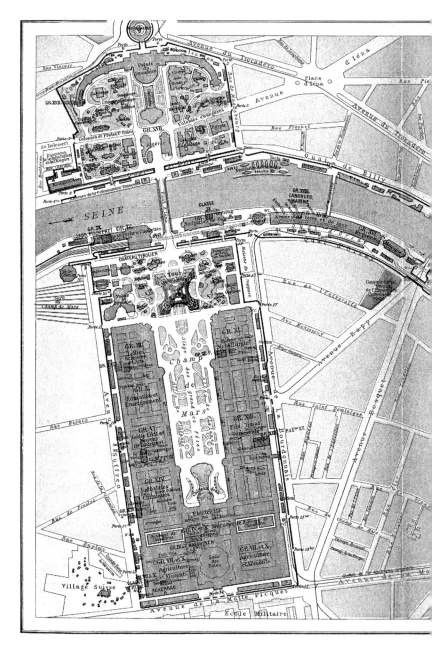

Figure 3.6   Official map of grounds and buildings of the Exposition Universelle Internationale de 1900 à Paris

Source: K.K. Österreichische General-Commissariate, *Berichte über die Weltausstellung in Paris 1900*, vol. 2, plate 1.

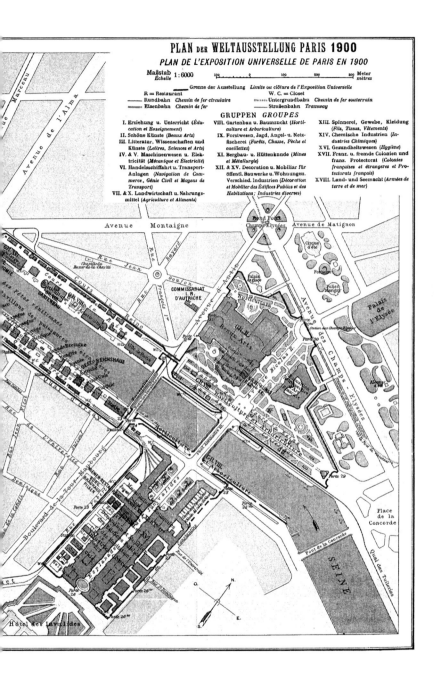

PLAN der WELTAUSSTELLUNG PARIS 1900

PLAN DE L'EXPOSITION UNIVERSELLE DE PARIS EN 1900

Figure 3.7   The *trottoir roulant* or 'moving sidewalk' in 1900, here shown at the foot of the
Eiffel Tower at the corner of Avenue de la Bourdonnais and the Quai d'Orsay. The building
on the left is the panorama *Tour du Monde*, while the replica of a lighthouse on the right
formed part of the Pavilion of the German Merchant Marine
Source: Courtesy of California State University, Fresno, Special Collections Research Center, Leighton
Collection, Nr. 182.

reported how he had felt – traveling through time and space and simultaneously
gazing at all the other passengers passing by – as if encountering a representative sample of humankind: 'Aha, those colorful appearances who pass by on the
runway are not just visitors to the exposition – no, they symbolize the whole of
humanity as it passes through time – brr, brr, brr – it almost seems to purr and
buzz continuously, and so it goes on and on and on...'[70] Taking the *trottoir roulant*
as a direct promise of future developments in urban passenger transport, commentators consequently expected that this 'novel mode of locomotion' would mark
a revolution in 'the future appearance of our cities, and that even in the lifetime
of those visiting Paris this year'.[71] Expected to solve evolving problems of urban
traffic and transport, soon afterwards it was supplanted by the automobile. Up
to a point, however, these enthusiastic passengers and optimistic critics were not
entirely mistaken, as moving sidewalks such as these constitute a direct precursor
of today's horizontal walkways, commonly used in airports for passengers to cover
ever-longer distances when moving from one gate to another.

Although less immediately connected to the organization of the exposition, another infrastructural measure proved of more lasting efficacy. On 19 July 1900 the first line of the *Chemin de fer Métropolitain* was opened, running from Porte Maillot in the west along the Champs-Elysées, the Palais Royal, the Hôtel de Ville and the Place de la Bastille to the Porte de Vincennes in the east – thus connecting the Trocadéro and the Champ de Mars with the exposition's annexe in Vincennes, even if the park could not be reached completely with the new Métro. Having been in the planning stage since the early 1880s but with its actual realization repeatedly delayed and postponed as a result of various bureaucratic conflicts and clashes of competence between the Parisian municipality and the French government, every effort was now made, and *ligne 1* was eventually completed to coincide with the mega-event's opening. 'It took nothing less', *l'Illustration* commented, without concealing its criticism, 'than the prospect of imperious needs created by the Exposition of 1900 to put an end to the conflict.'[72]

The widespread belief that Paris was in need of such infrastructural measures could be traced directly back to the 1889 exposition. Eleven years earlier it had become obvious that the public transport system was inadequate, especially during rush hour. Expositions and local traffic directly affected each other: for the former, the transport of thousands of visitors had to be organized, while the latter received incentives for further technical development. But, as symbols of urban status and municipal prestige, they also shared a structural similarity. Just as in the expositions themselves, mobility and electricity were regarded as signs of urban sophistication and modernity, and hence became the objects of fierce inter-urban competition. 'The Municipal Council did not want to give foreigners', the newspaper *Le Rappel* noted after the opening of the first Métro line, 'the awful spectacle they had witnessed in 1867, in 1878, and in 1889.'[73] A mutual relationship can be observed: both international expositions and the organization of public transport were instrumentalized to serve one and the same purpose, namely to demonstrate modernity. In this case, however, the reference city for inner-urban, international comparison was not Paris, but London, where the first underground system had already opened in 1863, with Budapest, Chicago, New York, Vienna and Berlin following soon after. The Parisian *Métropolitain* even derived its very name from the British metropolitan model and counterpart.[74]

Aspects and traces of these different vistas and modes of transport, traveling and mobility – internal and external, long and short distance, physical and imaginary – were combined in one extraordinary source, a map of the entire exposition grounds (Plate 3) that accompanied a souvenir set of 60 stereoscopic photographs taken at the venue.[75] The entire set could be purchased on the site itself, complete with a special mechanical hand-held device to watch these images through special lenses. Once the photographs had been inserted into the holder, the viewer could enjoy these images of the vistas of both the exposition proper and Paris itself as three-dimensional, for each photograph consisted of two shots of the same object taken from slightly different positions. The consumer-cum-spectator could then take this special version of the exposition's map in his or her hands, compare it to the official one (Figure 3.6), and exactly locate his or her imaginary position on the site as all photographs were numbered, with the beholder's viewpoint represented by little circles and the limits of his or her field of vision indicated by two diverging, straight red lines. Such an elaborate souvenir item was not so unusual by 1900. According to historian Jonathan Crary, with the exception of photographs, such stereoscopes provided the most significant form of visual imagery in the second half of the nineteenth century.[76] As popular consumer goods, they had been established much earlier and were more widely available than photographs. This particular set was produced and issued by Underwood & Underwood, an American company of Canadian origin founded in the 1880s which dominated the global market for news photos until well into the 1930s.

Yet, what makes this map so extraordinarily illuminating in the present context is the exactitude with which it combines within one single image different aspects central to this interpretation. It demonstrates how three distinct, yet related spatial fabrics – the city, the city within the city, and the visitor's pre-structured gaze on both – are superimposed on one another, and so literally and reciprocally inscribed on each other. Different meanings were ascribed on all three levels, often referring back and forth from one layer to the next. Moreover, the map formed part of an entire kit to be taken home as a souvenir item, thus allowing the visitor to consume the city and the exposition simultaneously, both during and after the grand show, while still in Paris or already back at home. It enabled its owner to recreate both the metropolis' and the exhibition's imaginative geographies regardless of where he or she was actually situated in space and time. Technically, however, the entire set of stereoscopic images was a mainstream product of a specific phase of development in late nineteenth-century media history – to be more precise, the history of a specific type of construction and reproduction of visual imagery. It comes as no surprise, then, that stereoscopes and world's fairs, both popular 'techniques of the observer', should have been combined in such an interdependent and mutually supportive way. If, as philosopher Lieven de Cauter has argued, world exhibitions were the 'spectacular version of the panoramic gaze, indeed the epitome of it, the panorama of panoramas', here a consumer-friendly replica of this all-encompassing experience could be taken home as a handy souvenir.[77]

The general incentive to present the world in a manner that was complete, picturesque, and well ordered was evident in the exposition's elaborate classification system. Approximately one-half of the available space was allotted to foreign countries. All exhibits were rubricated in 18 different groups, which were again subdivided into 120 classes. As the French organizers declared, education was considered the source of all human progress, and therefore ranked first in the hierarchy: 'At the head are education and teaching: this is how people enter social life; this is also the source of all progress.'[78] The guiding principle was that similar products should be displayed side by side, rather than according to their national origin. The choice of such a 'product'- or 'item'-oriented approach rather than a national principle of classification constituted a deliberate departure from established exhibition practices. 'The products of the whole world' were grouped 'in certain departments, thus presenting a condensed exhibition of the best of every clime', allowing for 'a ready comparison of the arts and industries of one country with the arts and industries of others.' Even more complexity resulted from the inclusion of historical samples in each group to demonstrate the progress achieved since 1800 and the emphasis on displaying dynamic production processes rather than finished – and hence static – products.[79]

Yet the introduction of this new classification system had unintended countereffects. It proved conducive to a further, unanticipated, 'nationalization' of the exhibition grounds. 'The principle of nationality, which underlies the whole conception, has been resurrected in the "national houses"', a critic commented. The so-called, hitherto prevalent pavilion principle was an invention of the 1870s. With the new classification system established here in Paris in 1900, participating nations had to exhibit on 18 different sites if they wished to show their exhibits in all the sections. In an effort to retain some national self-presentation, an entire *Rue des Nations* was created along the Seine between the Pont d'Alma and the Pont des Invalides, where all the buildings had been erected by workmen from the participating nations themselves. In addition, many of the participating foreign nations presented their respective colonies in the much-studied *Exposition coloniale*, located entirely in the garden of the Trocadéro on *rive droite*.[80]

Already for the 1889 Exposition Universelle, a section of the Esplanade had been taken over for a display of French colonies, including various ethnographic villages, populated by more than 400 'natives'. Yet colonization was not a distinct group in the official classification system as it would become 11 years later, and neither were individual exhibition pavilions built for each colony.[81] In 1900, the colonial exhibition was prominently placed in the Trocadéro gardens, the available space being divided into two equal areas, thus demonstrating the now greatly increased significance of such displays (Figure 3.8). The western half was reserved for pavilions of the French colonies, especially the two 'colonial crowns', Algeria and Tunisia, with two and five separate pavilions respectively that formed the focal points of the entire section, but also including free-standing buildings for Sudan, Senegal, the French East Indies, Dahomey, Indochina, Antilles, and New Caledonia. As the colonial minister's delegate →Jules Charles-Roux, a successful shipping magnate from Marseilles and organizer of the entire colonial section, explained, the altogether 28 pavilions and palaces had been located with a view to replicating their geographical affinity. Here a number of colonial restaurants and 'native villages' with altogether 476 'specimens' from places of origin as diverse as Tunisia, West Africa, Madagascar, and Indochina could be found, commonly described as producing a 'lively illusion of reality'. Further supplementary sections included a 'diorama of the colonies' and an official building by the French Ministry of the Colonies placed somewhat to the side. 'No other part of the exposition grounds', critics hailed, unsurprisingly, 'shows such a polyglot of nations, such a diversity in architecture or such a variety of exhibits.'[82]

In the opposite, eastern half of the Trocadéro grounds, the participating foreign powers presented 'their' colonies including British, Dutch and Portuguese possessions, but also countries such as Egypt, China and, in particular, Japan. 'Its presence here', one guide commented critically, 'contradicts the classification of this group as reserved for foreign colonies, a contradiction perhaps consolatory to the Transvaal

Figure 3.8   View onto the Eiffel Tower and the Champ de Mars, with the foreign colonial sections to the left (east), the French ones to the right (west), and the Trocadéro Park in the foreground. In the background across the Seine the Ferris Wheel and the Great Celestial Globe stand out
Source: Exposition universelle 1900, n.p.

and also to China.'[83] The British colonial section featured an Indian and Ceylon pavilion, in addition to two smaller buildings for all the other colonies and dominions. Painted in pure white and, unlike most other buildings, lighted by electricity after dark, it attracted more than six million visitors strolling in extensive 'Indian Tea Courts', gazing at several tableaux of life-size wild animals such as elephants, leopards and bears, or lunching nearby in a popular Indian and Colonial restaurant, privately opened on the Quai de Billy. Generally, however, critics regretted that the British Empire was not well presented. The principle, adopted throughout the entire exposition, that space assigned to France should be as large as that occupied by all other nations meant that many non-French colonies found the areas at their disposal inadequate, leading them to decline their participation in the exposition altogether.[84] German colonies, for example, were not on show at all. In the end, the entire colonial section followed an evident structure: Clearly distinguishing between French and non-French 'possessions', the section spatially reflected the colonies' position vis-à-vis the various European motherlands. Although set apart from them *and* the main grounds, the colonial pavilions nevertheless formed part of both.

Public reaction to the colonial exposition proved largely favorable, especially on the part of the numerous foreign visitors. Some, however, deplored the lack of novelty compared to other imperial expositions. →Otto N. Witt, for instance, a chemistry professor at the Technical University of Berlin, lauded the human diversity picturesquely staged in the Trocadéro gardens but could not help expressing a certain feeling of boredom caused by the repetitiveness. 'Everything has been erected very attractively, every pavilion has its own restaurant, in which colorfully dressed African girls present the products of their home countries', he wrote: 'Very dark negroes, Bedouins and others are represented here and there is no lack of black-eyed women and grubby children of every age. [...] Whoever has not been to the Orient is still familiar with such sights from the exhibitions in which they have reappeared for some decades.'[85] Anton Friebel, an Austrian teacher and school inspector, making an official inspection of the Paris exposition during his holidays on behalf of the Austrian Ministry of Culture and Education, did not differentiate between the hustle and bustle on the streets of the metropolis on the one hand, and the numerous strangers and foreign visitors – 'the most unusual types of people of foreign nationality never seen by me before' – on the other. The latter he 'studied' especially intensely within the exposition's colonial section:

> At first, one had to get used to the surge of people on the streets and squares, trams of all kinds, omnibuses crammed full of people; many, many motor cars, producing diverse, sometimes even irritating trumpet signals, bicycles, etc. were speeding through the roads in all directions. The mixture of Negroes, Arabs, Turks, Persians, and other nations presented a fascinating picture in their special national costume. These colorful teeming crowds were especially impressive in the area of the Trocadéro Palace, where the buildings and squares of the foreign colonial exhibition were located.[86]

Despite such enthusiastic accounts, the French organizers themselves were not entirely convinced that the colonies had been represented with the accuracy and the amount of space they – and their political cause – deserved. As historian William H. Schneider has noted, there was a constant tension between two different images of the French Empire – economic *mise en valeur* versus colonial exoticism – throughout the entire section and nowhere completely resolved.[87] Criticized even by colonial writers such as Marie Justin Maurice Coste (1850–1931), publishing under the pseudonym Maurice Talmeyr, the two Expositions Coloniales held in Marseilles in 1906, again under Charles-Roux's direction, and 1922, respectively, as well as the 1931 Exposition Coloniale must be regarded as attempts to simultaneously draw on and also correct some of the stale and not entirely satisfying exoticism so prevalent in 1889 and 1900.[88]

Further east along the venue, on the other side of the Seine, the so-called *Rue des Nations* was to be found (Figure 3.9). Here, on a 2.24-kilometer stretch, many of the participating foreign nations and all the great powers had erected special pavilions in two parallel rows of buildings. Contemporaries considered this one of the most significant features of the entire exposition. 'These residences of the foreign powers', a guidebook declared, 'could almost be called their "homes within the little exhibition city".' Calling it 'the most important part of the Exhibition', Vicomte H. de Kératry,

Figure 3.9   Westward panorama of the Seine in 1900 with the *Rue des Nations* (left) on its southern bank, and the pavilion of the *Ville de Paris* (right) on its northern bank; photograph taken from the Pont Alexandre III
Source: Courtesy of California State University, Fresno, Special Collections Research Center, Larson Collection.

author of an immensely successful British guidebook that went into several editions, informed potential visitors that the entire street would 'require to be seen minutely and carefully [...], and it would therefore be better to consecrate two days to it.'[89]

Located diagonally opposite the *Rue des Nations*, as part of the Cours la Reine on *rive droite*, was the so-called *Rue de Paris*, an area devoted to the City of Paris, both 'vieux' and 'moderne'. Often considered a 'veritable city unto itself', buildings here were placed in two rows, with one row bordering the Seine and the other the Cours la Reine and the Quai de Billy, thus running parallel with the river. Made entirely of wood, the *Pavillon de la Ville de Paris* claimed to be a faithful reproduction of the Hôtel de Ville, though the original was but a short distance away. Here the local municipality exhibited some of the metropolis' features, such as a miniature reproduction of the park of Versailles, and, above all different public works and infrastructural measures including water works, drains, sewers, lighting and schooling.[90] Gaston Bergeret (1840–?), for many years chief secretary in the Chamber of Deputies and author of a satirical account entitled *Journal d'un nègre à l'Exposition de 1900*, ridiculed the apparently jumbled conglomeration of exhibits. 'The pavilion of the City of Paris offers a tableau of life in this great capital. Here one sees a school desk, a hospital bed, a prison gate, water testing, portraits of various microbes – and of all the police prefects', he wrote.[91] Just like *Alt-Berlin* at the Gewerbeausstellung of 1896 and numerous other retrospectives at earlier exhibitions, the *Rue de Paris'* historical section – aptly called *Vieux Paris* – promised

Figure 3.10   The retrospective ensemble *Vieux Paris* in 1900, located on the northern banks of the Seine
Source: Courtesy of California State University, Fresno, Special Collections Research Center, Larson Collection.

its visitors an imaginary journey backward in time (Figure 3.10). Located only a short distance from the Trocadéro, 'it will be possible to step from amid the marvels of the present directly into the middle of the seventeenth century', where 'a most fascinating jumble of periods, buildings, customs and costumes' could be expected. So different guidebooks and journals described this veritable *pastiche*, carefully assembled and staged by the prolific author and celebrated artist →Albert Robida. Here, the visitor, ready to embark on a journey back in time could expect to find 'a whole village of the Middle Ages, but raised on piles and enclosing gatehouses and common lodgings, towers and barbicans, dwellings of the famous market stalls and a theater, palace halls and chapels, water wells and a pillory, shops and workshops, and numerous taverns', altogether a wholly functional miniature city within the city, as its creator proudly claimed, where people, appropriately costumed, 'lived the life of other days'.[92]

Yet, though divided into three distinct *quartiers*, *Vieux Paris'* exact location in historical time was even more vague than in the case of Berlin. While some parts, such as the Porte St Michel (Figure 3.11), were generally attributed to the fifteenth century, others, such as 'Les Halles', were described as representing the eighteenth, while further areas were claimed to represent mixtures of the seventeenth and eighteenth centuries, the Middle Ages, the Renaissance or even the time of Louis XIV. The various quarters, then, were not held together by an overarching

Figure 3.11   Porte St Michel, the main entrance to the *Vieux Paris* section at the 1900
exposition, facing the Place d'Alma
Source: Campbell, *Illustrated History*, 116.

historical narrative. Portrayed was an idealized, picturesque version of a city that
never existed and indeed had very little to do with the masses, the Revolution,
filth and crime that the streets of 'old Paris' would have evoked only a few decades
earlier.[93] Observers and critics were quick to realize that this exhibitionary feature
was far from being a conceptual innovation, but rather an import from other
West European exposition venues which now formed an integral part of the entire
medium, attempting to present a 'reader's digest' version of the city's idealized past.
Yet popular descriptions aiming at a wider audience did not consider it necessary
to differentiate over-much. '"Old Paris" adds a keynote of mediævalism and serves

Figure 3.12   The 'Salle des Illusions' inside the *Palais d'Electricité*, itself considered as modern as its subject matter
Source: Photograph taken by Helio Fortier-Marotte. Courtesy of California State University, Fresno, Special Collections Research Center, Leighton Collection, Nr. 171.

to link together the present and the past', noted one, while another labeled the hodge-podge hardly more precisely by naming it 'little Paris of ancient times'. A German guide rejoiced, writing 'to put it briefly: this little town takes us back completely to the good old times.' Others, however, claimed exactly the opposite, attributing the absence of any 'intimate sentiment' on actually entering the site to the replica's absolute lack of 'archaic faithfulness'.[94] False copies could not evoke true feelings.

One of the most striking sections that ran counter to the generally retrospective tone of the whole exposition – and which, perhaps for this reason, proved more successful than many of the other exhibits – was the *Palais d'Electricité*, located at the southern end of the Champ de Mars and designed by the exposition's principal architect →Eugène Hénard. In the form of a trilobate vault, containing the rococo *Château d'Eau* in the ensuing niche and entirely devoted to electricity and its applications, the *Palais* propagated the widespread use of a new technology considered a modern innovation at the nexus of global interest. In its center stood an allegorical statue of Electricity together with two fantastic beasts set against a huge metal sun; numerous mirrors inside the hall multiplied and reinforced the mysterious light effects (Figure 3.12). Outside, the *Palais'* roof was crowned with a huge, three-dimensional star that was illuminated at night, and water washed down grottoes powered by electrical generators hidden inside the building.[95] Although electricity as a new means of energy-transmission had already been the subject of a number of more specialized and far smaller exhibitions in Paris (1881), Munich (1882) and Frankfurt am Main (1891), it had never before been featured on such a scale in a universal exhibition with the sole exception of – once again – the 1893 Columbian Exposition in Chicago. Already during the exposition's run-up, critics were altogether enthusiastic, for example calling the palace 'the most dazzlingly, bewilderingly beautiful structure ever conceived by architectural mind', itself symbolizing 'something of the flashing and restless character of electricity', while others hailed it as 'new and modern as the element for which it stands'.[96]

In Paris, electricity was not only exhibited in the form of machines, lights and dynamos, but was also used extensively to drive machines and to illuminate elaborate displays at night, which, in turn, rendered the site in such an entirely new light that some observers spoke of a 'completely different exposition'. With electricity so widespread and the exposition's own main source of energy, it had technically become possible to apply a new classification system differentiating between production machines and power machines. The former fabricated goods, while the latter produced energy, which was in turn used to power the production machines. Moreover, electricity made illumination possible and thus prolonged the exposition's opening hours by 'two hundred nights'. It demonstrated that it was now possible to transport energy over distance, simply by applying it to itself. 'Electricity, veritable fairy of modern times, will preside over those destined for the ephemeral city born inside Paris', observed a contemporary journalist summarizing its twofold effect, on the exposition in particular and modern life in general: 'It will deposit in its cradle these living gifts of attraction and originality: light and movement.'[97] Electricity's importance to the entire exhibition was rated so high, that, according to one prolific art critic, →Georg Malkowsky, the central power station should be regarded as its 'very soul' – which was almost tantamount to nominating the *Palais* the exposition's *clou*. Still, the French poet and popular writer →Paul Morand went even further when declaring electricity as developing into the new religion of a dawning century: 'Electricity can be accumulated, condensed, transformed, put in bottles, stretched on wires, rolled onto coils, then discharged in water, on fountains, freed onto roofs, unleashed in trees – it is the plague, the religion of 1900.'[98] While the section's overt – and possibly inordinate – success can only be explained by the fact that the *Palais d'Electricité* was one of the few exhibits perceived as genuinely innovative, its central position at the southern end of the Champ de Mars further indicates that the exposition meta-medium not only generated novel forms of mass entertainment and spectacle but also swiftly incorporated those recently developed elsewhere, provided that they had proven successful in other exhibitionary contexts. Once integrated, these new features were then popularized and introduced to an international public. Both native villages and colonial sections must be seen as further examples of the medium's endogenous catalytic functions, exemplified by the *Palais d'Electricité*.

The heterogeneity that characterized the entire exposition extended not only to the 'serious' sections and state-sponsored displays, but also to the almost 60 commercially oriented and mostly privately run 'concessions'. These were known as *attractions* or *spectacles*, which, in the contemporary French sense, meant 'show' or 'entertainment'. Unlike at previous expositions, the attractions were scattered throughout the enclosure with the majority situated just below the Eiffel Tower and hence either directly on, or in the immediate vicinity of, the Champ de Mars, visible from the Seine and the right bank. In addition to scientifically minded attractions such as the *Palais de l'Optique* – featuring a huge telescope to study the moon and said to be so powerful 'that animals as large as an elephant should plainly be seen' on its surface – offers for more worldly, yet equally imagined, journeys abounded. The so-called *Maréorama* depicted a voyage on the Mediterranean Sea from Marseilles to Naples, Venice and Constantinople on a vast panorama slowly unfolding itself, while the *Cinéorama* offered an imaginary balloon trip inside the building itself, traversing one country after another.[99]

Two further buildings of a similar kind aroused even more attention in the official guides, if not necessarily among the paying public: both the *Globe céleste* and the *Panorama-Diorama du Tour du Monde* – often simply abbreviated as *Tour du Monde* – located at the angle of the Avenue de la Bourdonnais and the Quai d'Orsay, taught practical geography by offering imaginary travel both in space and time (Figures 3.13, right, and 3.7). While the former made a trip around the entire world possible inside a huge model of the earth, the latter – a *panorama animé* – simulated motion through voyage and offered a mélange of indigenous styles both inside and out. The *Magasin Pittoresque* explained the *Tour du Monde*'s promise to 'transport us successively by sight of various points of the globe' in more detail: 'Scenes appropriate to each country, represented in the foreground by natives in their costumes with the customs and habits of daily life, will complete the ensemble and will give each tableau an intensity of local color, which, put into relief by combined lighting effects, will give the impression of reality.' Countries 'visited' on the tour included Turkey, Syria, India and China, all subject to varying forms of European colonialism and hence not entirely unfamiliar to a largely European audience. The popularity of panoramas and dioramas around the turn of the century, an innovation of the early nineteenth century that culminated in film, has led contemporary observers and present-day historians alike to speak of '*fin-de-siècle* panoramania' and full-fledged 'ecstasy', with the *Tour du Monde* and its integration of painted panoramas with moving pictures and live performers as its pinnacle.[100]

Yet, although lauded by numerous commentators – 'This is a geography lesson, enriched by all the ingenious tricks and effects of our modern times', a critic enthused, for instance – the globe, this 'gigantic sphere' containing the 'universe in miniature' and featuring a unique 'pygmy world' went into bankruptcy after only a few weeks. Various other attractions included a 'Swiss Village' located just beyond the core site, a 'Venice in Paris' show and an entire section devoted to the subterranean world with imitations of mines, archeological reconstructions, replicated tomb-chambers and prehistoric caves.[101] All of them functioned on a similar principle of creating attraction through cultural difference, geographical

Figure 3.13 View from the Seine onto the Eiffel Tower and the Celestial Globe
Source: Olivares, *The Parisian Dream City* (9 August 1900), n.p.

remoteness and rampant exoticism. As such, they attempted to provide different perspectives on the 'world' with a degree of realism better even than reality itself. As was constantly emphasized, the grandest and the tiniest, the biggest and the smallest, the nearest and the most distant had all been gathered together and brought into a self-contained urban environment where they could all easily be consumed, without great expense or effort. 'A tour around the world in 24 minutes!', a second commentator exclaimed, hailing the exposition as 'the symbol of our age'.[102] Further southwest of the Champ de Mars was another spectacular and popular yet conceptually different feature, which, next to the Eiffel Tower, stood as the tallest structure on the site: the *Grande Roue* or Great Wheel. The wheel remained an unintentional legacy after the exposition's closure, staying in place until the First

World War, when its huge cars were removed to provide emergency housing units in the industrial north of France.[103]

One of the unexpected yet powerful structural consequences of a continuous 50-year French exhibition tradition was the widely shared assumption that each exposition must feature a distinct *clou*. The term referred to the respective exhibition's 'star attraction', whose aura and grandeur, it was hoped, would radiate out to other, less impressive sections and less striking displays. An *attraction*, though, was considered insufficiently serious to be a *clou*. Additionally, the term possessed an onomatopoeic dimension: a *clou* had to give a *clue* to make the internal, spatial functioning of the site comprehensible. While the *clou* was generally meant to be the pre-eminent exhibit, lording over a carefully established hierarchy, designed to provide the entire site with a central, clarifying perspective, it was usually among those few elements that were to become permanent structures after the exposition's closure. The ideal *clou* was designed to transcend the respective exhibition's present and reach out into the future – thereby negating the two fundamental exposition principles of transience and comprehensiveness – and eventually to develop into a monument which would demonstrate to posterity the great achievements of the exhibition. The ideal *clou* served a twofold function: first, it structured the exposition's internal space; second, in its planned permanence it provided a convincing reply to the oft-repeated 'day-after question'. Conceptually, however, the creation of a central perspective was paramount. It is unsurprising, then, that an increasing number of *clous* were observation posts and lookout towers from which one could survey the whole exposition.[104]

Though the concept of the *clou* was present even in the medium's mid-nineteenth-century origins, the term itself only emerged later, when it had become the medium-defining element. The French expression gained ground in the English and German languages as well, soon to become an established *terminus technicus*. 'All various world exhibitions have striven to feature buildings which are architectural focal points, in order to create an exposition with an unforgettable character', a German commentator summarized the previous development in the early 1890s, without directly referencing the term.[105] Famous examples *avant la lettre* include the Crystal Palace in 1851, the elliptic layout of the Parisian 1867 site, the Viennese Rotunda in 1873, the Trocadéro Palace in 1878 or the combination of the Eiffel Tower and *Galerie des Machines* at the Champ de Mars as the 1889 exposition's distinct double feature and companion *clous*.[106]

Yet did the Exposition Universelle of 1900 possess a *clou* proper? That such a question can be asked reveals the exposition's complexity. In the run-up to the exposition, this issue had been debated at length and with great care when considering different schemes and proposals. In August 1895, the aforementioned architectural journalist Planat summarized and ridiculed some of the submitted proposals, saying:

We are offered lakes to dig where there are mounds, hills where there are holes; we are offered balloons adapted to Russian mountains; they let us see the moon. Just as a tower 400 meters high does not offer many new surprises after one of 300, they invite us to dig holes that will descend much lower. [...] This obviously spares us sensations that are wholly different and absolutely new.[107]

Once opened, a major controversy about the exposition's central exhibit arose, and the question was never decided unanimously. Although it was known from the outset that the 1900 exposition would *not* feature anything comparable to that of 1889, at least five different positions on this question can be identified. The majority opinion, that of the largest group of commentators, observers and critics, argued that the exhibition had three, if not four, *clous* since the Avenue Nicolas II, the two *Palais des Beaux Arts*, and the Pont Alexandre III were all to survive as permanent reminders and 'fitting monument[s] to the glories of the year 1900'. 'The Alexandre III bridge', a French journalist decreed, 'should be considered as the "clou" of the Exposition', while a British guidebook briefly explained the entire principle to its readers:

> This exposition, like its predecessors, will leave Paris permanently enriched by the addition of something in the way of architecture. The fair of 1878 left a reminder of itself in the shape of the Trocadéro palace. The exposition of 1889 gave to Paris the Eiffel tower, and the exposition of 1900 contributes to the beauty of the region the Champ de Mars, the Alexander bridge and the art buildings.[108]

This stance was, however, fiercely challenged by a second group, which questioned whether the massive bridge, with its two groups of towers, surmounted by gilded Pegasus statues and recumbent female figures representing France in four different historical epochs, could be a *clou*. It would have been built whether or not there was an exposition, they claimed, and was opened well before the inauguration of the great event.[109] A third group suggested that another outstanding building, the aforementioned *Palais d'Electricité*, was one of the 'most attractive features of the exhibition', since it represented one of the century's most important achievements and was considered an emblem of modernity. Lessing, for example, agreed with his colleague Malkowsky. 'In front of this hall, there is a large Palace of Electricity', he drew his readers' attention to a particular architectural detail, 'which is to be enriched by the clou of this exhibition: electrically illuminated waterfalls', and some even went so far as to declare a single electric exhibit displayed in the *Palais*, which had only recently been developed and was here presented for the first time – the incandescent bulb – the actual and much-sought after *clou*.[110]

Others proposed different structures for this eminent position, such as the *Château d'Eau*, the *Deutsches Haus* or even the entire *Rue des Nations* along the Seine, the latter being 'on account of its special character [...] the most important part of the Exhibition', despite the fact that the concept was neither particularly new nor innovative. Even infrastructural measures such as the Métro, though planned well ahead of – and independently of – the exposition itself were suggested.[111] Or did the Seine itself possibly constitute the desperately desired *clou*? True, never before had the capital's river been incorporated so deliberately into the exposition grounds and layout; yet could a natural phenomenon really qualify as *the* highlight? The art historian →Julius Meier-Graefe, for instance, did not have the slightest doubt: 'The clou this time is an old, but no less charming one: it is the Seine, which always refreshes our eyes, even when they have become weary from all the sights.'[112] Citing this fierce debate, a fifth group of observers argued that the exposition as such lacked any *clou* at all. According to them, in assembling the century's final universal exposition, the 'city without a center' had created a fleeting entity echoing the capital, which also famously lacked an obvious center.[113] A genuine *clou* manifests itself and is, therefore, by definition evident. Conversely, while its meaning is obviously contingent, it does not require any general agreement or even a 'vote', and neither can the *clou* be the result of a lengthy decision-making process via public discussion. Even if it had been possible to settle these differences of opinion, the very fact of the debate proved their point that there simply was, in Paris in 1900, no genuine *clou*.[114]

No star attraction

A city w/o a soul? center?

An exposition in 1911?

Observers, visitors and critics alike were all intimidated by the exposition's sheer scale, which seemed to make an adequate overview virtually impossible – and led to a comprehensive debate on the question of the exhibition's principal 'imperceptibility'. When it was closed in November 1900, final reactions were varied, and conclusions drawn from this mega-event divergent. Critics bemoaned the immense and ever-increasing cost of more than 110 million francs – twice as much as 1889 – although the official deficit amounted to a modest two million francs.[115] In a long and moving passage, worth being quoted at length for its exceptional eloquence, chemistry professor Otto Witt, in one long breath, bid farewell to the exposition, its host city and the entire century alike, using an ascent to the Eiffel Tower to see things from a distance and hence in perspective:

> And now it is time to say farewell to the exposition. Whoever wants to let this giant portrait of life really take lasting effect should take one of the tireless lifts of the Eiffel Tower to the dizzy heights of the highest of all buildings. There they lie at our feet, all the shining palaces and wondrous buildings, seen in miniature as on a map. And on the spacious squares, thousands of people move like little black spots. The noise of the exposition is merely heard as a dull buzzing sound. Yet around the exhibition, even more imposing than that, appears Lutetia, the old city which has suffered so much but remains eternally young. There she lies, with her endless streets and incomparable buildings with their noble dimensions, with the shimmering domes and high towers. The town stretches as far as we can see, and through its dark masses of houses, appear the silvery twists and turns of the river. [...] What the exposition wants to tell us as a whole, it tells us here in its main part of the city: it gives us an overwhelming and splendid picture of the creativity and thirst for knowledge of humanity at the end of the nineteenth century. If it is acceptable to identify turning-points

in time, which exist more in the mind of men than in reality, and to mark these with festivals and events, then this could not happen in a more festive and splendid form than it does in relation to the nineteenth century with the one-year exposition, to which we now say goodbye.[116]

Numerous other visitors reacted with criticism and doubt rather than enthusiasm and solemnity. Quite frequently, the hope that this was the final international exhibition was expressed. 'Is this the last one?', writer Coste asked wearily – and replied: 'We hope so.'[117] In one of the last of his detailed reports on the Exposition Universelle, museum director Lessing came to a similar conclusion. International expositions had finally reached their absolute limits of growth, he argued, and any kind of further extension seemed simply inconceivable:

> One thing is really clear: an exposition of this kind is no longer feasible. Here in Paris, we have reached the absolute limits of a city's resources. Even now, there is hardly enough space. The streets are altogether too narrow and at many points there is a lack of light and air. If, in approximately ten years, we should consider another world exhibition, we will have to take into account that no city in the entire world offers the same resources as Paris. And Paris itself would have to make an even greater effort in order to resist harsh criticism, since a smaller version is definitely out of the question. Even if public transport increases and improves considerably: the interest that Paris shows in the exposition is of purely local nature. One would never spend millions just to allow foreigners to travel beyond the city limits. It is quite possible that this exhibition is not only a symbol for the end of this century but will also put an end to this type of world's fair.[118]

A fourth visitor expressed this position even more drastically. For him, it was evident that the spectacle staged here could not be topped. Since the drive to enlarge each successive exhibition was seen as absolutely essential to the medium's functioning, the only conclusion remaining logically possible was that here – in Paris in 1900 – the nineteenth-century exposition tradition had come to an irrevocable end:

> Even more floor space, even more diverse presentations cannot be offered by a future exposition, because human powers of comprehension could not deal with more. The time of world exhibitions has passed, and the epoch of competitive and specialized exhibitions has begun. Thus, we return to a path of action which should never have been abandoned.[119]

Even if the protests during the exposition's run-up and widespread feelings of exhaustion after the fact are taken into account, it seems, in retrospect, somewhat unexpected how quickly and with what little ado the Parisian 11-year tradition came to an end. The demolition process of the exposition's ephemeral structures

Figure 3.14 Panorama of the Champ de Mars in 1910. View from the Eiffel Tower, with the military school and the Great Wheel in the background
Source: Abercrombie, 'The Champ de Mars, Paris', plate 77.

was realized quite slowly and, when finally completed in 1902, the 'vast desert' of the Champ de Mars was quietly transformed into a park, now in possession of the Ville de Paris. The remaining *Galerie des Machines* was vehemently criticized as a nuisance, and already by 1891 the *Société des amis des monuments parisiens* demanded its immediate demolition since it hampered the view to the Ecole militaire.[120] With this legacy dismantled as well, the final remnants of the exposition were gone by 1909–10, and the site was transformed back into a park and upscale urban recreation area through 1928 (Figure 3.14). As a consequence of what town planner and architect →Sir Patrick Abercrombie called 'the first piece of Town Planning on a large scale [...] undertaken in Paris' since Haussmann, an uninterrupted vista, reaching from the Trocadéro across the Seine and through the Eiffel Tower's great arch to the Ecole militaire, was recreated.[121]

Interestingly, the year 1911 was never under serious discussion for a sixth Parisian Exposition Universelle. Apparently, the 11-year tradition had been invented in the early 1890s with a particular political object in mind, namely to legitimize the proposed 1900 exposition and to justify French claims to worldwide supremacy in this particular field. Although directly referring to this invented tradition when stating that 'France should not abandon a tradition

I wondered all along if this was the plan

that does it honor', the leftist *député* Lucien Cornet (1865–1922) suggested in
the *Chambre* that 1920, not 1911, be the date for the next Parisian universal
exhibition so as to coincide with the Third Republic's semicentennial.[122] Yet the
proposal met with negligible public response and was not revived until six years
later, though widespread reservations remained. In a national enquiry undertaken by the *Féderation des industriels et commerçants français*, 315 out of 477
communes declared themselves strictly opposed to such a plan. Yet, there were
also voices who carefully noted the great success such non-French international
exhibitions as the ones held in St Louis (1904), Liège (1905), or the Franco-
British Exhibition in London (1908) had achieved – the latter the subject matter
of the following chapter – which they considered 'excellent copies, that are very
successful, too' of the 'original works of art' that were the French nineteenth-
century *expositions*. Thus, inter-urban competition and the insistence on French
authorship for the global exposition medium ensured that the show went on in
Paris as well, despite growing practical, conceptual and theoretical doubts – and,
above all, the fact that alternative and more modern sites of modernity, such as
the cinema, would soon gain precedence. Large-scale expositions continued to
be held throughout the world, but their classical period had come to an irretriev-
able, if spectacular end.[123]

4

London 1908: Imre Kiralfy and the Franco-British Exhibition

Good old London's in a maze
With its very latest craze,
And ev'ry day in crowds we fight and push
On a motor'bus to climb
Twenty-seven at a time,
Or take the good old tube to Shepherd's Bush.
It's an Exhibition rare
That is drawing thousands there,
Ev'ry nation joining in the grand display,
So to see it you contrive,
But, directly you arrive,
The girlie hanging on your arm will say:

Chorus
Take me on the Flip Flap, Do, dear, do!
It looks so lovely down below
So you pay your money and up you go.
And though a queer sensation,
You wish it would never stop,
But down you slide on the other side,
With a Flip flap flop.

From each far off foreign land
There are tokens rare and grand
In ev'ry nook and corner placed on view.
And, all scattered round the place,
Of the girls of ev'ry race
You'll see some lovely exhibitions, too.
There are things you mustn't touch,
Though you'd like to, very much,
But suppose a little French girl comes your way,

Though you try to parlez-vous,
She won't parley long with you,
But with a saucy smile at one she'll say:

Chorus
Take me on the Flip Flap, &c.[1]

After the Great Exhibition's astounding success in 1851 and the almost complete failure of its designated successor, the International Exhibition, held 11 years later in South Kensington, no 'official' universal exposition was again held in the capital of the Empire. 'Since then, London has not been prepared to take on the burden of a true world exhibition', German museum director and art historian Julius Lessing noted in March 1900. Especially in comparison to Paris, the exposition movement had 'languished in London', Scottish biologist and town planner →Patrick Geddes noted at the same time, and a British architectural critic agreed when stating that 'the fascination of exhibitions on a large scale' had been 'strangely slow in seizing upon London'.[2] In 1852, the icon of the Great Exhibition and signum of the Victorian age, the Crystal Palace, was purchased by a private consortium for a nominal fee and relocated to Sydenham, a suburb in the south of London, approximately 15 kilometers from Trafalgar Square, where a remodeled and enlarged structure was re-erected and reopened in the summer of 1854. Beginning in the late 1880s, several exhibitions of limited size and scope were held there, culminating in the grand Festival of Empire celebrated in 1911. Although very popular at first and attracting millions of annual visitors, the reassembled building removed to Sydenham was subject to a steady demise and over time lost the original's 'nearly religious aura' almost completely. A letter published in *The Times* on the occasion of the Festival described the Palace as 'becoming dilapidated' before it eventually burned down in a dramatic fire on 30 November 1936.[3]

In London itself, numerous specialized, and often privately organized, exhibitions began to be held from the 1880s onwards. In addition to Sydenham and the old site in South Kensington, where →Sir Francis Philip Cunliffe-Owen organized between 1883 and 1886 a different exhibition each year on various themes, all of them took place at three different venues in west London: Earl's Court (1887–1908), Olympia (1891–99), and the White City (1908–14).[4]

The oldest of these three sites, Earl's Court, served as a permanent exhibition center from 1887 through the First World War. Originally occupied by a manor and grounds belonging to the earls of Oxford (hence its name), the land had become the property of the District Railway Company and was incorporated with the westward expansion of London's housing and rail communication in the early 1880s when businessman and impresario →John Robinson Whitley purchased the site. Whitley secured a triangular expanse of more or less derelict market gardens, ten hectares, between Earl's Court, West Brompton and West Kensington, with four railroad stations in their immediate vicinity, and transformed the site from a 'huge cabbage-garden' into a suitable exhibition ground, consisting of three distinct areas connected by enclosed bridges.[5]

Both the venue and its founder achieved public renown when a series of four national industrial exhibitions – American, Italian, French and German – held at Earl's Court between 1887 and 1891 proved great successes. Attracting 1.4 million visitors in only 133 days, the German Exhibition was actively supported by the *Verein Berliner Kaufleute und Industrieller* but not by the Kaiser. The French Exhibition, held a year earlier, in 1890, sought to present a 'best of' selection of the Parisian Exposition Universelle of 1889 to a British audience. 'France in Miniature' included a reduced replica of the Eiffel Tower, a stretch of gardens in the style of Versailles and an 'African jungle' with more than 100 'natives' on display. With its bi-national theme and enriched by its imperial setting, the French Exhibition is properly considered a direct precursor of the 1908 Franco-British Exhibition, the primary concern of this chapter. It is somewhat ironic however, that this exposition, an event so thematically similar to the Franco-British Exhibition, albeit on a smaller scale, was organized by a competitor a mere 18 years before.[6] In addition to the pleasure gardens and the many exhibitions, spectacles and pageants, Earl's Court featured three main permanent attractions: the Empress Theatre (1895–1950s), itself a remnant of the Colonial and Indian Exhibition of 1886, a gigantic, if temporary structure which had never been dismantled and derived its name from several visits by Queen Victoria (1819–1901); the Imperial Palace; and, finally, the 'Gigantic', wheel built in 1894. Exhibitions continued to be held annually through 1908, when Earl's Court went into bankruptcy since it could not compete with the White City's success. In 1937, a huge hall was built there, which, after a difficult start, became one of the country's largest indoor arenas and exhibition halls, and it remains so today.[7]

The second of the three London exhibition venues, directly competing with Earl's Court, was Olympia, likewise located in West Kensington, though further northwest. Planned in 1884, it opened two years later as a west London rival to the Royal Agricultural Hall in Islington. From 1908 through 1951, Olympia was home to the annual British Industries Fairs, including the annual Ideal Home Exhibition initiated and established by the *Daily Mail* newspaper. In general, the trade fairs held at Olympia were only open to the public at certain times and were largely of a more directly commercial and trade-oriented character; still, Olympia constituted the focal point for many of Britain's biggest promotions. In 1920, the *Builder* directly compared it to the Parisian *Grand Palais*, erected in 1900, as fulfilling the same kind of exhibition service for London.[8] It was here that the hero of this chapter – the Hungarian Imre Kiralfy – entered the British exhibition scene, at the invitation of →Harold T. Hartley, a producer of mineral water and chairman of a business enterprise. From 1891 till 1906, they organized numerous exhibitions at Olympia, where some early Kiralfy productions included the exhibition Modern Venice in London, complete with a spectacle show *Venice: The Bride of the Sea* (1891–93), and the exhibition India: A Grand Historical Spectacle (1895). Later in 1895, Kiralfy was named as director-general of Earl's Court and fashioned it as a 'centre of pageantry and imperial pride'. Other thematically similar exhibitions such as Briton, Boer and Black in Savage South Africa (1899) were later organized at Olympia without his direct involvement, though clearly trying to profit from the same *fin-de-siècle* fashion for colonial exoticism.[9]

A superman in the exhibition world

The third and most important exhibition site, the White City, was the brainchild of →Imre Kiralfy (Figure 4.1). Born in Budapest on 1 January 1845, the son of Jewish parents, Kiralfy soon gained an international reputation as one of the most prolific theater managers, entertainment impresarios and producers of numerous imperial spectacles, the majority of which, though not all, were held in London. Although largely forgotten today, leisure historians have gone so far as to call him the 'British Empire's public relations agent, glorifying imperialism'. Having been trained as a dancer and subsequently as a theater manager in Brussels, New York and Chicago, Kiralfy produced his first independent show in New York in 1874. He became better known in the late 1880s when he began to stage much bigger historical spectacles and pageants such as *Nero, or the Fall of Rome* (1889) or the already-mentioned 'aquatic pageant' *Venice: The Bride of the Sea*. In 1891, Kiralfy turned from spectacles to the organization of exhibitions in which pageants became integrated. 'Informative' exhibitions, and entertainment-oriented spectacles

Figure 4.1   Portrait of British exhibition impresario Imre Kiralfy (1845–1919), wearing Masonic medals
Source: Courtesy of Museum of London, Imre Kiralfy Collection, 82-232/490.

and historical pageants shared the same subject matter and thus ideally complemented one another. Until the end of his career, the impresario Kiralfy worked to join these two approaches, almost to the point of perfection.[10]

While Kiralfy's early productions were undertaken in cooperation with the American Barnum Circus Enterprises at Olympia, the first of the three sites, his newly established company, The London Exhibitions Ltd, took over Earl's Court, the second site, in 1894 and subsequently completely redeveloped the entertainment complex. Here, with Harold T. Hartley as managing director and →Paul Cremieu-Javal as chairman, Kiralfy staged nine expositions over the course of the next nine years. Through their concerted activities, Earl's Court became one of the most spectacular exhibition sights of Edwardian London, 'greatly adding to the gaiety of the imperial capital'. All of the exhibitions held there were devoted to imperial themes of different kinds and scope. Either they displayed typical products of single colonies (Empire of India Exhibition, 1895; Empire of India and Ceylon Exhibition, 1896; Greater Britain Exhibition, 1899), had the most comprehensive *omnium gatherum* theme possible (International Universal Exhibition, 1896) or presented a 'best of' selection from the 1900 Parisian Exposition Universelle (Paris in London Exhibition, 1902).[11] The Victorian Era Exhibition, staged in 1897, aimed at presenting a retrospective of Queen Victoria's life and times before they had actually come to an end. There was even a certain degree of international participation. In the Greater Britain Exhibition (1899), for example, a few smaller countries such as Switzerland or Belgium had separate sections.[12] But the vast majority of these Earl's Court exhibitions did not feature any official participants from abroad, and were at most bi-national. Their enormous popularity nonetheless made Kiralfy an expert in the public's eyes. Already a few years before his success with the White City, Imre Kiralfy's name had become a household word, and his work was highly praised. Kiralfy 'made it all real', as one observer put it. Eventually, the Franco-British Exhibition laid the foundations of his international renown. 'He has the reputation of being a very skilful and active businessman [...] and has, in other fields, gained much experience in exhibition work', a German diplomat reported. Even before the Franco-British Exhibition had actually opened, John George Campbell (1845–1914), ninth Duke of Argyll and the honorary president of the exhibition, had crowned the 'showman' *roi des fêtes*, alluding to the bi-national character of his most comprehensive exposition project, and others aggrandized him as 'one of the greatest living masters of form and colour'. After its closure, Kiralfy was likewise heralded 'superman in the exhibition world'.[13]

After resigning from his position as managing director of The London Exhibitions Ltd in 1902, Kiralfy moved in 1906 to the third venue in west London, the White City. Here, unlike at Earl's Court and Olympia, Kiralfy did not take over a pre-existing and well-established site but rather created and designed a new one for his own exhibition purposes. At the White City, Kiralfy produced seven expositions between 1908 and 1914.

In a self-congratulatory text entitled 'My Reminiscences', Kiralfy retrospectively described the largest of them, the Franco-British Exhibition of 1908 with 8.4 million visitors, as the 'summit of my life's achievements in the domain of public spectacle'. *The Strand Magazine,* which published this seven-page ego-document and referred to a planned autobiography, never to be written, extolled Kiralfy as 'by far the greatest living figure in the domain of public spectacle and mammoth entertainment'. In the article Kiralfy presented himself as in complete control over every possible situation, determined to bring about the largest spectacles possible, be they in Brussels, Philadelphia, New York, Chicago or London, characterizing himself as a truly global player. According to his own account, Kiralfy had experienced a deci- sive moment of revelation and personal awakening when first visiting the Paris Exposition Universelle of 1867 at the age of 22:

> But my mind was not made up nor my career fully determined until 1867, when [...] I went to Paris. The object of my visit was the International Exhibition in the Champs de Mars. This was the supreme achievement in the way of pageants and exhibitions. Not a single detail escaped me. I went about daily viewing this great spectacle, in whole and in parts from every point of view, and to my youthful mind the greatest man in the world then was the director-in-chief of that exhibition.[14]

Only one year later Kiralfy would begin to make his perceived personal destiny a reality by becoming director of a municipal fête in Brussels. Six years later, in 1873, he went to see the Viennese Weltausstellung. His depiction of a second, sim- ilarly revealing epiphany is even more telling. Though clearly a direct conceptual transfer from the 1893 World's Columbian Exposition in Chicago, the original White City, Kiralfy dramatically described how the vision of building a 'spotlessly white city' in London had suddenly appeared to him in a dream:

> One night I lay awake in bed and, as if by magic, I saw, stretched out in my mind's eye, an imposing city of palaces, domes, and towers, set in cool, green spaces and intersected by many bridged canals. But it had one characteristic which made it strangely beautiful. Hitherto I had dealt in colour in the shim- mering hues of gold and silver. The city was spotlessly white. I saw it all in an instant, and the next day I had jotted down the scheme of what London has learnt to know as the 'White City'.[15]

According to Kiralfy, it was only a matter of time and effort until this vision became reality, with the opening of London's version of the White City in 1908. The conclusion of his ego-document, written a year after the Franco-British Exhibition, was remarkably modest and formed a sharp contrast to the bulk of the self-confident, even blustering text. Not having mentioned any thematic concerns besides his own before, Kiralfy turned to the nation in order to retrospectively legitimize his life-long enterprise. It was a gratifying thought, Kiralfy concluded, that he might not only have helped to raise the standard of spectacular entertain- ment but also to have contributed something to the 'artistic needs' and 'gaiety of the nations'. When Imre Kiralfy died in Brighton on 27 April 1919, aged 74, he left the considerable fortune of £136,680, earned exclusively through the organization and production of imperial exhibitions and spectacular displays.[16]

Within a British context, Kiralfy had, over the course of two decades, turned the public medium 'exposition' into a private business enterprise. Yet how central the exhibitions' mostly imperial themes were to their popular success is difficult to ascertain. Although clearly dominant, they were by no means the sole focus. Other subject matters included antiquity, foreign countries and places, traveling and tourism. Simultaneously, imperially oriented themes were very much *en vogue* in numerous other venues and hence seem to have been easy to sell. Tellingly, Kiralfy's ego-document does not point to any kind of thematic agenda other than grandeur, exoticism and the most complete realism of representation possible.

It is clear that Kiralfy was successful in the process of controlling his public image. But more decisive in this context is the enormous number of different types of transnational networks in which Kiralfy actively participated and which had direct repercussions on the language of the spectacles he organized. Before analyzing the lavish 1908 Franco-British Exhibition in more detail, four of these networks will be briefly discussed, as they will allow the construction of an intertextual-interpretative framework: first, the international expositions that Kiralfy had visited himself; second, his personal contacts resulting from many of these visits; third, institutional overlappings; and fourth, direct conceptual transfers between various exposition venues.

Kiralfy had carefully studied elsewhere what he was to put on show in London. Before mounting the Franco-British Exhibition, he had visited three Parisian expositions over the course of 33 years, in 1867, 1889 and 1900. In addition, he saw a considerable number of other international exhibitions including Vienna in 1873, Philadelphia in 1876, Chicago in 1893, and the Berliner Gewerbeausstellung of 1896. In so doing Kiralfy sought to incorporate their cultural respectability into his own mass productions, sometimes quite literally: In Act III, Scene 4 of one of his patriotic spectacles organized within the framework of the 1893 World's Columbian Exposition in Chicago, the personified exposition itself appeared on stage, together with his favorite allegorical characters, 'Progress', 'Peace' and 'Liberty'. In addition, Kiralfy took on consultancy work with exhibition ventures in the early 1900s. In 1905 he was officially appointed *Commissaire général* of the British section at the Liège Exposition Universelle et Internationale; after his 1908 success, he became permanent advisor to the British government for foreign shows.[17]

While Kiralfy obviously had a great number of personal contacts, some of them were particularly crucial since they transcended institutional and national boundaries. He cooperated, for instance, with →Phineas Taylor Barnum, the great American impresario and circus showman; the aforementioned Pierre de Coubertin, the founder of the modern Olympic movement; and Lord Desborough (1855–1945), president of the British Olympic Council and later director of the sports section of the Franco-British Exhibition. In this regard, the association with Barnum – between 1888 and 1890 they had an official contract, Barnum died in early 1891 – was particularly important since Kiralfy would later take up and further refine a number of ideas first developed by him in the United States. Only personal contacts such as these made it possible for certain sections and key elements of his productions to be directly transferred and imported from one cultural context into another.[18]

After Athens 1896, Paris 1900 and St Louis 1904, the Quadrennial Olympic Games were combined with the Franco-British Exhibition in the first sports stadium expressly built for this purpose and dismantled only in the 1980s. Imre Kiralfy was not a strong advocate of the Olympic movement and by no means sought to make the Games the feature attraction of 1908. However, when the Italian government found itself unable to hold the Games in Rome in 1906 as originally planned due to the eruption of Mount Vesuvius in April 1906, Kiralfy embraced the opportunity and secured the Games as a sideshow to the Franco-British Exhibition, hoping that they would attract even larger crowds to the exhibition. Taking place during a fortnight in July 1908, the Games were neither part of the original plan nor even a feature attraction, but rather one of many sideshows. High admission costs and poor weather led to low attendance, and they made headline news only as a consequence of various rules disputes, the most controversial one including the Italian marathon runner Dorando Pietri (1885–1942) who was disqualified for being helped over the finishing line after having collapsed directly in front of it. It was only subsequently that the Olympic Games and world's fairs became two entirely separate institutions, with the former far superseding the latter. Although at this stage still subordinate to the exposition, Kiralfy's 1908 London Games did aid the Olympic movement in transforming it into a worldwide spectacle with international cooperation on all important issues, not the least because it was the first time that substantial new venues and facilities had been expressly built for the Olympics.[19]

Finally, many of Kiralfy's conceptual innovations were not new but rather copied and imported. Although presented as original ideas and unique innovations hitherto unseen at any other exhibition, in fact, Kiralfy took many of his creations directly from previous expositions where they had proved particularly successful. While some of these elements were of European origin, for example miniature ships and an emphasis on water from the Berliner Gewerbeausstellung, and a model for the structure of the Fine Arts Section from the 1900 Parisian Exposition Universelle, he imported and copied the majority of his ideas from the United States, in particular from the 1893 World's Columbian Exposition in Chicago. Examples include the Ferris Wheel at Earl's Court, central design elements of the White City such as the *Court of Honour*, and, of course, the White City's very name. While British newspapers such as *The Times* had initially praised the White City's whiteness as 'extremely brilliant and fairylike', in retrospect it grumbled when revealing the name's origins. It considered 'White City' 'both inept and commonplace': 'There have been and are dozens of "White Cities"', it wrote, 'the term has come to mean little more than a fancy pleasure resort', thus expressing disapproval.[20]

Not surprisingly perhaps, it is the *persona* of Imre Kiralfy that effectively provides a link between all the *fin-de-siècle* British imperial expositions dealt with in this volume – Olympia, Earl's Court, the White City and even the 1924 British Empire Exhibition in Wembley. In 1913, he became involved with →Lord Strathcona, one of the founders in 1897 of the British Empire League, with which Kiralfy had been associated since 1902 during the initial planning stages for the Wembley exhibition, possibly aiming to surpass the White City once again, just as Olympia and Earl's Court had themselves been surpassed. Despite their differences, the Franco-British Exhibition and the British Empire Exhibition held 16 years later shared the same point of origin.[21]

Dazzling whiteness

The 'biggest show' he ever organized, the Franco-British Exhibition of 1908 constituted the apogee of Kiralfy's work, though its import extended beyond his personal career. Its impact was unique: compared to other expositions hitherto mounted in the British capital, it attained an entirely new quality, with *The Times* going so far as to describe it as 'the greatest and in many respects the most remarkable exhibition ever held in the British Empire'. Moreover, it was not only in a British context that the Franco-British Exhibition constituted both a conceptual and an organizational novelty, in large part through its integration of a sports stadium into the venue's design. Unlike other exposition venues, the White City was, from its inception, designed as a permanent exhibition site, and all the principal buildings were constructed of steel frames and concrete.[22]

Inspired by the wish to bring out the project's size and grandeur in clear contrast to its historical predecessors, the organizers often compared the site's stadium – its largest single structure – with either the *Circus maximus* in ancient Rome or the Royal Albert Hall, a direct legacy of the Great Exhibition of 1851, though only completed 20 years later. Thus, they referred back to the post-1851 exhibition tradition which earlier British expositions had also evoked. With references to size, number of visitors and structure of the building complexes, the Crystal Palace exhibition always served as a benchmark against which to measure any of the subsequent expositions. The *Pictorial Guide*, for instance, predicted that the Franco-British Exhibition as the event of the year would make the entire nation reminiscent of 1851, 'only that this great undertaking occupies more space.' Yet, it was not only simply due to the time lag that the Great Exhibition played a diminishing role, losing its status as an absolute point of reference in evaluating an event held almost six decades later. In the interim, the medium's semantics had deviated so far from its origins, and its overall character changed to such an extent, that more explicit and further-reaching references than the common sense of belonging to the same medium were irrelevant. For the Franco-British Exhibition's architectural language, its bi-national and commercialized character were far more important than the repeatedly evoked references to a particular British exhibition tradition begun in 1851.[23]

The planning process for the Franco-British Exhibition had begun in 1902, six years before its opening, when two members of the British Empire League, Gerard Smith and →Sir John Cockburn, proposed a scheme for holding a comprehensive colonial and imperial exhibition in London. Established in 1894 as a successor organization of the Imperial Federation League, another imperial propaganda society and pressure group, the British Empire League's statutes set as its major objective the stabilization of the permanent unity of the Empire, by 'informing and educating the public mind' through a wide array of propagandistic activities. Inspired by both the success of the 1886 Colonial and Indian Exhibition and the Prince of Wales' 'epoch-making' 1901 journey through the entire British Empire, the advocates thought it time to organize another public assessment of the Empire's resources. The usual demonstration of imperial goods and products was to be supplemented by a 'display of the muscle and fibre of the British race'.[24]

When informed of this project, the French Chamber of Commerce in London supported the organization of such a joint exhibition 'to strengthen the friendship of the two nations and to encourage trade and commerce between them.' On the part of the French government the proposal received official support from the French ambassador in London, the French minister of commerce and the *Comité français des expositions à l'étranger*, the latter, established in 1885, being the official representative of the French government and French exhibitors at all foreign exhibitions with French participation, and hence solely responsible for organizing the French parts of the exhibition. On the British side, the Board of Trade officially certified the Franco-British Exhibition as international and coming under the provisions of the Patents, Designs, and Trade Mark Acts of 1883. Thus, in spite of all the official rhetoric before and after its opening, there could be no doubt about the enterprise's main objective right from the beginning: the commercial prosperity of the two nations. At a meeting held at the Mansion House in London on 11 July 1906, the organizing bodies decided that all potential profits should eventually be devoted to some public purpose and, accordingly, set up an executive committee. In an official letter of approval and support written on 4 February 1907, the King stressed precisely these two aspects: the project's private character *and* its commercial objective.[25]

The position of the British government remained ambivalent. On the one hand, the exposition was repeatedly certified as directly representing the interests of the state. Several times, the site was used for official purposes, as on the occasion of a much-publicized visit of the French president Fallières at the end of May 1908. Although a wholly private venture, some indirect governmental support was additionally called for in the form of notable or influential figures who formed numerous committees. Many of them were either members of the government or the League, →Frederick Arthur Stanley, sixteenth Earl of Derby, as president of both the League and the exhibition's Executive Committee, being the best example. The prestige of these committees was particularly influential in securing loan exhibits. They acted as guarantors of the importance and credibility of the exhibitions for the paying public. On the other hand, the government's direct involvement was minimal. Contrary to the usual practice in either the United States or France, successive British governments refused to directly finance the exhibition. While the French government, together with the Chamber of Commerce, subsidized the exposition with more than £80,000 through the *Comité*, its British counterpart provided only a guarantee fund. Thus, there was no direct financial involvement. No pavilion represented the British government, and the Prince of Wales' (the later George V, 1865–1936) involvement was likewise restricted to his active participation in the opening ceremony and a number of mostly private visits.[26]

The Executive Committee commissioned Imre Kiralfy and his company, Shepherds Bush Exhibitions Ltd, to project, conceptualize and realize the Franco-British Exhibition. Two of his sons, →Charles and →Albert Kiralfy, were among the directors of this company. Thus, the expert Kiralfy was charged directly with the organization of the exhibition, the design and layout of the site, and any subsequent exhibition to be held there. Kiralfy bore sole responsibility and appeared in public as the sole organizer. Eventually, there could be no doubt that Kiralfy as commissioner-general of the newly founded company Franco-British Exhibition Inc. was not the initiator, but rather the author of the exposition.[27]

The Franco-British Exhibition opened on 14 May 1908 and closed five and a half months later on 31 October. Total attendance was more than 8.4 million visitors, by no means an exceptionally high figure when compared to other international expositions held in the early 1900s (Figure 1.2) but unprecedented for a privately organized and financed venture in Great Britain. Equally unusual was the fact that the exhibition would pay for itself. With receipts totaling £1.2 million, it eventually made a profit of £38,902. The fact that all costs for developing the site and constructing the necessary infrastructure had thus amortized during the first season facilitated the future use of the White City venue for further exposition projects.[28]

The site selected in Shepherd's Bush in west London covered a total area of 57 hectares (Figure 4.2). Kiralfy had already purchased parts of the property in 1903, which he then sold to his own new company, and the location was clearly well chosen. Although still on the fringes of London, Shepherd's Bush in 1908 was hardly the remote rural backwater implied by *The Times* when speaking of its 'wilds'. The whole borough of Hammersmith had been an area of considerable house building for 30 years. The market-garden site of the exhibition was one of the few agricultural areas left in the borough when construction on the exhibition began. Moreover, it was well connected by public transport: though located somewhat outside London's centers, the site could be easily reached from every district of London by railway, tram and motor omnibuses. 'No part of the metropolis has so many methods of approach', boasted an official booklet. This was not entirely exaggerated: the first electric tramways in London had been built there in 1901. By 1908, there were four different stations, constructed partly with this purpose in mind, in immediate proximity and with connections to five different railway lines, making it possible to transport 70,000–100,000 visitors per hour to the exhibition (Figure 4.3).[29]

Kiralfy himself had carefully planned the egg-shaped exposition site (Plate 4) and its development, in close cooperation with the architects John Belcher (1841–1913) and Marius Tondoire. It followed a clear schedule. In order to do justice to the Franco-British Exhibition's main theme as a comparative stock-taking of the two nations and their achievements, a system of 17, later 19, different categories had been developed to classify the exhibits of the two countries. Likewise, according to a systematic set of criteria, the entire grounds were symmetrically divided.

Figure 4.2 Panoramic photograph of Shepherd's Bush, the site of the Franco-British Exhibition, with its main entrance at the venue's southern end in the foreground
Source: Courtesy of Museum of London, Imre Kiralfy Collection, 82-232/49.

In compliance with the exhibition's 'dual nature', the areas attributed to the two nations were of exactly the same size. Approximately one half of the 57 hectares were devoted to French displays. According to official propaganda, never before had more exhibits been displayed at any exposition outside Paris. This principle of national symmetry was continued throughout the site. While a large complex comprised of a huge machinery hall – the largest ever constructed in Britain until this time – stood on the grounds' western side, the eastern half was dominated by the sports stadium. 'The Stadium', hailed an architectural critic, 'is beyond all manner of doubt, the one great triumph of the exhibition. [...] Vast, splendid, monumental. It is the great achievement of the Franco-British Exhibition and of the engineering profession.'[30]

Kiralfy's spatial organization was particularly effective at medium range. Neither organized around a single building, as in 1851 or in 1867, nor primarily around national or single-themed pavilions, spatially the main structuring principle consisted of a series of 'courts', strung together and extending one after another in a straight line, with the buildings clustered around them. These included the *Court of Honour*, the *Court of Arts*, the *Court of Progress*, the *Garden of Progress* and the *Elite Gardens* in the area's center and the *Central Circus* further north, as well as more

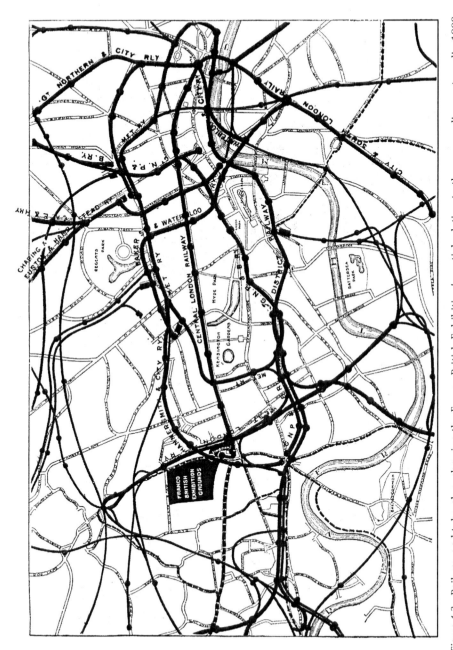

Figure 4.3 Railway and tube plan, showing the Franco-British Exhibition's spatial relation to the surrounding metropolis, 1908
Source: Courtesy of Geheimes Staatsarchiv Preußischer Kulturbesitz, Berlin, I. HA Rep. 120 MfHuG, E XVI 4 Nr. 2, vol. 1.

'traditional' sections such as the *Palace of Engineering* and a *Machinery Hall*. There were 20 pavilions devoted to British and French industry, and 120 other buildings; altogether the venue was comprised of 400 structures. Kiralfy himself allocated the sites before architects were consulted. If the entire layout seemed so much more orderly than in previous British cases – and hence easier to read in retrospect – this was clearly to be attributed to the fact that the exhibition's central planning was the work of a single person.

A central north–south axis cut through the entire White City site and constituted its 'backbone', as it was labeled in the *Pictorial and Descriptive Guide*. From south to north some of the most important buildings and pavilions lined this Central Avenue. Another import from the 1893 World's Columbian Exposition in Chicago was the so-called *Court of Honour* at the southern end. Although Kiralfy had sketched the exhibition's layout as a whole in addition to many of the 'amusements', this *Court of Honour* was the only building complex that he had also single-handedly designed, doing so in an architectural style loosely inspired by Indian examples. As was the case in Chicago, for the majority of visitors this was their first view of the exhibition as it opened directly from the entrance on Wood Lane. The visitor was greeted with an expanse of space: huge artificial lakes, ponds and waterways, snow-white buildings, and an emphasis on the vista. At night, the colored illuminations were especially spectacular. 'It was charming by day', a commentator found, 'but at night, lighted by thousands of electric lamps, it was exquisite.'[31]

The further north the attendee wandered, the more joyful, exotic and imperial the exposition became. Along the same main north–south axis, a *Court of Arts* and *Elite Gardens* followed the *Court of Honour*, directly leading to *Merryland*, the vast amusement area of the exhibition, including 'that weird and fascinating monster the Giant Flip-Flap'. While the southern half was generally devoted to the more serious and classical themes of arts, crafts and industry, the northern end consisted of 'a circular space from which divergent thoroughfares penetrate what may be described as the "hinterland" of the Exhibition, a spacious and more open area accommodating the Colonial exhibits and the native villages.' Here, Kiralfy had placed not only the amusement section but also all colonial displays. Beside a variety of rides such as the Spider's Web, a scenic railway, the Wiggle-Woggle and the Canadian Toboggan, here the Senegalese, Algerian, Irish and Ceylon Villages, the Indian Pavilion, the Australian Palace, the Canadian Palace, the New Zealand Pavilion and the Crown Colonies Pavilion were to be found. Thus, commercial amusement and colonial consumption took place at one and the same site and went hand in hand. Upon discovering the location of their buildings amidst the amusement section, the dominion and colonial governments lodged a strong protest, though to no avail.[32]

That the conceit of all-white buildings and pavilions, reminiscent of marble, was not original but rather copied and imported, did not hamper the White City's popularity in London. This optical effect, suggesting cleanliness, purity and wealth, was further reinforced by a complicated system of illuminations that, by night, threw the courts, palaces and pavilions into sharp contrast with the surrounding darkness.

By day and night, the White City's whiteness became an indispensable element of both its 'dazzling' beauty and popular appeal and hence a necessary precondition for its status as an artificial, paradisaic dream city. 'The prevailing colour is pure white', *The Times* wrote delightedly 'and the effect at night will be extremely brilliant and fairylike.'[33] One visitor described in stirring, almost dramatic words the vista opening up to him directly after entering the site. The sheer intensity of the hue seemed to dominate all other impressions:

> And then, all at once, there opens out before you a scene which seems incredible even as your eyes rest upon it. A white city indeed, milk-white and vast, with palaces to right and left, before you and behind, with towers and domes and cupolas standing in gleaming whiteness against the blue summer sky; with a river clear and green widening out into a miniature lake; with music and laughter mingling in the air; with half a dozen tongues in use wherever you go; and with distant view of more white palaces and golden domes, strange gateways, towers, turrets, all steeped in sun and morning light. It is almost too dazzlingly white, at first sight: a dream-city that has come true and to the sight of which the eyes of the Westerner in general, and the Londoner in particular, should be gradually accustomed.

'Is it possible', this overwhelmed visitor wondered, that this dream-city could be located in London, 'this pale fantastic City of the Plain?' Ironically, such an experience might eventually result in an unwelcome, indeed negative contrast effect for someone used to the metropolis' grey bleakness. 'And then you are back in London', he drastically described his reverse sense of culture shock when returning to the exhibiting city, 'and think that [it] is an even uglier place than you had imagined.'[34]

As all contemporaneous print media never tired of repeating, the official political motive for holding this bi-national exhibition was the signing of the *Entente cordiale* convention in April 1904 by the two former rivals, England and France, which had settled existing colonial disputes in North Africa and founded a colonial commonality of interests. The new union was to be cemented and celebrated by means of the exposition. 'The years which have passed since 1904', the *Daily Mail* praised the new relationship of the two powers, 'have confirmed the prudence and prescience of the negotiators of the understanding':

> It has been proved that England is not the 'perfidious Albion' which she was represented of old, prepared to abandon her friends at the first breath of danger or misfortune. It has been demonstrated that France is not fickle, or ready to forget her engagements.[35]

The *Illustrated London News* agreed: The exhibition, 'of its kind probably one of the greatest undertakings of modern times', marked the development of the 'great Anglo-French understanding that is to-day the keystone of the European political situation, and the most powerful instrument working for the maintenance of the world's peace.' Besides these broad political considerations, mentioned endlessly in public print discussion, though never in much detail, such a 'peg' proved meaningful for two reasons: First, this cooperation gave a certain 'flavour' to the 'whole affair' and provided the exhibition, at least officially, with a higher purpose than that of mere commercial competition. Second, it suggested the development of an unambiguous design concept. 'All exhibitions have their uses, and their social or educational side', the *Illustrated London News* commented on the practical utility of such an ostensible integration within a wider framework, 'but its promoters are justified in claiming for the Anglo-French Exhibition a larger sphere of utility than falls to the lot of the average undertaking of its class.'[36]

Its bi-national character, which was not reduced to a traditional rivalry between the two capital cities, characterized the entire exhibition and gave it a 'dual nature' – which is not to repeat the truism that the Franco-British Exhibition was, obviously, Franco-British. Even if the exposition and the choice of exhibits on display resulted from complex combinations of official intervening, personal autonomy and popular demand, this polarity was one of its main features and found direct expression in many of its sections and pavilions. As a mere occasion, the signing of the *Entente cordiale* was almost meaningless, and the relationship between the nations was thematized partly as cooperation, partly as competition. In view of this carefully enacted polarity it is not surprising that the exhibition, according to the official guide, demonstrated exactly this: 'distinguishing national characteristics' – classic circular reasoning. Yet, the most striking results were only to be gained, it continued, when 'leading racial characteristics and prominent industries' did not obscure but supplemented each other. Nowhere were the conditions for such harmonious and promising cooperation more favorable than in the case of the neighboring nations, Great Britain and France, whose national characteristics would complement one another almost ideally. 'When Anglo-Saxon energy blends with French savoir vivre, when British Empiricism is ordered by French method, when British solidity is adorned by French grace, a combination is reached which embraces the highest achievements of the human race', pointed out the official guide. Embedded in the exhibition's official rhetoric were concepts of nation, race and empire that were combined almost beyond recognition. Yet, whether its bi-national theme had any lasting effect on the rapprochement between the two nations is quite doubtful. Historians who emphasize the exposition's diplomatic significance and positive impact on international relations seem to take its official rhetoric at face value.[37]

The fate of the site was determined by the exhibition's bi-national character and its commercial orientation as it became clear that continued institutionalization beyond the exhibition medium proved impossible. Because the White City had been designed as a permanent exhibition site, the principal buildings were built with steel frames and concrete, avoiding the 'flimsy canvas and wood erections of which so many exhibitions are composed'.[38] Yet, the site's flexibility still proved remarkable: successfully inaugurated and established, its existing infrastructure could easily be used for further profitable projects. After a lavish closing ceremony in November 1908, subsequent exhibitions were, in accordance with the original plan, held annually until the First World War.

Constantly changing their configurations and layout, these expositions had broad themes of an imperial or national character (Imperial International Exhibition 1909, Coronation Exhibition of the British Empire 1911) or followed the bi-national pattern set in 1908 (Japan-British Exhibition 1910, Latin-British Exhibition 1912, Anglo-American Exhibition 1914), contrasting the British nation and its achievements with another. From season to season, the White City's architecture was altered only slightly to accommodate the new theme.[39] Nevertheless, the Franco-British Exhibition, with more than twice as many visitors than any subsequent exhibition at the White City, remained the most successful exhibition. Yet, the venue's spectacular fame and popularity with the public proved short-lived. Though used until 1914, by 1911 the site no longer had public appeal. 'The previously much-admired "White City" has lost much of its former nimbus with the present local public', an official German visitor noted in November 1911, 'and has sunk to the level of a trivial entertainment enterprise.'[40]

With the onset of the First World War, the White City was used by the government for the training and accommodation of military troops, later becoming, in turn, a medical inspection center, an airplane factory and eventually a dog track. 'With the succeeding years', *The Times* commented on the occasion of Kiralfy's death in 1919, 'most of the dazzling paint and of the glory that once caused people to flock to Shepherd's Bush have passed away.' In November 1922, the entire site was offered for sale by auction. Eventually, the London County Council acquired it in 1945 as part of a housing project. When the London Underground opened a tube station there in the 1950s, it was given this name as a reminder of the site's history. The White City stadium was the last surviving structure on the exhibition site, in continuous use until its demolition in 1985. The legacy bequeathed by the Franco-British Exhibition thus overshadowed the site and all later exhibitions and events held therein. To many Londoners, even long after its closure, the exhibition would simply remain 'the Franco-British'. Failing to transcend institutional boundaries, its long-term effects and impulses, though substantial, remained limited to the medium exposition itself.[41]

'Flip-Flap' versus 'native villages'

A few days after the opening ceremony, *The Times* endeavored to explain to its readers why the attractiveness and popularity of the Franco-British Exhibition was based more on 'various mechanical contrivances and other things' with such original names as Flip-Flap, Wiggle-Woggle, Hurley Burley and Roly Poly than the official announcements, with their rhetoric about the educational importance of the exhibition suggested. 'The Franco-British Exhibition', the newspaper stated, 'is no exception to the apparently universal rule that no exhibition, however high it may aspire as an exponent of art and commerce, can afford to dispense with amusements and attractions that are entirely innocent of any pretence at instruction.' Notwithstanding a certain continuing tension between the two constitutive poles – education and entertainment – the organizers in general and Kiralfy in particular had, much to *The Times'* regret, shifted the emphasis significantly to the latter. Indeed, the Franco-British Exhibition was the first British imperial exposition that was consistently organized as spectacle.[42]

The exhibition's bi-national nature was bridged by its dual commercial and spectacular character. Numerous attractions and side shows were to be found in *Merryland*, the upper portion of the site. Tellingly, these attractions also included the various ethnic displays and 'native villages' that were classified as such in all official publications. The crown jewel of *Merryland* was the Flip-Flap (Figure 4.4),

Figure 4.4 The Flip-Flap, one of the most outstanding spectacles of the Franco-British Exhibition
Source: Courtesy of London Transport Museum 2004/15705.

a counterpoised metal structure which was hailed as a means of 'physical refresh-
ment' and a great achievement in the realm of pleasure technology, and was
often celebrated as the Franco-British Exhibition's genuine 'specialty' or even
'wonder' – almost its *clou*. Because the building of an imperial tower, planned for
the southern half of the site, was abandoned at an early stage due to unforeseen
technical difficulties, the Flip-Flap was the exposition's only vertical structure of
considerable height.[43]

The Flip-Flap's functioning was as simple as it was effective: two huge steel
arms, 46 meters long and each holding up to 70 passengers in specially built
cabins at either end, rose from the horizontal and transcribed a semi-circle in
the air, thus 'flipping' up to the top, 'flapping' down the other side, and thereby
making 'terrifying' sounds. The Flip-Flap attracted enormous public attention,
caused widespread enthusiasm and, on the part of its passengers, a much-evoked
'thrill' which seemed inexplicable even to popular journals such as *The World's
Work*. 'To participate in this curious operation', the journal fell back on an accurate
technological explanation,

> one takes a seat in one of the pavilions swinging freely on the ends of two
> attenuated steel lattice-work arms which normally rest on either side in a hori-
> zontal direction, balanced on a common axle at their lower ends which are
> suitably weighted. The thrill consists of being swung from one platform to the
> other in a semicircle of some 300 ft. diameter, the two flaps moving in opposite
> directions simultaneously.[44]

For many, the Flip-Flap's most fascinating offering was the 'magnificent bird's-eye
view of the vast grounds of the Exhibition, and of a great portion of the Metropolis'
it provided, which over 1.1 million passengers enjoyed for two and a half to five
minutes after having paid their sixpence entrance fee. More interested in the vistas
offered than the machine's technology, one of these 'pleasure-seekers' described the
'art of Flip-Flapping' as switching one's gaze at the right point of time first from the
fellow passengers in the other cabin to the Crystal Palace in the distance, and then
back again to the White City itself – a short, fleeting moment, which apparently
provided an 'entirely new and extremely pleasant sensation':

> For the passenger, the thrill of seeing the other car pass in the wide
> air – those fellow adventurers across the deep gulf of space, mere dots behind
> the grille – remains above all else. There was an art in Flip-Flapping in know-
> ing just when to look at the distant view, in an effort to locate the Crystal
> Palace [...], just when to transfer the gaze (if you dared) at the wonder of the
> White City far beneath with its crawling specks. For the journey was none
> too long for the true air-voyager, so that your eyes had to hurry to get the
> full measure of impression. Many women flip-flapped with shut eyes and
> tightened hands, seeing nothing but mind-images of fear. For them was only
> the brave joy of saying they had been on the Flip-Flap. 'Of course we weren't
> going to miss *that*.'[45]

Its passengers often compared the Flip-Flap with the Eiffel Tower or the great wheels at other expositions, such as Chicago or at Earl's Court, where it had been demolished only three years earlier, while professional architectural critics sneered at its 'mechanical monstrosity'. Realizing that such a side-show had become an integral part of each exhibition, the critics ironically commented that the Flip-Flap at least marked a certain advance on previous, similar projects inasmuch as its appearance was intermittently obscured: 'Nevertheless this colossal pair of dividers is to be seen from time to time bisecting the heavens.' Another critic – partly amused, partly alluding to the song quoted in the epigraph to this chapter – considered it a 'monster-boomed thing' because 'it has achieved the crowning British honour of having a particularly inane music hall song written around it.'[46] The Flip-Flap's popular character should not lead one to underestimate the almost emblematic meaning of this genuine spectacle, properly analyzed only in light of its usage. In an almost ideal manner, the Flip-Flap supported the primary function of each colonial exhibition, that is, the visualization of empire. Yet, its specific function within the exhibitionary context went still further. Not only did it afford an unobstructed view of the entire exhibition venue – and hence the whole British Empire together with one of its major national competitors, complete with their respective colonies worldwide – but it also highlighted the site's spatial and imaginative placement within the metropolis. Almost too clichéd to be true, if weather permitted, the brave 'adventurer' could, from its top, make out the replica of the Crystal Palace in the distance – and thus the entire British exhibition tradition, preserved in Sydenham.

At the northern end of the exhibition, close to the Flip-Flap, yet set somewhat apart from the rest of the grounds, was the *Grand Avenue of the Colonies*, a semi-circular annexe featuring 'the wonders of the Colonial possessions of the two nations' gathered in a number of special buildings erected by the respective governments. The western half was devoted to the British colonies, the eastern to the French. Here, amusement and colonialism merged entirely. The former section featured displays from India, Gambia, the Gold Coast, Southern Nigeria, the Fiji Islands, Canada, Australia and New Zealand, as well as two so-called native villages, one Ceylonese and one Irish, and an open-air theater known as the 'Indian Arena'. French colonialism was represented by ten separate pavilions, and included Tunis, Algeria, French East Africa and Indochina, in addition to a general palace, a colonial bureau, various tea-houses, a war pavilion and a Senegalese village. Over the years, Kiralfy had developed a vast catalogue of strategies for displaying cultural exoticism in a manner that would appeal to the public. Political conceptions of imperialism and nationalism were carefully tied together with modern technologies of entertainment and spectacle in a semi-urban spatial setting. Exoticism was rendered a controlled event whose safeguarded appropriation would delight both visitors and spectators.[47]

Since the mid-1880s, so-called native villages and exotic sections had increasingly developed into a key element of every major exhibition's standard repertoire. Even thematically unrelated and much smaller and more specialized shows such as the

International Fire Exhibition organized by the British Fire Prevention Committee and held at Earl's Court in 1903 included an entire section Assouan: The Village of the Nile. Extolled as a 'graphic and real representation of life on the Sacred River', it had been specially brought from Egypt by permission of the government. The connection of such an exotic section with the exhibition's overall subject matter remained unclear, to say the least. In the Franco-British Exhibition, similar ethnographic ensembles were much more carefully orchestrated and closely integrated in its overall conceptualization. 'This will provide an extremely interesting section, for many of the pavilions are typical of the architecture of the country represented, and will be peopled by the inhabitants of these off-lands', Kiralfy declared, extolling the exoticism to be found in the colonial section before the exhibition's opening. The *Daily Telegraph* agreed, stating: 'With "villages" peopled by natives from far and near, the Exhibition is amply supplied.' While, for various reasons, some of the official pavilions attracted less public attention than expected, the 'native villages' proved a great success.[48]

The three villages – the Ceylon Village, the Senegalese Village and the Irish Village – were together classified as 'attractions' and, though they belonged to very different local, colonial and historical traditions, they were categorized together in the official guidebooks and catalogues. Thus, in the original conception they had been given a different status from the other pavilions and sections. Their immense popularity justified such a distinction: already, after three months, 750,000 visitors had toured the Senegalese Village, more than one million had visited the Ceylon Village, and one of Kiralfy's typical historical spectacles, held in the Indian Arena and entitled *Our Indian Empire*, had attracted no less than 700,000 spectators. With approximately two million paying visitors over the course of five and a half months, the Irish Village proved even more popular than the much-praised Flip-Flap with its 1.1 million passengers.[49]

Often incorrectly referred to as the Indian Village, the Ceylon Village constituted the only ethnic display that directly represented British overseas colonialism. Situated behind the Ceylon Tea House, where 'fascinating Cingalese damsels, daintily dressed in the native costume' served tea 'amidst an Oriental atmosphere', and located in the immediate vicinity of the Indian Palace, an entire ensemble of huts and houses had been erected, together with a pagoda and several bazaars in oriental style. In addition to praising the exotic bustling activities, the official guide somewhat mystifyingly hailed the 'clever' scheme of illumination, which, after nightfall, transformed the entire Ceylon Village into a 'perfect fairyland'.[50] Depicting his fascination in great detail, one visitor had no doubt at all about the realism and credibility of the 'oriental' life re-enacted in the Ceylon Village. In the end, the vision seemed so rounded and complete that a certain intrinsic value had to be conceded:

But the greed to see yet more drives you on, and, as if you turned a page in a picture-book, you stand, in another moment, in the centre of a Ceylon village, where the potter and the engraver, the carpet-worker and the embroiderer, ply their trades, steadily, lazily, with utmost dexterity. Little girls of five, with faces of

black angels, smoke cigarettes as other infants suck lollipops, the luminous eyes
of their mothers watching indulgently, approvingly; old men with tiny monkeys
lie in the dusty village street, waiting for halfpence, but without anxiety to display
their and their small apes' arts; the snake-charmer, in his corner, digs two luckless
cobras in the 'ribs' to make them raise their poor angry heads and show the more
than regal splendour of their scales; the elephants stand in long rows, munching
hay and keeping their keen small eyes upon the man in the neighbouring kitchen,
to whose bounty they owe occasionally a fistful of soft rice. The place is full of
life and brimful of gorgeous colour, the most beautiful tints of all being those of
the natives' brown satin skins shot with gold or daintiest rose pink. Steeped in
sunlight and shrill music, the village makes a picture of the East that could not
easily be bettered under the Western sun.[51]

The Ceylon Village was connected to the Indian Arena where more than 150
acrobats, sorcerers, wrestlers, 'dancing nautch girls', snake-charmers and other
indigenous actors, together with a variety of animals imported from India,
performed two or three times a day the spectacular play *Our Indian Empire*,
announced as 'a gorgeous spectacle depicting a Fair in the East', under the
direction of impresario Carl Hagenbeck and his Hamburg-based company. Each
performance culminated in a grand-scale tiger hunt, in the course of which not
only a mastiff in tiger disguise was caught by the native hunters, but also a dozen
elephants had to slide down a gigantic chute into a water basin at its foot in a
quite spectacular, though incongruous manner.[52]

It is almost impossible to find factual information regarding these indigenous
actors themselves. However, some conclusions may be drawn from another
group of similar size, composed of Indian, Ceylonese and Burmese artisans who
participated in Kiralfy's 1896 India and Ceylon Exhibition, presumably under
similar conditions. As becomes clear from the following contract, the autoch-
thonous actors were forced to accept very unfavorable legal working conditions.
In case of an unforeseen withdrawal, they were obliged to pay both a deficiency
compensation to the company and for their own return journey:

> Company agrees to convey employee to England and from England back to India.
> To board and lodge employee in England from time of arrival till his departure.
> To send him home by first steamer available after the close of Exhibition.
> Employee agrees to leave by such steamer and on such dates as Company may
>   notify.
> Company agrees to pay each employee Rs. [?] *per mensem* commencing from
>   date of departure from Bombay until his return to Bombay.
> Wages to be paid monthly at the rate of exchange.
> Company have right to deduct from pay all advances made to employee.
> Company agree to supply employee before leaving India with warm clothing
>   and suit of woollen clothing for voyage.
>   (1) Each employee contracts on his arrival in England that he will faithfully
>   and diligently serve the Company.

(2) To exhibit and demonstrate his trade of profession to the very best of his skill during each working day of 10 hours.

Company have the right for discharge any artisan who violates this contract by giving one week's notice and send him home at their own expense.

Each employee agrees to pay the Company the sum of Rs. 5000 as and for liquidated damages in the event of his leaving Company's service while in England before close of Exhibition.

In event of employee not performing his obligations under this Contract Company are absolved from continuing payment of monthly wages.[53]

With an average age of 30 years, the group was comprised altogether of 132 'natives' between 30 months and 60 years of age. Coming from different Indian, Ceylonese and Burmese provinces, mostly entire families had been recruited. While a vast majority of the group members were male and worked as musicians, weavers, jugglers, embroiderers, goldsmiths, painters, 'showmen', acrobats, snake-charmers, monkey trainers or tiger dancers, accompanied by a Buddhist priest from Burma, the few women were typically described as 'nautch', that is dancing- or 'gymnastic-girls'. Whether the entire group was on a tour through different European cities or performing periodically at the same location, by no means were these 'natives' always freshly imported on the occasion of the respective exposition. In 1909, one 'oriental juggler' proudly presented an official certificate stating that he had already participated in the 1886 Colonial and Indian Exhibition where Queen Victoria herself had taken personal pleasure in watching his artistic juggling.[54]

With a certain restraint, *The Times* disapproved of the import of these 'dusky children of Empire', since they were considered too poor and illiterate, and would hence create a wrong impression with the English audience who would take them for Indians while they were, in truth, mostly Tamils. Moreover, it was feared that the inhabitants themselves would be spoiled 'by the mixed and sometimes vulgar European crowds' and eventually sent back home entirely 'demoralized'. In the paper, a visitor from Ceylon who had just arrived bitterly complained along similar lines about the injustice done to Ceylon. 'The ill-clad, sleepy-looking women and children kept on show there have no connexion whatever with Ceylon', he wrote: 'The dirty and dismal enclosure has no resemblance to a Ceylon village. Whoever designed this village has done the greatest disservice to a flourishing colony with a bright and intelligent village population, and prosperous in planting and mercantile interests.'[55]

In the case of the Senegalese Village (Figure 4.5), located further east in the colonial section and north of the stadium, however, the newspaper seemed much less concerned about its denizens' well-being. Directly comparing the two villages, a reviewer noted contentedly that the visitor was offered 'good value for his money' in either place; yet, due to specific racial characteristics, he could naturally expect much less of the inhabitants of the Senegalese Village. The villages were clearly put in a hierarchy, with the 'negroes fall[ing] far behind the Tamils and the Ceylonese in artistic culture and skill, and in agility of mind.' Such an association was by no means the product of colonial rivalries. The Senegalese

Figure 4.5 Postcard of the Senegalese Village, located at the intersection of the *Algerian Avenue* and the *Grand Avenues of the Colonies* at the exhibition's northeastern end
Source: Courtesy of Hammersmith and Fulham Archives and Local History Centre, London.

Village with its 150 inhabitants was indeed situated in the eastern and, hence, the French part of the colonial section. Its inhabitants were under contract to two Frenchmen, Aimé Bouvier and Fleury Tournièr from the *Comité national des expositions coloniales*, to live in bamboo and palm huts, perform daily fetish worship rituals and ply the 'handicrafts associated with their existence' over the course of the summer. However, that Senegal, 'a fine colony', as *The World's Work* remarked, was itself a French colony rather than a British possession, was stated only indirectly in the vast majority of supplementary texts. Displaying sheer exoticism was valued more highly than colonial affiliation. Consequently, what was actually represented differed only in degree from what could be found in the Ceylon Village. Here, visitors could marvel at palm trees and bamboo huts, colorful exoticism as well as pseudo-authentic life, carefully staged and re-enacted daily on command. 'The primitive life of the occupants of the Sahara has never before been represented before Europeans', the official guide explained, going on to promise, in a manner hardly different from what it said about the Ceylon Village, 'but the Senegalese Village proves that the habits and customs of these negroes form a highly instructive picture.'[56]

Two sentences in the introduction to the special guide, *The Senegal Village*, encapsulated the entire metaphorical repertoire: mastering the unknown, escaping from modernity to mystery, and reaching a form of realism unparalleled and unattainable elsewhere, all by merely entering the village. The introduction presented the village as 'your invitation to penetrate the mysteries of the sunlit Continent, to transport yourself at a moment from the prosaic world in which you live to a land of mystery and romance. Behind these high walls another life is lived – a life which no reading of books and seeing of photographs can depict for you.'[57] The official guide balanced this rhetoric of sober rumination on the unknown with a more critical comment and explained: 'In a cruel-looking stockade, over a hundred men and women from the borders of the desert are now living exactly as they do in their native Africa. [...] The pleasures and amusements of these negroes are not neglected, and the visitor will hear and see with interest the weird chants and rhythmic dancing of the younger members of the tribe.'[58] Indeed, the best insight into this 'far-off land' and its inhabitants' 'living and loving, working and playing', as the special guide promised its gentle readers, was to be had at lunchtime when it would be possible to watch some of the female inhabitants prepare their food and recognize that the color of their hands was one 'that "won't come off"', while noting that during the ensuing meal the only forks used were the ones 'nature has generously given them'. At the same time the reader-spectators – themselves actor-performers in this highly choreographed setting – were warned not to overfeed the village's children with chocolates and candy for, unfortunately, sweets of all kinds were considered 'destructive of the very excellent digestions nature has given these fascinating little atoms of colour'. The analogies to feeding the animals in a zoo are obvious. Yet, although the village claimed to provide evidence of its inhabitants' (still) uncivilized nature, this proved a secondary goal. The exact geopolitical origin of these living exhibits was entirely irrelevant so long as they stemmed from some imagined 'corner of savage dark Africa' and fulfilled corresponding expectations. A strict hierarchy and classification of different concepts of race was of no particular importance provided that the section functioned as such within the exhibitionary context.[59]

At the northwestern end of the exhibition site behind the Canadian Pavilion was the Irish Village of Ballymaclinton (Figure 4.6), the third and largest of the ethnic displays. It promised to transport the visitor by a single escapist step 'from the whirl of London to the heart of Ireland' and simultaneously convey 'a real idea of Irish life'. The village presented a romantic but static image of rural Ireland, compiled of various structures from different Irish regions. There were more than 20 buildings in the village, many of them belonging to different historical periods. Around reproductions of some medieval ecclesiastical buildings and memorials evoking an age-old past such as a tiny ruined abbey, the replica of a round tower and an ancient St Patrick's Cross, a number of thatched cottages were arranged in which almost 200 young Irish women, so-called colleens, recruited from rural Ireland and employed on contract to inhabit the site for the season, lived and worked every day, weaving cloth and carpets and making lace and, in particular, soap. Ballymaclinton proved as popular as the other two villages, 'though the sixpence charged for admission brought it to the level of a "side-show"', as one visitor noted.[60] However, the 'realistic representation of what we may see any day in Ireland' found its definite limits in the village's very naming. By no means was Ballymaclinton, as many visitors assumed, named after some remote Irish settlement, but rather its main sponsor McClinton, an Irish soap company whose best-selling product was, significantly enough, called 'Colleen'. Thus, the emphasis on health and spotless cleanliness to be found in the press coverage not only suited

Model Cottage, Ballymaclinton.
Franco-British Exhibition, London, 1908

Figure 4.6   Postcard of Ballymaclinton, the Irish Village, located at the site's northwestern end across from the Ceylon Village, featuring a model cottage and living 'colleens'
Source: Courtesy California State University, Fresno, Special Collections Research Center, Larson Collection.

the organizers but the paying soap company as well. Nowhere else did the press coverage seem so carefully orchestrated and canonized as in this section: even the official guide declared that while the colleens' beauty was largely inherited, the 'softness and bloom of their cheeks' were certainly the result of the use of cosmetics. Additionally, all profits from the village were to go to a social program under the auspices of the Women's National Health Association of Ireland to help them fight the 'dread disease of consumption'.[61]

A second 'Western' counterpart to the ethnic displays could be found just north of the Flip-Flap. Here, the British equivalent of the German *Alt-Berlin* had been built: so-called *Old London*, complete with reproductions of London buildings from the fifteenth and sixteenth centuries and illustrated by a series of models including 'Old London Bridge', 'Cheapside', 'St Paul's Cathedral', 'Westminster Hall' and 'Parliament House': in short, a romanticized version of London before the Great Fire of 1666. 'Old London', the official guide declared, 'provides an exhibition in itself, even if there were no other wonders.' In a British context, domestic historical sections such as this had been first introduced at the International Health Exhibition, held in South Kensington in 1884. Likewise, the 1886 Colonial and Indian Exhibition held on the same site two years later featured an 'authentic' old London street with reproductions of medieval domestic architecture under the auspices of the same architect and museum curator, George H. Birch (1842–1904). By 1908, more than 20 years later, such a village had become a standard feature of the exhibition medium.[62]

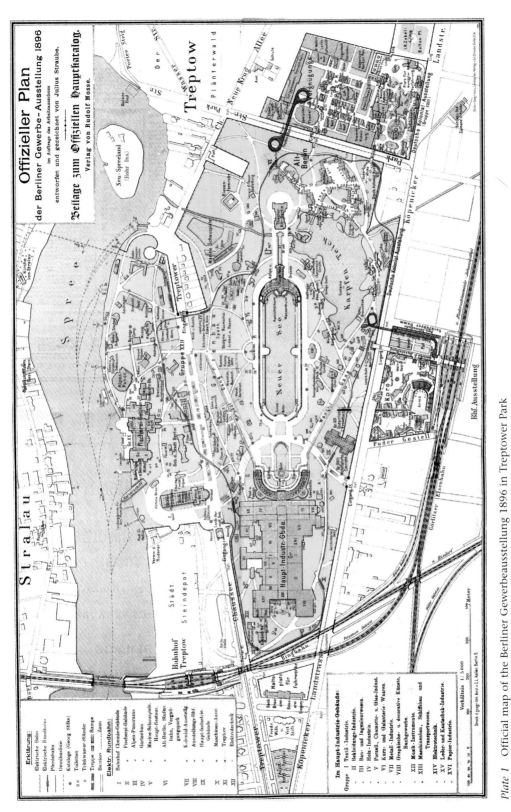

Plate 1   Official map of the Berliner Gewerbeausstellung 1896 in Treptower Park

Source: Courtesy of Zentral- und Landesbibliothek Berlin, Zentrum für Berlin-Studien.

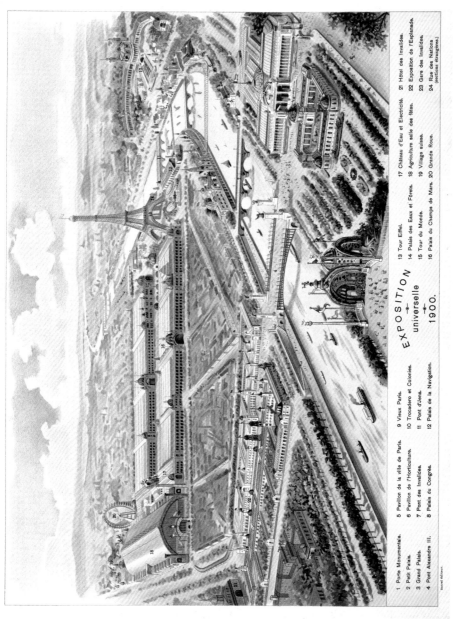

EXPOSITION
universelle
1900.

1 Porte Monumentale.
2 Petit Palais.
3 Grand Palais.
4 Pont Alexandre III.

5 Pavillon de la ville de Paris.
6 Pavillon de l'Horticulture.
7 Pont des Invalides.
8 Palais du Congrès.

9 Vieux Paris.
10 Trocadéro et Colonies.
11 Pont d'Iéna.
12 Palais de la Navigation.

13 Tour Eiffel.
14 Palais des Eaux et Forêts.
15 Tour du Monde.
16 Palais du Champs de Mars.

17 Château d'Eau et Electricité.
18 Agriculture salle des fêtes.
19 Village suisse.
20 Grande Roue.

21 Hotel des Invalides.
22 Exposition de l'Esplanade.
23 Gare des Invalides.
24 Rue des Nations
(sections étrangères)

Plate 2 Panorama of the Exposition Universelle, Paris 1900
Source: Courtesy of Musée Carnavalet/Roger-Viollet, Paris.

Plate 3 'A Trip Through the Paris Exposition 1900'. This map supplemented a souvenir set of 60 stereoscopic photographs that could be purchased in the exhibition city and later viewed at home
Source: Courtesy of California State University, Fresno, Special Collections Research Center, Donald G. Larson Collection.

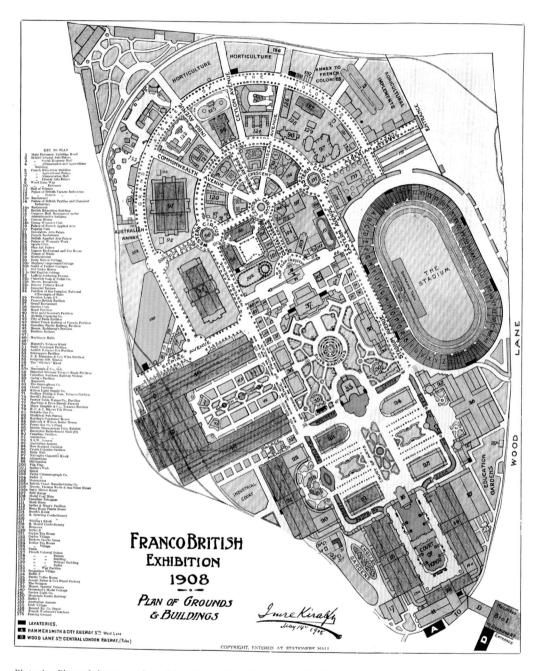

Plate 4   Plan of the grounds and buildings of the Franco-British Exhibition 1908, in Shepherd's Bush, west London

Source: Courtesy of Geheimes Staatsarchiv Preußischer Kulturbesitz, Berlin, I. HA Rep. 120 MfHuG, E XVI 4 Nr. 2, vol. 1.

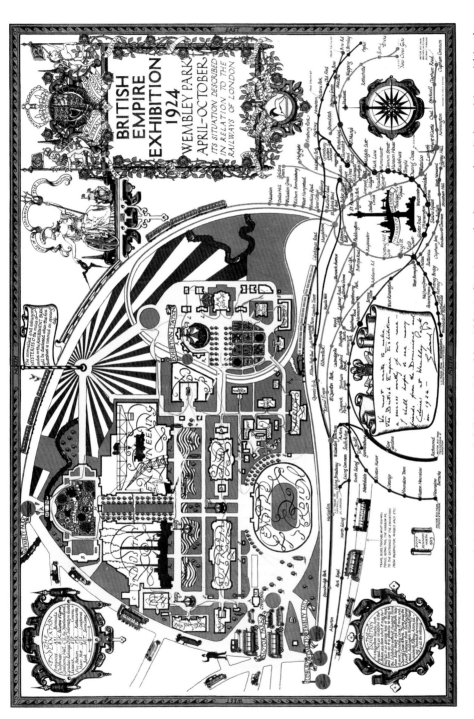

Plate 5 Stylized visitors' map of the British Empire Exhibition, Wembley 1924, indicating at the bottom the site's position within the greater London transport network and more specifically its relation to Trafalgar Square, the 'Heart of the Empire'

Source: London: Dobson, Molle and Co. Ltd, 1924. Courtesy of Brent Archive, London.

Plate 6 'Summer at Wembley', a poster in the popular 'Scenes of Empire' series, designed by Frank Newbould. The white building is the *Palace of Engineering*
Source: Weaver, Exhibitions and the Arts of Display, Plate CLVI/Fig. 360.

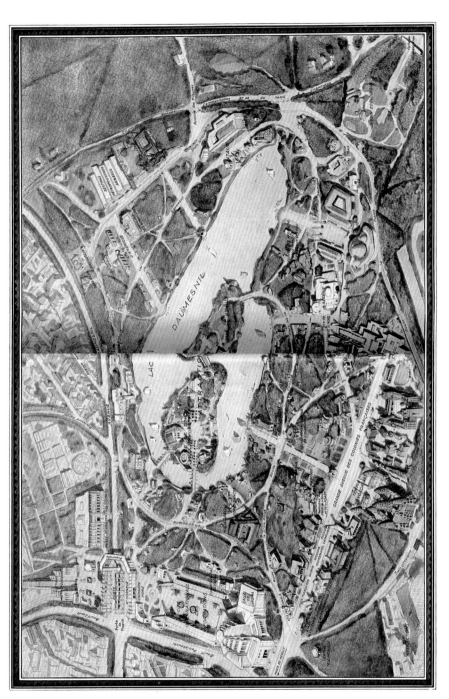

Plate 7 Panoramic plan of the Exposition Coloniale Internationale de Paris, 1931. In the foreground, the *Grande Avenue des Colonies Françaises* with a replica of the *Temple of Angkor Wat* and the 'West African Village', at left the *Cité des Informations* with the *Palais de la Section Métropolitaine* and the *Musée des Colonies*. The foreign sections and the zoological gardens were located in the north-east of Lac Daumesnil *Source*: Albert Tournaire, *L'Illustration* (July 1931), n.p. Courtesy of California State University, Fresno, Special Collections Research Center, Donald G. Larson Collection.

Plate 8 Artist's rendition of the reconstituted *Temple of Angkor Wat*, Exposition Coloniale Internationale de Paris, 1931
Source: *L'Illustration* (23 May 1931), n.p.

One visitor compared *Old London* directly to the contemporaneous surrounding metropolis, not without a certain sense of nostalgia:

> Constant complaints are heard of the rapidity with which London is falling into the rut of modern hustling methods, and those who especially deplore this metamorphosis can enjoy to the full the good old times that prevailed some two or three hundred years ago in the metropolis by a visit to 'Old London', where the capital city as it was in the sixteenth and as it is in the twentieth century, are brought into striking contrast. The gabled projecting timber-fronted houses with their mullioned windows, the rough uneven paving, dimly lighted streets, the picturesque costumes, the lackadaisical life, movement, and customs are all portrayed once inside the gate, which in the olden days cut off communication with the outer world after night-fall. Such a glimpse certainly comes as a relief to the hustle of this commercial age and the monotony of our prosaic bricks and mortar.

In a similar vein, *Old London* was thought to be of special interest to colonial visitors, as 'illustrations of the mother-city from which all our Colonial development sprung'.[63]

Although not a direct counterpart to *Old London*, the Pavilion of the City of Paris was, by contrast, decidedly contemporary and modern. While the London County Council, like the British government, had, after considering the expense involved, refrained from erecting its own pavilion, the municipality of Paris decided quite early to participate with a pavilion of its own displaying information on the many civic functions concerned with running an early twentieth-century city. Architecture was supposed to support this informative function: three sides of the pavilion were used to reproduce parts of famous Parisian buildings such as the Hôtel de Ville. The official guide called this architectural collage 'one of the most striking as well as one of the most beautiful structures in the whole exhibition'. In this section, the municipal authority tried to provide a picture as comprehensive as possible both of its own administrative activities and the City of Paris itself, ranging from police and prisons to lost-and-found services and animal shelters. Exhibits included visual representations and historical photographs, archival documents, tables of mortality, diagrams illustrating the work of the municipal sanitary authorities, plans and pictures of public buildings and parks, large-scale maps of Paris, as well as charts, statistics, models and sketches, showing the methods employed in supplying public utilities and in dealing with crime and regulating traffic. In addition to this rather static program, the Paris municipality also organized a social one by arranging numerous fêtes, receptions and visits on a number of different occasions.[64]

Thus, Ballymaclinton, *Old London* and the Pavilion of the City of Paris each added further extensions to the complex polarities of the Shepherd's Bush site. Popular versions of entire cultures with all their differences and similarities were condensed in sharply defined spaces while, in an effort to illustrate Western order and modern civilization, Ballymaclinton and *Old London*, were placed as a direct contrast to the exotic and 'primitive' of the various ethnic displays, while the City of Paris illustrated the marvels of modern administration. Matters were, however, further complicated not only by Ireland's contested political status but also by the different chronotopic configurations of these sections. The 'villages' represented far-off places lacking a past and with a static present, while Ballymaclinton and *Old London* stood for different national pasts, distinct but still connected, now overtaken by progress and hence improved, but with the old values conserved, as 'the ancient' was combined 'with the modern in a fascinating manner'. Paris, moreover, with its efficient bureaucracy and civic administration, epitomized a type of modernity that was still felt to be lacking in London. Thus, the primary contrast evoked in ever-varying configurations was between domestic and foreign space versus historical and present time.[65]

Seeing national beauty

Like all imperial expositions, the Franco-British Exhibition attracted a considerable amount of public attention. In a probably unintentional yet paradigmatic manner, the cover illustration of the satirical magazine *Punch, or the London Charivari*, published in June 1908, epitomized the different semantic concepts under discussion and their complex relationship to each other. Its frontispiece shows two figures, easily identifiable as Marianne and John Bull, about to happily embrace each other and carrying the other's national flag in their hands, obviously as a sign of goodwill (Figure 4.7). With the scene set in front of one of the larger ponds, so typical of the Franco-British Exhibition, and the modernist Flip-Flap and the *Court of Honour* with its curved, orientalist architecture in the backcloth, this image went far beyond merely illustrating the official *Entente cordiale* rhetoric of the public print discourse. Flip-Flap and the *Court of Honour* were not simply to be read as *partes pro toto* for the entire White City site; rather, they symbolized the imperial background only against which such a national encounter could be depicted. Quite literally, the image epitomized both the Empire and the communicative amusement technologies integrated into a national iconography, thus revealing the complex triangular relationship at the heart of the entire exhibition.

After its closure, the organizers repeatedly expressed satisfaction with the exhibition's course and results. The verdict of London and the entire nation was that the Franco-British Exhibition had successfully attained its object: it had proved an honor to the 'Capital of the Empire' and had effectively promoted the *Entente* between the two nations. Repeating the standard views of international exhibitions as demonstrating industrial achievement, promoting goodwill and strengthening commercial relations between nations – and hence forwarding global progress and fostering peace – the organizers stated that the anticipated strengthening of the *Entente cordiale* had effectively taken place, leading to immediate political repercussions involving bilateral relations.[66] Such an attribution, however, seemed based largely on trust in the exhibition medium rather than confidence in the *Entente* partner. Hopes that an exposition would have

PUNCH, OR THE LONDON CHARIVARI, JUNE 24, 1908.

Figure 4.7   Marianne and John Bull on the cover of the satirical magazine *Punch*
Source: *Punch* 134 (24 June 1908), cover illustration. Courtesy of Widener Library, Harvard College Library, Widener P 325.1 (134 1908).

a warming effect on German-British relations were misguided. On 28 October 1908, the very same day that a lavish banquet was organized in honor of Kiralfy with members of all the various committees present, the *Daily Telegraph* published its scandalous interview with Kaiser Wilhelm II, further alienating the German Reich from Great Britain on the eve of the First World War. On this occasion →Lord Blyth, the chairman of the Organization Committee, suggested that in the German-British case too, the mutual organization of a bi-national exhibition would, almost inevitably, lead to a peaceful settlement of all existing inter-governmental conflicts – in other words, civilizing expositions were considered a means of avoiding war.[67]

By and large, public criticism did not concern the medium's role in fostering international relations, but rather the exhibition's extravagant architecture. Well aware of the fact that by the early twentieth century, the fair-going public had come to expect a specific exhibition architecture with 'buildings quite impossible in any other surroundings', professional observers nevertheless agreed that the exhibition had possibly overdone it, with many of the admittedly spectacular buildings and pavilions 'overlaid with extraneous ornamentations to such a degree as to be almost lost'. In the *Architectural Review,* the critic Robert W. Carden deplored a lack of expressive originality. Although considering the results 'discouraging' in general, he could not help but voice a certain awe about the arrangement and layout.[68] The harshest criticism, however, came from a third reviewer, the distinguished architect J. Nixon Horsfield. His criticism was twofold. First, the British government had gambled away a great chance by exercising so little influence and control, thus missing the opportunity to organize an exhibition up to international standards. Compared to earlier events on a similar scale, such as the Paris 1900 Exposition Universelle, one had to feel ashamed in view of the numerous foreign travelers who had especially come to London on this occasion:

> Our friends from abroad will not experience a sense of welcome such as was expressed by the monumental entrance which graced the Place de la Concorde in 1900; they will miss the sense of breadth and freedom which was expressed by the uninterrupted lines stretching from the Trocadéro to the Cascades of the Electric Hall, and from the Champs-Elysées to the dome of the Invalides; and, above all, they will miss the sense of grandeur and importance which can be given only by extravagance of size and greatness of architectural scale, such as was maintained in St Louis.[69]

Moreover, Nixon Horsfield considered Kiralfy an architectural dilettante who would have done better to consult experts in the field rather than planning and laying down the entire design himself. He regarded the whole of the exhibition as less than the sum of its parts: 'Each building considered apart has distinct merits, but together they are lost. In the same way each division of the Exhibition grounds has merit, but that merit is not accumulated, and therefore does not tell.' From an architect's perspective, Nixon Horsfield presented himself as completely disillusioned. With his hope of great things unmet, one could only rely on future successes of the Parisian competitor; London had lost the age-old inter-urban competition once again:

> This country initiated the idea of an International Exhibition in 1851, and the unmistakable sky-line of the Crystal Palace may still be seen from the Downs, but it is doubtful whether we shall ever again have an international exhibition officially authenticated which will hold its own among the fairs of the world. It will certainly be unnecessary if Paris continues her series of exhibitions at intervals of a decade, as I sincerely hope she will, for there is nothing at Shepherd's Bush which will give her an excuse for omitting the Fair due in 1911.[70]

Precisely by considering certain elements of the bi-national polarity that the exhibition tried to bridge, if not to neutralize, this strong critique illustrated yet again the enormous tension between the two poles. At the same time, it could be read as an expression of disappointment that a professional outsider could so succeed. Despite Kiralfy's disregard for established architectural standards, the sheer number of visitors in itself confirmed the success of both his structural and thematic concept.[71]

The scope and impact of such conservative criticism seems, in any case, to have been limited. Negative reactions could hardly be found in the mass media. Above all, the Franco-British Exhibition – and with it, the White City – quickly proved a popular recreation area and an attractive destination for weekend outings for Londoners. For many, it was the high-point, indeed the signature event, of the entire year. As *The Times* declared: 'For more than five months the Exhibition has been a great fact in the life of London.' The recollections of individual visitors, together with the huge number of postcards mailed from the exhibition, testify to its enormous popularity. Most visitors seem to have used it as a pleasure resort for an affordable, if short, holiday. Phrases such as 'We had a nice time on Sat but it was very crowded', 'It is lovely, especially the Exhibition [...] is grand' or 'We are here & having a lovely time. It is beautiful to see all the illuminations' are typical of the primarily positive, yet rather apolitical and scarcely critical, response to the exhibition. Of course, due to the narrow limits the postcard medium places on potentially complex messages, these statements should not be overestimated.[72]

Even long after the exhibition closed, however, many visitors had fond memories of the Franco-British Exhibition because it had been the occasion for a particular, personally pleasing or otherwise meaningful moment in their individual biographies. At the age of 12, C. Hayward, for instance, had found his first employment as 'boy' with one of the participating companies; he remembered the entire site so vividly and in much detail because he kept that position for a number of years at the later White City exhibitions. A Mr and Mrs Boulton recalled their honeymoon experience at the site quite clearly, especially the spectacular vista of the city which, when the Flip-Flap failed at the top of its semi-circle and left its passengers stuck high above west London, they had more than two hours to appreciate. For a third visitor, the entire exhibition simply

Figure 4.8 View from the Flip-Flap, offering its passengers a spectacular panorama of the entire exposition city

Source: Courtesy of Geheimes Staatsarchiv Preußischer Kulturbesitz, Berlin, I. HA Rep. 120 MfHuG, E XVI 4 Nr. 2, vol. 2.

had a magical quality that later fairs never managed to recreate. All his expectations were completely fulfilled in 1908: 'Not only because most of us were young did those exhibitions which Kiralfy ran years ago have a magic about them [...]. A sense of entertainment, of we're-going-to-have-a-good-time, was in the air, and reached you at the moment the turnstile had been passed.' Given statements such as these, comments in the mass press which attempted to measure the event's significance by its meaning for the visiting crowds were not entirely unjustified. For many 1908 would indeed be remembered as the year when 'we went to the Franco-British'.[73]

Like all other imperial exhibitions, the Franco-British Exhibition aimed to present a visual version of the British Empire to a mass audience (Figure 4.8). Via carefully staged and highly spectacular events, it tried to transform its subject matter into an experience as immediate as possible. More so than any other exposition analyzed in this book, the Franco-British Exhibition constituted one enormous, centrally organized and timely spectacle. Although ubiquitous, the exhibition's dual nature both contextualized and obscured the spectacle in its entire tautology.[74] There were two overlapping polarities. First, the Franco-British Exhibition was characterized by an opposition between the two nations – precisely the exposition's 'dual nature' so often evoked by contemporaneous accounts. Second, this polarity stood out against the cooperation of the two nations abroad as racially similar rulers of their respective empires, in contrast to the indigenous cultures represented there in such a supposedly faithful manner. With its bi-national arrangement of all pavilions and the contrast between the White City and 'native villages', these double polarities were clearly identifiable in the site's spatial arrangement and directly reflected in its architectural forms. Presented in a quite conventional manner in the respective sections of the exhibition, only the prevailing commercialization and the predominance of spectacle concealed these tensions. From such a perspective, Kiralfy's towering Flip-Flap could then be read as the exhibition's genuine symbol, its *clou* and *pars pro toto* alike. Offering its passengers, with its bird's-eye view of a carefully designed image of the entire British Empire, the fiction of a fiction, it literally overcame the two topographical polarities by employing a third dimension.

5
Wembley 1924: The British Empire Exhibition as a Suburban Metropolis

> England is a small island. The world is infinitesimal [...]. But London is illimitable.
>
> (Ford Madox Ford)

> In its title the exhibition is merely a British enterprise, but in its character, in its dominant intention, it covers the world. The exhibition is a model of what we hope the whole world will one day become.
>
> (Winston S. Churchill[1])

The news was announced in the German press shortly before Christmas 1996, adding an ironic tinge to an ongoing German-British controversy. In an effort to increase its chances of hosting the Football World Cup in 2006, Britain's Sports Council had decided to demolish the world-famous Wembley Stadium (Figure 5.1) in northwest London in order to erect the 'most spectacular stadium in the world' (Tony Blair), a new 'superstadium', designed by the renowned architect Lord Foster and more expensive than any other sports arena in the world.[2] On the Internet, Foster declared that this marked the revival of a national symbol and momentous *lieu de mémoire*. 'The first Wembley was created for the 1920s', read the announcement: 'This Wembley is for the 21st century. At a moment when London is enjoying a renaissance as a world city, Britain's sporting leadership will be reasserted by a world-class Wembley stadium.' Likewise the local authorities took the opportunity to link the site to the nation's sense of itself, calling the stadium a 'national icon imprinted on the hearts and minds [...], and a mark of our identity abroad. Its history is our history.'[3] While German commentators referenced the still famous and controversial 1966 World Cup goal, numerous concerts and music festivals such as Live Aid in 1985 and the 1996 European Championship with Oliver Bierhoff's first (and last) 'golden goal', the British press preferred to remind readers of the legendary 'White Horse Final' between Bolton Wanderers and West Ham United on 28 April 1923. This game, the first Football Association Cup Final ever played in the stadium, attracted an estimated crowd of more than twice the stadium's 126,500 capacity, which Police Constable George Scorey alone, on his white horse 'Billie', managed to

Figure 5.1 The Empire Stadium in Wembley in 1924, with the renowned white twin towers in the foreground
Source: Courtesy of California State University, Fresno, Special Collections Research Center, Larson Collection.

subdue, subsequently elevating the two to almost mythical fame.[4] The British press also reminisced about a mega-event that was unknown to German commentators: the British Empire Exhibition of 1924–25 for which the stadium, with its prominent white twin towers, had originally been built. In different national contexts, one and the same site of memory can have very different meanings.

A sudden dismantling had not been foreseen when the stadium was constructed in the early 1920s. At that time, it was the largest sports arena in the world. Erected in less than 300 days, the so-called Empire Stadium – as it was known well into the 1950s – was opened to the public a year before the exhibition itself was launched, quickly becoming a national landmark and a veritable icon of Englishness. Although by the time the exhibition opened in 1924, it had 'already dominated the surrounding landscape for months', the stadium came to be seen as the central *clou* of the British Empire Exhibition.[5] It gave weight to the exposition's spatial structure and anchored its physical layout. While the sketches for the shape and size of the exposition venue changed considerably over the many years it was in the planning stage, the layout of the stadium as well as its exact location on the grounds remained remarkably consistent (Figure 5.2; compare with Figure 5.7). 'The shape, the size, the scale, and the dominating position of the Stadium pull

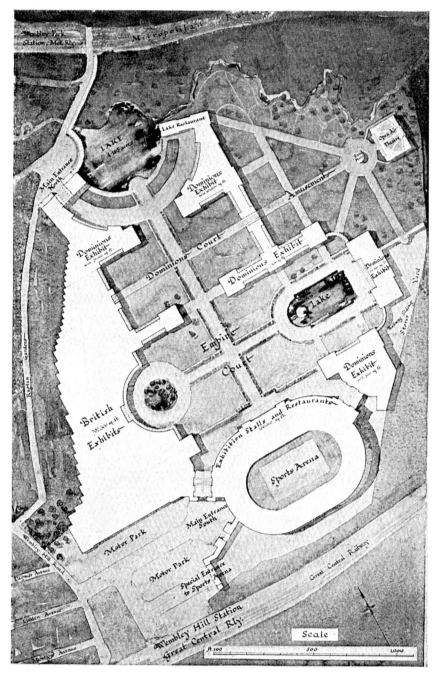

Figure 5.2 Proposed general plan of the British Empire Exhibition, designed by John W. Simpson and Maxwell Ayrton, *c.*1921
Source: Courtesy of The National Archives, Kew, BT 60/9/2.

the whole Exhibition grounds together', declared the *Journal of the Royal Institute of British Architects*, and 'reduce to some extent the little interfering excrescences dotted about here and there, and provide a quite fitting climax to a great Imperial adventure, an experiment and a success'.[6] As it was generally considered the greatest structure of its kind in existence, contemporaneous observers not only linked the stadium directly to the Crystal Palace as *the* legacy – both physical and conceptual – of yet another nationally significant exhibition, but also to other historical monuments of classical origins. In a grandiose manner, the building contractor Robert McAlpine, for example, repeatedly compared the stadium with the colosseum in Rome or the amphitheater in Nîmes, and pondered what would be the national significance of the world's largest structure 2000 years later. If Nîmes had outlasted the centuries, so too could the stadium, he posited, confident for a simple reason: 'Nothing more enduring than concrete has ever been used in building.'[7]

That such a structure for the ages was to last little more than three-quarters of a century, and that reinforced concrete did not prove as durable as experts had expected, was, in this case, not due to the innate transience of the exposition medium. In the interwar years, Wembley had not only become a 'national institution, but a name known in every country of the civilized world', as one of its first annalists stated in 1953.[8] Yet the exhibition's afterlife proved much less spectacular. At a private auction, the site and buildings were sold as they stood, with most of the pavilions then completely dismantled and others moved. The Burmese Pavilion, for instance, was shipped to Australia to form part of the Melbourne centenary celebrations. Factories in Glasgow, Letchworth and Ireland took over parts of various smaller pavilions. Only a very few of the original structures remained *in situ*. Already at the time of its official closure, one newspaper had described the site as being 'a vast white elephant, a rotting sepulchre of hopes and the graves of fortunes'. Although four complexes – the *Palaces of Art*, *Industry* and *Engineering*, and the British Government Building – had been intended to be permanent in addition to the stadium, grandeur and gravity rather than durability or sustainability were the main criteria at the time of their construction.

Only a year after the fair's closure, a visitor to the deserted site bemoaned how the grounds had fallen into decay, with the avenues leading to the stadium overgrown and a 'general air of desertion and forlornness' prevailing. In 1927, the entrepreneur and sports promoter →Arthur James Elvin eventually took over control of the Empire stadium, made it suitable for greyhound racing and had the so-called Empire Pool added, turning the whole complex into a national sports venue. Here, in 1948, the first Olympic Games after the Second World War were held, the so-called Austerity Games. In the 1970s, the site was transformed into an industrial park. The British Government Pavilion was demolished in 1973 and the *Palace of Engineering* six years later to make way for a warehouse development. However, built high upon a hill, the stadium continued to dominate the site just as it had, literally, in the mid-1920s towered over the entire exhibition venue. With the complete demolition of the original Wembley Stadium as its most central and mythical *pièce de résistance* in 2003, the final remains of the British Empire Exhibition were irretrievably swept away. Although all official contracts had included a special clause that made interfering with the use of the land or buildings for the purpose of another exposition at any time within a period of five years legally impossible, no further grand-scale exhibition was ever held at the Wembley site again. The first remained the last.[9]

While all this was debated in the British public print discourse *in extenso*, an even older layer of meaning of the site was never discussed: The Empire Stadium was built precisely on the site of the so-called Watkin's Folly, London's notorious imitation of the Eiffel Tower, itself an incomplete, but direct conceptual transfer from the Parisian 1889 Exposition Universelle. This largely forgotten episode demonstrates tellingly the complicated representational and symbolic interrelationships within the global exhibitionary network, between both single expositions on the one hand, and competing venues on the other. Already through the very choice of its site, the Wembley exhibition was, consciously or not, linked with the tradition of nineteenth-century French *expositions*.

The intricate genesis of Watkin's Folly goes back to the late 1880s. In the immediate aftermath of the French 1889 exposition, a public competition was held for a tower to be built in Wembley Park, a large estate in northwestern London. Aiming to open a railway line from his hometown of Manchester to Paris by way of a channel tunnel →Sir Edward Watkin, the initiator of this project and managing director of the Metropolitan Railway Company, made plain his intention to replicate the Eiffel Tower in London and to repeat its enormous commercial success in a different national setting. At the same time, Watkin proposed that the London version should be 'much more spacious and of greater altitude than the Eiffel Tower, with a view to its being still more useful, and to accommodate a larger portion of the public'. For him, the Eiffel Tower was primarily a matter of inter-urban competition and a national challenge to which London must respond. If Paris possessed such a 'tall tower', London simply could not do without if it was not to lag behind its continental rival. Given the Eiffel Tower's prominence in Watkin's original call for tenders, it did not come as a surprise, then, that the two winning designs both bore a striking resemblance to the Parisian original, looking almost like replicas of it, much to the disgust of professional journals such as *Engineering* (Figure 5.3).[10] Watkin had a second reason for pursuing his tower project. Inspired by the commercial success which a competitor, the District Railway Company, had achieved by renting out its land to the organizers of the Earl's Court exhibitions in the late 1880s, Watkin considered his plans for a spectacular pleasure park in Wembley – featuring sports grounds, tea pagodas, bandstands and a lake, together with the lookout tower as its central attraction – as an additional means of increasing inner-city tourism, thus providing his railway company with more passengers. In addition to his patriotic rationale, Watkin would profit doubly, not only from passengers' visits up and down the tower, but also from trips to and from the site.[11]

The building of a slightly smaller version of the winning design, though obviously still taller than its Parisian counterpart, an octagonal steel tower originally suggested by architects A. D. Stewart, J. M. McLaren and W. Dunn, was begun in June 1893, with a completion date in late 1894. However, despite its reduced height and modified design, London's replica of the Eiffel Tower was never realized beyond its first stages. When the tower had reached the height of only 47 meters – roughly

Die höchsten Turmbauten.

Die ausgestellten Pläne eines großen Turmes für London.

1. Turm von Otis (Höhe 1355'). — 2. Rinfel & Pohl (1250'). — 3. M. W. P. (1200'). — 4. E. S. Shaw (1400'). — 5. T. E. Clarke, J. Mayer & W. Hildenbrand (1280'). — 6. P. Campanaki (1100'). — 7. „Zeit ist Geld" (1200'). — 8. A. D. Stewart, J. M. Maclaren & W. Dunn (1200'), (1. Preis). — 9. Robert Wylie (1470'). — 10. E. Harper, H. A. H. Harper & J. Graham. — 11. Wyndham Baughan & Tomkins (1500'). — 12. Maram Ende (1550'). — 13. J. J. Webster & J. W. Haigh (1300'). — 14. Fox & G. E. Grayson (1300'). — 15. S. J. Fairfax (1296'). — 16. H. Davey (1250'). — 17. J. G. Read & L. A. Shuffrey (1250'). — 18. R. H. Smith & W. Henman (1400'). — 19. H. E. Stetschley (1193'). — 20. Lamont Young (440 m). — 21. T. W. Trew (1267'). — 22. Vegetarian (2007'). — 23. Anonyme (1600'). — 24. The Century Tower (1900'). — Der englische Fuß gleich 0,3048 m.

Figure 5.3 Twenty-four of the 68 submitted designs for a 'tall tower' to be built in London in the early 1890s, with proposals number 8 and 10 winning a prize
Source: 'Die ausgestellten Pläne eines großen Turmes für London', *Das Neue Universum* 12 (1891), 127. Courtesy of Staatsbibliothek zu Berlin – Preußischer Kulturbesitz.

a seventh of the planned 350 meters – in September 1895, the project had to be abandoned for want of funds and due to structural defects (Figure 5.4). Nonetheless, Watkin's Folly, as the site was soon nicknamed by the public, became a popular destination for weekend outings and remained open until 1902. In the meantime, the surrounding park had been laid out, including cricket and football grounds, a lake, fountains and several pavilions. The pleasure dome attracted 120,000 visitors in the 1895 season alone. Having been declared unsafe, Wembley Tower, in spite of its popular success, was closed to the public and eventually demolished in September 1907. Construction work for the Empire Stadium began 15 years later on exactly the same site. Thus, not only in its representational style, its use of architectural forms and its imperial imagery, but also the recent history of the site, the Wembley exhibition was – long before it actually opened – fully incorporated and integrated

Figure 5.4 One of the four 'legs' of the projected London Eiffel Tower, 1894. Construction had to be abandoned after the first stage
Source: Marsillon, 'La Tour Eiffel de Londres', 388.

into the complex exhibitionary networks of the late nineteenth and early twentieth centuries. Through a bizarre international and trans-metropolitan interaction, the British Empire Exhibition marked a further step in the age-old inter-urban competition between London and Paris.[12]

The following analysis is concerned not only with the site, its spatial structure and mental legacy, but, above all, with the exposition actually held there in 1924 and 1925. The British Empire Exhibition, though largely neglected by historians, has sometimes been referred to as an interwar propaganda ploy, an attempt to stimulate interest in the Empire and its achievements, and to counter post-war disillusionment by appealing to patriotic pride. Even a brief glance at contemporaneous press reports about the exposition, historian James Joll has suggested, would entirely suffice to 'understand what overweening efforts were involved in continually presenting London as the center of a worldwide empire'. Although not denying the legitimacy of such interpretations, a more nuanced reading is possible by further contextualizing and historicizing this mega-event while, at the same, acknowledging Wembley's particular position in the global exhibitionary networks.[13]

Never before had the imperial theme been so central and dominant in a European exposition of such a scale, and – as official and semi-official publications never tired of repeating – never before had an area as large been given to the dominions, colonies and 'dependencies' to present themselves in the metropolis. Yet, neither the exhibition's prevailing language nor its specific modes of representation were as unprecedented and unique as its promoters claimed. Indeed, one could diagnose both a representational and discursive 'hangover'. Signs of fundamental dissolution in both the 'medium of modern civilization' during the interwar years, as a prospectus glowingly described it, and this exposition's very subject matter could no longer be overlooked in 1924 and 1925.[14]

Setting the stage

Long before the opening of the British Empire Exhibition in Wembley in April 1924, full-page advertisements in all the daily newspapers had already alerted the public to the spectacle soon to be staged. London would, *The Times* assured, once again become 'host of the world' and Wembley the metropolis of the Empire. Other advertisements appealed to patriotism, stating 'Come to England, come to Wembley in 1924, and testify by your presence your pride in the past and your hope in the future!', and even usually rather restrained commentators declared themselves confident that Wembley would prove a 'landmark in our history'. A year and a half before the actual opening, a special newspaper, the *Empire Exhibition News*, was launched to manufacture the necessary publicity, while at the same time attracting the interest of commercial exhibitors, featuring strategic articles on topics such as 'Make Wembley your Advertisement' or 'How Exhibitions Vitalise Trade'.[15]

Just like the Parisian Exposition Coloniale of 1931, the Wembley exhibition had first been advanced long before the First World War, with a proposal by the British Empire League for holding an imperial exposition dating back to 1902, six years before the Franco-British Exhibition. The plan was again put forward by Lord Strathcona, Imre Kiralfy and the South African Captain Sir Pieter C. Van B. Stewart-Bam (1869–1928) at a public meeting in November 1910, a few years before Strathcona's death. Together, Strathcona and Kiralfy had organized comparable events, and Stewart-Bam had served as the chairman of the General Executive of the 1907 South African Exhibition. In 1910, the Wembley project still figured under the heading 'universal imperial exhibition' and was scheduled for 1915 to coincide with the Prince of Wales' coming of age.[16] Yet, the realization of these plans was delayed, first by organizational difficulties and then by the First World War, though interest persisted even after the start of the war. In April 1916, for example, an anonymous letter to the editor, published in the *Builder*, suggested that it would be wise to start preparing as soon as possible for such an event in the post-war period, when the eyes of the whole world would turn towards England, 'and then will be the time to show what we can do':

> For this purpose a showroom will be needed – a showroom worthy of the coun-try, worthy of the Empire – a showroom where our products of the past and present and our aims and intentions of the future may fittingly be exhibited. [...] This is a matter of such importance that it ought not to be left entirely to private enterprise, but should be national and subsidised by the Government.[17]

Once the war was over, the private initiators and the Board of Trade joined forces, a provisional committee was appointed, and the project eventually re-launched by the Prince of Wales – the future King Edward VIII (1894–1972) – at a meeting held under the auspices of the Lord Mayor of London at the Mansion House on 7 June 1920, thus creating a clear line of historical continuity within the exhibition medium. It was at this same place that Albert, the Prince Consort of Great Britain and Ireland (1819–1861), in March 1850, had first presented his genuinely epoch-making plans for organizing an international exhibition to the public. A year later, a second meeting was organized, this time with colonial secretary and future prime minister Sir Winston Churchill (1874–1965), with the mayors of numerous provincial towns present. The president of the exhibition's General Committee, the Prince of Wales, announced that the exhibition would feature a 'great national sports ground' as its centerpiece. Businessman and public servant →James Lord Stevenson was appointed chairman of the Board of Management, with →Sir Travers E. Clarke as deputy chairman and chief administrator.[18]

In the meantime, the scheme had also been approved by the Board of Trade, whose newly established Department of Overseas Trade led by civil servant and diplomat Sir William Henry Clark (1876–1952) was to become directly involved in the organization. Still, the government's position towards this project was at first hesitant. It arranged for a special guarantee fund by passing an Act of Parliament on 23 December 1920 to facilitate the private financing of the endeavor, and con-tributed £100,000, but otherwise proved reserved in its support. Above all, the gov-ernment did not initially provide any direct subventions or subsidies. It was only under the new Labour government, elected at the end of 1923, that the project was generally declared worthy of official promotion. The British Empire Exhibition was, therefore, neither government-initiated nor state-sponsored, though the government did increase its financial contribution several times and eventually actively participated. Indeed, a new policy was formulated by the Board of Trade's Exhibitions Branch, set up permanently on the recommendation of a 1907 survey committee, while the vast majority of colonies and dominions had agreed to take part with their own displays. Though the government eventually financed a spe-cial Government Pavilion on the site, in addition to those sections already exclu-sively devoted to the presentation of British exhibits, such as the *Palace of Industry* or the *Palace of Engineering*, it remained ambivalent about the undertaking.[19]

The motives for reviving these pre-war plans in early 1920 'on a really big scale', in the words of Lord Milner, were threefold. First, the First World War had led to an increased awareness of the Empire's domestic significance and, at the same time, of the fragility of its precariously maintained unity: 'What we have lost in Europe', Austin Frederic Harrison (1873–1928), editor of the *English Review*, concluded in 1922, 'we should be able to make up in the Empire', and went on to argue that a carefully staged, strategic instrumentalization of Britain's overseas possessions was imperative. Conceived as a major avenue for promoting commerce and industry throughout the Empire and at home, the exhibition was intended to ensure the Empire's stability after the First World War.[20] Second, such a large-scale endeavor could help the process of post-war demobilization and was envisaged as a means to counter wide-scale unemployment and threatening economic decline, providing a welcome opportunity to employ thousands of ex-soldiers in construction and to create jobs staffing the site itself.[21] The third and most momentous reason, however, was a consequence of London's twofold position as Britain's capital and the 'Empire's metropolis'. For much of the second half of the nineteenth century, the lack of both a centrally organized universal and major international exposition after 1862, with its own momentous and easily available venue such as the Parisian Champ de Mars, had been considered a major deficiency, in spite of numerous local, regional, national or bi-national events such as the Franco-British Exhibition of 1908. This failure seemed to reflect London's lack of confidence in the architectural quality of its monuments. Although often hailed as the world's greatest city, the capital of all cities or, simply, *the* great world city from whence the world's largest Empire was ruled, the architectural beauty and monumental dignity thought obligatory for a city of its size and status was felt to be lacking, resulting in a failure in self-presentation. 'The strangest thing is', →Sir Laurence Gomme, public servant and municipal administrator at the London County Council, pondered in 1912, 'that with a city such as London, capital of an Empire such as the British, there should be so little recognition of its position. Londoners do not recognize it; Parliament does not recognize it; statesmen do not recognize it. […] London is not London to the vast majority of Londoners, but a place.'[22] What seemed to contemporaries to be lacking was an effective 'city consciousness', the right spirit and attitude towards the capital on the part of its inhabitants. Thus, for the greater part of the nineteenth and early twentieth centuries, and despite its self-acclaimed and widely acknowledged role as an imperial metropolis and world city, London suffered from such a severe inferiority complex – in comparison to other European capitals, especially Paris – that it can be said to have suffered from its own variant of the 'capital question'. 'The only political organization which does not officially possess a capital, though practically it does, is the British Empire', Reginald Brabazon, the twelfth Earl of Meath lamented in 1921. The British Empire Exhibition in particular must, then, be interpreted as another, if transitory, attempt in a long line of comparable urban development projects to permanently alter and 'imperialize' London's character, thus ameliorating its inferiority complex with regard to continental competitors like Paris – an ailment that was representational in general and architectural in particular. In London, however, this undertaking would begin 'from the edges', that is from the suburban periphery, and then migrate inwards.[23]

Selecting a venue proved far less controversial and intricate than in previous instances and other national cases. Faced with the alternative of reusing a pre-existing site such as the Crystal Palace in Sydenham or the White City, or creating an entirely new venue, the latter was chosen, first and foremost for financial reasons. Although it would have been possible to make use of pavilions already built for the Festival of Empire held in 1911 at the Sydenham site, the Crystal Palace itself had already been in decline for some years. With trees and water in abundance from its previous function as a park, Wembley seemed a more suitable alternative, and was, in 1921, eventually chosen as the future exposition venue, in part because of its size and accessibility by rail. Indeed, contemporary observers carefully calculated that it would have taken three more minutes to reach the White City than to reach Wembley. Work on the exhibition grounds and the stadium began in early 1922. Some 18 months later, the *Builder* showed itself quite content with what had been achieved in the meantime. 'A year ago', the attentive observer could take note in its October 1923 issue, 'the site of the British Empire Exhibition [...] was open country except for the Stadium nearing completion [...]. Now about half of the site is covered with buildings either roofed in or in course of roofing.'[24]

This decision – as was also to be the case in 1931 – altered the venue's character permanently and effectively made Wembley, actually located in Middlesex, a functioning London suburb and a bustling satellite town, experiencing one of the highest population increases in the whole of England and Wales in the decade after 1921, accompanied and facilitated by a housing boom across Britain. From King's Cross, the newly built Wembley Park Station could be reached by fast train within 16 minutes, whence it was directly linked to the so-called Never-stop Railway, the exhibition's loop-shaped internal means of transport directly modeled on the Parisian *trottoir roulant*. This allowed for a smooth transition when moving through and then beyond the 'real' city, before entering its 'artificial' equivalent.[25]

Once again, a direct and immediate connection between the holding of an exhibition, processes of urban development and spatial restructuring, and the planned extension of a pre-existing system of public transport was apparent. While clearly taking the form of a city within a city, the site, although well connected by public transport, was 'some way out of London', as *The Times* had already noted in a leading article published in the fall of 1921, questioning whether the choice of Wembley Park was 'altogether judicious' (Figure 5.5). Though its relative remoteness was not mentioned by any of the numerous advertisements, other observers ruminated about 'the significance of an enterprise which will bring the Empire in miniature to the very *gates* of the Metropolis' – rather than into the city center itself.[26] Yet, the venue's relation to the host metropolis remained at best unclear. While it was often declared a new city in itself, Wembley lay outside the actual municipal area, thus forming part of a larger development, commenced much earlier. After the Colonial and Indian Exhibition of 1886, held in the Royal Horticultural Society

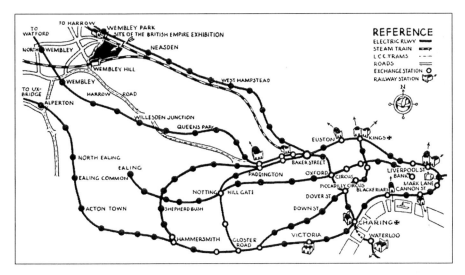

Figure 5.5 The site of the British Empire Exhibition in relation to the metropolis
Source: Courtesy of The National Archives, Kew, BT 60/9/2, 17.

Gardens in South Kensington, London exhibitions were increasingly driven to the outskirts, away from the city center, and thus, by and large, 'suburbanized'. It was only to be on the occasion of the 1951 Festival of Britain that town planners and urban designers realized its enormous potential for redevelopment and decided to bring the spectacle back into the city. Seen in this perspective, the British Empire Exhibition of 1924–25 constituted not only the peak but also the final turning away from a long-term movement to London's west.[27]

Although the original intention had been to open the exposition in May 1921, the date had to be postponed several times, first to 1923, and then, in the summer of 1922, to 1924, primarily to allow dominions and colonies more time for preparation and thus ensure their participation in the 'third great exhibition held in this country after the exhibition of 1851 and the comparatively unsuccessful exhibition of 1862' but, as the organizers emphasized, the 'first Empire Exhibition ever'. Although precise historical information is scarce, a 'rehearsal', albeit a largely independent exhibition, was held in Calcutta in 1923, in part to select the exhibits which Bengal would send to London. Unexpectedly, however, this enterprise met with certain local opposition, mostly on political grounds, so that some of the invited companies eventually refused to participate. Although the exhibition, held in Calcutta's Eden Gardens, contained exhibits from all parts of India, only a small portion of these were later transferred to London.[28] As a further means of international preparation and global promotion, in 1922 a special three-man mission, under the direction of →Major Ernest Albert Belcher – assistant general manager of the Wembley exhibition and later controller of general services – was sent for more than eight months on a publicity tour around the entire Empire to 'explain to the Dominions the spirit which underlies this great enterprise, and the essential characteristics which differentiate it from all previous exhibitions', and to secure their financial support and active participation.[29]

The eighth wonder of the world

King George V opened the British Empire Exhibition on 23 April 1924, Shakespeare's birthday as well as St George's Day, a national holiday, and it remained open until 1 November (Figure 5.6). The final words of his opening speech, 'I declare this exhibition open', was the first sentence by a head of state ever transmitted live on radio. Simultaneously a cablegram with this message was sent around the entire world, which then arrived back in Wembley, having, in the meantime, 'travelled the Empire in 80 seconds'. Thus, from the very day of its opening, the British Empire Exhibition took advantage of various technical achievements considered extremely modern, which caused a public stir similar to that produced by the Flip-Flap in 1908. Yet here, not only did their instrumentalization and integration in the overall concept go much further, but they also had a more inherent connection to this exhibition's specific version of the theme of globalization.[30]

The 17,403,267 visitors who came to see the Wembley exposition during its first 150 days guaranteed that it was a resounding success. But because a minimum of 25 million had been expected, the organizers made a loss of more than £600,000 before selling off the buildings. Speculation instantly began as to whether the exhibition would reopen in 1925, with the added intention of reducing the deficit accumulated during the first year. Although always having insisted that the exhibition was a private initiative and run by private enterprise, the government decided to step in. Because it considered the exposition a 'notable success' that had achieved much 'as an educational instrument and in stimulating a reasoned imperial sentiment', the government was willing to assume more financial responsibility, yet simultaneously asked for more direct control in return. Eventually, the new cabinet secured approval for the guarantee required to enable the exhibition to continue for a second year.[31] In consequence – and most unusually – the exhibition reopened the following year for another full season, from 9 May though 31 October 1925, with slight conceptual changes, some new pavilions and a number of extensions, yet without some of the colonies, such as India and Burma, who declined to participate in 1925 for financial reasons. Advertised as 'The Same Empire but a New Exhibition', and considered 'more spectacular than the previous year', Wembley's sequel was nevertheless unable to meet all expectations. Attendance figures dropped to 9,699,231, bringing the total over two seasons to 27,102,498. With construction and maintenance costs of more than 12 million British pounds, the exhibition ran a deficit of £1,581,905 over the two years, which had to be covered by private donations and the guarantee fund.[32] Hopes for a further, second continuation in 1926 or even 'something in the nature of a permanent institution' soon proved unrealistic. In spite of repeated claims on the part of the organizers and repeated assurances, in, for instance, the official guide, that Wembley was not an 'ephemeral structure designed to endure for a season and to pass thereafter into desolation or decay', its future was, at the time of the

Figure 5.6 Panorama of the British Empire Exhibition with the Empire Stadium in the background, here seen from the northern end where Wembley Park Station and the main entrance were located. The Government Pavilion is the building with two huge columns on the far left

Source: 'The Empire in Miniature', *Illustrated London News* 164 (24 May 1924), supplement. Courtesy of Widener Library, Harvard College Library, P229.10f.

exhibition, entirely unclear. Questions of sustainability and the introduction of infrastructural measures that would guarantee its endurance did not rank high on the agenda, though several buildings, including the two huge centrally located palaces and the Government Pavilion in the eastern section of the venue, had been erected as permanent structures.[33]

Like any other exposition, Wembley tried to create an imaginary structure by assigning both objects and people their correct place. 'The exhibition', an architectural critic observed, 'through its layout, becomes at once expressive of the Empire's attempt to produce order out of the chaos resulting from a century or more of uncurbed industrialism.'[34] Its spatial structure was strictly symmetrical (Figure 5.7 and Plate 5). The largely pyramid-shaped venue was 88 hectares in size and divided by a double axis in the form of a St Andrew's cross, with a large garden and the main entrance at its northern apex, and the Empire Stadium, the Pavilion of New Zealand and the Indian Pavilion at its southern, western and

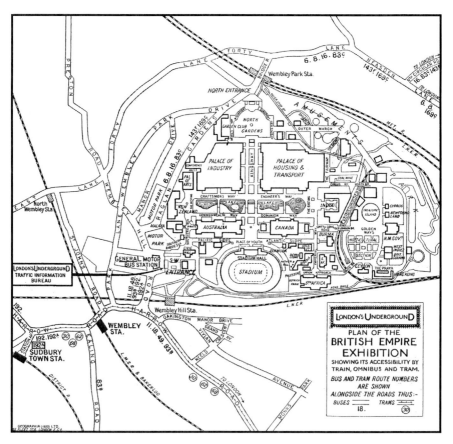

Figure 5.7   London Underground's plan of the British Empire Exhibition, 1925
Source: Courtesy of Brent Archive, London, 1924/PRI/2/4.

eastern ends respectively. The two largest buildings to be found on the entire site were the *Palace of Industry* and the *Palace of Engineering*, renamed *Palace of Housing and Transport* in 1925. A system of connected lakes and various parks divided the northern and the southern parts of the venue. Situated around these lakes and further gardens were exhibition pavilions of the four most important territories of the Empire: New Zealand, Australia, Canada and India. Of the 58 countries that comprised the British Empire at that time, 56 participated with displays and pavilions of their own, with only Ireland and Gibraltar missing. The majority of these colonies were located in the southern part of the venue. They included, from west to east, Malaya, Southern Rhodesia, the Bermudas, Sierra Leone, Nigeria, the Gold Coast, Palestine, South, West and East Africa, Burma, Ceylon and Hong Kong, to name but a few, and were all considered 'representative of the characteristic architecture of the different countries', although their architects and designers were more often than not of British rather than indigenous origin. 'In brief', as the official guide succinctly summarized the all-embracing global claims of the arrangement, 'from north to south, from east to west, Wembley presents the British Empire at the summit of its achievement.'[35]

Still further to the east, this rather 'serious' part of the exposition was supplemented by an amusement park, more than 19 hectares in size, with an abundance of 'fun-makers' and 'thrill-producers' including roller-coasters, merry-go-rounds and dancing halls for the pleasure-seekers among the visiting audience. Distractions with such resounding names as The Great Racer, The Devil's Bowl or Whirl of the World promised endless pleasure after all the intellectual exertion. Here, 'in this City of Excitement', an advertisement launched in the *Illustrated London News* promised, 'your children will grow wild with ecstasy'. Yet, even in entertainment a certain colonizing gesture was ever present. By no means should pure pleasure prevail. Rather, serious and genuine interest on the part of the 'amusement-loving Londoner' were to be rewarded with precious glimpses of exotic vistas, 'of strange places, [and] of scenic beauties in far lands', because there was 'instruction as well as amusement' to be found in this 'City of Pleasure'. Thus, the two distinct parts of the exhibition were meant to supplement, rather than to rival each other, both in conception and attractiveness. 'Wembley Park', one official summarized in the Royal Colonial Institute's journal, 'has been converted into a gigantic Empire Object Lesson and Pleasure Ground combined, and it only remains for the public to seize so unique an occasion, to their own benefit and that of the Empire at large'. While the much larger 'serious-minded' section provided the entire enterprise with its necessary legitimation, the prospects of pleasure and spectacle connected with the amusement park and the stadium were meant to arouse the visitors', spectators' and consumers' general interest and curiosity about the exposition.[36]

Yet, the carefully planned and well-organized enrichment of the entire site with additional, easily decipherable, Empire-laden symbolism went further and included more salient features such as the type of building material used, the naming of streets, and the exposition's overall design scheme. The predominant usage of reinforced concrete for the majority of pavilions was considered an outstanding and noteworthy feature, expressing the *dernier cri* in architectural achievement in particular, and urban modernity in general. Even the numerous flagstaffs and lamp-posts that dotted the venue were made of this material. Technology and modernity, artistic expressiveness and the exhibition's representational aims seemed to go hand in hand, indeed, to condition each other. 'The buildings erected', one critic wrote, 'must primarily be regarded as a most important and significant recognition of the claims of reinforced concrete to free outward expression', while the official guide chose rather to emphasize its emblematic qualities when proclaiming that 'no lesser foundation would serve the purpose of Empire'. Yet, architectural critics still debated whether the exhibition's design was actually as modernist as the building materials seemed to suggest. One commentator defended the comparatively restrained architectural approach by differentiating between the buildings' ultra-modern material and their neoclassicist appearance, arguing that they were 'at once new in treatment, for never in this country has such use been made of reinforced concrete, and yet they are redolent of national architectural character'. In this reading, form and function corresponded.[37]

Furthermore, in order to transform the exhibition both literally and materially into the 'Poem of Empire' – as numerous advertisements had praised it so flamboyantly – writer Rudyard Kipling (1865–1936) agreed to name the newly built gateways and bridges, ways and avenues, which, all in all, covered 24 kilometers of roadway. Kipling opted for a somewhat mixed bag of designations that were either historically relevant, politically correct or geographically reminiscent of the various participating nations, colonies and territories. The visitors' sense of direction in the venue was to be supplemented by feelings of imperial grandeur. Thus, directly behind the main entrance, 'Drake's Way' faced 'Anson's Way'. The pavilions of New Zealand and India were connected by both the 'Craftsmen's Way' and the 'Engineer's Way', as well as the 'Commonwealth Way' and the 'Dominion Way'. Leaving the 'Fairway of the Five Nations', the attentive visitor could stroll along the 'Imperial Way' and eventually reach the 'Atlantic Slope' or the 'Union Approach'. Most importantly, the vertical main axis, leading from the northern main entrance to the 'Place of Youth' in the south, situated immediately in front of the stadium with its white twin towers, was named 'Kingsway', the stadium being the exhibition's substitute for a royal palace.[38]

The name 'Kingsway' was particularly evocative, suggesting a double reference, both at home and abroad, and was chosen over alternative suggestions such as 'Empire Avenue' or 'King Edward VII Street'. 'Kingsway' referred not only to the last and greatest of the Victorian metropolitan improvements in London itself, the Kingsway-Aldwych project, which had led to a complete redevelopment of the Strand's eastern end during the early 1900s, resulting in a neoclassical circus called the Aldwych and a new north–south avenue regally named 'Kingsway'. Further, it could be read as an homage to the ceremonial King's Way (now Raj Path) built in imperial New Delhi after 1912, as part of the grandiose development scheme for the new Indian capital under the direction of →Sir Edwin Lutyens, the eminent architect who was responsible for the British Pavilion at the 1900 Exposition Universelle in Paris and a hall at the Esposizione Internazionale di Belle Arte held in Rome 11 years later.[39] Thus, even the naming of the streets was integral to the symbolic charge of the entire site, an effect carefully implemented by its organizers. Inspired by the wish to project the entire British Empire true to scale onto the site available in suburban London, the planners resorted to a multitude of terms, all stemming from highly different contexts, to connect the various British 'possessions' and the self-governing dominions with each other either concretely-spatially or abstractly-mentally. Somewhat surprisingly, the press did not comment on the artificiality of Kipling's rather strained metaphors. Just as the single colonies and 'possessions' would have been left to their own resources without those trade routes, cable lines and other means of communication supplied by Great Britain, the organizers provided the infrastructure which, at the same time, integrated all the colonies into a greater whole. In the end, though not due to Kipling's flowery naming of the streets, Wembley became, at least figuratively, 'the Empire's Metropolis' – and, thereby, London the 'host of the world', as numerous advertisements never tired of repeating time and again.[40]

A similar attempt to create a distinct corporate identity, and to prefigure and control all possible meanings a priori could also be observed in the marketing concept. The exhibition's modernist design was as elaborate as it was attractive. While previous expositions – the Berliner Gewerbeausstellung, for instance – had long experimented with specific color schemes, here the design was both more comprehensive and more consistently applied. In an attempt to contrast with these earlier venues in general and Kiralfy's White City in particular, different shades of color were used for the buildings' surfaces. 'The unpleasant and monotonous glare of pure white [...] is thus avoided', noted one approving professional critic, an innovation that unfortunately is not captured in the available black-and-white photographs.[41]

Responsible for much of Wembley's corporate design and aesthetic and hence a central figure for the entire exhibition was →Sir Lawrence Weaver, an architectural critic and, from 1910, editor of *Country Life*. Having visited several smaller expositions in the two preceding years, Weaver sought to achieve a new artistic exhibition standard by introducing a coherent arrangement of displays that emphasized the quality of the exhibits rather than merely displaying haphazardly assembled goods. The one decisive element in designing exhibitions, Weaver argued, was the central control of their overall layout and public presentation. At Wembley this included uniform lettering on all the displays throughout the entire exhibition which he implemented in the face of considerable opposition on the part of commercial exhibitors, the carefully-controlled designs of all smaller commercial pavilions and kiosks on the grounds, the popular 'Scenes of Empire' poster series used to advertise the exhibition, with its promise of imaginary travel through time and space (Plate 6), as well as the exhibition's powerful emblem, the ubiquitous Wembley lion (Figure 5.8).[42]

Existing in three different variants, one three-dimensional and two two-dimensional, the noble-lion logo was used as an official trade mark for the entire exhibition. Six huge concrete lions stood in front of the Government Pavilion

BRITISH EMPIRE
EXHIBITION 1924
LONDON

Figure 5.8   The Wembley lion, the exhibition's official emblem
Source: Weaver, *Exhibitions and the Arts of Display*, Plate CLIIA/Fig. 356.

(see also Figures 5.10 and 5.16). The same symbol, a somewhat schematic body-profile of a majestically poised lion, could be found on the award medal of the British Empire Exhibition, and another version was used for all publications and propaganda material. Although criticized as 'Assyrian, cowardly (because its tail hangs down instead of waving in the breeze), unnatural (lions at the Zoo were not like that)', and 'very un-English and, therefore, exceedingly disturbing', Weaver praised the emblem as 'an intensely significant and original symbol of the qualities we like to associate with the lion – dignity and unmenacing strength'. It was thought to simultaneously embody the values of the Empire such as 'might, dignity, power and prestige' as well as typically British characteristics like 'strength, honesty, simplicity'. By virtue of its design, the omnipresent logo helped to create a corporate identity for the exhibition, thus connecting otherwise thematically divergent, heterogeneous displays with the overall theme of empire, in part because it was to be found in different versions on numerous merchandising knick-knacks such as spoons, egg cups, tea caddies, ashtrays and mugs which could be purchased and taken home and that have, over time, become much sought-after collector's items.[43]

The heart of the heart of the heart

The exhibition's two main architects, →Sir John W. Simpson and →Sir Maxwell Ayrton, and its principal engineer, →Sir Owen Williams, had applied the standard pavilion system – widespread in the international exhibitionary system since the 1880s – to the explicit and officially exclusive subject matter of this exposition, the entire British Empire. Each colony was assigned its own pavilion. In those cases where this, usually for practical reasons, proved impossible, combined exhibits were assembled. Additionally there were a number of central and more comprehensive sections exclusively devoted to displaying British products and achievements, for instance the *Palaces of Industry* and *Engineering* and the Government Pavilion. Before turning to the representations of some of the foreign cultures participating on the Wembley site, it is necessary first to analyze and historicize these strictly domestic sections.

Classifying Wembley's status within the international exhibitionary networks is a more intricate task than it might first appear. Wembley was seldom, if ever, directly compared to any of the contemporaneous French *expositions*: neither the Exposition Nationale Coloniale held in Marseilles in 1922, nor the Exposition Internationale des Arts Décoratifs et Industriels Modernes, at that time in preparation for 1925, nor even the Exposition Universelle of 1900. On the contrary, the planners attempted to place and hence inscribe the British Empire Exhibition within the contingent and specifically national tradition, which had started in 1851 and stretched from the 1886 Colonial and Indian Exhibition to the Franco-British Exhibition of 1908. Soon after Wembley's official opening →Victor Christian Cavendish, the ninth Duke of Devonshire and one of the exhibition's main financial guarantors, enunciated this inheritance, praising Wembley as 'a triumph of imagination, art, organization and patriotic purpose': 'One thinks of the great International Exhibition of 1851, and realises how its achievement is exceeded by the British Empire Exhibition of 1924; one recalls some of the things said of the Indian and Colonial Exhibition in South Kensington in 1886, and feels that, however well warranted they were at the time, the significance of Wembley is infinitely greater.'[44] Such a process of self-historicization pursued a double objective. Principally, the medium of exhibition was presented as overcoming its innate transience by both participating in, and adding to, a historical continuum long in existence, thus demonstrating its very *raison d'être* and hence its legitimacy. Additionally, any progress achieved in the expositions' interim could be measured against historical predecessors and institutional precursors.

Critics and observers frequently emphasized that Wembley's area was ten times that of the Great Exhibition of 1851 in Hyde Park. On the opening day, *The Times* published a remarkable diagram to illustrate the site's size and define its historical position (Figure 5.9). Not only were two accurate scale maps of the two expositions placed next to each other, but the contour of the Wembley exhibition venue, together with the outlines of its two most massive structures, were also transplanted back into the metropolis' center and superimposed onto a map of London on the same scale, with Trafalgar Square as its imaginary nucleus. The image sought to visualize Wembley's complex position in both space and time, thus bringing home Wembley's 'greatness' – literally and figuratively – both topographically and historically. The choice of Trafalgar Square as a site in central London was by no means arbitrary. As Rodney Mace argued so perspicaciously more than 30 years ago, Trafalgar Square, central London's only large public place, had been designed

154

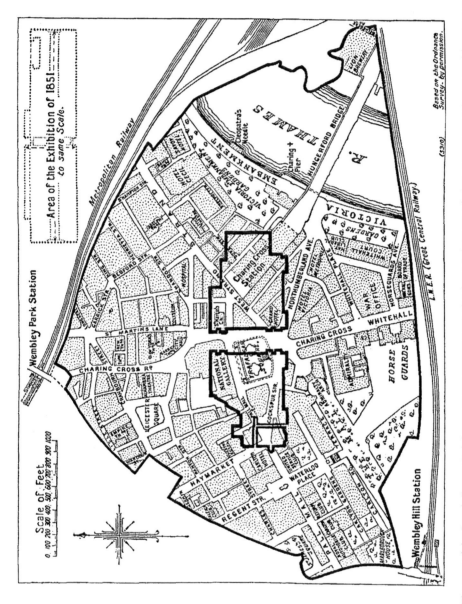

Figure 5.9 The area of the British Empire Exhibition in comparison with the Great Exhibition of 1851, superimposed onto Trafalgar Square in London
Source: The Times (23 April 1924), 16.

during the nineteenth century to be the most striking of the city's many imperial sites. With Lord Nelson's memorial column constructed in 1843, and completed in 1867, Trafalgar Square was subsequently regarded as a built manifestation of Empire and was transformed into England's foremost *place politique*. At the same time, the square was appropriated as *the* center for political meetings and anti-imperial demonstrations, and the place where today's protest marches still often terminate. Thus, the square's 'official' and 'unofficial' historical dimensions were obviously interdependent, not necessarily in a contradictory, but definitely in an ironic manner, with the Wembley exhibition both drawing on such a tradition and also adding to its imperial dimension.[45]

Compared with earlier international exhibitions, Wembley was, on the one hand, subject to precisely the same kind of universalizing and even globalizing relation vis-à-vis 'the world'. It was intended to collect, import, replicate, display and communicate what was considered the essence of the entire world in a strictly limited area within a dense Western metropolitan conglomeration during a clearly-defined time frame. Yet on the other hand, the 'entire world' on display at the Wembley site was reduced to its British imperial variant, that is, the British overseas dominions, colonies and possessions. There were no attempts to include other foreign countries or European nations in 1924–25 or to integrate them into a larger picture. Attributing to Wembley a *pastiche*-like quality in the *Illustrated London News*, well-known critics such as Gilbert Keith Chesterton (1874–1936) were fully aware that the world on display here was restricted to a consciously abridged version that excluded the entire European continent. 'The perilous illusion' maintained at Wembley, he commented, 'consists in looking on the Empire as the world – a sort of imaginative world made in our own image. It is looking into so large a looking-glass that we forget that we are not looking out of a window. It has in its heart the vague idea that we can forget Europe and only remember Empire.'[46] Chesterton feared that such a move would prove, as it were, a British diversion, if not an actual departure, from Europe and its affairs. While Wembley's globalized and globalizing character, partial and selective as it may have been, was emphasized time and again, potential claims to universalism, known from the discursive contexts of other expositions, inevitably proved more problematic. In order to make such claims and, at the same time, to maintain Wembley's position in the international exhibitionary network, the only rhetorical possibility lay in reversing the argument by emphasizing the enterprise's specific autarky and its self-sufficient character. 'Other great Exhibitions in the past have been open to all nations', *The Times* claimed retrospectively, defending and justifying the specifically 'isolationist' approach chosen here: 'Each was called a "World Exhibition" or an "Exposition Universelle"; but at Wembley no help was asked, no co-operation accepted, from outside. The resources of the Empire alone proved sufficient for the organization and staging of an Exhibition infinitely greater and more varied than the world had yet seen.'[47]

Together, the two largest buildings on the site, the *Palace of Industry* and the *Palace of Engineering*, represented Wembley's version of the standard machinery hall. First introduced at the Paris exposition of 1855, the idea of incorporating a pavilion solely devoted to machinery had been especially popular since the epoch-making Parisian *Galerie des Machines* of 1889, the world's largest iron struc-ture at that time, far surpassing St Pancras Station in London. Covering altogether no less than five hectares, the two Wembley palaces were by themselves already more than 12 times bigger than Trafalgar Square, the second of which was claimed to be the largest concrete building in the world. Here as well, differences as com-pared with earlier exhibitions – demonstrating internal and external progress alike – were achieved both historically and geographically. In the *Handbook of General Information*, for instance, the same twofold attempt at distinguishing the palaces from their historical models both at home and abroad can be observed:

> The Palace of Industry is twice the size of the corresponding building at Shepherd's Bush, and the Palace of Engineering is double the size of the build-ing used for the same purpose at the Franco-British Exhibition in 1908. The latter is, in fact, a great deal larger than was the Machinery Hall at the Paris Exhibition, which has hitherto been regarded as having reached the possible limits of dimensions.[48]

To many, the range of exhibits displayed in the two pavilions appeared excessive. While the *Palace of Engineering* was devoted to motors, transport, shipbuilding, marine, mechanical and general engineering, and had been organized by the British Engineers' Association, all other exhibits produced by British industries which did *not* fall under the rubric of engineering, such as textiles, jewelry, paper, furniture and so on, were housed in the *Palace of Industry*. The distinction did not prove sufficiently stable, however, as the collections were completely rearranged in 1925, the exhibition's second year, with the *Palace of Engineering* renamed the *Palace of Housing and Transport*. Here, Weaver's conceptual rationale was converted into exhibitionary practice in two different ways: first, displays were organized by representative associations of groups of firms, so that each type of industry was showcased in one joint exhibit, with similar goods from different producers in close proximity to each other; second, the palaces shared a common and cen-trally coordinated design scheme. 'The result', *The Times* wrote appreciatively, 'is an enormous improvement on the usual chaotic character of such exhibits where each individual exhibitor has his own sweet way in adorning his own little space.' Together with the adjacent *Palace of Arts*, featuring a lavish 'Queen's Doll's House', designed by Lutyens and now on display in Windsor Castle, these sections repre-sented the genuinely British parts of the exhibition. Conceptually and in terms of significance, however, they were both surpassed and held together by the British Government Pavilion, one of the most conspicuous buildings in the entire venue. If the Empire Stadium dominated the entire area architecturally and visually, then the Government Pavilion was Wembley's conceptual and organizational core, the 'focal point of the whole exposition', as Abercrombie declared (Figure 5.10).[49]

The Government Pavilion could be found further east on the site, towards the amusement park, where it was flanked by the sections of Fiji and Newfoundland on the one side, and the West Indies and British Guyana on the other. 'The

Figure 5.10   The British Government Pavilion at night, its entrance flanked by six majestic concrete lions
Source: The Pavilion of H.M. Government, 17. Courtesy of Centre Canadien d'Architecture/Canadian Center for Architecture, Montréal.

British Government Pavilion stands aside from other Pavilions not only in its actual position at Wembley, but in the purpose it serves', wrote the official guide, highlighting the striking contrast, especially at night, between the Government Pavilion and the other structures, characterizing it as the exhibition's 'Whitehall' or 'Downing Street'. Devoted neither to a specific territory nor a particular group of exhibits, but rather illustrating the British government's activities both at home and abroad, its objectives were more directly political and bluntly propagandistic. Designed by the exposition's two chief architects, John W. Simpson and Maxwell Ayrton under the direction of Lawrence Weaver himself, the Government Pavilion was intended to, as an official government document declared, 'epitomise the imperial idea and to place before the visitor the Empire's present, past and future'. A visitor described the building's ferro-concrete, two-story architecture 'of massive dignity' as 'almost classical with its imposing colonnaded doorway and the six majestic lions guarding the entrance'. Although entirely made of reinforced concrete, the pavilion was supposed to allude to the 'great monuments of antiquity'. While the ground floor was open to the public, an upper floor contained a royal

158

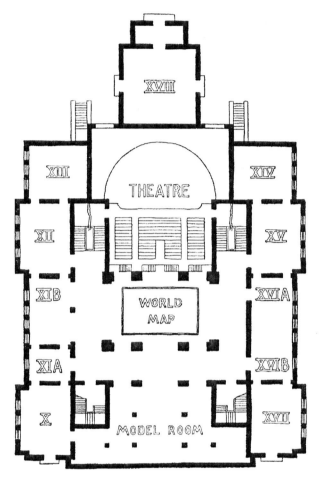

LOWER GROUND FLOOR.

X.   Oversea Settlement.
XIa.   Imperial Institute.
XIb.   Department of Overseas Trade.
XII.   Imperial Mineral Resources. Fuel Research.
XIII.   Ordnance, Hydrographic Survey. Geological Survey.
XIV.   Navy.
XV.   Navy and Air.
XVIa.   Air.
XVIb.   Army and Air.
XVII.   Army.
XVIII.   ANNEXE:
         Meteorological Office (Vestibule). Mint. Tropical Hygier

Figure 5.11   Lower ground floor of the British Government Pavilion, featuring the 'Admiralty Theatre' and a world map at its center
Source: The Pavilion of H.M. Government, 62. Courtesy of Centre Canadien d'Architecture/Canadian Center for Architecture, Montréal.

apartment, similar to that in the *Kaiserschiff Bremen* at the Berlin exposition of 1896. In the center of the building, the public floor opened onto a courtyard around which were grouped various galleries containing departmental exhibits (Figure 5.11).[50]

That the Wembley exposition should include such a pavilion at all could be considered the direct consequence of a new policy formulated by the Board of Trade's Exhibitions Branch, made permanent on the recommendation of a 1907 survey committee. Without any direct government participation in an 'exhibition of this magnitude', and no particular effort made 'to visualise to the public at home and in the Empire what H.M. Government is doing [...] for the public benefit', officials had feared, 'there would be somewhat of a gap', thus rendering the enterprise incomplete and open to criticism. Eventually, the Treasury granted the necessary funds. Although at first still reluctant, the Board of Trade also decided to participate actively, given that the vast majority of colonies and dominions had unanimously agreed to take part with their own displays. The fact that the government was represented by an official pavilion of its own was novel in a domestic British context, and is made even more surprising when one considers the government's general aloofness towards the semi-public, semi-private exhibition project and its initial uncertainties about the enterprise's justification. Like any other commercial exhibitor, the government even had to pay the exhibition organizers a substantial rent for the space allocated.[51]

Employing a wide variety of media, the Government Pavilion constituted a small, yet distinct exposition in itself. Here, 'all that we are and stand for as a nation' was exhibited, as *The Times* proclaimed. Various displays presented the 'achievements of modern civilization' in the fields of military defense, global communication, overseas migration and economic development. Military, aerial and naval displays were especially prominent, as was a staged performance in the 'Admiralty Theatre' where the famous 1918 'Raid on Zeebrugge' was re-enacted with model ships. Despite the fact that this proved one of the very few sites on the entire grounds where the First World War was at all thematized, this spectacle, 'extraordinarily popular amongst all ages and classes' and praised by visitors for being 'horribly realistic', was not Germanophobic. In the pavilion also hung a large oil painting by the British artist Henry Courtney Selous (1803–1890), on special loan from the Victoria and Albert Museum, portraying the opening of the 1851 exhibition by Queen Victoria.[52]

The nucleus and most important single exhibit in the pavilion's *Court of Honour*, however, immediately visible upon entrance, was a 'living', large-scale relief map of the entire world (Figure 5.12). Here, set in water, small model ships incessantly passed along the main ocean routes, moved from port to port and connected the various parts of the Empire with both the mother country and each other. As usual, the sections of the world 'belonging' to the British Empire were painted in a bright, transparent red, illuminated from beneath. According to the official guide, the ships served as a 'medium for the exchange of commodities between the manufacturing centres of overcrowded countries and the vast agricultural centres of the younger lands'. 'It is impossible', the *Guide* continued, obviously much impressed by this 'mobile-like' spectacle with its view to eliciting a desired

Figure 5.12   The *Court of Honour* in the British Government Pavilion, with an illuminated large-scale contour map of the world as its central exhibit
Source: 'With Ships Moving Along Empire Routes: The World in Contour', *Illustrated London News* 164 (24 May 1924), 939. Courtesy of Widener Library, Harvard College Library, P229.10f.

emotional reaction from spectators, 'to spend even a few moments watching the vessels in pursuit of their lawful occasions and the ever-changing lights which indicate the growth of this mighty empire without a sobering sense, not only of civilisation's vast achievement, but of its still vaster requirements.' Here, with the center of the British Government Pavilion as the entire exhibition's conceptual and intellectual 'headquarters', the promise was made that visitors would find themselves watching the 'beating of the heart of the Empire'. Interest in this 'dramatic lesson in Empire geography' proved so great that, according to official estimates, an average of 38 persons per minute were granted admission, amounting to approximately five million visitors in the first year alone and including 120,000 schoolchildren, during specially arranged morning performances.[53]

With its display of a wide range of British governmental activities and the superior state of the technologies employed for these purposes, the British Government Pavilion served not only as the contrast to the rest of the exhibition, but had above all a predominant, controlling function in comparison to the European commercial and industrial exhibits, and the non-European, colonial displays. At least temporarily, the pavilion was to provide the Empire with an otherwise lacking symbolic center, allowing its distant territories to be seen as a single unit, despite their different geographic locations or socio-cultural traditions, incorporating precisely the 'ideal of unity with variety', as one visitor noted.[54] London was intended to be to the entire Empire what the British Government Pavilion was to the exhibition. With such multiple layers of meaning, Wembley's symbolic structure became almost incomprehensibly complex. This represented a further attempt to domesticate the Empire, and, by implication, the entire world under British rule, by replicating, reducing and representing it as the centerpiece of the British Government Pavilion. The resulting relief map was the core of the British Empire Exhibition, standing at the heart of the Empire and 'the world's greatest metropolis', London. The 'heart of the heart of the heart of the heart' was displayed as a global network, with London as its natural hub. Thus, at the very center lay a map of the Empire. In a condensed passage published in the *Architectural Review* of June 1924, the critic and writer H. Barnes evoked several powerful, if divergent images and metaphors at once:

> Here the Government Pavilion occupies the same unobtrusive position as the Crown does in the Constitution, detached, retired, and yet the key to all. The visitor will be well advised if, after making the grand tour, he enters this building before any other. Here he will find, as it were, the index to the volume he is to read. Leaning over the balcony in the central hall, gazing down on the relief map of the world, following the uncanny persistency of the moving models that trace out the great ocean routes, he will be dull, indeed, if some awe is not stirred in him by a revelation of the order that may come out of a seeming chaos of individual desire and enterprise.[55]

Hence, the site was metaphorized as both a nation-state and a book to be read, and the spectator simultaneously transformed into a traveler, reader and interpreter, from whom an adequate emotional response was to be expected when confronted with this new world order.

With regard to other, less ambitious sections and displays, Wembley took part in the regular exhibitionary network of interdependent representations and intertextual quotations referring back to each other. Located between the Burmese Pagoda and the Indian Pavilion, and leading directly to the Government Pavilion, for instance, was the so-called *Old London Bridge* (Figure 5.13). It attempted to convey an impression of 'London in the old days'. 'After leaving the Burma Pavilion', a souvenir guide explained, 'with its lure of the Orient, its weird music, and wonderful dancers, we are confronted with Old London Bridge. Built of grey stone with green slate roof and a cobbled roadway, we are immediately transported from the mystic East to London in the Middle Ages.' However, a certain conceptual ambiguity remained as to the bridge's historical classification. Although officially labeled as 'the' *Old London Bridge* on the grounds and in the guidebooks alike, several critics caviled that *this* bridge was quite clearly not a true architectural reproduction of the 'real' old London Bridge, of which there had been several consecutive versions, the last constructed in 1823–31. A short visit to the London Museum would suffice to dispel this illusion entirely. Yet, in the exhibitionary context such a historically false attribution did not carry great weight. On the contrary, it was noteworthy that Wembley contained an equivalent to other 'old villages', such as the previously mentioned *Alt-Berlin*

Figure 5.13 The western entrance to the *Old London Bridge* on a crowded day. Leading to the British Government Pavilion, it was located between the Indian Pavilion (a fraction of which is visible on the left) and the Burmese Pagoda (on the right)
Source: Courtesy of California State University, Fresno, Special Collections Research Center, Larson Collection.

in 1896, *Vieux Paris* in 1900 or the *Old London Street* in 1908, thus implementing the retrospective principle established in the late 1880s.[56]

Signs of dissolution

What kind of imagery of far-flung territories and distinctly non-European spaces did 'the Empire City' actually evoke? If contemporaneous observers were correct in attributing to Wembley an 'atmosphere of Orientalism', how was such an atmosphere created and what kind of knowledge was provided, especially in the Indian and African sections at the Wembley site? With regard to the specific modes of representation employed, time and again numerous elements were transferred or further developed that had been popularized at earlier exhibitions. Wembley's unique position was rather due to the conflicts it provoked, albeit unintentionally. Although few in number, veiled and of little immediate consequence, these must be read as signs of dissolution in both the medium and its message.[57]

The Indian section was among the biggest of the non-European displays. In close proximity to the British Government Pavilion and next to the *Old London Bridge*, it was situated at the southeastern edge of the grounds and formed – together with New Zealand, Australia and Canada – part of the 'Dominions' Ring', even though India was technically still a colony. Traditionally the most important British possession overseas, with power to arouse deep emotions in the London audience, its pavilion played a crucial role in the conception of the British Empire Exhibition. Yet, at the same time, India's centrality to and dominance over similar earlier occasions such as the Colonial Exhibition and Indian Exhibition of 1886 or the Franco-British Exhibition had declined in the interim. 'The India that will be exhibiting at Wembley in 1924', the secretary of the Indian Advisory Committee warned the London audience in advance, 'is a very different thing from the India of 1851', because 'in every sense of the world she has found herself'.[58] With the emergence of the Indian National Congress in 1885, gradual concessions to repeated calls for Indian autonomy, the steady transference of decision-making authority to the individual provincial governments had proved necessary to sustain economic and military cooperation. By 1924, India was no longer a foil for the projection of European fantasies of colonial exoticism. For their part, the Indian authorities encountered significant obstacles to their participation. It was only after a controversial debate that the Indian Legislative Assembly decided on 25 March 1922 that India should be present at Wembley with an official pavilion, on condition that a preliminary exhibition be held in Calcutta and that the Indian section in Wembley would, for the first time ever, be organized by the government of India, in cooperation with the numerous provincial governments, rather than by the India Office in London.[59]

Such a political-cultural change found its direct expression in both the design and layout of displays and the pavilion itself, which was not a replica of one existing building but rather an 'original conception in the Indo-Saracenic style'. Designed by British architects, it featured a spacious forecourt, cupolas and minarets, as well as a central all-India court (Figure 5.14). 'The whole structure, with its lakes and fountains and peculiar architecture, based for the most part on [a] sixteenth-century Mogul building', a critic enthused, 'affords an interesting contrast between the architecture of the East and West.' A wide variety of exhibits were on display in numerous courts for the 27 different Indian provinces – ranging from the usual samples of raw materials, handicraft, carpets and metal working, to local newspapers, jungle exhibits and models of urban development plans for Bombay. This also included reproductions of edifices built by the British in India, for instance a large-scale painting of the Bombay Gateway, erected to commemorate the landing of King George V and Queen Mary on 2 December 1911, or a huge model of the recently completed, cathedral-like Victoria Memorial raised in Calcutta to impress the English and their inner-European rivals alike, while, at the same time, conveying a sense of active participation in a shared imperial enterprise to the Indian public.[60]

While the *Daily News Souvenir Guide* cautiously stated that 'India is changing rapidly and the change can be seen here', followed by a simple listing of all the painstakingly displayed indigenous products, Diwan Bahadur T. Vijayaraghavacharya (1875–1953), the official Indian exhibition commissioner,

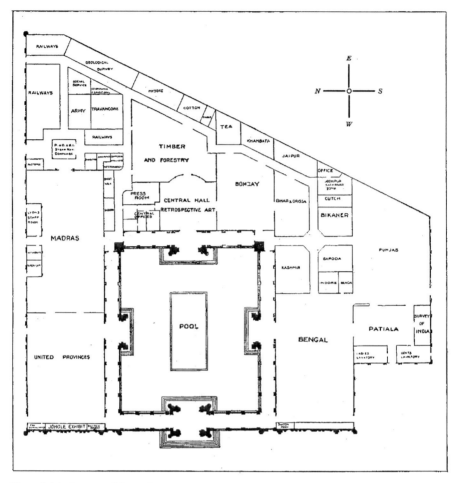

Figure 5.14 Layout of the Indian Pavilion at the British Empire Exhibition. It was situated at the southeastern edge of the grounds, in close proximity to the British Government Pavilion and next to the *Old London Bridge*
Source: *India: Souvenir of the Indian Pavilion and its Exhibits*, n.p.

proved much bolder. In describing his demystifying aims for the Indian section in the exhibition, Vijayaraghavacharya reminded his British audience of India's active military contribution during the First World War and stated bluntly: 'From a dependency India has grown to the status of a partner in the Empire', then confidently continued by emphasizing its self-perceived modernity:

> The India of the palm-trees, of the immemorial villages, of the rice-field and the bullock-cart is familiar enough to the world, but the India of the ballot-box, of elected Parliaments, of mills and factories, is hard to comprehend. It will be one of the objects of the Indian Section of the British Empire Exhibition

to bring home not only to people in England but to visitors from all parts of the world, more especially the rest of the Empire, the great changes that have happened in India.[61]

Despite such newly won self-confidence, at least after the exhibition's first year, chairman Lord Stevenson showed himself satisfied with what had been achieved. Praising the vista-like effect created by the pavilion, he declared: 'I have no hesitation in saying that the view of the Indian Pavilion looking down the lake from the far end, is one of the most beautiful which has ever been staged in connection with any Exhibition.'[62] Yet, that the Indian Pavilion did not pose any serious conceptual difficulties to the organizers had little to do with the pavilion's architecture or the fact that the usual displays of colonial exoticism – considered so desirable and entirely indispensable – had, literally, been given a different place on the venue. Rather, the references to changes in India and its growing independence could also be read differently, as a direct outcome of progress, of 'the gradual overcoming of difficulties, of a victorious fight against ignorance, famine, flood and pestilence', as the official guide formulated it, a state of affairs arguably spawned by the British.[63]

Yet, certain concessions to the audience's taste still proved imperative in order to attract sufficient visitors. Pains were taken to ensure that the traditional 'arts and crafts' exhibits did not dominate the gigantic, two-hectare pavilion because, as Vijayaraghavacharya cautioned, 'their undue preponderance in an exhibition is apt to produce an erroneous impression that India has little to show in the way of large industries or world-wide importance.' Instead, the audience was offered more 'direct' experiences through pseudo-authentic demonstrations of the Indian lifestyle. Thus, guests were served by Indian waitresses in an Indian restaurant where they could choose from an all-Indian menu, an entire section displayed the wild life of the jungle, and adjoined to the pavilion was a traditional Indian theater whose performers included Indian magicians, jugglers, a troupe of 'Tibetan devil's dancers' as well as numerous wild animals such as 'a real live cobra, slowly swaying its deadly hook'.[64]

In the end, then, the usual exoticism was supplied, but only to the extent seen as necessary not to jeopardize the whole section's general appeal. At the same time, consumer goods and commodities were displayed, business transactions made, and, according to an internal report, the organizers showed themselves satisfied with what had been achieved at this 'microcosm of India', despite all their expenses and the complicated negotiations between the government and the numerous provinces. However, considering India's reluctance and restraint both before and during the exhibition, the statement that it had been one of the 'earliest of the Dominions to throw itself heart and soul into the Exhibition', as assistant manager Belcher confidently claimed in an address delivered to the Royal Society of Arts in March 1923, was hardly accurate. Indeed, quite to the contrary: India's new self-confidence was demonstrated again in 1925, when it declined to participate in the exhibition's second run. Since the Indian government refused to grant the necessary funds to prolong its participation, India would be the only major colony not present during the exhibition's second year, much to the chagrin of the British organizers and public alike.[65]

As India could no longer be deemed a suitable backdrop for European fantasies of savagery, Africa – and in particular West Africa – became the focal point where conflicting ideas and representations of foreignness collided and exploded into controversy. In the exposition, the British colonies in Africa had been separated according to their geographical location. There, respective sections – one each for South, West and East Africa – were correspondingly situated on the exhibition grounds east of the Empire Stadium. For all three sections, collective exhibits under the control of group committees had been organized, with the two main architects in charge. *East Africa* comprised Kenya, Uganda, Zanzibar, Nyasaland, Somaliland, Sudan and the mandated territory of Tanganyika (the former *Deutsch-Ostafrika*), while Nigeria, the Gold Coast, Sierra Leone and Gambia together formed the so-called West African 'Walled City' – yet another city within a city within a city, in this case an 'exact replica of a typical city in the hinterland of West Africa'. Visitors praised the two sections as presenting 'both a contrast and a parallel' (Figure 5.15).[66]

Figure 5.15 The *East Africa* (on the left) and *West Africa* sections at Wembley. Together, Nigeria, the Gold Coast, Sierra Leon and Gambia formed the West African 'Walled City' (on the right)
Source: Courtesy of California State University, Fresno, Special Collections Research Center, Larson Collection.

The 'Walled City' comprised three 'native villages', each containing several huts with facilities for more than 70 occupants. For seekers of the exotic, this section was particularly attractive. 'Both inside and out, the walled city of West Africa is subtly different from all other parts of the Exhibition', the attentive visitor could, for example, read in the *Daily News Souvenir Guide*:

> Within the red mud walls, with the tang of wood smoke in the air, amid the thatched huts, with natives of many tribes passing to and fro, such far-off places as Sierra Leone and the fabled Gold Coast become fantastically real. Within the halls the same illusion is maintained. The dark dim lanterns in the mud-vaulted pavilion of the Gold Coast itself, the blue sunshine roof of the Nigerian hall, the mud and thatch of the Sierra Leone hut, all have a quality of reality.

In other words: 'This *is* West Africa.' Striving even to outdo reality itself, the same high quality of reproduction was also maintained in the 'African compound behind the bamboo gates', which, according to the same source, offered a faithful copy of 'native life': 'A real princess lives here', the *Guide* let it be known, 'and the natives carry on with their ordinary tasks much as if they were at home, weaving, making pots, weaving baskets and mats.' A self-proclaimed 'man in the street', careful to emphasize that he had never been to West Africa, considered the entire arrangement so convincing that he fully accepted the *Guide*'s claims, deducing that this was 'certainly not England [but] was somewhere in the outposts'. After traversing the 'Walled native City' even Major Sir Frederick Dealtry Lugard (1858–1945), the former Governor-General of Nigeria, found the design to be 'true'. Thus, the *Guide*, an ordinary visitor and a colonial representative alike all agreed on and, hence, contributed to the establishment of a hegemonic reading of this particular section of the Wembley site. According to them, there was not the slightest difference between *West Africa* and West Africa. In their interpretation, representation and reality had become identical.[67]

At the same time, however, the authority of such a reading was challenged. The public exposition of non-European peoples led, for the first time, to an open controversy, albeit short-lived and without lasting consequences. In May 1924 the Union of Students of African Descent (USAD), a London-based Christian group of approximately 120 students founded in 1917, took the publication of an article full of crude sexual allusions in the *Sunday Express* as an occasion to lodge an official complaint to the Colonial Office about the 'Holding up to public ridicule of African natives at Wembley' and sent additional letters of protest to the exhibition's authorities and to the Prince of Wales as its president.[68] Interestingly enough, though, the students did not criticize the inclusion of a 'native village' in the Nigerian section of the 'Walled City' per se but rather that 'some irresponsible London journalists' had tried to 'belittle African customs by misrepresenting in their journals interviews with the African workers at Wembley'. Such a protest is all the more surprising since the opinions about the exposition as expressed by various West African visitors to the site, many of them long-time London residents, were otherwise far from homogenous. While several described the exhibition as a 'wonderful affair' and thought the 'Walled City', in particular, so realistic that it made them feel home-sick when wandering through the various courts and pavilions, others vehemently disagreed. For them, 'the miniature reproduction of African life' clearly suffered from a 'European touch'. A third group went so far as to refuse to accept the ensemble in total, since it did not convey a sufficiently contemporary version of Nigerian life but rather the image of a past long gone. It was 'the West Africa of many years ago that we see at Wembley', one complained.[69]

However, in spite of these and other criticisms, it was this perceived misrepresentation of a secondary order, as it were, rather than the section itself or its inclusion in the Wembley exhibition, which triggered the students' objections. In the disputed article, entitled 'When West Africa Woos', a reporter had set out to write the 'story of love as it is made in Akropong'. For his investigation, the journalist had interviewed the putative 'princess' and questioned her bluntly about sexual practices and native marriage rituals. Though the civil servants of the Colonial Office instantly rejected the students' protest, brusquely arguing that the group had no 'earthly right to aggrandize itself this way' and that the Office had better things to do 'than to rush round in sympathy whenever a black "student" thinks his dignity is hurt', the African Village was consequently closed, first to the press only, then to the general public as well, obviously to the great disappointment of visitors.[70]

After consultations with the West African governments the 'Walled City' reopened the following year, this time without exciting any further public outrage. 'The lay public', one critic noted in 1925, 'is delighted [...] by the striking red walls which represent the colonies of Western Africa', and a government official joined him in this old, but now reiterated praise. Since the 'Walled City', 'went very near to giving visitors [...] the illusion that when within the walls they were actually in the countries that the "Walled City" represented', any criticism from Africans 'as regards the presentation of their countries at Wembley' was to be considered negligible, he argued, incisively rejecting any disapproval. Thus, these two critics, a journalist and a civil servant, helped to re-establish the hegemony of the once-dominant and still uncontested interpretation, yet only for the time being. From such a perspective, the concluding remarks of Edward Salmon (1865–1955) – long-time editor of the official journal of the Royal Colonial Institute, *United Empire*, and imperial propagandist by conviction – that 'notes first sounded or first heard at Wembley will long reverberate in British consciousness' could also be read in an ironic and even subversive way. Contrary to all expectations, Wembley epitomized the beginning of the Empire's end. Since the British Empire Exhibition had originally been planned to take place in a pre-war setting it was no longer appropriate when it eventually came about, with a lag of almost a decade and the first global war in between.[71]

Fact and fancy

On 10 June 1924, a certain Miss Laura Simson from Egmont, Cumberland, received a postcard from her friend Sally, sent the previous day from the Wembley premises. Having spent an exciting day at the exposition site, Sally had composed a little poem:

> Dear Laura,
>
> I've lit a cigar in Bermuda
> And sampled Australian fruit.
> And my tour was arranged to include
> A brief call at Newfoundland en route.
> I've lingered a moment in Burma,
> in Cyprus I've sheltered from rain.
> And I don't hesitate to affirm a
> desire to go Wembling again.
>
> Sally[72]

Sally sounded quite proud of her global achievements as an imperial consumer. In a single day, it seemed, she had traveled the entire world, enjoyed a variety of colonial products and seen a multitude of far-off places which she would probably never visit again, at least not in such rapid succession, unless she returned to the exposition venue. Sally was not the only spectator to define her experience at the Wembley site as an imaginary journey in time and space. Due to the vast number of divergent reactions, any attempt at a comprehensive analysis proves inadequate. Not only would it be in flagrant contradiction to the multifaceted character of every exposition, but it also could not do justice to the multitude and variety of meanings ascribed to it. Just to convey an impression of the myriad of possible voices: for the more than two million schoolchildren who saw the exhibition in the first year alone, the Royal Colonial Institute organized an essay competition with topics such as 'The British Empire Exhibition 1924' or 'The Value of Imperial Exhibitions'. Because it proved such a success, the competition was repeated the following year. After the exposition's closure the authorities themselves reported to have gathered and archived more than 200,000 newspaper cuttings and clippings of review articles. While such a number seems high, it is not necessarily exaggerated. Between November 1910 and the end of 1925, the London *Times* alone published altogether 4160 articles, notes, comments, reviews and announcements in connection with the Wembley event. Although the following analysis is based on research that unearthed a large number of visitor reports and hitherto unknown private accounts, for both qualitative and quantitative reasons an exhaustive analysis is not possible.[73] As such, this reading must be considered *cum grano salis*.

There were few 'serious' disputes about the British Empire Exhibition in the press, at least regarding its political status within the wider context of empire. Although agreeing to a large extent with the exhibition's general official objectives, the majority of newspaper critics presented a set of different arguments, seeking to demonstrate the desirability of such initiatives in general and the indubitable success of this project in particular. Most often they were specifically derived from 'official' interpretations already presented, and thus prefigured, by the organizers themselves in all kinds of official and semi-official publications such as guidebooks and souvenir volumes. These patterns of argument fell into certain types, all based on one another and presented time and again with only slight modifications. Without oversimplifying too much, the following four argumentative patterns can be isolated from the comprehensive press coverage:

1.   The first line of argument stated that the exhibition would act as a peace-time 'stocktaking of our Imperial position in production, manufacture and merchanting'. The holding of such an enterprise would help to consolidate and organize the Empire's resources, directly contribute to the advancement of the ailing British economy, and immediately result in an upturn in trade with the colonies (*Fostering Trade Argument*).[74]

2.   Moreover, the holding of such a 'family party' as a 'great agency of empire development' would strengthen the cohesion of the Empire and create a sense of unity. The exposition would constitute 'a most useful and effective means of bring-ing into closer association the people of this country and our brethren Overseas' and encourage mutual help and economic support under British leadership. In February 1924 →Lord Askwith, civil servant, industrial arbitrator and chairman of the Royal Society of Arts' council, for example, argued that Wembley would mark a historically significant step forward in comparison with earlier expositions such as the Great Exhibition of 1851 in which the colonies had been greatly underrep-resented, but also with regard to the Indian and Colonial Exhibition of 1886 or the Franco-British Exhibition of 1908. 'It is but fitting', he declared with a view to the First World War, 'that some stock should now be taken and education spread more widely than ever, to make us realize that the British Empire is a living and growing entity, bound together in a manner different from any other known to history' (*Bonds of Empire Argument*).[75]

3.   A third argument suggested that the exhibition would not only contribute to the improvement of the general living standard in Great Britain, but also have positive consequences for the welfare of humankind as a whole. The inexorable progress of science, the promotion of which formed an integral part of this expo-sition, made such results almost inevitable. In the end, the enterprise had to be regarded as a 'step towards ultimate understanding and co-operation between the nations of the world', nearly echoing the official rationale of the Prince Consort in 1851 that had since become part of the standard exposition rationale worldwide (*Unity of Mankind Argument*).[76]

4.   Lastly, a powerful argument was often advanced which, unlike the former arguments, sought to motivate individual visits, rather than simply justify the exhibition's contribution to the Empire as well as to modern civilization. For merely an 18-pence admission fee, a visit to the exhibition could replace an entire world tour. Frequently, the Wembley venue was described as offering a bewildering sequence of picturesque sights. There were, one critic noted, 'visions and vistas everywhere; a score of places striking the imagination and stirring the thought'. The visitor could easily transform him- or herself into an imaginary tourist just by wandering from one spot to another, thus creating a highly individual, even if pre-structured itinerary, according to personal predilection. This particular interpretation could be found in many variants, of which Sally's poem was only one. 'Visitors may thus take their lunch in South Africa, their tea in India, and finish the day by dining in Canada, Australia or New Zealand', wrote a journalist, describing the site's tourist attractions, while an architectural writer hailed the possibility of undertaking the classic grand tour 'without a costly journey round the world' (*Around the World in a Day Argument*) (Plate 6).[77]

Corresponding with the 'abridged' version of 'the world' on display at Wembley, none of the reactions distinguished between 'world' and 'empire'. Sometimes it was the former, sometimes the latter that was praised as the destination of the imaginary journey. The notions were completely congruent and entirely interchangeable. 'To visit the Exhibition is to visit every Continent of the earth', for instance George Clarke Lawrence stated succinctly, and an advertisement slogan – to be found under the heading 'All the World will be at Wembley' on the official tourist map – promised the sightseer a problem- and care-free panoramic insight into nothing less than the entire British Empire, by journeying around the globe:

> You have often wanted to travel around the world. At Wembley you will be able to do so at a minimum of cost, in a minimum of time, with a minimum of trouble, studying as you go to the shop windows of the British Empire. You will be able to go behind these windows and see how the goods are produced and meet the men and women who produce them. Every aspect of life, civilised and uncivilised, will be shown in an Exhibition which is the last word in comfort and convenience. You may go many times to the British Empire Exhibition at Wembley: you *must* go at least once.

This imaginary world tour in a restricted context was celebrated as a truly historic achievement and the logical end of a much older historical development. The exhibition promoted a democratization of travel in a politically correct and desirable – read, imperial – way. 'In the old days', began the official guide's introduction to the fair's overall objectives, 'the grand tour was the prize of the fortunate few. Young men of wealth and position devoted two or three years to travel, often in circumstances of acute discomfort, and came back having caught no more than a glimpse of Europe. [...] To-day the grand tour is within the reach of all, and the actual cost of it is just eighteen pence!' A development that, according to social historians of tourism such as John Towner, had begun with the decline of the romantic grand tour, seen together with the rise of a more organized tourist industry around 1820, and the subsequent, unsustainable increase in international exhibitions had reached its pinnacle. Tourism without travel was now possible. To adopt the tourist gaze no longer required leaving one's own home town. If Wembley and metropolitan London were not entirely spatially congruent, Wembley and the Empire most definitely were, at least in the contemporaneous imagination.[78]

Yet, how was the relationship between spectacle and imperial displays perceived and consumed by individual visitors, both private and official, domestic and foreign? First and foremost, the vast majority seem to have been immensely impressed, regardless of their social, cultural, educational or national background.

Figure 5.16   Private souvenir picture of a young boy standing by one of the six concrete lions in front of the British Government Pavilion
Source: Courtesy of Brent Archive, London.

In an oral history interview, Arthur Mason, the young son of a local butcher, reported that the exhibition was 'a big thing in our life'. Never having seen a non-European before, Mason was deeply moved by the completeness and remoteness of a world still in his hands and under his control:

> Every time you went you were entering into another world, a fascinating world. [...] The most vivid thing is the anticipation when you actually went in and paid your nine pence and you went through and you were, now this whole world was spread in front of you. All these pavilions and people, and, well, it was just like a fairy land really for a small boy.[79]

Ibrahim Ismaa'il wrote about a Wembley visit from the perspective of a young Somali who had been living in a socialist community near Cardiff. After a trip to the site he found himself confused and intimidated, but above all distanced from his European colonizers to whom the world seemed to belong:

> My friend told me of a place called Wembley where things from many parts of the world were to be seen, and we went there together. Here we saw big machines moving by themselves and all sorts of other strange and wonderful things. I felt overwhelmed by it all. It appeared to me as if the world had been made for Europeans, who had only to stretch out their hands to bring before them, as by magic, all the products of the Universe.[80]

Finally, Eric Pasold (1906–1978), the 18-year-old son of Bohemian industrialists whose parents had sent him to England to finish his education, and who later became a successful textile and clothing manufacturer there, felt equally 'overwhelmed' by the 'colourful, bustling spectacle' whose lasting impact on him could not be 'conveyed in words': 'The nostalgic picture of this mightiest of all empires as displayed at Wembley is so deeply engraved on my subconscious that its influence still lingers after all the years that have passed', he wrote later in his autobiography. At the same time, the visit to the Wembley site also left behind an ambivalent mixture of envy and admiration. Describing the reasons for this uneasiness in more detail than Ismaa'il, Pasold revealed why such feelings did not alter his wish to become a naturalized British subject, quite to the contrary:

> The more exotic the pavilions the more they thrilled me. [...] India held an irresistible fascination [...] Nigerians in their colourful robes, cowboys from Calgary, dusky East African beauties, Indians, Malays, Chinamen, Australians, New Zealanders and Fiji islanders in an endless variety of human types, colour of skin and national costume, and in a profusion of tongues with which the Tower of Babel itself could not have competed – yet all were members of one great Empire, united under one King and flag, linked by the English language, financed by sterling, ruled by British justice and protected by the Royal Navy. How proud they must all feel, I thought, and how I envied them.[81]

Visitors can be divided into four different subcategories: local sightseers and inhabitants of London; provincials undertaking a journey to the capital city on the occasion of the exposition; tourists from the European continent; and visitors and so-called colonialists from overseas, described by the *Builder* as 'pilgrims from all parts of the Dominions'. Detailed statistics as to their precise composition are unknown. Officials estimated that more than 5000 visitors from India alone came to see the exhibition, 'many of them leaving their native land for the first time for this purpose'. The chairman of the Committee for Government Participation, →Sir Henry Walter George Cole, rated Wembley's particular attractiveness to provincials higher than to Londoners (70 versus 30 per cent of visitors), much to the surprise of other commentators, and in contrast to data from the Franco-British Exhibition held 16 years earlier (40 versus 60 per cent). Incomplete and partial as they are, these figures say very little about individual visitors' travel routes, their places of origin, points of departure and especially their appropriation of the site. However, as the three examples discussed above – Mason, Ismaa'il and Pasold – demonstrate, exhibitions were attractive destinations for international, national, regional and even local tourists and visitors alike.[82]

European visitors to the site included the Neapolitan professor of arboriculture, Gaetano Briganti, who warmly recommended the British colonies to Italian emigrants on account of their wealth and unexploited resources; the Swiss-German tourist, Hans Eckinger, who combined a tour to Paris, London and Ostende in the summer of 1924 with a visit to Wembley whence he reported in somewhat eccentric verse on his 'journey around the world in two days'; and the government official, Camille Fidel, who reported from a French perspective. While the last proved one of the few critics who directly compared Wembley with the 1922 Exposition Nationale Coloniale held in Marseilles and found it less picturesque, more expensive and a typical example of the Anglo-American exhibition style, none of them expressed any fundamental doubts as to the general effectiveness of the exposition and its displays, especially when visited at night:

> And in the evening, in the gigantic stadium, spectacular performances exalted the imperial patriotism of innumerable spectators, who were already strongly impregnated with all they had seen and heard during the day, with a feeling of the immensity and inexhaustible wealth of the Empire. Wembley thus will have contributed, more than any other previous manifestation, to giving the British peoples an imperial mentality.

According to Fidel the exhibition had certainly succeeded in generating a specific feeling towards the Empire and creating an 'imperial mentality', whatever that may have been comprised of *en détail*.[83]

The German government decided to send not one but two official observers who were to report on their impressions in various lengthy communiqués. In addition, the German Embassy in London was asked to issue a special report on the representation of the former German colonies at the Wembley site. Contrary to all expectations, these fairly accurate and largely descriptive reports hardly proved revanchist. While civil servant Sommer and *Generalkonsul* Haug mildly criticized some technical aspects such as the site's disorderly spatial composition, the lack of a central perspective due to its having no central observation tower and the prevailing 'modern department store style' (*moderner Warenhausstil*) of many displays, they came to positive conclusions. Both expressed their deep admiration for such a 'unique achievement in content':

> If the main task of the exhibition had been to present the greatness and power of the British Empire in concentrated form to the whole world, it must be admitted that this aim has actually been largely achieved. […] The government's exhibition is consistent in its attempt to show, both to colonial and other visitors, the growth, development and importance of the English Empire as impressively as possible. It is imperialism in its purest form that is displayed here.[84]

Finally, Fritz von Hake, a former Prussian major, published his personal travelogue in a book aptly entitled *Wembley: Schein und Wahrheit* (Wembley: Fact and Fancy) (Figure 5.17). Having devoted an exhaustive, six-day visit to the exhibition site in September 1925 to distinguish between the 'appearance and reality' of the Empire as staged, he reached the by now familiar conclusion 'that one had, in just a few days, easily gained the same impression as if one had traveled through the entire far-flung British Empire', thus repeating the organizers' theme and chronotopic motto almost verbatim. Like the two German government officials, von Hake seemed surprised at not being able to detect signs of Germanophobia or feelings of post-war resentment. He concluded, apparently satisfied with both his expedition and the exposition, that 'it had given the public, in a clear and attractive form, an impressive picture of the British Empire worldwide'.[85]

Thus, the vast majority of domestic and foreign visitors alike were deeply impressed by the arrangement and the wide array of objects on display. Their immediate reaction to the multiplicity of objects and vistas was either overpowering or a diffuse imperial 'feeling' or 'sentiment', as the Earl of Meath put it – a diagnosis shared by numerous other commentators. 'Wembley has evidently succeeded in rousing an Imperial spirit', one of them stated, and another agreed that it had 'generated a sense of Empire in thousands who hitherto had given no thought to the Empire's story' and 'attracted so many people to London that the crowds of visitors have been hailed as proof of the popularity of the Metropolis as a holiday resort!', again emphasizing the exhibition's attraction as a center for promoting both internal tourism – the imaginary travel through different times and spaces, universes and empires *at* the site – as well as external tourism in the journey *to* the exposition venue.[86]

Exhibitions formed an integral part of both the material and mental urban environment, which they, in turn, helped to form, if not create. At times, however, the spatial relation between the exposition grounds and their urban context seemed in danger of being reversed. For the numerous foreign or colonial visitors – the aforementioned 'colonialists' – the metropolis itself constituted the actual exhibit, rather than the 'exported homes' at the exhibition site. For

Figure 5.17 'Wembley: Fact and Fancy'
Source: Hake, *Wembley*, frontispiece.

them, the distinction between the 'real world' outside the gates on the one hand, and the exhibition site on the other became blurred, with London being the de facto exhibit. Seen from this perspective, their experience could be considered complementary to the general tendency of importing and concentrating the entire world in the imperial center, thus reflecting the colonial situation itself, though in the metropolis.

At Wembley, as in other exhibitions, every effort was made to ensure the site's representational credibility. It is not an accident, then, that its 'native villages' came under public fire first. Their contribution *in situ* was of essential importance to the entire arrangement as only the displayed human beings could guarantee the authenticity of the reproduction and render virtual worlds 'real'. Yet, just like the 'hermits' hired to live in artificial caves and supply early nineteenth-century landscape gardens with the desired degree of authenticity, living 'natives' could not be copied. Thus, at Wembley, the temporary closure of the Nigerian 'native village' created a paradoxical situation. On the one hand, the decision to shut down the village to the public, as the exhibition authorities argued, was taken 'with a view to securing the privacy of the craftsmen and their families'. On the other hand, the inhabitants were of such conceptual significance that they could not simply be sent home, nor were they allowed to leave the 'Walled City' at all, 'except by special permission and under suitable escort'. The 'natives-turned-craftsmen-with-families' remained on display and hence were part of the overall arrangement, yet they were not allowed to be seen. If such attempts at staging authenticity failed, the exposition could finally do nothing but expose itself.[87]

Wembley's overall effect lay less in the knowledge gained from the exhibition than in its emotional mapping, the subjective creation of an imaginative topography. Some commentators assumed that this might have been meant as 'an act of faith, a gesture of confidence to the world' after the first global war.[88] Yet on closer inspection, clear signs of dissolution emerge. If all exhibitions function as *partes pro toto*, the inherent danger of tautological self-reflexivity had never before been so obvious, and indeed threatening. On the one hand, countless metaphorical variants for 'the empire *en miniature*' – a 'microcosm of the British Empire', 'the whole Empire in little', 'Empire City', an '*omnium gatherum*', an 'epitome of Empire', 'the Empire effort crystallised', the 'Empire in concrete', an 'Encyclopaedia Britannica of British Imperial industry', the 'Imperial *magnum opus*' [*sic*] and so forth – were fashioned and refashioned to describe and, literally, to come to terms with the exhibition's highly condensed and multi-faceted character. On the other hand, with the exhibition's overall premise being that 'The British Empire is the greatest the world has ever seen' and the British Empire Exhibition 'the most wonderful product of that Empire', contrary readings were, from the outset, virtually impossible. As a very few observers, among them Virginia Woolf, realized, spectacular tautology was the predominant form of representation at Wembley.[89]

In the end, Wembley's overall significance was deeply ambiguous. The exposition certainly served to renew and perpetuate the importance of Empire to the British in the interwar years. Never before had the imperial theme been so central and dominant in a European exhibition on such a scale, and, as official and semi-official publications endlessly repeated, never before had an area as large as this been given to the dominions, colonies and 'dependencies' to present themselves. In complete contrast to all expectations, however, Wembley simultaneously epitomized the symbolic beginning of the Empire's end. The first signs of dissolution in both the exhibitionary complex and the exposition's very subject matter could no longer be overlooked. Thus, while the British Empire Exhibition of 1924–25 represented yet another attempt at reinventing the Empire, it simultaneously foreshadowed the Empire's subsequent political disintegration. Taken together, the representations analyzed here stood for neither the Empire nor themselves. Rather, their meanings overlapped to such an extent that an unambiguous interpretation is not possible. The complete colonization of social life at the British Empire Exhibition proved tautological. Recalling his departure from the premises, Hans Eckinger rhymed:

> John Bull, du bist ein schlauer Mann,
> der gut Reklame machen kann.
> [...]
>
> Wir winken draußen eifrig noch
> und leiden Trennungsschmerzen doch;
> zwei Tage sind zu kurze Zeit
> für eine solche Herrlichkeit!
> Wir mußten manchmal galoppieren,
> um alles kurz zu inspizieren.
> Wir werden Wembley nie vergessen.
> Will sich ein and'res Volk vermessen,
> der Welt den gleichen Pomp zu bieten,
> wie diese Sappermenters-Briten?[90]

6
Vincennes 1931: The Exposition Coloniale as the Apotheosis of Imperial Modernity

Soleil soleil d'au-delà des mers tu angélises
la barbe excrémentielle des gouverneurs
Soleil de corail et d'ébène
Soleil des esclaves numérotés
Soleil de nudité soleil d'opium soleil de flagellation
Soleil du feu d'artifice en l'honneur de la prise de la Bastille
au-dessus de Cayenne un quatorze juillet

Il pleut il pleut à verse sur l'Exposition coloniale

(Louis Aragon)[1]

By 1931, six years after the British Empire Exhibition, the exposition medium had long attained a certain classicism. As strategies of display became increasingly refined, each succeeding exposition drew upon established architectural forms and a certain grammar, applying a wide range of modern technologies already tested and proven effective. Considered from an exclusively national perspective, the Exposition Coloniale Internationale de Paris, held on the capital's eastern fringes in the Bois de Vincennes, was the penultimate of the great French expositions in the twentieth century. While by no means the century's last international exhibition, this exposition constituted a preliminary endpoint in terms of scale, grandeur and impact.[2]

Ever since French historian Raoul Girardet interpreted the Exposition Coloniale more than 40 years ago as the 'apotheosis' of colonial France, drawing on the colonial minister →Paul Reynaud's inaugural speech, a number of French and American historians have followed suit, analyzing it as the apogee of French colonial propaganda at home and the locus of an emerging national identity.[3] Representations of the French Empire had played a major role in national and international expositions from the beginning of the Third Republic. Whilst the Expositions Universelles of 1878, 1889 and, in particular, 1900 had already featured significant colonial sections, the Exposition Coloniale of 1931 was the first Parisian exhibition solely devoted, and on such an ambitious scale, to the

179

theme of French overseas expansion. Additionally, the exposition grew out of a tradition of specialized fairs held in second-tier French cities such as Rouen in 1896, Strasbourg in 1924 and, in particular, Marseilles in 1906 and 1922, initiated and authored by Jean Charles-Roux, the organizer of the colonial section on the Trocadéro in 1900. 'Why not transpose once again and on a larger scale this vision of the East and Far East to the middle of Paris?', it was asked.[4]

However, while it is certainly possible to interpret the exposition as a 'primarily French event' that provided a 'hermetic world constructed within its own synchronous time', as architectural historian Patricia Morton has argued, such a reading is not exhaustive. The Exposition Coloniale was by no means limited to a central role within the web of interconnections and affiliations between colonized and colonizer. Rather, it simultaneously formed part of a multitude of other networks, standing firmly within the long-established tradition of its antecedents.[5] As its lengthy official title, 'Exposition Coloniale Internationale et des Pays d'Outre-Mer, Paris 1931', indicated, the fair's focus was much broader than either national and colonial: in fact, it was decidedly international. Belgium, Denmark, Italy, the Netherlands, Portugal and the United States accepted the invitation circulated by the French government as early as 1921–22 and built their own pavilions on the spacious Vincennes site.[6] Studies that concentrate exclusively on this one exposition as a single, supposedly isolated entity as well as a gigantic, unprecedented and manipulative propaganda machine tend to overemphasize its particularity within a French, European and global context. There is an urgent necessity to overcome the kind of bipolar readings largely based on the organizers' intentions, claims and official rhetoric, however carefully implemented and powerfully propagated they may have been. Such studies run the risk of replicating the very dichotomy between civilization and savagery that their writers mean to dissolve, merely transposing it into academic prose. Additionally, such analyses also risk disregarding the mega-event's multifarious character as well as the multiplicity of meanings that visitors and critics simultaneously ascribed to it. French (and other) colonial expositions held in the interwar period may have been primarily about the creation of a colonial 'other', yet their readings have often been limited to repeatedly emphasizing the obvious dichotomy between metropolitan civilization and colonial savagery. As a consequence, an originally powerful argument has regressed into a clichéd truism. When considering the complexity of international exhibitionary networks, these readings must be as multifaceted and protean as the objects of analysis themselves.

Paris versus Marseilles

As with Wembley, plans for a specifically colonial exposition to be held in Paris dated back to 1910, but were halted by the onset of the First World War. Originally scheduled to take place in 1916, the projected exposition met with fierce opposition from the provinces, motivated by objections to Parisian hegemony. The City of Marseilles, the nation's maritime center, its second largest city and proverbial 'port of the Empire', had suffered particularly from a sense of cultural domination by the capital. It demanded to hold another themed exposition of its own, thus attempting to demonstrate its difference by emulating the Parisian model: presenting itself to the world by means of exposition.[7]

Their 'fight for the colonial exposition' ended in a tie: in 1913, the government decided that the next national exposition after 1906 should be held in Marseilles, while Paris would host an international exhibition in 1920 or 1921. An identical debate between the two municipalities, repeated after the end of the war in early 1919, brought identical results: Marseilles would go ahead with its national exposition in 1922, but Paris would follow two years later with a more encompassing event that would include France's wartime allies. A law passed on 17 March 1920 eventually designated Paris as the host city for such an Exposition Coloniale Interalliée – as it was still called at this stage – to take place in 1925. Plans included the creation of a permanent *Musée des Colonies* as its *pièce de résistance*. Only in Paris, the 'capital of such great expositions', proponents argued, could 'the brilliance of these fairs' reach all of France, and 'indeed illuminate the universe'. Official invitations to foreign governments were issued shortly after.[8]

If these plans had been realized as envisaged, the exposition would have taken place concurrent with Wembley's second season. The long-projected event, however, had to be postponed six times, eventually being delayed by 11 years. In the interim, organizers had enlarged its *interallié* character to *international* so that other colonial powers, such as the Netherlands, could participate.[9] There are various explanations for such an unprecedented deferral. Some of the invited nations, first and foremost Great Britain (which ultimately participated only to a very limited degree), declared that sufficient time had not been granted for proper preparation, feared the potential costs, and bemoaned the rapid succession of comparable events in Wembley (1924–25), Paris itself (1925), Antwerp (1926, 1930), Barcelona (1929–30) and Liège (1930). Infrastructural projects such as the building of the colonial museum and the prolongation of the Métro line number 8 from the city center to Vincennes proved more time consuming than projected. Further administrative, organizational and financial difficulties were only overcome in 1927 when →Maréchal Hubert Lyautey, long-serving Governor of Morocco and a legendary French colonial hero, was appointed *Commissaire général* (Figure 6.1). It was the 77-year-old Lyautey who, together with *Délégué général* →Marcel Olivier, would shape the emerging exposition and leave his mark on this mega-event staged in a wooded park on the eastern edge of Paris through the summer and fall of 1931 – to such an extent that the enterprise was publicly nicknamed 'Lyauteyville'.[10]

Meanwhile, the Paris-based organizers were closely observing the planning, development and results of the successful Marseilles and Wembley expositions. The latter served in many ways as its British counterpart, held up as a model to which the so-called 'French' or 'Parisian Wembley' in Vincennes was often compared by French, British and other European visitors and critics. The structural similarities were striking indeed. Organizers of the two Marseilles expositions could rightly claim that it was there and not in Paris that the French exposition tradition was taken up again after the Exposition Universelle of 1900 and extended

Figure 6.1 Portrait of Hubert Lyautey (1854–1934), *Maréchal de France*, former colonial administrator in Morocco and general commissioner of the Exposition Coloniale Internationale de Paris, 1931
Source: L'Illustration (23 May 1931), n.p.

into the twentieth century, even if these detours made little lasting impact on the urban fabric of Marseilles.[11]

Although it was clear that the hosting of the 1931 exposition was the direct product of an inter-urban competition, both within France and across Europe, organizers declared that they would not be bothered by such petty rivalries. Rather, they argued that the planned exposition should be considered a meeting point of the civilized world in which to find a 'vision of the universe'. Two familiar claims were repeated: first, the exposition would have to be understood in the context of international expositions rather than local, regional or thematically specialized fairs; second, nothing less than the world would be on display in Vincennes. As a consequence of this broad vision, visitors were invited to transform themselves into 'pilgrims of the universe'.[12] To this end, 150,000 propaganda postcards were printed and distributed in France, the colonies and the rest of Europe during the run-up. Large advertising panels were bought and displayed in major European train stations and urban centers, such as Potsdamer Platz in Berlin, and advertisements were placed in international newspapers and journals as diverse as *Berliner Tageblatt*, *Münchner Neueste Nachrichten*, *Illustrated London News* and *The Times*. In some cases, advertisements extended to entire sponsored articles.[13] Catchy slogans such as 'Tour the World at the Paris Colonial International Exhibition, open until November 1931', 'Around the world in a day: The life of native people in the midst of Parisian Life' or 'The International Overseas Exhibition Paris 1931: A Million Lights … Fairy Sights … Exotic Nights …' promised travel through time and space identical to those of the Wembley exposition, echoing its rhetoric to the last imperialist detail.[14]

Emplacement

The Exposition Coloniale Internationale opened on 6 May 1931 in the presence of president Gaston Doumergue (1863–1937) and remained open for the next six months, attracting a total of 33 million visitors (Figure 6.2 and Plate 7). To put this figure in perspective, the highly successful Wembley exposition saw roughly the same number of attendances over the course of its two seasons (27 million).[15] Spatially, the vast exposition ground was organized around Lac Daumesnil in the Bois de Vincennes, the larger of the two major Parisian parks in the metropole's southeast. Its peripheral location meant that for the first – and last – time, a great Parisian exposition was detached from the symbolic Champ de Mars in the city center, expanding instead to an underdeveloped suburban district. 'This in itself is a new departure', contemporary observers noted, 'since international exhibitions of all kinds have hitherto been confined to the west end of Paris'.[16]

Comprising 934 hectares, the expansive Bois de Vincennes in the twelfth Parisian arrondissement was to its poorer east-end neighbors what the Bois de Boulogne was to affluent west-enders: a popular recreation ground. The Bois de Vincennes had been designed in the early 1860s by the same engineer as the Bois de Boulogne, Jean-Charles-Adolphe Alphand, on the orders of Emperor Napoléon III. The new park boasted three lakes: the small Lac de Saint Mandé in the north, the Lac des Minimes at its eastern end, and in its southwest the oval Lac Daumesnil featuring two islands, the Ile de Bercy and the Ile de Reuilly, around which the four large sections of the exposition would be arranged. After the park had opened to the public, it continued to be used as a drilling-ground for military exercises, as had the Champ de Mars. Another historical layer of spatial meaning was directly exposition-related: after the Bois de Vincennes had come under discussion as the site of the 1867 Exposition Universelle, albeit unsuccessfully, the park's western sections served as an annexe to the 1900 exposition. Large-scale exhibits of automobiles, machinery and houses for the working classes, and sports competitions were displayed here on a large stretch south of Lac Daumesnil.[17] Much as it had in 1900, the park's total area again eclipsed the 100-acre exposition venue, with large swathes of the grounds remaining unused. Additional portions of the site had been positioned within the belt of low-cost interwar housing built on a section of Paris' former defensive fortifications, east of the Boulevards Soult and Poniatowski and today covered by the Boulevard périphérique. Though this ring of massive walls was not knocked down until the early 1930s, its demolition had been decided upon as early as 1919.[18]

Architectural historians have parallelized the alleged socio-spatial remoteness of the site with that of the colonies themselves, likewise located on the physical and psychic

184

Figure 6.2 Panoramic photograph, north–south aspect, of the Exposition Coloniale taken from an airplane on inauguration day, 6 May 1931. On the left, the presidential motorcade can be seen, while crowds of visitors await its arrival in front of the *Temple of Angkor Wat*

Source: *L'Illustration* (25 July 1931), n.p.

edges of France, arguing that its selection doubled their marginality and led to the interrelated creation of 'loci of otherness'. In so doing, they have largely embraced the rhetoric of Lyautey and others. Lyautey only overcame his initial disdain for the selected venue by publicly exclaiming his intention to 'haussmannize' and reform the largely communist area in eastern Paris, creating a uniform *Quartier colonial* with a projected gigantic Avenue de la Victoire as its crowning achievement.[19] However, the marginality of the site was not equal to that of the colonies. While its social seclusion was indisputable, as it was part of the notorious Parisian 'red belt' famous for its left-wing politics, the venue's physical-spatial remoteness was insignificant when compared to other European expositions of the same period. Most, by this stage, had long ceased to occupy the center of their host cities. Both Treptower Park in 1896 and Shepherd's Bush in 1908 were situated nine kilometers away from their respective centers, while Wembley in 1924 was built a full 16 kilometers away. Vincennes, in contrast, was a relatively meager seven kilometers from the heart of the metropolis. Additionally, the Colonial Exposition was by no means isolated from Paris' urban and political life. Easily accessible by various means of public transport, Vincennes was served by a host of buses, trams and the new Métro extension from the Bastille to Porte de Charenton through Porte de Picpus or Porte Dorée, respectively (Figure 6.3). National and international critics repeatedly commented on both the continuous spatial expansion of

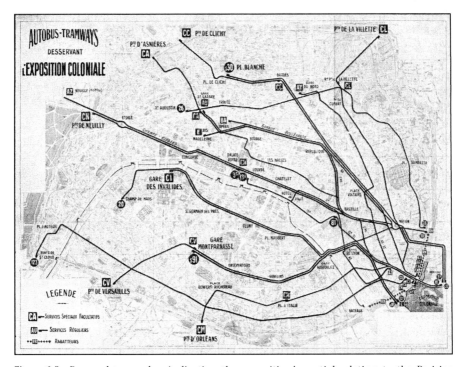

Figure 6.3 Bus and tram plan indicating the exposition's spatial relation to the Parisian metropolis
Source: Olivier, *Exposition coloniale internationale de Paris, 1931: Rapport général*, vol. 3, 188–9.

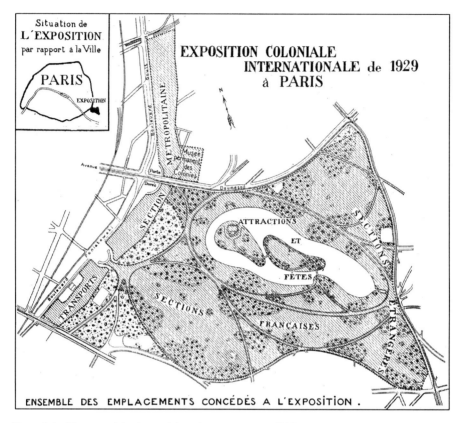

Figure 6.4   The exposition's quadripartite structure in 1927
Source: Courtesy of The National Archives, Kew, CO 323/977/6.

the urban fabric and the venue's questionable respectability – but not its geographical remoteness. 'Paris is a true exogen, increasing by successive additions to the outside arranged in concentric zones', wrote *The Times*, which described the exhibition grounds as 'within easy reach of the centre'. Similarly, →Sir Henry Cole (not to be mistaken for his grandfather by the same name, the executive commissioner for the Great Exhibition of 1851) considered the show 'as big as Wembley', only on the 'wrong side of Paris'.[20]

Dream city

Organized around three central pavilions – the huge *Cité des Informations*, the even larger *Palais de la Section Métropolitaine*, and the new *Musée Permanent des Colonies* – at the venue's western end facing the actual metropolis, the exposition ground was divided into three relatively distinct parts: a general, a colonial and an international section plus so-called attractions, dispersed over several locations on the site (Figures 6.4 and 6.5). The different parts were connected by a

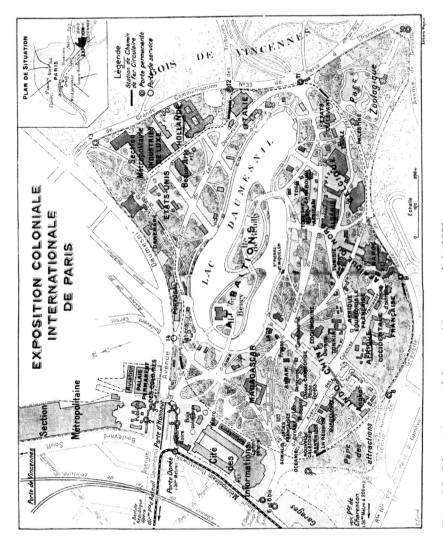

Figure 6.5 Schematic map of the exposition grounds in 1931
Source: Demaison, *A Paris en 1931*, 8–9.

Figure 6.6   The Porte d'Honneur, the exposition's monumental main entrance, here facing east. In the foreground, the new Métro entrance can be seen. A fraction of the *Musée Permanent des Colonies* is visible to the left; visitors to the *Cité des Informations*, the exposition's central media complex, turned right here
Source: Cloche, *60 aspects de l'Exposition Coloniale*, 1.

circular railroad that carried visitors around the Lac Daumesnil, stopping at the international pavilions, before depositing them in the colonial section proper. The organizational principle was straightforward: 'civilized' exhibits could be found in the west, the 'exotic' ones towards the east, and the international, non-colonial sections in the north. At the far southeastern end was a zoological garden modelled on Hagenbeck's famous 'natural' (that is, cageless and seemingly barrier-free) *Tierpark* in Hamburg-Stellingen; the *Parc zoologique de Paris* remains open to this day.[21]

Arriving at the new Métro station Porte Dorée and entering the grounds through architect Léon-Emile Bazin's (1900–1976) monumental Porte d'Honneur, one of the exposition's three main gates (Figure 6.6), visitors were welcomed by an imposing information center and media complex that served as an introduction to what they could expect to see and experience during their stay. On the right, this *Cité des Informations* featured orientation materials, production data, and statistical compilations detailing the colonial enterprise. Commercial services including travel agencies, banks and transport companies rented stands here, and a large 1500-seat movie theater held daily screenings of the latest products of imperial propaganda.

Figure 6.7 Postcard of the colonial museum. Planned as the only exposition structure to remain after its closure, the building now houses the *Cité nationale de l'histoire de l'immigration* (CNHI), a museum of French immigration opened in 2007
Source: Courtesy of Boston Public Library, Robert A. Feer Collection.

To visitors' left rose the *Section Métropolitaine*, dominated by a huge, 4.2-hectare large Art Deco hall for commercial exhibitors. If the *Cité* could be considered the Vincennes equivalent of the Government Pavilion at Wembley, the grand pavilion was built in the tradition of the exposition medium's former one-building-fits-all system. Though largely abandoned in the late 1870s, this feature could still be found in later examples such as the *Galerie des Machines* of Paris 1889 or the Berlin *Hauptgebäude* from seven years later. It was these two buildings, the *Cité des Informations* and the *Section Métropolitaine*, which – according to a contemporaneous architectural review – could explicitly 'be termed "modern"'.[22]

Further into the venue, visitors encountered one of the most momentous buildings on the entire site, the *Musée Permanent des Colonies*, a museum to represent both the metropolitan and the colonial side of French imperialism, the only non-transient structure and one of the two centerpieces of the entire arrangement (Figure 6.7). Architect →Albert Laprade had been at pains to design a specifically colonial museum that adequately represented 'la plus grande France' in a fitting national style, while abiding by the representational hierarchies established in other sections of the Colonial Exposition. Its organizational principle was bi-directional across space and time. A 'Section Rétrospective' on the entry floor showed the history of French colonial activities from the Crusades to the Second Empire including

Figure 6.8   The 'Allée des Nagas' leading to the *Temple of Angkor Wat*, the exposition's second *clou* in addition to the colonial museum, seen here from the north
Source: Cloche, *60 aspects de l'Exposition Coloniale*, 22.

their domestic impact, while a 'Section de Synthèse' on the second floor offered a summary of contemporary achievements abroad. One of the museum's items on display was a large-scale luminous map of the world, 12 meters in diameter, which observers compared to the Wembley equivalent, the illuminated contour map featured as the Government Pavilion's central exhibit. Although the inclusion of such a museum in the exposition's scheme had been one of Lyautey's stipulations upon being appointed *Commissaire général* in 1927, the idea as such was much older. As early as 1900, influential architect Charles Garnier (1825–1898) had demanded, in an open letter published in the *Figaro*, that two palaces in the Champs-Elysées be exclusively utilized as a colonial museum after the closure of the Exposition Universelle of that year.[23]

Unlike in 1900, the question of the exposition's *clou* did not arise. Indeed, there were two *chef-d'œuvres*: the colonial museum as well as a massive reconstruction of Angkor Wat, the famous Cambodian temple complex built in the twelfth century and abandoned in 1431, discovered in the jungle by French botanist and explorer Henri Mouhot (1826–1861) in 1860 (Figure 6.8 and Plate 8).[24] The centerpiece of Indochina's contribution, this detailed replica dominated Vincennes just as the pyramid had loomed over Treptower Park and the Empire Stadium over Wembley. The temple replica, in the center of the *Grande Avenue des Colonies Françaises*, dwarfed the venue's southern end. With its seven towers and huge stairways rising 55 meters into the sky, *Angkor Wat* proved so popular that organizers had to restrict public access on weekends. 'Along the axis of the avenue, at a perceptible distance, there is the grey and majestic silhouette of Angkor, an insidious and troubling sight', a contemporaneous observer noted, calling this vast monument with its 23 exhibition halls and displays of ethnographic objects a 'strange and grandiose spectacle' that was, in its imposing dimensions and monumentality, often compared to Notre Dame at the heart of the metropolis.[25]

The monumental scale of *Angkor Wat* was consistent with one of the medium's most enduring traditions. Though reconstructed at just one-quarter of its original size, the view from its top proved impressively intimidating. Providing a panoramic view and a central perspective, vantage points such as observation towers and Ferris Wheels had become a recurring feature since the erection of the Eiffel Tower in 1889, followed closely by the Ferris Wheel in Chicago in 1893. 'From the top of its monumental staircase, one discovers the whole Exposition', the same observer wrote of the replica's visual offerings.[26] Comparable simulacra of Angkor Wat, widely praised as speaking 'to us vividly of past civilisation', had been constructed for earlier French fairs, for instance in Paris in 1900 and in Marseilles in 1922, and would continue to be so in the future, for example at the 1937 Exposition Internationale des Arts et Techniques dans la Vie Moderne. Nowhere, however, was it as centrally featured as here, where *Angkor Wat* evoked an urban civilization far more ancient than the French, yet now under their imperial control. The whole site abounded in such imposing constructions, with altogether 17 vertical structures. The towers of *Angkor Wat* were not even the tallest: they were surpassed by the imposing central tower of the *Palais de la Section Métropolitaine* (85 m) and the Army's 'Bronze Tower' (82 m) at the opposite end of the *Avenue des Colonies*, which was the eastern terminus of this axis and close to the venue's margins.[27]

This *Grande Avenue des Colonies Françaises* cut through the grounds from one side to the other. Here, fairgoers could visit pavilions, palaces, native villages, mosques and temples from all the French colonies in Africa, the Near and Far East and Oceania. 'Before encountering in detail the palaces and pavilions, before being impregnated with the ambiance particular to each colony, before profiting from the attractions, the festivals, the nocturnal extravaganzas, an overall vision was necessary', the previously mentioned observer wrote, describing how he had walked along this avenue to prepare for further excursions: 'This preliminary promenade was made amid the indescribable vividness of the crowd, among natives of all races, the barbaric sounds of Africa, the perfumes of Asia, the Tahitian chants, the songs of the West Indies or Madagascar.'[28] Organizers ensured that no significant French colony would be omitted. There were even displays from some of the mandated territories such as Palestine and the Protectorates of Syria and Lebanon. Often taken *pars pro toto*, it was this particular section that was to justify the exposition's title. Here, buildings and pavilions could be found for each colony in what was assumed to be its respective architectural style, almost exclusively realized (and at times only too loosely interpreted) by French, and usually Parisian, architects whose task it had been to

Figure 6.9 Panoramic photograph of the western part of the *Avenue des Colonies* with, from left to right, the pavilions of New Caledonia (Pacific; only a fraction visible), Martinique and Réunion in the foreground. On the upper side of the street the pavilions of the French Indies (only a fraction visible), Guyana, the Protestant, and the Catholic Missions can be seen. On the right adjoined the grand replica of the *Temple of Angkor Wat*
Source: *L'Illustration* (23 May 1931), n.p.

interpret the 'many grades of civilization' found around the world.[29] Pavilions were strung along this major axis in no particular geographical, geopolitical or discernible hierarchical order, with neighboring buildings representing territories as far-flung as Somalia and the French Indies, New Caledonia in the Pacific and Martinique in the Caribbean, interspersed by pavilions of the various religious missions and the military (Figure 6.9). As at Wembley, all of Africa had been divided into different subcategories, including *French Northern, French Occidental* and *French Equatorial Africa* – dubious, if not entirely invented entities without any political counterparts such as French West Africa. 'This part of the Exposition is very important. It forms a distinct enclave, a recreated portion of the African Empire', the observer commented.[30]

The author of the exposition's official guide, →André Demaison, had declared in its preface that the organizers considered the visitor a 'man of good taste' who would find no 'vulgar displays that have brought discredit upon many other colonial expositions, but rather, reconstructions of tropical life with all its truly picturesque qualities and color', as well as the utmost realism, veracity and authenticity.[31] In order to offer such allegedly authentic experience, a reality-effect was evoked by exhibiting native inhabitants and setting up a mock school for imported indigenous people. Despite Lyautey's aversion to such colonial crudeness, displays of natives were omnipresent at the venue; according to contemporary sources, more than 3000 could be found on the site.[32] They were especially prominent in the sections of French West Africa, Madagascar, Somalia and the Pacific Austral Establishments including New Caledonia. While obviously included as ethnographic exhibits rather than equal participants, these poorly paid colonials were considered a functional necessity to guarantee the arrangement's overall realism and to prove its authenticity for most visitors. The sheer physical presence of their bodies was the only element that defied reproduction; if they were real, the rest must be as well. 'The Exhibition', reasoned the local correspondent of *The Times*, 'has introduced Paris to the colonies as well as the colonies to Paris', but he likewise commented with some surprise on the absence of a more excited reaction by the French public, which had been paying for decades to see similar spectacles in theaters, clubs and cabarets in other parts of the metropolis. 'The French', he wrote, 'do not regard the natives at Vincennes as a sort of "raree show." Annamites, Cambodians, Tuaregs, Saharans, Moroccans, Tunisians, and Algerians go about their daily business there without attracting curious attention. No attempt is made to prevent them from getting to know their European visitors.'[33]

As previously indicated, however, the exposition's scope was not limited to such displays of exotic otherness in the freak show tradition, ubiquitous and powerful as they may have been. Six foreign nations – Belgium, Denmark, Italy, the Netherlands, Portugal and the United States – had agreed to participate with their own exhibits. As historian Herman Lebovics has pointed out, the exposition planners were eager to demonstrate a newly won solidarity among the imperialist powers that might curtail international communism. Anything less, Lyautey declared, would be unworthy not only of the common enterprise but also of their rapprochement after a world crisis, bringing as it did a newly discovered, shared 'anxiety to co-operate practically in the finest work of civilisation and progress'.[34] With the exception of Belgium at the southeastern end of the site, all these foreign pavilions comprised the international section at the venue's northern end, altogether approximately half the size of the colonial portion at the opposite end. Especially noteworthy were the American and the Italian sections, though for very different reasons. This was the first time that the United States had agreed to an official representation at a European colonial fair. Under the supervision of Campbell Bascom Slemp (1870–1943), an American Republican politician and former presidential secretary, a full-size replica of George Washington's home at Mount Vernon was built, as had been the case on earlier exhibitionary occasions. This famous colonial-style American manse was considered highly representative and relatively easy to construct. The political reasoning was no less pragmatic: the American government expected the French in turn to participate in the next Chicago exposition planned for 1933. The Italian Fascist government, on the other hand, signaled its intention of reclaiming an ancient Roman imperial legacy for contemporaneous propagandistic purposes by erecting a rendering of the restored basilica which the second-century emperor Septimius Severus (145–211) had built in Leptis Magna, his North African hometown and since 1912 under Italian occupation.[35]

But international participation in the largest French colonial exposition ever held was equally noteworthy for the imperial powers that were *not* represented in Vincennes in 1931: Germany and Great Britain. The former had lost all colonial possessions as a result of its defeat in the First World War and was not among the invitees. The German government, for its part, decided not to prohibit the numerous large-scale poster advertisements for the exposition displayed in Berlin, among other places, but neither did it encourage participation in any of the numerous congresses and conferences organized around the event.[36] British non-participation was, by comparison, a more complex issue and led to repeatedly expressed 'great sadness' on the part of the organizers, who bewailed the fact that the 'greatest colonial Empire of the world' was missing – and that the idea of an international imperialist solidarity materializing in Vincennes was therefore doomed from the first. Great Britain had initially accepted France's invitation, leading the French authorities to earmark a huge, 12-hectare space on the grounds. But Britain eventually decided to withdraw to a large extent, though not completely, pleading financial constraints – at least officially.[37] The underlying reasons, however, were more charged. Given the number of times the exposition had been postponed, the British government seemed to have lost faith in the project's realization. Rather than invest in an enterprise which had continually fallen short of expectations, Britain preferred to contribute to the Antwerp exhibition of 1930. Perhaps more tellingly, it feared appearing diminished in a French colonial exposition where only a building of at least the size of the Government Pavilion at Wembley could do justice to 'Great Britain as the Metropolis of a great Empire'. Praised by *The Times* as 'small in extent, and highly specialized, [yet] very thorough and technically perfect', its ersatz offer to the organizers, a very limited participation in the form of an informational display housed in the *Cité des Informations*, proved surprisingly successful in 'attracting the crowds'.[38] 'After the massive propaganda of Wembley', a German critic commented, 'England probably assumed they had satisfied their obligation to the French invitation with this not entirely negative attitude.' Nonetheless, as London was Paris' main competitor for the title of 'capital of Europe', the British opinion was the one with which the French were the most concerned. As such the British cancellation was considered particularly painful. The void it caused led to considerable disappointment on the part of the organizers, who bemoaned that their 'great book of knowledge where everything relating to the world should be taught and pictured in the light of attractive settings' would be missing a key chapter.[39]

The truth about the colonies

It is a general feature of the exposition medium that the relationship between materialized and staged 'messages' on the one hand, and their consumption

and appropriation by the various groups of historical actors including participants, visitors and critics on the other is virtually impossible to investigate
without necessarily neglecting the desirable degree of historical precision and
analytical comprehensiveness. The number of voices is as vast as the multiplicity of meanings ascribed; every attempt to find any kind of unified meaning
is fatally flawed from the search's very beginning. Nonetheless, historians
frequently designate a particular exhibition a 'success' or a 'failure', generally based on more or less intensive readings of the extensive source material
available, and always at the risk of overhomogenizing divergent, possibly even
contradictory, reactions.

From such a perspective, the historical significance of the Parisian Exposition
Coloniale Internationale of 1931 is twofold. Although it was the most spectacular
and sumptuous of all the French colonial expositions, and as such on par with
the five preceding grand Parisian Expositions Universelles and the one held
afterwards, in 1937, the discrepancy between representation and perception was
wider than ever, both in a French and a European context. Despite its short-term
successes and the general contentment of the organizers, interested parties and
the media alike, the exposition signaled the beginning of the end of a particular
type of imperial modernity – just as Wembley had for Great Britain. In France,
it provoked a hitherto unheard of degree of criticism directed toward the official
rhetoric of authenticity, the exhibition's veracity of replication, and its displays
of human beings.

Superficially, however, any cracks in the representational system seemed negligible, at least for the time being. Exposing millions of visitors to the economic,
political, social and cultural significance of colonial imperialism, and with it the
recently revitalized vision of a 'Greater France' as both fact and ideal, the exposition's objectives directly corresponded with those of the British Empire Exhibition.
Intending to bring together the peoples of an Empire that had become the world's
second largest in the decades preceding the First World War and which covered
an area 22 times that of France itself, the exposition explicitly aimed at infusing
the French public with a colonial consciousness, a *mentalité coloniale* otherwise
considered dreadfully missing. 'To make the colonial idea succeed, we must create
the colonial spirit here at home', one of the numerous guidebooks summarized
the event's pedagogical key intent.[40] 'What is colonization but the extension to
another population of the benefit of a tradition or organization superior to its
own?', Lyautey asked on numerous occasions, replying by repeating the same
slogans time and again: 'To colonize is to civilize', he pronounced, 'our future is
overseas.' The exposition, Lyautey declared, 'will attest that for civilization there are
other fields of action than the fields of battle, that the nations of the twentieth
century might rival each other fairly and generously in works of peace and
progress. It will give a lesson in effective action, will be a site of practical teaching
for all those who want to inquire, to know, to achieve.'[41] An early memorandum
further specified the main objective of this 'synthesis of the French colonial effort
across many countries and through the ages' in less flowery terms, instead taking
the form of three distinct 'lessons' that it should teach: first, a 'history lesson

(memories and stages of our colonial conquests)'; second, a 'lesson in economic activity (promotion of the earth and what is under it; tools and means of transport; equipment of ports; commercial relations)'; and, third, a 'lesson in humanity (moral and social efforts; policies toward the indigenous)'. As the Wembley exhibition had been extolled as a 'Poem of Empire' because of Kipling's street names, Vincennes was to be nothing less than 'le plus beau poème de notre temps' – the finest poem of our times.[42]

In mainstream print discussion, the exposition was considered an enormous success. Not only did more people visit the Bois de Vincennes than had seen the Exposition Universelle of 1889, but the fair also made a significant profit of approximately 35 million francs. After only four months it was reported that more than 21 million visitors had already 'flocked here from all corners of the globe, captivated by a spectacle of unprecedented breadth, as endearing as it is suggestive, as rich in meaning as in images', thereby 'becoming familiar with the multiple faces of the colonial world in this dreamy atmosphere'. *Mutatis mutandis*, the four argumentative patterns identified in Wembley's press coverage (*Fostering Trade*; *Bonds of Empire*; *Unity of Mankind*; *Around the World in a Day*) could be found applied as well, in almost identical variations, especially the powerful and frequently evoked, if long familiar topos of a 'tour du monde en un jour'.[43] René Borelly, the oft-quoted observer, hailed the exposition for precisely this offer of an imaginary journey in space and the evocation of an otherwise abstract imperial reality when he stated:

> From this 'tour of the world' in a few hours […] an impression emerges, or rather a conviction. Tangible and real, it is 'a notion of Empire' of which we were still ignorant even yesterday. The French colonial Empire, the France of a hundred million souls, a geographical abstraction, becomes a reality.[44]

Although the standard orientalist rhetoric still proved effective enough to attract and awe large crowds, imperial expositions in *fin-de-siècle* Europe had passed their zenith. Two broad, directly opposed examples suffice to demonstrate the enormous and irreconcilable divergence between representation and consumption. Diametrical readings on the part of very different groups of visitors signaled yet another representational shift in the exhibitionary complex during the 1930s and resulted in a further loss of confidence in traditional forms of exhibiting exoticism. More than 130 letters of thanks survive from so-called *caravanes scolaires*, centrally organized excursions for approximately 10,000 schoolchildren from the provinces, who were sent on brief trips to visit the capital and the exposition to 'develop the colonial sense among the younger generations of schoolchildren' (Figure 6.10). In their program, the exposition figured more prominently than the capital: It allowed the students one day only to see all the important tourist sites and urban monuments, but three days to explore the exposition in-depth, culminating in a night-time visit to the spectacularly illuminated site on the evening before their departure. 'In a very few days we have been able to get to know the great city and its fine monuments, and especially (thanks to illuminating

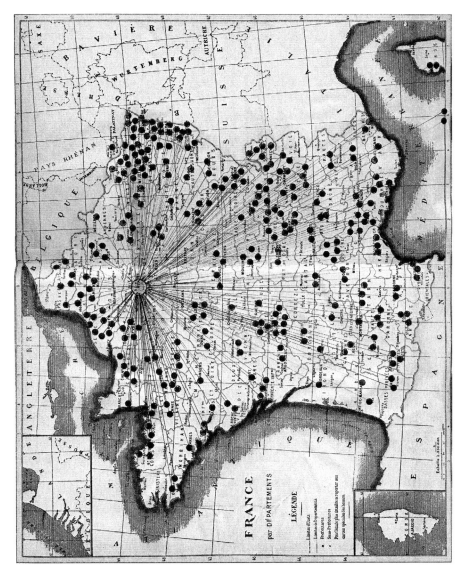

Figure 6.10 Schematic map of France detailing the provenances of the school groups visiting the Exposition Coloniale in 1931
Source: Courtesy of Archives de France, Archives nationales d'outre-mer, Aix-en-Provence, ECI/92, 16.

explanations) take an avid interest in the marvels of an imposing exposition that retraces the prodigious colonial effort accomplished by France and all nations', wrote one of the students in his thank-you letter to Monsieur Oudaille, the responsible superintendent: 'Such a visit has ravished our eyes at the same time as it enriched our minds with specific knowledge.'[45] 'A unique and unforgettable vision', as a schoolteacher from the Ecole Normale de Nîmes summarized her students' awe and collective learning experience,

> the colonial exposition has revealed to us the beauty of distant and unknown countries: the whiteness of the towns of Algeria, the perfumes of the Orient, the shimmering of the silk trade. [...] And later, when time passes slowly in our own little village, the memory of all this richness so prodigiously displayed will fill the soul with great sweetness, while we try to make live again before the eyes of our schoolchildren the colorful visions that we take back in order to convey to them a little of the enthusiasm and gratitude that animate us.[46]

At least in their teachers' words, for these students a visit to the Exposition Coloniale was a novel and eye-opening experience in which national, international and colonial contrasts were simultaneously enacted in the Bois de Vincennes, in particular the contrast between the metropolis and the province, and France and the wider world. As such, this three-dimensional 'great book, full of pictures spread open before the eyes' could indeed serve as a tangible supplement to the classroom maps so common in the 1920s and 1930s in which French imperial possessions were marked in pink.[47]

However, while the public exposition of non-European peoples had led to open controversy in Wembley, here protests took a new form and hitherto unprecedented intensity. Unlike in Wembley, the protesters themselves were not personally affected but rather politically and/or artistically motivated by causes that were largely inextricably intertwined. The Parti Communiste Français (PCF), since the Second Comintern Congress of 1920 strictly opposed to overseas expansion and actively supportive of revolutionary groups in the colonies, published a series of critical articles in their daily newspaper, *L'Humanité*, detailing colonial abuses and encouraging the French public to boycott the exposition.[48] Shortly after its opening in May 1931, a group of 12 notorious Surrealist artists including the writers André Breton (1896–1966), André Thirion (1907–2001) and Louis Aragon (1897–1982) as well as the poet Paul Eluard (1895–1952), the journalist Georges Sadoul (1904–1967) and the painter Yves Tanguy (1900–1955), many of whom had close connections to the Communist Party, distributed 5000 copies of a notorious two-page manifesto entitled *Ne visitez pas l'Exposition Coloniale*. They damned the 'entire bourgeoisie' for their 'complicity in the birth of a new and particularly intolerable concept: "Grande France"', and incriminated the exposition authorities: 'To implant this fraudulent concept, they have built the pavilions of the Vincennes exposition, in order to give the citizens of the homeland the property-owning awareness that they will need in order to hear the echo of distant fusillades without flinching. It is a matter of annexing the prospect of minarets and pagodas to the fine countryside of France, already uplifted pre-war by a song about a bamboo hut.'[49] A fire and complete destruction of the Dutch Pavilion on the night of 27 June 1931, together with its 'magnificent collection of native jewelry, paintings, sculpture, and rare fabrics', had the group publish a second, even more outspoken and inflammatory pamphlet headlined *Premier bilan de l'Exposition Coloniale*, likewise written by Breton. They blamed the organizers for recent massacres in Indochina, denounced the 'Luna-Parks in Vincennes' as a hypocritical celebration of imperialist subjugation and brutal exploitation, and mourned the loss of thousands of unique indigenous objects in the disastrous fire. Officially, it had been the loss of the container, 'The Netherlands Pavilion', that was bemoaned, not the irreplaceable objects – a fact that was, for the surrealists, a telling sign of the contempt the colonial powers had for the peoples under their self-acclaimed control, despite pious platitudes to the contrary.[50]

The anti-exhibitionist collaboration between communists and surrealists culminated in the opening of a counter-exposition under the heading of *La Verité sur les colonies* – 'The Truth about the Colonies'. Rejecting the idea of 'La Grande France' as an 'intellectual swindle', they questioned the officialized truth and aimed at substituting it with an alternative one. Largely overlooked for many years, within the last 10–15 years this little exposition in itself has garnered the attention of a number of French colonial historians and literary scholars, yet its greater significance within the wider exhibitionary networks has never been analyzed.[51] Co-organized by Thirion and Aragon, it opened much later than the exposition itself, on 20 September 1931, but remained open into December, long after the main event had closed. The counter-exposition was divided into three different sections spread over two floors. Thirion was responsible for organizing informative displays on the ground floor detailing the past and present of French colonialism as well as an upstairs room featuring Soviet propaganda artifacts, while Aragon and Sadoul curated the cultural exhibits on the upper floor, including indigenous art objects such as statues, masks and primitivist art, so-called *fétiches*. Contrasting ethnographic exhibits with pedagogic displays, the organizers sought to document the use of forced labor in the colonies and abuses of indigenous populations, and to juxtapose this with both 'authentic' artwork and Marxist-Leninist anti-colonial propaganda.

While the aesthetics of these displays vis-à-vis their official counterparts at the Vincennes site cannot be discussed here in detail, the counter-exposition's setting and location is of particular importance. For obvious reasons, it had to be held beyond the grounds of the Bois de Vincennes. Therefore, the protesters chose a former Soviet exposition pavilion, by then belonging to the French Communist Party. Originally used for the 1925 Exposition des Arts Décoratifs and vacant thereafter, this wooden structure had been moved to a lot on Avenue Mathurin-Moreau, close to the Parc des Buttes Chaumont, approximately six kilometers in a northwestern direction from the Vincennes site.[52] It was not only ironic that a counter-exposition would take place in a former exposition pavilion, and in a more centrally located site, but this fact simultaneously demonstrated the entrenched, yet contested, power of the exposition medium in the interwar years. Protests had now become possible, but their alleged subversiveness was limited, as it came largely from working within the representational system – capitalizing on the medium itself by adopting identical visual strategies rather than rejecting it altogether. Directly referring to 'several energetic protests', the Ministry of Colonies decided at the height of the Vincennes exposition in July 1931 to ban any future recruitment of human beings for public display purposes.[53]

The colonial exposition's winding down and liquidation was not spectacular, particularly in comparison with its intricate 21-year prehistory. Already in the first agreement between the Ministry of Colonies and the City of Paris, signed on 26 July 1921, it was stipulated that the Bois de Vincennes was to be entirely restored to its *status quo ante* including the replanting of fallen trees after the exposition's closure. By the spring of 1932, all traces had been removed.[54] Only a single one of the numerous structures erected was left *in situ* and remains open to this day: the *Musée des Colonies*. Hailed during the exposition as one of its two *clous* and origi- nally a major incentive to hold yet another mega-event, the building fell into neglect and lost its prominence as a tourist attraction. Serving for many years as a bizarre and somewhat haunted relic in still underprivileged eastern Paris, it was only the aquarium contained in the basement which over the years continued to attract schoolchildren and other visitors, thus keeping the building from sinking into complete oblivion. Reflecting a general shift away from any kind of colonial rhetoric, the museum changed its name several times, first to *Musée de la France d'Outre-Mer* in 1935, then to *Musée des Arts africains et océaniens* in 1960. As a con- sequence of former president Jacques Chirac's endeavor to concentrate all exhib- its of non-European art in a new museum complex on the Quai Branly in western Paris, close to the Champ de Mars, the building reopened in 2007 as a museum of French immigration, the *Cité nationale de l'histoire de l'immigration* (CNHI).[55] Today, a visit to the partially rededicated site still evokes a sense of unease. All that remains from France's most elaborate colonial exhibition is one of its two *clous*, indelibly marked with the visual remnants of the fleeting summer of 1931 – a story read in the strikingly exotic images literally carved into the building's walls. Monument to the apotheosis of French imperial modernity, the Exposition Coloniale Internationale did leave a physical, if limited, vestige on the fabric of eastern Paris. Long disregarded as a historical site, yet still standing, the building continues to serve as a reminder of the cracks within the representational system that characterized this bygone, but hardly concluded imperial past.

7
Conclusion: Exhibition Fatigue, or the Rise and Fall of a Mass Medium

> The exposition exposes itself.
>
> (Umberto Eco)[1]

By the beginning of the twentieth century, around the time of the Parisian Exposition Universelle of 1900, the medium of world and imperial exhibitions as technologies of a society's visual-spatial self-representation had achieved quasi-canonical status. With general strategies of representation constantly refined, particularly through the early stages of inter-urban Franco-British competition, a tradition of architectural forms with its own particular system of grammar, semantics and imagery became well established in public life. Indeed, universal, industrial and imperial expositions were held regularly in most Western European nations, as well as in the United States, and attracted ever-growing audiences.

Parallel to the medium's meteoric rise over the course of the second half of the nineteenth century, a transnational public discourse had developed with regard to the meaning and function of exhibitions in society, as well as their effects on culture at large. By the turn of the century, this debate was characterized by two contrasting and competing discursive strands, one of earlier and the other of more recent origin. On the one hand, from the initial emergence of the medium, a theoretical, quasi-'scientific' rationale had been elaborated according to which detailed assessments were made of the medium's effects on, and reception by, the public and were used to justify significant expenditure and the extensive use of various human and material resources. On the other hand, the curious topos of *Ausstellungsmüdigkeit* – 'exhibition fatigue' – was introduced in the 1880s to describe both criticism of the medium as well as a reluctance to participate on the part of visitors and organizers alike, bundling together a heterogeneous set of arguments against holding further expositions. While visitors complained that traversing and comprehending the ever-vaster exhibition areas had become increasingly arduous, leading to hitherto unknown symptoms of physical fatigue, commercial organizers seemed less and less inclined to bear the spiraling costs of extensive and lavish displays of whose usefulness they were no longer convinced.

Examining this discourse and its institutional consequences in a broader context, this concluding chapter reflects on the ways in which a theorizing of

European *fin-de-siècle* exposition practices might be achieved, simultaneously adopting a historical and a heuristic perspective. By analyzing a heterogeneous body of both prescriptive and analytical texts by writers, urban theorists and cultural critics on exhibitions in London, Paris and Berlin, such as Georg Simmel, Patrick Geddes, George F. Barwick, Julius Lessing and Werner Sombart – to name the most prominent – the chapter reconstructs the historical expectations and socio-cultural assumptions embedded in the vast majority of expositions. Did the general strategies of representation and visualization used by one of the most typical nineteenth-century media change under the altered conditions of the early twentieth century and its transformed media landscape? Where is the counter-discourse on exhibition fatigue located historically? Its international institutional consequences are then examined by analyzing the respective conferences held and organizations founded to address so-called *Ausstellungsmissbräuche* – 'exhibition abuses' – and the general, oft-lamented *indifférence* toward the entire medium. The fourth section uses the work of the French Marxist philosopher Henri Lefebvre to analyze temporal structures and spatial legacies, elaborating a theoretical perspective that is applicable beyond the five expositions examined in the preceding chapters. Finally, in an effort to disentangle the major principles of representation employed by the medium, the last section identifies three key elements of a theory of European exposition practices.

Peace, progress, prosperity

Broadly seen as a 'superb publicity medium', international exhibitions were considered to demonstrate and justify progress and modernity and, as 'enterprises of national importance', to foster common understanding and world peace, while simultaneously exerting a broad 'civilizing influence' on humankind. 'An Exhibition', declared a commissioner describing the global function of the medium in 1883, 'is a field for general competition – nation against nation, industry against industry – it is the great battlefield of peace, progress, and prosperity.' Expositions had to be regarded, as another commentator put it, as 'flash photographs of civilisation in [*sic*] the run', thus linking one prototypical nineteenth-century medium to the other via metaphor.[2] Almost parallel to its inception, a theoretical, quasi-'scientific' rationale was developed that ascribed a number of well-defined functions to the medium, including detailed assessments of its presumed societal impact. International exhibitions were in many ways materialized manifestations of the Enlightenment belief that reason made possible the creation of a comprehensive and accurate archive of knowledge of the world and everything in it, and that such an archive could be adequately replicated and displayed for the general public in a clearly defined urban space. The objects were ordered in ever-varying and increasingly complex systems of classification, thus allocating for each a precise location in an ideally ordered world. Their partisans never tired of repeating that expositions, as endorsements of reason, were indispensable agents in the inexorable 'march of progress', and hence both catalysts and proof of self-ascribed modernity. Once established and developed, this discursive formation remained stable throughout the second half of the nineteenth century.

Such a rationale could be found, for example, in various encyclopedia entries.[3] Aiming to explain the medium's unexpected success and breathtaking rise in a historical perspective, these articles referred to the Franco-British rivalry of the late eighteenth and early nineteenth centuries, and their respective, almost identical, assertions of having organized the first large-scale national trade exhibition. The British based their claims on a small trade fair organized in London by the Society for the Encouragement of Arts, Manufactures and Commerce in 1756, whereas the French cited the 1798 trade fair held on the Champ de Mars.[4] By rendering the medium international, the Great Exhibition of 1851 resolved this bi-national conflict and gave expositions an entirely new quality. The establishment of representational competition among cities and between nations in turn gave rise to entirely new rivalries and ambitions. Such competition was believed to be the driving force behind the vaunted 'march of progress'. 'In reviewing the history of international exhibitions', →George F. Barwick, keeper of printed books in the British Museum and an early British exhibition theorist, wrote towards the end of the century, 'we see that they have performed a great work in the past by bringing the nations together, and enabling them to compare each other's methods of work, mechanical appliances, artistic ideals, and scientific progress.'[5]

Completing a classical *circulus vitiosus*, expositions were considered central to progress, progress was considered central to Western civilization, and hence expositions central to each individual nation. H. Georges Berger, for instance, stressed the competitive nature itself as the driving force behind progress, characterizing, only a few years later than Barwick, the core idea of the exposition as that which

> results in gathering in a fixed place artifacts and products arranged according to the order of their species, their genres, and their provenances, and to display them to visitors so as to give the impression of a competition. [...] [Expositions] appear as manifestations of the human spirit by which peoples contribute to the general progress by instructing others in them and by learning themselves.[6]

For this reason, especially at the early expositions, the role and functions of juries were held to be of considerable importance. Juries were supposed to guarantee an exclusively procedural order among all participants, and their decisions were therefore considered crucial for the direction which progress would take in the near future.

Yet, starting with 1851, exhibitions were considered not only catalysts of international progress in so far as they fostered competition in a national context, they themselves became subject to the very same mechanism of constant self-reproduction and continuous expansion. Writing in an early issue of the *Zeitschrift für Socialwissenschaft*, →Lambertus Otto Brandt, an industrialist involved in organizing a local trade fair in Düsseldorf in 1902, described the spiral-like process of development which had led to one exposition after another after the medium's emergence in mid-century. 'Any world exhibition was always on an increasingly ambitious scale than the last', he stated, 'one more elaborate than the other, and aimed at offering a more and more impressive picture of cultural development.' In the end, Brandt argued, such a development would inevitably lead to the creation of an entire 'encyclopedia of the civilized world'.[7] Therefore, just as general progress was, by definition, inexorable and infinite, succeeding exhibitions had to become bigger and better, more expansive and expensive than previous ones, and also more spectacular and all-encompassing. 'It is said that each world exhibition should out-do the previous one', a German report commented laconically on this unwritten rule in 1882, and towards the end of the century the journalist Albert Montheuil summarized 50 years of French exposition history with the simple device 'de plus fort en plus fort' (from strength to strength). Such a general development was reminiscent of the three classic Olympic dimensions *citius, altius, fortius* – faster, higher, greater – translating as a faster sequence, higher buildings and structures, and wider sites. It is no coincidence, then, that the modern Olympic Games, the analogous twentieth-century-institution – with their notorious though obligatory 'the best games ever' – are still subject to the same rationale of constant growth and relentless progress, with one mega-event after the other being obliged to outdo all preceding ones.[8]

The possibility of comparing national achievements in material formed directly 'on the spot' was supposed to lead inevitably to an increasing 'self-knowledge of nations', to a 'more just estimate of their own resources' and therefore – eventually – to create and contribute to progress via international comparison, transfer and adjustment. In later encyclopedia articles, when many expositions had become dominated by their highly commercialized character, the similarities between this particular medium and advertising were often emphasized. 'National and commercial exhibitions', one architect wrote in 1933, adjusting the rationale to the altered situation, 'are really advertisements in three dimensions.'[9]

The 'religion of World's Fairs' found numerous prophets and believers who gave explicit expression to the far-reaching expectations they trusted expositions to fulfill.[10] While Lawrence Weaver did not launch his 'first attempt at a coherent philosophy of exhibition making' before the mid-1920s, their theoretical potential had already been recognized in 1877 by Sir Patrick Geddes, the Scottish biologist and noted sociologist who was also one of the first city planners. Long before he fully developed his philosophy of urban planning in *City Development* (1904), which he was to summarize in *Cities in Evolution* (1915), Geddes devoted his first book-length manuscript to the problem of *Industrial Exhibitions and Modern Progress*, published in 1887. 'The spectacle', so Geddes described their intellectual appeal, 'of not only grown men but intelligent chiefs of industry, naïvely working up their contributions to a museum of production into the exact likeness of the ornaments made in every kindergarten, is as instructive from an educational and anthropological point of view as it is grotesque from the artistic and utilitarian.' Geddes himself would maintain a lifelong interest in expositions: in 1900, he took the participants of his annual Edinburgh summer school to the Paris exposition of that year and gave a full account of their visit afterwards. Later, in 1913, Geddes set up his own Cities and Town Planning Exhibition based on material collected since 1892 in his personal Edinburgh museum, the so-called Outlook Tower, but which was lost at sea a year later on its way to India.[11]

Expositions were regarded not only as catalysts but also as active agents in the ongoing struggle for 'peace, progress, and prosperity' as well as for the unity of mankind that they were supposed to communicate through encyclopedism, education and – albeit to a much lesser extent – entertainment. The year 1851 played a crucial role in this scenario. The Great Exhibition's unprecedented success established 1851 simultaneously as a standard point of reference and narrative template, especially but by no means exclusively in the British context. Museum director Julius Lessing also invoked the Crystal Palace as the place where everything began, writing in 1912 that '[i]n this nostalgic movement to return to old historic forms, we see from the floor of the most up-to-date creation of the Crystal Palace a spiral development which seems to go both upwards and downwards.'[12] That the Great Exhibition developed into both an epoch-making and unsurpassed founding myth of the entire medium was not only the result of its immense, broadly-based social success and effective self-invention of bourgeois society, but also the direct consequence of a skilful *mise en scène* by its organizers, labeled by contemporaries the 'generation of 1851'. Architect →Joseph Paxton's mythologized career and the aura of the iconic Crystal Palace became central and highly transfigured symbols that elevated the Great Exhibition to the meta-narrative of the entire world exhibition genre and would shape the new medium profoundly. It was 'not a blueprint but a prototype', literary scholar Thomas Richards has rightly suggested, a model on which later stages of development were based and against which they could be judged.[13]

Many of the vague and grand 'ideas of 1851' lingered in the public imagination well into the twentieth century, particularly in Great Britain, and were easily reactivated for later exhibitions. In the British context, 1851 defined the medium's rules until the turn of the century and dictated the practical, technical, organizational and intellectual standards applied to later expositions. In 1907, the year before the opening of the Franco-British Exhibition, an advertising brochure set 1851 as its reference point in the increasing internationalization of the entire medium:

> Industrial Exhibitions, after a varied existence of a century and a half, have now established a distinct claim to recognition in history, and from being content in the long ago with a pedlar's pack, or a wandering show-van, or a booth at the fair, they have waxed rich and important and have settled down into a permanent institution. Commencing with what could only be described as parochial displays, they gradually attained the dignity of the designation of National, but it was long before the growingly progressive spirit of the age allowed them to become International. And, this ideal once realised, it would be difficult to determine the great influence wrought by the periodical holding of the immense expositions which are, in this twentieth century, looked for annually.[14]

Although the Franco-British Exhibition was by definition bi-national, it was still necessary to emphasize its international character. Similar to the organizers of the Berliner Gewerbeausstellung, Kiralfy considered it essential, largely for reasons of credibility, that the enterprise be viewed within the context of great – read: international – exhibitions. Fourteen years later, when the entire White City grounds were to be sold at auction, a prospectus characterized the medium's distinctive place in society as family-friendly, class-transcending and, at the same time, as offering education, entertainment and outdoor leisure:

Class-Transcending [handwritten annotation in left margin]

> No medium of modern civilisation so enters into the life of people as to enable entire families of toilers to gather together for a few pence and enjoy, in common with Royalty, the aristocracy, and others generally, the beauties of Art, the wonders of Science, the romance of Industry, the marvels of Manufacture, the advantages of Education and World Progress in general, and all this under highly congenial architecture, beautiful gardens, delightful music, combined with the pleasures of healthy open-air enjoyment of recreation.[15]

Once again it was argued that the 'medium of modern civilisation' was to impart education directly through entertainment, in order to promote international understanding and to advance 'World progress in general'. However, written to advertise and to enhance the site in Shepherd's Bush to potential buyers, such a statement was, by 1922, rather anachronistic. By that time the formerly hegemonic discursive rationale had long been under severe attack – especially by organizers, exhibitors and critics – and was by no means as self-evident as it had seemed mid-century.

Exhibition fatigue

Had the European *Exhibitionskultus* (exhibition cult) come to an irrefutable end by the turn of the century? Had the medium's heyday passed? Had the 'art of display' deteriorated, as it were, into sheer 'exhibitionism'? There is plenty of evidence to support the existence of a widespread discursive crisis in *fin-de-siècle* Europe. 'Increasingly', the French economist Georges Gérault lamented in 1901, 'universal expositions are losing their prime characteristic and becoming enterprises of pleasure. The interest of industry and commerce is no more than a pretext, amusement is the goal.' German chemist Otto Witt opened the very first of his letters on the Parisian exposition of 1900 by declaring that the world was 'tired of exhibitions'. The well-known journalist Alfons Paquet devoted an entire chapter of his PhD thesis in political economy to the problem. Georg Simmel diagnosed a comparable discrepancy between 'a complete paralysis of the senses, a true hypnosis' caused 'by the richness and diversity of what is offered', and a not yet entirely developed consumer culture. And the equally influential German economist Werner Sombart conjectured in 1908 that 'exhibitions had reached their pinnacle in all respects, when in Paris this great symbol of modern culture: the Eiffel Tower, was imposed as a final touch.' Subsequently, Sombart argued, as an institution the exhibition had increasingly been exploited by big business and capitalism, with trade fairs becoming heavily commercialized. With the expansion of the 'democratic omnibus-principle', the entire 'idea of the exhibition' had been irretrievably corrupted and fallen prey to complete capitalization and commercialization.[16]

Beginning in the 1880s, under the heading of *Ausstellungsmüdigkeit*, a new rationale proved increasingly dominant in the international exposition discourse, primarily originating from, but by no means limited to, Germany. Threatening first to undermine, and subsequently to supersede the older exposition rationale of 'peace, progress and prosperity', the codification of the medium's assumed effects on and function in society were accompanied by a perceived decline and an increasing sense of disillusionment. Approximately 30 years after its invention and institutionalization, the exposition medium seemed to have entered a grave state of crisis that only worsened through 1900 (Figure 7.1).

Present-day historians have readily taken up this argument. The idea of a general decline has become *the* hidden, yet central, leitmotiv of a large part of the recent historiography on exhibitions. It is commonly argued that the expositions of the twentieth century rapidly degenerated into sites for mere consumption and

Figure 7.1 Exhibition fatigue in the summer of 1900
Source: *Encyclopédie du siècle*, vol. 2, 221.

amusement, deprived of any serious content or political meaning, and that their overtly commercialized character led to a hitherto-unknown spectacularization of objects, displays and ensembles. Different contemporary authors have given different answers to the question of when exactly this point of no return was reached, with suggestions ranging from the second Parisian Exposition Universelle in 1867 to the First World War. Yet, a majority agrees that the Parisian Exposition Universelle of either 1889 or 1900 represents an irreversible break, for only at this point could a complete change of the meanings ascribed and functions attributed to a long-established medium be recognized. By that time, Parisians had come to refer to the exposition as 'La Foire' – the fun fair.[17]

However, these scholars overlook the fact that complaints about the incomprehensibility and transience of the items on display were as old as the medium itself. The huge public discourses inspired by each exposition generated significant critical attention. Yet, complaints increased and intensified in the course of time, and, as they became more radical, attacked the very principle of holding large expositions. With the German expression *Ausstellungsmüdigkeit*, a new all-embracing signum emerged in the light of which the grave crisis affecting the whole medium was discussed. But what exactly was the content of this 'new dogma', as Otto Witt termed it? What kind of critique was subsumed under the catchword 'exhibition fatigue'? And how is it to be explained that similar debates in France and the United Kingdom were, in comparison, initially far less trenchant than those in Germany?

The diaries of the German engineer, agricultural technician, popular poet and internationally active exhibition expert →Max Eyth are helpful in tracking the gradual evolution of this counter-discourse *avant la lettre*, long before the notion of *Ausstellungsmüdigkeit* was invented in the early 1880s. Born in Swabia in 1836, Eyth moved to London at the age of 25 where he worked as the official representative of a machinery company owned by Sir John Fowler (1817–1898), one of the inventors of the steam engine. Eyth traveled widely, and was in charge of his company's stand at international expositions held in London in 1862, Vienna in 1873 and Paris in 1878. Having returned to Germany, Eyth founded in 1885 the still existent *Deutsche Landwirtschafts-Gesellschaft* (DLG), modeled on the British Royal Agricultural Society, and, until his death in 1906, organized small-scale exhibitions, mainly trade fairs.[18] His diaries are full of enthusiastic and yet increasingly critical observations of the numerous expositions, big and small, in which he participated throughout his life. As early as 1862, at the second international exhibition ever held in London, complaints of individual fatigue and saturation were an important theme in his writing, even if, in retrospect, Eyth considered the seven months spent at the site the most fulfilling of his life. Yet, in one of his letters Eyth noted how 'sick and tired of all this greatness and splendor' he felt:

> In fact, I am enormously tired of all this colorful confusion. As often happens in London, one loses all sense of large and small among all these thousands of impressive sights and the endless succession of commonplace exhibits.

We all, of course, have our personal conception of such phenomena – as seen through our own eyes. One can absorb a certain amount of impressions but then comes the point when this ability is exhausted. I have really had enough of it all.[19]

Eleven years later, on the occasion of the Viennese Weltausstellung of 1873, Eyth's bewilderment had increased, and so had the harshness of his verdict. His inability to come to terms with this 'latest horizontal Tower of Babel' led him, for the first time, to question the general viability of the medium. Eyth bluntly declared exhibitions obsolete because technologies of international communication and global exchange had advanced so considerably:

The usefulness of world exhibitions has decreased tremendously. Precisely that which made them possible, that is, the swift daily traffic between the nations, makes them more and more superfluous. They have nothing new to offer so that nobody waits for a world exhibition to present their own achievements. They only promote trade and industry at certain points and to a certain extent, just as any customary annual fair. As to their contribution to world peace, even the most simple-minded among us know what nonsensical chatter this is. [...] What we are doing here, will be completely forgotten in five years.[20]

Some five years later in Paris in 1878, Eyth had hardly changed his opinion, ironically comparing the ever-recurring exhibitions to a chronic fever. Yet now he adopted a more distant position from which to assess this latest mega-event, above all wondering at the expositions' frequency and repetitiveness. Why were his contemporaries enamored, again and again, of something so insipid? Why was it that each generation seemed to require its own exhibition? 'It is both interesting and difficult to discover what motivates nations and individuals to repeat such experiments on this increasingly large scale', he wrote:

Never have more splendid buildings been erected to show the riches of our world. [...] Perhaps this is the secret of the seductiveness of these giant modern mayflies [*modernste Rieseneintagsfliegen*]. Nobody actually calls for them and they are loathed like mosquitoes, yet they glitter in the summer sun just like false diamonds. It is an inevitable reaction: the whole world applauds for a moment and this is enough to make this strange kind of fever chronic. Occasionally it is asked where and when it will break out again. [...] The enormous impression, left by the Great Exhibition of 1851, cannot be repeated again.[21]

Again, for Eyth there was nothing novel in the exhibition, yet far too much on display, a fact which made it entirely impossible to comprehend this replica of the world, with the question of *cui bono* remaining particularly unclear. While Eyth had been far more critical at an earlier stage than most of his contemporaries, he now felt completely overwhelmed, sated and exhausted, and not exclusively in a physical sense. On the eve of the closing ceremony of the Parisian exposition of that year, Eyth moaned that it, in fact, embodied 'sheer pathos in form and color. It is like a dazzling bubble of soap, in which the five continents are reflected, before it bursts at six o'clock tomorrow evening.' An active exhibition organizer himself, Eyth would return to Paris in 1900, six years before his death. By that time, he had entirely capitulated: the multifarious exposition had become, despite a new classification system, entirely unmanageable. Hence, he readily joined those critics who vehemently demanded a sudden and definitive end to all world exhibitions. Criticizing the 1900 mega-event as an overstretched *Riesen-Ganzes* (huge entity), Eyth fatalistically predicted an imminent collapse in his diary in August of the same year, fearing that '[i]n this way world exhibitions destroy themselves, and perhaps this is the best they can do at the present time.'[22]

Thus, the argument preceded the invention of the notion *Ausstellungsmüdigkeit* itself, which would structure the smoldering debate and give it a new quality by subsuming existing criticism. The term's gradual emergence and historical development can be observed – and hence dated – with surprising precision. Analyzing the sources, it is startling how persistently the argument was advanced in the aftermath of the Paris 1878 exposition in which Germany had not even participated, with the dispute reaching a fever pitch in the winter of 1879–80. Alternative notions, many equally graphic, were tried, but none became widely accepted. They included *Überflüssigkeit* (superfluousness) and *Schädlichkeit* (harmfulness). In November 1879 the term *Erkaltung* (cooling off) was used several times during a debate in the *Deutscher Handelstag*, and *Erkaltung* was also the key term in an official declaration made shortly after. Such official use had the paradoxical effect of granting previously rather loosely presented objections a new kind of legitimacy, thus unintentionally contributing to a rapid loss of confidence in the medium.[23]

The next stage of development in the genesis of the idea can be observed in two articles published in early 1880 by →Egbert Hoyer, a professor for mechanical technology, drawing on a lecture he delivered on 10 November 1879 at the *Polytechnischer Verein* (Polytechnic Association) in Munich entitled 'Über die Praxis der Ausstellungen'. Here, the idea of *Ausstellungsmüdigkeit* was used to link previous doubts as to the medium's overall utility with objections about the frequency and burgeoning scales of the sites, which made complete visits all the more exhausting. In the article's very first sentence, this argument was already fully developed even though the appropriate term had not yet been found:

When the papers break the news of a new exhibition project, many people exclaim automatically: 'Another exposition? Haven't we had enough expositions?' It is hardly any time since the Philadelphia and the Paris expositions have closed their doors, that we are considering an Australian one. Why should there only be new exhibitions in Munich, Düsseldorf, Leipzig, Stuttgart etc.?[24]

Two pages further in the same article, Hoyer gave an oft-used arithmetical example to elucidate the practical consequences of the constantly growing sites for the 'common' visitor:

> 53,000 exhibitors participated in the Paris exposition of 1878. If somebody had planned to visit this exhibition with the intention of devoting a single minute to every exhibitor, he would have needed 53,000 minutes to achieve this. If he spent five hours per day on this task – and for this he would have needed the stamina of an especially enthusiastic exhibition hunter – it would have taken 180 days or six months. Of course, nobody would dream of visiting every exhibitor; but even if we assume that a tenth part of it all should be inspected, it would have taken 18 days, a period of time which is seldom exceeded by any visitor.[25]

The third and final step was then taken on the next page, half way through the entire article, when Hoyer spoke of 'a further reason, based on facts and experience, for the apparent *fatigue* in great exhibitions'. This was the very first time that the two terms 'exhibition' and 'fatigue' were brought and discussed together, with the latter meant to emphasize dramatically the former's current state.[26]

Yet, it was still another decade, before, in 1892, the notion *Ausstellungsmüdigkeit* was fully established in public discourse and gained undisputed centrality. Counter-reactions to this counter-discourse did not take very long to appear. While some tried to popularize the antonym *Ausstellungslust* (exhibition lust) to offer at least some counter-resistance in the ensuing debate, others went even further, speaking of a 'fundamental hostility', a 'surfeit', a 'general antagonism' or even a whole 'exhibition plague' instead of mere fatigue. The bigger *Ausstellungsfrage* was, right from the beginning, the subject of this second debate on *Ausstellungsmüdigkeit*, as both issues were discussed with particular intensity during the same three distinct phases in public print culture: the early 1880s, 1891–92, and between 1907 and 1910 (cf. Figure 2.1 above). Before 1900, the contemporary standard argument was *not* to abandon the medium of exhibition entirely, but rather to reduce its size and frequency, to make expositions more specialized and differentiated, and to establish an international institution which would be exclusively responsible for urgently needed regulation.[27]

In France, a debate of such large scope was unheard of, and criticism limited to a brief yet intense period of discussion, largely in national newspapers during the run-up to the 1900 Exposition Universelle. On this occasion a certain amount of opposition was, for the very first time, expressed and justified by a general indifference towards the medium, but objections remained largely haphazard and soon died down. Berger, for instance, summarized this novel development, observing with bewilderment 'the growing hostility to expositions, even on the part of persons who were formerly passionate admirers of similar solemnities'. 'It is certain', he wrote, 'that the project of the Exposition of 1900 has raised objections that previous Exposition projects did not.'[28] In comparison, however, the debate remained limited and seems to have come from abroad, rather than originating domestically.

Foreign journals stated in 1895 that the 'tide of opposition' to international exhibitions had finally reached France as well, with French newspapers declaring themselves 'tired of exhibitions' and the British *Builder* deeming the 1900 exposition a 'mere spectacle', an anachronistic and entirely obsolete remnant from a now distant past:

> For the purposes of education and intellectual enjoyment it is doubtful if the day of international exhibitions is not over. Those who desire to see particular subjects, either mechanical or artistic, can do so better at small exhibitions of particular things. Moreover, now that people can move about the world so easily, the products of a country can be seen in it by those who desire to be acquainted with them, so that the *raison d'être* of collecting everything from everywhere in one spot is very largely a thing of the past.[29]

Writing with more restraint, Pierre de Coubertin put the existing criticism in a broader perspective. By no means an uncritical observer, de Coubertin still judged the French *fin-de-siècle* opposition to the medium as comparatively modest and largely negligible, particularly when seen in an international context: 'In France, each time the subject has been discussed, and notably regarding the expositions of 1889 and 1900, objections have been formulated', he wrote: 'Although these objections have been discussed in the Chamber and voiced by various deputies, it cannot be said that the idea has ever met with any serious opposition.'[30]

In the end, this diagnosis is no less counter-intuitive than it was in the German context: If complaints about *Ausstellungsmüdigkeit* must largely be considered as counter-reactions to the excessive number and disproportionate frequency of expositions, one would assume the complaints to be particularly strong in France, also at a comparatively early stage. Yet, this was clearly not the case. After the first objections had been raised during the run-up to the 1900 exposition, harsh criticism was voiced again after the event had closed, leading to an interruption of the invented 11-year tradition and a deferment of the next exposition. This, however, can be easily interpreted as an act of definite *Ausstellungsmüdigkeit*, albeit *sans la lettre* and despite a certain time lag.[31]

The debate in Great Britain was less virulent than in Germany, but more prominent than in France. After the two great exhibitions held in 1851 and 1862, the considerably smaller scope and more specialized focus of the mostly privately organized expositions forestalled complaint. Nonetheless, similar arguments were made from the mid-1880s onwards. In 1886, for instance, during an official meeting of the royal commission for the Colonial and Indian Exhibition, the aforementioned Lord Derby – at that time still Secretary for Colonies, but later to be appointed president of the Board of Trade, president of the British Empire League and, just before his death in 1908, president of the Executive Committee for the Franco-British Exhibition – remarked that there had been 'a time, a few years ago, when it was said exhibitions were played out, and it would be well [...] to discontinue them'. Yet, according to Lord Derby this temporary crisis had now entirely passed and interest in exhibitions, 'whatever the ostensible object', was again 'unabated and ever increasing'. In 1900, Patrick Geddes diagnosed a 'feeling of widespread distrust of Exhibitions and their promises altogether'. Similarly, George F. Barwick reported prevalent fears that universal exhibitions had become unmanageable and that grave disadvantages were to be feared. Enumerating them, he mentioned 'the constantly increasing space necessary for the growing emulation of nations; the lessening interval between the exhibitions; their too short actual duration, and the extra charges put on everything in the town where they were held, without any apparent prospect of again reducing the prices'. According to Barwick, however, experience had not justified any of these fears. In spite of so many expositions having been held, he insisted, they had lost nothing of their vitality, and the movement would continue to grow 'with ever-increasing vigour', even if they would become increasingly specialized in the future.[32]

Similar complaints were repeated time and again. Calling exhibitions generally a 'moribund institution', on the occasion of the Parisian Exposition Universelle of 1900, A. Anderson stated in the *Architectural Review* that the institution of international exhibitions had 'latterly shown unmistakeable symptoms of approaching decrepitude'. In 1910, →George Collins Levey alluded to a comparable feeling of exhaustion when he concluded his *Encyclopedia Britannica* entry by saying that 'it might well be thought that the evolution of this type of public show had reached its limits', and a few years later, an American observer also summarized that 'in Great Britain there has long been growing a disinclination for international exhibitions'.[33] Participation, it was generally argued, was no longer worthwhile. Although a specific *terminus technicus* equivalent to the German *Ausstellungsmüdigkeit* was never found, the issue remained widely discussed, even throughout the 1920s. The arguments advanced in Great Britain were very much the same as in other national contexts: a perceived oversupply leading to apathy toward the entire medium.

How is this type of fundamental and extensive criticism to be historically located and adequately contextualized? For three reasons the diagnosis seems utterly paradoxical. First, general exhibition criticism is presumably as old as the exhibition tradition itself. 'Lately, a lot has been said about exhibition fatigue', Brandt stated in his seminal 1904 article, 'but since 1856, the recurrent outcry about the excessive number of such events has had no effect at all, as it seemed at first.'[34] Second, despite these and similar complaints, never were more and vaster exhibitions held in Europe than in the period between 1880 and 1910, with almost 50 over the course of only three decades. In addition to numerous smaller fairs, eight large-scale international expositions were held world-wide, seven of them in Europe: in Paris in 1900, in St Louis in 1904, in Turin in 1902, in Liège in 1905, in Milan in 1906, in London in 1908, in Brussels in 1910 and again in Turin in 1911. Many more had already been announced for the near future. Contemporary observers such as the ever-critical journalist Alfons Paquet registered this discrepancy quite clearly. 'In face of the profound economic effects of general exhibitions of such great and ever greater dimensions', he commented in 1909, 'it becomes clear that the frequently heard opinion that world exhibitions had outlived themselves [...] has not proved true. On the contrary, the number of national and international exhibitions [...] has, in fact, increased.'[35] Third, the particularly German origins of this discourse are noteworthy. Nowhere else does the debate seem to have been as early and as intense as in Germany. A telling indication is the lack of a term equivalent to *Ausstellungsmüdigkeit* in both English and French. That Germany should have played such a central role in the critical-theoretical assessment of national and international *fin-de-siècle* expositions comes as yet another surprise – given that the Berliner Gewerbeausstellung was the only large-scale imperial exhibition ever held there – and further complicates Germany's already intricate position in the global exhibitionary network. This is only to be explained if one is ready to accept the term's prominence as merely another sign of the exhibitionary network's trans- and international character, in which Germany participated in a more direct and significant way than hitherto acknowledged. These fierce debates may not have been felt abroad to their full extent, but it is evident that German observers and critics were well aware of the most recent international developments, on which they constantly commented and aimed to influence within their own, however limited, realms of possibility.

Taken in both an active and a passive sense, all these Western European authors traced back a certain reluctance to participate in great exhibitions to a general oversupply, which caused waning interest on the public's part and diminished confidence in the medium's overall effectiveness. The vast majority of articles and pamphlets reacted *against* the term *Ausstellungsmüdigkeit* and the reproach it implied – quite frequently in a critical manner – rather than endorsing the critique. Thus, criticism of the exhibitionary system was more often criticized than advanced. As a consequence, partisans and advocates are particularly difficult to identify. On the other hand, the notion's very vagueness added to its attractiveness. The fact that its addressees, those deplorable victims who had fallen prey to such fatigue, remained ambiguous expanded the term's scope and made it all the more applicable. Two different target-groups can be distinguished: the exhibition-going public and big industry. Examples can easily be found for both types of usage. According to the historian Hans Delbrück, it would be equally possible to lament over a widespread 'labor fatigue', while a civil servant elucidated how physical fatigue necessarily led to mental exhaustion and eventually even apathy on the part of the visitors.[36] On the occasion of the Berliner Gewerbeausstellung, →Paul Lindenberg, for instance, felt first lost, then alienated and eventually exhausted – and feared thus to have missed the most significant exhibit:

> Where is the beginning, where is the end? How often has this question been asked by those, who put foot on the exhibition grounds for the first time, who let their eyes wander around both in admiration and yet questioningly, who pause frequently because they do not know where to go first. [...] Even those, who feel at home in the midst of the seething world crowds, will experience a feeling of loneliness and strangeness, will wander about without any plan and

destination, and visit this and that, in order to pause tiredly – without having seen, perhaps, the most important exhibits.[37]

Second, around the turn of the century, even previously enthusiastic industrialists adopted this dismissive attitude. For instance, in a debate in April 1886, Werner von Siemens (1816–1892) lamented that, 'the great benefit, which world exhibitions used to produce formerly, when industry was not as developed as today, could not be repeated by the last world exhibitions. I can only say: I think world exhibitions have outlived themselves.' In 1900, the Essen-based industrialist Friedrich Alfred Krupp (1854–1902) – whose enormous cannons and ever-growing blocks of cast steel had been a constant *pièce de resistance* of subsequent international exhibitions since 1851 – candidly declared that, as far as he was concerned, no more exhibition publicity was needed, and the organization of any further exhibition was both entirely useless and senseless.[38]

A parallel can be observed here to the term *Materialermüdung* – 'industrial' or 'material fatigue' – which in the mid-nineteenth century had already acquired a second, technical connotation apart from its original physiological meaning, so aptly demonstrated by cultural historian Wolfgang Schivelbusch. Once imported into the realm of applied science and technology, the everyday concept of fatigue was given a precise technical definition, carefully described, quantified and made acceptably scientific by material research and testing. Having completed an epistemological detour, *Ermüdung* then re-emigrated back into physiology as an exact, clearly defined notion that, purged of its vagueness, was to become part of the standard vocabulary in industrial medicine.[39] Such a process of scientizing the popular, and of subsequent linguistic re-integration was, of course, impossible in the exhibition realm, not least due to its very subject matter. Rather than making the discourse more specific, a number of quite different debates were subsumed under one and the same metaphorical and dramatic buzzword – *Ausstellungsmüdigkeit* – including the *Hauptstadtfrage* and the *Ausstellungsfrage*, as well as the overarching question of international regulation and institutional reform. It is for this reason that it proves so taxing to disentangle the different strands of this debate and to assess their stakes today. In the end, the term served as an organizing concept under which the grave crisis affecting the entire medium could be discussed, without ever having to define the problem.

Ausstellungsmüdigkeit found another, more direct counterpart in the notion of *Ausstellungsschwindel* (exhibition swindle), coined at about the same time in the early 1880s. The term could be applied in the same double sense. On the one hand, exhibition swindle referred to a widespread fear on the exhibitors' part that competitors had obtained *their* medals, prizes and diplomas by devious and illegal means, including bribery and simple payment. On the other hand, from the organizers' perspective, the swindle referred to fears of so-called 'wild', 'unofficial' or 'illegitimate' exhibitions, which unscrupulous, fraudulent entrepreneurs organized as copycats in the shadow of the greater enterprises merely for the sake of profit. That *Ausstellungsmüdigkeit* and *Ausstellungsschwindel* should actually preclude each other – for why would it make any sense at all to complain bitterly about widespread exhibition swindle if one had long grown weary of expositions anyhow – remained largely unnoticed.[40]

Although frequently exaggerated, in retrospect such fears were not unjustified and are further testimony to the seriousness with which expositions, the nineteenth century's central medium, were received and discussed. When an unauthorized and uncoordinated Anglo-German Exhibition, held at the Crystal Palace in Sydenham between May and October 1913, came to the notice of German officials, they circulated a letter of warning and recommended extreme caution in case any German industrialist intended to participate. They also contacted Imre Kiralfy himself to ascertain his precise relation to the event. Kiralfy replied instantly and expressed his disapproval that 'the splendid opportunity which a real German-Anglo Exhibition would have offered in London' should have been lost due to an unauthorized undertaking of this kind. Yet, at the same time, Kiralfy seized the opportunity by offering to organize such an exposition himself, to be held at the White City in 1916. 'A Great Anglo-German Exhibition in these critical times', Kiralfy wrote, could be a 'matter of great significance for the preservation of peace' in Europe, and hence be more than just a commercial enterprise.[41] However, for both strategic and professional reasons, such an exhibition was unwanted on the part of the German *Ausstellungskommission*. Concerning possible cooperation with the British 'superman', the commission had been warned early on by the local German consul general in London. In November 1911, he articulated three distinct reasons for his opposition to Chancellor Theobald von Bethmann Hollweg (1856–1921), the first relating specifically to the White City, the second, a personal worry regarding Kiralfy's suspect reputation as an entrepreneur, and the third, a general concern as to the entire medium's suitability for diplomatic purposes:

The highly praised 'White City', as Mr. Kiralfy wants his exhibition to be called, [...] has lost much of its earlier aura in public opinion and has sunk to the level of simple entertainment. To my mind, it is not worthy of the German reputation if German exhibits were to be presented on these sites and in these buildings which have been used so often for this purpose. In the meantime, as I may mention confidentially, many suspicions have been voiced about the entrepreneur Kiralfy which present him in the light of a somewhat inconsiderate businessman, with whom it would be better not to conclude agreements and contracts if one wants to avoid unpleasant surprises. I also would like to voice my own opinion that the enterprise of an English-German industrial exhibition would not be a suitable means to improve German-English relations.[42]

Against this background, Kiralfy's proposal was rejected. When the dispute about the dubious Anglo-German Exhibition had finally been settled, the Foreign Ministry, in almost militaristic language, expressed its satisfaction with 'the energetic, fast and appropriate procedure' with which the commission had succeeded in rendering this event harmless. 'Swindle exhibitions' were a serious cause well worth fighting against – on the condition that the necessary, specifically responsible institutions existed to remedy existing international misgovernment.[43]

Counter-reactions, institutional and international

Given France's central position in the global exhibitionary network, it does not come as a surprise that forms of permanent institutionalization and self-organization independent of the respective – always only temporary – organizing committees were first developed there. Yet, it is not without irony that these resulted from private initiatives in which neither the state nor the government played any decisive role. Already in 1885, in the aftermath of the 1878 Parisian Exposition Universelle, a *Comité d'initiative des expositions françaises à l'étranger* had been founded by various groups of private individuals, mostly businessmen, to organize French participation in foreign exhibitions, with G.-Roger Sandoz of Nice named its first president and later secretary general. 'Les expositions aux exposants', they declared clearly and firmly, thus advancing their claims for more direct influence during all phases of organization and realization. Afterwards, the *Comité* changed its organizational structure several times (1895, 1901, 1903), finally becoming the *Comité français des expositions à l'étranger*.[44] With a *décret* dated 12 June 1901, president Emile Loubet (1838–1929) confirmed the *Comité*'s status as a public and charitable organization, declaring it of 'public utility'. As already indicated by its name, the *Comité* had as its object the development of the industrial and commercial expansion of France – either by organizing French expositions abroad or in the French colonies, or by supporting, participating in and organizing French sections at international, universal or specialist exhibitions outside France. A year later, the *Comité* fused with *La Réunion des jurys et des comités des expositions universelles* under the auspices of Georges Berger.[45]

A comparable German commission was the first to follow the example thus set. Here, however, the public debates on exhibition fatigue and swindle proved decisive for the foundation of a *Ständige Ausstellungskommission für die deutsche Industrie* (Permanent Exhibition Commission for the German Industry) in 1906, and no traces of direct conceptual transfers from a French into a German exhibitionary-organizational context can be confirmed in the sources. Anxieties were perceived as pressing enough to render the 'battle against the deplorable state of affairs in exhibitions' one of the major aims of the newly founded organization, even more so than the 'support of promising exhibition projects'. Therefore, from the outset the commission's objectives were first and foremost of a defensive character, even if the *Journal of the Society of Arts* explained to its British readers that the new organization's purpose was, above all, to 'obtain exact data as to the aims, extent, and possibilities of each exhibition planned', in order to be in a position 'to give precise practical directions to inquirers, with the object of promoting German manufactures and trade'.[46]

Organized as a private amalgamation of various industrial and trade associations, including the *Centralverband Deutscher Industrieller*, the *Centralstelle für Vorbereitung von Handelsverträgen* and the *Bund der Industriellen*, and with permanent representatives delegated by a number of ministries and official bureaus, the *Ständige Ausstellungskommission für die deutsche Industrie* started work on 1 January 1907 with Max Ludwig Goldberger appointed as its first president and remaining so through October 1913. Less than a year after its inception, the committee was fully functional, obtaining expert advice, sending agents to remote fairs and receiving many queries from potential exhibitors. With several changes of name – in 1920, 1923, 1927 and 1934 – its ensuing institutional and organizational history was as complex as that of its French counterpart. While the commission was neither a private foundation (as in the French case) nor officially attached to any ministry or state institution, but was rather a self-governing organ of, and financed by, German industry, the government nonetheless committed itself to consulting the *Ausstellungskommission* during any future decision-making processes concerning industrial exhibitions, trade fairs and universal expositions, and to take the commission's opinion into account. Conversely, government representatives were granted a number of permanent seats in the commission's various sub-committees.[47]

In this context, two aspects are of further interest. First, the urgency and necessity of reforming the entire exhibition system was initially recognized by the last quarter of the nineteenth century. Demands for a transnational agreement, providing binding regulations and issuing obligatory restrictions on frequency, had been raised for the first time in Germany during one of the early debates of the *Deutscher Handelstag* in the fall of 1879, and were repeated whenever the notorious *Weltausstellungsfrage* flared up. In the fall of 1882, the *Verein zur Beförderung des Gewerbefleißes* proposed as well that a permanent department or central office in charge of all exhibition matters should be installed and passed a resolution 'to persuade our government to agree with foreign governments through diplomatic means, that world exhibitions should not recur too frequently and that we are prepared to organize such an event in our own country'.[48] Finally, ten years later, →Friedrich Reusche, the self-proclaimed editor of a so-called *Deutsche Weltausstellungs-Bibliothek*, expressed the same thought more poetically, linking it directly to the debate on *Ausstellungsmüdigkeit*, at that time in its most heated phase, when demanding that the 'tree of the exhibition industry must be freed of all its destructive shoots and deformed branches and must be *thoroughly reformed*. Then it will become clear that the industrial world is by no means weary of exhibitions.'[49] Thus, the commission's foundation was, in the end, yet another direct consequence of the intricately intertwined discourses on exhibition fatigue and the German *Ausstellungsfrage*. Second, a direct connection can be found here with the *Bureau International des Expositions*, established in the early 1930s as an independent and supranational mediating non-governmental organization.

Exhibition policy also changed in Great Britain, yet later than in France or Germany. In October 1906, which was, ironically, the first time such a policy had been explicitly formulated, public discussion of the problem had become so widespread and criticism so fierce that it demanded a response. As such, the British government appointed a Special Committee on Great International Exhibitions under the chairmanship of →Sir Alfred Bateman,

> to enquire and report as to the nature and extent of the benefit accruing to British Arts, Industries and Trade, from the participation of this country in

Great International Exhibitions, whether the results have been such as to warrant His Majesty's Government in giving financial support to similar exhibitions in future; and, if so, what steps if any, are desirable in order to secure the maximum advantage from any public money expended on this object.[50]

The ensuing 377-page report, compiled after 30 meetings during which 8022 questions were posted to 56 witnesses, was divided into three parts: First, it discussed the general effects of exhibitions on British arts, industries and trade; second, it analyzed British participation in past expositions; third, it gave recommendations as to how exhibitions could be organized more effectively. Sharing with the medium's critics the diagnosis that the 'reluctance to exhibit has undoubtedly increased considerably in recent years' and that the novelty of expositions had 'to a large extent worn off', the report still insisted on the overall necessity of effective advertising. It described the fundamental role of exhibitions in fostering peace and progress in the older hegemonic sense. Though the Committee registered a tendency towards shorter, sectional and non-public fairs – 'the big show is not wanted just now', they groaned – they argued vehemently that Great Britain could not afford to abstain from participation in international expositions, even if the medium's impact on culture and society at large remained somewhat unclear. In the end, it was felt that Great Britain could not afford *not* to exhibit vis-à-vis the other global exhibitionary powers. 'The representation of British arts and industries at the more important Exhibitions will remain a national necessity', the committee concluded. While it did not recommend the organization of an international exposition in Great Britain, it suggested the establishment of a special branch of the Board of Trade, responsible for all kinds of possible 'exhibition work' including organization and conduct, to ensure the continuation of preparation considered essential for effective representation at any exhibition abroad.[51]

Eventually, the Board of Trade elected to follow the Committee's recommendations, deciding not to organize another international exhibition in London, which would have been the first official universal and international exhibition since 1862, but rather to appoint a special permanent 'Exhibitions Branch' to ensure a degree of governmental control over a still rapidly expanding field and to redirect and concentrate public spending. Noting the successful work of the French *comité* on the occasion of the Franco-British Exhibition, the British press was much in favor of establishing a similar institution in Great Britain.[52] In 1908, the Committee was founded as a branch of the Board's Commercial Department, and was charged with matters relating to the participation of the United Kingdom in international expositions and with supervising the organization of British exhibits therein. The branch sought, first, to ensure the adequate and appropriate representation of the nation, and, second, to lighten the organizational burden of individual exhibitors. For exhibitions upcoming in Brussels in 1910, as well as Turin and Rome in 1911, special royal commissions were formed. →Ulick Wintour, who had served as secretary to the Special Committee, was appointed the newly established branch's inaugural director in 1908. Later, Wintour was to be promoted to the post of general manager and first director of the British Empire

Exhibition, until he was replaced by Lord Stevenson in June 1923 after a brief period of managerial crisis.

Commenting on this unusual replication of administrative structure within the European exhibition network, a committee member wrote, '[i]n this and other respects, the British government, for the first time in the annals of International Exhibitions, will follow the example of foreign governments in directly helping exhibitors to display their goods to the best advantage.' Thus, one of the few lasting effects of the German debate on exhibition fatigue and swindle vis-à-vis the proposed imperial exposition in Berlin was administrative reform in Great Britain, in its own mind still the motherland of the global exhibition movement. Given that the British commission was the only committee in Europe created and operated by the state rather than by private enterprise, there is clear irony.[53]

In the early twentieth century, the international debate was characterized by the same tendency towards increased state control of expositions with an eye to limiting their frequency. With a number of similar national exhibition committees established in Belgium (1903), Italy (1905), Hungary (1907), Denmark (1908), Switzerland (1908) and Austria (1910), it seemed logical for them to join forces and expand their activities to the international level. Attempts at international collaboration and subsequent standardization were not, however, a new phenomenon but went back to the late 1860s, to the foundation of an *Association internationale pour le développment des expositions* on 25 November 1867, a first, albeit largely ineffectual, effort. Yet even when negotiations between the different national bodies began anew in the late 1900s, it would take another 20 years until final agreement could be reached.[54]

Three large international conferences were held in Paris in November 1907, in Berlin in October 1912 and again in Paris in November 1928 to solve the most pressing organizational problems. The explicit object of the first two conferences was to find a way 'to limit the number of great international exhibitions and to establish a uniform code of regulations with a view to reforming their organization and administration'. In accordance with the vast majority of national committees, the ensuing, unpublished report recommended limiting exhibitions held under government supervision and allowing for a minimum of time to elapse between them. In the end, the participating countries of the second conference agreed on the foundation of the *Fédération internationale des comités permanents d'expositions* in Brussels, with French Senator →Emile Dupont as its first chairman.[55] Yet, a convention resulting from this conference, although signed by 15 European countries in addition to Japan, was, as a consequence of the First World War, never ratified and so proved ineffective. Only at a third conference, after more than 20 years of diplomatic preparation, was an official 'Convention Relating to International Exhibitions' signed on 22 November 1928 by the representatives of 23 of the 38 attending countries. While it had already proven a complex task to define what type of enterprise should be covered and regulated, and what precisely constituted an 'international exhibition', the new convention introduced a clear *definiens* in Article 4, section II for the so-called 'First category': 'those [exhibitions] in which the countries invited to participate are obliged to construct national pavilions'.

Thus, the so-called pavilion system or principle, dating back to the 1876 world's fair held in Philadelphia, had become, more than 50 years later, *the* defining element for each official international exhibition.[56]

As a part of this convention, the official *Bureau International des Expositions* (BIE) was established in Paris as a central, supranational and independent organization henceforth exclusively responsible for mediating between governments intending to organize an exhibition and ensuring that regulations were followed, in particular during the newly established application process for potential host cities and nations. After various consultations with the member states, in December 1933 the BIE proposed a revised set of regulations to be adopted by the organizing countries, intending to further a process of 'natural evolution' by which regulations were to become both more uniform and precise. This supplement to the 1928 convention was meant to increase standardization and to simplify the organizational process. In the end, the BIE effectively countered the oft-lamented 'rank growth' in the exhibitionary system with a number of regulatory and administrative measures, thus putting a definitive end to the previous debates on *Ausstellungsmüdigkeit*, *Ausstellungsschwindel* and the like. As a direct consequence of these trenchant organizational reforms, the overall number of expositions held both in Europe and the United States declined dramatically in the post-war period.[57]

Only after the war does new regulation limit Expos [handwritten margin note]

Sites, cities, sights

International expositions held in *fin-de-siècle* Europe resembled their surrounding metropolitan areas in numerous ways. Frequently, they were considered cities within the city. To use Louis Wirth's classic attributes of urbanism, both kinds of cities – the 'real' and the 'artificial' – were large, spatially dense and socially heterogeneous conglomerates. Unlike their 'real' environs, however, there was very little that was incidental about these expositions. One of their essential, much-discussed features was their transitory, ephemeral character. Expositions were conceived as fleeting microcosms of national self-representation that had to be situated both physically and mentally within the metropolis. First reflecting the meanings with which they were charged, and then condensing and catalyzing them, they interacted both with the surrounding urban development and its intellectual context, themselves often assuming a symbolic character. Exhibitions were not only an integral part of the urban environment, both materially and cognitively, but also contributed to its shaping. They were 'agents of change'.[58] *Agents of Change* [handwritten margin note]

International expositions can be considered 'paradigmatic places' in three ways.[59] First, they represented various kinds of global spaces in a strictly limited locale situated within an urban agglomeration. Second, in their respective *mise en scène*, expositions ascribed to the surrounding city a specific dramaturgical role. Finally, as spaces of representation themselves, they formed part of the surrounding metropole which they, at the same time, partially transformed. Thus, writing the history of expositions requires the analytical bridging of three different types of space, extending from the micro-context of the single exhibit within the exposition site, including the space between those exhibits, to the middle ground of the adjacent urban ground and up to the global macro-context of collecting, selecting, shipping and displaying objects considered representative in the metropolis.

The present analysis concentrates on this middle ground. While endeavoring not to lose sight of the other two spatial contexts, it focuses on the relationship between the sites of these ephemeral expositions and the ways in which they wove themselves permanently into the urban fabric, adopting a theoretical, as opposed to a merely empirical, perspective. Underlying this analysis is Henri Lefebvre's clear distinction between physical space, social space and mental space, as described in his classic *La Production de l'espace*. While spatiality could by no means be completely separated from physical and psychological spaces, Lefebvre argued, it had first and foremost to be theorized as socially produced. He identified three distinct moments – a 'trialectic' – which served as his main conceptual tools and are also applied here: direct spatial practices (*perçu*), representations of space (*conçu*), and spaces of representation (*vécu*). Whereas Lefebvre considered spatial practices as a constant in social life, he found that there was a notable shift from actually lived spaces to imaginary spaces, from spaces to their conceptualization, with 'things, acts and situations [...] forever being replaced by representations'.[60]

Applying Lefebvre's conceptual triad to the history of expositions allows a clear distinction to be drawn between the various explicit or implicit statements that expositions made about themselves, their position in the capital city, and the relationship between the host city and the wider world. Such an approach represents a welcome means to overcome the theoretically wanting hermeneutics for which exhibitions, as dense, materialized textures extended over time, inevitably call. Demanding several different kinds of contextualization, both spatial and other, this approach requires thinking beyond simple dichotomies, while also allowing for considering mutual influences, perceptual interdependencies and transnational interrelations in both an historical and analytical perspective. An analysis of the relationship between ephemeral exposition sites and the ways in which they wove themselves into the urban fabric thus operates on three distinct levels: the exposition and the city, the exposition as city, and the city as exposition.

The exposition and the city

European *fin-de-siècle* expositions had a catalytic effect on the city in which they were held, changing and affecting their urban environments to a considerable degree both materially and mentally. Exhibitions and their urban environments were interdependent in two ways: first, due to organizational requirements including infrastructure, transport, accommodation and catering for a huge number of visitors, large exhibitions could only be held in big urban conglomerates, chiefly capital cities. Since the Great Exhibition of 1851, this rule held for almost 40 years. The first two European international expositions, which were *not* organized in their respective capitals, were the 1888 Exposición Universal de Barcelona and the Belgian 1905 Exposition Universelle et Internationale, held in Liège. Second, the importance of hosting expositions on a frequent basis was of considerable significance for a capital's image of itself, and had repercussions, both obvious and more hidden, on its concrete appearance. The Viennese Weltausstellung of 1873, for example, provided a welcome opportunity to present the impressive vistas and splendid buildings of the recently completed Ringstraßen-complex to an international audience. Additionally, only through the infrastructural transformation of the entire city was it possible to realize a hallmark event on such a scale. The exposition also served as an organizational framework within which to publicly present the possible future of the city-enlargement project, not scheduled for completion until 1913 with the erection of the Kriegsministerium and the Neue Hofburg, as well as a venue to foster its progress by staging various laying-of-the-foundation-stone ceremonies. The educated Parisian classes of the Third Republic were especially aware that the position of their metropolis as a world city was closely linked to its role as the premier world exhibition city. Therefore, plans for the next exposition were made as far in advance as possible, with proposals for the 1900 exhibition beginning as early as 1892. The fierce competition between the European capitals for exhibitions thus comes as no surprise, nor do the number of unrealized attempts to organize an international exposition in Berlin after 1878.

Among the three European metropoles analyzed in this book, Berlin played the most underestimated, if ultimately least important, role in the global exhibitionary network for one simple reason: a major world exhibition was never held in Germany, and a large-scale event such as the Berliner Gewerbeausstellung of 1896 was never repeated. Yet in spite of the failure to realize any other major German exposition project, the same argumentative mechanisms as in Paris or London were at work. In order to demonstrate the city's newly acquired world-class status, Berlin tradesmen had been exerting enormous pressure to organize an exposition on a comparable international scale. When the long-awaited event finally came about with the Gewerbeausstellung, contemporary observers like Georg Simmel praised it precisely as evidence of Berlin's *Großstadt* character and as an unmistakable sign of the city's now irreversible modernity. What these critics did not realize, however, was that British and French rivals had demonstrated their respective modernity half a century earlier, and that the Berliner Gewerbeausstellung could therefore be read in precisely the opposite way than had been intended.[61]

In London the relationship between the venue and the city generally developed very differently. Here, the newly created exhibition spaces were quickly incorporated into the ever-growing urban fabric and effectively digested. Since the South Kensington site, where both great exhibitions of 1851 and 1862 had been held, was, soon after the 1851 Great Exhibition, enriched by prestigious institutions such as the South Kensington Museum, the Natural History Museum and the Royal Albert Hall – together forming an entire 'city of museums' or 'treasure casket', as the writer Paul Morand formulated it – consecutive expositions moved to the northwest.[62] Subsequent fairs became increasingly specialized. As largely private enterprises with little, if any formal state support, they were driven further and further to the periphery, first to the southeast (Sydenham, today in the borough of Bromley), then to the west and northwest (Earl's Court, Olympia, White City, Wembley), and thus by and large suburbanized. It was only on the occasion of the 1951 Festival of Britain held on London's South Bank between County Hall, Waterloo Bridge, the Thames and York Road, that town planners and urban designers under the auspices of the London County Council realized the enormous possibilities for urban redevelopment. They decided to bring the spectacle back into the city center in the form of a new riverside waterfront which London 'had not had for a couple of hundred years', as the *Architectural Review* put it in 1949. 'We made', chief architect →Sir Hugh Maxwell Casson explained two years later in a short film entitled *Brief City*, 'this exhibition to be part of London', with the Thames itself being 'part of the show'. In 2000, Richard Rogers's Millennium Dome with its specially built Jubilee Line extension attempted the same feat, though in an easterly direction, integrating itself into a 150-year old exposition tradition.[63]

Nowhere, however, was the relation between exhibition and city as close and as marked as in Paris.[64] As the venue of the five most important Expositions Universelles held in Europe during the nineteenth century, Paris was often referred to as the 'Queen City of Expositions'. The 'Fair City [...] in which everything seems to have been planned with a view to beauty', as a tourist put it in 1890, exemplified for contemporaneous observers the entire institution. 'France, or rather her capital, Paris, has been called the foster mother of the International Exposition, or, as she loves to call it, the Exposition Universelle', another explained:

> The title is not a mere euphemism nor empty flattery. It is a truism, warranted by all the conditions that enter into the origin and assure the success of such an institution. Letting Paris stand for France and the French people, it is a centre at which the continents can gather with a minimum of travel and expense.[65]

With the exception of the 1931 Colonial Exposition, all French exhibitions were centered around the Champ de Mars. First used for such a purpose on a very small scale in the aftermath of the 1789 Revolution, this square developed over the course of the second half of the nineteenth century into the prototypical exhibitionary space of transitory yet recurrent festive character. 'No other city in the world', a comprehensive guidebook to Paris and the Exposition Universelle of 1900 alike enthused over its uniqueness, 'contains in its very center an equal area available for a great exposition.'[66]

However, the *tabula rasa*'s uninscribed character was to be drastically altered – at first temporarily, for only 20 years, but then permanently – with the building of the *Tour de 300 mètres* in 1889. As the *clou* of the exposition of that year, the iron tower was meant both to symbolize and literally to stand for the political and industrial dual revolution, in celebration of the former's centennial and as a product of the latter. It was, in fact, a special clause in engineer →Gustave Eiffel's contract, stating that the tower should not be demolished after the exhibition's closure, which triggered fierce controversy and sparked heated debate even before construction had even begun. Various pamphlets and articles critical of the project had already been published throughout 1886, when, on 14 February 1887, with ground just broken for the tower's foundation, a most excited and later notorious petition appeared in *Le Temps*, vehemently protesting 'against the erecting in the very heart of our capital of the useless and monstrous Tour

Eiffel'. The almost 50 signatories – among them many artists such as the composer Charles Gounod, the architect Charles Garnier, the painters Léon Bonnat, Jean-Louis Ernest Meissonier and William-Adolphe Bouguereau, and noted writers such as Alexandre Dumas, Sully Prudhomme, Charles Marie René Leconte de Lisle and Guy de Maupassant – feared the ruin of their beloved capital's beauty. They saw in the future not only the site, but the entire city dominated by 'the odious shadow of the odious column of bolted sheet-metal', day after day spreading across its surface 'like an ink-stain': 'Moreover, it suffices to imagine for an instant a vertiginously ridiculous tower dominating Paris, like a black and gigantic factory chimney-stack, crushing with its barbarous mass [...] all our humiliated monuments, all our belittled architectural buildings, which will disappear in this stupefying dream.'[67] The minister replied that, much to his regret, contracts had already been signed and that, consequently, it was too late to save from profanity 'that incomparable square of sand, known as the Champ de Mars, so worthy of inspiring poets and of seducing landscape painters'. Gustave Eiffel himself, on the other hand, reacted to the artists' reproaches in quite a restrained manner. In an interview in the same issue of *Le Temps*, he defended the tower's particular beauty and aesthetic originality by summing up his artistic doctrine. As an engineer, his task had been to create elegance as well as ensure solidity and durability, and his primary concern in designing the tower had been maximum wind-resistance rather than any grand theory of art. Apart from that, he wrote, 'there remains in the colossal an attraction, a proper charm to which ordinary theories of art are scarcely applicable'. Eiffel could not resist upholding his own sensibilities. By following nature's hidden rules of harmony, he felt that he had given the tower a very special beauty of its own.[68]

Once construction was completed, criticism rapidly dropped off, not least because of the tower's enormous success with the fair-going public. 1,953,122 visitors made the ascent during the six months of the 1889 exposition (Figure 7.2). Shortly after its opening, guidebooks already began to hail the tower as 'the feature of the Exhibition, and the new landmark of Paris'. 'It is the future observatory of civilization', one of them boldly declared, directly linking the site to its history, 'Paris in 1789 demolished the Bastille; in 1889 she rears the Eiffel Tower. Both performances are characteristic and original. To have made the ascent of the Eiffel Tower is one of the regulation performances of the year. The sensation is novel.'[69] There were countless further attempts to make sense of the 'gigantic and black chimney-stack'. The British *Builder* called it a 'foolish and costly piece of brag', and other foreign commentators, such as Friedrich Reusche, agreed in their resolute condemnation of the tower's ugliness. He thought it only fitting that the sinful Babel on the Seine had eventually received the tower it deserved. 'The Eiffel Tower', Reusche wrote, 'is a brutal iron monster, a monument of bad taste, but also of the artistic decline of our century even though it is a symbol of technical progress. This tower has not enriched the world with any new thought.' Tourists often described their ascent as a breathtaking experience. To them, the tower served as a focal point for both the exposition and for all of Paris. Guidebooks recommended that, on their very first tour through the grounds, visitors should

226

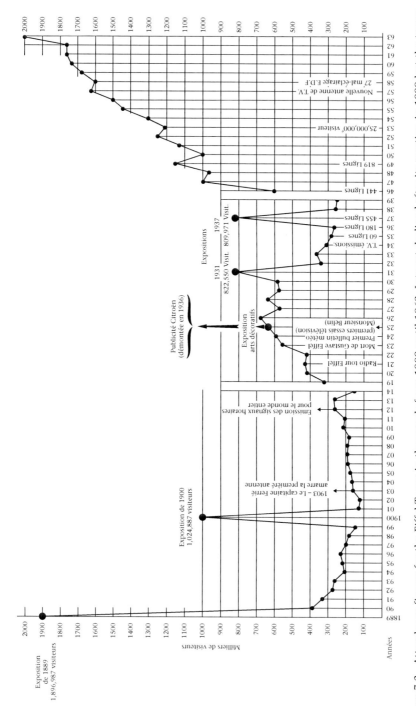

Figure 7.2 Attendance figures for the Eiffel Tower in thousands from 1889 until 1963. Interest declined after its erection in 1889 but the tower remained a focal point of subsequent Parisian expositions before it was officially declared a historical monument in 1964. Today, it receives almost seven million visitors per year

Source: Braibant, *Histoire de la Tour Eiffel*, Fig. 2, 168–9. Courtesy of Widener Library, Harvard College Library, Widener Fr 7505.6.

place themselves under the center of the Eiffel Tower to find their bearings and to 'know how to locate [themselves] at [their] next visit'. Just by climbing the tower, one could gain a different world-view – literally a new *Weltanschauung* – of the exposition and, mediated through it, of the entire 'world' itself.[70]

During the half-century after its construction, the tower was far from being the popular site that it is today. Its conceptual significance had already changed from 1889 to 1900. Serving as the *clou* and the absolute innovation of the former exposition, by 1900 it had become a structural and visual necessity as it organized the vastly enlarged grounds and provided visitors with an overall perspective. As the 'core of the entire area' and 'the focal point of the exhibition site', the Eiffel Tower was functionally essential to see all the sites and sights. Between 1901 and 1914, attendance figures were at a historical low, with no more than 120,000 to 260,000 visitors per year.[71]

The tower's popularity increased with the expositions of 1925, 1931 and 1937, but it was not until the end of the Second World War that a process of codification set in, eventually transforming it into the very symbol of modernity. In the end, it was Roland Barthes's 1964 semiotic analysis of the Eiffel Tower which, at least in an academic context, succeeded in establishing a widely known and still convincing argument of the tower being synonymous with Paris and the whole of France. According to Barthes, the interpretative key to the monument, seen as both object and symbol, was to be found in its inherent uselessness and lack of specific function, even if to call it 'empty' (as Michelet had done with the Champ de Mars, which, ironically, had forever lost that void-like quality through the erection of the tower) still seemed exaggerated, inaccurate and a factual mistake: 'As a matter of fact, the Tower is *nothing*, it achieves a kind of zero degree of the monument', Barthes stated. The urban omnipresence of *la Tour de 300 mètres*, with its visual inescapability throughout Paris, enabled the tower and the city to fuse together metonymically: the one created the incentive to visit the other as they were viewed and visited at the same time. From one, tourists and travelers could not help but see and experience the other. In this way, the *clou* of the 1889 exposition eventually developed into *the* joint symbol of Paris, and subsequently of France – what Barthes called 'a symbolic couple [...] articulated on the opposition of the past and the present, of stone, old as the world, and metal, sign of modernity'.[72]

Barthes proved, however, to be by no means the first thinker to grasp and depict this complex relationship between exposition, tower, city and nation and their complementation both in representation and meaning. In 1889, the *Pall Mall Gazette* exposition guide had described the complementary character of site and city in very similar terms. 'The Eiffel Tower, of course, you see everywhere, by night and by day', it declared. 'It is the great fingerpost of the Exhibition, the unmistakable landmark of Paris. [...] Unlike all other monuments, it is visible from almost every part of Paris, while from its summit you obtain a great panoramic view of the heart of France.'[73] Even if that description was far less trenchant than Barthes's poetic interpretation, its point was equally clear: site and city were inextricably intertwined, each providing the other with a 'sight' that was impossible, but essential, to overlook. The Exposition Universelle of 1889 equipped Paris with a seemingly natural and literally outstanding pivot, a new and unsurpassable center of gravity, and a focal point in an otherwise heterogeneous city. The exhibition served as a direct mediator between the two, leaving a legacy that was to alter the city's character forever. Thus, the tower's overwhelming success with the public obscured the fact that Gustave Eiffel had fundamentally erred in the 1887 controversy. It was not his but the protesters' prediction that 'the Paris of sublime Gothic buildings, the Paris of Jean Goujon, of Germain Pilon, of Puget, of Rude, of Barye, etc., will have become the Paris of Monsieur Eiffel' which proved, in retrospect, more accurate than any other comment.[74] From such a perspective, Barthes's influential reading eventually helped the protesters achieve their right: in 1909, 20 years after opening, the tower became the property of the state. For 41 years, until the Chrysler Building was erected in Chicago in 1930, the Eiffel Tower remained the world's tallest man-made structure and today still attracts almost seven million visitors per year. In 1964 – the same year in which Barthes's essay was published – it was finally declared an official 'historic monument'.

Including such technologies of overview was considered necessary not only for large-scale exhibitions such as the Parisian mega-event of 1900. All expositions analyzed in this study possessed vertical structures. A smaller fair, Imre Kiralfy's 1896 Empire of India and Ceylon Exhibition, had already included three of them – a captive balloon which would take visitors up to an altitude of 300 meters, a Great Wheel and the Belvedere Tower, a 'diminutive Eiffel tower' of only 60 meters in height. Special balloons were not only made available in Paris in 1900, but also in Berlin four years earlier, where visitors had been able to embark on a steerable 'Aerostat' to gain both an overall view of the exhibition city and the surrounding metropolis. Likewise, a so-called Imperial Tower had been planned for the Franco-British Exhibition in addition to the Flip-Flap, but was never built.[75]

After the complete failure of Watkin's Folly, other attempts to embellish London with a monumental tower to rival the Parisian original were also unsuccessful. In 1923, 18 years after the removal of Kiralfy's Ferris Wheel, the inclusion of yet another Imperial Tower, the 275-meter-tall 'Flywheel of Wembley' was briefly envisaged. When *The Times* published details of the projected tower in April 1923, comparing it to the Nelson Column in Trafalgar Square rather than its French competitor, a flurry of letters to the editor ensued. One reader, T. W. Littleton Hay from Hampstead, took the occasion of the Imperial Tower projected for Wembley to discuss all these grand projects – the original Eiffel Tower in Paris, Watkin's Folly and even the Crystal Palace at Sydenham – at once, clearly aware of the complicated exchanges between the various projects, and most decidedly denouncing another Wembley 'folly':

The original Wembley enlargement of the Eiffel Tower, which fortunately never advanced above the first stage, and had subsequently to be dynamited out of existence, was sufficiently hideous in design; the proposed structure would be still more monstrous. It has often been said that, when one is travelling southward from London, it is only safe to open one's eyes when Croydon is reached so that there may be no chance of shock to one's æsthetic sense by a sight of the dreadful Crystal Palace towers; but, if the gigantic cylinder be erected at Wembley, northward travellers will do well to be blindfolded until Bletchley be passed.[76]

The Fascist Party leader Sir Oswald Mosley (1896–1980) brought this issue to the House of Commons, where Lieutenant-Colonel Buckley, parliamentary secretary of the Overseas Trade Department, replied to Mosley's question by stating that the construction of such a tower had not yet been officially suggested to the exhibition authorities. With considerable protests expressed at this early stage and financing plans unclear, the project came to a halt. Since ultimately the British Empire Exhibition lacked a genuine observation tower from which it was possible to see things in perspective, the stadium had to take over such a function. To 'enjoy the magnificent panorama of the whole Exhibition', to gain 'at once a sense of proportion' and thus to 'survey the Empire in miniature', the official guide recommended that each tour through the grounds should begin with the splendid view from its terrace.[77] In Berlin, at exactly the same time, the *Funkturm* was being built and opened to the public two years later, in September 1926, on the occasion of the Dritte Große Deutsche Funkausstellung. Its architect, Heinrich Straumer (1876–1937), did not try to conceal the fact that his design was, from the outset, indebted to the Eiffel Tower, even if the Berlin copy, at 150 meters, attained only half its height (Figure 7.3). Unsurprisingly, soon afterwards the new tower was nicknamed the 'Eiffelturm von Berlin' by the local public.[78]

Although a moving machine and hence a less permanent structure, the Ferris Wheel, specifically developed with a view to rivaling the *Tour des 300 mètres*, presents a final example of trans-exhibitionary – and in this case transatlantic – exchange not only directly comparable to the Eiffel Tower and its numerous imitations, but also subject to the same inter-urban competition. Linking the 'established' exhibition cities of Chicago and Vienna, London and Paris through a complex exchange process, it was first designed and invented by the American civil engineer George Washington Gale Ferris (1859–1896) for the so-called Midway Plaisance, the amusement section of the World's Columbian Exposition in Chicago 1893. Dubbed the Midway Nuisance, it was later transferred to the 1904 Louisiana Purchase International Exposition and became the prototype for even bigger big wheels at other fairs, including the Earl's Court exhibitions in London and the *Grande Roue* at the Paris exposition of 1900 (Figure 7.4). Here, contemporary critics and observers such as Friedrich Naumann interpreted it as a second pole, whence it was possible to survey and comprehend the entire exhibition. Even if he found it lacking compared with the Eiffel Tower, Naumann still saw its 'long thin spokes' as expressing 'a new kind of elegance' superior to the 'excessive accumulation of the muses, fates and angels or all the other useless figures with or without wings' to be found elsewhere on the site.[79]

None other than the omnipresent Imre Kiralfy commissioned the British engineer Walter B. Bassett to construct another Ferris Wheel, called the 'Great' or even the 'Gigantic' wheel, on the occasion of the complete restructuring of the Earl's Court exhibition grounds in London in the fall of 1894 (Figure 7.5). After considerable delay, it was opened on the occasion of the Empire of India Exhibition

Figure 7.3 The Eiffel Tower and the *Funkturm* in Berlin, in comparison but not drawn to scale
Source: Berliner Messe-Amt, *Der Berliner Funkturm*, 6–7.

in July 1895. Kiralfy's Ferris Wheel, the first of many copies, had an altitude of more than 90 meters and was even higher than the one in Chicago (80 meters), though somewhat smaller than the entirely illuminable *roue* erected for the 1900 Paris exposition. It featured a more sophisticated and durable design. One revolution of the wheel was to last between eight and 40 minutes, depending on the number of stoppages, and afforded passengers, as *The Times* reported, 'ample opportunity [...] to enjoy the panoramic view of London to the east and north, and the country to the west'.[80] Outspoken as ever and recognizing the new structure's relevance in inter-urban competition, the *Builder* did not leave the slightest doubt that it considered the wheel at Earl's Court an interesting technological challenge, though entirely superfluous: 'We have as little sympathy with this foolish kind of sensational toy as we have with Eiffel towers, but no doubt the construction of such a wheel so as to provide for all the enormous and varying strains brought upon the structure in the course of revolution is practically a very interesting engineering problem'. Commenting on Kiralfy's latest creation and eventually

Figure 7.4   Postcard of the *Grande Roue*, the 'Big' or Ferris Wheel, at the Parisian Exposition Universelle of 1900
Source: Courtesy of California State University, Fresno, Special Collections Research Center, Larson Collection.

Figure 7.5   Over 90 meters high, the Great Wheel at Earl's Court dominated the west London skyline through 1907 and offered panoramic views of the city. On a clear day, its promoters boasted, one could see Windsor Castle
Source: Photograph by Charles and George Washington Wilson, 1898. Courtesy of Museum of London.

even denouncing avowed admirers and potential passengers of this 'foolish kind of sensational toy' as 'fools' themselves, the magazine continued: 'It is only a pity that all the ability and cost expended in its construction should not be devoted to some more useful end than carrying coach-loads of fools round a vertical circle.'[81]

Kiralfy's wheel dominated the west London skyline until 1907 when it was partially demolished and transferred to Blackpool, the British working-class seaside resort. Despite the *Builder's* firm disapproval, a ride on the wheel seems to have made both positive and lasting impressions on its numerous passengers. 'Above you towered the Great Wheel, one of the wonders of London', theater manager and historian Walter Macqueen-Pope (1888–1960) nostalgically recalled a visit to Earl's Court several decades later, 'at night it was a thing of mystery, as it crept slowly round, a vast circle of points of light, with its brightly lit carriages hanging from their crossbars; at day, a huge spider's web of iron bars, of satisfying strength and ingenuity. It was an adventurous trip which every Londoner took at least once in his life.' And since it could be seen from far away, 'dominating the approaches from the West and South West', the Great Wheel became a landmark, a *pars pro toto* overlooking the metropolis and symbolizing the whole of London, just as the Eiffel Tower had done in Paris. Yet, unlike its French counterpart, this metonymy was not complete – not only because it did not last, but above all because it remained unilateral. London's symbolic representation did not exhaust itself with the Great Wheel. Three years later Kiralfy's Flip-Flap attempted to rival both his own Great Wheel and the Eiffel Tower, yet it proved less successful. Despite its oft-praised sense of danger and enormous popularity with the fair-going crowds, the Flip-Flap never reached the status of a unique urban landmark, nor did it capture the imagination to the same extent as *la Tour*.[82]

The exposition as city

International expositions in London, Paris, Berlin and elsewhere presented themselves as complex, well-organized conglomerations, composed of numerous sections and subsections. Despite the differences between individual cases, all these expositions aimed at introducing a reduced, but nonetheless accurately reproduced replica of a European version of 'the world' into the metropolis' center, where it was presented to large audiences composed of local, national and international visitors, spectators and tourists. It did not escape these audiences' attention, however, that this act of appropriation often led to an enormous heterogeneity of exhibits and objects on stage, and in fact increasingly assumed the form of a city within the city. To cite three paradigmatic examples, one each for Berlin, London and Paris, in order to demonstrate the widespread character of this equation: 'The exhibition', journalist Kerr enthusiastically celebrated the Gewerbeausstellung in his famous *Berliner Briefe* in which he extensively covered the mega-event held in Treptower Park 'is simply grandiose. It is not a village but a city that has been created here; perhaps it is even better to say it comprises various little cities. Nevertheless, the central point of the exhibition does not seem urban. In fact, it resembles a world spa [*Weltbadeort*].' Lord Stevenson explained in April 1925 that the creation of Wembley had been equivalent to 'the building of a huge new city', while a journalist likewise considered 'it an education in itself to walk through the almost innumerable ways and avenues and passages of the unprecedented City of the Exhibition at Wembley'.[83] Finally, a young American tourist in Paris, standing on the far bank of the Seine and admiring the Champ de Mars, thinking 'of all the great events which have enlivened that desolate stretch', noted:

> Its permanent condition is that of perfect emptiness and aridity, but occasionally it is the scene of wonderful concentrations of humanity. Great International Exhibitions have flourished there and disappeared; armies have drilled there which now lie mouldering under the earth. As I looked over it, it seemed that I could almost see the Emperor Napoleon seated on his throne, with hundreds of thousands of cheering Frenchmen round about. It was an experience worth having, merely to stand there and give way to one's imagination, and it was late when I went to bed that night.[84]

This metaphor could be extended further, as entire subsections were perceived as little secluded cities. In 1896 the official guide declared that 'Kairo and Old Berlin, like a fun fair, are complete cities, offering in themselves a great number of sights', and even otherwise critical observers such as Paul Lindenberg readily accepted this equation when commenting on the oriental, dreamlike quality of the *Sonder-Ausstellung Kairo*, hailing it 'a city full of wonders, which has been built on the prosaic sandy soil of Brandenburg, appearing like a dream, a *fata morgana* from the Orient.' Numerous other metaphors were sought to come to terms with each exposition's problem of perception, that is its inherent and increasing *indescriptibilité* and the ensuing 'paralysis of the senses' that resulted from the ever-increasing vastness of their venues, but none was as frequently evoked.[85]

   While the relationship between the exhibiting city and the exhibition site had, from the beginning, been characterized by both a certain tension and permeability, its problematic nature became more acute over time with the constant growth of subsequent exhibitions (Figure 7.6). Increasingly, exhibitions were described as 'cities within the city'. Such an equation pursued a double aim. On the one hand, it helped to grasp the sites' continuous enlargement historically. With regard to Paris, contemporaneous observers dated the beginnings of this process as far back as 1867, when Napoléon III moved the exposition of that year for the first time to the Champ de Mars, eventually, over the course of the nineteenth century, transforming this former swamp into *the* prototypical exhibitionary space of transitory though recurrent festive character. By the mid-1880s, it had become commonplace to describe international expositions as generally developing into quasi-industrial cities, and later to depict them, especially the 1900 Exposition Universelle, as 'part of the city itself'.[86] After careful international and comparative studies, the *Verein zur Beförderung des Gewerbefleißes* described the general state of the art in international exhibition design in 1886 as 'a powerful melting pot of all industrial mass articles; a kind of industrial city emerges, which cannot be ignored or systematically described. Nobody is capable of finding his way in it and every single achievement is swallowed up by the mass of exhibits.'[87]

   Yet, to describe an exposition as a self-contained city was also a means of coming to terms with the increasing complexity of the various sites – both internally,

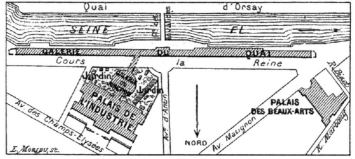

1855. — Superficie : 16 hectares.
Dépenses : 11,500.000 fr. — Recettes : 3,200,000 fr. — Visiteurs : 5,160,000.

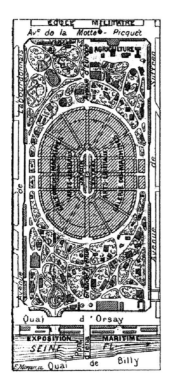

1867. — Superf. 46 hectares
(avec l'île de Billancourt)
68 hectares.

Dépenses : 23,440,000 fr.
Recettes : 10,765,000 fr.
Visiteurs : 11,000,000.

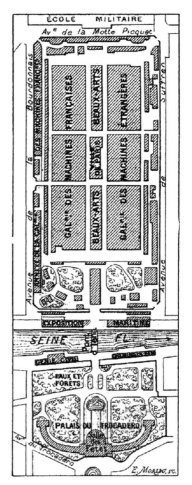

1878. — Superficie : 74 hectares.
Dép. 55,400,000 fr. ; Rec. 23,700,000 fr.
Visiteurs : 16,100,000.

Figure 7.6 Continued

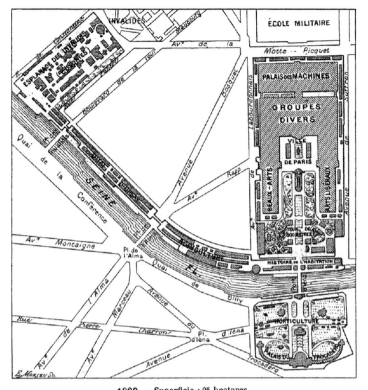

1889. — Superficie : 95 hectares.
Dépenses : 40,000,000 fr. — Recettes : 50,000,000 fr. — Visiteurs : 28,000,000.

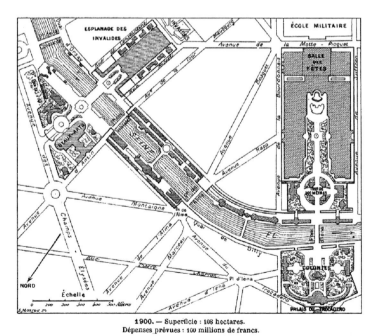

1900. — Superficie : 108 hectares.
Dépenses prévues : 100 millions de francs.

Figure 7.6 Sites and layouts of the five Expositions Universelles held in Paris between 1855 and 1900, with their sizes multiplying from 16 to 108 hectares over the course of 45 years
Source: Montheuil, 'Les Expositions universelles 1855–1900', *L'Illustration* 54 (8 February 1896), 118.

with regard to their spatial structure and layout, and externally, in relation to the surrounding city. Depicting the venue as just as complex and protean as a city was to transfer a familiar concept from one context to another. At the same time, such a rhetorical maneuver was the equivalent of surrendering to the oft-lamented problem of the sites' general *indescriptibilité*, a much more familiar topos within the contemporaneous study of urban conglomerations. As one author remarked in 1901 with regard to the British metropolis, 'topographically, Modern London is essentially Protean [*sic*], and there can be no finality in its depiction'. Each exposition posed the same problem anew, namely the enormous, physical and mental difficulties of coming to terms with an indeterminable number of objects and people on display.[88]

The city as exposition

The final key distinction between the city and the exposition site is determined by their respective pace of development. The relationship between the transitory exhibition and the permanent – by no means fixed, but certainly more stable – surrounding city was always one of the medium's crucial features, even if the respective degree of this ratio varied. Quite a few observers realized that this correlation was not as simple as it prima facie seemed. Paris, 'this wonderful city', Otto N. Witt remarked in one of his letters on the Exposition Universelle of 1900, 'is the most beautiful object in the exposition. One will never come to an end in taking in all these impressions', and the Swiss tourist Karl Böttcher noted a similar mutual permeability, stating '[t]he city and the exhibition, the exhibition and the city: they intertwine so that it is hardly possible to distinguish one from the other.' Making the identical argument already 11 years earlier in 1889, on the occasion of the Exposition Universelle of that year, the *Pall Mall Gazette* had put it even more drastically. 'There are many things to see in Paris', it strongly advised its readers, 'but the most important thing is to see Paris itself. Paris is more than any Exhibition. [...] There is only one Paris, but there are many Exhibitions. Paris, therefore, is the first thing to be seen, before even the Exhibition.'[89]

International expositions were soon considered welcome tourist attractions, commonly classified in widely read and commercially successful guidebooks such as *Baedeker*, *Michelin* or *Guide Bleu*, and presented as tourist attractions and travel destinations. Frequently, expositions became the object of special guidebook editions issued for the occasion – which then did not differentiate between the sections devoted to the respective host city and the ones regarding the specific exhibition. For the sake of simplicity, one such guide just called itself 'Exhibition Paris'. Not only did sections in these books overlap; they were often intertwined. Even in their accompanying literature, instructions and manuals, exhibition and city merged.[90]

In fact, ever since Thomas Cook, in cooperation with several railroad companies, had organized special low-cost excursions – including transport, accommodation and breakfast – to the 1851 exhibition and also to London in general for the British working classes from all parts of the country, an easily repeatable pattern was set. A newspaper specially launched for that purpose, *The Excursionist and Exhibition Advertiser*, combined articles with factual information regarding the journey with hints on how to visit both exhibition and metropolis, and simultaneously served to market Cook's package tours. Once refined for later expositions in London, Paris

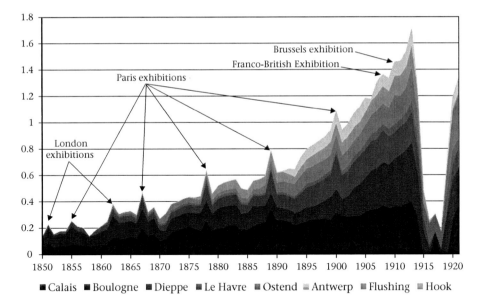

Figure 7.7 Number of passengers in millions embarking or disembarking at French, Belgian and Dutch ports connecting with Great Britain from 1850 until 1921
Source: Courtesy of The National Archives, Kew, RAIL 633/425, 411/655.

and elsewhere, this method of attracting tourists could simply be revived, though obviously on a much larger scale. An already well-promoted, popular product like the Great Exhibition suited the nascent tourism industry perfectly, and it is with these excursion trains that the democratization of English leisure is said to have begun. At the same time, employers frequently provided special travel grants to reward a few select groups of workers and to foster their 'industrial education'. These, in turn, were given the opportunity to embark on a journey about which they had to write lengthy and often detailed reports on their return. Thus, for instance, the Royal Society of Arts sent up to 200 carefully chosen artisans to Paris in both 1867 and 1878, and the Mansion House Committee did the very same 11 years later. It comes as no surprise, then, that exhibitions were mediated, communicated and popularized through the same kind of advertisements, newspapers, travel literature, guidebooks, picture postcards and other ephemera as was 'normal' tourism. Both, therefore, comprised part of the fast-developing universe of mass tourism and commercially organized group travel.[91]

It is difficult to obtain precise numbers with which to illustrate this interdependent relationship between large-scale universal, industrial or imperial exhibitions, and mass tourism. According to contemporaneous estimates, the total number of persons who visited Paris during the Exposition Universelle of 1878 amounted to 571,792, that is 308,974 more than had come to the French metropolis during the entire year of 1877, and the organizers of the Gewerbeausstellung estimated that more than 581,300 *Fremde* (foreigners) had booked hotel rooms in Berlin before the end of September 1896.[92] Figure 7.7 shows the number of passengers embarking or disembarking at eight different French, Belgian and Dutch ports connecting with Great Britain from 1850 until 1921. Four trends are particularly striking: First, the number of passengers grew almost exponentially over the course of more than 60 years; second, until 1900, the holding of exhibitions always produced clearly distinguishable peak points in the growth curve; third, after 1900, with the overall number of passengers several times higher than in 1850, the peaks became less distinct, hidden as a consequence of comparatively lower growth rates behind the general growth curve, but were nonetheless still recognizable; and fourth, the First World War led to a dramatic collapse in passenger numbers which, however, swiftly recuperated once the hostilities had ceased.[93]

At times, the relation between the exposition grounds and their urban contexts seemed in danger of being reversed far more fundamentally. All of London, →Ford Madox Ford augured in his *Survey of a Modern City* published in 1905, 'does without any architecture, because in essentials it is [...] a permanent world's fair', and that at a time when the last large exhibition held in the British metropolis had taken place several years before. The very same argument can be found for Paris in the writings of authors as different as →George Augustus Sala, well-known *Daily Telegraph* correspondent, or the protesters from the *Ligue Lorraine*. While the former attributed to the French capital the quality of 'a perpetual and kaleidoscopic Fair', the latter emphasized the city's permanently spectacular character. 'Paris with its warehouses of all the major French industries and its splendid display windows the length of the grand avenues', they wrote, 'constitutes a permanent Exposition.' Even the author of a popular contemporaneous history book reflected in like manner on the complex and interdependent, by no means fixed and stable ratio between the two spatial textures, stating that one could not 'separate the exposition from the city – Paris' and that the fair had to be considered 'an illustrated appendix to the great city that created it.[94]

Yet, the interchangeable relation between such an appendix – thus evoking and transposing another popular metaphor, namely the exhibition as a vast picture-book of encyclopedic scope – and the 'great city that created it' went further than merely attributing the characteristics of a permanent exposition to the big city itself.[95] Especially for the numerous foreign or colonial visitors, the so-called colonialists, the metropolis itself constituted the actual exhibit, rather than their 'exported' and frequently even self-built 'homes' on the exhibition site. For them, the relation between the 'real world' beyond the gates on the one hand, and the exhibition site on the other was blurred, if not entirely inverted. From such a perspective, their experience could be considered as complementary to the general trend of importing and concentrating the entire world in the imperial center, thus reflecting the colonial situation *in nuce* in the imperial metropolis rather than in the exposition itself.

In sum, how could the whole world be encompassed in a strictly limited area within the metropole, both materially and mentally? And how were these spaces of representation – temporarily, but still literally – woven into the urban fabric? When comparing the different, yet fragile, relations between exhibiting city and exhibition city, including the former's respective after-life and sustained usage after closure in Europe at large, three different patterns of movement can be loosely distinguished. The various nineteenth century exhibition sites in Paris, London and Berlin:

1. *either* were completely integrated into the city by gradually taking on additional functions, or by being transformed into comparable visual institutions such as museums of different kinds. While it had, together with the surrounding Albertopolis complex, already developed into a key symbolic space of London by 1862, the South Kensington site itself, with its own museum (opened in 1857 and in 1899 renamed The Victoria and Albert Museum) is the best example of how international expositions can actively contribute to imbuing urban sites with specific, yet stable meaning. Another example is the Esposizione Internazionale del Sempione, held in Milan in 1906, whose only permanent structure consisted of a huge aquarium, 'intended to stand as a memorial of the Exhibition in future years'.[96]

2. *or* they were used solely for subsequent expositions, with or without lasting dramatic alterations being made to the surrounding urban landscape. The White City in Shepherd's Bush, for example, gradually developed into a semi-permanent exhibition site until it was sold at auction in the early 1920s and redeveloped; yet, the legacies it left behind were limited, hardly transcending the medium exposition.[97] The most telling case in this second category is probably the Champ de Mars: on the one hand, it was and remained *the* French, if not global exhibitionary space par excellence and was thus of transitory but recurrent celebratory character; on the other hand, together with the Eiffel Tower it soon came to dominate both the appearance and image of the entire city of Paris, with its metonymical function thus maintained over time.

3. *or* the sites were specifically designed only for one time use, but nonetheless acquired symbolic significance after the actual event was over, as in the cases of Wembley with the Empire Stadium or Vincennes with the *Musée des Colonies* and the zoological garden. The Berliner Gewerbeausstellung, on the other hand, left almost no visible traces on the urban fabric, since its venue, Treptower Park, was afterwards restored almost completely to its *status quo ante*.

The second dimension, also reinforced by a conceptual apparatus developed by Henri Lefebvre, concerns the 'representation of space' embodied in the actual exhibitions. Being such complex constructs, most expositions experimented with a variety of forms of represented spaces. Often the City of London or Paris, for example, was exhibited in a so-called *Metropolitan Section* or *Section Métropolitaine*, such as the *Rue de Paris*, representing parts of a larger 'city' (i.e., the surrounding exhibition site as a whole) in addition to exhibits of the works carried out by the respective municipality within the 'real' city of London, Paris, Berlin or Vienna. While the same principle also applied to the representation of different regions, countries, nations or colonies, it showed itself most clearly in specific town-planning exhibitions, such as those held in Dresden in 1903, in Berlin in 1910 or in Ghent in 1913; on the latter, Patrick Geddes reported extensively.[98] Here, the city itself, as the spatial context, was not only implicitly but also explicitly and exclusively the theme and subject matter of the exhibition itself. It was therefore not by chance that, as briefly mentioned above, one of the most influential articles in the social sciences in general, and in urban anthropology in particular, that is Georg Simmel's essay on the 'mental life of the metropolis', was written and published on the occasion of such a specific urban planning-related exposition, in this case the 1903 Dresden Städteausstellung. Once again, this coincidence reveals the perennially precarious and unstable relation between city and exposition, whether in the form of exhibition city, exhibiting city or – in this latter case – the city-planning exhibition.[99]

Theorizing European exposition practices

'Exhibitions', the *Pall Mall Gazette* noted on the occasion of the 1889 Parisian exposition, 'are all more or less modeled on the same pattern'. Some decades later, a British critic agreed when noting in the *Saturday Review* that 'all exhibitions are alike in that they are advertisement disguised as entertainment, instruction, or amusement, [while] they differ chiefly in extent and scale'.[100] Even if the medium was subject to its own fashions and trends, such far-reaching resemblances and a comparatively slow pace of change resulted from a defined set of applied rules about how to put which items on what kind of display. First developed through inner-European, inter-urban competition in the course of the second half of the nineteenth century, this led to the increasing codification of a standard repertoire and the gradual development of a special exhibition language.[101] Such a repertoire consisted of certain exhibits and specific sections featuring the oft-discussed, inevitable *clou*, and included repeated assumptions about the enormous importance of exhibitions for society and culture, shared by organizers, visitors and critics alike.

The following attempt to theorize exhibition practices proceeds from the observation that expositions structurally resembled each other. A large degree of interaction among the internationally well-connected and well-informed groups of exhibition professionals led to transnational adjustments in consecutively organized fairs. Once successfully introduced at any exposition, new elements and novel features were quickly transferred across borders and integrated into later ones, often regardless of the respective specifically national context. Far-reaching international similarities, increasing codification and a high level of inertia can only be explained by the widespread networks and extensive personal connections between the distinctly internationalized and enormously mobile actors in this field. Already a quick glance at the detailed listings of *dramatis personae* enclosed in the Appendix of this book – detailing all available biographical information, career paths and participation in national and international expositions of the most important European organizers, participants and critics – will reveal the large degree of transnational entanglements and interconnections, both professional and personal.

When asked, on the occasion of Expo '67 in Montreal, about the fair's meaning and how to interpret it adequately, Umberto Eco responded that there were many possible answers,

> depending on the point of view from which we look at the phenomenon. We could give an interpretation in terms of cultural history, in sociological terms, in architectural terms, or from the point of view of visual, oral, or written communication. Since an exposition presents itself as a phenomenon of many facets, full of contradictions, open to various uses, we are probably entitled to interpret it from all these points of view. Perhaps in the end we shall discover that though the interpretations are different, they are complementary and not contradictory.[102]

In this book, such high hopes of a final merging of all imaginable and plausible forms of ascribed meanings and possibilities of interpretation are not shared. Expositions are too protean and polymorphous, and can be read in too many divergent directions at the same time. Such versatility enhances the fascination of the mass-medium exhibition, yet it also increases its complexity for historical analysis. Of transitory character, without a narrative of their own or a predetermined single, compelling central perspective, a pre-given chronology or a simply decipherable hierarchy of meanings, exhibitions present both a complex historical phenomenon and a historiographical challenge.

Expositions can be seen as closely knit textures spread over time that reveal multiple perspectives for interpretation. They were intended to represent contingent versions of the global in local contexts and constituted, in the words of Georg Simmel, 'momentary centers of world civilization'.[103] Eco had to concede that expositions must be seen as complex technologies and media of communication: 'The exposition [...] does not display goods, or if it does, it uses the goods as a means, as a pretext to present something else', he stated: 'And this something else is the exposition itself. [...] The exposition expose[s] itself.'[104] Even if the modern exposition had, in the final analysis, only itself as a subject, one must differentiate very sharply between their intention, realization and consumption. How successfully this broad image of a culture is communicated via media, then, becomes the main question, and an analysis of their horizontal and vertical patterns of reception and the ways in which they were appropriated a *conditio sine qua non*. It is for this reason that the innumerable varieties of metaphors evoked to explain the functioning of expositions are of such considerable historiographical interest.

Historically, the full realization of the medium's inherent self-referentiality can be precisely located in time: only eight years after the invention of the respective technological process, more than 150 calotype photographs of the Great Exhibition of 1851 were already included in the deluxe edition of the four-volume jury reports, making them one of the earliest photographically illustrated publications (Figure 7.8).[105] In 1900, less than five years after the first public presentation of film by the brothers Auguste and Louis Lumière in Paris, films of the exposition produced at the venue itself were also shown on the exhibition grounds. The Exposition Universelle of

Figure 7.8 One of more than 150 original calotype photographs of the Crystal Palace in London's Hyde Park that were taken in 1851
Source: Exhibition of the Works of Industry of All Nations, vol. 4, 819.

1900 became the subject of various newsreels, so-called *actualités*, which had been produced jointly by the brothers Lumière themselves and the American motion-picture company of Thomas Alva Edison. These short films showed some of the, then still unfinished, pavilions, but focused primarily on the various *pièces de résistance*, including the *Rue des Nations*, the *Palais d'Electricité*, the *trottoir roulant* and, obviously, the ascent up the Eiffel Tower.[106] Thus, in addition to the visitors, spectators and consumers actually on the site, there were those who participated in this mega-event via mass media. Distances were bridged both within the exhibition venue and beyond. For the first time ever, the 1900 Exposition Universelle included a separate retrospective section in the *Petit Palais* entirely devoted to the history of the Expositions Universelles themselves. Plans to turn it into a permanent exhibition museum came to naught. Even if the exposition is, as Eco suggested, a medium which generally exposes itself, such inherent self-referentiality had eventually come full-circle by the year 1900.[107]

Reconstructing these enterprises' general assumptions can help to identify them as precisely that: rhetorical strategies advanced by the organizers with the intention of depicting, comprehending, advertising and also justifying the respective exposition, rather than as an historical vocabulary to be used to support historiographical analysis. The rationale behind this conceptual move is to distinguish any historiographical reading of expositions from contemporaneous ones, thus counterbalancing them with a clear, independently developed terminology, specifically introduced for historiographical purposes. The three concepts suggested here – the exhibitions' transitional nature, their spatial context within the European metropolis, and their chronotopic character – mark necessary, albeit still incomplete elements within a theory of exposition practices.

First, international exhibitions of the nineteenth and twentieth centuries were fundamentally characterized by their transitory character. The vast majority of all structures, including buildings and pavilions, were planned with a view to immediate demolition after the event's closure. Although such transience was intrinsic to the entire medium, organizers and audience alike discussed time and again how it might be overcome, whether by transferring all exhibits directly into a museum after the exhibition's close as in the case of 1900, or, more often, by suggesting that the entire site should be preserved *in toto*. The medium's transitoriness frequently provoked the wish on the part of the participating public that an enduring feature should be included to prolong the memory of the exhibition – a *clou*, as it were, that would, in due time, become a *souvenir*. However, that the medium's transience was one of its constitutive elements and therefore, by definition, impossible to overcome, was registered by architects and critics alike. The former in particular often opposed this widespread attitude and wondered why the 'permanent-building idea' proved, over and over again, so popular with the public. Writing in 1901, an architect gave expression to his complete bewilderment and disapproval of such a repeated subject of debate, and recommended modesty and reliance on personal memory instead:

> Why have anything material by which to 'remember an exposition'? Why spoil the mental picture? Certainly, no reality can compare with the vision our minds will preserve of these passing splendors, as year by year adds to its charm. For memory is 'always kind'; under her touch staff is as marble, and the errors of artists and architect go unrecorded. The monument she raises to the beautiful work of the world may not be more enduring than brass, but it far surpasses any commemorative thing that our hands can fashion. If only we could be satisfied with it![108]

Barwick also vehemently rejected the idea of erecting permanent exhibition sites as a fundamental violation of Simmel's 'exhibition principle'. 'Their great value', he wrote indignantly when faced with such a proposal, 'would be completely lost, and it is certain, from their very nature, that they could not be of a permanent character.' Only in recent years, under the now ubiquitous heading of sustainability, has the exact opposite principle of an ideal of a continuous, sustained and intensive usage of the site and its structures after the respective exposition's closure come to dominate contemporary exhibition theory and practice.[109]

Second, all expositions were characterized by contrasts and tensions between spaces, places and their representation. Internally, strategies of representation and various levels of meaning overlapped with one another and formed a multitude of different spaces that were all highly condensed, yielding what geographer David Harvey considers a central and characteristic feature of modernity.[110] Space was by no means annihilated, but rather compressed and made consumable for individual visitors through prefabricated itineraries that led through the exhibition grounds, as, for instance, at the 1931 Exposition Coloniale (Figure 7.9). A visit would start with the French colonial possessions, then stop at the pavilions of the foreign nations participating, with a brief interruption at the zoological garden *en route* before concluding at the amusement section, thus circling the Lac Daumesnil in a day. As they moved across the grounds, sightseers could avail themselves of the numerous offers of imaginary, substitutive travel, both in time and across the whole globe.

Externally, space could be transformed into place, and despite the permeability between the exposition venue and the surrounding city, the possibilities for exchange led to a complete inversion. As is often argued, space and place differ precisely in the degree to which they are imbued with meaning and emotion. According to a widely accepted definition, place, unlike space, is subject to a

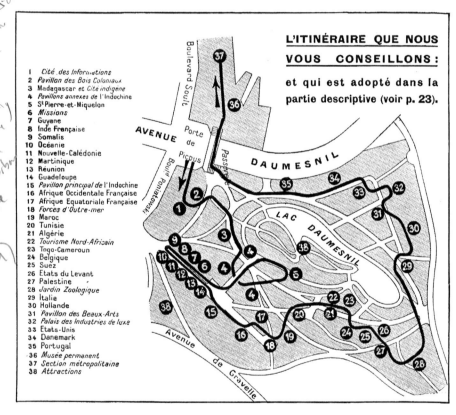

Figure 7.9 Officially suggested itinerary for a trip through the 1931 Exposition Coloniale in Paris
Source: Demaison, *A Paris en 1931*, 10–11.

specific 'aura'. Places are conceptualized as objects to which one feels emotionally attached. They have a meaning for an individual, a social group or an entire culture, and, hence, contrast with the uniform infinity of abstract space.[111] With the single exception of the Berliner Gewerbeausstellung all expositions closely read in this book constituted, in one way or the other, specific moments of transition from space to place. Albeit with different degrees of success, all contributed to the endowment of a particular urban site with such a multiplicity of divergent meanings, transforming it from abstract space into a concrete place. Once again, the best example is the Champ de Mars. This transformative power was further complicated by the fact that expositions were not only spaces of representation but featured themselves as representations of space.

Third, *fin-de-siècle* expositions exhibited 'frozen times' and distant places in an urban setting, and opened up undreamt-of opportunities of traveling in time and space for their visitors. 'Tour the World at the Paris Colonial International Exhibition open until November 1931', an advertisement heralded.[112] While similar offers for imaginative traveling had been present since 1851, the so-called retrospective principle became much more explicit and prevalent towards the end of the nineteenth century, from the mid-1880s onwards. Thus, the 1884 Esposizione Generale Italiana, held in Turin, featured a replica of an entire medieval castle which remained *in situ* for more than a decade, while the 1889 Exposition Universelle included a reproduction of the entire Bastille. The so-called *Old London Street*, forming part of the Colonial and Indian Exhibition held in South Kensington in 1886, already consisted of more than 20 different buildings, all together presenting a *tour de force* journey through English history from Roman occupation to the Great Fire of 1666.[113] Soon after, similar pseudo-historic, often self-contained ensembles – aptly labeled *Old London*, *Oud Antwerp*, *Vieux Paris*, *Alt-Wien* and *Alt-Berlin* – were integral and often very popular parts of each exhibition's standard repertory. For approximately half a century, such imaginary journeys remained limited to traveling backwards in time. Explicit offers for prospective travel in the future were only introduced much later, in an international context at the New York World's Fair of 1939 (whose motto was 'Building the World of Tomorrow') or, in a distinctly European context, at the 1951 Festival of Britain.

To characterize this central feature of *fin-de-siècle* European imperial expositions, this book suggests applying Bakhtin's suggestive 'chronotope' concept. Chronotopes are fictional sites where different times and spaces are brought together, thickened and highly compressed, where activities, stories and events belonging to those different times and spaces are simultaneously staged and enacted, and where they are, ultimately, sold to visitors, spectators and consumers. 'The chronotope', as Bakhtin's editor, Michael Holquist, puts it, 'is an optic for reading texts as x-rays of the forces at work in the culture system from which they spring.' The concept makes it possible to comprehend exhibitions according to the character and ratio of both their temporal and spatial categories without favoring either. Further, it can serve as a tool to isolate and describe the distinct yet contingent set of presuppositions about both time and space that each of these representational mega-events made and remade, and to

Chronotype?.

thematize the time-space ratio materialized in the exhibitions themselves. At the same time, the chronotope helps to locate and contextualize the expositions both diachronically and synchronically – which then, in turn, creates an almost ideal situation to connect a historiography of structures with that of events.[114]

These times and spaces varied in their agendas as much as the political 'messages' which the expositions were supposed to communicate. Implied in these contrasting displays were different political stances concerning historical achievements, the state of civilization and, especially in the case of colonial exhibitions, different stages of progress and prospects for both the mother country and its colonies. Despite such differences, similar offers for time and space traveling were omnipresent and frequently evoked. As a result of the overall, ongoing differentiation of the entire medium over time, these offers became increasingly explicit and elaborate.

Emphasizing the chronotopic character of imperial exhibitions allows for two different strategic moves, opening up further fields of study related to distinct forms of movement and mobility, and thus also to Lefebvre's 'lived' spatial practices. First, it becomes essential to distinguish between various forms of tourism – namely *external* tourism (i.e., traveling *to* the exhibition site) as well as *internal* tourism (i.e., the imaginary journeys *on* the site itself) – and to relate them to questions of consumption and perception on the part of the exhibition-going public. Second, it helps to explain why so much attention was devoted to the creation of both vertical constructions (for instance the Eiffel Tower, the Flip-Flap in London, the projected 'Flywheel' of Wembley or *Angkor Wat* in Vincennes) and horizontal structures (the *trottoir roulant* in Paris, the *Stufenbahn* in Berlin or the 'Never-stop Railway' at Wembley) that tried to combine the organization of perception with movement in space. These techniques for overview were as crucial for the exposition site's internal functioning as they were for providing an otherwise lacking central perspective. Thus, there was a triple movement in time and space. First, exposition venues rotated, with exhibitions held in one different urban location after another. Second, displays, pavilions and sections were situated differently with regard to their representations of time and space. Third, masses of visitors reproduced these pre-structured movements by traveling to, from and on the sites, yet found their individual way on the grounds both horizontally and vertically, embarking on all kinds of imaginary 'tours'. In the end, then, such mobilization of perception corresponded with its temporalization.

While expositions could easily be added to the many similar heterotopic sites where, according to Michel Foucault, 'history unfolds', namely the cemetery, the theater, the cinema, the garden, the zoo, the museum, the library, the brothel, barracks and, of course, the prison, they nevertheless differ from all of these locations through a single common factor of utmost importance: their transient character.[115] The fact that their organizers tried to overcome the medium's inherently fleeting character by issuing thick catalogues and innumerable single volumes, bequeathing carefully designed architectural residuals or incorporating all the exhibits in a museum before the actual exhibition had even been inaugurated, is by no means contradictory. Since 1851, the question of the 'day after' has constituted a highly controversial issue. Yet, what is evident for its spatial characteristics also holds true for the medium's temporal structures. There was a general tendency to overcome its definite limitations and, eventually, to transcend them for good. With regard to the city, it was the exposition that first made use of its spatial context before this relationship was later deliberately inverted. Over time, representation and consumption became increasingly distinct. As Georg Simmel had already argued in his seminal 1896 essay, an increasing specialization in the exhibition field was not accompanied by a similar differentiation on the supply side. Although the medium prefigured its various and contingent meanings and messages, it did not determine its consumption.

Coda: Pictures at an Exhibition

An Weltausstellungen ist es ein eigenthümlicher Reiz, daß sie ein momentanes Centrum der Weltcultur bilden, daß die Arbeit der ganzen Welt sich, wie in einem Bilde, in diese enge Begrenzung zusammengezogen hat.

(Georg Simmel)[1]

Fleeting cities required fixation, if not *in situ* then in pictures. With the precipitous rise of the exposition medium after 1851 came a corresponding surge in pictorial representations of unimaginable scope and variety. These included not only sketches, engravings, oil paintings, billboard advertisements, diagrams and maps, but also photographs, stereoscopic cards, newsreels and films. Only a few years after the invention of photography, the Great Exhibition's official report already contained more than 150 daguerreotype and calotype pictures taken both inside and outside the Crystal Palace. Brief films and newsreels, so-called *actualités*, were first featured 50 years later, at the Paris exposition of 1900. By the interwar period, moving images had become part and parcel of each such mega-event and were an integral element of the global exhibitionary system. Organizers, artists and journalists alike sought to fix and document, communicate and convey their experiences and impressions to a wider public. In order to remember and share these autobiographically momentous occasions, visitors invested in lavishly illustrated souvenir volumes and sent rapturous letters and picture postcards to friends and families at home, even if the visual accuracy of these tangible representations was always open to question.

   The total number of images generated around national and international expositions held in the late nineteenth and early twentieth centuries is mind-boggling. Their sheer existence testifies to the fact that, time and again, the visual character of expositions was overpowering, calling for instant representation and commemoration with the help of the most modern media available. It is these pictorial records that make imaginary visits, such as those undertaken in this study, possible. Featuring a wealth of unpublished or recovered images, the book itself benefits from the existence of a parallel universe of exposition paraphernalia while also promulgating the circulation of these crucial visual remnants.

Images were selected with a view to several criteria. Rather than simply depicting buildings, attractions and sites, their very form serves to argue for the centrality of visuality within the exposition medium. They illustrate, support and supplement the argument made in this text of which they form part. Taken in their entirety, they also convey a multifaceted impression of the expositions' visual character. Ranging from maps to panoramas, from picture postcards to billboard posters, these images represent the variety of pictorial types generated by each exhibition. As a consequence of long exposure times, pictures featuring individual human beings only began to appear in the early decades of the twentieth century, lending the previous corps of images a particular effect of stark monumentality. Pictures taken by private visitors seem to have been less frequent in Europe before the First World War than, for instance, in the United States, where the World's Columbian Exposition of 1893 proved an early, popular picture spot for amateur photographers.

Striving for grandeur and impressive effect, expositions provided an overbearing, and at times overwhelming, visual experience for their consumers. Ultimately, each one eluded adequate and complete representation in the available formats. But while much of their allure escaped documentation, these exhibitions collectively formed a powerful meta-medium that drove the trans-European spectacularity of the *fin-de-siècle* metropolis. As Georg Simmel knew, transience and visuality went hand in hand; both were key features within the rhetoric of imperial modernity. For this reason, expositions became its primary technology, both in Europe and beyond.

Appendix

National and international expositions, 1750–1951, with an emphasis on Western Europe

By chronology

1750–1849

1757	London
1761	Exhibition of Agricultural and other Machines. London
1798	Paris, Champ de Mars
1801	Paris, Louvre
1802	Paris, Louvre
1806	Paris, Palais des Invalides
1819	Paris, Louvre
1820	Ghent
1822	Ausstellung vaterländischer Fabrikate. Berlin
1823	Paris, Louvre
1827	Preußische Gewerbeausstellung. Berlin, Akademiegebäude Unter den Linden
1827	Paris
1830	Brussels
1834	Paris, Place de la Concorde
1835	Liège
1839	Paris, Champs-Elysées
1844	Allgemeine Deutsche Gewerbeausstellung. Berlin, Königliches Zeughaus
1844	Exposition des Produits de l'Industrie Française. Paris, Champs-Elysées
1845	Free Trade Bazaar. London, Covent Garden Theatre
1849	Berliner Gewerbeausstellung. Berlin
1849	Paris, Champs-Elysées

1850–59

1851	Great Exhibition of the Works of Industry of All Nations. London, Hyde Park
1854	Allgemeine Ausstellung Deutscher Industrie- und Gewerbe-Erzeugnisse. Munich
1855	Exposition Universelle des Produits de l'Agriculture, de l'Industrie et des Beaux-Arts. Paris, Champs-Elysées

1860–69

1861	Esposizione Italiana Agraria, Industriale ed Artistica. Florence
1862	International Exhibition of Industry and Art. London, South Kensington
1867	Exposition Universelle. Paris, Champ de Mars

1870–79

1872	London International Exhibition. London, South Kensington
1873	Weltausstellung. Vienna, Prater
1874	International Exhibition of Art and Industry. London, South Kensington
1876	Centennial Exhibition. Philadelphia, Fairmount Park
1878	Exposition Universelle. Paris, Champ de Mars

| 1879 | Berliner Gewerbeausstellung. Berlin-Moabit, Lehrter Bahnhof |
| 1879–80 | International Exhibition. Sydney |

1880–89

1880	Allgemeine Kunst- und Gewerbe-Ausstellung. Düsseldorf
1880–81	International Exhibition. Melbourne
1881	Esposizione Nazionale. Milan
1881	Exposition d'Electricité. Paris, Champs-Elysées, Palais de l'Industrie
1882	Elektrotechnische Ausstellung. Munich
1883	Internationale Koloniale en Uitvoerhandel Tentoonstelling. Amsterdam
1883	Ausstellung auf dem Gebiete der Hygiene und des Rettungswesens. Berlin
1883	Fisheries Exhibition. London, South Kensington
1883–84	International Exhibition. Calcutta
1884	International Health Exhibition. London, South Kensington
1884	Esposizione Generale Italiana. Turin
1885	Inventions Exhibition. London, South Kensington
1885	Exposition Universelle. Antwerp
1886	Colonial and Indian Exhibition. London, South Kensington
1886	Jubiläums-Ausstellung der Bildenden Künste. Berlin
1887	The American Exhibition. London, Earl's Court
1888–89	Centennial International Exhibition. Melbourne
1888	The Italian Exhibition. London, Earl's Court
1888	Exposición Universal. Barcelona
1888	Grand Concours Internationale des Sciences et de l'Industrie. Brussels
1889	Exposition Universelle Internationale. Paris, Champ de Mars

1890–99

1890	The French Exhibition. London, Earl's Court
1890	Nordwest deutsche Gewerbe- und Industrie-Ausstellung. Bremen
1890	International Exhibition of Mining and Metallurgy. London, Crystal Palace at Sydenham
1891	The German Exhibition. London, Earl's Court
1891	Internationale Elektrotechnische Ausstellung. Frankfurt am Main
1891–93	Venice in London. London, Olympia
1892	International Horticultural Exhibition. London, Earl's Court
1892	Electrical Exhibition. London, Crystal Palace at Sydenham
1893	World's Columbian Exposition. Chicago
1893	Photographic Exhibition. London, Crystal Palace at Sydenham
1893	Forestry and Gardening Exhibition. London, Earl's Court
1893	Constantinople. London, Olympia
1894	Exposition International d'Anvers. Antwerp
1894	Exposition Internationale et Coloniale. Lyon
1894	Industrial Exhibition. London, Earl's Court
1895	India: A Grand Historical Spectacle. London, Olympia
1895	Empire of India Exhibition. London, Earl's Court
1895	Wereldtentoonstelling. Amsterdam
1895	South African Exhibition. London, Crystal Palace at Sydenham
1896	Berliner Gewerbeausstellung. Berlin, Treptower Park
1896	Empire of India and Ceylon Exhibition. London, Earl's Court
1897	Victorian Era Exhibition. London, Earl's Court

1897	Exposition Internationale. Brussels
1897	Allmänna Konst- och Industriutställningen. Stockholm, Djurgården
1897	Imperial Victorian Exhibition. London, Crystal Palace at Sydenham
1898	International Universal Exhibition. London, Earl's Court
1898	Esposizione Nazionale Italiana. Turin
1899	Greater Britain Exhibition. London, Earl's Court
1899	Briton, Boer and Black in Savage South Africa. London, Olympia
1899	Savage South Africa Spectacle. London, Earl's Court

1900–09

1900	Exposition Universelle et Internationale. Paris, Champ de Mars
1900	Women's Exhibition. London, Earl's Court
1901	Military Exhibition. London, Earl's Court
1901	Naval and Military Exhibition. London, Crystal Palace at Sydenham
1902	Paris in London Exhibition. London, Earl's Court
1902	Industrie- und Gewerbeausstellung für Rheinland, Westfalen und benachbarte Bezirke, verbunden mit einer deutsch-nationalen Kunst-Ausstellung. Düsseldorf
1902	Esposizione Internazionale d'Arte Decorativa Moderna. Turin
1903	Deutsche Städteausstellung. Dresden
1903	International Fire Exhibition. London, Earl's Court
1904	Italian Exhibition (Venice by Night). London, Earl's Court
1905	Indian and Colonial Exhibition. London, Crystal Palace at Sydenham
1905	Naval, Shipping and Fisheries Exhibition. London, Earl's Court
1905	Exposition Universelle et Internationale. Liège
1906	Exposition Coloniale. Marseilles
1906	Imperial-Royal Austrian Exhibition. London, Earl's Court
1906	Food, Health and Hygiene Exhibition. London, Crystal Palace at Sydenham
1906	Esposizione Internazionale del Sempione. Milan
1907	Palestine in London Exhibition/The Balkan States. London, Earl's Court
1907	Deutsche Armee-, Marine- und Kolonialausstellung in Berlin. Berlin-Schöneberg
1908	Franco-British Exhibition. London, White City
1908	Hungarian Exhibition. London, Earl's Court
1909	Africa and the East. London, Royal Agricultural Hall at Islington
1909	Imperial International Exhibition. London, White City

1910–19

1910	Exposition Universelle et Internationale. Brussels
1910	Allgemeine Städtebau-Ausstellung. Berlin
1910	Japan-British Exhibition. London, White City
1911	Coronation Exhibition of the British Empire. London, White City
1911	1. Internationale Hygiene-Ausstellung. Dresden
1911	Festival of Empire. London, Crystal Palace at Sydenham
1911	Esposizione Internazionale delle Industrie e di Lavoro. Turin
1911	Esposizione Internazionale di Belle Arte. Rome
1912	Latin-British Exhibition. London, White City
1913	Imperial Services Exhibition. London, Earl's Court
1913	Exposition Universelle et Internationale/Wereldtentoonstelling. Ghent
1913	Jahrhundertausstellung. Breslau
1913	National Gas Exhibition and Congress. London, White City
1914	Anglo-American Exhibition. London, White City

1920–29

1922	Exposition Nationale Coloniale. Marseilles
1923	Jubilee Exhibition. Gothenburg
1923	Calcutta Exhibition
1924	Exposition Coloniale, Agricole et Industrielle. Strasbourg
1924–25	British Empire Exhibition Wembley. London, Wembley
1925	Exposition Internationale des Arts Décoratifs et Industriels Modernes. Paris, Champ de Mars
1925	Colonial Exhibition. New Zealand
1926	Antwerp Colonial and International Fair. Antwerp
1926	GESOLEI. Düsseldorf
1927	Colonial Exhibition. Edinburgh
1929–30	Exposición Internacional. Barcelona

1930–39

1930	2. Internationale Hygiene-Ausstellung. Dresden
1930	Exposition Internationale. Antwerp and Liège
1930	Stockholmsutställningen. Stockholm, Djurgården
1931	Exposition Coloniale Internationale. Paris, Vincennes
1933	Deutsche Kolonialausstellung des Reichskolonialbundes. Berlin
1935	Exposition Universelle et Internationale. Brussels
1936	British Empire Exhibition. Johannesburg, South Africa
1936	Deutsche Kolonial-Ausstellung des Reichskolonialbundes. Breslau
1937	Reichsausstellung 'Schaffendes Volk'. Düsseldorf
1937	Exposition Internationale des Arts et Techniques dans la Vie Moderne. Paris, Champ de Mars
1938	Empire Exhibition Scotland. Glasgow, Bellahouston Park
1939	Deutsche Kolonial-Ausstellung. Dresden
1939	Exposition Internationale de l'Eau. Liège
(1942)	Esposizione Universale di Roma (EUR). Rome

Post-1945

1951	Festival of Britain. London, South Bank
1958	Exposition Universelle et Internationale. Brussels

By location (in London, Paris, Berlin)

London

South Kensington

1851	Great Exhibition of the Works of Industry of All Nations
1862	International Exhibition of Industry and Art
1872	London International Exhibition
1874	International Exhibition of Art and Industry
1883	Fisheries Exhibition
1884	International Health Exhibition
1885	Inventions Exhibition
1886	Colonial and Indian Exhibition

Crystal Palace at Sydenham

1890	International Exhibition of Mining and Metallurgy
1892	Electrical Exhibition

1893   Photographic Exhibition
1895   South African Exhibition
1897   Imperial Victorian Exhibition
1901   Naval and Military Exhibition
1905   Indian and Colonial Exhibition
1906   Food, Health and Hygiene Exhibition
1911   Festival of Empire

Olympia Exhibitions

1891–93   Venice in London
1893   Constantinople
1895   India: A Grand Historical Spectacle
1899   Briton, Boer and Black in Savage South Africa

Earl's Court Exhibitions

1887   The American Exhibition
1888   The Italian Exhibition
1890   The French Exhibition
1891   The German Exhibition
1892   International Horticultural Exhibition
1893   Forestry and Gardening Exhibition
1894   Industrial Exhibition
1895   Empire of India Exhibition
1896   Empire of India and Ceylon Exhibition
1897   Victorian Era Exhibition
1898   International Universal Exhibition
1899   Greater Britain Exhibition
1899   Savage South Africa Spectacle
1900   Women's Exhibition
1901   Military Exhibition
1902   Paris in London Exhibition
1903   International Fire Exhibition
1904   Italian Exhibition (Venice by Night)
1905   Naval, Shipping and Fisheries Exhibition
1906   Imperial-Royal Austrian Exhibition
1907   Palestine in London Exhibition/The Balkan States
1908   Hungarian Exhibition
1913   Imperial Services Exhibition

White City Exhibitions

1908   Franco-British Exhibition
1909   Imperial International Exhibition
1910   Japan-British Exhibition
1911   Coronation Exhibition of the British Empire
1912   Latin-British Exhibition
1913   National Gas Exhibition and Congress
1914   Anglo-American Exhibition

Paris

1798	Champ de Mars
1801	Louvre
1802	Louvre
1806	Palais des Invalides
1819	Louvre
1823	Louvre
1827	Paris
1834	Place de la Concorde
1839	Champs-Elysées
1844	Exposition des Produits de l'Industrie Française. Champs-Elysées
1849	Champs-Elysées
1855	Exposition Universelle des Produits de l'Agriculture, de l'Industrie et des Beaux-Arts. Champs-Elysées
1867	Exposition Universelle. Champ de Mars
1878	Exposition Universelle. Champ de Mars, Trocadéro, Quai d'Orsay
1881	Exposition de l'Electricité. Champs-Elysée, Palais de l'Industrie
1889	Exposition Universelle Internationale. Champ de Mars, Trocadéro, Quai d'Orsay, Esplanade des Invalides
1900	Exposition Universelle Internationale. Champ de Mars, Trocadéro, Quai d'Orsay, Cours la Reine, Esplanade des Invalides, Chaillot, Seine, Vincennes
1925	Exposition Internationale des Arts Décoratifs et Industriels Modernes. Champ de Mars, Trocadéro, Champs-Elysées, Place de la Concorde
1931	Exposition Coloniale Internationale. Vincennes
1937	Exposition Internationale des Arts et Techniques dans la Vie Moderne. Champ de Mars, Chaillot, Île de Cygnes, Esplanade des Invalides

Berlin

1822	Ausstellung vaterländischer Fabrikate
1827	Preußische Gewerbeausstellung. Akademiegebäude Unter den Linden
1844	Allgemeine Deutsche Gewerbeausstellung. Königliches Zeughaus
1849	Berliner Gewerbeausstellung
1879	Berliner Gewerbeausstellung. Moabit, Lehrter Bahnhof
1883	Ausstellung auf dem Gebiete der Hygiene und des Rettungswesens
1886	Jubiläums-Ausstellung der Bildenden Künste
1896	Berliner Gewerbeausstellung. Treptower Park
1907	Deutsche Armee-, Marine- und Kolonialausstellung. Schöneberg
1910	Allgemeine Städtebau-Ausstellung
1933	Deutsche Kolonialausstellung des Reichskolonialbundes

Sites, *clous* and residuals, 1851–1951

Date	Venue	Official Title	Site	Clou	Surviving?	Residuals
1851	London	Great Exhibition of the Works of Industry of All Nations	Hyde Park	Crystal Palace	In Sydenham until 1936 when it burned down	South Kensingon/Albertopolis
1855	Paris	Exposition Universelle des Produits de l'Agriculture, de l'Industrie et des Beaux-Arts	Champs-Elysées, Cours la Reine, Carré Marigny, Avenue Montaigne, Champ de Mars	Palais de l'Industrie/Galerie des Machines	Until 1897 when it was demolished for two new Palais des Beaux Arts for the 1900 exposition	Rue de Rivoli
1862	London	International Exhibition of Industry and Art	South Kensington	Industrial Palace	Torn down after the exhibition's closure	South Kensington
1867	Paris	Exposition Universelle	Champ de Mars	Palais d'Exposition	Torn down after the exposition's closure	Champ de Mars
1873	Vienna	Weltausstellung	Prater	Industrial Palace with Rotunda	Burned down in 1937	'New' Prater
1878	Paris	Exposition Universelle	Champ de Mars, Trocadéro, Quai d'Orsay	Palais de l'Industrie/Palais du Trocadéro	Dismantled and recycled after the exposition's closure/remained *in situ* until 1934 when it was replaced by the Palais de Chaillot for the 1937 exposition	–

1886	London	Colonial and Indian Exhibition	South Kensington	Durbar Hall, Indian Palace	No	–
1888	Barcelona	Exposición Universal	Parc de la Ciutadella	Hotel Internacional/Triumphal Arch	Yes	Park
1889	Paris	Exposition Universelle	Champ de Mars, Trocadéro, Quai d'Orsay, Esplanade des Invalides	Eiffel Tower/Galerie des Machines	Yes/demolished in 1910	–
1895	London	The Empire of India Exhibition	Earl's Court	Ferris Wheel/Empress Theater (after 1905 Empress Hall)	No/until 1950s	–
1896	Berlin	Berliner Gewerbeausstellung	Treptower Park	Hauptgebäude	No	Archenhold observatory
1897	Brussels	Exposition Internationale	Parc du Cinquantenaire, Tervuren	–	–	Palais des Colonies was reopened as the Musée du Congo in 1898; processional avenue between Brussels and Tervuren
1900	Paris	Exposition Universelle et Internationale	Champ de Mars, Trocadéro, Quai d'Orsay, Cours la Reine, Esplanade des Invalides, Chaillot, Seine, Vincennes	Grand Palais/Petit Palais/Gare d'Orsay	Yes/yes/yes	Pont Alexandre III, Avenue Nicolas II, Métro

(Continued)

Date	Venue	Official Title	Site	Clou	Surviving?	Residuals
1905	Liège	Exposition Universelle et Internationale	Les Vennes, La Boverie, La Fragnée	–	–	Palais des Beaux Arts (Musée d'Art Moderne et d'Art Contemporaine), Parc d'Acclimatation
1906	Milan	Esposizione Internazionale del Sempione	Parco Real, Piazza d'Armi	Galleria del Sempione	No	(Simplon tunnel)
1908	London	Franco-British Exhibition	White City, Shepherd's Bush	White City/ Stadium	No, but in use as an exhibition venue until 1914/ stadium until 1985	–
1910	Brussels	Exposition Universelle et Internationale	Parc de Solbosch, Bois de la Cambre, Tervuren	Galerie des Machines	No	Gardens
1911	London	Festival of Empire	Crystal Palace and park, Sydenham	Crystal Palace at Sydenham	Burnt down in 1936	–
1913	Ghent	Exposition Universelle et Internationale	Quartier St Pierre	Palais du Congo Belge	No	–

1924–25	London	British Empire Exhibition	Wembley	Empire Stadium	Demolished in 2002	–
1925	Paris	Exposition Internationale des Arts Décoratifs et Industriels Modernes	Champ de Mars, Trocadéro, Champs-Elysées, Place de la Concorde	Grand Palais (from 1900 exposition)	Yes	–
1929–30	Barcelona	Exposición Internacional	Montjuïc Park	Palacio Nacional/sports stadium/German Pavilion (Mies van der Rohe)	Yes/yes (refurbished for the 1992 Olympics)/dismantled after the fair but reconstructed in the 1980s	Park, smaller pavilions, Via Reina Maria Cristina, Plaçe d'Espanyu
1931	Paris	Exposition Coloniale Internationale	Vincennes	Angkor Wat/Musée des Colonies/zoological garden	No/yes/yes	Métro Porte Dorée

(Continued)

Date	Venue	Official Title	Site	Clou	Surviving?	Residuals
1935	Brussels	Exposition Universelle et Internationale	Plateau du Heysel	Grand Palais/ Stadium	Yes/yes	Tram
1937	Paris	Exposition Internationale des Arts et Techniques dans la Vie Moderne	Champ de Mars, Chaillot, Île de Cygnes, Esplanade des Invalides, Grand Palais	Palais de Chaillot/Palais Tokyo	Yes/yes	Musée d'Art Moderne
1938	Glasgow	Empire Exhibition	Bellahouston Park	Tower of Empire (Tait Tower)	Demolished in July 1939	Palace of Art
1951	London	Festival of Britain	South Bank	Dome of Discovery/ Skylon	No/no	Royal Festival Hall, redevelopment of South Bank

Dramatis personae[1]

Name	*/†	Biographical Information and Exposition Participation
Abercrombie, Sir Leslie Patrick	1879–1957	British town planner. Long-time editor of *Town Planning Review*. 1915–35 Lever Professor of Civic Design at Liverpool University, 1935–46 Professor of Town Planning at University College, London. President of Town Planning Institute. Prepared large-scale post-war schemes for rebuilding and planning London after the Second World War (County of London Plan, 1943; Greater London Plan, 1944). Noted architectural critic and often compared to →Sir Patrick Geddes.
Allen, Col. Hon. Sir James	1855–1942	Politician in New Zealand. 1891–1920 MP for Bruce, New Zealand; 1912–20 Minister of Defense, New Zealand; 1912–25 Minister of Finance and Education; 1919–20 Minister of External Affairs and Finance; 1920–26 high commissioner in London for New Zealand; 1920–26 member of Legislative Council in New Zealand. Member of Board of British Empire Exhibition (chairman: →Lord Stevenson); representative of the high commissioners for overseas dominions. Championed imperial cooperation and the sanctity of British imperialism.
Alphand, Jean-Charles-Adolphe	1817–1891	French engineer, administrator and town planner. Worked in Bordeaux until Georges-Eugène Haussmann made him move to Paris where he worked as one of his closest collaborators. 1857 *Ingénieur en chef*; 1861 *Directeur administratif des promenades*; 1867 *Directeur de la voie publique et des promenades*; 1869 *Inspecteur général des ponts et chaussées*. 1891 member of the *Académie des beaux-arts*. Responsible for numerous urban development programs. Participated in Paris 1855 exposition; principal organizer of Paris expositions 1867 and 1878. Together with →Georges Berger and →Alfred Picard one of the three *Directeurs générals* at Paris 1889 exposition (*Directeur général des travaux*).
Angoulvant, Gabriel	1872–1932	First general governor of *Afrique equatoriale française*. First *Commissaire général* of Paris 1931 exposition, but resigned later and then suceeded by →Maréchal Lyautey.
Askwith, George Ranken, Lord	1861–1942	Civil servant and industrial arbitrator. Held numerous international positions for British government as one of its leading conciliator and adviser on industrial relations: 1907 assistant secretary, Board of Trade; British plenipotentiary to International Congress on Copyright at Berlin 1908; 1911 chief industrial commissioner. Head of the Board of Trade's Commercial Department to which the Exhibitions Branch was attached, hence superior of →Sir Alfred Edmund Bateman and →Ulick Wintour. Chairman of Council of the Royal Society of Arts (1922–24), Treasurer (1925–27), and vice-president (1927–41).

(Continued)

Name	*/†	Biographical Information and Exposition Participation
Ayrton, Ormrod Maxwell	1874–1960	Together with →John W. Simpson architectural director of the British Empire Exhibition; designed Empire Stadium and British pavilion for the Exposiçao Internacional do Centenario do Brasil, held in Rio de Janeiro in 1922–23.
Barnum, Phineas Taylor	1810–1891	American impresario and circus showman, mostly based in New York City. Organized a wide variety of popular spectacles, engaged in so-called freak shows and made – after having it imported from the Royal Zoological Society in London – the African elephant Jumbo an all-American star. In 1889, Barnum moved to London, where he exhibited his show at Olympia and collaborated with →Imre Kiralfy; cooperated also with →Carl Hagenbeck.
Barrès, Maurice	1862–1923	Conservative French politician, writer and journalist. 1889–93 *député* in Nancy. Opposed Paris 1900 exposition. Since 1906 member of the *Chambre* and the *Académie française*. Self-declared nationalist.
Barwick, George Frederick	1853–1931	Museum curator, editor and Keeper of Printed Books in the British Museum, London. Published one of the first articles on theoretical aspects of exhibitions.
Bateman, Sir Alfred Edmund	1844–1929	British barrister, civil servant and writer. Joint manager of the Imperial Institute 1905–16. Chairman of the International Exhibitions Committee set up by the Board of Trade in 1906–07. British chairman at Exhibitions Conference in Berlin 1912.
Belcher, Major Ernest Albert	1871–1949	Major in the military and exhibition organizer. Assistant general manager and later Controller of General Service of the British Empire Exhibition 1924–25.
Benjamin, Walter	1892–1940	German philosopher, critic, writer. One of the most influential cultural critics of the early twentieth century. Independent scholar and author in Berlin before emigrating to Paris in 1933. His planned *opus magnum Passagen-Werk* was to assemble the collective phantasmagorias of the past metropolitan world. Threatened with extradition to Nazi Germany, Benjamin committed suicide in Port Bou in 1940.

Berger, Paul Louis Georges	1834–1910	French engineer. Collaborated with →Frédéric Le Play in organizing the 1867 Paris exposition. Organized foreign sections at Paris 1878 exposition. Together with →Jean-Charles-Adolphe Alphand and →Alfred Picard one of the three *Directeurs générals* in 1889. *Membre de la commission supérieure* at Paris 1900 exposition. Organized Exposition d'Electricité 1881 in Paris, and presided over French sections at Amsterdam exhibition 1869, Melbourne exhibition 1880–81, Amsterdam exhibition 1883 and Antwerp exhibition 1885. After 1889 *député* in Paris. Frequent contributor to professional journals such as *Génie civil*.
Berger, H. Georges	?	French lawyer. Wrote his *Thèse pour le doctorat* on historical and legal aspects of French Expositions Universelles. Son of →Georges Berger, one of the three *Directeurs généráls* at Paris 1889 exposition.
Birdwood, Sir George Christopher Molesworth	1832–1917	British administrator in India, colonial civil servant and writer. MD and member of Royal College of Surgeons, later member of India Office. In charge of the Indian exhibits at Paris 1867 exposition; responsible for Indian collections at South Kensington exhibitions and all principal international exhibitions of the period. Friend of and historical advisor to →Imre Kiralfy.
Blyth, Arthur, Lord	?	Chairman of the Organization Committee at →Imre Kiralfy's London 1908 and 1910 exhibitions; vice-president of the British Empire Exhibition 1924–25.
Bobertag, Georg	?	Advocate for a German universal exhibition; former mayor.
Bouvard, Joseph Antoine	1840–1920	French architect. Designed *Pavillon de la Ville de Paris* at Paris 1878 exposition, the *Dôme central* at Paris 1889 exposition and director of architectural works at Paris 1900 exposition.
Brandt, Lambertus Otto	1868–1927 (?)	Syndic of chamber of commerce in Düsseldorf, industrialist and member of municipal council. Involved in organizing trade fair held in Düsseldorf in 1902; published important article on the history of expositions in 1904.
Brockhoff, Albert	?–1902	German journalist in Berlin, wrote for *Berliner Lokalanzeiger*.

(Continued)

Name	*/†	Biographical Information and Exposition Participation
Bucher, Lothar	1817–1892	German journalist; later statesman and civil servant. Political refugee in London where he worked as correspondent for the *National-Zeitung*. Participant observer in London 1851 on which he reported extensively in the German press; collected articles later published as *Kulturhistorische Skizzen aus der Industrieausstellung aller Völker*.
Carden, Robert Walter	?–1926	British architect and architectural critic. Published on Esposizione Internazionale del Sempione, held in Milan in 1906, and on the 1908 Franco-British Exhibition.
Casson, Sir Hugh Maxwell	1910–1999	British architect and architectural writer. Joined the Ministry of Town and Country Planning in 1944. Director of Architecture for the 1951 Festival of Britain held in London. Knighted in 1952 for his work on the Festival. 1960–83 member of the Royal Fine Arts Commission; 1975–84 president of the Royal Academy.
Cavendish, Victor Christian William, 9th Duke of Devonshire	1868–1938	Politician and Governor-General of Canada (1916–22); 1922–25 secretary of state for the Colonies. 1891–1908 MP for west Derbyshire. Succeeded →Earl of Derby in 1908 as president of the British Empire League. Involved in the organization of the British Empire Exhibition and one of its principal financial guarantors.
Chardon, Henri	1861–1939	French administrator and *maître des requêtes* of the *Conseil d'Etat*. *Secrétaire général* and delegate to the Fine Arts Section at Paris 1900 exposition. Close collaborator of →Alfred Picard; presented first project for construction of Pont Alexandre III as well as *Grand* and *Petit Palais*.
Charles-Roux, Jules	1841–1918	*Ancien député*, businessman, banker, provincial legislator and president of the *Société de géographie de Marseilles*; *Délégué des ministères des affaires étrangères et des colonies* and main organizer of colonial section at Paris 1900 exposition; *Commissaire général* of colonial exposition in Marseilles 1906.
Clarke, Lieut.-Gen. Sir Travers Edward	1871–1962	Lieutenant-General and transport expert; participated in First World War. 1919–23 Quartermaster-General to the Armed Forces and member of the Army Council. 1923–25 deputy chairman of the Board and chief administrative officer of the British Empire Exhibition (chairman: →Lord Stevenson).

Cockburn, Sir John Alexander	1850–1929	Physician and colonial politician. Born in London, settled in South Australia in 1875. Mayor of Jamestown; Minister of Education and Agriculture. Representative of South Australia at numerous international congresses, conferences and expositions. Vice-chairman of the Executive Committee of the Franco-British Exhibition; member of the Executive Council of the British Empire Exhibition.
Cole, Sir Henry [pseud. Felix Summerly]	1808–1882	British civil servant and editor. 1838–73 Senior Assistant Keeper of Public Record Office. Chairman of the Council of the Society for the Encouragement of Arts, Manufacture, and Commerce. Executive Commissioner for the Great Exhibition of 1851; general adviser to the exhibition of 1862; acting commissioner and secretary to the Royal Commission for Great Britain at Paris expositions 1855 and 1867; acting commissioner for South Kensington international exhibitions 1870–74. At the center of the group which organized the 1851 exhibition. Worked for 20 years to make South Kensington/Albertopolis complex a national center for the arts and sciences. By the time of his retirement in 1873, it consisted of the Museum, various schools, the Albert Hall, and the gardens of the Royal Horticultural Society, with Cole himself being nicknamed 'King Cole' by the general public.
Cole, Sir Henry Walter George	1870–1932	Grandson of →Sir Henry Cole. Lieutenant-Colonel. British commissioner general at International Exhibition Rio de Janeiro 1922; chairman of the Committee for Government Participation at British Empire Exhibition 1924. Director of the Exhibition Divisions of the Department of Overseas Trade in 1924. British commissioner general for Paris 1925 and Antwerp 1930 exhibitions.
Coubertin, Pierre Baron de	1862–1937	Initiated campaign for revival of Olympic Games in 1887. Secretary of the French Union of Athletic Sports and subsequently founder of the modern Olympic movement; long-term president of the *Comité international olympique*. Participated in Paris 1900 exhibition.
Cremieu-Javal, Paul	1857–1927	British Foreign consul-general. Chairman of The London Exhibitions Ltd. Collaborated with →Harold T. Hartley and →Imre Kiralfy in establishing Earl's Court as an exhibition center after 1894.

(Continued)

Name	*/†	Biographical Information and Exposition Participation
Cunliffe-Owen, Sir Francis Philip	1828–1894	British exhibition organizer and museum director. 1857 Deputy general superintendent of the newly established South Kensington Museum; 1860 assistant director, subordinate to →Henry Cole with whom he closely collaborated and whom succeeded in the directorship of the museum (1873–93). Superintendent of the British section of the Paris 1855 exposition; director of Foreign Sections at London 1862 exhibition; assistant executive commissioner for Paris 1867 exposition; secretary of the Royal Commission appointed to represent Britain at Vienna 1873 exhibition; executive commissioner for Great Britain at Philadelphia 1876 world's fair; secretary of the Royal Commission at Paris 1878 exposition; director of South Kensington exhibitions held in London 1883–86; commissioner for India and secretary of the Royal Commission for the Colonial and Indian Exhibition in London 1886.
Delbrück, Hans G.L.	1848–1929	Prussian historian and professor of history at Friedrich-Wilhelms-Universität, Berlin (1881 *Habilitation*; 1885 chair). 1882–85 member of Prussian parliament; 1884–90 member of *Reichstag*; 1883–1919 editor of *Preußische Jahrbücher*. Outspoken opponent of German *Weltausstellungsfrage* and convinced critic of expositions.
Delbrück, Rudolf von	1817–1903	Prussian civil servant, statesman and one the principal architects of Prussian economic policy. Participated at New York 1853 world's fair, Paris 1855 exposition, London 1862 exhibition and Paris 1867 exposition as president or vice-president of the respective Prussian commissions.
Demaison, André	1883–1956	French colonial author and journalist who wrote introduction to 1931 *Guide officiel*. Known as the 'French Kipling'.
Démy, Adolphe	?	French consul, writer and author. Published one of the first comprehensive surveys on international exhibitions, the 1100-page long *Essai historique sur les Expositions universelles de Paris* (1907).
Dupont, Emile-Adrien	1848–1922	French politician and company owner. Commissioner at Paris expositions 1899 and 1900, main organizer of the French section at St Louis world's fair 1904. Senator of Oise after January 1906. First vice-president, then president of the *Comité français des expositions à l'étranger*; first chairman of the *Fédération internationale des comités permanents*.
Eiffel, Gustave Alexandre	1832–1923	French engineer (but not an architect). Specialized in constructing metal works, and received a *Grand Prix* at Paris 1878 exposition. 1886 winner of competition for 1889 exhibition; created *La Tour de 300 mètres*. Authored numerous scientific works attempting to prove the usefulness of the Eiffel Tower for research.

Eitelberger, Rudolf von	1817–1885	Austrian art historian, since 1852 professor. Initiator and subsequently director of Österreichiches *Museum für Kunst und Industrie* in Vienna. Influential art critic.
Elvin, Sir Arthur James	1899–1957	British entrepreneur and sports promoter. Cigarette salesman at the British Empire Exhibition 1924–25. Took over control of the entire site in 1927, supervised demolition process, and closely collaborated with chief engineer →Owen Williams in transforming Wembley stadium into a sports ground especially known for its greyhound races. Had Williams build the Empire Pool in 1933–34. Having visited the 1936 Olympic Games in Berlin, Elvin aimed at organizing them in Wembley which he finally achieved in 1948.
Exner, Wilhelm Franz	1840–1931	Austrian civil servant, publicist, critic and member of parliament. Since 1875 professor in Vienna; founder and first director of *K.K. Technologisches Museum für Industrie und Gewerbe* in Vienna. Commissioner and jury member of London 1862 exhibition and Paris 1867 exposition. Commissioner general for Austria at Paris 1900 exposition. Visited exhibitions include London 1862, Paris 1867, Vienna 1873, Paris 1878, Paris 1900.
Eyth, Max	1836–1906	Engineer, technician and writer. Committee member of *Deutsche Landwirtschaftsgesellschaft* (DLG), which he had founded in 1895. Organized numerous agricultural touring exhibitions. Represented British machinery companies at exhibitions in London 1862, Vienna 1873, Paris 1878; participated in Paris 1900 exposition.
Felisch, Bernhard	1839–1913	Architect and member of Prussian parliament since 1895. Together with →Fritz Kühnemann and →Ludwig Max Goldberger vice-chairman of the Berliner Gewerbeausstellung's *Arbeitsausschuss*.
Ford, Ford Madox	1873–1939	German-British writer, close collaborator of writer Joseph Conrad. Born Ford Madox Hueffer. Published *The Soul of London: A Survey of a Modern City* in 1905.
Geddes, Sir Patrick	1854–1932	Renowned Scottish biologist, sociologist, and pioneer of modern urban planning. Held a chair in botany at the University of Dundee, Scotland (1889–1919); after 1919 Professor of Sociology and Civics at the University of Bombay. Visited and wrote on numerous expositions such as Paris 1878, Paris 1900 and Ghent 1913. Set up his own Cities and Town Planning Exhibition in 1911. 'Revolutionary conservative' (Helen Meller) who was strongly influenced by →Le Play in his thinking on human society and in the development of his own theory of 'civics'.

(Continued)

Name	*/†	Biographical Information and Exposition Participation
Giedion, Sigfried	1888–1968	Swiss art historian. Founder-member of the *Congrès Internationaux d'Architecture Moderne* (CIAM) in Zurich and from 1938 Professor of Art History at Harvard University. Published standard work *Space, Time, and Architecture* in 1941 (numerous editions) and directly involved in debate on 'exhibition fatigue'.
Goldberger, Ludwig Max	1848–1913	German banker, involved in economic policy. *Geheimer Kommerzienrat* and 1892–1901 president of the *Verein Berliner Kaufleute und Industrieller*. Together with →Fritz Kühnemann and →Bernhard Felisch vice-chairman of the *Arbeitsausschuss* of the Berliner Gewerbeausstellung in 1896. Had an audience with the president of the French Republic on the occasion of Paris 1900 exposition where non-civil servant Germans were received for the first time after 30 years (23 May 1900). Published metaphor-inventing book *Das Land der unbegrenzten Möglichkeiten* on the United States in 1903 after extensive period of traveling. First and long-term president of the *Ständige Ausstellungskommission für die deutsche Industrie* (1906–13).
Gomme, Sir George Laurence	1853–1916	Public servant, municipal administrator and folklorist. Joined Metropolitan Board of Works in 1873, then worked for the newly created LCC, after 1900 as its clerk, or chief administrative officer. Secured the LCC's participation in the Survey of London and was involved in setting up the commemorative blue plaque scheme (1901). Wrote several books on London.
Grisebach, Hans	1848–1904	German architect; together with →Karl Hoffacker and →Bruno Schmitz one of the three main architects of the Berliner Gewerbeausstellung.
Grothe, Hermann	1839–1885	Civil engineer, editor and member of German *Reichstag*. Managing director of *Centralverband Deutscher Industrieller*. Visited more than 30 expositions including the Philadelphia world's fair of 1876.
Hagenbeck, Carl	1844–1913	Hamburg-based animal trader, entrepreneur and impresario. Organizer of numerous *Völkerschauen* and founder of his own zoological garden in Hamburg-Stellingen in 1907. Cooperated with →Phineas Taylor Barnum. Participated at exhibitions in Chicago 1893, Berlin 1896, St Louis 1904 and London 1908. Company participated also in Paris 1931 exposition where it advised the organizers on the enclosures and their construction, and supplied animals to the zoo.

Hartley, Harold T.	1851–1943	British magazine publisher, art collector, mineral water-producer and exhibition expert. Invited →Imre Kiralfy to emigrate from USA to Europe, and to found and establish with him Earl's Court as an exhibition center. Organized majority of exhibitions held there between 1895 and 1908 together with →Paul Cremieu-Javal and continued to do so after Kiralfy had left their company in 1906. Director of London exhibitions such as Venice in London (1891–93), India (1895), Victorian Era (1897), Greater Britain (1899), Military (1901). Published his memoirs *Eighty-Eight Not Out* in 1939.
Haussmann, Georges-Eugène	1809–1891	French administrator. 1853–70 *Préfet de la Seine* in Paris und Napoléon III, from 1857 member of the *Sénat*. Most influential nineteenth-century Parisian 'town planner' *avant la lettre* who completely restructured the city's geography, within 17 years, through the building of grand avenues, the design of the two *bois* and the creation of a circular railway line around Paris to allow for better communication.
Hénard, Gaston Charles Eugène	1849–1923	French architect and one of the first specialists in town planning and urbanism. One of the main architects at Paris expositions of 1889 and 1900. Had obtained first prize in 1895 competition for proposing the prolongation of the *Invalides* axe by building a new bridge (Pont Alexandre III), leading up to the junction with the Champs-Elysées; held an appointment in the *Travaux de Paris*, the office that directed public works. Designed *Palais d'Electricité* and *Salle des Illusions* in 1900. Participated in London Town Planning Conference in 1910, and at exhibitions held in Berlin 1910, Turin 1911 and Düsseldorf 1912.
Hillger, Hermann	1865–1945	Writer, editor of journal *Die Gegenwart* and author of a much-praised book on the Chicago 1893 exhibition where he had served as the German secretary general. Triggered third and final phase of German *Weltausstellungsfrage* in 1909. 1925–32 member of Prussian parliament.

(Continued)

Name	*/†	Biographical Information and Exposition Participation
Hoffacker, Karl	1856–1919	Renowned German exhibition architect and engineer. Participated and designed sections at Chicago world's fair 1893 (member of the German *Reichskommission*; designed German section/ *Deutsches Dorf*); Berlin 1896 exhibition (designed *Thor-Gebäude, Gebäude für Wohlfahrt und Unterricht, Verwaltungsgebäude, Gebäude für Fischerei und Nahrungsmittel, Alt-Berlin*, amongst numerous others), Paris 1900 exposition (arts and crafts; member of the German *Reichskommission*), Düsseldorf 1902 exhibition and St Louis 1904 world's fair. Together with →Hans Grisebach and →Bruno Schmitz, one of the three main architects of 1896 Berliner Gewerbeausstellung.
Hoyer, Egbert Ritter von	1836–1920	1877–1900 Professor for Mechanical Technology at Technische Hochschule München, 1894–1900 director. 1877 involved in revision of patent law and in promotion of industry.
Huber, Franz Caspar	1851–1913	Civil servant and professor. Secretary of chamber of commerce in Stuttgart. Prolific author and exhibition critic.
Jaffé, Franz	1855–1937	German architect and interior designer. Decorated German sections at Melbourne 1888–98, Chicago 1893 and Paris 1900 expositions, reported on Berlin 1896 exhibition in various national newspapers and published a lengthy encyclopedia article on exhibition buildings and their architecture in 1906.
Jaussely, Léon	1875–1932	French architect. Trained at the *Ecole des Beaux-Arts* in Toulouse and winner of the 1903 *Prix de Rome d'architecture* who did pioneering work as an urban designer before 1914. First chief architect of Paris 1931 exposition, before he became too ill, so that →Albert Tournaire was appointed as his successor in 1927. Designed various early schemes and, together with →Albert Laprade, the *Musée des colonies*. Long-term president of the *Société des architectes urbanistes français*.
Kerr, Alfred	1867–1948	German journalist, feature writer and theater critic. Reported extensively on 1896 Berliner Gewerbeausstellung in his letters published regularly in the *Breslauer Zeitung*.
Kiralfy, Albert Enrico	1878–1967	→Imre Kiralfy's second son, involved in organizing spectacle plays and exhibitions since 1898.
Kiralfy, Bolossy	1847–1932	Producer of spectacles, especially at Olympia. Brother of →Imre Kiralfy.

Kiralfy, Charles I.	?	→Imre Kiralfy's first son. Assisted in stage productions; associated with Kiralfy's shows since the early 1890s.
Kiralfy, Imre	1845–1919	Exhibition organizer and impresario. Hungarian, married to an Englishwoman. Lived in Brussels, New York City, Chicago and London where he eventually became director-general at Earl's Court in 1895. Created and designed White City in west London (1908) and the stadium (1908–86) for the Olympic Games. Visited Paris 1867 exposition, Philadelphia 1876 world's fair, Paris 1889 exposition, Chicago 1893 world's fair and Berlin 1896 exhibition. Collaborated, among others, with →Phineas Taylor Barnum and →Pierre Baron de Coubertin. Had three sons: →Charles I. Kiralfy, →Albert E. Kiralfy, and Gerald A. Kiralfy.
Koch, Alexander	1860–1939	German publisher, editor and art critic. Together with →Hermann Muthesius, →Friedrich Naumann and many others involved in the foundation of the *Deutscher Werkbund* in 1907 which he had already suggested in 1901.
Kraemer, Hans	1870–1938 (?)	German writer, publisher and industrialist. Edited best-selling works such as *Das XIX. Jahrhundert in Wort und Bild* (4 vols, 1900). Since 1906 member of the *Ständige Ausstellungskommission für die Deutsche Industrie*. President of the *Deutsches Ausstellungs- und Messeamt*.
Kühnemann, Max Eugen Fritz	1840–1917	Civil servant, industrialist and *Geheimer Regierungsrat*. Main organizer of 1879 Berlin trade fair. Together with →Ludwig Max Goldberger and →Bernhard Felisch chairman of *Arbeitsausschuss* of 1896 Berliner Gewerbeausstellung.
Laprade, Albert	1883–1978	French architect. Gained firsthand experience with Moroccan architecture while serving under →Lyautey's protectorate between 1915 and 1919. Designed the Morocco pavilion and, with →Léon Jaussely, the *Musée des colonies* at Paris 1931 exposition. 1932–60 chief architect for civil buildings and national edifices in Paris.
Lessing, Julius	1843–1908	Art historian and director of the Berliner Kunstgewerbemuseum after 1872. Visited and published on Paris 1867 exposition, Vienna 1873 exhibition, Paris 1878 exposition (having previously written a pamphlet entitled *Ein Wort gegen das Projekt der Pariser Weltausstellung*), Berlin 1896 exhibition and Paris 1900 exposition. The same year his *Das halbe Jahrhundert der Weltausstellungen* appeared, a general interim report after 50 years of universal exhibitions.

(Continued)

Name	*/†	Biographical Information and Exposition Participation
Levey, George Collins	1835–1919	Journalist, compiler, editor and member of the Legislative Assembly in Victoria, Australia. Commissioner for Victoria at exhibitions in London 1873, Vienna 1873, Melbourne 1875, Philadelphia 1876, Paris 1878, Sydney 1879, Melbourne 1880–81, Amsterdam 1883; secretary to Colonial Committee of British Royal Commission to Paris Exhibition 1900.
Lindenberg, Paul	1859–1943	German journalist (*Deutsche Rundschau*), writer and editor. Reported on numerous major expositions between 1880 and 1914. War correspondent during First World War.
Lüders, Karl Wilhelm	1823–1896	German merchant, ethnographer und director of Museum für Völkerkunde in Hamburg. Intervened in German debate on *Weltausstellungsfrage*.
Lutyens, Sir Edwin Landseer	1869–1944	Influential and internationally renowned British architect. Designed British pavilions for Paris 1900 exposition and for Rome 1911 exhibition (subsequently rebuilt as the British School); member of Committee to advise government of India on site of (New) Delhi in 1911–12; architect for Government House, Imperial Delhi; one of principal architects for the Imperial War Graves Commission (1917 'War Stone' and Cenotaph; 1927–32 memorial to the missing of the Somme at Thiepval). Designed Queen's Doll's House for British Empire Exhibition 1924–25. Among the fellow architects who praised his work in public long before Lutyens had become a national figure were →Hermann Muthesius (in 1904) and →Lawrence Weaver (in 1913).
Lyautey, Louis Hubert Gonzalve	1854–1934	*Maréchal de France*. Participated in the conquests of several of France's most important colonies including Indochina, Madagascar and Morocco. Colonial administrator of Morocco (1912–25). The so-called Lyautey method stood for pacification and/or security, but also respect for local beliefs, traditions, habits and political alignments. 1916 French Minister for War. *Commissaire général* at Paris 1931 exposition.
Malkowsky, Georg	1851–1921	German art critic and writer. Published lavishly illustrated volume on Paris 1900 exposition with numerous contributions.
Meier-Graefe, Julius Alfred	1867–1935	German writer and art historian. Involved in numerous art exhibitions such as the Jahrhundertausstellung deutscher Kunst held in Berlin in 1906. Lived in Paris and published extensively on the Paris exposition of 1900.

Meinecke, Gustav Hermann	1854–1903	German colonial politician and writer. Propagandist for German colonial cause; 1887–99 editor of *Deutsche Kolonialzeitung*. Published official report on colonial section of Berlin 1896 exhibition and wrote a popular guide to that section.
Morand, Paul Emile Charles Ferdinand	1888–1976	French diplomat, poet and screenwriter. Served at various French embassies in London, Rome, Madrid and Siam. 1939–40 *Chef de la mission française économique* in the United Kingdom. Active supporter of the Vichy regime. 1944 ambassador in Bern, Switzerland. Wrote on Paris expositions of 1900 and 1931.
Muthesius, Hermann	1861–1927	German architect, writer and one of the founders, later secretary (until 1916) of the *Deutscher Werkbund* which he had set up in 1907 together with →Friedrich Naumann, →Alexander Koch and many others. 1891 *Regierungsbaumeister* in Berlin; 1896–1903 architectural attaché to the German embassy in London, afterwards appointed by Wilhelm II to the Ministry of Finance. Reported on Paris 1900 exposition. Inspired by the British arts and crafts-movement, he contributed to building of *Gartenstadt Hellerau* in Dresden (1910).
Naumann, Friedrich	1860–1919	German pastor, political theorist, liberal journalist and politician (member of the *Reichstag*), with pronounced interest in social and Christian issues. Founded in 1896 the *Nationalsozialer Verein* and subsequently edited its official organ *Die Hilfe*. Together with →Hermann Muthesius, →Alexander Koch and many co-founder of the *Deutscher Werkbund* in 1907. Visited exhibitions in Berlin 1896, Paris 1900, Düsseldorf 1902 and Brussels 1910. Published an important article *Die Kunst im Zeitalter der Maschine* (1904) and reported extensively on a number of national and international exhibitions in his *Ausstellungsbriefe* (1909).
Olivier, Marcel	1879–1945	Colonial military officer, in French West Africa and Governor General in Madagascar from 1924 to 1930 (for an account of his experiences there, see his *Six ans de politique sociale à Madagascar*). Delegate general at the 1931 Paris exposition and responsible for editing its multi-volume *rapport général*.
Paquet, Alfons	1881–1944	German economist, author, publisher, journalist and correspondent of *Frankfurter Zeitung*. Author of influential dissertation on history of European expositions prior to 1908. Visited and wrote on St Louis 1904 world's fair and Liège 1905 exposition. Extensive number of publications up to his death. Wrote important PhD thesis *Das Ausstellungsproblem in der Volkswirtschaft* (1908).

(Continued)

Name	*/†	Biographical Information and Exposition Participation
Paxton, Sir Joseph	1803–1865	British landscape gardener and architect; became known for his design of the Crystal Palace, built in Hyde Park on the occasion of the 1851 Great Exhibition. Superintended re-erection of altered version in Sydenham between 1853 and 1854, later becoming director of gardens there.
Picard, Alfred-Maurice	1844–1913	French engineer, administrator and civil servant; member of the *Conseil d'Etat* since 1881; since 1885 president of the Parisian Departments of Public Works, Agriculture, and Commerce. Participated in Paris 1878 exposition. Together with →Jean-Charles-Adolphe Alphand and →Georges Berger one of the three *directeurs généraux* at Paris 1889 exposition; as its official historian he wrote an influential report in ten volumes. *Commissaire général* at Paris 1900 exposition. 1908 Minister of Naval Affairs. 1912 vice-president of *Conseil d'Etat* (as a reward for his work in 1889 and 1900).
Planat, Paul	1839–1911	*Rédacteur en Chef* of *Construction Moderne*. Reported extensively on Paris 1900 exposition.
Le Play, Pierre Guillaume Frédéric	1806–1882	French economist, engineer, social scientist and politician. Organized and responsible for Paris 1867 exposition. Convinced Saint-Simonian.
Poppović, Alexander	?	Austrian commissioner and assistant delegate at Paris 1900 exposition and St Louis 1904 world's fair.
Reuleaux, Franz	1829–1905	Engineer, 'machine philosopher' and professor, first in Zurich (1856), then in Berlin (1868) where he became director of the Berliner Gewerbeakademie. Exhibitions which he visited include London 1862, Paris 1867, Vienna 1873, Philadelphia 1876, Sydney 1879 and Melbourne 1880–81. Official commissioner for German sections at Philadelphia world's fair 1876, Sydney exhibition 1879 and Melbourne exhibition 1880–81. Caused huge public controversy when condemning German section in Philadelphia 1876 as 'billig und schlecht' (cheap and nasty) in one of his *Ausstellungsbriefe* (1877).
Reusche, Friedrich		Author, critic and editor of *Deutsche Weltausstellungs-Bibliothek*.
Reynaud, Paul	1878–1966	French lawyer and prominent politician in the interwar period; *député* (Paris 1919–24), Minister of Finance (1930, 1938–40) and of Justice; Minister of the Colonies at the time of Paris 1931 exposition. Penultimate Prime Minister of the Third Republic and vice-president of the Alliance démocratique.

Name	Dates	Description
Richter, Max	1856–1921	*Geheimer Oberregierungsrat* and undersecretary of state in the Prussian Ministry of Commerce, then of the Interior. General commissioner for Germany at Chicago 1893 world's fair and Paris 1900 exposition.
Robida, Albert	1848–1926	Prolific French author, artist, caricaturist and designer who played a central role in the French conservation and architectural heritage movement, and who also wrote several early science fiction-novels. Responsible for *Vieux Paris* at Paris exposition of 1900. Published two guidebooks to accompany the display.
Roche, Jules	1841–1923	French economist, journalist and politician; Minister of Commerce and Industry in 1892.
Sala, George Augustus	1828–1895	Victorian journalist, writer and artist; educated in France. Wrote numerous books, several of which, including *The House that Paxton Built* (1851) on the Crystal Palace, carried what was to become his familiar *nom de plume*, G.A.S., a household name. Worked for Thackeray and Dickens. Visited and published extensively on London 1851 exhibition, London 1862 exhibition, Paris 1867 exposition, Paris 1878 exposition, London 1886 exhibition and Paris 1889 exposition as special foreign correspondent for *Daily Telegraph* and *Illustrated London News*.
Schmitz, Bruno	1858–1916	Together with →Hans Grisebach and →Karl Hoffacker one of the three main architects of 1896 Berliner Gewerbeausstellung (responsible for *Hauptgebäude* and *Haupthalle*). Designed nationalist monuments such as *Deutsches Eck* in Koblenz (1894–97) and *Völkerschlachtdenkmal* in Leipzig (1898–1913).
Schweinitz und Krain, Hans-Hermann Graf von	1865–1929	General and Commander of German colonial troops. Chairman of the special *Arbeitsausschuss* of the colonial exhibition 1896 in Berlin; president of the Colonial Committee of the *Ständige Ausstellungskommission für die Deutsche Industrie* in 1914.
Simmel, Georg	1858–1918	German sociologist and cultural philosopher, and one of the founders of sociology as an academic discipline. After considerable difficulties 1900 supernumerary professor (*extraordinarius*) for philosophy of history at Friedrich-Wilhelms-Universität in Berlin; since 1914 professor in Strasbourg. Monographs include classics such as *Die Philosophie des Geldes* (1900) and *Soziologie* (1908). Published seminal article on Berliner Gewerbeausstellung in 1896.

(Continued)

Name	*/†	Biographical Information and Exposition Participation
Simpson, Sir John William	1858–1933	British architect. Together with →Maxwell Ayrton main architect of 1924 British Empire Exhibition where he was responsible for the general layout, the Empire Stadium, and the palaces of industry and engineering. Also designed British pavilion for the Exposiçao Internacional do Centenario do Brasil, held in Rio de Janeiro in 1922–23. Wrote an introduction to a book by →Lawrence Weaver (1911).
Sombart, Werner	1863–1941	German economist and sociologist, and one of the founders of sociology as an academic discipline. 1888–90 syndic of Bremen chamber of commerce where he organized the Nordwestdeutsche Industrie- und Gewerbeausstellung (1890). 1890 professor in Breslau, 1917 in Berlin. Wrote numerous, partly best-selling sociological monographs, culminating in his three-decade long study of the genesis and evolution of modern capitalism and the capitalist spirit (*Der moderne Kapitalismus*, 1902/16); edited *Archiv für Sozialwissenschaft und Sozialpolitik* jointly with Max Weber. Visited Paris 1889 exposition. Wrote on relation between exhibitions and advertising.
Spielmann, Sir Isidore	1854–1925	British exhibition organizer, government advisor and art critic. British commissioner for art at numerous exhibitions between 1897 and 1925, in particular secretary and delegate of the British Fine Art Section, Royal Commission at Paris 1900 exposition. Member of Departmental Committee to inquire into British participation in international expositions, 1907; commissioner for art London 1908. Member of International Exhibitions Committee; in 1908 appointed honorary director for British art at international exhibitions. Council member of British Empire Exhibition 1924.
Stahl, Fritz	1864–1928	Pseudonym of writer and art critic Siegfried Lilienthal, journalist and art critic for *Berliner Tageblatt*. Triggered third phase of German *Weltausstellungsfrage* in 1907 and wrote influential book on Paris (1928) which ran into numerous editions up to the 1960s.
Stanley, Frederick Arthur, 16th Earl of Derby	1841–1908	British politician, civil servant and Governor-General of Canada. 1865–68 MP for Preston; 1868–85 MP for north Lancashire. 1878–80 secretary for war; 1885–86 secretary for colonies; 1886–88 president of Board of Trade; 1888–93 governor general of Canada. Active in colonial pressure groups, becoming president of the British Empire League in 1904 (succeeded by →Victor Cavendish, the Duke of Devonshire in 1908) and of the Executive Committee of the Franco-British Exhibition in 1908.

Stevenson, James, Lord	1873–1926	Businessman and public servant. Left position as joint managing director of whisky company John Walker to work under Lloyd George for the Ministry of Munitions during the First World War. 1921 personal advisor to Winston Churchill, then secretary of state for the colonies. Went on to serve on various advisory councils during the 1920s. 1923 chairman of the Board of Management of the British Empire Exhibition (deputy chairman: →Sir Travers Clarke), replacing →Ulick Wintour. Considered the 'man who "ran" Wembley' (*Daily Sketch*, 11 June 1936). He was created a baronet in 1917 and made G.C.M.G. in 1922; in recognition of his work for the British Empire Exhibition, peerage was conferred in May 1924.
Strathcona, Donald Alexander Smith, Lord	1820–1914	Canadian financier, politician and businessman who worked 30 years for Hudson's Bay Company and played important role in the capitalization and construction of the Canadian Pacific Railway; 1871–96 member of Canadian parliament; 1896–1911 high commissioner for Canadian Dominion in London; director of various railway companies; honorary president of the Bank of Montreal. So-called empire builder and said to have been the wealthiest Canadian of his time. Member of British colonial committee at 1900 exposition. Later associated with →Imre Kiralfy; chairman at complimentary banquet in October 1908; one of the founders of the British Empire League. Directly involved in London exhibition 1908 and said to have first developed idea of holding Wembley exhibition.
Tournaire, Joseph Albert	1862–1958	French architect. Trained at the *Ecole des Beaux-Arts* in Paris and winner of the 1888 *Prix de Rome d'architecture*. Designed palace and buildings for 1895 colonial exposition in Bordeaux. Chief architect for the 1931 exposition in Paris after →Léon Jaussely had become ill.
Vogüé, Eugène Marie Melchior, Vicomte de	1848–1910	French diplomat, traveler, historian and literary scholar. Best known for his work as a critic.

(Continued)

Name	*/†	Biographical Information and Exposition Participation
Watkin, Sir Edward William	1819–1901	British railroad promoter. 1863–94 chairman of the Manchester, Sheffield and Lincolnshire Railway Company and 1872–94 managing director of Metropolitan Railway Company. MP for Hythe and Folkestone Kent. One of the first promoters of the idea of a channel tunnel (1872; plan withdrawn in 1893); chairman of the Channel Tunnel Company. Initiator of an Eiffel Tower replica in northwest London (Watkin's Folly). Friend of Prime Minister William Ewart Gladstone whose visit to the Paris 1889 exposition he arranged.
Weaver, Sir Lawrence Walter William	1876–1930	British architect, architectural writer and critic; civil servant. 1910–16 architectural editor of *Country Life*; 1918 commercial secretary to the Board of Agriculture; 1919–22 director-general of Land Department and assistant secretary in the Ministry of Agriculture. 1922–25 general staff officer, later director-general United Kingdom Exhibits (including the Palace of Arts) at the British Empire Exhibition. Book publications include *Exhibitions and the Arts of Display* (1925) and *The Place of Advertising in Industry* (1928), following his experience at Wembley.
Wermuth, Adolf	1855–1927	German politician and diplomat; civil servant in the Ministry of the Interior; Mayor of Berlin between 1912 and 1920. German general commissioner at Melbourne exhibition 1888–89 and Chicago world's fair 1893.
Whitley, John Robinson	1843–1922	British trade exhibitions instigator and resort promoter. Visited numerous international exhibitions including Paris 1867 and 1878. Founded exhibition venue Earl's Court in London, and organized four national exhibitions there between 1887 and 1891.
Williams, Sir Owen	1890–1969	British civil engineer and architect, central to early British motorway design. Consulting Civil Engineer to British Empire Exhibition, responsible for the Palace of Industry, and the introduction of reinforced concrete for large-scale building projects; also designed the *Parc des Attractions* in Paris 1925, the Wembley Empire Pool in 1933–34 and subsequent installations for the 1948 Olympic Games, on behalf of sports promoter →James Elvin. Work for British Empire Exhibition earned him knighthood.

Wintour, Ullick Fitzgerald	1877–1947	British civil servant; appointed to Board of Trade in 1904. 1906 secretary to the Committee on Great International Exhibitions; 1908 director of the Exhibitions Branch of the Board of Trade. British commissioner-general at Brussels 1910 exhibition, Turin 1911 exhibition, Ghent 1913 exhibition. General manager and first director at British Empire Exhibition in 1924; in June 1923 superseded by →Lord Stevenson, then adviser to the Board of the exhibition.
Witt, Otto Nikolaus	1853–1915	German chemist, *Geheimer Regierungsrat* and professor at Königliche Technische Hochschule, Berlin. Editor of official German catalogues of Chicago 1893 world's fair and Paris 1900 exposition; published so-called *Ausstellungsbriefe* on the latter.
Wood, Sir Henry Trueman	1845–1929	British civil servant, exhibition promoter and writer. Brother of women's rights activist Annie Besant (1847–1933). First secretary, then treasurer, then chairman of Council of the Royal Society of Arts (1879–1917) and editor of its journal. Officially connected with and involved in the organization of the South Kensington exhibitions held 1883–86, especially the 1884 'Healtheries'. British commissioner in Paris 1889; secretary to the Royal Commission for Chicago 1893 world's fair. Compiled comprehensive list of British exhibitions (1851–1907) and authored 'official' history of the Royal Society of Arts (1913).

National exhibitions committees and international treatises

France: Comité français des expositions à l'étranger (CFEE)

1885–95	*Comité d'initiative des expositions françaises à l'étranger*
1895	*Comité d'initiative des expositions françaises à l'étranger* and *Comité national des expositions coloniales* merged by official decree; newly founded as *Comité français des expositions à l'étranger*
1903	*Comité d'initiative des expositions françaises à l'étranger* fused with *Réunion des jurys et comités des expositions universelles*

Germany: Ständige Ausstellungskommission für die deutsche Industrie/ Ausstellungs- und Messeausschuss der Deutschen Wirtschaft (AUMA)

1907	*Ständige Ausstellungskommission für die deutsche Industrie* founded by *Centralverband Deutscher Industrieller*, *Centralstelle für Vorbereitung von Handelsverträgen* and *Bund der Industriellen*
1908	Exhibition conference held in Düsseldorf
1913	Goldberger's resignation as president
1916	*Leipziger Messeamt*
1920	*Ständige Ausstellungskommission* renamed *Ausstellungs- und Messeamt der Deutschen Industrie*
1920	*Reichsmessekonferenz* held in Berlin
1927	*Ausstellungs- und Messeamt der Deutschen Indust*rie renamed *Deutsches Ausstellungs- und Messeamt*
1928	Conference in Cologne
1930	Conference in Dresden
1934	*Ausstellungs- und Messeamt* renamed *Ausstellungs- und Messeausschuss der Deutschen Wirtschaft* (AUMA)
1949	AUMA re-founded
1951	AUMA headquarters moved to Cologne
1961	'Empfehlungen für das Ausstellungs- und Messewesen' published

Great Britain: Exhibitions Branch of the Board of Trade

Oct. 1906	*Special Committee on Great International Exhibitions*
1908	*Exhibitions Branch* of the *Board of Trade*
1916	*Exhibitions Branch* and *Commercial Intelligence Branch* merged into *Department ot Commercial Intelligence*, still forming part of the Board of Trade
1918	*Exhibitions Division* of the *Department of Overseas Trade*

International: Bureau International des Expositions (BIE)

Nov. 1867	*Association Internationale pour le Développment des Expositions* founded in Paris
Nov. 1907	First international conference held in Paris
8–26 Oct. 1912	Second international conference held in Berlin, *Fédération Internationale des Comités permanents d'expositions* founded
1925	*Union des Foires Internationales*
12–22 Nov. 1928	Third international conference held in Paris, with representatives of 38 nations present
22 Nov. 1928	'Convention Relating to International Exhibitions' signed in Paris

Georg Simmel, Berliner Gewerbe-Ausstellung/The Berlin Trade Exhibition (1896)[2]

Karl Lamprecht erzählt in seiner Deutschen Geschichte, daß gewisse ritterschaftliche Bünde des Mittelalters allmählich ihre praktisch-sachlichen Zwecke eingebüßt, aber als bloß gesellige Vereinigungen zu Vergnügungszwecken weiter existiert hätten. Damit ist ein Typus sociologischer Entwicklung bezeichnet, der auf den verschiedensten Gebieten gleichmäßige Verwirklichung findet. Der Doppelsinn von 'Gesellschaft' drückt es symbolisch aus, wie sehr das gesellige Vergnügen mindestens als ein Nebenproduct jede Vergesellschaftung begleitet, wie es den Berührungspunkt der heterogensten Interessengruppen bildet und so als eine zusammenführende Kraft übrig bleibt, wenn die sachlichen Gründe und Reize der Vereinigung ihre Wirkung verloren haben. An der Geschichte der Weltausstellungen, anhebend von ihren Vorgängern, den Jahrmärkten, tritt die Unvermeidlichkeit dieses Grundtypus aller menschlichen Vergesellschaftung in die klarste Erscheinung, und die Stärke, in der er die Berliner Gewerbe-Ausstellung charakterisiert, läßt schon für sich allein diese in die Familie der Weltausstellungen gehören. Hier ist die Fülle und Divergenz des Gebotenen, die als schließlichen Einheitspunkt und farbegebendes Charakteristicum nur das Amüsement bestehen läßt. Die nachbarliche Enge, in die die heterogensten Industrieproducte gerückt sind, erzeugt eine Paralyse des Wahrnehmungsvermögens, eine wahre Hypnose, in der der einzelne Eindruck nur noch die obersten Schichten des Bewußtseins streift und schließlich nur die am häufigsten wiederholte Vorstellung als Sieger über den Leichen unzähliger würdigerer, aber in ihrer Zersplitterung schwacher Eindrücke im Gedächtnis zurückbleibt: die Vorstellung, daß man sich hier amüsieren soll. Ein sehr kleinlich erscheinendes Arrangement dient dieser Reduction des Ganzen auf den Generalnenner Vergnügen in psychologisch feiner Weise: alle paar Schritte nämlich wird für eine besondere Schaustellung oder sonstige Darbietung ein kleines Eintrittsgeld erhoben. Dadurch wird die Neugier immer von neuem gespannt, jedes einzelne Vergnügen erscheint durch die dafür gemachte Aufwendung gewichtiger und betonter, das Viele, an dem man vorbeigehen muß, erregt die Vorstellung, daß hier noch vielerlei Überraschungen und Vergnügungen aufgespeichert bleiben, kurz die Abtönung auf das leitende Motiv: Amüsement – wird durch diese steten, nur durch ein kleines Opfer zu überwindenden Hemmungen gründlicher erreicht, als wenn eine einmalige höhere Eintrittszahlung einem alles gleichmäßig zugängig machte, dafür aber dem 'Vergnügungssinn' jene fortwährenden kleinen Reizungen versagte.

Jeder feiner empfindliche Sinn aber wird sich durch die Massenwirkung des hier Gebotenen vergewaltigt und derangiert fühlen, wie andererseits doch nicht geleugnet werden kann, daß dem Aufregungsbedürfnis überreizter und ermatteter Nerven gerade diese Fülle und Buntheit vorüberhastender Eindrücke angemessen ist. Während nämlich steigende Cultur zu immer größerer Specialisierung und häufigerer Einseitigkeit der Leistungen führt, zu immer engerer Beschränkung auf das zugewiesene Gewicht – *entspricht dieser Differenzierung der Production keineswegs eine ebensolche der Consumtion*; sondern im Gegenteil: es scheint, als ob der moderne Mensch für die Einseitigkeit und Einförmigkeit seiner arbeitstheiligen Leistung sich nach der Seite des Aufnehmens und Genießens hin durch die wachsende Zusammendrängung heterogener Eindrücke, durch immer rascheren und bunteren Wechsel der Erregungen entschädigen wolle. Die Differenzierung der activen Provinzen des Lebens ergänzt sich offenbar durch umfassende Mannigfaltigkeit seiner passiven und rezeptiven. Die Ungeduld vielfältiger Kräfte, durch die die Menschenseele ein Mikrokosmos ist und der die Differenzierung des modernen Arbeitens keine volle Entfaltung gewährt, sucht sich an der Vielseitigkeit, den Unterschiedsreizen, den zusammengedrängten Entgegengesetztheiten des Empfangens und Genießens auszuleben. Keine Erscheinung des modernen Lebens kommt diesem Bedürfnis so unbedingt entgegen, wie die großen Ausstellungen, nirgends sonst ist eine große Fülle heterogenster Eindrücke in eine äußere Einheit so zusammengebracht, daß sie der durchschnittlichen Oberflächlichkeit doch als zusammengehörig erscheinen und gerade dadurch jene lebhafte Wechselwirkung unter ihnen erzeugt wird, jene gegenseitige

Contrastierung und Steigerung, die dem ganz beziehungslos Nebeneinanderliegenden versagt ist.

Nun wird hier eine Einheit des Ganzen allerdings in sehr wirkungsvoller und interessanter Weise durch die Idee getragen, daß diese Unübersehbarkeit von Objecten in *einer* Stadt producirt sind. So wenig sie diesen Ursprung etwa in einer Gleichmäßigkeit des Stiles oder durchgehender Tendenzen zum sichtbaren Ausdruck bringen, so sehr er vielmehr nur als darüber schwebende Idee eine psychologische Wirksamkeit üben kann – so ist diese doch nicht zu verkennen. An Weltausstellungen ist es ein eigenthümlicher Reiz, daß sie ein momentanes Centrum der Weltcultur bilden, daß die Arbeit der ganzen Welt sich, wie in einem Bilde, in diese enge Begrenzung zusammengezogen hat. Hier umgekehrt hat sich eine einzige Stadt in die Gesammtheit der Culturleistungen verbreitet. Es fehlt kein Typus wesentlicher Producte, und so sehr das Material und die Muster dieser aus der ganzen Welt zusammengeholt sind, so haben sie doch hier die abschließende Form erhalten, jedes ist erst hier ein Ganzes geworden. So wird denn hiermit recht klar, was 'Weltstadt' bedeutet und daß Berlin, trotz allem, eine ist: eine Stadt, der die ganze Welt die Stoffe ihres Arbeitens liefert und die diese zu allen wesentlichen Formen gestaltet, die irgendwo in der gegenwärtigen Culturwelt erscheinen. Vielleicht ist nach dieser Richtung hin die Berliner Ausstellung eine ganz einzige Erscheinung; vielleicht ist es noch niemals so anschaulich gemacht worden, wie sehr die Form der modernen Cultur gestattet, sie an einem Platze zu verdichten und zwar nicht, wie die Weltausstellung es thut, durch mechanisches Zusammentragen, sondern durch eigene Production, mit der die Stadt sich als Abbild und Auszug der gewerblichen Kräfte der Culturwelt überhaupt darbietet.

Es ist von großem culturhistorischem Interesse, die Herausbildung eines eigenartigen Stiles für solche Darbietungen zu verfolgen. Am markiertesten tritt hier in den Baulichkeiten der specifische Ausstellungsstil hervor. Eine ganz neue Proportion zwischen Festigkeit und Vergänglichkeit mußte nicht nur in der verborgenen Structur, sondern auch in dem ästhetisch Beurtheilbaren herrschend werden. Indem das Material und seine inneren technischen Bedingungen einen ganz harmonischen Ausdruck in der äußeren Formgebung gewonnen haben, ist eine der letzten und tiefsten Forderungen aller Kunst erfüllt. Die Mehrzahl der Baulichkeiten, insbesondere gerade die Hauptgebäude, tragen durchaus den Charakter einer Schöpfung für die Vergänglichkeit; weil ihnen dieser unmißverständlich aufgeprägt ist, wirken sie absolut nicht unsolid; denn der Eindruck der Unsolidität entsteht nur, wo das Vergängliche dem Anspruch auf Dauer und Widerstandskraft genügen soll. Im Ausstellungsstil kann die Phantasie des Architekten von dieser Forderung befreit walten und so Anmuth und Würde in ganz eigenen Maßen mischen. Es ist die bewußte Verneinung des Monumentalstiles, die hier eine ganz neue positive Gestaltung ergeben hat. Wenn es sonst der Sinn aller Kunst ist, an vergänglichem Materiale die Ewigkeit der Formen zu verkörpern, wenn gerade in der Baukunst sonst das Ideal der Dauer zur Verwirklichung und zum Ausdruck strebt – so formt hier der Reiz und Duft der Vergänglichkeit einen eigenen Stil, und, um so charakteristischer, aus einem Material, das doch wieder auf nicht beschränkte Dauer angelegt scheint. Und wirklich ist es den Architekten unserer Ausstellung gelungen, daß man diesen Gegensatz gegen das historische Ideal der Baukunst nicht als Widersinn und Stillosigkeit, sondern nur als eine jener Entwicklungen empfindet, in denen der letzterreichte Punkt erst an dem Ausgangspunkt, wie an einem anders gefärbten Hintergrund, die Betonung seines Sinnes erhält und indem er ihn zu verneinen scheint, dennoch in eine Reihe mit ihm gehört. Nach der architektonischen Seite hin bezeichnet diese Ausstellung vielleicht den Gipfelpunkt dessen, was das Ausstellungsprincip bisher in ästhetischer Productivität geleistet hat. Nach einer anderen Seite seiner Fruchtbarkeit hin steht sie wenigstens auf einer relativen Höhe: ich meine die durch die Ausstellungen hervorgerufene Steigerung dessen, was man die Schaufenster-Qualität der Dinge nennen könnte. Die Warenproduction unter der Herrschaft der freien Concurrrenz und mit dem durchschnittlichen Übergewichte des Angebots über die Nachfrage muß dazu führen, den Dingen über ihre Nützlichkeit hinaus noch eine verlockende Außenseite zu geben.

Wo die Concurrenz inbezug auf Zweckmäßigkeit und innere Eigenschaften zu Ende ist –
und oft genug schon vorher – muß man versuchen, durch den äußeren Reiz der Objecte,
ja sogar durch die Art ihres Arrangements das Interesse der Käufer zu erregen. Dies ist der
Punkt, an dem gerade aus der äußersten Steigerung des materiellen Interesses und der bit-
tersten Concurrenznoth eine Wendung in das ästhetische Ideal erwächst. Das Bestreben,
dem Nützlichen auch einen Reiz für das Auge zu geben, wie es den Orientalen und den
Romanen ganz natürlich ist, entspringt bei uns aus dem Kampfe um den Abnehmer – das
Anmuthigste aus dem Anmuthlosesten. Die Ausstellung, in der überhaupt, ihrer Betonung
des Vergnügens zufolge, eine neue principielle Synthese zwischen dem äußerlichen Reiz und
der sachlichen Zweckmäßigkeit der Dinge gesucht wird, stellt die äußerste Steigerung dieses
ästhetischen Superadditums dar. Das banale Bestreben, die Dinge 'ins rechte Licht zu setzen',
läutert sich aus dem marktschreierischen Vordrängen zu den interessantesten Versuchen,
ihnen durch das Arrangement ihres Zusammenseins neue ästhetische Bedeutsamkeiten zu
verleihen – wie die gemeine Reclame zur Placatkunst vorgeschritten ist. Es ist überhaupt
sehr merkwürdig: der einzelne Gegenstand innerhalb einer Ausstellung zeigt dieselben
Beziehungen und Modificationen, wie sie dem Individuum innerhalb der Gesellschaft
eigen sind: einerseits Herabdrückung durch den anders qualificierten Nachbar, andererseits
Hervorhebung auf Kosten ebendesselben; einerseits Nivellierung und Vergleichgiltigung
durch die gleichartige Umgebung, andererseits die Steigerung, die das und der Einzelne
gerade durch die Summierung der Eindrücke erfährt; einerseits ist das Einzelne nur Element
eines Ganzen, nur Glied einer höheren Einheit, andererseits tritt es doch mit dem Anspruch
auf, selbst ein Ganzes und eine Einheit zu sein. So spiegeln die Eindrücke der in einem
Rahmen vereinten Dinge mit ihren wechselseitig erregten Kräften, ihren Widersprüchen
wie ihrem Zusammengehen, die objectiven Verhältnisse socialer Elemente wieder. Dies
eigenthümliche Relief, das die Dinge so durch ihre Wechselwirkungen, ihr Vor- und
Zurücktreten gewinnen, gilt es nun, in der Ausstellung ästhetisch auszunützen, wie es in
der Gesellschaft gilt, eben die entsprechenden Verhältnisse ethisch auszunützen. Deutsche,
insbesondere norddeutsche Ausstellungen können in dieser Hinsicht mit den Franzosen
nur schwer concurrieren, bei denen die Fähigkeit, den Reiz der Erscheinungen mit allen
Mitteln herauszuarbeiten, eine viel längere Geschichte und viel breitere Gelegenheiten hat.
Immerhin ist in dieser Ausstellung das Bestreben sichtbar und nicht immer erfolglos, die
ästhetischen Chancen auszubauen, die das 'Ausstellen' der Waren ihrer Anziehungskraft
hinzufügen kann. Gewiß sind gerade die Geschmacksqualitäten die mangelhaftesten an
den Einzelheiten dieser Ausstellung. Allein von der 'praktischen Vernunft' Berlins, die sich
in dieser Ausstellung objectiviert und verkörpert hat, ist zu hoffen, daß sie wenigstens jene
ästhetischen Impulse weiterentwickeln wird, die aus der Ausstellung als solcher, als einer
besondern Form der Darbietung von Arbeitsproducten quellen.

* * *

In his *Deutsche Geschichte* Karl Lamprecht relates how certain medieval orders of knights
gradually lost their practical purpose but continued as sociable gatherings. This is a type of
sociological development that is similarly repeated in the most diverse fields. The double
meaning of the word 'society' symbolizes this twin sense. Alongside the very process of
sociation there is also, as a byproduct, the sociable meaning of society. The latter is always
a meeting-point for the most diverse formation of interest groups, thus remaining as the
sole integrating force even when the original reasons for consocation have lost their effectiveness. The history of world exhibitions, which originated from annual fairs, is one of
the clearest examples of this most fundamental type of human sociation. The extent to
which this process can be found in the Berlin exhibition alone allows it to be placed in the
category of world exhibitions. In the face of the richness and diversity of what is offered,
the only unifying and colorful factor is that of amusement. The way in which the most
heterogeneous industrial products are crowded together in close proximity paralyzes the

senses – a veritable hypnosis where only one message gets through to one's consciousness: the idea that one is here to amuse oneself. Through frequency of repetition this impression overwhelms countless no less worthy impressions, which because of their fragmentation fail to register. The sense of amusement emerges as a common denominator due to a petty but psychologically subtle arrangement: every few steps a small entry fee is charged for each special display. One's curiosity is thus constantly aroused by each new display, and the enjoyment derived from each particular display is made to seem greater and more significant. The majority of things which must be passed creates the impression that many surprises and amusements are in store. In short, the return to the main motif, amusement, is more effectively achieved by having to make a small sacrifice, which overcomes one's inhibitions to indulge, than if a higher entry price, giving unrestricted access, was charged, thereby denying that continuous small stimulation.

Every fine and sensitive feeling, however, is violated and seems deranged by the mass effect of the merchandise offered, while on the other hand it cannot be denied that the richness and variety of fleeting impressions is well suited to the need for excitement for overstimulated and tired nerves. While increasing civilization leads to ever-greater specialization and to a more frequent one-sidedness of function within an evermore limited field, in no way does this differentiation on the side of production extend to consumption. Rather, the opposite: it appears as though modern man's one-sided and monotonous role in the division of labor will be compensated for by consumption and enjoyment through the growing pressure of heterogeneous impressions, and the ever-faster and more colorful change of excitements. The differentiation of the active side of life is apparently complemented through the extensive diversity of its passive and receiving side. The press of contradictions, the many stimuli and the diversity of consumption and enjoyment are the ways in which the human soul – that otherwise is an impatient flux of forces and denied a complete development by the differentiations within modern work – seeks to come alive. No part of modern life reveals this need as sharply as the large exhibition. Nowhere else is such a richness of different impressions brought together so that overall there seems to be an outward unity, whereas underneath a vigorous interaction produces mutual contrasts, intensification and lack of relatedness.

Now this unity of the whole creates a stronger impression and becomes more interesting when one considers the impossibility of surveying the objects produced in a single city. It is only as a floating psychological idea that this unity can be apprehended since in its origins the styles and emerging trends receive no clear expression. It is a particular attraction of world fairs that they form a momentary center of world civilization, assembling the products of the entire world in a confined space as if in a single picture. Put the other way round, a single city has broadened into the totality of cultural production. No important product is missing, and though much of the material and samples have been brought together from the whole world, they have attained a conclusive form and become part of a single whole. Thus it becomes clear what is meant by a 'world city' and that Berlin, despite everything, has become one. That is, a single city to which the whole world sends its products and where all the important styles of the present cultural world are put on display. In this sense perhaps the Berlin exhibition is unique; perhaps it has never been so apparent before how much the form of modern culture has permitted a concentration in one place, not in the mere collection of exhibits as in a world fair, but how, through its own production, a city can represent itself as a copy and a sample of the manufacturing forces of world culture.

It is a point of some cultural historical interest to follow how a particular style for such exhibitions has developed. The specific exhibition style is seen at its clearest in the buildings. An entirely new proportion between permanence and transience not only predominates in the hidden structure but also in the aesthetic criteria. In doing this the materials and their intrinsic properties have achieved a complete harmony in their external design, so satisfying one of the most fundamental demands of all art. The majority of the buildings, in particular the main ones, look as if they were intended for temporary purposes; because this lack of permanence is unmistakable they are absolutely ineffective as unsolid buildings. And the impression of lack of solidity works only where the temporary can claim permanence and durability. In the exhibition style the imagination of the architect is freed from the stipulation of permanence, allowing grace and dignity to be combined in their own measure. It is the conscious denial of a monumental style that has produced a new and positive shape. Elsewhere, it is the meaning of art to incorporate the permanence of form in transient materials, and the ideal of architecture is to strive to give expression to the permanent, whereas here the attraction of the transient forms its own style and, even more characteristically, does this from material that doesn't appear as if it was intended for temporary use. And in fact the architects of our exhibition have succeeded in making the opposition to the historical ideal of architecture not a matter of absurdity or lack of style; rather, they have taken the point last reached in architecture as their starting-point, as if only this arrangement would allow its meaning to emerge fully against a differently colored background and yet be seen as part of a single tradition. It is on the architectural side that this exhibition reaches its acme, demonstrating the aesthetic output of the exhibition principle. From another point of view its productivity is at least as high: and here I refer to what could be termed the shop-window quality of things, a characteristic which the exhibition accentuates. The production of goods under the regime of free competition and the normal predominance of supply over demand leads to goods having to show a tempting exterior as well as utility. Where competition no longer operates in matters of usefulness and intrinsic properties, the interest of the buyer has to be aroused by the external stimulus of the object, even the manner of its presentation. It is at the point, where material interests have reached their highest level and the pressure of competition is at an extreme, that the aesthetic ideal is employed. The striving to make the merely useful visually stimulating – something that was completely natural for the Orientals and Romans – for us comes from the struggle to render the graceless graceful for consumers. The exhibition with its emphasis on amusement attempts a new synthesis between the principles of external stimulus and the practical functions of objects, and thereby takes this aesthetic superadditum to its highest level. The banal attempt to put things in their best light, as in the cries of the street trader, is transformed in the interesting attempt to confer a new aesthetic significance from displaying objects together – something already happening in the relationship between advertising and poster art. Indeed, it strikes one as curious that the separate objects in an exhibition show the same relationships and modifications that are made by the individual within society. On the one side, the depreciation of an otherwise qualified neighbor, on the other, accentuation at the expense of the same; on the one side, the leveling and uniformity due to an environment of the same, on the other, the individual is even more accentuated through the summation of many impressions; on the one side, the individual is only an element of the whole, only a member of a higher unity, on the other, the claim that the same individual is a whole and a unity. Thus the objective relation between social elements is reflected in the impression of things in unison within a single frame yet composed of interactively excited forces, and of contradictions, yet also their confluence. Just as in the exhibition, the contours of things in their interactive effects, their moving to and fro undergoes an aesthetic exploitation, so in society the corresponding patterns allow an ethical use. German, in particular north German, exhibitions could compete only with difficulty with French ones where the ability to accentuate by all means possible the stimulus of appearance has a much longer history and wider applicability. Nevertheless, this exhibition shows the attempt, often successful, to develop aesthetic opportunities which, through display, can contribute to their attractiveness. Certainly, the qualities of taste are mostly lacking in the individual items of the exhibition. Aside from the practical motive of Berlin's exhibition, it is to be hoped at the least that the aesthetic impulse is encouraged beyond the exhibition itself and becomes part of the way products are presented.

Notes

Chapter 1 Introduction: How to Read an Exposition

1. 'EXPOSITION: The nineteenth century's subject of delirium'. Flaubert, *Le Dictionnaire des idées reçues*, 78.
2. Simmel, 'Berliner Gewerbe-Ausstellung', 59; the German original and an English translation of this article can be found in the Appendix. Although more pivotal to this problematic than any other single text I have come across in the course of my research, Simmel's dauntingly rich text has been largely overlooked by exposition historians. The exception to the rule is Rowe, 'Georg Simmel and the Berlin Trade Exhibition of 1896', here 216–19.
3. When a proper name is quoted for the first time, an arrow ('→') in front of it denotes that additional bio-bibliographical information is to be found in the section *Dramatis personae* in the Appendix. Simmel, 'Berliner Gewerbe-Ausstellung'; and 'Die Großstädte und das Geistesleben'. Written and published on the occasion of yet another local exhibition, this 1903 text is – together with Louis Wirth's 'Urbanism as a Way of Life', published in 1938 – arguably one of the most widely known treatises in the social sciences in general and a founding text for urban anthropology in particular. Simmel had published on art exhibitions before; see his 'Über Kunstausstellungen'; and Hannerz, *Exploring the City*, 59–63. See also Nolte, 'Georg Simmels Historische Anthropologie der Moderne'; Yengoyan, 'Simmel, Modernity, and Germanisms'; and Jazbinsek, 'The Metropolis and the Mental Life of Georg Simmel', here 109–10.
4. Moonen, *Exhibitions*, 9.
5. Simmel, 'Soziologie des Raumes', 229: 'Die Grenze ist nicht eine räumliche Tatsache mit soziologischen Wirkungen, sondern eine soziologische Tatsache, die sich räumlich formt.' This famous formula does *not* refer to the city in particular but the boundary more generally, as numerous English-speaking scholars have wrongly assumed, following David Frisby's 1984 translation (Frisby, *Georg Simmel*, 131).
6. Simmel, 'Berliner Gewerbe-Ausstellung', 59: 'Es ist von großem culturhistorischem Interesse, die Herausbildung eines eigenartigen Stiles für solche Darbietungen zu verfolgen.' Yengoyan, 'Simmel, Modernity, and Germanisms', 621–2.
7. Charles Baudelaire, 'Le Peintre de la vie moderne' [1863], in his *Œuvres complètes*, vol. 3, 453–507, here 468–7: 'La modernité, c'est le transitoire, le fugitif, le contingent, la moitié de l'art, dont l'autre moitié est l'éternel et l'immuable.' For an English translation, see Charles Baudelaire, 'The Painter of Modern Life', in *The Painter of Modern Life and Other Essays*, ed. Jonathan Mayne, London: Phaidon, 1964, 1–41, here 13. The literature is vast and cannot be discussed here in detail; but see in this context Lefebvre, *Introduction à la modernité*; Berman, *All That Is Solid Melts Into Air*; and Clark, *The Painting of Modern Life*. It is not a coincidence that Lefebvre refers to exhibitions on the very first page of his introduction, that Berman discusses the Crystal Palace *in extenso* (235–49), and that Clark features the Parisian Expositions Universelles of 1867 and 1878 in his classic study on Impressionism, Paris, and the rise of art criticism (60–6, 72–5, 259). See also Yack, *The Fetishism of Modernities*.
8. Lessing, *Das halbe Jahrhundert der Weltausstellungen*, 7.
9. Driver, 'Geography's Empire', 35. On the spatial turn, see classics such as Harvey, *The Urban Experience*; Soja, *Postmodern Geographies*; and Gregory, *Geographical Imaginations*. For various influential conceptual approaches, see Massey, 'Places and Their Pasts'; Blackbourn, *A Sense of Place*; Osterhammel, 'Die Wiederkehr des Raumes'; Schlögel, *Im Raume lesen wir die Zeit*; and Geppert, Jensen and Weinhold, *Ortsgespräche*, the latter with

numerous suggestions for further reading. In the interim, anthologies on the spatial turn have become legion.

10. Reusche, *Chicago und Berlin*, 8; Bennett, 'The Exhibitionary Complex', and *The Birth of the Museum*, 59–88; Kriegel, 'After the Exhibitionary Complex'.
11. Simmel, 'Berliner Gewerbe-Ausstellung', 60.
12. This is one of several new avenues of research recently suggested by Robert Rydell, 'New Directions for Scholarship about World Expos', 21.4–5.
13. John Forbes Watson, 'International Exhibitions', *Times* (28 December 1872), 10.
14. The *Oxford English Dictionary* defines 'exhibition' as 'a public display (of works of art, manufactured articles, natural productions, etc.); also, the place where the display is made. In early quots. often *spec.* the exhibition of pictures of the Royal Academy; now applied *esp.* to those exhibitions on a large scale of which the "Great Exhibition" held in London in 1851 was the first and typical example'. Cf. with the OED's respective entry for 'exposition', defining the latter concurrently as 'the action of putting out to public view; an instance of this; a display, show, exposure', or equating the two terms even directly as 'After mod. French use; = Exhibition'. The notion 'fair' ('A periodical gathering of buyers and sellers, often with shows and entertainments. [...] More recently also *spec.* an exhibition, esp. one designed to publicize a particular product or the products of one industry, country, etc.'), on the other hand, additionally connotes commerce and selling, rather than solely displaying goods. *Oxford English Dictionary*, 2nd edn, Oxford: Clarendon, 1989, vol. 5, 537, 579, 670. See also Wallace, 'Empire Exhibitions and Fairs', 213–14, for a detailed definitional discussion.
15. Sombart, 'Die Ausstellung', 249; Lenger, *Werner Sombart*, 169–70.
16. In a letter dated 15 May 1851 to his younger friend, the German-born but Oxford-based orientalist and philologist Friedrich Max Müller (1823–1900), here quoted after Démy, *Essai historique*, 53 ('das poetischste und weltgeschichtlichste Ereignis der Zeit'); *Bemrose's District Railway Guide to the Irish Exhibition in London*, 11.
17. Haltern, *Die Londoner Weltausstellung*, 352; Nord, 'London and the World', 133; Breckenridge, 'The Aesthetics and Politics of Colonial Collecting', 201.
18. For instance 1851, 1862, 1908 and 1924–25 in London; 1855, 1867, 1878, 1889, 1900, 1925, 1931 and 1937 in Paris; 1858, 1864, 1870, 1871, 1884, 1898 and 1911 in Turin; 1873 in Vienna; 1885, 1894 and 1930 in Antwerp; 1888 and 1929–30 in Barcelona; 1879 and 1896 in Berlin; 1897 and 1930 in Stockholm; 1874, 1888, 1897, 1910, 1935 and 1958 in Brussels; 1879, 1881, 1894 and 1906 in Milan; 1905 in Liège; 1853–54, 1918 and 1939–40 in New York; 1876 and 1926 in Philadelphia; 1893 and 1933–34 in Chicago; 1904 in St Louis; 1915 and 1939–40 in San Francisco; 1879–80 in Sydney; and 1854, 1880–81 and 1888–89 in Melbourne.
19. On the development of these taxonomies over time, see Benedict, 'The Anthropology of World's Fairs', 27–41, esp. 28.
20. Data contained in Figures 1.1 and 1.2 have been compiled from a variety of different sources. For a comprehensive list of international, industrial and technical expositions held between 1851 and 1907, see Wood, 'International Exhibitions'. One of the most accurate exposition listings can be found on the web page of the Special Collections Research Center at California State University, Fresno: http://www.fresnostate.edu/library/subjectresources/specialcollections/worldfairs/listbycity.html (accessed 22 May 2013). But see also 'Appendix B: Fair Statistics', in Findling and Pelle, *Encyclopedia of World's Fairs and Expositions*, 413–17; and Daniloski, *The World's Fair and Exposition Information and Reference Guide*. Cf. Rembold, 'Exhibitions and National Identity', 223, for a comparable graph. See also the Appendix to this volume.
21. For a detailed list, see Lowe, *Four National Exhibitions in London and Their Organiser*, 29.
22. Olivier, *Rapport général*, vol. 1, 5.
23. Geddes, 'The Closing Exhibition', 667.
24. 'Über Bedeutung und Werth der Ausstellungen', 106; see also Behrens, 'Über Ausstellungen', 34: 'Heute leben wir im Zeitalter der Ausstellungen.' Démy, *Essai historique*.

In addition see, for example, Geddes, *Industrial Exhibitions and Modern Progress*; Barwick, 'International Exhibitions and Their Civilising Influence'; Huber, *Die Ausstellungen und unsere Exportindustrie*; Lessing, *Das halbe Jahrhundert der Weltausstellungen*; Berger, *Les Expositions universelles internationales*; Brandt, 'Zur Geschichte und Würdigung der Weltausstellungen'; Paquet, *Das Ausstellungsproblem in der Volkswirtschaft*.

25. Rydell, *All the World's a Fair*; Greenhalgh, *Ephemeral Vistas*; Mitchell, 'The World as Exhibition'; Rebérioux, 'Au tournant des expos', 4 n. 4; see also Rebérioux, 'Approches de l'histoire des Expositions universelles à Paris du Second Empire à 1900'; Brain, 'Going to the Exhibition', 117–18.

26. Bennett, 'The Exhibitionary Complex'. According to Bennett, the 'exhibitionary complex' encompasses museums of art, history and natural science; dioramas and panoramas; national and international exhibitions; arcades and department stores, serving as 'linked sites for the development and articulation of new disciplines (history, biology, art history, anthropology) and their discursive formations (the past, evolution, aesthetics, man) as well as for the development of new technologies of vision' (ibid., 73). See also Bennett, *The Birth of the Museum*, 59–88.

27. Rydell, 'The Literature of International Expositions', 10, 42; more recently Rydell, 'New Directions for Scholarship about World Expos'. See Geppert, 'Welttheater', for a comprehensive review of the pertinent scholarly literature with an emphasis on Europe.

28. All calculations are based on Geppert, Coffey and Lau, *International Exhibitions, Expositions Universelles and World's Fairs*, a comprehensive and regularly updated bibliography that currently (3rd edition as of 1 November 2006) lists 1868 references and covers expositions from 24 countries. Although inevitably incomplete, this is the most comprehensive bibliography on the topic that exists. In calculating annual publication figures, journals and internet resources were not included, leaving 1718 publications over 55 years. While some details may be inexact as, for instance, contributions to an edited volume were generally counted as one entry, the accuracy of the overall development is beyond question. Further, though it might seem that the figures reflect a slight decline in recent years, this may also be due to delays in data recording.

29. The first term was coined by Richard Rorty in 1967 (*The Linguistic Turn*), the second by W. J. T. Mitchell in 1992 ('The Pictorial Turn'), the third by Edward Soja in 1998 (*Postmodern Geographies*, 39). See Bachmann-Medick, *Cultural Turns*, for an astute analysis of these subsequent and partially overlapping turns.

30. These seminal studies include Poirier, *Des Foires, des peuples, des expositions*; Rydell, *All the World's a Fair*; Leprun, *Le Théâtre des colonies*; Greenhalgh, *Ephemeral Vistas*; Wesemael, *Architecture of Instruction and Delight*; Sigel, *Exponiert*; Morton, *Hybrid Modernities*; Hoffenberg, *An Empire on Display*, with an emphasis on English, Indian and Australian exhibitions before the First World War; and Großbölting, '*Im Reich der Arbeit*'. In a broader context, see in particular Rearick, *Pleasures of the Belle Epoque*; Walkowitz, *City of Dreadful Delight*; Coombes, *Reinventing Africa*; Fritzsche, *Reading Berlin 1900*; Burton, *At the Heart of the Empire*; Schwartz, *Spectacular Realities*; Schneer, *London 1900*; Driver and Gilbert, *Imperial Cities*; and Dennis, *Cities in Modernity*. The best starting-point for any kind of exposition-related research is Findling and Pelle, *Encyclopedia of World's Fairs and Expositions*, even if its statistical and factual data are far from reliable.

31. Little known and hardly ever cited in the English-speaking world, the landmark study on the London exhibition of 1851 remains Haltern, *Die Londoner Weltausstellung*; but cf. also Richards, *The Commodity Culture of Victorian England*, 17–72; Auerbach, *The Great Exhibition*; Purbrick, *The Great Exhibition of 1851*; Bosbach and Davis, *Die Weltausstellung von 1851*; as well as Auerbach and Hoffenberg, *Britain, the Empire, and the World at the Great Exhibition of 1851*. On the Parisian exposition of 1889, see Schön, 'Der Triumph des Industriezeitalters'; Rebérioux, *Mise en scène et vulgarisation*; and Plato, *Präsentierte Geschichte*, 209–60. Despite an overabundance of literature on the 1893 world's fair in Chicago (Geppert, Coffey and Lau, *International Exhibitions, Expositions Universelles and World's Fairs*, list nearly twice as many publications on this exposition as for the second-best

researched exposition, the Great Exhibition of 1851) the *locus classicus* remains Rydell, *All the World's a Fair*, here 38–71. However, Rydell's central argument that the World's Columbian Exposition became the 'standard with which every subsequent fair would be compared' (ibid., 71) holds true only when strictly limited to an American context. In addition, see also Gilbert, *Perfect Cities*; Oppenheimer Dean, 'Revisiting the White City'; and Lewis, *An Early Encounter with Tomorrow*. Various European and American expositions have been the subject of popular fiction; see, for instance, Doctorow, *World's Fair*, on the 1939 world's fair in New York City; Mendoza, *La ciudad de los prodigios*, which treats the 1929–30 international exhibition held in Barcelona; Larson, *The Devil in the White City*, a fascinating international bestseller that revived public interest in the Chicago 1893 fair; as well as Orsenna, *L'Exposition coloniale*, and Daeninckx, *Cannibale*, both focused on the 1931 exposition in Paris.

32. MacKenzie, *Propaganda and Empire*, 97.
33. Hoffenberg, *An Empire on Display*, xvii.
34. At the core of this body of literature is Timothy Mitchell's justifiably much celebrated article 'The World as Exhibition', even if the idea of the entire 'world as exhibition' is per se less innovative than it might appear. In 1960, art historian Werner Hofmann had already spoken of 'die Welt als Schaustellung', and Utz Haltern chose the exact phrase as the title for a comprehensive article published in 1973. Cf. Hofmann, *Das irdische Paradies*, 151; Haltern, 'Die "Welt als Schaustellung"'. Other outstanding and methodologically inspiring essays include De Cauter, 'The Panoramic Ecstasy'; and Niquette and Buxton, 'Meet Me at the Fair', the former with an emphasis on the rise and fall of the panoramic gaze as the modern form of representation, the latter focusing on visitors' experience at the 1893 world's fair in Chicago through an analysis of cartoons.
35. Jaworski, 'Alte Postkarten als kulturhistorische Quellen'; Sweet, 'International Exhibition Postcards'; and Schor, '*Cartes Postales*' discuss postcards as a historical and hitherto undervalued source, the latter with a particular emphasis on the iconography of *fin-de-siècle* Paris.
36. Harvey, *Hybrids of Modernity*, 19. For a comparable distinction between a horizontal extension of exhibitions – more of the same products – and a vertical extension – a larger number of participating countries, more but different products – see Askwith, 'Exhibitions', 3.
37. For this notion, see Weaver, *Exhibitions and the Arts of Display*.
38. For a beginning, see Cockx and Lemmens, *Les Expositions universelles et internationales en Belgique*; more recently Tilly, 'Du 19ème au 20ème siècle'; and Stanard, 'Selling the Empire between the Wars'.
39. But see Espuche et al., 'Modernization and Urban Beautification'; Meller, *European Cities*, 47–55; and Baumeister, 'Alteuropäische Städte auf dem Weg in die Moderne' on Barcelona. On Turin and Milan, see ibid.; Romano, 'Le esposizioni industriali italiane'; Misiti, 'L'Italia in mostra'; Della Coletta, *World's Fairs Italian-Style*; and Pellegrino, '"Il gran dimenticato"'.
40. Harvey, *Hybrids of Modernity*, 127.
41. See, for instance, McArthur, 'The Dialectic of National Identity', 199–22; Greenhalgh, *Ephemeral Vistas*, 112–41; Benedict, 'International Exhibitions and National Identity'; Lebovics, *True France*, xi–xvi; Wörner, *Vergnügung und Belehrung*, 4; Rembold, 'Exhibitions and National Identity', 222–3; Kaiser, 'Vive la France! Vive la République?', 228–30; Maxwell, *Colonial Photography and Exhibitions*, 7–14; Auerbach, *The Great Exhibition*, 165–79; Hoffenberg, *Empire on Display*, xiv, 27, 144; Hale, *Races on Display*, 1–3, 22. For a detailed critique of this conceptual deficiency, see Geppert, 'Exponierte Identitäten?'; and more generally Niethammer, *Kollektive Identität*.
42. Chartier, *Cultural History*, 9–13, here 8–9. Chartier defines representation as 'the establishment of a relation between a present image and an absent object in which the one is a valid equivalent of the other because it is in conformity with it'. See also Chartier, 'Le Monde comme représentation', here 1514, and 'The Powers and Limits of

Representation', in Chartier, *On the Edge of the Cliff*, 90–103, here 100–1. The German
equivalent to the concept of appropriation – *Aneignung* – was coined by historian Alf
Lüdtke. See, for instance, Lüdtke, 'Alltagsgeschichte: Aneignung und Akteure'.
43. On the concept of field reconnaissance, see Lynch, *The Image of the City*, 15, 143–5. Paris
as the capital of the nineteenth century is, of course, Walter Benjamin's famous phrase,
see 'Paris, die Hauptstadt des XIX. Jahrhunderts'.

Chapter 2   Berlin 1896

1. Wilhelm II to Graf von Caprivi, 20 July 1892, in Rich et al., *Die Geheimen Papiere
Friedrich von Holsteins*, 376; ('There ain't going to be no exhibition, as my Berlin
friends would put it'); Herzfeld, 'Berlin als Kaiserstadt und Reichshauptstadt', 168–9;
Spranger, *Berliner Geist*, 11 ('In 1896, Berlin became a world city. Until then, it was
only a European provincial town. The watershed event is the trade exhibition in
Treptower Park').
2. Sigel, *Exponiert*, 21–4. So far the Berliner Gewerbeausstellung has not received
the kind of scholarly attention it deserves. Two catalogues for one and the same
historical exhibition organized by the Heimatmuseum Treptow on the occasion of
the exposition's centennial allow for the most instructive access. See Bezirksamt
Treptow von Berlin, *Die verhinderte Weltausstellung*, and *Die Berliner Gewerbeausstellung
1896 in Bildern*. See also Thiel, 'Berlin präsentiert sich der Welt'; Mieck, 'Berlin als
deutsches und europäisches Wirtschaftszentrum', esp. 133–9; Reuter, 'Die Große
Berliner Gewerbeausstellung 1896 im Treptower Park'; Rowe, 'Georg Simmel and the
Berlin Trade Exhibition of 1896'; Müller, 'Eine Parade der Produktion'; and Geppert,
'Weltstadt für einen Sommer'. There is a confusing abundance of official and semi-
official catalogues, publications and reports. As is often the case, the main catalogue
(Arbeitsausschuss der Berliner Gewerbe-Ausstellung, *Offizieller Haupt-Katalog der
Berliner Gewerbe-Ausstellung 1896*) was issued before the fair's actual opening and
is far from reliable. The official final report was published as Arbeitsausschuss der
Berliner Gewerbe-Ausstellung, *Berlin und seine Arbeit*; a second edition, issued in
1910, included a financial report. The only official guide available for visitors was
the *Illustrierter Amtlicher Führer*. Semi-official publications include Lindenberg, *Pracht-
Album*; and Kühnemann, *Groß-Berlin*.
3. This question has been largely overlooked, but see Schultze, 'Warum es in Berlin
nicht zu einer Weltausstellung kam'; Kroker, *Die Weltausstellungen im 19. Jahrhundert*,
194–8; Bohle-Heintzenberg, 'Berlin und die Weltausstellung'; Erhard Crome,
'Berliner Gewerbeausstellung 1896', in Bezirksamt Treptow von Berlin, *Die verhinderte
Weltausstellung*, 14–16; Großbölting, '*Im Reich der Arbeit*', 394–9; and Geppert,
'Ausstellungsmüde'. The only known list of 'fairs that never were' is limited to the
twentieth century and has a certain North American bias; see Findling and Pelle,
Encyclopedia of World's Fairs and Expositions, 428–34.
4. On the 1844 trade fair, see *Amtlicher Bericht über die allgemeine Deutsche Gewerbe-
Ausstellung zu Berlin im Jahre 1844*; Brennglas, *Die Berliner Gewerbe-Ausstellung*; Bonnell,
'Die Deutsche Gewerbeausstellung zu Berlin im Jahre 1844'; and Geitel, 'Hundert
Jahre deutsches Ausstellungswesen'. On the 1879 fair, see Maurer, *Officieller Katalog
zur Berliner Gewerbe-Ausstellung im Jahre 1879*. With a permanent exhibition building
erected for the Jubiläumskunstausstellung of 1886, the site was later (1892–1932) used
for the annual Große Berliner Kunstausstellung until being entirely dismantled in
1951–52; see Steinle, 'Das Moabiter Ausstellungsgelände'. 'Die Eröffnung der Berliner
Ausstellung', *Vossische Zeitung* (1 May 1896, MA), 1.
5. Bobertag, *Eine Weltausstellung in Deutschland*, GStA PK, I. HA Rep. 120 MfHuG, E XVI 2,
Nr. 13 F: 'Veranstaltung einer Weltausstellung in Berlin', vol. 1, 187–238, 15; Schwankl,
Das württembergische Ausstellungswesen, 278; and Cleve, 'Dem Fortschritt entgegen'.

For a broader context, see Thomas Großbölting's study *'Im Reich der Arbeit'* on German nineteenth-century trade exhibitions, in particular in Mainz, Berlin, Munich, Düsseldorf and Hanover, here esp. 124–5 and 258–9.

6. Examples for raising the question of organizing an international exhibition in the aftermath of the 1878 exposition include Lohren, 'Mitteilungen von der Pariser Weltausstellung', 177; and 'Das Projekt einer Weltausstellung zu Berlin im Jahre 1885'.

7. Franz C. Huber subdivides the controversy until 1895 into four different phases: February 1880, April 1881, May 1885 and April 1891; see Huber, *Die Berliner Welt-Ausstellung*, 4. L. Otto Brandt, however, distinguishes between two phases only, at the beginning of the 1880s and in the early 1890s; see Brandt, 'Zur Geschichte und Würdigung der Weltausstellungen', 91–2.

8. On the latter, see Biggeleben, 'Kontinuität von Bürgerlichkeit im Berliner Unternehmertum', and *'Bollwerk des Bürgertums'*, 143–9. Unfortunately, Biggeleben ignores the Gewerbeausstellung almost entirely in his otherwise painstaking study of the association's social and economic history. *Illustrierter Amtlicher Führer*, 29; 'Verwendung des Ueberschusses der Berliner Gewerbe-Ausstellung 1879', *Deutsche Bauzeitung* 15 (19 January 1881), 36. For a report of Goldberger's activities during the ten years of his chairmanship, see Goldberger, *An die Mitglieder des Vereins Berliner Kaufleute und Industrieller*, here 32–9.

9. Lindenberg, *Pracht-Album*, 9; Arbeitsausschuss der Berliner Gewerbe-Ausstellung, *Offizieller Haupt-Katalog der Berliner Gewerbe-Ausstellung 1896*, i–xvii.

10. Reuleaux, *Briefe aus Philadelphia*, 3–5. For more detailed biographical information, see Zopke, *Professor Franz Reuleaux*; and Pöschl, *Franz Reuleaux*; on the scandal itself Braun, 'Franz Reuleaux und der Technologietransfer zwischen Deutschland und Nordamerika am Ausgang des 19. Jahrhunderts'; Radkau, *Technik in Deutschland*, 148–55; Krutisch, '"...billig und schlecht!"'; and Bonnell, '"Cheap and Nasty"'. 'Der Schluß der Gewerbe-Ausstellung', *Berliner Morgen-Zeitung und Tägliches Familienblatt* (16 October 1896), 1; 'Beschlußfassung über die Anträge des technischen Ausschusses', 102; Pollard, '"Made in Germany"'. The fact that Reuleaux triggered this debate and coined its key term did not impair his professional position, personal reputation and future career as one of the most outspoken and distinguished German exhibition professionals. Reuleaux continued to publish on expositions, though carefully avoided mentioning the scandal; see Reuleaux, 'Die Anfänge des Ausstellungswesens'; 'Ausstellungswesen 1851–1899'; and 'Die Entwicklung des Ausstellungswesens'.

11. Pohl, 'Die Weltausstellungen im 19. Jahrhundert', 424; Lohren, 'Mitteilungen von der Pariser Weltausstellung', 177.

12. The building was not erected but the two architects constructed another semi-permanent exhibition pavillion that was used for two consecutive smaller expositions in Berlin, the Ausstellung auf dem Gebiete der Hygiene und des Rettungswesens (1883) and the Jubiläums-Ausstellung der bildenden Künste (1886). Messel, 'Ausstellungsbauten', 501–9; 'Die Architektur auf der diesjährigen Ausstellung der Akademie der Künste zu Berlin', *Deutsche Bauzeitung* 13 (4 October 1879), 402–5, here 404; Lüders, 'Das Project einer Weltausstellung zu Berlin im Jahre 1885', 614–15; 'Verein deutscher Eisen- und Stahlindustrieller', *Glaser's Annalen für Gewerbe und Bauwesen* 5 (1 December 1879), 415. The ensuing debate is documented in GStA PK, I. HA Rep. 120 MfHuG, E XVI, 2, Nr. 13 U: 'Die Errichtung eines allgemeinen Ausstellungsgeländes in Berlin, 1880–1890'.

13. Präsidium des Deutschen Handelstages an die Deutschen Handelskammern und die zum Deutschen Handelstage gehörigen wirthschaftlichen Vereine, 15 January 1880, GStA PK, I. HA Rep. 120 MfHuG, E XVI 2, Nr. 13 F, vol. 1, 41–7, here 41–2; 'Berliner Weltausstellung'. On the question of international regulation, see Chapter 7.

14. Kühnemann, *Die wünschenswerthe Gestaltung einer demnächstigen größeren Ausstellung in Berlin*, 19; Reuleaux, 'Eine deutsche Weltausstellung?', 17.

15. Scheffler, *Berlin – ein Stadtschicksal*, 15: 'die zur Millionenstadt und Reichshauptstadt gewordene Siedelung germanischer Ackerbauern und wendischer Fischer'.

16. Lüders, 'Das Project einer Weltausstellung zu Berlin im Jahre 1885', 619–20, and 'Eine Weltausstellung in Berlin'; Brockhoff, *Eine Weltausstellung in Berlin*; Vogel, 'Bericht, betreffend das Ausstellungswesen', 254.

17. *Stenographische Berichte über die Verhandlungen des Reichstages: V. Legislaturperiode, 1. Session 1881–82*, 36. Sitzung am 27. Januar 1882, 1008–10; Hermann, 'Bericht über Ausstellungen und Ansichten über eine Weltausstellung in Berlin', 153.

18. 'Weltausstellungs-Pläne', *Deutsche Bauzeitung* 24 (4 October 1890), 481–6, here 483, 485–6; Bobertag, *Eine Weltausstellung in Deutschland*, 10; Simon, 'Über eine im Jahre 1894 in Berlin zu veranstaltende Allgemeine deutsche Gewerbausstellung', 134.

19. 17. Deutscher Handelstag: 1. Sitzung, 15 January 1892, GStA PK, I. HA Rep. 120 MfHuG, E XVI 2, Nr. 13 F, vol. 1, 121–4: 'Der deutsche Handelstag hält [...] es für geboten, daß die nächste Welt-Ausstellung in Berlin veranstaltet werde, um auf diese Weise auch der deutschen Gewerbethätigkeit diejenigen Vortheile zu sichern, welche eine im eigenen Lande veranstaltete Welt-Ausstellung gewährt.' For a detailed chronology, see Bobertag, *Eine Weltausstellung in Deutschland*, 79–88, here 81.

20. 'Zur Gewinnung des Entwurfes eines allgemeinen Lageplans für eine in Berlin zu veranstaltende Weltausstellung', *Centralblatt der Bauverwaltung* 12 (25 May 1892), 228. As early as March 1881, the association had organized a similar, but smaller architectural contest which, however, came to no consequence. See 'Architekten-Verein zu Berlin', *Deutsche Bauzeitung* 15 (12 March 1881), 126. '[International Exhibition in Berlin]', *Builder* 62 (19 November 1892), 390; [Berlin Exhibition], ibid. 62 (23 April 1892), 319.

21. 'Preisbewerbung um den Entwurf des Lageplans für eine Weltausstellung in Berlin', 485–6, 502.

22. Ibid., 551; 'Entwurf des allgemeinen Lageplans einer in Berlin zu veranstaltenden Weltausstellung'.

23. This was roughly the area in Berlin-Wedding today covered by the Volkspark Rehberge. Braun, *Panorama der Berliner Weltausstellung*, 136–49. A copy of this rare pamphlet can be found in GStA PK, I. HA Rep. 120 MfHuG, E XVI 2, Nr. 13 F, vol. 2.

24. This was meant quite literally: 'Instead, a tower could be built here with one foot on the left and the other on the right bank of the Spree; this would quite outdo the Paris Eiffel Tower in every respect'; Reiländer, *Ausstellungen der Zukunft*, 33. See also *Builder* 58 (22 February 1890), 128.

25. Braun, *Panorama der Berliner Weltausstellung*, 18–21. See also J. Knöfel to Handels-Ministerium, 8 August 1892, GStA PK, I. HA Rep. 120 MfHuG, E XVI 2, Nr. 13 F, vol. 3, 54; 'Der wahre Grund der Haltung des Herrn Reichskanzlers in Sachen der Berliner Weltausstellung', 8 August 1892, ibid., 55–6.

26. For instance Reuleaux, 'Eine deutsche Weltausstellung?', 18; Grothe, 'Bericht über Ausstellungen und Ansichten über eine Weltausstellung in Berlin', 157; Vogel, 'Bericht, betreffend das Ausstellungswesen', 263: 'Wir haben lange genug Gastrollen auf fremden Weltausstellungen gegeben, wir sind jetzt einmal verpflichtet, Gastfreundschaft zu üben. Das ewige Schnorrertum ist des deutschen Volkes unwürdig.'

27. For instance 'Das Projekt einer Weltausstellung zu Berlin im Jahre 1885', 18; Grothe, 'Bericht über Ausstellungen und Ansichten über eine Weltausstellung in Berlin', 150; Delbrück, 'Die Berliner Weltausstellung', 236; Lessing, 'Die Berliner Gewerbe-Ausstellung 1896', 279: 'zu Deutschlands neuerlangter Weltstellung gehört eine Weltausstellung'; Hillger, *Die Deutsche Welt-Ausstellung von 1897: Eine Forderung und ein gutes Recht der deutschen Nation!*; Simon, 'Über eine im Jahre 1894 in Berlin zu veranstaltende Allgemeine deutsche Gewerbeausstellung', 140, 148.

28. Vogel, 'Bericht, betreffend das Ausstellungswesen', 262; Brockhoff, *Eine Weltausstellung in Berlin*, 19: 'Berlin [...] muß internationalen Cercle halten. [...] Berlin wird alte Vorurtheile, die gegen das ehemalige wendische Fischerdorf bestehen, zerstreuen, es wird selbst die Reste seiner kleinbürgerlichen Vergangenheit abschütteln und sich als Weltstadt fühlen lernen.' The parallels between this process of 'capitalization' and a similar one roughly a hundred years later are more than obvious. The eventually unrealized 1993 plans to hold

the Olympic Games of 2000 in Berlin were largely motivated by comparable hopes for unifying repercussions on the metropolis' self-image and self-perception. See the contributions to Körner and Weigand, *Hauptstadt*, especially the essay by Wolfram Siemann, 'Die deutsche Hauptstadtproblematik im 19. Jahrhundert', 249–60.

29. 'Exhibitions', 23–4; Bobertag, *Eine Weltausstellung in Deutschland*, 23; Reusche, Chicago und Berlin, 53; L'Ambassadeur de la République française à Berlin à S. Exc., M. le Ministre des Affaires Etrangères à Paris, 20 May 1892, CARAN F12 4993; 'Weltausstellung und Revanchekrieg', *Allgemeine Zeitung* (8 July 1892, MA), 1; 'The Rival International Exhibitions', *Times* (5 July 1892), 5; 'The Exhibition of 1900', ibid. (6 September 1895), 3.

30. See Chapter 7 for an extensive discussion of *Ausstellungsmüdigkeit*.

31. Reiländer, *Ausstellungen der Zukunft*, 1: 'Ihre heutige Gestalt stempelt sie zu Luxus-Passionen, die sich nur ein industriell und mercantil überleistungsfähiges, an Fluctuationen gewöhntes und mit der erforderlichen Elasticität begabtes Gemeinwesen unbedenklich gestatten kann.'

32. See, for instance, Lüders, 'Das Project einer Weltausstellung zu Berlin im Jahre 1885', 615; 'Germany', *Times* (14 November 1885), 5.

33. Bobertag, *Eine Weltausstellung in Deutschland*, 9: 'lokalpatriotische Eifersüchteleien und die leider noch immer eine so unschöne Rolle spielende Voreingenommenheit gegen den "Wasserkopf" Berlin.'

34. Brandt, 'Zur Geschichte und Würdigung der Weltausstellungen', 91; Reusche, *Chicago und Berlin*, 55; Borges, 'On Rigor in Science'.

35. *Reichs-Anzeiger* (13 August 1892): 'Daß dem Plane einer Weltausstellung in Berlin von Reichs wegen nicht näher zu treten sei.' Wilhelm II. to Graf von Caprivi, 20 July 1892, in Rich et al., *Die Geheimen Papiere Friedrich von Holsteins*, 375–6: 'Der Ruhm der Pariser läßt den Berliner nicht schlafen. Berlin ist Großstadt, Weltstadt (vielleicht?), also muß es auch seine Ausstellung haben! [...] Paris ist nun mal – was Berlin hoffentlich nie wird – das große Hurenhaus der Welt, daher die Anziehung auch außer der Ausstellung. In Berlin ist nichts, was den Fremden fesselt als die paar Museen, Schlösser und die Soldaten. [...] Ich will die Ausstellung nicht, weil sie meinem Vaterland und -Stadt Unheil bringt! [...] Ausstellung is nich, wie meine Herren Berliner sagen.'

36. See Alfred von Kiderlen-Wächter to Holstein, 13 July 1892, ibid., 372, for a similar statement.

37. 'Das Ende der deutschen Weltausstellungs-Träume', *Deutsche Bauzeitung* 26 (20 August 1892), 401–2, here 401; 'Germany', *Times* (15 August 1892), 3; see also 'Die Pläne der Wettbewerbung um den Lageplan einer Weltausstellung in Berlin', *Centralblatt der Bauverwaltung* 12 (24 December 1892), 567.

38. A wealth of material can be found in BArch R 901/694.

39. On the Ständige Ausstellungskommission, see Chapter 7. *Jahresberichte des Vereins Berliner Kaufleute und Industrieller* (1906), 56; 'Die Berliner Weltausstellung 1913', *Berliner Tageblatt* (21 March 1907, AA); Hermann Hillger to Auswärtiges Amt, 28 April 1909, BArch R 901/694, 64, and 'Eine Weltausstellung in Berlin'; *Verhandlungen des Deutschen Reichstages*, 200. Sitzung, 6 February 1909, 6742.

40. 'Der Kaiser gegen eine Berliner Weltausstellung', *Berliner Lokal-Anzeiger* 551 (29 October 1910, AA); *Temps* (31 October 1910); 'Der Kaiser gegen die großen Weltschauen', *Berliner Tageblatt* (30 October 1910, MA).

41. Fritz Stahl, 'Berliner Weltausstellung', *Berliner Tageblatt* (2 November 1910); see also Stahl, 'Die Berliner Weltausstellung', *Berliner Tageblatt* (11 March 1907).

42. After the international success of the 1936 Olympic Games, Hitler intended to hold a German Weltausstellung in the capital once Germany had emerged victorious from the war and Berlin had been rebuilt. Apparently after a conversation with Hitler, Joseph Goebbels noted in his diary on 3 March 1937: 'World's fair in Berlin not yet to be planned. Not before Berlin's building plans have been realized, in 15 years. Furthermore, Führer is of the opinion that the year 1943 is too risky in terms of war and security politics. Thus, to be postponed.' Goebbels, *Tagebücher*, vol. 3: *1935–1939*, 1052.

43. Reif, 'Hauptstadtentwicklung und Elitenbildung'.
44. Paquet, *Das Ausstellungsproblem in der Volkswirtschaft*, 281; Budde, 'Über Ausstellungswesen', 301.
45. 'Projekt einer Weltausstellung in Berlin', *Deutsche Bauzeitung* 16 (1 February 1882), 50; Grothe, 'Bericht über Ausstellungen und Ansichten über eine Weltausstellung in Berlin', 157–9; Vogel, 'Bericht, betreffend das Ausstellungswesen', 257–8.
46. For instance Grunow, *Der Kaiser und die Kaiserstadt*, 49–50; Stremmel, *Modell und Moloch*, 57–63; Röhl, *Wilhelm II*, 513–15.
47. *Illustrierter Amtlicher Führer*, 5: 'Das Sehnen nach einer großen Ausstellung war in Berlin alten Datums'; 'Die Anlage und die Bauten der Berliner Gewerbe-Ausstellung des Jahres 1896 I', 209; Paquet, *Das Ausstellungsproblem in der Volkswirtschaft*, 292. For a concise summary of the exhibition's prehistory from the organizers' perspective, see Arbeitsausschuss der Berliner Gewerbe-Ausstellung, *Offizieller Haupt-Katalog der Berliner Gewerbe-Ausstellung 1896*, ii–xvii.
48. Delbrück, 'Die Krisis des deutschen Weltausstellungsplans', 358: 'Die nationale Ausstellung theilt mit der Weltausstellung den Fehler der Unübersichtlichkeit, die Versuchung zu Blendwerk und Schwindel. Die entbehrt aber die Vorzüge jener: die imponirende Größe, den Glanz, die Stärke der Contraste, die Vollständigkeit der Belehrung, die Anziehungskraft für die Fremden, die Deutschland kennen und schätzen lernen sollen.' XX, 'L'Exposition de Berlin', 887; Charles Bonnefon, 'L'Exposition de Berlin', *Figaro* 42 (5 May 1896), 5.
49. *Jahresberichte des Vereins Berliner Kaufleute und Industrieller* (1890–91), 8; ibid. (1891–92), 3; 'Anlage No. 2 betr. Berliner Weltausstellung und Berliner Gewerbeausstellung 1896', ibid. (1892–93), 10, 26–7; 'Reichskanzler Gr. Caprivi an das Präsidium des Vereins Berliner Kaufleute und Industrieller, 3 June 1892', ibid., 27; 'Germany', *Times* (23 May 1892), 5.
50. 'Öffentliche Versammlung zur Diskussion der Frage einer Berliner Ausstellung 1896–97 abgehalten am 10. November 1892 im grossen Saale des Kaiserhofes', *Jahresberichte des Vereins Berliner Kaufleute und Industrieller* (1892–93), 28: 'Berlin hat, was es der Welt zeigen darf, deshalb will Berlin der Welt einmal zeigen, was es hat!' See also Richard Schott, 'Wie die Ausstellung zu Stande kam', in Kühnemann, *Groß-Berlin*, 15–21, here 19.
51. 'Aufruf Berliner Gewerbe-Ausstellung', *Jahresberichte des Vereins Berliner Kaufleute und Industrieller* (1892–93), 33–5; 'Berliner Gewerbe-Ausstellung 1896: Bestimmung für die Beschickung der Ausstellung', 25 January 1894, BArch R 1001/6332, 77. See also Verein Berliner Kaufleute und Industrieller, *Berlins Aufstieg zur Weltstadt*, 162–6.
52. XX, 'L'Exposition de Berlin', 891.
53. 'Preisbewerbung um den Entwurf des Lageplans für eine Weltausstellung in Berlin', 503; 'Wo soll die Weltausstellung hin?', 394; 'Die Platzfrage zur Berliner Gewerbe-Ausstellung', *Berliner Tageblatt* (19 May 1894, MA); Leopold Rosenow, 'Vorgeschichte und Vorbereitung der Berliner Gewerbe-Ausstellung 1896', in Arbeitsausschuss der Berliner Gewerbe-Ausstellung, *Berlin und seine Arbeit*, 27–84, esp. 45–54; Braun, *Panorama der Berliner Weltausstellung*, 11; 'Germany', *Times* (30 July 1895), 3.
54. *Jahresberichte des Vereins Berliner Kaufleute und Industrieller* (1896–97), 26; Klinke, 'Die Verkehrs-Verhältnisse der Berliner Gewerbe-Ausstellung 1896', *Deutsche Bauzeitung* 30 (22 February 1896), 101–2; 'Die Erweiterung der Stadt- und Ringbahn, namentlich inbezug auf die Berliner Gewerbe-Ausstellung', ibid. (9 September 1896), 459–60; 'Die Berliner Gewerbeausstellung 1896 III', *Centralblatt der Bauverwaltung* 16 (28 March 1896), 137–9, here 138; XX, 'L'Exposition de Berlin', 890.
55. Arbeitsausschuss der Berliner Gewerbe-Ausstellung, *Berlin und seine Arbeit*, 98; Schulz, 'Der Treptower Park', 198–9; Arbeitsgemeinschaft 'Junge Historiker', *Das Treptower Ehrenmal*; *Das Sowjetische Ehrenmal in Berlin-Treptow*; Ladd, *The Ghosts of Berlin*, 1, 194–5.
56. XX, 'L'Exposition de Berlin', 893; 'Die Einnahmen der Berliner Gewerbe-Ausstellung', *Berliner Morgen-Zeitung und Tägliches Familienblatt* (18 October 1896); Arbeitsausschuss

der Berliner Gewerbe-Ausstellung, *Berlin und seine Arbeit*, 151, 181; *Vossische Zeitung* (9 May 1896, MA): 'Man muß doch auf der Ausstellung gewesen sein; denn wer sie nicht besucht hat, gilt gleichsam als nicht existenzberechtigt; er darf nicht mitreden, wird am Stammtisch über die Achseln angesehen und von den strafenden Blicken seiner Herren Söhne und Fräulein Töchter verfolgt, denen er noch nicht Gelegenheit gegeben hat, die Schaustellung in Treptow zu sehen.'

57. XX, 'L'Exposition de Berlin', 889.
58. 'Die Berliner Gewerbeausstellung 1896', *Centralblatt der Bauverwaltung* 15 (13 April 1895), 153–6, here 153; ibid., 16 (22 February 1896), 77–9; Zetsche, 'Die Architektur', *Berliner Tageblatt* (16 May 1896): 'So entstand hier aus der gärtnerischen Anlage die Grundrißdisposition, statt daß wie sonst die Architektur in großer ungehinderter Massenentwicklung zunächst die Gesammtwirkung [sic] anstreben und dann zur Abrundung und Ausschmückung des Bildes die gärtnerischen Anlagen hinzufügen durfte.'
59. 'Die Sonderausstellung der Stadt Berlin auf der Berliner Gewerbe-Ausstellung 1896', *Deutsche Bauzeitung* 30 (19 September 1896), 475–6; 'Die Berliner Gewerbeausstellung VIII', *Centralblatt der Bauverwaltung* 16 (25 July 1896), 330–3.
60. 'Die Anlage und die Bauten der Berliner Gewerbe-Ausstellung des Jahres 1896 I', 209; 'Die Bautechnik auf der Berliner Gewerbe-Ausstellung 1896', *Deutsche Bauzeitung* 30 (25 July 1896), 382–3.
61. 'Die Anlage und die Bauten der Berliner Gewerbe-Ausstellung des Jahres 1896 I', 209; 'Die Berliner Gewerbeausstellung VI', *Centralblatt der Bauverwaltung* 16 (4 July 1896), 294–8, here 294; *Illustrierter Amtlicher Führer*, 31: 'der Brennpunkt des Ganzen'. On the *Hauptgebäude*'s architecture, see also Großbölting, 'Im Reich der Arbeit', 265–9, 358–9.
62. 'Die Berliner Gewerbeausstellung IV', *Centralblatt der Bauverwaltung* 16 (18 April 1896), 171–4, here 172; XX, 'L'Exposition de Berlin', 894: 'The building [...] evokes for a Frenchman the memory of the Trocadéro. The semi-circular colonnade decorating the façade completes the analogy. But as in most Berlin monuments, the breadth is too exaggerated for the height, and the ensemble looks heavy.'
63. 'Die Anlage und die Bauten der Berliner Gewerbe-Ausstellung des Jahres 1896 II', 226; 'Die Eröffnung der Berliner Ausstellung', *Vossische Zeitung* (1 May 1896, MA), 1: 'Die Berliner Gewerbeausstellung wird einen Ehrenplatz in der Geschichte deutscher Arbeit, deutschen Fleißes behaupten.'
64. Kühnemann, *Groß-Berlin*, 21.
65. 'Statuten der Deutschen Kolonial-Ausstellung: Gruppe XXIII der Berliner Gewerbe-Ausstellung', BArch R 1001/6333, 130, §2; Daniela Schnitter, 'Zur ersten Deutschen Kolonialausstellung im Rahmen der Berliner Gewerbeausstellung 1896', in Bezirksamt Treptow von Berlin and Heimatmuseum Treptow, *Die verhinderte Weltausstellung*, 115–24. See also the contributions to Kundrus, *Phantasiereiche*.
66. Arbeitsausschuss der Deutschen Kolonial-Ausstellung, *Deutschland und seine Kolonien*, 6; Roland Richter, 'Die erste Deutsche Kolonialausstellung 1896: Der "Amtliche Bericht" in historischer Perspektive', in Debusmann and Riesz, *Kolonialausstellungen*, 25–42.
67. 'Aufruf des Arbeitsausschusses für die Kolonialabtheilung auf der Berliner Gewerbeausstellung 1896', *National-Zeitung* (2 June 1895): 'Um eine allgemeine Theilnahme für diese erste deutsche Kolonial-Ausstellung im größeren Stil zu erwecken, müssen alle Kräfte zur Bethätigung an der Ausstellung in Bewegung gesetzt werden. Der Arbeitsausschuß richtet daher an alle Kolonialabtheilungen, an die interessirten Industriekreise, an die Behörden, an die Vertreter der Wissenschaft, nicht zum wenigsten aber an die große Anzahl unserer Afrikaforscher die Aufforderung, sich an der Kolonial-Ausstellung zu betheiligen und in ihren Kreisen zur Bethätigung derselben nach Kräften zu wirken, damit durch eine in allen Theilen möglichst vollkommen ausgestaltete Kolonial-Ausstellung das Interesse für weitere Kolonien auch in den weitesten Volksschichten erwacht.'
68. Gustav Meinecke, 'Einleitung', in Arbeitsausschuss der Deutschen Kolonial-Ausstellung, *Deutschland und seine Kolonien*, 1–3: 'ein Gebot nationaler und kultureller Pflicht'; 'Was in Europa Grossmacht ist [...], das ist auch Kolonialmacht.'

69. *Illustrierter Amtlicher Führer*, 155–61; Richard Schott, 'Die Berliner Gewerbe-Ausstellung 1896: Die Deutsche Kolonial-Ausstellung', in Kühnemann, *Groß-Berlin*, 253–63; Programm für die Ausstellung der Kolonialabtheilung i. J. 1896, BArch R 1001/6333, 23; 'Ein Rundgang durch die Kolonialabtheilung der Gewerbeausstellung', *Vossische Zeitung* (13 May 1896, AA); 'Die deutsche Kolonialausstellung', *Berliner Neueste Nachrichten* 16 (23 May 1896, MA).

70. Arbeitsausschuss der Deutschen Kolonial-Ausstellung, *Deutschland und seine Kolonien*, 17; Lindenberg, *Pracht-Album*, 52.

71. Arbeitsausschuss der Berliner Gewerbe-Ausstellung, *Berlin und seine Arbeit*, 151; Arbeitsausschuss der Deutschen Kolonial-Ausstellung, *Deutschland und seine Kolonien*, 355–6.

72. According to the official guide there were 90 'natives' (24 from Cameroon, 20 from Togo, 6 from New Guinea and approximately 40 from East Africa); according to the section's official report, the group comprised 103 persons. See *Illustrierter Amtlicher Führer*, 155–61; Eugen Neisser, 'Das Leben und Treiben der Eingeborenen', in Arbeitsausschuss der Deutschen Kolonial-Ausstellung, *Deutschland und seine Kolonien*, 25–42, for detailed listings. On their fate after the exposition's closure, see BArch R 1001/6349.

73. Reubauer, 'Die deutsche Kolonialausstellung (Schluß)', *Berliner Neueste Nachrichten* 16 (24 May 1896, MA): 'Es lag in der Absicht, dem Beschauer der Kolonialausstellung in natura eine Reihe von Ansiedlungen vorzuführen, wie sie für die Haupttheile unserer Kolonialgebiete charakteristisch sind, und diese Ansiedlung zu bevölkern mit Menschenmaterial aus den Kolonien selbst.'

74. Arbeitsausschuss der Deutschen Kolonial-Ausstellung, *Deutschland und seine Kolonien*, 11.

75. Ibid., 23: 'In dieses Bild der tropischen Kolonien brachten die Eingeborenen ein buntbewegtes Leben. Sie verpflanzten mitten hinein in die Weltstadt mit ihren verfeinerten Sitten, ihren Modemenschen, ihrer stolzen Pracht, ein Stück natürlicher Wildheit, rohester Kultur. Gerade diese Gegensätze, zum erstenmal in engem Rahmen nebeneinander mit greifbarer Deutlichkeit vorgeführt, machten die Ausstellung so fesselnd und reizvoll für jedermann.'

76. The literature is ever-growing. See, for instance, Zippelius, 'Der Mensch als lebendes Exponat'; Çelik and Kinney, 'Ethnography and Exhibitionism at the *Expositions universelles*'; Corbey, 'Ethnographic Showcases'; Mathur, 'Living Ethnological Exhibits'; Bancel et al., *Zoos humains*; Gründer, 'Indianer, Afrikaner und Südseebewohner in Europa'; Abbattista, 'Torino 1884'; and Dreesbach, *'Gezähmte Wilde'*.

77. 'Die deutsche Kolonialausstellung', *Berliner Neueste Nachrichten* 16 (23 May 1896, MA); 'Ausstellungen', 9.

78. The substantial body of literature on Carl Hagenbeck now includes Reichenbach, 'Carl Hagenbeck's Tierpark and Modern Zoological Gardens'; Thode-Arora, *Für fünfzig Pfennig um die Welt*; Dittrich and Rieke-Müller, *Carl Hagenbeck*; Pelc, 'Hagenbeck auf den Weltausstellungen'; Rothfels, *Savages and Beasts*, 81–142; and Kuenheim, *Carl Hagenbeck*. See also Leutemann, *Lebensbeschreibung des Thierhändlers Carl Hagenbeck*.

79. Although such recruitment was legally banned in 1901, there continued to be numerous exceptions. The later held *Deutsche Afrika-Schau* was independent of Hagenbeck and was closed down in 1940, only at the Propaganda Ministry's direct instigation. See Strauch, 'Zur Frage der Ausfuhr von Eingeborenen aus den deutschen Kolonien zum Zwecke der Schaustellung', *Deutsche Kolonialzeitung* 13 (1900), 500–1, 511–12, 520; and Forgey, '"Die große Negertrommel der kolonialen Werbung"', 25. Corbey ('Ethnographic Showcases', 358) errs in this respect.

80. 'Die deutsche Kolonialausstellung', *Berliner Neueste Nachrichten* 16 (23 May 1896, MA); Wilhelm Gronauer, 'Gesundheitszustand und Krankheiten der Eingeborenen', in Arbeitsausschuss der Deutschen Kolonial-Ausstellung, *Deutschland und seine Kolonien*, 43–9, here 43, 47–8; 'Von den Eingeborenen der Kolonial-Ausstellung', *Berliner Morgen-Zeitung und Tägliches Familienblatt* (15 October 1896), 243; Graf von Schweinitz, 12 October 1896, BArch R 1001/6340, 43; Brief des Präsidenten der Deutschen Kolonialgesellschaft an das Auswärtige Amt, Kolonial-Abteilung, BArch R 1001/6348/6, 36.

81. Haarmann, *Vor dem Rubicon*, 13–14: 'Was den Pariser Ausstellungen das internationale und in gewisser Beziehung exotische Gepräge gab, waren hauptsächlich die ethnographischen und kolonialen Abtheilungen, welche eine fast unumschränkte Entfaltung fremdartiger Erscheinungen und pomphafter Aufzüge ermöglichten. Will man derartige Zuthaten durchaus für eine Nothwendigkeit ansehen, so hindert uns offenbar nichts, durch die Veranschaulichung des Lebens, der Verhältnisse und der Erzeugnisse der deutschen Schutzgebiete und durch die sicherlich nicht vergebens anzurufende Mitwirkung der Reichsangehörigen in fremden Ländern, nach dieser Richtung auch einer deutsch-nationalen Ausstellung ein Gepräge der Internationalität zu geben, welches dem Sensationsbedürfnis des Publicums ausreichende Befriedigung zu gewähren vermöchte. Die Einbeziehung der deutschen Schutzgebiete würde obendrein das, beiläufig vom nationalen wie vom volkswirthschaftlichen Gesichtspunkte gewiß nicht unwillkommene, Mittel bieten, das Interesse für unsere kolonialen Unternehmungen in alle Schichten des Volkes zu tragen.'

82. Arbeitsausschuss der Berliner Gewerbe-Ausstellung, *Berlin und seine Arbeit*, 3 (emphasis in original). This difference in scope was also emphasized by the sheer naming of the two different catalogues: Arbeitsausschuss der Deutschen Kolonial-Ausstellung, *Deutschland und seine Kolonien*, for the colonial sections versus Arbeitsausschuss der Berliner Gewerbe-Ausstellung, *Berlin und seine Arbeit*, for the general exhibition.

83. A precursor to the Parisian Cairo street could be found at the Vienna exposition of 1873. See Gléon, *La Rue du Caire*; and, especially, Mitchell's seminal article 'The World as Exhibition'. Hans Resener, 'Kairo in Berlin', *Berliner Neueste Nachrichten* 16 (28 June 1896, MA), 1–2; *Illustrierter Amtlicher Führer*, 212.

84. Ibid., 12: 'feenhafte Schöpfung aus dem Morgenlande'; Krug, *Offizieller Führer durch die Spezial-Abtheilung Kairo*, 10, 3, 101; Charles Bonnefon, 'L'Exposition de Berlin', *Figaro* 42 (5 May 1896), 5.

85. *Illustrierter Amtlicher Führer*, 212; Carl Stangen, 'Kairo in Berlin', in Kühnemann, *Groß-Berlin*, 129–41.

86. Krug, *Offizieller Führer durch die Spezial-Abtheilung Kairo*, 14, and 'Die Sonder-Ausstellung Kairo', in Arbeitsausschuss der Berliner Gewerbe-Ausstellung, *Berlin und seine Arbeit*, 867–73, here 873.

87. *Berliner Illustrirte Zeitung* (3 May 1896); 'Die Anlage und die Bauten der Berliner Gewerbe-Ausstellung des Jahres 1896 VII', 365; 'Die Berliner Gewerbeausstellung VI', *Centralblatt der Bauverwaltung* 16 (4 July 1896), 294–8, here 296: 'Schmitz hat […] mit dem Ton des Fremdländischen, Märchenhaften angeschlagen, den Ton, der zur Eintagserscheinung paßt, der bei Schaustellungen anlockt und durch seine Außergewöhnlichkeit auf die Sinne wirkt; – nicht umsonst ist "Kairo" das unausbleibliche Zubehör unserer Ausstellungen.'

88. Naumann, *Ausstellungsbriefe*, 36; Eyth, *Tagebücher*, 556.

89. *Berliner Tageblatt* (29 June 1896); *Berliner Lokal-Anzeiger* (2 July 1896).

90. 'Rundschau der wichtigsten Ausstellungen des Jahres 1896', 233; George, 'Die Ausstellung Alt-Berlin'.

91. Reuleaux, 'Ausstellungswesen 1851–1899', 194–5; Jaffé, 'Ausstellungsbauten', 635, 727–9; Witt, 'Naturwissenschaftlich-technische Ausstellungen', 456–8; Korn, *Hanseatische Gewerbeausstellungen im 19. Jahrhundert*, 144.

92. Brendicke, 'Bericht über die Sitzungen des Vereins', and *Führer durch die Sonder-Ausstellung von Berolinensien*. Geppert, 'Weltstadt für einen Sommer', 442–4.

93. *Illustrierter Amtlicher Führer*, 201–6; Maximilian Rapsilber, 'Die Sonder-Ausstellung Alt-Berlin', in Arbeitsausschuss der Berliner Gewerbe-Ausstellung, *Berlin und seine Arbeit*, 861–6, here 864; and Zelljadt, 'Presenting and Consuming the Past'.

94. 'Alt-Berlin auf der Berliner Gewerbe-Ausstellung', n.d., GStA PK, I. HA Rep. 120 MfHuG, E XVI 2, Nr. 13 Af, vol. 1, 141–56/1–31.

95. 'Die Berliner Gewerbeausstellung XIII', *Centralblatt der Bauverwaltung* 16 (10 October 1896), 450: 'Thore, Ringmauern und wehrhafte Thürme, winklige Gassen und

Gässchen, der Markt mit Rathhaus und Gerichtslaube, die holländische Mühle, alle die traulichen, malerischen Häuser und Häuschen der ehrenfesten Berliner Patricier und Ackerbürger mit ihren Ein- und Ausbauten, ihren Erkern und Thürmchen und Wetterfahnen, ihren herausgebauten Treppen und heimlichen Laubensitzen sind wiedererstanden und versetzen uns in die Zeit, in der das Leben den Altvordern beschaulich dahinfloß, die aber gleichwohl die Keime legte zu dem gewaltigen Aufschwunge, den das bescheidene mittelalterliche Städtchen im Laufe der Jahrhunderte nehmen sollte.'

96. Alt-Berlin G.m.b.H. (Berliner Gewerbeausstellung 1896), 'Unter dem Protektorate des Vereins für die Geschichte Berlins', *Mittheilungen des Vereins für die Geschichte Berlins* 12.7 (7 July 1895), 72–3, here 73; *Illustrierter Amtlicher Führer*, 201.

97. 'Die Anlage und die Bauten der Berliner Gewerbe-Ausstellung des Jahres 1896 VII', 365: 'Seine Hauptbestimmung liegt in der künstlichen und künstlerischen Zurückversetzung des Besuchers in Zeiten, in welchen im Vergleich zu heute das Leben des Einzelnen dahinfloss wie ein ruhiger Strom, dessen Rauschen dem Nachbar kaum bemerkbar war und der selten die ihm gezogenen Ufer durchbrach. Das ist heute anders, und in diesem bei dem Besuche Alt-Berlins zum Bewusstsein kommenden Gegensatze liegt die Anziehungskraft dieser Veranstaltung.'

98. *Mittheilungen des Vereins für die Geschichte Berlins* 13.3 (1896), 34.

99. Franz Jaffé, 'Die Bauten', *Berliner Neueste Nachrichten* 16 (29 April 1896, MA); Richard Schott, 'Alt-Berlin', in Kühnemann, *Groß-Berlin*, 81–9, here 81.

100. XX, 'L'Exposition de Berlin', 897. For positive reviews from a British perspective, see 'The Berlin Industrial Exhibition', *Builder* 69 (7 December 1895), 419; and ibid. 71 (10 October 1896), 281–3.

101. For this, see Sweet, 'International Exhibition Postcards', 08.1; Arbeitsausschuss der Berliner Gewerbe-Ausstellung, *Berlin und seine Arbeit*, 198.

102. Kerr, *Wo liegt Berlin?*, and *Warum fließt der Rhein nicht durch Berlin?*

103. Kerr, *Wo liegt Berlin?*, 141, 148, 167; *National-Zeitung* (16 October 1896), 1. Beiblatt; 'Veröffentlichungen betreffend die Berliner Gewerbe-Ausstellung 1896, bestimmt für a.) Berliner Presse, b.) Auswärtige Deutsche Presse, c.) Versendungen durch Vermittlung des Auswärtigen Amtes', SBB-PK, 4° Oo 3766/28.

104. Simmel, 'Berliner Gewerbe-Ausstellung'; see the Appendix for the article's full text in German and English.

105. See Chapter 1. These seven plus one arguments are: form and spectacle; spectacle and perception; production and consumption; the exhibiting city and the exhibition city; transience; aesthetics; exhibit and exhibition/individual and society; and Berlin is not Paris.

106. Simmel, 'Berliner Gewerbe-Ausstellung'.

107. Richard Schott, 'Berliner Gewerbe-Ausstellung 1896: Ein erster Besuch', in Kühnemann, *Groß-Berlin*, 42–7, here 44: 'Ich sah all diese stolzen Gebäude mit tausend und abertausend Gästen aus aller Herren Länder sich bevölkern, ich sah wie alle nur bewunderten und mit Freuden ihre Portemonnaies hervorzogen, um von den dargebotenen Herrlichkeiten soviel wie möglich mit sich fortzunehmen, und mir war, als ginge über dem ganzen Ausstellungswerke eine Sonne des Segens auf, die ihre Strahlen über das gesamte Berlin und noch viel, viel weiter über das ganze deutsche Vaterland entsendete.'

108. Lessing, 'Die Berliner Gewerbe-Ausstellung', 289, 293. See also Franz Jaffé, 'Ein Rückblick', *Berliner Neueste Nachrichten* (27 September 1896, MA).

109. In 1909, Naumann's collected letters were published again, this time in book format. See Naumann, *Ausstellungsbriefe*, here 8, 67, 10 ('Die Aufgabe des Besuchers heißt: sehen! Hier muß man mit den Augen trinken'), 42–3, 45.

110. 'The Berlin Industrial Exhibition', *Times* (2 May 1896), 9; 'The Berlin Exhibition', ibid. (16 October 1896), 3; 'Not an Impressive Fair', *New York Times* (17 May 1896), 6; XX, 'L'Exposition de Berlin', 901.

111. Arbeitsausschuss der Berliner Gewerbe-Ausstellung, *Offizieller Haupt-Katalog der Berliner Gewerbe-Ausstellung 1896*, xvi: 'Für die Berliner Gewerbe-Ausstellung 1896 ist es schwer,

den rechten Masstab zu finden.' Wilhelm II. to Graf von Caprivi, 20 July 1892, in Rich et al., *Die Geheimen Papiere Friedrich von Holsteins*, 375–6; *Jahresberichte des Vereins Berliner Kaufleute und Industrieller* (1895–96), 25–6; 'Vereinigung Berliner Architekten', *Deutsche Bauzeitung* 30 (23 December 1896), 658–9, here 658.

112. *Illustrierter Amtlicher Führer*, 10; 'Nach Schluß der Ausstellung', *Vossische Zeitung* (16 October 1896, MA), 1; 'Weltausstellung und Treptower Ausstellung: Ein Interview mit Professor Reuleaux', *Berliner Tageblatt* (20 July 1896, AA), 1; Kerr, *Wo liegt Berlin?*, 215.

113. Reif, 'Hauptstadtentwicklung und Elitenbildung', 684; Lindenberg, *Pracht-Album*, 22: 'Da besann Berlin sich seiner selbst'; Brendicke, 'Zur Gewerbe-Ausstellung in Berlin', 68; 'Der Schluß der Gewerbe-Ausstellung', *Berliner Morgen-Zeitung und Tägliches Familienblatt* (16 October 1896), 1: 'das Unternehmen, das den ganzen Sommer über die Signatur der Stadt Berlin gebildet hatte'; 'Einpacken!', ibid. (17 October 1896), 1; Simmel, 'Berliner Gewerbe-Ausstellung', 60.

Chapter 3   Paris 1900

1. 'The exposition will constitute the synthesis, will determine the philosophy of the nineteenth century'. Roche, 'L'Exposition de 1900', 1–2; *Exposition universelle internationale de 1900 à Paris. Actes organiques*, 7. 'Perhaps one hits on the essential point when one says that this world exhibition is of the most magnificent unity in its foundational idea, yet of bewildering multiplicity in its realization and outward appearance.' Poppović, *Pariser Eindrücke*, 57, and 'Impressions parisiennes', 223.

2. For recent examples, see Jones, *Paris*; Higonnet, *Paris*; Harvey, *Paris, Capital of Modernity*; Prochasson, *Paris 1900*; Willms, *Paris*.

3. To be precise, with the exception of the first one, the intervals were always a decade each, with the exposition held during the eleventh year.

4. Poppović, 'Impressions parisiennes', 223, and *Pariser Eindrücke*, 57.

5. 'Exhibitions: Their History and Purpose', *Builder* 118 (9 April 1920), 431; Coubertin, 'Building up a World's Fair in France', 115.

6. Kidder, 'First View of the Exposition of 1900', 232.

7. According to official figures, total attendance was 50,860,801 with 48,368,504 in Paris and 2,492,297 at the Vincennes annexe; 'Statistique comparée des précédentes expositions', *Magasin Pittoresque* 68 (1900), 478; T. A., 'Statistique de l'Exposition', *Nature* 2 (1900), 407–9.

8. For initial reflections on how to conceptualize a history of Parisian expositions, see Rebérioux, 'Approches de l'histoire des Expositions universelles à Paris du Second Empire à 1900'. Surprisingly, the 1900 Exposition Universelle has attracted less scholarly attention than many other French fairs, in particular that of 1889. In many ways, Richard Mandell's classic 1967 study (*Paris 1900*) is still unsurpassed, but see also Williams, *Dream Worlds*; Wilson, 'Consuming History'; Bennett et al., *1900: The New Age*; Mabire, *L'Exposition universelle de 1900*; and Wesemael, *Architecture of Instruction and Delight*, 333–440. For an influential reading of the 1900 exposition as the culmination of a decade-long searching for a French craft Art Nouveau, see Silverman, *Art Nouveau in Fin-de-Siècle France*, 284–314.

9. For example, Henry Trueman Wood, 'The Paris Exhibition of 1900', *Times* (14 September 1895), 8; and Zeldin, *Histoire des passions françaises*, vol. 3, 388: 'The Exposition of 1900 was the most magnificent of all those ever organized, but it carried to an extreme the tensions apparent during previous manifestations.'

10. Roche, 'L'Exposition de 1900', 2.

11. Campbell, *Illustrated History*; Lessing, *Weltausstellung Paris 1900*, KB-SMB; Boyd, *The Paris Exhibition of 1900*, 9; Aflalo, 'The Promise of International Exhibitions', 830.

12. *The Nineteen Hundred*, 5; Plato, *Präsentierte Geschichte*, 261.

13. Bennett, *Report on Current European Fairs and Suggestions Arising from Attendance*, 15. Cf. also the Appendix in this volume.

14. Nora, *Les Lieux de mémoire*. While the conceptual applicability of Pierre Nora's term *lieu de mémoire* seems beyond doubt, it must nonetheless be considered all the more astonishing that, with the exception of the Eiffel Tower and the 1931 Exposition Coloniale, neither the Champ de Mars nor the various infrastructural legacies of the other seven expositions are examined in his mammoth *œuvre*.

15. Laulan, *Le Champ-de-Mars et ses origines*, 2; Riollot and Laulan, *Le Champ-de-Mars avant la Révolution*, 1. See also Baillehache, *L'Ecole militaire*.

16. Maindron, *Le Champ de Mars*, 1–2.

17. See the map appendix in Boullet, *Etudes de transformation, translation et restauration du Champ-de-Mars*; Faucheur, *Le Champ de Mars*.

18. Michelet, 'Préface', 32.

19. Morrison, *How I Worked My Way Around the World*, 148; Jourdain, 'L'Architecture au Champ-de-Mars'; and especially, albeit for an earlier period, Fride, 'L'Organisation spatiale de trois fêtes nationales révolutionnaires'.

20. Nelms, *The Third Republic and the Centennial of 1789*, 11–63, here 18.

21. On the reasons for Germany's non-participation in 1878, see 'Berliner Weltausstellung'; 'Die Betheiligung Deutschlands an der Pariser Weltausstellung'; and especially Pohl, 'Die Weltausstellungen im 19. Jahrhundert', 404–15.

22. Maindron, *Le Champ de Mars*, 2.

23. Nelms, *The Third Republic and the Centennial of 1789*, 11–13.

24. Lessing, *Das halbe Jahrhundert der Weltausstellungen*, 5.

25. 'Champ-de-Mars', in *Larousse du XXe siècle en six volumes*, vol. 2, Paris: Librairie Larousse, 1929, 118.

26. Pilz, *Paris amüsirt sich*, 182; Lohren, 'Mitteilungen von der Pariser Weltausstellung', 175.

27. Démy, *Essai historique*, 227–8: 'Le choix du Champ de Mars s'imposait. [...] C'est qu'en effet Paris en prenant avec les siècles une extension prodigieuse a conservé – fait unique peut-être dans l'histoire des capitales de l'Europe, – les caractères de sa constitution première et cet espace libre qui du centre allait s'élargissant toujours d'un même côté vers sa circonférence.' Maindron, *Le Champ de Mars*, 394; Berger, *Les Expositions universelles internationales*, 67–8.

28. 'Der Platz für die Pariser Weltausstellung des Jahres 1900', *Deutsche Bauzeitung* 27 (24 May 1893), 253–5, here 253.

29. 'L'Exposition de 1900', *Construction Moderne* 8 (8 April 1893), 314–15; 'The Competitive Schemes for the General Arrangement of the Exposition of 1900', *The American Architect and Building News* 47 (9 February 1895), 62-4; '[Sites proposed for the exhibition of 1900]', *Builder* 64 (4 February 1893), 83. The early disputes about the question of emplacement are reviewed in Calonne, 'L'Exposition de 1900 à Paris: Programme et concours'.

30. Jourdain, 'Le Concours de l'Exposition universelle de 1900'; 'Letter from Paris', *Builder* 65 (4 November 1893), 333; *Construction Moderne* 8 (18 March 1893), 288.

31. As on similar earlier occasions in 1876, 1880 and 1890, the utilization of the Champ de Mars was the subject of an agreement between the organizers on the one hand, and the City of Paris and the state (i.e., Ministry of War) on the other. Eventually, the City would acquire the entire site. Martayan, 'Les Rapports entre l'Etat et la Ville de Paris', 56, and 'L'Ephémère dans la ville', 44 n. 8.

32. Quoted after 'L'Exposition de 1900', *Construction Moderne* 8 (4 March 1893), 264.

33. Ibid.

34. Berger, *Les Expositions universelles internationales*, 145.

35. 'Exhibitions', 24.

36. Barrès, *Pas d'Exposition en 1900*; 'Objections contre l'Exposition de 1900', *Journal des Débats* (30 August 1895); Berger, *Les Expositions universelles internationales*, 145-8. Mandell is the only historian who discusses some of this opposition, see *Paris 1900*,

40–51. Comprehensive material in GStA PK, I. HA Rep. 120 MfHuG, E XVI 4, Nr. 3H, vol. 1.

37. Maurice Barrès, 'On peut éviter l'Exposition de 1900', *Figaro* 41 (2 August 1895). In a brief note, the *Figaro* clearly distanced itself from Barrès by calling itself 'too Parisian in its essence and in its program' not to support the exposition.

38. Emile Beer, 'Contre 1900!', *Figaro* 41 (22 August 1895), 1.

39. Méline, 'Faut-il faire l'Exposition de 1900?'.

40. Maurice Barrès, 'Sur l'Exposition de 1900: Note en réponse à M. Picard', *Figaro* 41 (24 August 1895), 1, and *Pas d'Exposition en 1900*.

41. Planat, 'Plus d'Expositions universelles'.

42. Maurice Barrès, 'Les Parisiens et l'Exposition', *Figaro* 41 (23 September 1895).

43. Paul Leroy-Beaulieu, 'Les Grands inconvénients des foires universelles et la nécessité d'y renoncer', *Economiste français* 23 (7 December 1895), 729–31.

44. Mirbeau, 'Pourquoi des Expositions?'.

45. Mauclair, 'Enquête logique sur l'Exposition de 1900'.

46. Chardon, 'L'Exposition de 1900'.

47. Planat, 'L'Exposition universelle de 1900', 291.

48. Méline, 'Faut-il faire l'Exposition de 1900?'.

49. Ibid.: 'First of all they allow us to observe that their resistance is appearing rather late; it is quite difficult to turn back a current that has been allowed to spring up, to grow, and to assume a regular course, instead of stopping it at its source. The project of a universal exposition already dates back several years, and if the League wanted to oppose it with a movement of public opinion strong enough to arrest its flow, it should have acted earlier and not waited to act until the affair was already underway and counted upon by powerful interests.'

50. Daix, *Die Wunder der Weltausstellung*, 8. But see also Lessing, *Das halbe Jahrhundert der Weltausstellungen*, 29; Jaffé, 'Ausstellungsbauten', 561; and Stanton, 'The International Exhibition of 1900', 314, for the same argument.

51. Statham, 'The Paris Exhibition', 132.

52. Boyd, *The Paris Exhibition of 1900*, 571; André Drevon, 'Paris 1900', in Findling and Pelle, *Encyclopedia of the Modern Olympic Movement*, 27–32, here 27.

53. 'The Competitive Schemes for the General Arrangement of the Exposition of 1900', *The American Architect and Building News* 47 (9 February 1895), 62–4, here 63; Sigel, *Exponiert*, 25–32.

54. Lessing, *Weltausstellung Paris 1900*, KB-SMB, n.p.

55. *Les Merveilles de l'Exposition de 1889*, 12.

56. Napoléon III, quoted after Mainardi, *Art and Politics of the Second Empire*, 40. Paul Strauss, 'L'Exposition de 1900', *Revue Bleue* (15 June 1895), 738–42; *Concours pour les deux palais des Champs-Elysées*; Macquoid and Macquoid, *In Paris*, 120. On the *Grand* and *Petit Palais*, see Silverman, *Art Nouveau in Fin-de-Siècle France*, 293–4.

57. The difference between 'intentional' and 'unintentional' monuments has been further developed by the Austrian art historian Alois Riegl, *Der moderne Denkmalkultus*. See also Anderson, 'The Paris Exhibition and Some of its Buildings', 30; and E. Rümler, 'Le Condamné', *Construction Moderne* 12 (9 January 1897), 169–70.

58. Levin, 'The Eiffel Tower Revisited', 1054; 'Eiffel Tower', *Builder* 75 (12 November 1898), 423; Loyrette, 'La Tour Eiffel', 496.

59. Roche, 'L'Exposition de 1900', 2; 'Dépôt d'un projet de résolution tendant à décréter une Exposition universelle pour l'année 1900', *Journal Officiel de la République Française* (1892), V/1434; 'Exposition universelle de 1900: Préparation de l'Exposition universelle de 1900 sur l'emplacement et les moyens de transport', ibid. (1893), I/5589. There is more than ample historical documentation for the 1900 Exposition Universelle. Basic information is provided in Boyd, *The Paris Exhibition of 1900*; Campbell, *Illustrated History*; Figaro Illustré, *L'Exposition de 1900*; Geddes, 'The Closing Exposition'; Lindenberg, *Paris und die Weltausstellung 1900*; Malkowsky, *Die Pariser Weltausstellung*

in Wort und Bild; Meier-Graefe, *Die Weltausstellung in Paris*; and *The Nineteen Hundred*. For comprehensive and partially annotated bibliographies, see Wendté, 'Reading List of Magazine Articles on the Paris Exposition, 1900'; Signat, *Bibliographie analytique*; and Mandell, *Paris 1900*, 122–39.

60. Robert W. Brown, 'Paris 1900', in Findling and Pelle, *Encyclopedia of World's Fairs and Expositions*, 149–57, here 149. There is no recent biography of Picard, but see Ryckelynck, 'Les Hommes de l'Exposition universelle de 1889', esp. 38–42.

61. Valona, 'L'Exposition de 1900', 180; Coubertin, 'Building up a World's Fair in France', 117.

62. Mandell, *Paris 1900*, 34–5. Picard, *Exposition universelle internationale de 1889 à Paris*; 'Historique sommaire des expositions universelles françaises de 1789 à 1849', in ibid., 3–102; and 'Historique sommaire des expositions universelles françaises de 1851 à 1888', in ibid., 105–300. Subsequent to the 1900 exposition, Picard published two voluminous official works, the *Rapport général administratif et technique* in eight volumes, and *Le Bilan d'un siècle* in six.

63. 'Exposition universelle de 1900', *Journal Officiel de la République Française* (1894), I/2674; 'Exposition universelle de 1900', ibid. (1895), IV/2444; 'Exposition universelle de 1900', ibid. (1896), IV/124, 164, 463, 485, 503, 529, 536, 542; Coubertin, 'Building up a World's Fair in France', 117. For a critical synopsis of the 112 schemes submitted, see 'The Competitive Designs for the Paris Exhibition of 1900', *Builder* 67 (29 December 1894), 465–7. Eventually, no single one was chosen, but rather a mixture of suggestions taken from the prize-winning proposals was realized.

64. 'The Rival International Exhibitions', *Times* (5 July 1892), 5; 'France and Germany', ibid. (6 July 1892), 5.

65. Eckmann, *Der Weltjahrmarkt Paris 1900*, 27, 34; 'Temporary Architecture', *Builder* 78 (9 June 1900), 560. See Wesemael, *Architecture of Instruction and Delight*, 382–3, figs 20 and 21, for a comparison of the planned with the later realized spatial settings.

66. Lucas, 'Notes sur les palais de l'Exposition de Paris en 1900', 159.

67. Butler, 'The Moving Pavement', 271; Daix, *Die Wunder der Weltausstellung*, 50.

68. Campbell, *Illustrated History*, 5, 134.

69. Ibid.; Butler, 'The Moving Pavement', 276.

70. Böttcher, *Weltausstellungs-Glossen*, 16; see also M. S., 'The Paris Fair as an American Sees It', *New York Times* (19 August 1900), 18.

71. Butler, 'The Moving Pavement', 271.

72. 'L'Ouverture du métropolitain', *L'Illustration* (14 July 1900).

73. *Le Rappel* (20 January 1904), 1. By 1913, the bulk of today's Métro system had been completed.

74. Barker and Robbins, *A History of London Transport*. The second European underground system was only opened in 1896 in Budapest, 30 years later than in London.

75. *A Trip Through the Paris Exhibition*; a complete kit forms part of the Larson collection, CSU Fresno (EXP 900a.26c).

76. Crary, *Techniques of the Observer*, 116–17.

77. De Cauter, 'The Panoramic Ecstasy', 5.

78. For a chart of the classification system see Quantin, *L'Exposition du siècle*, xii–xiii; *Exposition universelle internationale de 1900 à Paris: Actes organiques*, 77; Benedict, 'The Anthropology of World's Fairs', 28–9.

79. *Twelve Tours to the Paris Exposition of 1900*, 28; Eastman and Mayer, *Paris*, 89.

80. Poppović, *Pariser Eindrücke*, 61; Schneider, 'Colonies at the 1900 World Fair', and *An Empire for the Masses*, esp. 174–201; Przyblyski, 'Visions of Race and Nation at the Paris Exposition, 1900'; Vanessa Ogle, 'La colonizzazione del tempo: Rappresentazioni delle colonie francesi all'Esposizione Universale di Parigi del 1889 e 1900', in Geppert and Baioni, *Esposizioni in Europa tra Otto e Novecento*, 191–209; Hale, *Races on Display*, 14, 32–45, 53–66. Contemporary semi-official accounts include Charles-Roux et al., *Exposition universelle de 1900: Section des Colonies et Pays de Protectorat*;

Charles-Roux et al., *Colonies et pays de protectorats*; ibid., 'Les Colonies à l'Exposition de 1900'; ibid., *Les Colonies françaises: Introduction générale*; and *Les Colonies françaises: L'organisation*.

81. *Groupe XVII: Colonisation*, classes 113–15. It is noteworthy that the Berliner Gewerbeausstellung with its *Gruppe XXIII: Deutsche Kolonial-Ausstellung* had taken part in – if not anticipated – such a general trend, although a reversed German-French conceptual transfer is unlikely.

82. Charles-Roux, 'Les Colonies à l'Exposition de 1900', 24, and *Les Colonies françaises: L'organisation et le fonctionnement de l'Exposition des colonies et pays et protectorat*, 216. For an extensive description, see Kératry, *Paris Exposition*, 33–48, here 44; Campbell, *Illustrated History*, 96.

83. Kératry, *Paris Exposition*, 40.

84. *Report of His Majesty's Commissioners for the Paris International Exhibition 1900*, vol. 1, 14–15, 53–61; Shaw, 'Paris and the Exposition of 1900', 688.

85. Witt, *Pariser Weltausstellungsbriefe*, 44, 52, 53.

86. Friebel, 'Skizzen von meiner Studienreise zur Pariser Weltausstellung', 6.

87. Schneider, *An Empire for the Masses*, 182–5, and 'Colonies at the 1900 World Fair', 36.

88. Talmeyr, 'L'Ecole du Trocadéro'.

89. Daix, *Die Wunder der Weltausstellung*, 33; Kératry, *Paris Exposition*, 70.

90. Ibid., 25–6; for a detailed listing of all Parisian exhibits, see Coyecque, 'Paris à l'Exposition universelle de 1900'.

91. Bergeret, *Journal d'un nègre à l'Exposition de 1900*, 9. For a detailed discussion of this combined diary, semi-fictional tale and guide to the exposition, see Smalls, '"Race" as Spectacle in Late-Nineteenth-Century French Art and Popular Culture', 351–8.

92. *Twelve Tours to the Paris Exposition of 1900*, 34; Lucas, 'Notes sur les palais de l'Exposition de Paris en 1900', 161; Herman J. Hall, 'Unique Features of the Paris Exposition', *The Western World and American Club Woman Illustrated* 16.9 (1900), 17–22, here 20; Emery, 'Protecting the Past', 70; Peixotto, 'Some Picturesque Sides of the Exposition', 523. See also Robida, *Le Vieux Paris*; Saunier, 'Les Curiosités de l'Exposition'; 'Visite des Amis des monuments aux chantiers de la reconstitution du "Vieux Paris" par Robida'; 'Description de la reconstitution du "Vieux Paris" à l'Exposition universelle de 1900'; 'Souvenirs des rétrospectives de l'Exposition universelle'; and 'Visite aux chantiers de la reconstitution du "Vieux Paris"'.

93. Kératry, *Paris Exposition*, 29–30; Eastman and Mayer, *Paris*, 73; Brown, 'Albert Robida's Vieux Paris Exhibit', 430, 437.

94. See, for instance, Poppović, *Pariser Eindrücke*, 66; Pilz, *Paris amüsirt sich*, 186. Campbell, *Illustrated History*, 117, 58; Daix, *Die Wunder der Weltausstellung*, 82; 'Alt-Paris, das Schweizerdorf und andere kleinere Veranstaltungen', *Deutsche Bauzeitung* 34 (1 September 1900), 425–8, here 426.

95. Lucas, 'Notes sur les palais de l'Exposition de Paris en 1900', 176; Corday, 'La Force à l'Exposition'; Silverman, *Art Nouveau in Fin-de-Siècle France*, 297–9.

96. *Twelve Tours to the Paris Exposition of 1900*, 25; Schricker, 'Die Pariser Weltausstellung', 292; Statham, 'The Paris Exhibition', 142; Peixotto, 'Some Picturesque Sides of the Exposition', 521; Gentsch, *Die Weltausstellung in Paris*, 45–53. Other, partly earlier electricity exhibitions are discussed in Bensaude, 'En flânant dans les expos'; Beltran, 'La "Fée Electricité"'; Carré, 'Expositions et modernité'; Gugerli, 'Technikbewertung zwischen Öffentlichkeit und Expertengemeinschaft'; and Beauchamp, *Exhibiting Electricity*.

97. Corday, 'La Force à l'Exposition', 437, 439.

98. Malkowsky, *Die Pariser Weltausstellung in Wort und Bild*, 26; Morand, *1900*, 77: 'L'Electricité, on l'accumule, on la condense, on la transforme, on la met en bouteilles, on la tend en fils, on l'enroule en bobines, puis on la décharge sous l'eau, sur les fontaines, on l'émancipe sur les toits, on la déchaîne dans les arbres; c'est le fléau, c'est la religion de 1900.'

99. Cf. Debord, *The Society of the Spectacle*. Wilson, 'Consuming History', 144; *Twelve Tours to the Paris Exposition of 1900*, 27; Quantin, *L'Exposition du siècle*, 347–53; Meusy, 'L'Enigme du Cinéorama de l'Exposition universelle de 1900'.

100. Robert Hénard, 'Le Panorama-diorama du Tour du monde à l'Exposition de 1900', *Magasin Pittoresque* 67 (1899), 316–18; Schwartz, *Spectacular Realities*, 150, 165, 171–6; and De Cauter, 'The Panoramic Ecstasy', esp. 14–17. The *locus classicus* on these 'vision machines' remains Oettermann, *Das Panorama*.

101. Naumann, *Ausstellungsbriefe*, 99: 'eine Geographiestunde mit allen Chikanen der Neuzeit'; *Paris Exposition Reproduced from the Official Photographs*, n.p.; *Twelve Tours to the Paris Exposition of 1900*, 33; E.-A. Martel, 'Le Monde souterrain à l'Exposition', *Nature* 28.2 (1900), 22–5; L. de Launay, 'Le Monde souterrain à l'Exposition de 1900', *Monde Moderne* (1900), 800–10.

102. *The Nineteen Hundred*, 5.

103. *Exhibition Paris, 1900*, xviii–xxxvi; Mandell, *Paris 1900*, 152 n. 11. The *Grande Roue* serves as a perfect example to demonstrate the transnational and intra-European interconnections of various exhibition sites and the different kinds of – literally – 'outstanding' accessories with which they enriched the metropolis; cf. the last chapter.

104. On the history of lookout towers between 1870 and 1914, see Schmoll, 'Der Aussichtsturm'; De Cauter, 'The Panoramic Ecstasy', 17–18.

105. See Reusche, *Chicago und Berlin*, 16–17: 'Es hat sich bei allen Weltausstellungen das Bestreben gezeigt, in den Bauten selbst Ausstellungsobjecte zu bieten, architektonische Mittelpunkte zu schaffen, die der betreffenden Weltausstellung einen bestimmten bleibenden Charakter geben sollten.'

106. 'Vereinigung Berliner Architekten', *Deutsche Bauzeitung* 30 (23 December 1896), 658–9, here 658. See the Appendix.

107. Planat, 'Les Clous de l'Exposition universelle', 532.

108. Thomson, *The Paris Exhibition of 1900*, i; Pierre Leroy-Beaulieu, 'Les Travaux de l'Exposition', *Economiste français* (1 April 1899), 409–11; Campbell, *Illustrated History*, 43.

109. Laske, *Bericht über die Pariser Welt-Ausstellung*, 4, 8.

110. Macquoid and Macquoid, *In Paris*, 123; Lessing, *Weltausstellung Paris 1900*, KB-SMB, n.p., and *Das halbe Jahrhundert der Weltausstellungen*, 28; Schricker, 'Die Pariser Weltausstellung', 292; Woodward, 'The Exposition of 1900', 474. Deborah Silverman's argument that the Porte Binet, a gigantic entryway named after its architect and crowned by a large statue of *La Parisienne*, constituted the 'main attraction' of the 1900 exposition could not be confirmed by the sources consulted for this study. Cf. Silverman, *Art Nouveau in Fin-de-Siècle France*, 288–93.

111. Kératry, *Paris Exposition*, 70.

112. Jaffé, 'Ausstellungsbauten', 621; Meier-Graefe, *Die Weltausstellung in Paris*, 20; Peixotto, 'Some Picturesque Sides of the Exposition', 515. See also Martayan, 'L'Ephémère dans la ville', 49.

113. Laske, *Bericht über die Pariser Welt-Ausstellung*, 8. For the 'city without a center', see Stierle, *Mythos von Paris*, 122: 'Stadt der Dezentriertheit, wo alles Mittelpunkt werden kann.'

114. The fierce debate that arose before and after the building of the Eiffel Tower is not an exception to this rule. Of course, the tower's appearance and functionality were the subject of much controversy, but its capacity as the central attraction and major exhibit in 1889 was never questioned.

115. Gide, 'La Liquidation de l'Exposition universelle', 676; 'Les Attractions de l'Exposition et les capitaux', *Revue scientifique* 4.13 (14 April 1900), 478–9; 'Le Budget de l'Exposition', *Temps* (16 December 1900), 2. The exact figures indicated in the literature differ considerably.

116. Witt, *Pariser Weltausstellungsbriefe*, 143–5.

117. Talmeyr, 'L'Ecole du Trocadéro', 198; Laske, *Bericht über die Pariser Welt-Ausstellung*, 4: 'Hoffentlich und voraussichtlich aber ist die Ausstellung dieses Jahres überhaupt die *letzte* Weltausstellung gewesen.'
118. Lessing, *Weltausstellung Paris 1900*, n.p.
119. Schricker, 'Die Pariser Weltausstellung', 295.
120. Jules Cardane, 'Le Squelette de l'Exposition', *Magasin Pittoresque* 69 (1901), 306–10; Planat, 'Le Champ de Mars'; 'Le Champ de Mars'.
121. Abercrombie, 'The Champs de Mars', 251.
122. See 'Proposition de résolution tendant à décréter une exposition universelle à Paris', *Journal Officiel de la République Française* (1904), IV/88; and 'Dépôt d'un projet de résolution tendant à inviter le Gouvernement à décréter une exposition universelle à Paris', ibid. (1910), III/1785.
123. Gelbert, 'Une Nouvelle Exposition universelle', 95; Planat, 'Les Expositions universelles et la manière de s'en servir', and 'L'Exposition universelle de 1920', 121: 'Nous détenons les œuvres originales dont les autres sont d'excellentes copies, très réussies d'ailleurs.'

Chapter 4   London 1908

1. 'Take me on the Flip Flap!', written by Charles Wilmott, composed by Hermann E. Darewski, London: Francis Day & Hunter, 1908, HFALHC, H 606.1 HAG.
2. Lessing, *Das halbe Jahrhundert der Weltausstellungen*, 17; Geddes, 'The Closing Exhibition', 654; Carden, 'The Franco-British Exhibition', 83. On the 1862 exhibition, considered by many a national disgrace, see in particular 'The Exhibition Building of 1862'; and Bradford, 'The Brick Palace of 1862'.
3. Hoffenberg, *Empire on Display*, 5; Herbert W. Matthews, 'The Crystal Palace', *Times* (22 September 1911), 9. On the Crystal Palace in Sydenham consult, above all, Piggott, *Palace of the People*, esp. 166–83; but see also Auerbach, *The Great Exhibition of 1851*, 206–13; Atmore, 'Utopia Limited', esp. 189–91, 209–10; and Kay, 'Villas, Values and the *Crystal Palace Company*'. On the 1911 exhibition, see Moore, 'The 1911 Festival of Empire'. Two years after the Festival, the Palace was in such a deplorable state that *The Times* deemed it necessary to launch a fund-raising appeal for its preservation; see 'Failure of Crystal Palace Fund', *Times* (30 June 1913), 8; and 'Wanted, £90,000', ibid., 9.
4. See, for instance, Hart, 'The International Health Exhibition', 36–7; Watson, 'International Exhibitions'; and in particular TNA CO 323/436/3769. This series consisted of the Fisheries Exhibition (popularly called the 'Fisheries'; 1883), the International Health Exhibition (or 'Healtheries'; 1884), the Inventions Exhibition (1885), and the Colonial and Indian Exhibition (the 'Colinderies') in 1886. So far only the last of these four expositions has found some, if limited, historiographical interest; see Mathur, 'Living Ethnological Exhibits'.
5. Lowe, *Four National Exhibitions in London and Their Organiser*, 58–9; 'Earl's Court before 1900'; Colby, 'Noble Origins of Earl's Court'. See also Greenhalgh, 'Education, Entertainment and Politics', 79–81; and Schneer, *London 1900*, 94–5, for brief discussions of Earl's Court.
6. Lowe, *Four National Exhibitions in London and Their Organiser*, 373, 309; *Jahresbericht des Vereins Berliner Kaufleute und Industrieller* (1890–91), 6–7; *Album de l'Exposition française ouverte à Londres le 17 Mai 1890; French Exhibition in London: Official Guide*.
7. Langdon, *Earls Court*, 5, 99–100. Langdon took control of the Empress Theatre in 1935 and transformed it into a vast sports stadium, especially known for its indoor ice arena, while the rest of the area remained an exhibition center. For an atmospheric picture of Earl's Court immediately after the Kiralfy years, see the opening passages 'Before the War' of Angus Wilson's novel *No Laughing Matter*, 11–35. Gregory, *The Spectacle Plays and Exhibitions of Imre Kiralfy*, 368; 'Earl's Court Exhibition'; 'The London Exhibitions Limited: Sixteenth Report of the Directors', 8 July 1910, TNA BT 31/15403.

8. E. T. Swann, 'Britain's "Shop Window"', *The British Manufacturer* (April 1962), 21–3, 35; 'Exhibitions: Their History and Purpose', *Builder* 118 (9 April 1920), 431; Ryan, *The Ideal Home Through the 20th Century*.

9. Campbell, *Briton, Boer and Black in Savage South Africa at Olympia*; Johnson, 'Briton, Boer and Black in Savage South Africa'.

10. Barker, 'Imre Kiralfy's Patriotic Spectacles', 175; *Venice: The Bride of the Sea*; Altick, *The Shows of London*, 507–9. On Kiralfy himself, see Gregory, *The Spectacle Plays and Exhibitions of Imre Kiralfy*; Hotta-Lister, *The Japan-British Exhibition of 1910*; and Javier Pes, 'Kiralfy, Imre (1845–1919)', in *Oxford Dictionary of National Biography*, Oxford: Oxford University Press, 2004: http://www.oxforddnb.com/view/article/53347 (accessed 10 March 2009).

11. Fletcher and Brooks, *British Exhibitions and their Postcards*, vol. 1, 17–19; Knight, *The Exhibitions*, 5–6; Colby, 'Noble Origins of Earl's Court', 1273. For a comprehensive compilation of press reactions, see 'Empire of India Exhibition, Earl's Court, London, S.W.', 1895, 35–40, ML IKC; extensive material ibid., 1/1/0, 1/1/A–E.

12. Kiralfy, *Victorian Era Exhibition; The Empire of India Exhibition 1895: Earls Court London; Souvenir of the Greater Britain Exhibition; Military Exhibition Earl's Court 1901; Paris in London 1902*. In his autobiography *Eighty-Eight Not Out*, Harold T. Hartley provides a lively picture and detailed information on all exhibitions held at Earl's Court between 1891 and 1908. Likewise, Walter Macqueen-Pope devotes an entire chapter of his autobiography (*Ghosts and Greasepaint*, 239–54) to the Earl's Court exhibitions in general and the 1899 Greater Britain Exhibition in particular.

13. Beavan, *Imperial London*, 475; Macqueen-Pope, *Carriages at Eleven*, 216; Johannes: 'Die Französisch-Britische Ausstellung in London', 18 May 1908, GStA PK, I. HA Rep. 120 MfHuG, E XVI 4, Nr. 2, vol. 1, 2; unidentified newspaper clipping Philip Page, 'What Wembley Wants' (*c.* 1925), ML IKC, 9/2/A/4–5; Blathwayt, 'London's Great Exhibition'; 'Opening by the Prince', *Times* (15 May 1908), 8.

14. 'Imre Kiralfy on The London Exhibitions', *Times* (12 January 1904), 10; Kiralfy, 'My Reminiscences', 646–9. Unlike his brother Bolossy Kiralfy, who successfully published his own memoires (Kiralfy, *Creator of Great Musical Spectacles*), Imre Kiralfy's planned autobiography remained unfinished. Only a synopsis of chapters and some fragmentary notes exist, apparently written in March 1918; see 'Autobiographical Notes', ML IKC, 82.232.

15. Kiralfy, 'My Reminiscences', 649. On the myth and memory of Chicago's White City, see Harris, 'Memory and the White City'; Oppenheimer Dean, 'Revisiting the White City'; and Miller, 'The White City'.

16. Kiralfy, 'My Reminiscences', 649; 'Death Certificate', ML IKC, 9/0/B/17; 'Bio Sheet Imre Kiralfy', ibid., 9/0/B/1; 'Death of Imre Kiralfy, Exhibition Organiser', *Times* (29 April 1919), 9; Gregory, *The Spectacle Plays and Exhibitions of Imre Kiralfy*, 454.

17. Ibid., 373.

18. On de Coubertin, see MacAloon, *This Great Symbol*; and the contributions in Clastres, *Pierre de Coubertin*; on Barnum, above all, Harris, *Humbug*, here 245.

19. On the relationship between expositions and other hallmark or mega-events such as the Olympic Games, see in particular Chalkley and Essex, 'Urban Development through Hosting International Events', here 375, 390. On the 1908 Games, see James Coates, 'London 1908', in Findling and Pelle, *Encyclopedia of the Modern Olympic Movement*, 51–6; Matthews, 'The Controversial Olympic Games of 1908 as Viewed by the *New York Times* and the *Times* of London'; and Jenkins, *The First London Olympics*.

20. Hartley, *Eighty-Eight Not Out*, 81; Spielmann, *Souvenir of the Fine Arts Section*, 9; 'The Franco-British Exhibition', *Times* (2 April 1908), 4; 'The Next Exhibition at Shepherd's Bush', ibid. (23 November 1908), 15.

21. Gregory, *The Spectacle Plays and Exhibitions of Imre Kiralfy*, 442. According to other sources the League had made such a proposal only in 1904. See Lord Sydenham to the president of the Board of Trade, 19 May 1920, TNA BT 60/9/2: 'In the year 1904, a proposal was made by this League that a British Empire Exhibition should be held in London. For State reasons the proposal was postponed, and when revived, it took the form of the

Franco-British Exhibition, held in 1908. The proposal for a British Empire Exhibition was never lost sight of, and on the Armistice being signed, in November 1918, a Resolution was passed by the Executive Committee of the League in favour of such an Exhibition.'

22. 'The Franco-British Exhibition, 1908', *Times* (8 May 1908), 20. The limited body of existing scholarly literature on the Franco-British Exhibition includes Greenhalgh, 'Art, Politics and Society at the Franco-British Exhibition of 1908'; Coombes, 'The Franco-British Exhibition', and *Reinventing Africa*, 187–213; and Cornick, '"Putting the Seal on the *Entente*"'. For a contemporary survey, see Cockburn, 'The Franco-British Exhibition'; and an interview with Imre Kiralfy, 'A Great London Playground'. Helpful also is the comprehensive three-volume French report by Guyot et al., *Rapport général de l'Exposition franco-britannique de Londres 1908*, esp. vol. 2.

23. *A Pictorial and Descriptive Guide to London and the Franco-British Exhibition, 1908,* S; *The Pictorial Guide to the Franco-British Exhibition*, 5–7; 'Progress at Shepherd's Bush', *Weekly Express and West End Press* (12 July 1907).

24. Murray, 'The British Empire League', 437, according to whom the White City would never have been constructed without the League's initiative. Information provided by various contemporary publications as to the spectacle's origins is often contradictory and frequently seems glorified, but see 'The Exhibition in the Making', here 53.

25. Will Darvillé, 'Expositions à l'étranger', *Construction Moderne* 22 (27 October 1906), 48; 'Franco-British Exhibition', *Times* (1 February 1907), 10; F. E. G. Ponsonby for the King, 4 February 1907, in *Franco-British Exhibition 1908, Shepherd's Bush*, 5, 14; *Franco-British Exhibition, London, 1908: Official Guide*, 2–3.

26. Murray to F. G. Ogilvie, 18 November 1907, V&A AAD, S.F. 277, FBE; F. E. G. Ponsonby to Duke of Argyll, *Observer* (February 1907). Other sources mention a sum five times higher. The colonies' expenses amounted to £150,000, while the Indian government and the City of Paris subsidized the enterprise with £15,000 and £12,000 respectively. *Times* (12 December 1907), 15; 'The Exhibition in the Making', 58; Paul Cambon to Imre Kiralfy, 18 September 1909, ML IKC, 2/1/15; 'The Great Exhibition. To-Day's Opening of the Prince', *Daily Graphic* (14 May 1908); HFALHC, H 606.12, HM83/2473.

27. Publicity Brochure/Biography of Albert Kiralfy, ML IKC, 2/1/16.

28. Founded in 1753, the British Museum, by comparison, saw altogether 754,872 visitors over the whole of 1912, the Natural History Museum 433,618. See *Times* (2 August 1913), 8. 'Summary of Receipts and Attendances for Season 1908', ML IKC, 3/0/2; 'Balance Sheet and Revenue Account', 30 April 1908, ibid., 3/0/27; 'Exhibition Attendances', *Journal of the Royal Society of Arts* 56 (5 June 1908), 733.

29. 'The Close of the Exhibition', *Times* (31 October 1908), 11; *Maps and Plans of the Franco-British Exhibition*, 1; Gregory, *The Spectacle Plays and Exhibitions of Imre Kiralfy*, 469; Porter, *London*, 312–15; 'Brief Particulars of the White City', n.d., HFALHC, H 606.1, HM83/2472, 1; 'Particulars of the World-Renowned, Valuable and Highly Important Property Well Known as the White City', 1922, ibid., H 606.1, WHI/H60 X49.

30. Carden, 'The Franco-British Exhibition', 96–7.

31. Dumas, *The Franco-British Exhibition Illustrated Review*, 6.

32. *A Pictorial and Descriptive Guide to London and the Franco-British Exhibition*, D–F, J; *Franco-British Exhibition, London: Official Guide*, 4–8; 'The Franco-British Exhibition', *Times* (2 April 1908), 4.

33. Luckhurst, *The Story of Exhibitions*, 148; Carden, 'The Franco-British Exhibition I/II', 35; 'The Franco-British Exhibition', *Times* (2 April 1908), 4.

34. H. F., 'In Lightest London', *Westminster Gazette* (30 May 1908).

35. 'The Outlook: The Future of the Entente', *Daily Mail* (27 May 1908).

36. Dumas, *The Franco-British Exhibition Illustrated Review*, 5; 'The Franco-British Exhibition', *Illustrated London News* 132 (16 May 1908), 711.

37. *Franco-British Exhibition, London: Official Guide*, 2; Cornick, '"Putting the Seal on the *Entente*"'.

38. *Maps and Plans of the Franco-British Exhibition*, 2.
39. Shepherd's Bush Exhibition Estate, London, *A City for Sale*, 2–3, HFALHC, H 606.1, WHI/HQM537, 4.; ML IKC, 7/B–C, 8/0, 8/A–B.
40. Johannes to von Bethmann Hollweg, 8 November 1911, GStA PK, I. HA Rep. 120 MfHuG, E XVI 4, Nr. 2, vol. 3.
41. 'Death of Imre Kiralfy', *Times* (29 April 1919), 9; Macqueen-Pope, *Carriages at Eleven*, 219. In 1985 Pete Townshend of The Who released a solo album named after the White City.
42. 'The Franco-British Exhibition: The Lighter Side', *Times* (19 May 1908), 16; 'Particulars of the World-Renowned, Valuable and Highly Important Property Well Known as the White City', 1922, HFALHC, H 606.1, WHI/H60 X49, 7.
43. 'Aspects of the Great Fair'; 'How Visitors Are Amused'; 'London May Now Flip the Flap', *Daily Graphic* (6 August 1908); *Franco-British Exhibition, London, 1908: Daily Programme*, 4–7; Charles Kiralfy to Albert Kiralfy, 6 May 1922, ML IKC, 2/1/19; 'Franco-British Exhibition, Shepherd's Bush', *Builder* 93 (28 September 1907), 343; *Times* (29 April 1908), 3; 'A Great London Playground'; Imre Kiralfy, 'The Great Exhibition: A Preliminary Sketch', *Daily News* (7 May 1908).
44. 'How Visitors Are Amused', 101–2; 'Particulars of the World-Renowned, Valuable and Highly Important Property Well Known as the White City', 1922, HFALHC, H 606.1, WHI/H60 X49, 7; Shepherd's Bush Exhibition Estate, London, *A City for Sale*, 20; Mutsu, *The British Press and the Japan-British Exhibition*, ii. For technical details, see 'Engineering at the Franco-British Exhibition', *Builder* 95 (18 July 1908), 61–2.
45. Dumas, *The Franco-British Exhibition Illustrated Review*, 292; *Franco-British Exhibition, London, 1908: Official Guide*, 59–60.
46. 'The Franco-British Exhibition', *Times* (13 December 1907), 9; Nixon Horsfield, 'The Franco-British Exhibition of Science, Art and Industries', 554; Dumas, *The Franco-British Exhibition Illustrated Review*, 291.
47. Ibid., 8; 'Aspects of the Great Fair', 23; *The Pictorial Guide to the Franco-British Exhibition*, 20–1; 'French Colonial Section', *Times* (29 May 1908), 17; Coombes, 'The Franco-British Exhibition', 154–6.
48. *International Fire Exhibition*, 10; 'Getting into Order', *Daily Telegraph* (16 May 1908). In the case of India, for instance, this was primarily due to organizational difficulties. Because the Indian government had decided to officially participate only belatedly, and placed much less funding at the organizer's disposal than expected, its pavilion was much smaller than planned. 'The Indian Section', *Times* (28 May 1908), 5; Dumas, *The Franco-British Exhibition Illustrated Review*, 270; 'The Palace of India', *Morning Post* (8 June 1908).
49. 'Statistics of Attendances', *Times* (31 October 1908), 13; 'Franco-British Exhibition: Success of the Sections and Side Shows', *Evening Standard* (12 August 1908). According to a different source the Senegalese Village had found only 459,024 paying visitors between 16 May and 10 October. See Brunet, *Exposition Franco-Britannique Londres 1908*, 437–8; 'Statement Showing Amount Received by the London and South Western Bank, Holland Park Branch from Various Shows and Concessions', 11 January 1916, ML IKC, 3/0/25.
50. 'How Visitors Are Amused', 105; 'India', Westminster Gazette (31 July 1908); *Franco-British Exhibition, London, 1908: Daily Programme*, 3; *Franco-British Exhibition, London, 1908: Official Guide*, 56.
51. H. F., 'In Lightest London', *Westminster Gazette* (30 May 1908).
52. This led to a controversial debate in the press. See 'Jumbo's Joy in the Hot Weather: Elephants Shooting the Chute at the Franco-British Exhibition', *Illustrated London News* 133 (4 July 1908); 'How Visitors Are Amused', 104–5; 'The Indian Arena', *Times* (5 June 1908), 12.
53. 'Summary of Native Contract', 29 November 1910/1896, ML IKC, 1/B/2. Information on the exact amount of these wages is not available.
54. 'Indian Artisans of the India and Ceylon Exhibition', 29 November 1910/17 July 1896, ML IKC, 1/B/2; *Imperial International Exhibition: Official Guide,* 59–60.

55. 'The Ceylon Village', *Times* (10 June 1908), 9; W. A. de Silva, ibid. (3 July 1908), 19.
56. 'The Senegal Village', *Times* (12 June 1908), 8; *Franco-British Exhibition, London, 1908: Official Guide*, 66–7.
57. Ibid.; Bouvier and Tournièr, *Franco-British Exhibition: The Senegal Village*, 3.
58. *Franco-British Exhibition, London, 1908: Official Guide*, 67.
59. Bouvier and Tournièr, *Franco-British Exhibition: The Senegal Village*, 3, 8–9, 11; *Franco-British Exhibition, London, 1908: Daily Programme*, 6; 'Editorial Notes', *Journal of the African Society* 7 (1907–08), 434–5; MacKenzie, *Propaganda and Empire*, 115–17.
60. *Times* (14 May 1908), 5; 'To Fight Consumption in Ireland', *Morning Leader* (13 May 1908); 'Two Nations Show Products in London', *New York Times* (24 May 1908), C3; Dumas, *The Franco-British Exhibition Illustrated Review*, 8, 287–8.
61. 'How Visitors Are Amused', 100; *Guide to and Souvenir of Ballymaclinton*, 1, 28; 'Ireland at Shepherd's Bush', *Daily Graphic* (1 May 1908); 'The Irish Village', *Times* (27 May 1908), 10–11.
62. Dumas, *The Franco-British Exhibition Illustrated Review*, 295; *Franco-British Exhibition, London, 1908: Official Guide*, 66; *International Health Exhibition*, 43–6; Adams, 'The Healthy Victorian City'; George H. Birch, 'The "Old London" Street', in Cundall, *Reminiscences of the Colonial and Indian Exhibition*, 98–101; *Colonial and Indian Exhibition: Official Catalogue*, lxxxix. Margaret Richardson, 'Birch, George Henry (1842–1904)', in *Oxford Dictionary of National Biography*, Oxford: Oxford University Press, 2004: http://www.oxforddnb.com/view/article/31891 (accessed 10 March 2009).
63. 'How Visitors Are Amused', 103; 'Models of Old London', *Builder* 93 (19 October 1907), 405.
64. 'Franco-British Exhibition, 1908', *Builder* 93 (14 December 1907), 650; *Franco-British Exhibition, London, 1908: Official Guide and Description Sommaire de l'Exposition*, 42–3; *Franco-British Exhibition in London 1908: Catalogue of the Special Exhibition of the City of Paris and of the Department of the Seine*; Dumas, *The Franco-British Exhibition Illustrated Review*, 281–4.
65. *Franco-British Exhibition, London, 1908: Daily Programme*, 5.
66. 'Franco-British Exhibition 1908: Report of Proceedings', 28 October 1908, 16, HFALHC, H 606.12 FRA.HAM 500; 'Industry and Peace', *Westminster Gazette* (15 May 1908); Arthur A. Beckett, 'The "White City" and the Colonies', *Morning Post* (15 August 1908) and the reply, ibid. (22 August 1908). This was immediately confirmed by the Foreign Office. Harpinge/Penshurst to Lord Blyth, ML IKC, 2/1/15.
67. 'Franco-British Exhibition 1908: Report of Proceedings', 28 October 1908, HFALHC, H 606.12, FRA.HAM 500, 15–16. Lord Blyth repeated this opinion in a letter published a few days later in *The Times* (2 November 1908), 6.
68. 'Aspects of the Great Fair', 12; Carden, 'The Franco-British Exhibition I/II', 33.
69. Nixon Horsfield, 'The Franco-British Exhibition of Science, Art and Industries', 547–8.
70. Ibid., 552, 556.
71. Directly reacting to this article and taking up the criticism it contained, the *Builder* vehemently announced itself against a further Parisian exhibition in 1911, claiming that it would spoil a great deal of Paris for years after, if not permanently. 'The Next Paris Exhibition', *Builder* 95 (1 August 1908), 123.
72. 'The Close of the Exhibition', *Times* (31 October 1908), 11. This impression is based on an unsystematic analysis of a comprehensive collection of historical postcards contained in HFALHC, H 606.12, SSR 362, 709, 1506, 1667, 1820.
73. C. Hayward, 'Transcript of a Cassette on the White City Exhibitions', ibid., H 606.1, HAY. Hayward made a telling mistake: he described a life-size model of King Edward, completely made out of butter. Such a figure, however, was only to be found 16 years later in the Canadian Pavilion at the British Empire Exhibition. 'A Bit of a Flap or More Reasons why Father did not know Lloyd George', HFALHC, H 606.1, HAG; Philip Page, 'What Wembley Wants', unidentified newspaper cutting (*c.* 1925), ML IKC, 9/2/A/4–5;

'The Outlook: Success of the White City', *The Daily Mail Special Exhibition Number* (July–October 1908), 6.

74. *Franco-British Exhibition, London, 1908: Official Guide*, 5; Landon, 'The Exhibit of the Empire Builders'.

Chapter 5   Wembley 1924

1. Ford, *The Soul of London*, 15; Churchill, 'The British Empire Exhibition', 3464.
2. 'Für den Bau einer neuen Arena: Das Wembley-Stadion wird abgerissen', *Frankfurter Allgemeine Zeitung* (18 December 1996), 38.
3. http://www.cec.wustl.edu/~djr4/wembley.html; http://www.brent.gov.uk/wembley/srb/wemstad.html (both sites are now defunct). Popular histories of the stadium include Low, *Wonderful Wembley*; Watt and Palmer, *Wembley*; and Barclay and Powell, *Wembley Stadium*. For the sport stadium's general significance as an architectural feature of urban modernity, see the contributions to Bale and Moen, *The Stadium and the City*; and Marschik et al., *Das Stadion*. The landmark study remains Verspohl, *Stadionbauten von der Antike bis zur Gegenwart*, but for an analysis of this particular context, see especially Hill and Varrasi, 'Creating Wembley'.
4. See the police reports in TNA HO 45/11627.
5. *A Pictorial and Descriptive Guide to London and the British Empire Exhibition*, E [sic].
6. Corlette, 'The British Empire Exhibition Buildings', 665.
7. *The Story of the Building of the Greatest Stadium in the World*, 1, 4; *The New Wembley 1925*; Hastings, *Wembley Empire Stadium and Sports Arena*, 1.
8. Low, *Wonderful Wembley*, 11–12, 39–46.
9. 'Future of Wembley Site', *Times* (4 March 1926), 14; Bennett, *Report on Current European Fairs and Suggestions Arising from Attendance*, 1; Hastings, *Wembley Empire Stadium and Sports Arena*, 3–4; E. Owen Williams, 'The XIV Olympiad: Work at Wembley Stadium', *Builder* 174 (30 July 1948), 130–1, 186–7; Gillian Darley, 'Relics of an Empire', *Building Design* 327 (10 December 1976), 12–13.
10. Lynde, *Descriptive Illustrated Catalogue*, 5–6; 'The Great Tower in London', 544.
11. Lowe, *Four National Exhibitions in London and Their Organiser*, 58–9; Hodgkins, *The Second Railway King*; 'Sir Edward Watkin', *The Manchester Guardian* (15 April 1901), 10; C. W. Sutton, 'Watkin, Sir Edward William, first baronet (1819–1901)', rev. Philip S. Bagwell, in *Oxford Dictionary of National Biography*, Oxford: Oxford University Press, 2004: http://www.oxforddnb.com/view/article/36762 (accessed 10 March 2009).
12. 'The Proposed "Eiffel Tower" for London', *Builder* 59 (5 July 1890), 9, 12; 'An Eiffel Tower for London', *Times* (27 July 1891), 12; 'Wembley Park Tower'; Marsillon, 'La Tour Eiffel de Londres'; Richards, 'A Tower for London'; Wilson and Day, 'A London Rival to the Eiffel Tower'; Jenkins, 'Harbingers of Eiffel's Tower'; Jay, 'Taller than Eiffel's Tower'.
13. Joll, 'Die Großstadt', 38. Unlike most other imperial expositions of the same size, scale and significance, the British Empire Exhibition has hitherto received surprisingly little scholarly attention. But see Knight and Sabey, *The Lion Roars at Wembley*; MacKenzie, *Propaganda and Empire*, 96–120, esp. 107–12; Walthew, 'The British Empire Exhibition of 1924'; Woodham, 'Images of Africa and Design at the British Empire Exhibitions between the Wars'; Hill and Varrasi, 'Creating Wembley'; Cohen, 'The Empire from the Street'; Clendinning, 'Exhibiting a Nation'; as well as Hughes, 'Kenya, India and the British Empire Exhibition of 1924'. A vast number of contemporary exhibition guidebooks and catalogues can be found in BA BEEC, Gen. I/II. In this case, the exhibition authorities did not produce a comprehensive official report.
14. *British Empire Exhibition 1924: Handbook of General Info*rmation, 10; Shepherd's Bush Exhibition Estate, London, *A City for Sale*, 4.
15. See 'Wembley: The Empire's Metropolis', *Times* (16 April 1923), 19; 'Wembley, the Gateway of Empire', ibid. (23 April 1924), i; *United Empire* 14.4 (1923), xix; Harrison, 'The British Empire Exhibition, 1924', 451.

16. 'Proposed Imperial Exhibition in 1915', *Times* (11 November 1910), 11; 'A London Exhibition in 1921', ibid. (21 May 1919), 7; 'An Empire Exhibition', ibid. (8 June 1920), 15; *Journal of the Royal Society of Arts* 60 (1912), 667; Lord Sydenham to the president of the Board of Trade, 19 May 1920, TNA BT 60/9/2; 'Wembley: To-Day's Opening Ceremony', *Times* (23 April 1924), 15.

17. Voyageur, 'After the War! A British Empire Exhibition', *Builder* 110 (21 April 1916), 296.

18. 'Memorandum on Official Policy Towards Exhibitions', 24 November 1920, 10, TNA BT 60/6/3; 'An Empire Stadium', *Times* (1 July 1921), 9; 'The Prince's Appeal', ibid. (13 October 1921), 5; Albert, 'Speech at the Banquet'.

19. TNA BT 60/50/1, 7657; 'B.E.E. 1924 and 1925 Wembley Report', January 1928, TNA BT 60/14/2; *The Pavilion of H.M. Government*.

20. 'Resources of the Empire: London Exhibition in 1923', *Times* (8 June 1920), 19; Harrison, 'The British Empire Exhibition, 1924', 446–7.

21. Of the more than 2000 workers already employed at Wembley Park in March 1923, 72 per cent were ex-servicemen. See 'The British Empire Exhibition', *United Empire* 14.3 (1923), 144.

22. Gomme, *The Making of London*, 240.

23. The Earl of Meath, 'London as the Heart of Empire', 252. See also a leading article on 'Imperial London', *Builder* 102 (5 January 1912), 11–13. Deploring the difficulties of creating an imperial quarter in the center of London, the Earl of Meath nonetheless demanded that London be prepared in case it became the seat of a 'Federated Imperial Government' one day. Important studies in this area include Driver and Gilbert, 'Heart of Empire?', and *Imperial Cities*; and Schneer, *London 1900*, esp. 17–36. However, it seems more than doubtful whether Londoners truly enjoyed 'an indelible if ambiguous identity which distinguished them from residents of other great cities', as Schneer nevertheless claims, without bringing any other European 'nexus of empire' into comparative view (ibid., 10). For insightful historiographical critiques of this scholarship, see Hall, 'Cities of Empire'; and Nord, 'London and the World'.

24. 'The British Empire Exhibition', TNA BT 60/9/2, 17–18; memorandum by Frederick Butler, 11 July 1919, ibid.; 'Site of Empire Exhibition', *Times* (25 October 1921), 8; 'British Empire Exhibition, Wembley', *Builder* 125 (19 October 1923), 615.

25. *Metro-Land*, 29; Hewlett, *A History of Wembley*, 188, 191.

26. 'The British Empire Exhibition', *Times* (13 October 1921), 11; 'The Exhibition and Its Ways', *United Empire* 15.3 (1924), 135–6, here 135 (my emphasis). See also Stevenson, *British Empire Exhibition*, 16: 'The building of Wembley was the building of a huge new city. That it was a beautiful city, no one denies.'

27. Such a process of suburbanization had already begun in 1854 with the Crystal Palace's transfer to Sydenham. Although certainly a significant exhibition site in London, internationally it received far less attention. The same holds true for the Glasgow Empire Exhibition of 1938. Studies on the 1951 Festival of Britain include Banham and Hillier, *A Tonic to the Nation*; and Conekin, *The Autobiography of a Nation*.

28. Askwith, 'Exhibitions', 9; *Calcutta Exhibition 1923*, 25–27; *Journal of the Royal Society of Arts* 68 (1920), 638. A first international exhibition had been held in Calcutta in 1883–84.

29. 'British Empire Exhibition Mission', *United Empire* 13.2 (1922), 96–9, here 97; 'Successful Mission', *Times* (2 December 1922), 10, 13.

30. 'The King's Speech', *Times* (24 April 1924), 14. For the quotation in this section's heading, see *Illustrated London News* 164 (3 May 1924), 811. The official exhibition film bore the same title; see *Times* (5 July 1924), 12. *Empire Exhibition News: The Organ of the British Empire Exhibition (1924)*, Wembley, Wembley 1922–24.

31. 'The Total Attendances', *Times* (2 November 1925), 11. It was estimated that these 17 million admissions represented approximately eight million individuals; see Clarke, 'The British Empire Exhibition', 175. In comparison, the Crystal Palace at Sydenham was seen by 2,290,719 visitors during the 17 months after its reopening in June 1920;

'Public and Crystal Palace', *Times* (15 November 1921), 5. William Lunn, 'The Future of the British Empire Exhibition', 31 July 1924, TNA BT 61/22/2, E 6801, here 4, 11; Amery, *My Political Life*, vol. 2, 340.

32. In the following, changes from the first to the second year are indicated only where necessary. 'Another Year of Wembley', *Times* (6 June 1924), 9; 'Wembley Next Year', *United Empire* 15.12 (1924), 666; 'The New Wembley', *Saturday Review* 139 (9 May 1925), 480–1; *The New Wembley 1925*; 'Report on HMG Participation at the BEE Wembley 1924 and 1925', TNA BT 60/14/2; 'British Empire Exhibition: What's Fresh in 1925? The New Wembley', 1925, BA BEEC, Gen I.

33. 'A Second Year of the Exhibition', *United Empire* 15.10 (1924), 570–1; Lawrence, *The British Empire Exhibition*, 13; Henry Walter George Cole, 'Scheme for Using Wembley in the Future [11 November 1924]', TNA BT 60/5/4.

34. Birnstingl, 'Architecture at the British Empire Exhibition', 29.

35. 'The Area of the Exhibition', *Times* (23 April 1924), 16; reply by the Parliamentary Secretary to the Overseas Trade Department, Lieut.-Colonel Buckley, to a question posed by Viscount Sandon, House of Commons, 23 April 1924; quoted after *Journal of the Royal Society of Arts* 71 (1922–23), 449. Lawrence, *The British Empire Exhibition*, 15.

36. 'The Eighth Wonder of the World', *Illustrated London News* 164 (3 May 1924), 811; *The Spirit of Carnival: All the Fun of the Fair at Wembley*, BA BEEC, Gen. I; Clarke, 'The British Empire Exhibition', 178; McLeod, 'The British Empire Exhibition', 201.

37. Brangwyn, 'The Architecture of the British Empire Exhibition'; Lawrence, *The British Empire Exhibition*, 13; Ayrton, 'A Note on Concrete Buildings'; Birnstingl, 'Architecture at the British Empire Exhibition', 32. The same argument also applies to the Canadian Pavilion, which featured a full-sized model of the Prince of Wales together with a horse, both completely made of butter, to simultaneously emphasize both Canada's production capacities in this particular field and its royal loyalty. The Prince of Wales in butter 'was the one feature', a schoolgirl later remembered, 'that captured everybody's imagination'. Noel-Jackson, BA BEEC, Gen. II. See also 'A Butter Prince of Wales', *Illustrated London News* 164 (24 May 1924), 937; and Wagner, *Das Material der Kunst*, 200.

38. 'Street Names at Wembley', *Times* (6 February 1924), 7.

39. On the Kingsway-Aldwych project, see, among others, Schubert and Sutcliffe, 'The "Haussmannization" of London?'; Schneer, *London 1900*, 19–27; and Rappaport, 'Art, Commerce, or Empire?'. On the making of imperial Delhi, see Metcalf, *An Imperial Vision*, 211–39; and Volwahsen, *Imperial Delhi*, 74–7. At the Glasgow Empire Exhibition of 1938 one of the three main axes would also be called Kingsway, featuring the pavilions of the United Kingdom government, the City of Glasgow itself, and an exhibit on the women of the Empire; see Crinson, *Modern Architecture and the End of Empire*, 92–3.

40. *Times* (16 April 1924), 19; ibid. (23 April 1924), 33. Not a single site in the exhibition was named after Kipling himself.

41. Birnstingl, 'Architecture at the British Empire Exhibition', 30.

42. From the experience gained at Wembley, Weaver later published two influential volumes, *Exhibitions and the Arts of Display* and *The Place of Advertising in Industry*, both indicating his growing concern with commercial affairs. Weaver's contribution to the Wembley exposition earned him the designation as 'National Professor of Commonsense Art' among the public. 'Sir Lawrence Weaver', *Times* (11 January 1930), 12, 14. For additional information see the biography by a previous collaborator, the coordinating architect for the *Palace of Industry*, Bertram Clough Williams-Ellis, *Lawrence Weaver*; a 'biographical sketch' by his grandson Lawrence Trevelyan Weaver, in idem, *Lawrence Weaver*, 12–16; and Christopher Hussey, 'Weaver, Sir Lawrence Walter William (1876–1930)', rev. Catherine Gordon, in *Oxford Dictionary of National Biography*, Oxford: Oxford University Press, 2004: http://www.oxforddnb.com/view/article/36792 (accessed 10 March 2009).

43. Weaver, *Exhibitions and the Arts of Display*, 91–4 ('A Footnote on Exhibition Lions and the Display of Medals'), here 92; 'Triumph of Advertising: Making Wembley Popular',

Daily Telegraph (28 October 1924); 'How Wembley was Advertised', *Times* (28 October 1924), 10; Lawrence, *The British Empire Exhibition*, 103.

44. Devonshire, 'The Empire in Concrete', 277.
45. Mace, *Trafalgar Square*, 15–16; see also Schneer, *London 1900*, 17.
46. Chesterton, 'Our Notebook'.
47. 'Wembley Exhibition in Retrospect', *Times* (1 November 1924), 13.
48. *Metro-Land*, 15; *British Empire Exhibition 1924: Handbook of General Information*, 15. On the *Galerie des Machines*, see Stamper, 'The Galerie des Machines of the 1889 Paris World's Fair'; and Stamper and Mark, 'Structure of the Galerie des Machines'.
49. Lawrence Weaver, 'The Palace of Industry', in *British Empire Exhibition: Official Catalogue 1924*, 11–12; 'Vast Palace of Industry: A Wembley Triumph', *Times* (15 April 1924), 12; 'What to See at Wembley', ibid. (12 May 1925), 7; Abercrombie, 'The Planning of the British Empire Exhibition', 904; *Daily News Souvenir Guide*, 61.
50. Lawrence, *The British Empire Exhibition*, 45; 'Report on HMG Participation at the BEE Wembley 1924 and 1925', TNA BT 60/14/2, D; *British Empire Exhibition 1924: Handbook of General Information*, 8–9; *The Pavilion of H.M. Government*, 7, 10; Grimsditch, 'The British Government Pavilion and the Basilica at Wembley'; Hake, *Wembley*, 20; *A Pictorial and Descriptive Guide to London and the British Empire Exhibition*, x. See Crinson, *Modern Architecture and the End of Empire*, 75–8, for an analysis of its architecture.
51. Smith, 'Should Britain Take Part in International Exhibitions?', 986–7; 'Participation by Government Departments in the B.E.E.', 20 November 1922, TNA BT 60/50/1, 2; 'Original Version of a Draft to the Secretary', January 1923, TNA BT 60/5/1. In the document, 'visualise' was later manually replaced with 'demonstrate'. 'Participation by Government Departments in the British Empire Exhibition: Minute Sheet', 27 February 1923, ibid., 5.
52. 'Wonders of Wembley', *Times* (3 April 1924), 16; *The Raid on Zeebrugge*; *Daily News Souvenir Guide*, 47; 'Report on HMG Participation at the BEE Wembley 1924 and 1925', TNA BT 60/14/2, F; B. B. Cubitt to Maclagan, 14 April 1925, V&A AAD, S.F. 277, BEE, 3046.
53. Lawrence, *The British Empire Exhibition*, 44–5; *Daily News Souvenir Guide*, 47; 'With Ships Moving Along Empire Routes'; 'Report on HMG Participation at the BEE Wembley 1924 and 1925', TNA BT 60/14/2, C9. The famous phrase 'the heart of the Empire' was the title of an influential collection of critical essays edited by the liberal politician and radical journalist Charles F. G. Masterman (1874–1927) and published in 1901.
54. Barnes, 'The British Empire Exhibition, Wembley', 212.
55. Ibid., 215.
56. *A Short Description of Burma*; *Souvenir of the British Empire Exhibition*; Maxwell, *Wembley in Colour*, 56.
57. Richmond, 'The Lure of Wembley', 312, 315; Chesterton, 'Our Notebook'.
58. Kendall, 'The Participation of India and Burma in the British Empire Exhibition, 1924', 647, and 'India's Part in the British Empire Exhibition', 213. In addition to the London exhibitions of 1851, 1862, 1886 and 1908, India had also participated in the three Parisian Expositions Universelles of 1867, 1878 and 1889, the American Centennial Exhibition held in Philadelphia in 1876, and the 1883 Internationale, Koloniale en Uitvoerhandel-Tentoonstelling in Amsterdam. Breckenridge, 'The Aesthetics and Politics of Colonial Collecting'; Hoffenberg, *An Empire on Display*, 151–65.
59. Kershaw, 'The British Empire Exhibition', 80; *Calcutta Exhibition 1923*, 20.
60. *India*; Birnstingl, 'Architecture at the British Empire Exhibition', 30; Metcalf, *An Imperial Vision*, 203–10.
61. *Daily News Souvenir Guide*, 56; Vijayaraghavacharya, 'India and the British Empire Exhibition', 142–3, and *British Empire Exhibition*.
62. Stevenson, *British Empire Exhibition*, 13.
63. Lawrence, *The British Empire Exhibition*, 62.

64. Unfortunately, no record was kept of the number of visitors to the Indian section. Vijayaraghavacharya, 'India and the British Empire Exhibition', 142–3, and *British Empire Exhibition*, 36–49; 'India at Wembley', *Times* (11 March 1924), 16; *Daily News Souvenir Guide*, 56–7.

65. Vijayaraghavacharya, *British Empire Exhibition*, 52; Belcher, 'The Dominion and Colonial Sections of the British Empire Exhibition, 1924', 390; Vijayaraghavacharya to William Clark, 19 July 1924, TNA BT 61/22/2; 'India's Non-Participation in the British Empire Exhibition', TNA T 172/1462; 'Report on HMG Participation at the BEE Wembley 1924 and 1925', TNA BT 60/14/2.

66. *British Empire Exhibition 1924: Handbook of General Information*, 12; Corlette, 'The British Empire Exhibition Buildings', 662.

67. 'West African Conditions', *Times* (4 September 1923), 7; *Daily News Souvenir Guide*, 72, 74 (emphasis in original); 'This Strange, Alluring Fragment of Africa', *West Africa* (24 May 1924), 51; F. D. Lugard, 'Tropical Africa at Wembley', ibid., 3–7, here 3.

68. Charles Graves, 'When West Africa Woos', *The Sunday Express* (4 May 1924), 7; C. F. Hayfron-Benjamin, 'The Union for Students of African Descent', *West Africa* (25 October 1924), 1179–80; Minutes, 17 May 1924, TNA CO 554/64, 169–325. The incident is briefly mentioned in MacKenzie, *Propaganda and Empire*, 110–11.

69. Union of Students of African Descent, *West Africa* (4 October 1924), 1050; 'The Walled City as Seen by an African', ibid. (24 May 1924), 57–9.

70. TNA CO 554/64, here 169. C. T. Lawrence, 'Nigeria at the British Empire Exhibition', *West Africa* (15 November 1924), 1283–4. 'Gold Coast Official Sessional Papers XVII', CUL RCSAC, L448, 5: 'In 1924 the public, for various reasons, were not admitted to the Village until the last month of the Exhibition and then only after the departure of the Craftsmen and their wives from Wembley.'

71. Edward Shanks, 'Reflections on Wembley', *Saturday Review* 140 (11 July 1925), 36–7; 'Report of the Chairman of the West African Exhibition Committee Covering the Period January to November, 1925', Gold Coast, Accra 1925, CUL RCSAC, L448, 4–5; Salmon, 'Has the Exhibition Justified Itself?', 583.

72. Postcard from Sally to Laura Simson, 10 June 1924, GL, Noble Collection, C 67.1.

73. Fidel, *Publicité et vulgarisation coloniales*, 5; 'Essay Competition', *United Empire* 15.1 (1924), 63 and 15.12 (1924), 716–17; Stevenson, *British Empire Exhibition*, 1. Unfortunately, neither the essays nor the collection of newspaper clippings have survived in the archives.

74. For instance Clarke, 'Is British Empire Economic Unity Possible?', 19, and 'The British Empire Exhibition', 180; 'A London Exhibition in 1921', *Times* (21 May 1919), 7.

75. 'British Empire Exhibition Mission', *United Empire* 13.2 (1922), 96–9, here 96; Lord Askwith, 'Empire Exhibition', *Daily Telegraph* (4 February 1924); Young, 'At Wembley', *Saturday Review* 137 (29 March 1924), 317–18; Harrison, 'The British Empire Exhibition, 1924'; Gerald Barry, 'A Day at Wembley', *Saturday Review* 137 (17 May 1924), 502–3.

76. 'The Meaning of Wembley'; Lawrence, 'The British Empire in Miniature'.

77. Barnes, 'The British Empire Exhibition, Wembley', 215; Kershaw, 'The British Empire Exhibition', 80–1; Corlette, 'The British Empire Exhibition Buildings', 654.

78. Lawrence, *The British Empire Exhibition*, 13, 15; *British Empire Exhibition 1924*, GLRO, 35.8 (BRI); Towner, 'The Grand Tour', 314, 325. The history of tourism has flourished for over a decade. See, for instance, Buzard, *The Beaten Track*, for an early and brilliant study; Baranowski, 'An Alternative to Everyday Life?', for a comprehensive review essay; and, especially in a British context, the various contributions to Berghoff et al., *The Making of Modern Tourism*.

79. Interview with Arthur Mason, 2 February 1996, GMCH. See also various visitors' reports in BA BEEC, Gen. II; H. Duncan Hendry, 'Looking Back: Some Memories of Eighty Changing Years', ibid., Gen. I; and Hose, *Fifty Years of Romance*, 255.

80. Ismaa'il, 'The Life and Adventures of a Somali', 378–9. Although a part of Somalia (British Somaliland) had come under British rule in 1884, it was not represented by a pavilion of

its own, but rather collectively together with a few other East African states. Even though it seems unlikely that he did not visit it, Ismaa'il did not mention the section *East Africa*.

81. Pasold, *Ladybird, Ladybird*, 77–9; on Pasold himself, see D. C. Coleman, 'Pasold, Eric Walter (1906–1978)', in *Oxford Dictionary of National Biography*, Oxford: Oxford University Press, 2004: http://www.oxforddnb.com/view/article/48092 (accessed 10 March 2009).

82. 'The British Empire Exhibition', *Builder* 126 (8 February 1924), 216; 'Report on HMG Participation at the BEE Wembley 1924 and 1925', TNA BT 60/14/2; McLeod, 'The British Empire Exhibition', 199; H. W. G. C. [→Sir Henry Walter George Cole], 'Scheme for Using Wembley in the Future', 11 November 1924, BT 60/5/4, 3–4; Pasold, *Ladybird, Ladybird*, 75–6.

83. Briganti, *Additiamo agli emigranti italiani*; Eckinger, *Eine Reise nach Paris, London, Wembley und Ostende*, 88–126; Fidel, *Publicité et vulgarisation coloniales*, 5.

84. Sommer, 'Bericht über Eindrücke von einer Reise nach London zur Besichtigung der Britischen Empire-Ausstellung', 25 July 1924, GStA PK, I. HA Rep. 120 MfHuG, E XVI 4, Nr. 2, vol. 5; Generalkonsul Haug, 'Bericht über die britische Reichsausstellung zu Wembley', n.d., ibid.; 'Bericht der Deutschen Botschaft London über die früheren deutschen Schutzgebiete auf der Wembley-Ausstellung', 25 June 1924, BArch R 1001/6370, 195–200, here 3, 10.

85. Hake, *Wembley*, 9 ('so daß man in wenigen Tagen bequem fast den gleichen Eindruck erhielt, als hätte man eine Reise durch das erdumspannende britische Imperium gemacht'), 48 ('Auf verhältnismäßig kleinem Raum hat sie [die Ausstellung] in übersichtlicher, ansprechender Form der Allgemeinheit ein imposantes Bild des weltumfassenden britischen Imperiums gegeben'). For a similar mixture of simultaneous admiration, envy and awe, see the review by A. Baerwald, 'British Empire Exhibition', *Zentralblatt der Bauverwaltung* 44 (1924), 427–30.

86. Meath, 'London as the Heart of Empire', 252–3; Mathias, 'Locating Rhodesia', *United Empire* 15.10 (1924), 609; Salmon, 'Has the Exhibition Justified Itself?', 581.

87. C. T. Lawrence, 'Report on Nigerian Section, British Empire Exhibition', *West Africa* (1 November 1924), 1212–16, here 1212.

88. 'The Meaning of Wembley', 428.

89. 'The Exhibition', *United Empire* 15.5 (1924), 269; Maxwell, *Wembley in Colour*, 8; 'The Meaning of Wembley', 428; 'Wembley Exhibition in Retrospect', *Times* (1 November 1924), 13; 'British Empire Exhibition', *Builder* 126 (2 May 1924), 721–4, here 721; *Daily News Souvenir Guide*, 43, 7; Churchill, 'The British Empire Exhibition', 3464; Woolf, 'Thunder at Wembley'.

90. John Bull, you are a clever man / to publicize yourself so well. / Outside we are eagerly waving / yet already feel the separation aching; / two days are too short a time / for magnificence so sublime! / At times we had to gallop / for it all briefly to inspect. / Never will we forget Wembley. / How could another people presume / to show the world such pomp / as these Blimey-Brits? Eckinger, *Eine Reise nach Paris, London, Wembley und Ostende*, 117, 125. The expression 'the complete colonization of social life' is from Debord, *The Society of the Spectacle*, 29.

Chapter 6   Vincennes 1931

1. Sunshine sunshine beyond the seas you angelize / the excremental beard of the governors / Sunshine of coral and of ebony / Sunshine of numbered slaves / Sunshine of nudity sunshine of opium sunshine of flagellation / Sunshine of fireworks in honor of the storming of the Bastille / above Cayenne one July 14 / It is raining it is pouring on the Colonial Exposition. Aragon, 'Mars à Vincennes', 216.

2. Leprun, *Le Théâtre des colonies*, 12. Other important European interwar expositions include the Exposition Internationale 1930 in Antwerp and Liège, the Stockholmsutställningen 1930 in Stockholm, the Exposition Universelle et Internationale 1935 in Brussels, the

Reichsausstellung 'Schaffendes Volk' 1937 in Düsseldorf, the Exposition Internationale des Arts et Techniques dans la Vie Moderne 1937 in Paris, the Empire Exhibition in 1938 in Glasgow and the Exposition Internationale de l'Eau 1939 in Liège; see Norton, 'World's Fairs in the 1930s'. For the various American expositions held during the Great Depression, in particular 1933–34 in Chicago, 1935–36 in San Diego, 1939–40 in San Francisco and 1939–49 in New York, see, above all, Rydell, *World of Fairs*.

3. Girardet, 'L'Apothéose de la "plus grande France"', 1085; Reynaud, *Mémoires*, 301–12. Despite considerable differences in quality of analysis, the 1931 Exposition Coloniale is better researched than the other four expositions read in this book; therefore, its discussion is kept significantly shorter. Major historiographical accounts include, in chronological order, Ageron, 'L'Exposition coloniale de 1931'; Leprun, *Le Théâtre des colonies*; Vigato, 'Die Architektur der französischen Kolonialausstellungen'; Hodeir and Pierre, *L'Exposition coloniale*; Lebovics, *True France*, 51–97; Miller, 'Hallucinations of France and Africa in the Colonial Exhibition of 1931'; Ezra, 'The Colonial Look'; Norindr, 'Representing Indochina', and *Phantasmatic Indochina*, 14–33; Hodeir, 'Decentering the Gaze at French Colonial Exhibitions'; and, above all, Patricia Morton's grand study, *Hybrid Modernities*, the latter written from the perspective of a historian of art and architecture. See Demissie, 'Displaying Race and Exhibiting Empires in the 1930s', for an extensive review essay. For the broader context consult, in particular, Wright, *Politics of Design*; Aldrich, *Greater France*; Wilder, 'Framing Greater France Between the Wars'; and the numerous valuable, even somewhat repetitive and largely undertheorized anthologies edited by Pascal Blanchard and the members of the *Association pour la connaissance de l'histoire de l'Afrique contemporaine* (ACHAC), for instance Blanchard and Lemaire, *Culture coloniale*, or *Culture coloniale en France*. For comprehensive reviews of this ever-growing body of literature, see Sherman, 'The Arts and Sciences of Colonialism'; Berenson, 'Making a Colonial Culture?'; and Jennings, 'Visions and Representations of French Empire', esp. 702–5.

4. Olivier, *Rapport général*, vol. 1, xii. On the Marseilles expositions, see Yaël Simpson Fletcher, '"Capital of the Colonies": Real and Imagined Boundaries between Metropole and Empire in 1920s Marseilles', in Driver and Gilbert, *Imperial Cities*, 136–54; Meller, *European Cities*, 169–73; Hale, *Races on Display*, 86–9; and, for a brief architectural review, Beldimano, 'The Colonial Exhibition at Marseilles'. On lesser known colonial expositions in the French provinces, for instance in Strasbourg in 1924, see Goerg, 'Exotisme tricolore', and 'The French Provinces and "Greater France"', in Chafer and Sackur, *Promoting the Colonial Idea*, 82–101.

5. Morton, *Hybrid Modernities*, 323–4 n. 16, and 81, 8; but see also Norindr, *Phantasmatic Indochina*, 21–4.

6. Letter from W. J. Glenny, 17 November 1922, TNA CO 323/895/31, 270.

7. Although the City of Marseilles was larger, the title of 'la seconde ville de France' was traditionally held by Lyon; Démy, *Essai historique*, 489. *Exposition coloniale internationale de Paris 1931: Colonies et pays d'Outre-Mer*, 5; Masson, 'Marseilles port colonial', and 'Marseilles et la colonisation française'.

8. 'Kampf um die Kolonialausstellung: Marseilles – Paris 1916', 16 May 1931, GStA PK, I. HA Rep. 120 MfHuG, EXVI 4 Nr. 3, vol. 6. Olivier, *Rapport général*, vol. 1, xi–xiv, and 'Les Origines et les buts de l'Exposition coloniale', 46–9; 'Draft Brief for Ministers Imperial Conference', 1926, TNA CO 323/977/6; Wirtschaftspolitische Abteilung der Deutschen Botschaft Paris to Auswärtiges Amt, 18 October 1927, BArch R 1001/6387, 68–9.

9. *Recueil des textes organisant l'Exposition coloniale internationale Paris 1931*, 1. Exact wordings of the diverse *lois* and *décrets* can be found in the *Journal Officiel de la République Française*, beginning in 1919.

10. The first *Commissaire général*, →Gabriel Angoulvant, was forced to resign in 1927 because of these difficulties; Camp and Corbier, *A Lyauteyville*. On Lyautey, see Durosoy, *Lyautey*; Homo, 'Lyautey et l'Exposition coloniale internationale de 1931'; Singer, 'Lyautey'; and Rabinow, *French Modern*, 104–25, 277–319, in particular on his activities in Morocco,

where Lyautey realized his colonial town-planning visions by constructing new districts in Rabat and Casablanca, earning him the nickname 'Lyautey Africanus'.

11. G. W., 'Travel by Land, Sea and Air: The French Colonial Exhibition', *The Field* (14 March 1931), 369; 'The French Colonial Exposition: Unique and Picturesque Display', ibid. (26. September 1931), 488. Rydell, *World of Fairs*, 64.

12. Joseph Trillat, 'Les Harmonies du monde exotique', in *Exposition coloniale internationale Paris 1931: Le plus beau voyage à travers le monde*, 2: 'Universelle puisqu'elle nous découvre la vision de l'univers, l'Exposition est internationale par les concours qu'elle a groupés, par l'élan de sympathie fervente qu'elle a provoqué chez tous les peuples civilisés. L'œuvre coloniale s'avère animée d'un besoin de comprendre et d'aimer plus impérieux que le souci de dominer et d'unifier.'

13. For instance, to have a laudatory article 'Die Internationale Kolonial- und Überseeausstellung, Paris 1931' printed in the German *Illustrierte Industrie- und Handelszeitung* [(25 April 1931), 28–9, 32], 148,92 Reichsmarks were directly transferred through the French Ambassador in Berlin. See correspondence between the paper's editorial office and the Ministère des Colonies de la République Française, 12 May 1931 and 9 June 1931, ANOM ECI 26/2.

14. See the extensive material and numerous examples in ANOM ECI 26/1 and 26/2/5.

15. The exact number was 33,489,902 visitors; see Olivier, *Rapport général*, vol. 3, 570; and J. R. Cahill to L. M. Hill, 31 October 1933, TNA BT 60/25/1, 312. A. de Gobart, 'Des chiffres sur l'Exposition', *L'Intransigeant* (8 November 1931), 1, gives 30,683,778 paying visitors. As always, these official figures should be treated with a certain caution as they represent the total number of attendances rather than individual visitors. Other sources speak of eight million visitors only – four million from Paris and its surroundings, three million from the provinces, and one million from abroad. See Hodeir and Pierre, *L'Exposition coloniale*, 101, which unfortunately provides no evidence for such a claim.

16. 'Exhibition for Paris', *Times* (3 December 1928), 15.

17. *Exhibition Paris, 1900*, 283.

18. On the park's history, see Champion, *Le Bois de Vincennes*; Sarafian, *Le Bois de Vincennes*; and Derex, *Histoire du Bois de Vincennes*, esp. 240–6. On the 1900 annexe, see Macquoid and Macquoid, *In Paris*, 96; and *Guide Lemercier*, 250–2.

19. Morton, *Hybrid Modernities*, 130–74, here 131, 133, 145; Leblond, 'L'Exposition coloniale dotera-t-elle Paris d'une avenue de la Victoire qui par Vincennes ira vers la Marne et Strasbourg reconquise?'; Stovall, *The Rise of the Paris Red Belt*.

20. 'The Growth of Paris', *Times* (13 July 1931), 11; 'Lessons of the Exhibition', ibid., (23 July 1931), 13: 'Had the Exhibition been held 15 miles [= 24 km] outside Paris it is doubtful whether the number of visitors would have been half as large.' 'Participation of Colonies, etc. in Imperial and International Exhibitions', TNA CO 323/977/6, 15.

21. Its site was moved from the southeastern end to north of Lac Daumesnil; Henry Thétard, 'Le Parc zoologique de l'Exposition coloniale', *L'Art vivant* 7 (1931), 407.

22. *La Cité des Informations*, 23 (ANOM SOM Br. 10057 C); Vaillat, 'A l'Exposition coloniale'; Cayla, 'The International Colonial Exhibition of Paris', 560–1; Antony Goissaud, 'Où est-on? La Cité des Informations', *Construction Moderne* 46 (22 February 1931), 332–6, and 'La Cité des Informations', ibid. 46 (2/9 August 1931), 690–8, 713–19; A. F. Wickenden, 'Experimental Architecture: Progressive Work at the Paris Exhibition', *Builder* 141 (23 October 1931), 659–60, here 660.

23. *L'Exposition coloniale internationale de Paris*, 2; Boudot-Lamotte, 'La Métropole à l'Exposition coloniale', 229–40; G. W., 'Travel by Land, Sea and Air', 369; *The Nineteen Hundred*, 6; Cornilliet-Watelet, 'Le Musée des Colonies et le Musée de la France d'Outre-Mer'. For a brilliant reading of the museum's architecture and its decorative program, see Morton, *Hybrid Modernities*, 272–312, and her largely identical article 'National and Colonial', here esp. 360–3. Another example of an ethnographic museum originating from an exposition is the Belgian Koninklijk Museum voor Midden-Afrika (KMMA), the vestige of the 1897 colonial exhibition held in Tervuren; Corbey, 'Ethnographic Showcases', 357.

24. *Album-souvenir de l'Exposition coloniale internationale de Paris*, n.p.: 'Le *Temple d'Angkor-Vat* doit être considéré comme le clou de l'Exposition et chacun admire l'habilité des mouleurs, des staffeurs qui ont si bien copié l'original, et, en particulier, des peintres qui ont donné au plâtre la patine de la latérite.' Antony Goissaud, 'Le Temple d'Angkor reconstitué', *Construction Moderne* 46 (16 August 1931), 723–35, here 735.
25. Borelly, *Promenade à l'Exposition coloniale*, 19.
26. Ibid., 25; Bazin, 'La Reconstitution du temple d'Angkor à l'Exposition coloniale de 1931'; Lebovics, *True France*, 59–61.
27. Beldimano, 'The Colonial Exhibition at Marseilles'; Herbert, *Paris 1937*, 16, 174; Vigato, 'Die Architektur der französischen Kolonialausstellungen', 30–4. Other towers included three in the West African section; the respective minarets of Algeria, Tunisia and the Somalian Coast; the bell-tower of the Catholic mission; and the towers of the pavilions of Madagascar and Guadeloupe.
28. Borelly, *Promenade à l'Exposition coloniale*, 29.
29. See the lists in ANOM ECI 1/2/11; and 'The Colonial Exhibition, Paris', *Builder* 141 (3 July 1931), 7.
30. Morton, *Hybrid Modernities*, 26, 42; Borelly, *Promenade à l'Exposition coloniale*, 20–1.
31. Demaison, *A Paris en 1931*, 18: 'Mais vous ne trouverez pas ici une exploitation des bas instincts d'un public vulgaire. Le nom même de l'homme qui préside aux destinées de cette exposition est un gage de grandeur incontestée. M. le maréchal Lyautey, et avec lui, M. le gouverneur général Olivier et tous leurs collaborateurs, vous ont considéré, cher Visiteur, comme un homme de bon goût. Point de ces bamboulas, de ces danses du ventre, de ces étalages de bazar, qui ont discrédité bien d'autres manifestations coloniales; mais des reconstitutions de la vie tropicale avec tout ce qu'elle a de vrai pittoresque et de couleur.'
32. Goldman and Dickie, 'The International Colonial Exposition in Paris', 526.
33. 'Lessons of the Exhibition', *Times* (23 July 1931), 13. About the natives on display in 1931, see in more detail Lebovics, *True France*, 78–83; Henningham, '"The Best Specimens in all our Colonial Domain"'; Dauphine, *Canaques de la Nouvelle-Calédonie à Paris en 1931*; Morton, *Hybrid Modernities*, 111–20; and Hale, *Races on Display*, 108–10, 133–5. Didier Daeninckx' 1998 novel *Cannibale* is entirely written from the perspective of such a living exhibit named Gocéné, a Kanak from New Caledonia shipped to Paris together with 100 other members of his tribe and forced to live up to his ethnic group's savage and cannibalistic reputation. Some time after he and his friend Badimoin have managed to escape from the guarded complex in the middle of Vincennes zoo, the latter is shot by the French police during a communist protest.
34. Lebovics, *True France*, 83–6; Lyautey, 'France and the International Colonial Exhibition', 538.
35. NARA RG 43/1316/11. Similar replicas of Mount Vernon had been exhibited at earlier American world's fairs, in particular at the World's Columbian Exposition in Chicago in 1893 and the Panama-Pacific International Exposition in San Francisco in 1915. After the exposition's closure, this exemplar was moved to Vaucresson in the western suburbs of Paris, where it can still be visited today. For extended analyses of the US and Italian sections, respectively, see Rydell, *World of Fairs*, 62–3, 72–82; and Maddalena Carli, 'Ri/produrre l'Africa romana: I padiglioni italiani all'*Exposition Coloniale Internationale*, Parigi 1931', in Geppert and Baioni, *Esposizioni in Europa tra Otto e Novecento*, 211–32, here 223–9.
36. Minister für Handel und Gewerbe, 18 June 1931, BArch R 1001/6388, 78–9; GStA PK, I. HA Rep. 120 MfHuG, E XVI 4, Nr. 3, vol. 7; Hardy, 'Die internationale Kolonialausstellung in Paris', 559.
37. Lyautey, 'France and the International Colonial Exhibition', 538.
38. See TNA BT 13/41, BT 60/25/1 and CO 323/977/6; 'International Exhibitions in France and Belgium 1919–1930', ibid.; 'The Royal Visit to Paris', *Times* (20 July 1931), 11; extract of personal letter to Mr Reeve, 1 August 1931, TNA BT 60/25/1; see also Crinson, *Modern Architecture and the End of Empire*, 83.

39. Hardy, 'Die internationale Kolonialausstellung in Paris', 559: 'Nach der großen Propaganda von Wembley glaubte England wohl, mit dieser nicht völlig ablehnenden Haltung der französischen Einladung gegenüber Genüge getan zu haben.' Claire Hancock, *'Capitale du plaisir*: The Remaking of Imperial Paris', in Driver and Gilbert, *Imperial Cities*, 64–77, here 70; Cayla, 'The International Colonial Exhibition of Paris', 563.

40. *La Cité des Informations*, 27 (ANOM SOM Br. 10057 C): 'Pour faire aboutir l'idée coloniale, il reste à créer chez nous l'esprit colonial.' *Exposition coloniale internationale de Paris 1931: Colonies et pays d'Outre-Mer*, 7; Cayla, 'The International Colonial Exhibition of Paris', 559; Discours du Marechal au diner de clôture de l'Exposition Coloniale, 14 November 1931, ANOM ECI 1/2/Div/14. On the contradictory figure of 'la plus grande France' as both real and imagined, see Wilder, 'Framing Greater France Between the Wars', 202–6.

41. *L'Exposition coloniale internationale de Paris*, 2 (ANOM SOM Br. 9588 C): 'Elle [l'Exposition] attestera qu'il y a pour la civilisation d'autres champs d'action que les champs de bataille, que les nations du vingtième siècle peuvent rivaliser loyalement, généreusement dans les œuvres de paix et de progrès. Elle donnera une leçon d'action réalisatrice, sera un foyer d'enseignement pratique pour tous ceux qui veulent s'enquérir, savoir, conclure.'

42. 'Propagande Métropolitaine/Schéma de Conférence/plan développé No. 1: Synthèse de l'effort: L'Exposition colonial français', ANOM ECI 1/2/Div/13, 1; *L'Exposition coloniale internationale de Paris*, 2 (ANOM SOM Br. 9588 C).

43. Joseph Trillat, 'Les Harmonies du monde exotique', in *Exposition coloniale internationale Paris 1931: Le plus beau voyage à travers le monde*, 1–2. See Chapter 5 in this volume; cf. with Geppert, 'True Copies'; Morton, *Hybrid Modernities*, 16–69; and Furlough, 'Une Leçon des choses', 447–50.

44. Borelly, *Promenade à l'Exposition coloniale*, 30: 'De ce "tour du monde" en quelques heures […] une impression se dégage, une conviction plutôt. Tangible, réelle, cette "notion d'empire" qu'hier encore nous ignorions s'impose. L'Empire colonial français; la France de cent millions d'âmes, abstraction géographique, devient réalité.'

45. Olivier, *Rapport général*, vol. 4, 299–303, here 302; letter from André Muller, Chambéry, 1 August 1931, ANOM ECI 92, 414: 'Nous avons pu en très peu de jours connaître la grande ville et ses beaux monuments et surtout, grâce à des explications éclairées, nous intéresser vivement aux merveilles d'une exposition grandiose qui retrace le prodigieux effort colonial accompli par la France et toutes les nations. Une telle visite a ravi nos yeux en même temps qu'elle enrichissait notre esprit de connaissances précises.' See also 'Adoption d'une proposition de résolution tendant à organiser la visite de l'Exposition coloniale par les élèves des écoles primaires de France', *Journal Officiel de la République Française* (2 July 1931), 3598.

46. Letter to M. le Sénateur Messimy, 2 December 1931, ANOM ECI 92, 1; J. Bourgues to Monsieur Oudaille, ibid., 422: 'Vision unique et inoubliable, l'exposition coloniale nous a révélé la beauté de pays lointains et inconnus: blancheur des villes d'Algérie, parfums d'Orient, chatoiement de soieries. […] Et, plus tard, quand dans notre petit village, l'heure passera lente, le souvenir de toutes ces largesses si amplement prodiguées nous remplira l'âme d'une grande douceur, tandis que nous essaierons de faire revivre devant les yeux de nos petits élèves des visions colorées que nous emportons avec nous pour leur communiquer un peu de l'enthousiasme et de la reconnaissance qui nous animent.'

47. Lyautey, 'France and the International Colonial Exhibition', 529.

48. Ezra, *The Colonial Unconscious*, 28–9.

49. Breton, Eluard, Péret et al., *Ne Visitez pas l'Exposition coloniale*, 195, 451.

50. Tanguy, Sadoul, Aragon et al., *Premier Bilan de l'Exposition Coloniale*; copies of both pamphlets and additional material in ANOM ECI 27/Divers. On the fire, see 'Fire at Paris Colonial Exhibition', *Times* (29 June 1931), 11; 'New Dutch Pavilion Opened', ibid. (19 August 1931), 9; and Reynaud, *Mémoires*, 309, who mentions an array of exposition details in his autobiography, yet remains entirely silent on critical issues such as the protests.

51. The most detailed discussion of the counter-exposition by a literary scholar can be found in Norindr, *Phantasmatic Indochina*, 59–71; but see also Ageron, 'L'Exposition coloniale

de 1931', 571–3; Hodeir and Pierre, *L'Exposition coloniale*, 125–34; Lebovics, *True France*, 56, 105–10; and Morton, *Hybrid Modernities*, 98–110. Most of what is known about the counter-exposition is based on brief autobiographical accounts by the two co-organizers, André Thirion and Louis Aragon, as well as several articles in the communist newspaper *L'Humanité*, in spite of the difficulties that such a limited source base entails. See Thirion, *Révolutionnaires sans révolution*, 312–21; Aragon, 'Une Préface morcelée'; and 'L'Exposition anti-impérialiste se prépare: elle montrera la vérité sur les colonies', *L'Humanité* (4 July 1931), 4. For information on a visit by the communist politician and journalist Marcel Cachin (1869–1958) on Friday, 23 October 1931, see Cachin, *Carnets*, 608.
52. Thirion, *Révolutionnaires sans révolution*, 319–20.
53. Quoted after Jennings, 'Visions and Representations of French Empire', 712–13 n. 23.
54. Olivier, *Rapport général*, vol. 1, 44, 56, 93; vol. 2, 55–6. For various *ex post* assessments, see Mousset, 'L'Exposition coloniale'; Vatin-Pérignon, 'Le Bilan de l'Exposition coloniale'; as well as Lyautey and Olivier, 'Après l'Exposition coloniale'.
55. See Cohen, 'Musée des Arts africains et océaniens', 74, for a brief iconographic analysis; Viatte and François, *Le Palais des colonies*.

Chapter 7   Conclusion: Exhibition Fatigue, or the Rise and Fall of a Mass Medium

1. Eco, 'A Theory of Expositions', 296.
2. Moonen, *Exhibitions*, 8; Barwick, 'International Exhibitions and Their Civilising Influence', 313; Woodward, 'The Exposition of 1900', 479. George Macaulay Trevelyan would apply this very first notion to the Crystal Palace in 1922, while historian Richard Mandell echoed the second statement almost verbatim, arguing that expositions 'offer a sort of comprehensive, though variously distorted, flash picture of world civilization at its particular epoch'. See Trevelyan, *British History in the Nineteenth Century*, 295; and Mandell, *Paris 1900*, x. See also Auerbach, 'The Great Exhibition and Historical Memory', 96.
3. See, for instance, Roscher, 'Die Industrieausstellungen, ihre Geschichte und ihr Einfluß auf die Culturentwickelung'; Emminghaus, 'Märkte und Messen'; Schäffle, 'Industrie-ausstellungen'; Reuleaux, 'Die Anfänge des Ausstellungswesens', and 'Die Entwicklung des Ausstellungswesens'; Messel, 'Ausstellungsbauten'; Huber, 'Ausstellungen'; Jaffé, 'Ausstellungsbauten'; G. C. L., 'Exhibition'.
4. The Society for the Encouragement of Arts, Manufactures and Commerce is identical with the previously mentioned Royal Society of Arts, with the prefix 'Royal' being granted in 1908.
5. Barwick, 'International Exhibitions and Their Civilising Influence', 313. Cf. also Smith, 'Should Britain Take Part in International Exhibitions?', 884; and Boyd, *The Paris Exhibition of 1900*, 5–6: 'The International Exposition has come to be one of the most potential of civilizing agents. [...] The genius of man has not been able to invent a more general, complete and wholesome appeal to the refining and elevating instincts of individuals, communities and nations than the International Exposition. [...] What institution grander and more-embracing than this! What higher evidence of liberality and enlightenment! What so conducive to universal peace and progress!'
6. Berger, *Les Expositions universelles internationales*, 1–2.
7. Brandt, 'Zur Geschichte und Würdigung der Weltausstellungen', 83.
8. Vogel, 'Bericht, betreffend das Ausstellungswesen', 259; Montheuil, 'Les Expositions universelles 1855–1900', 118; Reusche, *Chicago und Berlin*, 15. See also Allwood, *The Great Exhibitions*, 8; and De Cauter, 'The Panoramic Ecstasy', 7, for the same observation.
9. Gloag, 'Advertising in Three Dimensions'; see also Ford, 'Expositions, International', 24: 'a world's fair is but an extension and sublimation of window dressing and display advertising, with its own rules and techniques.'

10. Adams, *Education*, 465.
11. Weaver, *Exhibitions and the Arts of Display*, v; Geddes, *Industrial Exhibitions and Modern Progress*, 26. See also Weaver, 'The Closing Exposition', and 'Man and the Environment', both on the 1900 exposition. On Geddes himself, see Meller, *Patrick Geddes*; and Welter, *Biopolis*.
12. Lessing, 'Kunst- und Kunstgewerbeausstellungen', 429: 'In dieser Rückbewegung nach den alten historischen Formen von dem Boden der allermodernsten Schöpfung des Kristallpalastes heraus sehen wir jene Schraubenbewegung der Entwicklung, die scheinbar zu einem früheren Punkte zurückkehrt, aber doch immer aufwärts strebt.'
13. John Forbes Watson, 'International Exhibitions', *Times* (28 December 1872), 10; Richards, *The Commodity Culture of Victorian England*, 71. See Breckenridge, 'The Aesthetics and Politics of Colonial Collecting', 201, for an identical argument. Similarly, Lutchmansingh speaks of a 'logic of commodification and universalization promoted in 1851' that shaped the 'entire apparatus of art practice and exhibition'; Lutchmansingh, 'Commodity Exhibitionism at the London Great Exhibition of 1851', 213. See Auerbach, 'The Great Exhibition and Historical Memory', for an insightful analysis of the Great Exhibition's changing meanings over time, according to him 'one of the most misinterpreted events in modern British history' (ibid., 97).
14. *London's Great Exhibition, 1907*, LMA, P.35.8 LON, 1.
15. Shepherd's Bush Exhibition Estate, London, *A City for Sale*, 4.
16. Bucher, *Kulturhistorische Skizzen aus der Industrieausstellung aller Völker*, 19; Gérault, *Les Expositions universelles au point de vue économique*, 204; Witt, *Pariser Weltausstellungsbriefe*, 1; 'Exhibitions'; Paquet, *Das Ausstellungsproblem in der Volkswirtschaft*, 287–97; Simmel, 'Berliner Gewerbe-Ausstellung', 59; Sombart, 'Die Ausstellung', 254: 'Und es schien fast, als habe schon 1889 die Ausstellung in jeder Form ihr Ende erreicht, als in Paris das Wahrzeichen der modernen Kultur: der Eiffelturm aufgepflanzt und in der Tat eine unerreicht glänzende Veranstaltung in der Jubiläumsausstellung verwirklicht worden war.' Brandt, 'Zur Geschichte und Würdigung der Weltausstellungen'; Kollmann, 'Zur Reform des Ausstellungswesens'.
17. Statham, 'The Paris Exhibition', 131. The Swiss-American art historian Sigfried Giedion was the first to advance such an argument in 1937 ('Sind Ausstellungen noch lebensfähig?', 76) and further developed it in his pathbreaking *Space, Time, and Architecture*, here 243–90. Following Giedion, quite a few authors argue for 1889 as a decisive turning point in the international exhibitionary system. See, for example, Kalb, *Weltausstellungen im Wandel der Zeit*, 23; and Plato, *Präsentierte Geschichte*, 211. However, for the counter-argument of such a break having been reached in 1900, see, among others, Mandell, *Paris 1900*, xiv; Schmidt, 'Die frühen Weltausstellungen und ihre Bedeutung für die Entwicklung der Technik', 169; De Cauter, 'The Panoramic Ecstasy', 14, 20–1; Wörner, *Vergnügung und Belehrung*, 1; and Sigel, *Exponiert*, 14. Kretschmer (*Geschichte der Weltausstellungen*, 118–19, 131) identifies an entire phase of decline, lasting from 1873 through 1900. It seems absurd to see such a decline as already setting in with the fifth international exposition ever held, that is, in Paris in 1867, and hence declare a 'turning point' in the history of exhibitions, but cf. Reusche, *Chicago und Berlin*, 10; Kroker, *Die Weltausstellungen im 19. Jahrhundert*, 30 n. 33, 11; and Volker Barth, 'Paris 1967', in Findling and Pelle, *Encyclopedia of World's Fairs and Expositions*, 37–44, here 43. See also Wesemael, *Architecture of Instruction and Delight*, 651–3.
18. There is no comprehensive biography of Eyth, but see Ebner, *Max Eyth*; Thiel, *Max Eyth zum Gedächtnis*; Weihe, *Max Eyth*; and, more recently, Harbusch, *Mit Dampf und Phantasie*.
19. Eyth, *Im Strom unserer Zeit*, vol. 2, 64–5 (15 August 1862).
20. Ibid., 324–5 (17 June 1873).
21. Ibid., 436–8 (9 November 1878): 'Darin liegt vielleicht das Verführerische dieser modernsten Rieseneintagsfliegen. Niemand wünscht sie herbei; die meisten fürchten sie wie Moskitos; aber sie glänzen in der Sonne eines Sommers falschen Diamanten

zum Trotz. Man kann nicht anders: die ganze Welt jubelt einen Augenblick. Und das scheint zu genügen, um das eigenartige Fieber chronisch zu machen. Heute fragt man da und dort, wo und wann es das nächstemal ausbrechen werde. [...] Der mächtige Eindruck, den die Weltausstellung von 1851 zurückgelassen hat, ist heute nicht mehr zu erzielen.' Also Paquet, *Das Ausstellungsproblem in der Volkswirtschaft*, 287–8, refers to this passage in his discussion of *Ausstellungsmüdigkeit.*

22. Eyth, *Im Strom unserer Zeit*, vol. 2, 438 (9 November 1878); Reitz, *Hinter Buch und Schreibtisch*, 171: 'In dieser Weise vernichten diese Weltausstellungen sich selbst, was vielleicht in unseren Tagen das Beste ist, was sie tun können.'

23. Lüders, 'Das Project einer Weltausstellung zu Berlin im Jahre 1885', 615; Präsidium des Deutschen Handelstages, 'Antrag für die Ausschuss-Sitzung am 21. November 1879: Anlagen I/II', GStA PK, I. HA Rep. 120 MfHuG, E XVI 2, Nr. 13 F, vol. 1, 42; Hoyer, 'Über die Praxis der Ausstellungen', 334; 'Berliner Weltausstellung', *Glaser's Annalen für Gewerbe und Bauwesen* 5 (15 November 1879), 381.

24. Hoyer, 'Über die heutige Praxis der Ausstellungen', 16, and 'Über die Praxis der Ausstellungen', 333. The articles are almost identical, with the former apparently slightly revised for print.

25. Hoyer, 'Über die heutige Praxis der Ausstellungen', 18–19, and 'Über die Praxis der Ausstellungen', 334.

26. Ibid.: 'die offenbar eingetretene *Ermüdung* an grossen Weltausstellungen' (my emphasis). This is the earliest usage that could be traced. According to Albert Brockhoff (*Eine Weltausstellung in Berlin*, 3), the term was called into existence in the immediate aftermath of the Paris exposition of 1878, while A. Haarmann (*Vor dem Rubicon*, 42) linked its origins to the post-1885 *Weltausstellungsfrage.*

27. See Chapter 2 in this volume. Simon, 'Über eine im Jahre 1894 in Berlin zu veranstaltende Allgemeine deutsche Gewerbeausstellung', 148; Arbeitsausschuss der Berliner Gewerbe-Ausstellung, *Berlin und seine Arbeit*, 25; Pistor, *Die Ständige Österreichische Ausstellungskommission*, 70; Budde, 'Über Ausstellungswesen'; Hoyer, 'Über die Praxis der Ausstellungen'.

28. Berger, *Les Expositions universelles internationales*, 145.

29. 'The Paris Exhibition', *Builder* 79 (29 September 1900), 265. Cf. also 'Exhibitions', here 23: 'Not only the English papers declare themselves tired of exhibitions; there are not wanting Frenchmen who consider the exhibition needless, and even hurtful to the interests of France.'

30. Coubertin, 'Building up a World's Fair in France', 123.

31. 'L'Exposition universelle de 1920', *Construction Moderne* 26 (7 January 1911), 172–3.

32. Lowe, *Four National Exhibitions in London and Their Organiser*, 30; Geddes, 'The Closing Exhibition', 654; Barwick, 'International Exhibitions and Their Civilising Influence', 310–11.

33. Anderson, 'The Paris Exhibition and Some of its Buildings', 29; G. C. L., 'Exhibition', 71; I. W. Chubb, 'Great Britain and International Exhibitions', *American Machinist* 39 (18 August 1913), 378; Askwith, 'Exhibitions', 3. See also *Report of His Majesty's Commissioners for the Paris International Exhibition 1900*, vol. 1, 4–5.

34. Brandt, 'Zur Geschichte und Würdigung der Weltausstellungen', 88.

35. Paquet, *Das Ausstellungsproblem in der Volkswirtschaft*, 286; Budde, 'Über Ausstellungswesen', 297.

36. Delbrück, 'Die Krisis des deutschen Weltausstellungsplans', 354; Laske, *Bericht über die Pariser Welt-Ausstellung*, 6.

37. Lindenberg, *Pracht-Album*, 28.

38. 'Beschlußfassung über die Anträge des technischen Ausschusses betreffend die für das Jahr 1888 vorgesehene deutsche Gewerbeausstellung in Berlin', 102; Krupp quoted after Giedion, 'Sind Ausstellungen noch lebensfähig?', 77.

39. Schivelbusch, *Geschichte der Eisenbahnreise*, 113–16.

40. Bobertag, *Eine Weltausstellung in Deutschland*, 190; Boenigk, *Die Unlauterkeit im Ausstellungswesen*; Chiger, *Ausstellungs-Mißbräuche*; Paquet, *Das Ausstellungsproblem in der Volkswirtschaft*, 298–307. For an extensive discussion, see Stüber, *Das Ausstellungswesen und seine Organisation*, ch. 4 (n.p.).

41. 'Eine englisch-deutsche Ausstellung', *Kölnische Zeitung* (15 June 1912); Imre Kiralfy to Ständige Ausstellungskommission für die Deutsche Industrie, 17 March 1913, GStA PK, I. HA Rep. 120 MfHuG, E XVI 4, Nr. 2, vol. 4.

42. Johannes to von Bethmann Hollweg, 8 November 1911, ibid., vol. 3.

43. Busley to Kiralfy, 20 March 1913, ibid., vol. 4; 'Protokoll der Plenar-Vorstandssitzung der Ständigen Ausstellungskommission für die Deutsche Industrie', 29 April 1913, GStA PK, I. HA Rep. 120 MfHuG, E XVI 4, Nr. 2, vol. 4, 6: 'das energische, schnelle und sachgemässe Vorgehen der Kommission und vornehmlich ihres Präsidenten, durch das es ihr gelungen sei, die Veranstaltung noch in ihren ersten Stadien unschädlich zu machen und so dem bisherigen Kampfe gegen das Ausstellungswesen einen neuen Erfolg anzureihen.'

44. For a comprehensive report on the committee's activities and involvement in various expositions (among others Barcelona 1888, Brussels 1897, Glasgow 1901, St Louis 1904, Liège 1905, Milan 1906, London 1908) during its first two decades of existence, see Comité français des expositions à l'étranger, *Historique*; Mandell, *Paris 1900*, 37–8, 118–19.

45. Comité français des expositions à l'étranger, *Historique*; 19, 55; Paquet, *Das Ausstellungsproblem in der Volkswirtschaft*, 317; 'The Exhibition in the Making', 54–5; 'Comité Français des Expositions à l'Etranger', *Construction Moderne* 18 (15 November 1902), 81.

46. BArch R 901/18187-18191; ibid., R 3101/609-610; Ständige Ausstellungskommission für die Deutsche Industrie, *Zusammensetzung, Ziele und Zwecke*, here 21: 'Bekämpfung der Mißstände im Ausstellungswesen' and 'Förderung von aussichtsvollen Ausstellungen'; 'The Utilisation of Exhibitions in Germany', *Journal of the Society of Arts* 55 (26 April 1907), 645.

47. BArch R 3101/609, 38–40; GStA PK, I. HA Rep. 120 MfHuG, E XVI 4, Nr. 3, vol. 3; Paquet, *Das Ausstellungsproblem in der Volkswirtschaft*, 318–23; Ständige Ausstellungskommission für die Deutsche Industrie, *Jahrbücher/Jahresberichte*, Berlin 1914–22, and *Zusammensetzung, Ziele und Zwecke*; *Rückblick auf ein halbes Jahrhundert*. Both the commission's extensive library and most of the relevant archival material were lost during the Second World War; personal communication Markus Seumer, BDI, 5 May 2000. See also Großbölting, '*Im Reich der Arbeit*', 164–5.

48. Präsidium des Deutschen Handelstages, 'Antrag für die Ausschuss-Sitzung am 21. November 1879: Anlage II: Notizen betreffend die in Aussicht genommene Weltausstellung in Berlin', GStA PK, I. HA Rep. 120 MfHuG, E XVI 2, Nr. 13 F, vol. 1, 47; Grothe, 'Referat über die staatliche Organisation des Ausstellungswesens', 289–90; Vogel, 'Bericht, betreffend das Ausstellungswesen', 268. Earlier that year, the problem had also been discussed in parliament where a quick solution was expected. See von Boetticher, 36. Sitzung am 27. Januar 1882, *Stenographische Berichte über die Verhandlungen des Reichstages: V. Legislaturperiode, 1. Session 1881–82*, Berlin: Verlag der 'Norddeutschen Allgemeinen Zeitung', 1882, 1009.

49. Reusche, *Chicago und Berlin*, 9 (emphasis in original).

50. International Exhibitions Committee, *Report of the Committee Appointed by the Board of Trade*, iv; an abbreviated version can be found in TNA BT 13/41/13; for a comprehensive interim report, see H. Llewellyn Smith to Secretary of the Treasury, 14 November 1911, TNA BT 13/49/3.

51. International Exhibitions Committee, *Report of the Committee Appointed by the Board of Trade*, 3, 9–11; 'International Exhibitions Committee', *Builder* (19 October 1907), 404–5.

52. 'The Exhibition in the Making', 54–8.

53. Smith, 'Should Britain Take Part in International Exhibitions?', 987; 'International Exhibitions Committee', *Builder* (1 August 1908), 143; 'International Exhibitions at Brussels, Rome, and Turin', ibid. (27 March 1909), 383; BArch R3101/610, 9; Pistor, *Die Ständige Österreichische Ausstellungskommission*, 33. See also Hoffenberg, *An Empire on Display*, 89–90, who attributes the establishment of the Committee exclusively to complaints from British exhibitors and overseas commissioners.

54. Comité français des expositions à l'étranger, *Historique*, 50; Kraemer, 'Die internationale Regelung des Ausstellungswesens'; Heiman, 'Internationale und nationale Regelung des Ausstellungs- und Messewesens'; Piat, *Les Expositions internationales relevant du Bureau International des Expositions*, 12–13; Galopin, *Les Expositions internationales au XXe siècle et le Bureau International des Expositions*, 35–89; Exner, *Die neuesten Fortschritte im Ausstellungswesen in Beziehung*, 144; Kroker, *Die Weltausstellungen im 19. Jahrhundert*, 193.

55. Askwith, 'Exhibitions', 5; 'International Exhibitions', *Builder* 103 (1 November 1912), 499; 'Participation in International Exhibitions', TNA BT 60/6/3; 'Projet de loi portant approbation de la convention relative aux expositions internationales, signée à Berlin le 26 octobre 1912', *Journal Officiel de la République Française* (4 November 1931), annexe 3138/161–7.

56. Locock, 'The Diplomatic Conference of Paris on International Exhibitions', 37; F. Crowe, J. R. Cahill and H. W. G. Cole to Secretary for Foreign Affairs, 20 December 1928, TNA 30/76/246; 'Convention Relating to International Exhibitions', 22 November 1928, ibid.; *The 1928 Convention Governing International Exhibitions*, 10.

57. *Draft of General Regulations Applying to International Exhibitions*, 2. For the current version of this international convention, see Scherpenberg, *Weltausstellungen*, 23–38.

58. Wirth, 'Urbanism as a Way of Life', 8: 'For sociological purposes a city may be defined as a relatively large, dense, and permanent settlement of socially heterogeneous individuals'; see also Fischer, 'Urbanism as a Way of Life'. Hoffenberg, *An Empire on Display*, 27.

59. Gregory, 'The Geographical Discourse of Modernity', 58.

60. Lefebvre, *La Production de l'espace*, 48–50, and *The Production of Space*, 38–41, 311. Edward Soja has rendered this 'trialecticts of spatiality' as firstspace (perceived), secondspace (conceived), and thirdspace (lived), see his *Thirdspace*, 10. Lynn Stewart ('Bodies, Visions, and Spatial Politics', 610 n. 2) is right in arguing that 'spaces of representation' should be preferred over 'representational spaces' as in the English translation, since it is closer to the French original, less confusing and more suggestive.

61. Simmel, 'Berliner Gewerbe-Ausstellung'.

62. Morand, *Londres*, 161–2.

63. Cullen, 'Bankside Regained', 15. *Brief City*, dir. Maurice Harvey and Jacques B. Brunius, London: Massingham Productions Ltd, 1951.

64. For a brief survey, see Martayan, 'L'Ephémère dans la ville'.

65. Blake, *A Summer Holiday in Europe*, 39, 105; Boyd, *The Paris Exhibition of 1900*, 6.

66. Campbell, *Illustrated History*, 14.

67. Meissonier et al., 'Les Artistes contre la tour Eiffel': 'Il suffit, d'ailleurs, pour se rendre compte de ce que nous avançons, de se figurer un instant une tour vertigineusement ridicule, dominant Paris, ainsi qu'une gigantesque et noire cheminée d'usine, écrasant de sa masse barbare [...] tous nos monuments humiliés, toutes nos architectures rapetissées, qui disparaîtront dans ce rêve stupéfiant.'

68. Ibid.; Eiffel, 'L'Achèvement de la tour Eiffel'. For various histories of the tower, see Braibant, *Histoire de la Tour Eiffel*; Harris, *The Tallest Tower*; Levin, 'The Eiffel Tower Revisited'; Loyrette, 'La Tour Eiffel'; Kowitz, *La Tour Eiffel*; Kohle, 'Der Eiffelturm'; and, above all, Thompson, '"The Symbol of Paris"'. For recent visitor numbers, see: http://www.parisinfo.com/uploads/9e//chiffres-cles-2009.pdf, 24 (accessed 10 March 2009).

69. *Paris and its Exhibition*, 36.

70. 'Eiffel Tower', *Builder* 56 (8 June 1889), 425; Reusche, *Chicago und Berlin*, 18: 'Der Eiffelthurm ist ein brutales Eisenungeheuer, ein Monument der Geschmacklosigkeit, zwar des technischen Fortschrittes, aber des künstlerischen Rückschrittes unseres Jahrhunderts.

Dieser Thurm hat die Welt um keinen neuen Gedanken bereichert, es sei denn um den sehr naheliegenden, daß das Seine-Babel auch seinen Babelthurm haben müsse!' (emphasis in original); Davenport, *'Going On Me Own'*, 29; Kératry, *Paris Exposition*, 18.

71. Lessing, *Weltausstellung Paris 1900*, KB-SMB, n.p.; Daix, *Die Wunder der Weltausstellung*, 67–8; Blake, *A Summer Holiday in Europe*, 106–8; Braibant, *Histoire de la Tour Eiffel*, 168–9; Loyrette, 'La Tour Eiffel', 497.

72. Barthes, *The Eiffel Tower*, 7, and *Tour Eiffel*, 73: 'Any other monument [...] referred to a certain usage; only the Tour was nothing other than something to visit; its very emptiness made it symbolic and the prime symbol it was meant to arouse, by logical association, could only be what was "visited" at the same time, to wit Paris: the Tour has become Paris by metonymy.' This passage is not contained in the English translation. Thompson, '"The Symbol of Paris"', 1137–8.

73. *Paris and its Exhibition*, 32, 36.

74. Meissonier et al., 'Les Artistes contre la tour Eiffel'.

75. 'The "New" India: This Year's Exhibition at Earl's Court', *Westminster Gazette* (25 April 1896); *Exhibition Paris, 1900*, 301; Bezirksamt Treptow von Berlin, *Die Berliner Gewerbeausstellung 1896 in Bildern*, 22; Carden, 'The Franco-British Exhibition I/II', 109–10.

76. T. W. Littleton, *Times* (24 April 1923), 15; 'Rival to Eiffel Tower', ibid. (11 April 1923), 16; Edward Rew, 'Proposed London Tower', ibid. (12 April 1923), 8; E. G. Swain, 'Proposed Wembley Tower', ibid. (19 April 1923), 13; F. H. Fox, ibid. (21 April 1923), 12.

77. 'Exhibition Tower at Wembley', *Times* (24 April 1923), 8. Lawrence, *The British Empire Exhibition*, 33–5. However, the Glasgow Empire Exhibition of 1938 featured a Tower of Empire as its *clou*.

78. See Berliner Messe-Amt, *Der Berliner Funkturm*; and Brentano, 'Der Eiffelturm von Berlin'. For the venue's history in Berlin-Charlottenburg, see Escher, 'Berlin und seine Ausstellungen', 432–5; and Hoffmann, 'Das Ausstellungsgelände am Funkturm', 101–8.

79. Robert Hénard, 'La Grande roue de l'Exposition de 1900', *Magasin Pittoresque* 66 (1898), 261–2; Kératry, *Paris Exposition*, 91. Other sources (e.g., Pilz, *Paris amüsirt sich*, 188) claim that, with a diameter of 100 meters, it was the largest Ferris wheel ever built. Naumann, *Ausstellungsbriefe*, 74: 'So ungeschickt als Konkurrenz des Eiffelturmes das "große Rad von Paris" sein mag, so ist es doch voll von Idee und Leben gegenüber den Bauwerken der Umgebung, denn in den dünnen, langen Speichen dieses Rades redet eine neue Eleganz, die eleganter ist als die Anhäufung von Musen, Parzen, Engeln oder sonst welchen zwecklosen Wesen mit oder ohne Flügel.' On the history of big wheels, see William H. Searles, 'The Ferris Wheel', *Journal of the Association of Engineering Societies* 12 (12 December 1893), 614–16; Beck, *Das Wiener Riesenrad*; Kouwenhoven, 'The Eiffel Tower and the Ferris Wheel'; Anderson, *Ferris Wheels*; and De Cauter, 'The Panoramic Ecstasy', 17–20. The only one of these big wheels still in use today is the famous *Riesenrad* at the Prater amusement park in Vienna. Also developed by Bassett, it was constructed only three years later than the American original (in 1896–97), for the Venedig in Wien exhibition, to offer a movable vantage point just like the Flip-Flap; see Rubey and Schoenwald, *Venedig in Wien*.

80. 'The Great Paris Wheel', *Current Literature* 25 (1899), 245; 'The Great Wheel', *Times* (8 July 1895), 9.

81. 'The Wheel at Earl's Court', *Builder* 67 (13 October 1894), 266.

82. Macqueen-Pope, *Carriages at Eleven*, 217; 'The Great Wheel at Earl's Court', *Times* (19 April 1907), 10; 'The Franco-British Exhibition', ibid. (13 December 1907), 9.

83. Kerr, *Wo liegt Berlin?*, 150; Stevenson, *British Empire Exhibition*, 16; 'The Exhibition', *West Africa* (26 April 1924), 373.

84. Morrison, *How I Worked My Way Around the World*, 149.

85. *Illustrierter Amtlicher Führer durch die Berliner Gewerbe-Ausstellung 1896*, 34; Lindenberg, *Pracht-Album*, 43; Simmel, 'Berliner Gewerbe-Ausstellung', 59.

86. Weigert, 'Weltausstellungen', 40; Boyd, *The Paris Exhibition of 1900*, 8; *A Pictorial and Descriptive Guide to London and the Franco-British Exhibition, 1908*, E [*sic*]: 'It is hardly an

exaggeration to describe the Exhibition as a city in itself, and whole days will hardly suffice for a thorough inspection.'

87. 'Beschlußfassung über die Anträge des technischen Ausschusses betreffend die für das Jahr 1888 vorgesehene deutsche Gewerbeausstellung in Berlin', 102: 'Es ist jetzt eine Weltausstellung ein gewaltiger Zusammenfluß von allen möglichen industriellen Massenartikeln, es entsteht eine Art Industriestadt, man kann sie nicht mehr übersehen, kann sie nicht mehr systematisch ordnen, niemand kann sich noch in ihr zurecht finden und jede Einzelleistung verschwindet in den ausgestellten Massen.'

88. Beavan, *Imperial London*, preface.

89. Witt, *Pariser Weltausstellungsbriefe*, 1–2; Böttcher, *Weltausstellungs-Glossen*, 5; *Paris and its Exhibition*, 10.

90. For example, *Exhibition Paris, 1900*; *Guide dans l'Exposition*.

91. Aflalo, 'The Promise of International Exhibitions', 838. See Rancière and Vauday, 'Going to the Expo'; Geppert, 'Exponierte Identitäten?'; and Pellegrino, '"Il gran dimenticato"'. Reulecke, 'Kommunikation durch Tourismus?'.

92. G. C. L., 'Exhibition'; Arbeitsausschuss der Berliner Gewerbe-Ausstellung, *Berlin und seine Arbeit*, 182–3.

93. Tissot, 'How did the British Conquer Switzerland?', 29–30.

94. Ford, *The Soul of London*, 13; Sala, *Paris Herself Again in 1878–9*, vol. 1, 11; Barrès, *Pas d'Exposition en 1900*: 'Qu'au surplus, Paris, avec ses dépôts de toutes les grandes industries françaises et ses splendides étalages le long des grandes voies constitue une Exposition permanente'. See also Berger, *Les Expositions universelles internationales*, 146. Numerous further examples could be given for this most central *topos*. Campbell, *Illustrated History*, 70.

95. See, for instance *Empire Exhibition Scotland 1938*, 72–3, for the metaphor of the exhibition as a 'text book whose pages and chapters have been opened before us'; Boyd, *The Paris Exhibition of 1900*, 5.

96. Barringer, 'The South Kensington Museum and the Colonial Project'; Wainwright and Gere, 'The Making of the South Kensington Museum'; Carden, 'The Milan International Exhibition', 358.

97. 'Industrial Exhibitions', *Builder* 122 (7 April 1922), 122.

98. Geddes, 'Two Steps in Civics'; Sutcliffe, *Towards the Planned City*, 165–73; Welter, 'Stages of an Exhibition'; and Meller, 'Philantrophy and Public Enterprise'.

99. Simmel, 'Die Großstädte und das Geistesleben'; Woodhead, 'The First German Municipal Exposition'; Wurm, 'Der deutsche Städtetag und die deutsche Städteausstellung'; Wuttke, *Die deutschen Städte*.

100. *Paris and its Exhibition*, 10; Filson Young, 'At Wembley', *Saturday Review* (29 March 1924), 317.

101. See Harvey, *Hybrids of Modernity*, 129, for the identical observation of noteworthy stability over time. For an analysis of Anglo-French rivalries and inter-urban competition at early great exhibitions, see Wildman, 'Great, Greater? Greatest??'.

102. Eco, 'A Theory of Expositions', 291. That an exposition should be a 'hybrid institution that for better or worse carries clear traces of its origins' – as Penelope Harvey has objected to Eco's argument – is a truism and hence entirely indisputable; see Harvey, *Hybrids of Modernity*, 108–9.

103. Simmel, 'Berliner Gewerbe-Ausstellung', 59.

104. Eco, 'A Theory of Expositions', 296.

105. But not in the *Descriptive Catalogue*, which was adorned by the usual engravings. Harvard, 'The Great Exhibition was Photographed'; *Exhibition of the Works of Industry of All Nations, 1851*.

106. G. Mareschal, 'Le Cinématographie à l'Exposition de l'enseignement de la Ville de Paris', *Nature* 28.2 (1900), 273–4; Toulet, 'Le Cinéma à l'Exposition universelle de 1900'; Abel, *The Ciné Goes to Town*, 17, 91. At least 17 different *actualités* made by the brothers

Lumière are known; some of them have been made available to the public by the Library of Congress and can be found at http://memory.loc.gov (accessed 10 March 2009).

107. Démy, *Essai historique*, 565–6.
108. Thomas R. Kimball, 'The Management and Design of Expositions', *The American Architect* 74 (26 October 1901), 29–31, here 31.
109. Barwick, 'International Exhibitions and Their Civilising Influence', 313; Fesche, 'Räumliche Effekte von Weltausstellungen', 148. However, the French philosopher and socialist Pierre-Joseph Proudhon (1809–1865) suggested already in 1865 transforming the *clou* of the Parisian 1855 exposition, the famous *Palais de l'Industrie*, into a perpetual exposition center, largely comparable to a department store; see Proudhon, 'Société de l'Exposition perpétuelle'.
110. Harvey, *The Urban Experience*.
111. Tuan, *Space and Place*, 4, 18.
112. ANOM ECI 26/2/5.
113. *Colonial and Indian Exhibition*, lxxxix–xciii, here lxxxix. The *Street* did not fail to impress foreign visitors; see Reuleaux, 'Die Entwicklung des Ausstellungswesens', 4.
114. Bakhtin, 'Forms of Time and the Chronotope in the Novel: Notes toward a Historical Poetics' [1937], in *The Dialogic Imagination*, 84-258, here 84 and 246. As Bakhtin puts it: 'We will give the name *chronotope* (literally, 'time space') to the intrinsic connectedness of temporal and spatial relationships that are artistically expressed in literature. [...] In the literary artistic chronotope, spatial and temporal indicators are fused into one carefully thought-out, concrete whole. Time, as it were, thickens, takes on flesh, becomes artistically visible; likewise, space becomes charged and responsive to the movements of time, plot and history.' As a short introduction, Kinser, 'Chronotopes and Catastrophes'; Morson and Emerson, *Mikhail Bakhtin*, esp. 366–432.
115. Foucault, 'Of Other Spaces', 25.

Coda   Pictures at an Exhibition

1. 'It is a particular attraction of world fairs that they form a momentary center of world civilization, assembling the products of the entire world in a confined space as if in a single picture.' Simmel, 'Berliner Gewerbe-Ausstellung', 59.

Appendix

1. Information in this table has been compiled from a variety of different sources, general encyclopedias, and biographical dictionaries including *Allgemeine Deutsche Biographie*; *American National Biography*; *Archives biographiques françaises*; *British Biographical Archive*; *British Biographical Index*; *Deutsche Biographische Enzyklopädie*; *Deutscher Biographischer Index*; *Deutsches Biographisches Archiv*; *Deutsches Biographisches Jahrbuch*; *Dictionary of American Biography*; *Dictionary of National Biography*; *Dictionnaire de biographie française*; *Index biographique français*; *Journal of the Royal Society of Arts*; *Neue Deutsche Biographie*; *Oxford Dictionary of National Biography*; *Times*; *Who's Who* 1897–1996; *Who Was Who*; and *World Biographical Information System*. See also Findling and Pelle, *Encyclopedia of World's Fairs and Expositions*, 418–21; and Hoffenberg, *An Empire on Display*, 281–5.
2. Georg Simmel, 'Berliner Gewerbe-Ausstellung', *Die Zeit: Wiener Wochenschrift für Politik, Volkswirtschaft, Wissenschaft und Kunst* 8.95 (25 July 1896), 59–60; Sam Whimster's translation first appeared in *Theory, Culture and Society* 8.3 (1991), 119–23. It is reproduced here by permission of Sage Publications Ltd.

Bibliography

Archival sources

Archives de Frances, Centre d'accueil et de recherche des Archives Nationales, Paris (*CARAN*)

F12 11933–8	Exposition coloniale internationale de 1931 à Paris
F12 3757–4055*	Exposition universelle de 1889
F12 4056/A–4456*	Exposition universelle de 1900
F12 4984	Londres 1886
F12 4993	Berlin 1896
F12 7538–40	Exposition universelle de Paris, 1900
F12 7574–7575	Londres, Exposition franco-britannique de 1908
F12 7576–7577	Expositions franco-coloniales, 1902–12
F14 13065	Londres, Exposition franco-britannique
F14 9155	Métropolitain de Paris: Projet Deligny et Vautier (1879–96) Etudes pour l'Exposition universelle de 1900 (1892–96)

Archives de France, Archives nationales d'outre-mer, Aix-en-Provence (*ANOM*)

Colonies, généralités, Instruction publique: Exposition permanente des colonies, Expositions universelles (1851–1902)

Annam R1	Exposition coloniale de Marseilles (1906); Exposition internationale de Vienne et Exposition de la Société coloniale des artistes françaises (1929)
ECI	Exposition coloniale internationale
A.O.F. II 2–4	Expositions (1899–1907)
A.O.F. Q 26 à 47	Participation aux expositions (1854–1916)
A.E.F. II 1–9	Expositions et congrès (1913–16)

Bibliothèque historique de la Ville de Paris (*BHVP*)

Boston Public Library (*BPL*)

Robert A. Feer Collection of World's Fairs

Brent Archive, London (*BA*)

British Empire Exhibition Collection (BEEC)

Bromley Public Libraries, London (*BrPL*)

Crystal Palace Collection, Archives Section

Bundesarchiv Berlin (*BArch*)

R 43	Reichskanzlei
R 901	Auswärtiges Amt

R 1001	Reichskolonialamt (Aktengruppe Kongresse, Ausstellungen, Kolonialpropaganda)
R 3101	Reichswirtschaftsministerium (Aktengruppe Ausstellungssachen)
R 8023	Deutsche Kolonialgesellschaft (Aktengruppe Ausstellungen, Kongresse und Tagungen)

Bureau International des Expositions, Paris (*BIE*)

California State University, Special Collections Research Center, Fresno (*CSU*)

Donald G. Larson Collection of International Expositions and Fairs
George R. Leighton Collection

Cambridge University Library, Cambridge (*CUL*)

Royal Commonwealth Society Archives and Collections (RCSAC)

Geheimes Staatsarchiv Preußischer Kulturbesitz, Berlin (*GStA PK*)

| I. HA Rep. 120 MfHuG | Ministerium für Handel und Gewerbe, Aktengruppe XVI: 'Ausstellungen und Messen' |

Grange Museum of Community History, London (*GMCH*)

Oral History Interviews

Guildhall Library, London (*GL*)

Noble Collection of Cuttings and Ephemera
Photograph and Postcard Collection

Hammersmith and Fulham Archives and Local History Centre, London (*HFALHC*)

| H 606.1–12 | White City Exhibitions |

Kunstbibliothek Berlin – Staatliche Museen zu Berlin (*KB-SMB*)

Julius Lessing, Weltausstellung Paris 1900: Ausschnitte aus der National-Zeitung, Berlin, 1900

Landesarchiv Berlin (*LAB*)

| STA-Rep. 045–05/6 Nr. 28 | Berliner Gewerbe-Ausstellung (1896–97) |
| Photograph Collection | |

London Metropolitan Archives, London (*LMA*)

35.8	Exhibitions: Trade
41.5	Festival of Britain
43.5	Crystal Palace

London Transport Museum (*LTM*)

Photograph Collection

Museum of London (*ML*)

Imre Kiralfy Collection (IKC)
Photograph Collection

Royal Institute of British Architects, London (*RIBA*)

11.2.2	Exhibitions Joint Committee Minutes and Papers, 1921–27
11.2.3	Exhibition Record Files, 1921–72
10.4	Art Standing Committee Minutes and Papers, 1886–1939

Staatsbibliothek zu Berlin – Preußischer Kulturbesitz (*SBB-PK*)

Staats- und Universitätsbibliothek Hamburg, Handschriftenabteilung (*SUB-HH*)

Cod. Hans. II, 184   Weltausstellung zu Paris 1900: Berichte der Stipendiaten

Technische Universität Berlin (*TUB*)

Map Collection

The National Archives, Kew, London (*TNA*)

BT 13/41	International Exhibitions Committee
BT 13/49	International Exhibitions Committee
BT 22	Railway Dept: Correspondence and Papers, 1867–1900
BT 237	Export Promotion Department: Exhibition and Fairs Branch, 1937–57
BT 31/15403	The London Exhibitions Ltd
BT 31/40546	The International and Colonial Commercial Company Ltd/ Shepherd's Bush Exhibition Ltd
BT 60	Department of Overseas Trade Correspondence and Papers, 1918–46
BT 61	Department of Overseas Trade Establishment Files, 1918–46
BT 80/20	The Results of Wembley
BT 90/20	British Empire Exhibition: Results Attained by Exhibitors and Prospects
CO 323	Colonies, General: Original Correspondence, 1689–1952
CO 378	Colonies, General: Register to Correspondence, 1852–1952
CO 554	West Africa Original Correspondence, 1911–65
CO 555	West Africa Register of Correspondence, 1889–1951
CO 573	Colonies General Supplementary Original Correspondence, 1759–1955
HLG 4	Planning Scheme Files, 1905–51
HLG 52/897	British Empire Exhibition 1924: Housing and Town Planning Exhibits
HO 144/906/176565	Exhibition Titles
PRO 1/177	PRO General Correspondence
RAIL 267/267/389	Great Western Railway Company: Special Reports, 1845–1940
RAIL 268/222–3	Great Western Railway Company: Publications, 1898–1951
T 1	Treasury Board Papers
T 161	Treasury Supply Files
T 172/1462	India's Non-Participation in the British Empire Exhibition

United States National Archives and Records Administration, College Park, MD (*NARA*)

RG 79/800	Paris Colonial Overseas Exposition, 1931–33
RG 43/1316–20	Records of the Commission Representing the United States at the International Colonial and Overseas Exposition at Paris, 1930–32
RG 43-EX/4	United States Exhibits at International Expositions, 1888–1934

University of Sussex Library, Special Collections, Brighton (*USL*)

James Stevenson Papers

Victoria and Albert Museum, Archive of Art and Design, London (*V&A/AAD*)

S.F. 274   United Kingdom: Indian and Colonial 1886
S.F. 277   Exhibitions London Various
Nominal File Franco-British Exhibition 1908
Wembley British Empire Exhibition 1924: Correspondence, Minutes and Catalogues, 1921–24

Journals, newspapers and serials

Allgemeine Zeitung
American Architect and Building News
Annales de Géographie
Les Annales Politiques et Littéraires
The Architects' Journal
Architectural Forum
Architectural Record
Architectural Review
L'Architecture
L'Art vivant
Asiatic Review
Atlantic Monthly
Der Bär
Berliner Börsen-Courier
Berliner Börsenzeitung
Berliner Lokal-Anzeiger
Berliner Merkur
Berliner Morgen-Zeitung und Tägliches Familienblatt
Berliner Neueste Nachrichten
Berliner Politische Nachrichten
Berliner Tageblatt
Black and White: A Weekly Illustrated Record and Review
Builder
Centralblatt der Bauverwaltung
La Construction Moderne
Daily Telegraph
Deutsche Bauzeitung
Deutsche Kolonialzeitung
Deutsche Kunst und Dekoration
Deutsche Oekonomist
Deutsche Revue
Deutsche Rundschau
Deutsche volkswirthschaftliche Correspondenz
Deutsches Wochenblatt
Die Zukunft
East Africa
Empire Exhibition News: The Organ of the British Empire Exhibition
Engineering
English Review
Entwürfe: Erfunden und herausgegeben von Mitgliedern des Architekten-Vereins zu Berlin

Evening Standard
Le Figaro
Fortnightly Review
Frankfurter Zeitung
Freisinnige Zeitung
Germania
Glaser's Annalen für Gewerbe und Bauwesen
Grande Revue
Hamburger Nachrichten
Hamburgischer Correspondent
Illustrated London News
L'Illustration
Jahresberichte des Vereins Berliner Kaufleute und Industrieller
Journal des Débats
Journal of the Royal Institute of British Architects
Journal of the Royal Society of Arts
Journal Officiel de la République Française
Das kleine Journal
Kölnische Zeitung
Kreuzzeitung
Literary Digest
Magasin Pittoresque
Mittheilungen des Vereins für die Geschichte Berlins
Le Monde Moderne
Morgen: Wochenschrift für deutsche Kultur
Münchener Allgemeine Zeitung
Münchner Neueste Nachrichten
Museums Journal
National Review
National-Zeitung
Neue Freie Presse
Neue Preußische Zeitung
New York Times
New-Yorker Handels-Zeitung
Nineteenth Century
Norddeutsche Allgemeine Zeitung
Nouvelle Revue
Officielle Ausstellungs-Nachrichten
Ostpreußische Zeitung
Outre-Mer: Revue Générale de Colonisation
Papier-Zeitung
Le Petit Journal Illustré
Preußische Jahrbücher
Punch; or, the London Charivari
Questions Diplomatiques et Coloniales
Reichsbote
Revue de Paris
Revue des Deux Mondes
Revue Maritime et Coloniale
Revue Scientifique
Revue Universitaire
Saturday Review of Politics, Literature, Science and Art
Schlesische Zeitung
The Scotsman

Sitzungsberichte des Vereins zur Beförderung des Gewerbefleißes in Preußen
South African Railways and Harbours Magazine
Staatsbürger-Zeitung
Ständige Ausstellungskommission für die Deutsche Industrie: Jahrbücher/Jahresberichte
Studio
Der Tag
Le Temps
Times of London
Town Planning Review Quarterly
United Empire: The Royal Colonial Institute Journal
Vorwärts
Vossische Zeitung
West Africa
Westdeutsche Allgemeine Zeitung
World's Work
Zeitschrift des Vereines deutscher Ingenieure

Primary sources

1900: Paris Exposition. Guide pratique du visiteur de Paris et de l'Exposition, Paris: Hachette, 1900.

Abercrombie, Patrick, 'The Champs de Mars, Paris', *Town Planning Review* 1.3 (1910), 251–5.

——, 'The Planning of the British Empire Exhibition: A Symbolical Lay-Out', *The Architects' Journal* 59 (28 May 1924), 903–5.

Adams, Henry, *The Education of Henry Adams* [1907], Boston: Houghton Mifflin, 1974.

Ador, Gustav, *Weltausstellung in Paris 1900: Administrativer und technischer Bericht des Schweizerischen Generalkommissariats*, Geneva: Kündig, 1901.

Aflalo, F. G., 'The Promise of International Exhibitions', *Fortnightly Review* 73 (1900), 830–9.

Albert, Prince Consort of Victoria, Queen of Great Britain, 'Speech at the Banquet Given by the Right Hon. the Lord Mayor, Thomas Farncombe, to Her Majesty's Ministers, Foreign Ambassadors, Royal Commissioners of the Exhibition of 1851, and the Mayors of One Hundred and Eighty Towns, at the Mansion House [March 21st, 1850]', in *The Principal Speeches and Addresses of His Royal Highness the Prince Consort*, ed. Arthur Helps, London: Murray, 1862, 109–14.

Album de l'Exposition française ouverte à Londres le 17 Mai 1890, London: Courrier de Londres et de l'Europe, 1890.

Album-souvenir de l'Exposition coloniale internationale de Paris: 12 Dessins représentant les principaux Palais. Une description de l'Exposition coloniale, Charenton: Imprimerie Moderne, 1931.

Allix, André, 'The Geography of Fairs: Illustrated by Old-World Examples', *Geographical Review* 12.4 (1922), 532–69.

Almanach in Wort und Bild der Berliner Gewerbe-Ausstellung 1896: Unter dem Protectorat Sr. Kgl. Hoheit d. Prinzen Friedrich Leopold von Preussen, Berlin: Schmidt, 1896.

Das Alpenpanorama: Bergfahrt im Zillerthal zur "Berliner Hütte" der Section Berlin des D. u. Ö. Alpenvereins auf der Berliner Gewerbeausstellung 1896, Berlin: Tietz, 1896.

Alt-Berlin auf der Berliner Gewerbe-Ausstellung 1896, Berlin: Kufahl, 1895.

Amery, Leo S., *My Political Life*, vol. 2: *War and Peace 1914–1929*, London: Hutchinson, 1953.

Amtlicher Bericht über die allgemeine Deutsche Gewerbe-Ausstellung zu Berlin im Jahre 1844, Berlin: Karl Reimarus, 1845.

Anders, N. J. [pseud. Nathan Jacob], *Lehmann und Müller in der Berliner Gewerbe-Ausstellung: Eine komische Ausstellungs-Geschichte in acht Abtheilungen*, Berlin: Weichert, 1896.

Anderson, A., 'The Paris Exhibition and Some of its Buildings', *Architectural Review* 7 (1900), 29–37.

Angoulvant, Gabriel, 'Les Palais et les pavillons: L'Afrique occidentale française', *Revue des Deux Mondes* 101 (15 August 1931), 834–54.

'Die Anlage und die Bauten der Berliner Gewerbe-Ausstellung des Jahres 1896 I–VII', *Deutsche Bauzeitung* 30 (25 April/2 May/9 May/23 May/30 May/20 June/18 July 1896), 209–11, 225–7, 237–8, 265, 277, 317–18, 365–6.

Annalist [pseud. Charles Whibley], *Musings Without Method: A Record of 1900–01*, Edinburgh: Blackwood, 1902.

Ansichten von Berlin mit der Gewerbe-Ausstellung 1896, Dresden: Kunstanstalt, [1896?].

Ansichten von Kairo in der Berliner Gewerbeausstellung 1896, Berlin: Kaufmann, 1896.

Aragon, Louis, 'Une Préface morcelée: L'an 31 et l'envers de ce temps', in *L'Œuvre poétique*, vol. 5: *1930–1933*, Paris: Livre Club Diderot, 1975, 177–84.

——, 'Mars à Vincennes', in *L'Œuvre poétique*, vol. 5: *1930–1933*, Paris: Livre Club Diderot, 1975, 212–16.

Arbeitsausschuss der Berliner Gewerbe-Ausstellung, ed., *Offizieller Haupt-Katalog der Berliner Gewerbe-Ausstellung 1896*, Berlin: Mosse, 1896.

——, ed., *Berlin und seine Arbeit: Amtlicher Bericht der Berliner Gewerbe-Ausstellung 1896, zugleich eine Darstellung des gegenwärtigen Standes unserer gewerblichen Entwicklung*, Berlin: Reimer, 1898 (2nd edn 1901).

Arbeitsausschuss der Deutschen Kolonial-Ausstellung and Gustav Meinecke, eds, *Deutsche Kolonial-Ausstellung 1896: Gruppe XXIII der Berliner Gewerbe-Ausstellung 1896. Offizieller Katalog und Führer*, Berlin: Mosse, 1896.

Arbeitsausschuss der Deutschen Kolonial-Ausstellung: Graf v. Schweinitz, C v. Beck, F. Imberg, Gustav Meinecke, eds, *Deutschland und seine Kolonien im Jahre 1896: Amtlicher Bericht über die erste Deutsche Kolonial-Ausstellung*, Berlin: Reimer, 1897.

Archimbaud, Léon, 'L'Indochine et la cause de la colonisation française à l'Exposition coloniale de Paris en 1931', *Revue du Pacifique* 1.4 (1930), 193–9.

L'Architecture à l'Exposition universelle de 1900, Paris: Librairies-Imprimeries Réunis, 1902.

'Architecture at International Exhibitions', *Journal of the Royal Institute of British Architects* 46 (7 November 1938), 33–4.

Askwith, Lord, 'Exhibitions', *Journal of the Royal Society of Arts* 72 (23 November 1923), 2–14.

'Aspects of the Great Fair', *The World's Work* 12 (June 1908), 9–28.

'Ausstellungen', *Die Zukunft* 40 (4 July 1896), 1–10.

Ausstellungs- und Messe-Ausschuss der Deutschen Wirtschaft, ed., *AUMA: 75 Jahre im Dienst der Messewirtschaft (1907–82)*, Cologne: Heider, 1982.

Ayrton, Maxwell 'A Note on Concrete Buildings', *Journal of the Royal Institute of British Architects* 31 (22 March 1924), 298–302.

Bablet, G., *La Rage en Indochine*, Saigon: Portail, 1931.

Baedeker, Karl, *Paris and Environs with Routes from London to Paris: Handbook for Travellers*, Leipzig: Karl Baedeker, 1900.

Baillehache, Marcel de, *L'Ecole militaire et le Champ-de-Mars*, Paris: Charles, 1896.

Barnes, H., 'The British Empire Exhibition, Wembley', *Architectural Review* 55 (1924), 206–17.

Barnicoat, Constance A., 'England Seen Through French Eyes', *Fortnightly Review* 83 (1908), 1027–37.

Barrès, Maurice, *Pas d'Exposition en 1900*, Nancy: Aux Bureaux de la Ligue Lorraine de Décentralisation, 1895.

Barthélemy, A., 'L'Exposition universelle de 1900', *Grande Revue* (1 April/1 May 1900), 194–211, 451–67.

Barwick, George F., 'International Exhibitions and Their Civilising Influence', in *The Civilisation of Our Day: A Series of Original Essays on Some of Its More Important Phases at the Close of the Nineteenth Century. By Expert Writers*, ed. James Samuelson, London: Sampson Low, Marston, 1896, 301–13.

Baudelaire, Charles, *Œuvres complètes*, 3 vols, Paris: Club français du livre, 1961.

Bazin, Germain, 'La Reconstitution du temple d'Angkor à l'Exposition coloniale de 1931', *L'Architecture* 43.4 (1930), 131–40.

Beavan, Arthur Henry, *Imperial London*, London: Dent & Dutton, 1901.

Beck, Friedrich, *Das Wiener Riesenrad: Fernsicht und Beschreibung*, Vienna: Beck, 1937.

Behrens, Peter, 'Über Ausstellungen', *Die Rheinlande* 1.1 (1900), 33–4.

Behrens, S., *Krebsschaden des Ausstellungswesens*, Berlin: n.p., 1907.

Belcher, Ernest Albert, 'The Dominion and Colonial Sections of the British Empire Exhibition, 1924', *Journal of the Royal Society of Arts* 71 (20 April 1923), 388–96.

Beldimano, W., 'The Colonial Exhibition at Marseilles', *The Graphic* (8 July 1922), 43–4.

Bemrose's District Railway Guide to the Irish Exhibition in London, London: Bemrose, 1888.

Bénard, Charles and Jules Charles-Roux, eds, *Rapport général: Exposition coloniale de Marseilles 1906*, Marseilles: Barlatier, 1907.

Bennett, Helen M., *Report on Current European Fairs and Suggestions Arising from Attendance: The Exposition of the British Empire, Wembly Park, London, 1926* [sic]; *the Leipsig Trade Fair, Leipsig, 1928; the International Press Exhibition, Cologne, 1928; Swiss Exhibition of the Work of Women, Berne, 1928; Site of Special International Fairs, Paris,* Chicago [?]: n.p., 1928.

Berger, H. Georges, *Les Expositions universelles internationales: Leur passé, leur rôle actuel, leur avenir*, Paris: Arthur Rousseau, 1902.

Bergeret, Gaston, *Journal d'un nègre à l'Exposition de 1900*, Paris: Conquet, 1901.

Berichte über den Besuch der Pariser Welt-Ausstellung 1900, erstattet von den durch die Handwerkskammer für das Herzogtum Braunschweig zur Ausstellung entsandten Handwerksmeistern, Braunschweig: n.p., 1901.

Berichte über die Welt-Ausstellung in Paris im Jahre 1900, Berlin: Grunert, 1902.

Berliner Gewerbe-Ausstellung 1896: Organe der Ausstellung, Berlin: Otto von Holten, 1896.

Berliner Messe-Amt and Karl Vetter, eds, *Der Berliner Funkturm: Worte und Bilder zum Werden und Wirken*, Berlin: Berliner Messe-Amt, 1926.

'Berliner Weltausstellung', *Glaser's Annalen für Gewerbe und Bauwesen* 5 (15 November 1879), 381.

Bernard, B., *Anglo-Saxon Guide to the Paris Exhibition, 1900*, London: Boot, 1900.

Bertrand, Louis, 'A Travers les sections de l'Exposition coloniale: L'Algérie', *Revue des Deux Mondes* 101 (15 June 1931), 825–37.

'Beschlußfassung über die Anträge des technischen Ausschusses betreffend die für das Jahr 1888 vorgesehene deutsche Gewerbeausstellung in Berlin', *Sitzungsberichte des Vereins zur Beförderung des Gewerbefleißes* 65 (5 April 1886), 100–25.

Beste, Th., 'Märkte, Messen, Ausstellungen', in *Staatslexikon*, vol. 3: *Kapitulationen bis Panslawismus*, ed. Hermann Sacher, 5th edn, Freiburg im Breisgau: Herder, 1929, 1158–68.

'Die Betheiligung Deutschlands an der Pariser Weltausstellung', *Die Gegenwart* 10 (18 November 1876), 321–2.

Birnstingl, H. J., 'Architecture at the British Empire Exhibition', *The Architectural Forum* 41.1 (1924), 29–32.

Blake, Mary Elizabeth, *A Summer Holiday in Europe*, Boston: Lee & Shepard, 1890.

Blake, William Phipps, *Great International Expositions: Their Objects, Purposes, Organization, and Results. An Address Delivered Before the American Centennial Commission*, Philadelphia: Markley, 1872.

Blathwayt, Raymond, 'London's Great Exhibition: A Chat with Mr. Imre Kiralfy', *Black and White* (25 January 1908), 108.

Bobertag, Georg, *Eine Weltausstellung in Deutschland: Beiträge zur Geschichte des Berliner Weltausstellungsplanes*, Berlin: Maschning, Winkler, 1892.

Boenigk, Otto Freiherr von, *Die Unlauterkeit im Ausstellungswesen*, Halberstadt: Verlag der Handelskammer, 1893.

Bohnstedt, 'Die Pariser Weltausstellung im Jahre 1900 I/II', *Centralblatt der Bauverwaltung* 15 (26 January/2 February 1895), 46–7, 51–2.

Bonnell, Waldemar, 'Die Deutsche Gewerbeausstellung zu Berlin im Jahre 1844', *Mitteilungen des Vereins für die Geschichte Berlins* 4 (1893), 35–9.

Borelly, René, *Promenade à l'Exposition coloniale*, 3rd edn, Paris: L'Association de maîtres imprimeurs, 1931.

Böttcher, Karl, *Weltausstellungs-Glossen: Kritisches Geplauder über die Pariser Weltausstellung, besonders im Vergleich mit der Chicagoer*, Zurich: Schröter, 1900.

Boudot-Lamotte, Emmanuel, 'La Métropole à l'Exposition coloniale', *L'Architecture* 44.7 (1931), 219–40.

Boullet, Ernest, *Etudes de transformation, translation et restauration du Champ-de-Mars*, Rennes: Oberthur, 1859.

Bouvier, Aimé and Fleury Tournièr, *Franco-British Exhibition: The Senegal Village*, London: n.p., 1908.

Boyd, James P., *The Paris Exhibition of 1900: The Century's Last and Grandest All-World Exposition. A Vivid Descriptive View and Elaborate Scenic Presentation of the Site, Plan and Exhibits*, Chicago: Dominion, 1900.

Brandt, L. Otto, 'Zur Geschichte und Würdigung der Weltausstellungen', *Zeitschrift für Socialwissenschaft* 7.2 (1904), 81–96.

Brangwyn, Frank, 'The Architecture of the British Empire Exhibition', *Studio 87* (15 May 1924), 249–52.

Braun, Rudolph (im Auftrage des Comités für das Weltausstellungs-Terrain im Norden Berlins), *Panorama der Berliner Weltausstellung*, Berlin: Cassirer und Danziger, [1892?].

Brendicke, Hans, *Führer durch die Sonder-Ausstellung von Berolinensien des Vereins für die Geschichte Berlins in der Heiliggeistkirche zu Alt-Berlin auf der Gewerbe-Ausstellung zu Berlin 1896*, 2nd edn, Berlin: Verein für die Geschichte Berlins, 1896.

——, 'Bericht über die Sitzungen des Vereins', *Mittheilungen des Vereins für die Geschichte Berlins* 13.3 (1896), 34.

——, 'Zur Gewerbe-Ausstellung in Berlin', *Mittheilungen des Vereins für die Geschichte Berlins* 13.6 (1896), 66–8.

Brennglas, Adolph, *Die Berliner Gewerbe-Ausstellung: Genre-Bild*, Leipzig: Bernhard Hermann, 1844.

Brentano, Bernhard von, 'Der Eiffelturm von Berlin', in *Wo in Europa ist Berlin? Bilder aus den zwanziger Jahren*, Frankfurt am Main: Insel, 1981, 125–7.

Breton, André, Paul Eluard, Benjamin Péret, Georges Sadoul, Pierre Unik, André Thirion, René Crevel, Aragon, René Char, Maxime Alexandre, Yves Tanguy and Georges Malkine, *Ne Visitez pas l'Exposition coloniale*, Paris: n.p., 1931 [Reprinted in *Tracts surréalistes et déclarations collectives*, ed. José Pierre, vol. 1: *1922–1939*, Paris: Terrain Vague, 1980, 194–5].

Brevan, E. de, 'Liste sommaire des publications du Comité français des expositions à l'étranger 1895–1916', *Bulletin officiel: Comité français des expositions à l'étranger* 1–10 (1916), 23–32.

Briganti, Gaetano, *Additiamo agli emigranti italiani le ricche colonie britanniche: Visitando l'esposizione di Wembley,* Piacenza: Federazione Consorzi Agrari, 1925.

Brisson, Adolphe, *Scènes et types de l'Exposition*, Paris: Montgrédien, 1900.

British Empire Exhibition 1924 Wembley, London April–October: Handbook of General Information, London: n.p., 1924.

British Empire Exhibition 1925: Opening Ceremony by H.M. the King Accompanied by H.M. the Queen. Wembley May 9th 1925, London: Fleetway, 1925.

British Empire Exhibition Wembley, 1924–1925: Catalogue of the Palace of Arts, London: Fleetway, 1924.

British Empire Exhibition: Official Catalogue 1924, London: Fleetway, 1924.

Brockhoff, Albert, *Eine Weltausstellung in Berlin*, Berlin: Oswald Seehagen, 1880.

Brunet, J. L., *Exposition Franco-Britannique Londres 1908: Les colonies françaises*, 2nd edn, Paris: Comité National des Expositions Coloniales, 1909.

Bucher, Bruno, 'Die Ausstellungs-Frage', *Westermann's Illustrirte Deutsche Monats-Hefte* 50 (1881), 79–90.

——, *Zur Reform des Ausstellungswesens: Aus den Blättern für Kunstgewerbe*, Vienna: Waldheim, 1880.

Bucher, Lothar, *Kulturhistorische Skizzen aus der Industrieausstellung aller Völker*, Frankfurt am Main: Lizius, 1851.

Budde, E., 'Über Ausstellungswesen', *Deutsche Revue* 33.1 (1908), 295–303.

Butler, Herbert E., 'The Moving Pavement', in *The Paris Exhibition of 1900*, ed. David Croal Thomson, London: Virtue, 1901, 271–6.

Cachin, Marcel, *Carnets 1906–1947*, vol. 3: *1921–1933*, ed. Denis Peschanski, Paris: CNRS, 1998.

Calcutta Exhibition 1923: Official Guide and Handbook, Calcutta: n.p., [1923?].

Calonne, Alphonse de, 'L'Exposition de 1900 à Paris: Programme et concours', *Revue des Deux Mondes* 65 (15 January 1895), 354–71.

——, 'The French Universal Exposition of 1900', *Architectural Record* 5.3 (1896), 217–26.

——, 'L'Exposition de 1900: Les deux palais', *Le Correspondant* 186 (1897), 751–62.

Camp, Jean and André Corbier, *A Lyauteyville: Promenades sentimentales et humoristiques à l'Exposition coloniale*, Paris: Société Nationale d'Editions Artistiques, 1931.

Campbell, James B., *Illustrated History of the Paris International Exposition Universelle of 1900: A Presentation of the World's Achievements in Literature, Science, Industry, Art and Architecture, as Shown at the Paris Exposition at the Close of the Nineteenth Century*, Chicago: Omaha, 1900.

Campbell, Lady Colin, ed., *Briton, Boer and Black in Savage South Africa at Olympia: Libretto and Programme (Combined). Savage Africa, the Eskimo Encampment, the Zulu Kraal, the Soudanese Village and Behind the Scenes*, London: Hill, 1899.

Carden, Robert W., 'The Milan International Exhibition', *Architectural Record* 20.5 (1906), 353–68.

——, 'The Franco-British Exhibition I/II', *Architectural Review* 24 (1908), 32–7, 108–11.

——, 'The Franco-British Exhibition', *Architectural Record* 24.2 (1908), 83–97.

Cassel's Guide to Paris and the Universal Exhibition of 1900: With Two Plans and Numerous Illustrations, London: Cassel, 1900.

Caster, Louis de, 'L'Exposition de 1900: L'Annexe de Vincennes', *Monde Moderne* (1900), 527–31.

——, 'L'Exposition de 1900: Les Palais de Champ de Mars', *Monde Moderne* (1900), 91–8.

Cayla, Léon, 'L'Exposition coloniale de Paris en 1931, son but et son organisation', *Bulletin de la Société d'Encouragement pour l'Industrie Nationale* (1929), 691–9.

——, 'The International Colonial Exhibition of Paris, 1931', *Asiatic Review* 26 (1930), 558–63.

Cervisy, 'L'Exposition de 1900: Le Château-d'Eau et les fontaines lumineuses', *Monde Moderne* (1900), 225–38.

La Chambre de Commerce de Paris à l'Exposition universelle de 1900, Paris: Chambre de Commerce, 1900.

'Le Champ de Mars', *Bulletin de la Société des Amis des Monuments Parisiens* 4/5 (1891), 91–3.

Champion, Pierre, *Le Bois de Vincennes: Promenade parisienne*, Paris: Commission du Vieux Paris, 1929.

Chardon, Henri, 'L'Exposition de 1900', *Revue de Paris* 3 (1 February 1896), 630–57.

——, 'Souvenirs d'exposition', *Revue Bleue* (27 March/3 April 1909), 405–9, 438–41.

——, *Souvenirs de 1900*, Paris: Perrin, 1910.

Charles-Roux, Jules, 'Les Colonies à l'Exposition de 1900', *Bulletin de la Société de Géographie de Marseilles* 24 (1900), 7–30.

——, *Les Colonies françaises: Introduction générale. Exposition universelle de 1900. Publications de la commission générale chargée de préparer la participation du Ministère des Colonies*, Paris: Challamel, 1901.

——, *Les Colonies françaises: L'organisation et le fonctionnement de l'Exposition des colonies et pays de protectorat. Rapport général*, Paris: Imprimerie Nationale, 1902.

——, *Nos Colonies et l'Exposition de 1900*, Paris: n.p., 1901.

——, *Rapport général de l'Exposition coloniale internationale de Marseilles, 1906*, Marseilles: Barlatier, 1907.

Charles-Roux, Jules, Marcel Saint-Germain, Yvan Broussais, Victor Morel and Frédéric Basset, *Colonies et pays de protectorats, Paris: Alcan-Lévy, 1900*.

——, *Exposition universelle de 1900: Section des colonies et pays de protectorat. Album commémoratif*, Paris: Chevajon, 1900.

Charmes, Francis, 'Chronique de la quinzaine', *Revue des Deux Mondes* 70 (15 April/1 May/1 October 1900), 947–58, 229–40, 709–20.

Chesterton, Gilbert Keith, 'Our Notebook', *Illustrated London News* 164 (24 May 1924), 930.

Chiger, Siegmund, *Ausstellungs-Mißbräuche, deren Ursachen, Folgen und Verhinderungsmaßregeln*, Munich: Schnitzler, 1895.

Chiger, Siegmund, *Praktische Winke für alle Ausstellungsbetheiligten*, Breslau: n.p., 1896.

Churchill, Winston S., 'The British Empire Exhibition (International Advertising Convention Banquet, Savoy Hotel, London, 14 July 1924)', in *His Complete Speeches 1897–1963*, vol. 4: *1922–1928*, ed. Robert Rhodes James, London: Chelsea House, 1974, 3463–4.

La Cité des Informations, Paris: n.p., 1931.

Clarette, Jules, 'L'Exposition – le champ de bataille', *Les Annales Politiques et Littéraires* (11 February 1900), 83–4.

Clarke, Travers, 'Is British Empire Economic Unity Possible?', *Nineteenth Century* 94 (1923), 19–24.

——, 'The British Empire Exhibition – Second Phase', *Nineteenth Century* 97 (1925), 175–82.

Cloche, Maurice, *60 aspects de l'Exposition Coloniale*, Paris: Arts et Métiers Graphiques, 1931.

Closing Ceremony Programme and Souvenir: British Empire Exhibition Wembley October 31st, 1925, London: n.p., 1925.

Cockburn, Sir John A., 'The Franco-British Exhibition', *Journal of the Society of Arts* 56 (29 November 1907), 23–32.

Coggin, F. G., 'The Ferris and Other Big Wheels', *Cassier's Magazine* 6 (1894), 215–22.

Cogniat, Raymond, 'L'Exposition coloniale', *L'Architecture* 44.9 (1931), 317–40, 365–86, 389–401.

Cole, Henry, *Fifty Years of Public Work of Sir Henry Cole, K.C.B. Accounted for in his Deeds, Speeches and Writings*, 2 vols, London: Bell, 1884.

Colmont, Achille de, *Histoire des Expositions des produits de l'industrie française*, Paris: Guillaumin, 1855.

Colonial and Indian Exhibition: Official Catalogue, London: Clowes, 1886.

'The Colonial and Indian Exhibition', *Westminster Review* 126 (1886), 29–59.

'Colonial Exhibitions and Their Use', *Journal of the Society of Arts* 57 (22 October 1909), 995–6.

Les Colonies aux expositions: Foires et manifestations de 1942, Paris: Larose, 1942.

Comité français des expositions à l'étranger, *Historique, 1890–1910*, Paris: Bourse de Commerce, 1910.

——, *Conférence diplomatique concernant les expositions internationales, Berlin 1912*, Paris: Comité français des expositions à l'étranger, 1913.

Comité français des expositions et Comité nationale des expositions coloniales, *Cinquantenaire, 1885–1935*, Asnières: S.I.M.A.G., 1936.

Concessions: Règlement relatif aux concessionnaires de l'Exposition coloniale internationale de Paris, Paris: Imprimerie Nationale, 1929.

Concours pour les deux palais des Champs-Elysées (Exposition universelle de 1900): Projets exposés au Palais de l'Industrie, Paris: Bernard, 1896.

Congrès de la lutte contre les ennemis des cultures, 19 juin 1931: Organisé par la ligue nationale de lutte contre les ennemis des cultures, Abbeville: Paillart, 1931.

Convention Relating to International Exhibitions, Paris: n.p., 1928.

Cook, Marjorie Grant and Frank Fox, *The British Empire Exhibition, 1924: Official Guide*, London: n.p., 1924.

Corday, Michel, 'Les Etrangers à l'Exposition', *Revue de Paris* 6 (1 December 1899), 557–80.
——, 'La Force à l'Exposition', *Revue de Paris* 7 (15 January 1900), 435–81.
Corlette, Hubert C., 'The British Empire Exhibition Buildings', *Journal of the Royal Institute of British Architects* 31 (18 October 1924), 653–65.
Cornély, Edouard, ed., *Le Livre d'or de l'Exposition de 1900*, Paris: n.p., 1900.
Coste, Adolphe, 'Impressions de l'Exposition', *Revue Internationale de Sociologie* 8.12 (1900), 884–99.
Coubertin, Baron Pierre de, 'Building up a World's Fair in France', *The Century* 57.1 (1898), 114–27.
Courthion, Pierre, 'L'Architecture à l'Exposition coloniale', *Art et Décoration* 60 (1931), 37–54.
Coyecque, Ernest, 'Paris à l'Exposition universelle de 1900: Expositions décennale et centennale, exposition rétrospective de la Ville de Paris', *Mémoires de la Société de l'Histoire de Paris et de l'Ile-de-France* 27 (1900), 39–100.
Cullen, Gordon, 'Bankside Regained: A Scheme for Developing the South Bank of the Thames with an Eye to the 1951 Exhibition', *Architectural Review* 105 (1949), 15–24.
Cundall, Frank, ed., *Reminiscences of the Colonial and Indian Exhibition*, London: Clowes, 1886.
Cunha, A. da, 'Les Ports de Paris et leur transformation en vue de l'Exposition de 1900', *Nature* 2 (1898), 387–90.
——, 'Les Pavillons étrangères à l'Exposition universelle', *Nature* 2 (1900), 199–200, 259–62.
——, *Les Travaux de l'Exposition de 1900*, Paris: Masson, 1900.
D'Ydewalle, Charles, 'Les Palais et les pavillons: Le Congo Belge', *Revue des Deux Mondes* 101 (1 October 1931), 617–27.
Daily News Souvenir Guide to the British Empire Exhibition: With Maps and Photographs, Concise 'Where Is It' Index and Complete Train, Tram and Bus Guide, London: Daily News, 1924.
Daix, V., ed., *Die Wunder der Weltausstellung 1900: Praktischer Wegweiser durch die 'Ausstellungsstadt'*, Paris: Internationales Repraesentationsbureau für die Weltausstellung, 1900.
Dary, Georges, *A travers l'électricité*, 2nd edn, Paris: Nony, 1901.
Davenport, Esther Chaddock, *'Going On Me Own': The Trifling Summer Adventures of a Woman Abroad*, Buffalo: Matthews-Northrup, 1900.
Davidge, W. R., 'The Growth of London', *Architectural Review* 44 (1918), 98–104.
Delamotte, Philip Henry, *Photographic Views of the Progress of the Crystal Palace*, Sydenham, London: n.p., 1855.
Delbrück, Hans, 'Die Berliner Weltausstellung', *Preußische Jahrbücher* 70.2 (1892), 229–36.
——, 'Die Krisis des deutschen Weltausstellungsplans', *Preußische Jahrbücher* 70.3 (1892), 350–9.
Demaison, André, *A Paris en 1931: Exposition coloniale internationale. Guide Officiel*, 2nd edn, Paris: Mayeux, 1931.
——, *L'Exposition coloniale internationale de 1931: Edition de luxe du Guide Officiel*, Paris: Mayeux, 1931.
Démy, Adolphe, *Essai historique sur les Expositions universelles de Paris*, Paris: Picard, 1907.
Derôme, J., 'A propos du trottoir roulant', *Nature* 2 (1900), 165–6.
'Des Prinzen von Preußen Reise zur Londoner Weltausstellung 1851', *Deutsche Revue über das gesamte nationale Leben der Gegenwart* 20.4 (1895), 129–39, 257–70.
'Description de la reconstitution du "Vieux Paris" à l'Exposition universelle de 1900', *L'Ami des Monuments et des Arts* 13 (1899), 214–18, 292–308.
Desplanques, Emile, 'L'Exposition de 1900: Les palais des Champs-Elysées', *Construction Moderne* 12 (17/31 July 1897), 494–6, 517–18, 531–2.
——, 'Les Travaux de l'Exposition', *Construction Moderne* 13 (23/30 October 1898), 40–1, 51–2.
Devonshire, Duke of, 'The Empire in Concrete', *United Empire* 15.5 (1924), 277–9.
Döring, Wilhelm, Bruno Tietz and Hans Georg Döring, eds, *Handbuch der Messen und Ausstellungen: In Zusammenarbeit mit dem Ausstellungs- und Messe-Ausschuss*

der Deutschen Wirtschaft und dem Deutschen Städtetag, Darmstadt: Verkehrs- und Wirtschaftsarchiv, 1956.

Draft of General Regulations Applying to International Exhibitions: Translated and Issued by the Department of Overseas Trade/Draft of General Regulations Applying to International Exhibitions, London: H.M. Stationery Office, 1934.

Droege, Ottokar A., *Chicago? Warum und wie müssen wir dort ausstellen? Eine transatlantische Skizze*, Berlin: Hoffschläger, 1891.

Du Vivier de Streel, Edmond, *Les Enseignements généraux de l'Exposition coloniale*, Paris: Musée social, 1932.

Dubois, Marcel and Auguste Terrier, *Les Colonies françaises: Un siècle d'expansion coloniale*, Paris: Challamel, 1901.

Dumas, François Guillaume, ed., *The Franco-British Exhibition Illustrated Review*, London: Chatto & Windus, 1908.

Dunkel, Ulrich, *Tierfänger Johannes erzählt: Für Hagenbeck in Afrika*, Stuttgart: Kreuzl, 1953.

'Earl's Court before 1900', *Architectural Review* 52 (1937), 162–4.

'Earl's Court Exhibition', *The Architects' Journal* 86 (12 August 1937), 253–6.

Eastman, Barrett and Frédéric Mayer, *Paris, 1900: The American Guide to the City and Exposition. Written for the Information of Travelers who Carry Travelers' Letters of Credit Issued by the Northern Trust Company Bank, Chicago, and Obtain Their Funds From Its Correspondents in All Parts of the World*, Chicago: Northern Trust Company Bank, 1899.

Ebner, Theodor, *Max Eyth: Der Dichter und Ingenieur. Ein schwäbisches Lebensbild*, Heidelberg: Winter, 1906.

Eckinger, Hans, *Eine Reise nach Paris, London, Wembley und Ostende im Sommer 1924. In Versen erzählt*, Bassersdorf-Zurich: n.p., 1925.

Eckmann, Otto, *Der Weltjahrmarkt Paris 1900*, Berlin: Fischer, 1900.

Eiffel, Gustave, 'L'Achèvement de la tour Eiffel', *Temps* (2 April 1889).

——, *La Tour Eiffel en 1900*, Paris: Masson, 1902.

Emminghaus, A., 'Märkte und Messen', *Fauchers Vierteljahrsschrift für Volkswirtschaft und Kulturgeschichte* 5.1 (1867), 61–84.

Empire Exhibition Scotland 1938: Official Guide, Glasgow: Empire Exhibition Scotland, 1938.

'Empire in Miniature', *Illustrated London News* 164 (24 May 1924), supplement.

Empire of India and Ceylon Exhibition: Official Programme, London: n.p., 1896.

The Empire of India Exhibition, 1895: Earls Court London. The Conception, Design and Production of Imre Kiralfy. Plan of Exhibition Buildings Queens Court, Showing Arrangements of Exhibits, London: n.p., 1894–95.

The Empire of India Exhibition, 1895: Plan of Imperial Palace, Showing Arrangements of Exhibits, London: n.p., 1895.

Empire of India Exhibition: Illustrated Guide to the Jungle, London: Clowes, 1895.

Empire of India Exhibition: Official Guide, London: Keliher, 1895.

Empire of India Exhibition: Official Programme, London: Keliher, 1895.

Encyclopédie du siècle: L'Exposition de Paris de 1900, publiée avec la collaboration d'écrivains spéciaux et des meilleurs artistes, 3 vols, Paris: Montgrédien, 1900.

'England and France in 1908: An Editorial Interpretation', *The World's Work* 12 (June 1908), 1–8.

'The Exhibition in the Making', *The World's Work* 12 (June 1908), 53–8.

Exhibition of the Works of Industry of All Nations, 1851: Reports by the Juries on the Subjects in the 30 Classes into which the Exhibition was divided, 4 vols, London: Spicer, 1852.

Exhibition Paris, 1900: A Practical Guide containing Information as to Means of Locomotion, Hotels, Restaurants, Cafés, Theatres, Shops, Museums, Buildings and Monuments, Daily Life and Habits, the Curiosities of Paris and the Exhibition, London: Heinemann, 1900.

'Exhibitions', *Literary Digest* 11 (5 October 1895), 23–4.

Exner, Wilhelm Franz, *Der Aussteller und die Ausstellungen: Erörterungen über den Nutzen der letzteren; geschichtliche Notizen; Rathschläge für die Sicherheit des Ausstellungsgutes, Zweckmäßigkeit und Schönheit der Exposition; Bemerkungen über permanente und Arbeiterausstellungen; offizielle*

Aktenstücke der Ausstellungen: Paris 1867, Havre 1868, Brüssel 1868, Breslau, Frankfurt a. M. etc. und Wien 1873; ein Buch für Gewerbetreibende, Industrielle, Künstler, Weimar: Voigt, 1866.

——, *Studien über die Betheiligung Deutsch-Österreichs an der Weltausstellung in Paris 1867*, Vienna: Hilberg, 1867.

——, *Die neuesten Fortschritte im Ausstellungswesen in Beziehung auf Sicherheit, Zweckmäßigkeit und Schönheit: Geschichtliche und sachliche Notizen über temporäre Industrie- und Arbeiterausstellungen sowie über Gewerbsmuseen*, 2nd edn, Weimar: Boigt, 1868.

'L'Exposition coloniale de 1931', *La Vie* 18.1 (1 January 1929), 30.

Exposition coloniale internationale de Paris 1931: Album de 154 pages comprenant les matières parues dans les numéros de 'L'Illustration' des 23 mai, 27 juin, 25 juillet, 22 août et 28 novembre 1931, Paris: L'Illustration, 1931.

Exposition coloniale internationale de Paris 1931: Cité internationale des informations, Paris: Imprimerie Nationale, 1931.

Exposition coloniale internationale de Paris 1931: Colonies et pays d'outre-mer, Paris: Imprimerie Nationale, 1930.

Exposition coloniale internationale de Paris 1931: Liste officielle des exposants, Paris: Mayeux, 1931.

Exposition coloniale internationale de Paris 1931: Section du Ministère des colonies. But et organisation, Paris: Imprimerie Nationale, 1930.

Exposition coloniale internationale de Paris 1931: Section rétrospective française. But et organisation, Paris: Imprimerie Nationale, 1928.

Exposition coloniale internationale de Paris 1931: Son but, son organisation. Allocutions prononcées à l'occasion du 25e anniversaire de la Fédération des industriels et commerçants français le samedi 23 juin 1928, Nancy: Rigot, 1928.

Exposition coloniale internationale Paris 1931: Le plus beau voyage à travers le monde. Album de 40 vues, Paris: Braun, 1931.

'L'Exposition de 1900: Les palais de l'Esplanade des Invalides', *Monde Moderne* (1900), 217–24.

L'Exposition de 1900 par l'image, Poissy: Lejay, 1900.

Exposition franco-britannique de Londres en 1908: Catalogue de l'Exposition spéciale de la Ville de Paris et du département de la Seine, Paris: Chaix, 1908.

Exposition universelle 1900, Paris: n.p., 1900.

Exposition universelle de 1900: Catalogue officiel de la section allemande, Berlin: Stargardt, 1900.

Exposition universelle de 1900: Catalogue officiel illustré de l'Exposition rétrospective de l'art français, des origines à 1900, Paris: Lemercier et Baschet, 1900.

Exposition universelle de 1900: Développement historique de la place de la Concorde, des Champs-Elysées et de l'esplanade des Invalides, Paris: Imprimerie Nationale, 1896.

Exposition universelle de 1900: Section des colonies et pays de protectorat. Album commémoratif dressé... par les soins de M. Scellier de Gisors, Paris: n.p., 1900.

Exposition universelle internationale de 1900 à Paris: Actes organiques, Paris: Imprimerie Nationale, 1895.

'L'Exposition: Le Pavillon royal de la Grande-Bretagne', *Les Annales Politiques et Littéraires* (21 October 1900), 261.

Eyth, Max, *Vergangenheit und Zukunft der Wanderausstellungen der Deutschen Landwirtschafts-Gesellschaft: Vortrag gehalten in der Hauptversammlung am 20. Februar 1896*, Berlin: Unger, 1896.

——, *Im Strom unserer Zeit: Aus Briefen eines Ingenieurs*, 3 vols: 1: *Lehrjahre*; 2: *Wanderjahre*; 3: *Meisterjahre*, Heidelberg: Winter, 1904–05.

——, *Tagebücher 1882–1896*, ed. Rudolf Laïs, Frankfurt am Main: DLG, 1975.

Faber, Oscar, 'The Concrete Buildings at Wembley', *Architectural Review* 55 (1924), 218–21.

Faucher, Julius, *Vergleichende Culturbilder aus den Vier Europäischen Millionenstädten (Berlin-Wien-Paris-London)*, Hanover: Rümpler, 1877.

Faucheur, Théodore, *Le Champ de Mars depuis son origine jusqu'à l'Exposition universelle de 1867*, Paris: Dentu, 1867.

Festival of Empire, London 1911: Official Guide and Catalogue, London: Bemrose, 1911.

Fidel, Camille, *Publicité et vulgarisation coloniales: Emigration, expansion au dehors. Enquêtes en Grande-Bretagne et en Allemagne*, Paris: Société des études coloniales et maritimes, 1925 [*Revue des Questions Coloniales et Maritimes* 49, 137–56].

Fidelio, *Baron Mikosch's Erlebnisse auf der Berliner Gewerbe-Ausstellung 1896*, Berlin: Haebringer, 1896.

Figaro Illustré, L'Exposition de 1900, Paris: Manzi, Joyant, 1900.

Flament, Albert, 'Tableaux de l'Exposition Coloniale', *Revue de Paris* 38 (1 July 1931), 211–28.

Flaubert, Gustave, *Le Dictionnaire des idées reçues et le catalogue des idées chic* [1913], Paris: Librairie Générale Française, 1997.

Fleury, V. Charles, 'Les Palais et les pavillons: Participations étrangères', *Revue des Deux Mondes* 101 (15 October 1931), 794–803.

Fonssagrives, Jean, *Notice sur le Dahomey: Publiée à l'occasion de l'Exposition universelle de 1900, sous la direction de M. Pierre Pascal*, Paris: Alcan-Lévy, 1900.

Ford, Ford Madox, *The Soul of London: A Survey of a Modern City*, London: Alston Rivers, 1905.

——, 'The Future in London', in *London Town Past and Present*, ed. W. W. Hutchings, vol. 2, London: Cassell, 1909, 1094–110.

Ford, Guy Stanton, 'Expositions, International', in *Encyclopedia of the Social Sciences*, ed. Edwin R. A. Seligman and Alvin Johnson, vol. 6, New York: Macmillan, 1937, 23–7.

Fort, Paul, 'Paris sentimental', *Mercure de France* 31.1 (1902), 59–87.

'Die Frage der Berliner Weltausstellung', *Sitzungsberichte des Vereins zur Beförderung des Gewerbefleißes* 71 (13 June 1892), 223–7.

'France and Her Colonies: The Paris Exhibition', *The Scotsman* (7 February 1931), 16.

'The Franco-British Exhibition at Shepherd's Bush: Interview with Mr. Imre Kiralfy', *Review of Reviews* 37 (May 1908), 454–7.

Franco-British Exhibition in London 1908: Catalogue of the Special Exhibition of the City of Paris and of the Department of the Seine, Paris: Central Printing-Office and Library of the Chemins de Fer, 1908.

Franco-British Exhibition 1908, Shepherd's Bush, London, W.: Prospectus, London: General Offices, 1907.

Franco-British Exhibition 1908: Report of Proceedings at the Complimentary Banquet at the Garden Club of the Franco-British Exhibition in Honour of Mr. Imre Kiralfy, the Commissioner General, Wednesday, 28th October 1908, London: n.p., 1908.

The Franco-British Exhibition Official Souvenir, London: Hudson & Kearns, 1908.

Franco-British Exhibition, London, 1908: Daily Programme, London: Bemrose, 1908.

Franco-British Exhibition, London, 1908: Official Guide and Description Sommaire de l'Exposition, 4th edn, London: Bemrose, 1908.

Franco-British Exhibition: Irish Art Gallery, Ballymaclinton, London: Ballantyne, 1908.

'The Franco-British Exhibition', *Burlington Magazine for Connoisseurs* 13 (1908), 193–200.

The Franco-British Pictorial: Black and White's Special. An Illustrated Record of the Great Exhibition at Shepherd's Bush 1908, London: Black & White, 1908.

'The French Colonial Exposition: Unique and Picturesque Display', *Field* (26 September 1931), 488.

French Exhibition in London: Official Guide, London: Waterlow, 1890.

Frères Neurdein, eds, *Exposition universelle de 1900*, Paris: n.p., [1900?].

Friebel, Anton, 'Skizzen von meiner Studienreise zur Pariser Weltausstellung', *Jahresberichte der K.K. II. Deutschen Staats-Realschule in Prag-Kleinseite* 28 (1901), 3–22.

Führer durch die Berliner Gewerbe-Ausstellung 1896: Nebst einem Anhange, enthaltend: die zur Ausstellung führenden Verkehrswege, sowie die Sehenswürdigkeiten, Kunst- und wissenschaftliche Institute, Vergnügungs-Etablissements, Verkehrs-Anstalten etc. etc. der Reichshauptstadt, Berlin: Hirschberg, 1896.

G. C. L. [George Collins Levey], 'Exhibition', in *Encyclopedia Britannica*, vol. 9, 13th edn, London: Encyclopedia Britannica, 1926, 67–71.

'La Galerie des machines', *Construction Moderne* 16 (1 December 1900), 101–3.

Gally, J. M., *Das Ausstellungswesen und sein Wert: Erfahrungen, Erlebnisse und Reformvorschläge*, 2nd edn, Vienna: Spielhagen und Schurich, 1911.

Gas-Louraine, 'Les Leçons d'une exposition', *Grande Revue* 136 (1931), 189–222.

Gautier, Henri, ed., *L'Exposition universelle 1900: Bulletin des lois, décrets et documents officiels relatifs à l'Exposition*, Paris 1896–1900.

Geddes, Patrick, *City Development: A Study of Parks, Gardens, and Culture-Institutes*, Bournville, Birmingham: Saint George, 1904.

——, *Industrial Exhibitions and Modern Progress*, Edinburgh: Douglas, 1887.

——, 'Man and the Environment: A Study from the Paris Exposition', *International Monthly* 2 (1900), 169–95.

——, 'The Closing Exhibition: Paris, 1900', *Contemporary Review* 78 (1900), 653–68.

——, 'Two Steps in Civics: "Cities and Town Planning Exhibition" and the "International Congress of Cities". Ghent International Exhibition, 1913', *Town Planning Review* 4.2 (1913–14), 78–94.

——, *Cities in Evolution: An Introduction to the Town Planning Movement and to the Study of Civics*, London: Williams & Norgate, 1915.

Geitel, Max, 'Hundert Jahre deutsches Ausstellungswesen', *Glaser's Annalen für Gewerbe und Bauwesen* 81 (1 September 1917), 60–2.

Gelbert, A., 'Une Nouvelle Exposition universelle', *Construction Moderne* 20 (19 November 1904), 94–5.

Gentsch, Wilhelm, *Die Weltausstellung in Paris 1900 und ihre Ergebnisse in technisch-wirthschaftlicher Beziehung*, Berlin: Heymanns, 1901.

Gentsch, Wilhelm, ed., *Amtlicher Bericht über die Internationale Ausstellung in Mailand 1906*, Berlin: Reichsdruckerei, 1908.

George, Richard, 'Die Ausstellung Alt-Berlin', *Der Bär* 22 (20 June 1896), 291–4.

——, 'Die Sonder-Ausstellung von Berolinensien in der Heiliggeistkirche zu Alt-Berlin', *Der Bär* (1896), 459–62.

Gérault, Georges, *Les Expositions universelles au point de vue économique*, Thèse pour le doctorat, Faculté de droit, Université de Dijon, Dijon, 1901.

Gers, Paul, *En 1900*, Corbeil: Editions Crété, 1900.

Gervais, A., 'Les Expositions nationales et universelles 1799–1889', *Revue Bleue* (24 August 1889), 238–46.

Gide, Charles, 'La Liquidation de l'Exposition universelle', *Revue d'Economie Politique* 15.6 (1901), 674–7.

Girard, André G., *L'Architecture Moderne aux Expositions Belges de 1930*, Paris: Frèal, 1930.

Gleize, Jules, 'L'Exportation française et les expositions', *La Nouvelle Revue* 35 (15 July 1906), 195–202.

Gléon, Delort de, *La Rue du Caire: L'Architecture arabe des Khalifes d'Egypte à l'Exposition universelle de Paris en 1889*, Paris: Plon, Nourrit et Cie., 1889.

Gloag, John, 'Advertising in Three Dimensions', *Architectural Review* 74 (1933), 109–16.

Goebbels, Joseph, *Tagebücher 1924–1945*, 5 vols, Munich: Piper, 1992.

Goecke, Theodor, 'Allgemeine Städtebau-Ausstellung Berlin 1910', *Der Städtebau* 7.7/8 (1910), 73–92.

Goldberger, Ludwig Max, *An die Mitglieder des Vereins Berliner Kaufleute und Industrieller und an die Delegirten zum Generalausschuss hiesiger kaufmännischer, gewerblicher und industrieller Vereine*, Berlin: Ullstein, 1901.

——, *Das Land der unbegrenzten Möglichkeiten: Beobachtungen über das Wirtschaftsleben der Vereinigten Staaten von Amerika*, Berlin: Fontane, 1903.

Goldman, Golda M. and Francis Dickie, 'The International Colonial Exposition in Paris: A Mighty Display of Advancing Civilizations', *The World Today* 57.6 (1931), 524–35.

Gomme, Sir Laurence, *The Making of London*, Oxford: Clarendon, 1912.

Graves, Charles, 'When West Africa Woos', *Sunday Express* (4 May 1924), 7.

'A Great London Playground: The Coming "Entente" Exhibition', *Pall Mall Gazette* (22 December 1906).

'The Great Telescope of the Paris Exhibition', *Literary Digest* 18 (11 March 1899), 283.

'The Great Tower in London', *Engineering* 49 (2 May 1890), 542–4.

Griffin, Lepel, 'An Imperial City', *Pall Mall Magazine* 1 (1893), 656–68.

Grimsditch, Herbert B., 'The British Government Pavilion and the Basilica at Wembley', *Studio* 88 (July 1924), 27–32.

Grothe, Hermann, *Die Americanische Industrie und die Ausstellung in Philadelphia 1876: Zwei Vorträge, gehalten in der Polytechnischen Gesellschaft zu Berlin*, Berlin: n.p., 1877.

——, 'Ausstellungsbericht', *Sitzungsberichte des Vereins zur Beförderung des Gewerbefleißes* 59 (1 November 1880), 239–50.

——, 'Bericht über Ausstellungen und Ansichten über eine Weltausstellung in Berlin', *Sitzungsberichte des Vereins zur Beförderung des Gewerbefleißes* 61 (3 April 1882), 125–62.

——, 'Referat über die staatliche Organisation des Ausstellungswesens', *Sitzungsberichte des Vereins zur Beförderung des Gewerbefleißes* 61 (6 November 1882), 288–98.

Guerrier de Haupt, Marie, *Les Enfants à l'Exposition de Paris*, Paris: Librairie Artistique de la Jeunesse Rituelle, 1900.

Guide Armand Silvestre de Paris et de ses environs et de l'Exposition de 1900, Paris: Didier et Méricant, 1900.

Guide dans l'Exposition: Paris et ses environs, 7th edn, Paris: Delarue, 1889.

Guide Lemercier: Exposition universelle de 1900. Publié par les concessionnaires du Catalogue officielle, Paris: Baschet, 1900.

Guide Officiel de la Section Italienne à l'Exposition coloniale, Paris: de Rosa, 1931.

Guide Peterson de l'Exposition coloniale Marseilles 1906: French and English, Marseilles: Guiraud, 1906.

Guide to and Souvenir of Ballymaclinton (Irish Village) at the Franco-British Exhibition 1908, London: Bemrose, 1908.

Guide to the Pavilion of His Majesty's Government: British Empire Exhibition 1925, London: H.M. Stationery Office, 1925.

Guy, Camille, *Exposition universelle 1900: Les Colonies françaises. Notice sur les établissements français de l'Inde*, Paris: Levé, 1900.

——, 'Les Enseignements de l'Exposition coloniale (Conférence)', *Bulletin de la Société de Géographie de Lyon et de la Région Lyonnaise* 17 (1901), 32–5.

Guyot, Yves, G.-Roger Sandoz, Paul Bourgeois and Léo Claretie, eds, *Rapport général de l'Exposition franco-britannique de Londres 1908*, 3 vols, Paris: Comité français des expositions à l'étranger, [1917].

Haake, Rudolf, *Das städtische Messe- und Ausstellungswesen*, Stuttgart: Kohlhammer, 1938.

Haarmann, A., *Vor dem Rubicon: Ein letztes Wort der Beherzigung zur Ausstellungsfrage*, Berlin: Deutsche Verlags- und Buchdruckerei-Actien-Gesellschaft, 1892.

Hagenbeck, Carl, *Von Tieren und Menschen: Erlebnisse und Erfahrungen*, 2nd edn, Berlin: Vita, 1909.

Hake, Fritz von, *Wembley: Schein und Wahrheit*, Weimar: Fink, 1926.

Hallays, André, *En flânant: A travers l'Exposition de 1900*, Paris: Perrin, 1901.

Hanslick, Eduard, 'Pariser Musikzustände während der Weltausstellung 1878', *Deutsche Rundschau* 16 (1879), 137–45, 316–25.

Hardy, Hugo, 'Die internationale Kolonialausstellung in Paris 1931', *Zeitschrift für Geopolitik* 8.7 (1931), 557–61.

Harley Moseley, C. H., *Southern Nigeria: Description and Catalogue of Exhibits at the Franco-British Exhibition*, London: n.p., 1908.

Harper's Guide to Paris and the Exposition of 1900: Being Practical Suggestions concerning the Trip from New York to Paris; a Comprehensive Map and Guide to the City of Paris; a Complete Description and Guide to the Exposition, with French Phrases Translated; and Maps, Diagrams, Plans, and Illustrations, New York: Harper, 1900.

Harrison, Austin, 'The British Empire Exhibition, 1924', *English Review* 35 (1922), 446–51.

Hart, Ernest, 'The International Health Exhibition: Its Influence and Possible Sequels', *Journal of the Society of Arts* 33 (28 November 1884), 35–58.

Hartley, Harold T., *Eighty-Eight Not Out: A Record of Happy Memories*, London: Muller, 1939.

Hartt, Rollin Lynde, 'Things France Can Teach Us', *The World's Work* 12 (June 1908), 29–34.

Harvard, Charles, 'The Great Exhibition was Photographed', *Architectural Review* 85 (1939), 299–300.

Hassall, John, *The Light Side of the Exhibition*, London: n.p., 1908.

Hastings, H. C., *Wembley Empire Stadium and Sports Arena: Sports Centre of the Empire*, London: Pitkins, 1956.

Hayfron-Benjamin, C. F., 'The Union for Students of African Descent: Its Work in London for Africa', *West Africa* (25 October 1924), 1179–80.

Heiman, Hanns, 'Internationale und nationale Regelung des Ausstellungs- und Messewesens', in *Ausstellung und Messe in Recht und Wirtschaft der Zeit: Vorträge gelegentlich der 2. Mitgliederversammlung des Deutschen Ausstellungs- und Messe-Amtes am 24. Mai 1930 in Dresden*, Berlin: Deutsches Ausstellungs- und Messe-Amt, 1930, 13–48.

Heine, H., *Professor Reuleaux und die deutsche Industrie: Eine Skizze auf Grundlage amerikanischer sowie deutscher Beobachtungen und Erfahrungen*, 2nd edn, Berlin: Seydel, 1876.

Hénard, Eugène, *L'Exposition de 1900 devant le parlement*, Paris: Delarue, 1896.

——, *Etudes sur les transformations de Paris*, vol. 4: *Le Champ de Mars et la Galerie des Machines*, Paris: Librairies-Imprimeries Réunies, 1904.

Hendry, H. Duncan, *Looking Back: Some Memories of Eighty Changing Years*, London: n.p., n.d.

Henop, C., *Die Wahrheit über Paris 1900: Ein Rückblick auf die Pariser Weltausstellung 1900*, Vienna: n.p., 1900.

——, *Das Finale der Pariser Weltausstellung 1900: Ergänzung und Schluss der Schrift 'Die Wahrheit über Paris'*, Vienna: n.p., 1901.

Hermann, 'Bericht über Ausstellungen und Ansichten über eine Weltausstellung in Berlin', *Sitzungsberichte des Vereins zur Beförderung des Gewerbefleißes* 61 (3 April 1882), 125–62.

Hillger, Hermann, *Die Deutsche Welt-Ausstellung der Zukunft*, Berlin: Fischer, 1892.

——, *Die Deutsche Welt-Ausstellung von 1897: Eine Forderung und ein gutes Recht der deutschen Nation!* Berlin: Steinitz, 1892.

——, *Amerika und die Columbische Welt-Ausstellung, Chicago 1893: Geschichte und Beschreibung*, Chicago: Columbian History Company, 1893.

——, 'Eine Weltausstellung in Berlin', *Die Gegenwart* 38 (1909), 289–91.

Hinneberg, Paul, ed., *Die Kultur der Gegenwart: Ihre Entwicklung und ihre Ziele*, Teil 1, Abt. 1: *Die Allgemeinen Grundlagen der Kultur der Gegenwart*, 2nd edn, Berlin: Teubner, 1912.

Hirth, Georg, ed., *F. Reuleaux und die deutsche Industrie auf der Weltausstellung zu Philadelphia: Eine unparteiische Sammlung der durch die ersten vier Briefe des Herrn Prof. Reuleaux hervorgerufenen wichtigeren Streitschriften*, Leipzig: Hirth, 1876.

'Die höchsten Turmbauten', *Das Neue Universum* 12 (1891), 126–9.

Hose, Charles, *Fifty Years of Romance and Research or a Jungle-Wallah at Large*, London: Hutchinson, 1927.

'How Visitors Are Amused: Sideshows at the Exhibition', *The World's Work* 12 (June 1908), 99–106.

Hoyer, Egbert, 'Über die Praxis der Ausstellungen: Vortrag gehalten am 10. November 1879 im Polytechnischen Verein zu München', *Glaser's Annalen für Gewerbe und Bauwesen* 6 (1 April 1880), 333–6.

——, 'Über die heutige Praxis der Ausstellungen', *Zeitschrift für deutsche Volkswirtschaft* 1 (1880), 16–23.

Huber, Franz C., *Die Ausstellungen und unsere Exportindustrie*, Stuttgart: Neff, 1886.

——, *Die Berliner Welt-Ausstellung*, Stuttgart: Grüninger, 1892.

——, 'Ausstellungen', in *Handwörterbuch der Staatswissenschaften*, ed. Johannes Conrad, Ludwig Elster, Wilhelm Lexis and Edgar Loening, vol. 2, 2nd edn, Jena: Fischer, 1899, 51–61.

——, 'Industrieausstellungen', in *Handwörterbuch der Staatswissenschaften*, ed. Johannes Conrad, Ludwig Elster, Wilhelm Lexis and Edgar Loening, vol. 5, 3rd edn, Jena: Fischer, 1910, 616–28.

Hutchings, W. W., *London Town Past and Present: With a Chapter on the Future in London by Ford Madox Hueffer*, London: Cassell, 1909.

Illustrated Souvenir of the Palace of Arts: British Empire Exhibition (1924) Wembley, London, London: Fleetway, 1924.

Illustrierter Amtlicher Führer durch die Berliner Gewerbe-Ausstellung 1896: Mit einer Übersichts-Karte der Ausstellung, Berlin: Verlag der Expedition des Amtlichen Führers, 1896.

Imperial International Exhibition: Official Daily Programme, London: n.p., 1909.

Imperial International Exhibition: Official Guide, London: n.p., 1909.

Imperial International Exhibition: Shepherd's Bush London 1909, London: n.p., 1909.

Imperial Victorian Exhibition: Daily Programme, London: Riddle & Couchman, 1897.

Imperial Victorian Exhibition: Official Catalogue, Sydenham: Crystal Palace, 1897.

Imre Kiralfy's India: Libretto and Official Guide, London: Keliher, 1895.

India: Souvenir of the Indian Pavilion and its Exhibits, Wembley: British Empire Exhibition, 1924.

Indian Court: Festival of Empire, 1911. Guide Book and Catalogue, London: Bemrose, 1911.

'Industrielle Wanderungen durch die Pariser Weltausstellung', *Berliner Tageblatt und Handels-Zeitung* (23 June 1900).

Informator für die Besucher von Paris (zur Weltausstellung 1900): Mit 1 Plan und Hilfsbuch für Deutsche auf französischem Sprachgebiete, Berlin: Steinitz, 1900.

Insley, Edward, 'Paris in 1900 and the Exposition', *Harper's Monthly Magazine* 101 (1900), 485–97.

International Exhibitions Committee, *Report of the Committee Appointed by the Board of Trade to Make Enquiries with Reference to the Participation of Great Britain in Great International Exhibitions, together with the Appendices Thereto*, London: H.M. Stationery Office, 1907.

'International Exhibitions from 1851 to 1874: A Retrospect', *Practical Magazine* 4 (1875), 448–54.

International Exposition Paris 1900: Official Catalogue Exhibition of the German Empire, Berlin: n.p., 1900.

International Fire Exhibition: Daily Programme, London: Gale and Polden, 1903.

International Health Exhibition: Official Guide, London: Clowes, 1884.

Die Internationalen Verhandlungen und Vereinbarungen über Ausstellungen und Messen: Ein Rückblick und ein Ausblick, Berlin: Deutsches Ausstellungs- und Messe-Amt, 1928.

Isaac, Maurice, *Les Expositions en France et dans le régime international*, Paris: Larousse, 1928.

Ismaa'il, Ibrahim, 'The Life and Adventures of a Somali: Presented and Annotated by Richard Pankhurst', *Africa: Rivista trimestrale di studi e documentazione dell' Istituto Italo-Africano* 32.2/3 (1977), 159–76, 355–84.

Jaffé, Franz, 'Ausstellungsbauten', in *Handbuch der Architektur*, 4. Teil, 6. Hbbd., Heft 4: *Gebäude für Sammlungen und Ausstellungen: Archive, Bibliotheken und Museen; Pflanzenhäuser und Aquarien; Ausstellungsbauten*, 2nd edn, Stuttgart: Kröner, 1906, 559–744.

Jähnl, Wilhelm, *Die Entwicklung und Bedeutung der Handelsmessen bis zum Jahre 1914*, Leipzig: Grumbach, 1922.

Jannasch, R., 'Die Weltausstellung zu Berlin', *Export* 14 (1892), 481–5.

Jentzen, E., *Professor Reuleaux' Urteil über die Leistungen unserer deutschen Industrie auf den Weltausstellungen zu Philadelphia und Chicago kritisch beleuchtet*, Dresden: Gerhard Kühtmann, 1894.

Jessett, F. A. Chetwynd, *British Empire Exhibition: What You Want to Know about the Exhibition*, Wembley: Hugh Whitwell, 1924.

Joubert, Louis, 'Fin de rêve: L'Exposition universelle de 1900', *Le Correspondant* 201 (24 November 1900), 771–84.

Jourdain, Frantz, 'L'Architecture au Champ-de-Mars', *Construction Moderne* 8 (29 April 1893), 349–50, 373–4.

——, 'Le Concours de l'Exposition universelle de 1900', *L'Illustration* 52 (22 December 1894), 522–5.

——, 'L'Architecture à l'Exposition universelle: Promenade à bâtons rompus', *Revue des Arts Décoratifs* 20 (1900), 245–51, 326–32, 342–50.

K.K. Österreichische General-Commissariate, ed., *Berichte über die Weltausstellung in Paris 1900*, 2 vols, Vienna: Gerold, 1902.

Keary, C. F., 'Pictures at the Paris Exhibition: The New Movement in Art', *Edinburgh Review* 192 (1900), 182–207.

Keim, Albert, 'Ce que sera l'Exposition coloniale', *Voyages à travers l'actualité mondiale* 8 (15 April 1930), 236–43.

——, *Manuel de l'Exposition coloniale internationale de Paris*, Paris: n.p., 1931.

Kellen, Tony, *Ratgeber für Aussteller: Die Industrie- und Gewerbeausstellungen, ihre Geschichte, Bedeutung und Organisation. Zugleich eine Anleitung, wie man ausstellen soll*, Leipzig: Klasing, 1902.

——, *Lehrbuch der kaufmännischen Propaganda, im besonderen der Anzeige- und Reklame-Kunst*, 2nd edn, Leipzig: Moderne kaufmännische Bibliothek, 1911.

Kendall, Austin, 'The Participation of India and Burma in the British Empire Exhibition, 1924', *Journal of the Royal Society of Arts* 71 (3 August 1923), 645–57.

——, 'India's Part in the British Empire Exhibition', *Asiatic Review* 20 (1924), 212–18.

Kératry, Vicomte Helarion de, *Paris Exposition, 1900: How to See the Exposition Alone. Cicerone*, 3rd edn, London: Simpkin, Marshall, Hamilton, Kent, 1900.

Kerr, Alfred, *Wo liegt Berlin? Briefe aus der Reichshauptstadt 1895–1900*, ed. Günther Rühle, Berlin: Aufbau, 1997.

——, *Warum fließt der Rhein nicht durch Berlin? Briefe eines europäischen Flaneurs 1895–1900*, ed. Günther Rühle, Berlin: Aufbau, 1999.

Kershaw, J. B. C., 'The British Empire Exhibition', *Scientific American* (1924), 80–1, 168–9, 222–3, 254, 291–2.

Kick, Friedrich, 'Über die Weltausstellungen vom allgemeinen technischen Standpunkt', *Technische Blätter* (1879), 25–31.

Kidder, F. A., 'First View of the Exposition of 1900', *Cosmopolitan* 29.3 (1900), 227–41.

Kiesslings praktischer Führer durch die Berliner Gewerbe-Ausstellung 1896, Berlin: Kiessling, 1896–97.

Kiralfy, Bolossy, *Constantinople or The Revels of the East: A Grand Terpsichorean, Romantic and Lyric Spectacle, and Aquatic Pageant, In Two Acts and Six Tableaux*, London: Olympia, 1894.

——, *Dramatic Stories of Dreams and Realisations: In Four Parts*, London: n.p., 1908.

——, *Creator of Great Musical Spectacles: An Autobiography*, ed. Barbara M. Barker, Ann Arbor: UMI Research Press, 1988.

Kiralfy, Imre, *My Life's Ambition*, New York: n.p., 1888.

——, *India: An Operatic-Historical Production in Two Acts*, London: n.p., 1895.

——, *Imre Kiralfy's India: Libretto and Official Guide. Empire of India Exhibition, 1895: Earl's Court London, S. W.*, London: Keliher, 1895.

——, *Victorian Era Exhibition, 1897, Earl's Court London, S. W. Catalogue, Historical and Commemorative Sections*, London: Riddle & Couchman, 1897.

——, *Paris in London Exhibition: Daily Programme*, London: Gale & Polden, 1902.

——, 'My Reminiscences', *Strand Magazine* 37 (1909), 643–9.

Klary, C., *La Photographie d'art à l'Exposition universelle de 1900*, Paris: Gauthier-Villars, 1900.

Kley, Wilhelm, *Was lehren uns die Weltausstellungen der letzten Jahre (Chicago und Paris)? Volkswirtschaftlicher Plaudervortrag*, Hanover: Meyer, 1904.

Koch, Alexander, 'Reformen im Ausstellungs-Wesen', *Deutsche Kunst und Dekoration* 7 (1900–01), 28–40.

——, *Eine deutsche Welt-Ausstellung?* Darmstadt: n.p., 1910.

Kollmann, J., 'Das Projekt einer internationalen Verkehrsausstellung in Berlin 1910', *Deutsche Wirtschafts-Zeitung* (1906), 486–92.

——, 'Zur Reform des Ausstellungswesens', *Technik und Wirtschaft* 2.6/7 (1909), 241–55, 289–303.

——, 'Zur Technik des Ausstellungswesens', *Technik und Wirtschaft* 3.8 (1910), 449–65.

Konrad, A. M., *Bunte Blätter der Berliner Gewerbe-Ausstellung 1896*, Berlin: Pasch, 1896.

Korheer, Richard, 'Berlin', *Süddeutsche Monatshefte* 27 (1930), 365–412.

Körner, Erich, 'Von der pariser [*sic*] Weltausstellung: Die Maschinen', *Illustrirte Zeitung* 114 (1900), 753–5.

Kraemer, Hans, Heinrich Lux and Albert Neuburger, eds, *Die Ingenieurkunst auf der Pariser Weltausstellung 1900*, Berlin: Bong, 1900.

Kraemer, Hans, 'Die internationale Regelung des Ausstellungswesens', *Die Wirtschaft und das Recht* 3.11 (1928), 889–920.

Krug, Karl, *Offizieller Führer durch die Special-Abtheilung Kairo der Berliner Gewerbe-Ausstellung 1896*, Berlin: Verlag des 'Kleinen Journal', 1896.

Kühnemann, Albert, ed., *Groß-Berlin: Bilder von der Ausstellungsstadt*, Berlin: Pauli's Nachfolger, 1896–97.

Kühnemann, Fritz, *Die wünschenswerthe Gestaltung einer demnächstigen größeren Ausstellung in Berlin: Mit sich daran anschließender Debatte und Resolution*, Berlin: Lehmann, 1881.

La Revue de l'Exposition de 1900, Paris: Sanard, 1900.

Lair, M., 'Après l'Exposition', *La Réforme Sociale* 41 (1 February 1901), 233–50.

Lambert, Pierre and Joris-Karl Huysmans, 'L'Exposition Universelle de 1889 et la Tour Eiffel jugées par Huysmans d'après des lettres inédites et un texte retrouvé', *Bulletin de la Société J.-K. Huysmans* 37 (1959), 358–65.

Landes, Gaston, *Notice sur la Martinique publiée à l'occasion de l'Exposition universelle de 1900*, Paris: Lévy, 1900.

Landon, Perceval, 'The Exhibit of the Empire Builders: English and French Colonies. Contrasts and Comparisons', *The World's Work* 12 (June 1908), 35–9.

Langdon, Claude, *Earls Court*, London: Stanley Paul, 1953.

Lapauze, H., Max de Kansoutry, A. Da Cunha, H. Jarzuel, J. Vitoux and L. Guillet, *Le Guide de l'Exposition de 1900*, Paris: Flammarion, 1900.

Laprade, A., 'Avant-promenade à travers l'Exposition Coloniale', *L'Architecture* 44.4 (1931), 109–25.

Laske, Friedrich, *Bericht über die Pariser Welt-Ausstellung 1900: In Verfolg des Erlasses des Herrn Ministers der geistlichen pp. Angelegenheiten vom 30. Juli 1900*, Potsdam: Müller, 1900.

Laulan, Robert, *Le Champ-de-Mars et ses origines: Les emplacements de la future exposition*, Paris: n.p., n.d.

Lawrence, George Clarke, 'The British Empire in Miniature: A Preliminary Survey of Next Year's Great Exhibition in Wembley', *The World's Work* 42 (October 1923), 429–32.

Lawrence, George Clarke, ed., *The British Empire Exhibition 1924: Official Guide*, 4th edn, London: Fleetway, 1924.

Lawrence, Major C. T., 'Report on Nigerian Section, British Empire Exhibition', *West Africa* (1 November 1924), 1212–16.

——, 'Nigeria at the British Empire Exhibition (Second Report on the Nigerian Section, by the Commissioner)', *West Africa* (15 November 1924), 1283.

Leblond, Marius-Ary, 'La Représentation picturale des colonies à l'Exposition', *Mercure de France* (1900), 270–82.

——, 'L'Exposition coloniale dotera-t-elle Paris d'une avenue de la Victoire qui par Vincennes ira vers la Marne et Strasbourg reconquise?', *La Vie* 18.1 (1929), 2–6.

Lefebvre, Théodore, *Notes et impressions d'un natif du Finistère à l'Exposition et dans Paris*, Châteaulin: Goff, 1900.

Leon, Alfons, 'Über die Mailänder Ausstellung im Jahre 1906', *Der Bautechniker* 26 (7/14 December 1906), 1061–4, 1081–6.

——, *Die erste italienische Weltausstellung, ihr Schauplatz und ihre Vorgeschichte: Skizzen*, Vienna: Hölder, 1907.

Lessing, Julius, *Das Kunstgewerbe auf der Wiener Weltausstellung 1873*, Berlin: Wasmuth, 1874.

——, 'Die Berliner Gewerbe-Ausstellung', *Deutsche Rundschau* 23.11 (1896), 276–94.

——, *Das halbe Jahrhundert der Weltausstellungen: Vortrag gehalten in der Volkswirthschaftlichen Gesellschaft zu Berlin, März 1900*, Berlin: Simion, 1900.

——, *Ein Wort gegen das Projekt der Pariser Weltausstellung 1878*, Berlin: Wasmuth, 1876.

——, 'Kunst- und Kunstgewerbeausstellungen', in *Die Kultur der Gegenwart: Ihre Entwicklung und ihre Ziele, Teil 1, Abt. 1: Die Allgemeinen Grundlagen der Kultur der Gegenwart*, ed. Paul Hinneberg, 2nd edn, Berlin: Teubner, 1912, 421–41.

Leutemann, Heinrich, *Lebensbeschreibung des Thierhändlers Carl Hagenbeck*, Hamburg: n.p., 1887.

Lienau, H., 'Unlauterer Wettbewerb: Medaillenunwesen und Ausstellungsschwindel', *Markenschutz und Wettbewerb* 6.5/7 (1907), 61–6, 78–81, 93–9.

Lieuze, Jean, 'Les Allemands à l'Exposition de 1900', *Figaro* 43 (31 October 1897).

Lindenberg, Paul, *Pracht-Album Photographischer Aufnahmen der Berliner Gewerbe-Ausstellung 1896 und der Sehenswürdigkeiten Berlins und des Treptower Parks: Alt-Berlin, Kolonial-Ausstellung, Kairo etc.*, Berlin: Werner, 1896.

——, *Paris und die Weltausstellung 1900: Zur Führung und zur Erinnerung*, Minden in Westfalen: Bruns, 1900.

Le Livre d'or de l'Exposition coloniale internationale de Paris, 1931: Publié sous le patronage officiel du Commissariat Général de l'Exposition, Paris: Champion, 1931.

Locock, Guy H., 'The Diplomatic Conference of Paris on International Exhibitions', *World Trade* 1 (1929), 35–45.

Loftie, W. J., *Souvenir of Old London*, London: Old London, 1908.

Lohren, 'Mitteilungen von der Pariser Weltausstellung', *Sitzungsberichte des Vereins zur Beförderung des Gewerbefleißes* 57 (7 October 1878), 175–8.

Lomas, Sophie C., ed., *Festival of Empire: Souvenir of the Pageant of London*, London: Bemrose, 1911.

London's Great Exhibition, 1907: At the New International Exhibition Grounds, Shepherd's Bush, London, W., London: n.p., 1905.

Low, Archibald Montgomery, *Wonderful Wembley*, London: Paul, 1953.

Lowe, Charles, *Four National Exhibitions in London and Their Organiser*, London: Fisher Unwin, 1892.

Lucas, Charles, 'Notes sur les palais de l'Exposition de Paris en 1900', *Journal of the Royal Institute of British Architects* 7 (24 February 1900), 149–77.

Lüders, Karl, 'Das Project einer Weltausstellung zu Berlin im Jahre 1885', *Preußische Jahrbücher* 44 (1879), 614–27.

——, 'Eine Weltausstellung in Berlin', *Westermann's Illustrirte Deutsche Monatshefte* 26 (1881–82), 400–11.

Lüders, Richard, *Die Weltausstellungen: Sind Ausstellungen ein Bedürfnis? Zur Reform des Ausstellungswesens*, Görlitz: n.p., 1893.

Ludwig Salvator, Erzherzog von Österreich: *Einiges über Welt-Ausstellungen*, Prague: Mercy, 1911.

Lyautey, Hubert, *Discours prononcé le 5 novembre 1928 par le Maréchal Lyautey à l'occasion de la pose de la première pierre du Musée permanent des colonies*, Paris: n.p., 1928.

——, 'France and the International Colonial Exhibition', *Nineteenth Century* 109 (1931), 529–39.

Lyautey, Hubert and Marcel Olivier, 'Après l'Exposition coloniale', *Revue des Deux Mondes* 103 (1 January 1933), 50–60.

Lynde, Frederick Charles, ed., *Descriptive Illustrated Catalogue of the Sixty-Eight Competitive Designs for the Great Tower of London*, London: Industries, 1890.

Macdonald, John F., *Paris of the Parisians*, London: Richards, 1900.

Macqueen-Pope, Walter, *Carriages at Eleven: The Story of the Edwardian Theatre*, London: Hutchinson, 1947.

——, *Ghosts and Greasepaint: A Story of the Days That Were*, London: Hale, 1951.

Macquoid, Katharine S. and Gilbert S. Macquoid, *In Paris: A Handbook for Visitors to Paris in the Year 1900*, London: Methuen, 1900.

Magistrat zu Berlin, ed., *Berliner Gewerbe-Ausstellung von 1896: Katalog für die Sonder-Ausstellung der Stadtgemeinde Berlin*, Berlin: Mosse, 1896.

Maindron, Ernest, *Le Champ de Mars, 1751–1889*, Lille: Daniel, 1889.

Malkowsky, Georg, ed., *Die Pariser Weltausstellung in Wort und Bild*, Berlin: Kirchhoff, 1900.

Malo, Henri, 'L'Exposition coloniale', *Figaro Illustré* 125 (1900), 171–92.

Les Manifestations qui auront lieu à l'Exposition coloniale internationale, Paris, avril-novembre 1931, Paris: n.p., 1931.

Mann, Heinrich, 'Weltstadt und Großstädte', *Das Zwanzigste Jahrhundert* 6.1 (1895–96), 201–13.

Maps and Plans of the Franco-British Exhibition, London, 1908, London: Bemrose, 1908.

Marshall, E. J., *Notes of Lectures Given in the Conference Room of the Colonial and Indian Exhibition, and Specially Adapted for Lectures to Working Men's Clubs by the Head Master of Brighton Grammar School*, London: Clowes, 1886.

Marshall, Sir James, ed., *Colonial and Indian Exhibition, 1886: Handbook to the West African Court, Gold Coast, Lagos, Sierra Leone, Gambia*, London: Clowes, 1886.

Marsillon, Ch., 'La Tour Eiffel de Londres', *Nature* 22.2 (1894), 387–90.

Martin, Alexis, *Une Visite à Paris en 1900: La ville et l'exposition en quinze jours*, Paris: Hennuyer, 1898.

Masson, Paul, 'Marseilles port colonial', *Bulletin de la Société de Géographie de Marseilles* 23.1 (1899), 7–30.

——, 'Marseilles et la colonisation française', *Questions diplomatiques et coloniales* 10 (1900), 129–41, 321–32.

Masterman, Charles F. G., ed., *The Heart of the Empire: Discussions of Modern City Life in England*, London: Fisher Unwin, 1901.

Matschoß, Conrad, *Preußens Gewerbeförderung und ihre großen Männer: Dargestellt im Rahmen der Geschichte der Vereins zur Förderung des Gewerbefleißes 1821–1921*, Berlin: Verein Deutscher Ingenieure, 1921.

Mauclair, Camille, 'Enquête logique sur l'Exposition de 1900', *Nouvelle Revue* 97 (1895), 550–74.

Maurer, J. H., *Officieller Katalog zur Berliner Gewerbe-Ausstellung im Jahre 1879: Im Auftrage des Central-Comités*, 6th edn, Berlin: Goldschmidt, 1879.

Maxwell, Donald, *Wembley in Colour: Being Both an Impression and a Memento of the British Empire Exhibition of 1924 as Seen by Donald Maxwell, with Over One Hundred Sketches in Colour and Monochrome*, London: Longmans, Green, 1924.

McLeod, Charles, 'The British Empire Exhibition', *United Empire* 15.4 (1924), 199–201.

'The Meaning of Wembley', *Saturday Review* 137 (26 April 1924), 428.

Meath, the Earl of, 'London as the Heart of Empire', in *London of the Future*, ed. Aston Webb, London: Fisher Unwin, 1921, 251–8.

Meier-Graefe, Alfred Julius, *Die Weltausstellung in Paris 1900: Mit zahlreichen photographischen Aufnahmen, farbigen Kunstbeilagen und Plänen*, Leipzig: Krüger, 1900.

Meile, Wilhelm, *Die Schweiz auf den Weltausstellungen*, Freiburg: Fragnière, 1913.

Meissonier, Ernest, Ch. Gounod, Charles Garnier, Robert Fleury, Victorien Sardou, William-Adolphe Bouguereau, Alexandre Dumas fils, François Coppée, Leconte de Lisle, Sully Prudhomme, Guy de Maupassant et al., 'Les Artistes contre la tour Eiffel', *Temps* (14 February 1887).

Méline, Jules, 'Faut-il faire l'Exposition de 1900?', *La République française* (24 August 1895), 1.

'Mémoire sur le projet d'exposition de Paris à travers les âges par MM. Lucien Leblanc et Charles Normand, architectes', *L'Ami des Monuments et des Arts* 8 (1894), 319–25.

Merchier, A., 'Les Colonies françaises à l'exposition (Conférence)', *Bulletin de la Société de Géographie de Lille* 35 (1901), 14–35.

Messel, Alfred, 'Ausstellungsbauten', in *Handbuch der Architektur*, ed. Josef Durm, Hermann Ende, Eduard Schmitt and Heinrich Wagner, 4. Teil, 6. Hbbd., 4. Heft: *Gebäude für Sammlungen und Ausstellungen: Archive und Bibliotheken, Museen, Pflanzenhäuser, Aquarien, Ausstellungsbauten*, Darmstadt: Bergsträsser, 1893, 472–534.

Metro-Land: British Empire Exhibition Number, London: n.p., 1924.

Michelet, Jules, 'Préface' [31 January 1847], in *Histoire de la Révolution française*, Paris: Flammarion, 1868, 31–46.

Military Exhibition Earl's Court 1901: Programme, London: Keliher, 1901.

Mirbeau, Octave, 'Pourquoi des Expositions?', *Revue des Deux Mondes* 65 (15 December 1895), 888–908.

Molitor, Jacques, *Illustrirter Führer durch Paris und die Weltausstellung 1900*, 2nd edn, Strasbourg: Strassburger Druckerei und Verlags-Anstalt, 1900.

Montheuil, Albert, 'Les Expositions universelles 1855–1900', *L'Illustration* 54 (8 February 1896), 118.

Moonen, Leo, *Exhibitions: Their Origin, Aim, Influence, and Results; and the Utility of a Prominent Exhibition Commission. A Paper Read at the Special General Meeting of the Victorian Chamber of Manufactures, Monday, August 6, 1883*, Melbourne: Troedel, 1883.

Moore, Harras, *The Marlborough Pocket Guide to the Empire Exhibition at Wembley, 1924*, London: Marlborough Printing, 1924.

Morand, Paul, *1900*, 32nd edn, Paris: Collection 'Marianne', 1931 [*1900 A.D.*, New York: Farquhar Payson, 1931].

——, 'Le Champ de Mars et la tour Eiffel en 1925' [1927], in *Chroniques 1931–1954*, Paris: Grasset, 2001, 350–5.

——, 'Rien que la terre à l'Exposition coloniale', *Revue des Deux Mondes* 101 (15 July 1931), 329–45.

——, *Londres*, Paris: Plon, 1933.

Morgenroth, Wilhelm, 'Ausstellungen', in *Handwörterbuch der Staatswissenschaften*, ed. Johannes Conrad, vol. 2, 4th edn, Jena: Gustav Fischer, 1924, 47–55.

Morrison, Harry Steele, *How I Worked My Way Around the World: The Romantic Story of a Young American who Traveled Fifty Thousand Miles by Land and Sea, Interviewed Crowned Heads and other Notabilities, and Returned Home with Both Money and Experience, having Literally Worked His Way Around the World*, New York: Bible House, 1903.

Mössner, K. E., 'Die Mustermesse, ihre begrifflichen Grundlagen, allgemeinen Probleme und geschichtliche Entwicklung', *Jahrbücher für Nationalökonomie und Statistik* 168 (1956), 251–79.

Mousset, Paul, 'L'Exposition coloniale: Un bilan', *Le Correspondant* 325 (1931), 641–6.

Murray, C. Freeman, 'The British Empire League', *United Empire* 6.6 (1915), 431–9.

Mutsu, Hirokichi, ed., *The British Press and the Japan-British Exhibition*, 4 vols, London: Imperial Japanese Commission, 1910.

Nansouty, Max de, *Premières visites à l'Exposition de 1900*, Paris: Flammarion, 1900.

Naumann, Friedrich, *Ausstellungsbriefe*, Berlin-Schöneberg: Buchverlag der 'Hilfe', 1909 [*Im Reiche der Arbeit: Neue unveränderte Auflage der Ausstellungsbriefe*, 2nd edn, Berlin: Reimer, 1913].

Neumann-Spallart, F. X. von, 'Rückblicke auf die Pariser Weltausstellung', *Deutsche Rundschau* 18/19 (1878–79), 247–77, 432–48, 79–94.

The New Wembley 1925: British Empire Exhibition May–October. The Same Empire but a New Exhibition, London: n.p., 1925.

Nicoll, Edna L. and Suzanne Flour, *A Travers l'Exposition coloniale*, Paris: E. L. Nicoll, 1931.

The Nineteen Hundred: Illustrated Journal of the Paris Exposition, Paris: Mayer & Bernhardt, 1895–1900.

The 1928 Convention Governing International Exhibitions [What You Should Know About the 1928 Convention Governing International Exhibitions], Paris: n.p., 1959.

Nixon Horsfield, J., 'The Franco-British Exhibition of Science, Art and Industries', *Journal of the Royal Institute of British Architects* 15 (25 July 1908), 546–56.

Norton, Richard, *Die Epoche der Begriffsverwirrung*, 2nd edn, Berlin: Steinitz, 1881.

Nouveau Plan de Paris monumental, industriel et commercial, avec la reproduction des jardins et palais de l'Exposition universelle de 1900, Paris: n.p., 1900.

O'Brien, Sophie, 'The Lessons of the Colonial Exhibition in Paris', *Irish Monthly* 59 (1931), 634–8.

Official Daily Programme: British Empire Exhibition 1925, London: n.p., 1925.

Olivares, José de, *The Parisian Dream City: A Portfolio of Photographic Views of the World's Exposition at Paris Comprising its Marvelous Architectural, Sculptural, Artistic, Mechanical, Agricultural, Industrial, Archaeological, Ethnological, Historical and Scenic Attractions. Also Presenting and Describing the Magnificent Vistas, Water-Ways, Natural Scenery and Landscape Effects All Conveying Authentic Realistic Impressions as Received by the Actual Visitor*, St Louis: Thompson, 1900.

Olivier, Marcel, *Six Ans de politique sociale à Madagascar*, Paris: Grasset, 1931.

——, 'Les Origines et les buts de l'Exposition coloniale', *Revue des Deux Mondes* 101 (1 May 1931), 46–57.

——, 'Philosophie de l'Exposition coloniale', *Revue des Deux Mondes* 101 (15 November 1931), 278–93.

——, *Exposition coloniale internationale de Paris, 1931: Rapport général*, 7 vols, Paris: Imprimerie Nationale, 1932–34.

Oncken, August, 'Die Wiener Weltausstellung 1873', *Deutsche Zeit- und Streitfragen* 2 (1873), 1–80.

'Organisation de l'Exposition coloniale en 1927', *Bulletin municipal officiel de la Ville de Paris* (31 December 1923), 5625–30.

Organisation générale des services de l'Exposition coloniale internationale de Paris (1929), Paris: Imprimerie Nationale, 1927.

Le Palais de la femme à l'Exposition de 1900, Paris: Chaix, 1900.

Le Panorama 1900: Exposition universelle Paris, 2 vols, Paris: Baschet, 1900.

Panorama von Berlin für die Gewerbe-Ausstellung 1896, Berlin: n.p., 1896.

Pantlen, R., 'Märkte und Messen', in *Handwörterbuch der Staatswissenschaften*, ed. Ludwig Elster, Adolf Weber and Friedrich Wieser, vol. 6, 4th edn, Jena: Fischer, 1925, 481–96.

Paquet, Alfons, *Das Ausstellungsproblem in der Volkswirtschaft*, Jena: Fischer, 1908.

——, 'Das Wesen der Ausstellung', *Zeitschrift für Handelswissenschaft und Handelspraxis* 7.2 (1914), 34–8.

——, 'Wandlung und Entwicklung im Ausstellungswesen', in *Ausstellung und Messe in Recht und Wirtschaft der Zeit: Vorträge gelegentlich der 2. Mitgliederversammlung des Deutschen Ausstellungs- und Messe-Amtes am 24. Mai 1930 in Dresden*, Berlin: Deutsches Ausstellungs- und Messe-Amt, 1930, 49–71.

——, 'Die Stadt als Schaufenster: Vom Reiz und Nutzen der sehenswürdigen Dinge', *Frankfurter Zeitung* (5 May 1937, 2. MA), 4.

Paris and its Exhibition, London: Pall Mall Gazette, 1889 [*Pall Mall Gazette Extra* 49 (26 July 1889)].

A Paris en mai 1931: L'Exposition coloniale internationale ouvre ses portes, Paris: De Plas, 1931.

Paris Exhibition 1900: Catalogue of the British Fine Art Section, London: St Stephen's House, 1900.

Paris Exposition Reproduced from the Official Photographs Taken under the Supervision of the French Government for Permanent Preservation in the National Archives, New York: Peale, 1900.

Paris in London 1902: Guide and Catalogue, London: Gale & Polden, 1902.

Parville, Henri de, 'Les Premiers travaux de l'Exposition universelle', *Nature* 1 (1897), 81–2.

The Pavilion of H.M. Government: A Brief Record of Official Participation in the British Empire Exhibition, Wembley, 1924, London: H.M. Stationery Office, 1924.

Pasold, Eric W., *Ladybird, Ladybird: A Story of Private Enterprise*, Manchester: Manchester University Press, 1977.

Peck, Ferdinand W., 'The United States at the Paris Exposition in 1900', *North American Review* 168.1 (1899), 24–33.

Petermann, Theodor, ed., *Die Großstadt: Vorträge und Aufsätze zur Städteausstellung*, Dresden: von Zahn und Faensch, 1903.

Peixotto, E. C., 'Some Picturesque Sides of the Exposition: An Artist's Impressions', *Scribner's Magazine* 27.5 (1900), 515–26.

Philips' Picture Map of London: Exhibition Souvenir. Places of Interest to Visitors, London: n.p., 1908.

Picard, Alfred, 'Historique sommaire des expositions universelles françaises', in *Exposition Universelle de 1889 Paris: Rapport général et technique*, Paris 1891–92: Imprimerie Nationale, 3–102, 105–300.

Picard, Alfred, ed., *Exposition universelle internationale de 1889 à Paris: Rapport général et technique*, 8 vols, Paris: Imprimerie Nationale, 1891–92.

——, *Rapport général administratif et technique de l'Exposition universelle internationale de 1900 à Paris*, 8 vols, Paris: Imprimerie Nationale, 1902–03.

——, *Le Bilan d'un siècle (1801–1900)*, 6 vols, Paris: Imprimerie Nationale, 1906.

A Pictorial and Descriptive Guide to London and the British Empire Exhibition, 1925, 45th edn, London: Ward, Lock, 1924.

A Pictorial and Descriptive Guide to London and the Franco-British Exhibition, 1908, London: Ward, Lock, 1908.

The Pictorial Guide to the Franco-British Exhibition: With Easy Plan. Showing How to Get There From Any Terminus or Principal Station in London, What to See Easily When There; Also Particulars of Some of the Interesting Side Shows, London: Larby, 1908.

Pietri, François, 'Les Colonies françaises à la veille de l'Exposition', *Les Conférences et Lectures populaires: Revue Mensuelle de la Société Nationale des Conférences Populaires* 32 (1930), 74–9.

Pilz, Hermann, *Paris amüsirt sich: Intimes aus der Stadt der Welt-Ausstellung*, Leipzig: Weigel, 1900.

Pinon, René, 'A l'Exposition coloniale: le pavillon des missions et ses enseignements', *Revue d'Histoire des Missions* 4 (1931), 481–92.

'Pioneers, O! Pioneers: The Walled City as Seen by an African', *West Africa* (24 May 1924), 57–9.

Piper, August, 'Bericht über einen vierzehntägigen Aufenthalt in Paris während der Weltausstellung', in *Jahresberichte des Grossherzoglichen Realgymnasiums zu Schwerin über das Schuljahr Ostern 1900 bis Ostern 1901*, Schwerin: Sengebusch, 1901, 1–19.

Pistor, Erich, *Bericht über das Ausstellungswesen und seine Regelung an den Export-Ausschuß der Kammer*, Vienna: Niederösterreichische Handels- und Gewerbekammer, [1908–09?].

——, *Die Ständige Österreichische Ausstellungskommission: Entstehungsgeschichte und Bericht über die Jahre 1910 und 1911*, Vienna: Handels- und Gewerbekammer, 1912.

Les Plaisirs de Paris: Guide du 'Rire' dans Paris et à l'Exposition de 1900, Paris: Juven, 1900.

Planat, P., 'L'Exposition de 1889 et la tour de 300 mètres', *Construction Moderne* 1 (27 May 1886), 397–9.

——, 'La Tour, le ministre et le règlement de l'Exposition universelle', *Construction Moderne* 1 (4 September 1886), 565–6.

——, 'Les Clous de l'Exposition universelle', *Construction Moderne* 10 (10 August 1895), 532–4.

——, 'Plus d'Expositions universelles', *Construction Moderne* 10 (31 August 1895), 565–7.

——, 'L'Exposition universelle de 1900', *Construction Moderne* 11 (21 March 1896), 291–3.

——, 'La Galerie des machines', *Construction Moderne* 16 (1 December 1900), 101–3.

——, 'Le Champ de Mars', *Construction Moderne* 18 (6 December 1902), 111–12.

——, 'Les Expositions universelles et la manière de s'en servir', *Construction Moderne* 25 (24 September 1910), 613–15.

——, 'L'Exposition universelle de 1920', *Construction Moderne* 26 (10 December 1910), 121–3.

——, 'L'Exposition universelle de 1920', *Construction Moderne* 26 (7 January 1911), 172–3.

Pontzen, Alfred, *Der Ausflug des Aachener Gewerbe-Vereins in den Tagen vom 25. Juli bis 3. August 1900 zur Weltausstellung nach Paris*, Aachen: Deterre, 1900.

Poppenberg, Felix, 'Folies universelles', *Neue Deutsche Rundschau* 11.8 (1900), 878–991.

Poppović, Alexander, *Pariser Eindrücke im Frühling 1900*, Vienna: Hartleben, 1900.
——, 'Impressions parisiennes', *Nouvelle Revue* 8 (1901), 223–32.
Popular Guide to the Franco-British Exhibition: Shepherd's Bush, London 1908, London: Bemrose, 1908.
Pöschl, Theodor, *Franz Reuleaux: Rede gehalten bei der von der Technischen Hochschule Karlsruhe und dem Bezirksverein Karlsruhe des Vereines deutscher Ingenieure am 31. Oktober 1929 veranstalteten Gedenkfeier*, Karlsruhe: Müller, 1929.
'Preisbewerbung um den Entwurf des Lageplans für eine Weltausstellung in Berlin', *Centralblatt der Bauverwaltung* 12 (12/26 November 1892), 485–6, 501–3.
'Die Preisbewerbung um den Lageplan einer in Berlin zu veranstaltenden Weltausstellung', *Deutsche Bauzeitung* 26 (9 November 1892), 549–51.
Prévost, Marcel, 'Réflexions sur l'Exposition coloniale', *Revue de France* 11 (1 September 1931), 42–9.
'Das Projekt einer Weltausstellung zu Berlin im Jahre 1885', *Deutsche Bauzeitung* 14 (10 January 1880), 17–18.
'Promenade à travers l'Exposition: Le Musée permanent des colonies', *Miroir du Monde* 2 (1931), 587.
Proudhon, Pierre-Joseph, 'Société de l'Exposition perpétuelle: Projet', in *Théorie de la propriété*, 2nd edn, Paris: Librairie Internationale, 1866, 294–308.
Proust, Antonin, *Les Sections étrangères à l'Exposition de 1900: Allemagne, Autriche, Espagne, Italie, Pays-Bas, Russie, Suède*, Paris: Per Lamm, 1901.
Pudor, Heinrich, ed., *Ausstellungs-Jahrbuch*, Berlin: Pudor, 1906–08.
Quantin, A., *L'Exposition du siècle*, Paris: Le Monde Moderne, 1900.
The Raid on Zeebrugge: An Illustrated Souvenir of the Model Display in the Admiralty Theatre of H.M. Government Pavilion. British Empire Exhibition, London: H.M. Stationery Office, 1924–25.
Rapsilber, Maximilian, *Offizieller Führer durch die Spezial-Ausstellung Alt-Berlin: Mit einem Plan und 25 Abbildungen nach Originalzeichnungen*, Berlin: Verlag des 'Kleinen Journal', 1896.
Rathenau, Walter, 'Die schönste Stadt der Welt', *Die Zukunft* 26 (7 January 1899), 36–48.
Recueil des textes organisant l'Exposition coloniale internationale Paris 1931, Paris: Crouzet, 1929.
Règlement général pour l'Exposition coloniale internationale de 1931 à Paris, Paris: Imprimerie Nationale, 1927.
Regnier, Noël, *L'Industrie française au XIXe siècle: Revue et examen des expositions nationales et internationales en France et à l'étranger depuis 1878 jusqu'à 1878*, Paris: Sault, 1878.
Reichskommissariat für die Weltausstellung in Paris 1900, ed., *Amtliches Verzeichnis der zur deutschen Abtheilung der Weltausstellung in Paris 1900 zugelassenen Aussteller*, Berlin: Mosse, 1899.
Reiländer, Stefan, *Ausstellungen der Zukunft: Berlin 1900? Ein 'greifbarer Plan'*, Düsseldorf: Wolfrum, [1892?].
Reise-Berichte der städtischen Beamten über den Besuch der Pariser Weltausstellung, Düsseldorf: Schwann, 1901.
Reitz, Adolf, ed., *Hinter Buch und Schreibtisch: Vergessene Tagebücher von Max Eyth*, Ulm: Hess, 1961.
Report of His Majesty's Commissioners for the Paris International Exhibition of 1900, 3 vols, London: Clowes, 1901.
Reuleaux, Franz, *Briefe aus Philadelphia*, Braunschweig: Vieweg, 1877.
——, 'Eine deutsche Weltausstellung?', *Friedrich Georg Wieck's Deutsche illustrirte Gewerbezeitung* 47.3 (1882), 17–18.
——, 'Die Entwicklung des Ausstellungswesens', *Allgemeine Zeitung* (4/5 November 1896), 1–5, 3–6.
——, 'Die Anfänge des Ausstellungswesens', in *Das XIX. Jahrhundert in Wort und Bild: Politische und Kultur-Geschichte*, ed. Hans Kraemer, vol. 2: *1840–1871*, Berlin: Bong, 1900, 131–44.

——, 'Ausstellungswesen 1851–1899', in *Das XIX. Jahrhundert in Wort und Bild: Politische und Kultur-Geschichte*, ed. Hans Kraemer, vol. 3: *1871–1899*, Berlin: Bong, 1900, 185–202.

——, 'Die Entwicklung des Ausstellungswesens', in *Deutsche Industrie, deutsche Kultur*, ed. Julius Eckstein and J. J. Landau, Berlin: Fischer, 1900–02, 13–22.

Reusche, Friedrich, *Chicago und Berlin: Alte und neue Bahnen im Ausstellungswesen*, Berlin: Carl Ulrich, 1892.

Reynaud, Paul, *L'Empire français: Discours prononcé à l'inauguration de l'Exposition coloniale*, Paris: Guillemot et de Lamothe, 1931.

——, *Mémoires: Venu de ma montagne*, Paris: Flammarion, 1960.

Richards, J. M., 'A Tower for London', *Architectural Review* 88 (1940), 141–4.

Richmond, Leonard, 'The Lure of Wembley', *Studio* 87 (15 June 1924), 312–17.

Riegl, Alois, *Der moderne Denkmalkultus: Sein Wesen und seine Entstehung*, Vienna: Braumüller, 1903 ['The Modern Cult of Monuments: Its Character and Its Origin', *Oppositions* 25 (1982), 21–51].

Riemerschmid, Richard, 'Ausstellungen als ein Mittel zum Zweck', in *Die Durchgeistung der deutschen Arbeit: Wege und Ziele in Zusammenhang von Industrie/Handwerk und Kunst*, Jena: Diederichs, 1912, 38–44.

Riollot, Jules and Robert Laulan, *Le Champ-de-Mars avant la Révolution: Annales de 1750 à 1790*, Paris: Librairie de l'Armée, 1936.

Robida, Albert, 'L'Exposition de 1900', *Monde Moderne* (1896), 97–117.

——, 'Le Vieux Paris à l'Exposition de 1900', *Monde Moderne* (1900), 63–74.

——, *Le Vieux Paris: Etudes et dessins originaux*, Paris: Lemercier, 1900.

——, *Le Vieux Paris: Guide historique, pittoresque, et anecdotique*, Paris: Ménard et Chaufour, 1900.

Roche, Jules, 'L'Exposition de 1900', *Le Rappel* (15 July 1892), 1–2.

Rogers, Joseph M., 'Lessons from International Exhibitions', *Forum* 23.4 (1901), 500–10.

Roscher, Wilhelm, 'Die Industrieausstellungen, ihre Geschichte und ihr Einfluß auf die Culturentwickelung', *Die Gegenwart: Eine encyklopädische Darstellung der neuesten Zeitgeschichte für alle Stände*, vol. 12, Leipzig: Brockhaus, 1856, 470–534.

Rosenkranz, Karl, *Die Topographie des heutigen Paris und Berlin: zwei Vorträge*, Königsberg: Bornträger, 1850.

Royal Commission for the Colonial and Indian Exhibition, ed., *Report of the Reception Committee*, London 1886.

——, *Report of the Royal Commission for the Colonial and Indian Exhibition*, London: Clowes, 1887.

'Round the World at the Paris Exposition', *Atlantic Monthly* 40 (1879), 41–8.

Rückblick auf ein halbes Jahrhundert: Von der Ständigen Ausstellungskommission zum Ausstellungs- und Messe-Ausschuß der Deutschen Wirtschaft e.V., Cologne: Ausstellungs- und Messeausschuß der Deutschen Wirtschaft, 1957.

'Rundschau der wichtigsten Ausstellungen des Jahres 1896', *Jahrbuch der Berliner Morgen-Zeitung* (1897), 223–41.

Sala, George Augustus, *Paris Herself Again in 1878–9*, 2 vols, 2nd edn, London: Remington, 1879.

Salmon, Edward, 'Has the Exhibition Justified Itself?', *United Empire* 15.10 (1924), 581–3.

Sander, A., 'Die gewerbliche Entwickelung Berlins: Eine Ausstellungs-Betrachtung', *Neue Deutsche Rundschau (Freie Bühne)* 7.1/2 (1896), 561–9.

Saunier, Charles, 'Les Curiosités de l'Exposition: Le vieux Paris par Robida', *Revue des Arts Décoratifs* 20 (1900), 193–6.

Schäffle, Albert, 'Industrieausstellungen', in *Deutsches Staats-Wörterbuch*, ed. Johan Caspar Bluntschli, vol. 5, Stuttgart: Expedition, 1857–70, 313–17.

Scheffler, Karl, *Berlin – ein Stadtschicksal*, Berlin: Reiss, 1910.

Schick, Adolf, 'Das Ausstellungs- und Messewesen in der Reichshauptstadt: Ein Rückblick – Ausblick', *Mitteilungen der Industrie- und Handelskammer zu Berlin* 25 (10 July 1927), 601–5.

Schopfer, Jean, 'Amusements of the Paris Exposition', *Century Magazine* 60.4/5 (1900), 483–95, 643–54.

Schricker, A., 'Die Pariser Weltausstellung', *Deutsche Rundschau* 104/105 (1900), 76–80, 290–5.

Schulze-Smidt, Bernhardine, *Bleistift-Skizzen: Erinnerungen an die Pariser Weltausstellung von 1889*, Bremen: Kühtmann, 1890.

Schweizerischer Gewerbeverein and Werner Krebs, eds, *Fach-Berichte über die Pariser Weltausstellung im Jahre 1900*, Bern: Buechler, 1901.

Searles, William H., 'The Ferris Wheel', *Journal of the Association of Engineering Societies* 12 (12 December 1893), 614–16.

Séguy, René, 'Dialogue à propos de l'Exposition coloniale de 1931', *Revue Hebdomadaire* (1929), 1–8.

Seidel, Paul, ed., *Die Kunstsammlung Friedrich's des Großen auf der Pariser Weltausstellung 1900*, Berlin: Giesecke und Devrient, 1900.

Serre, Edouard, 'Les Questions ouvrières à l'Exposition de 1900', *Grande Revue* (1 August/ 1 September 1900), 320–55, 620–53.

Shaw, Albert, 'Paris and the Exposition of 1900', *American Monthly Review of Reviews* 21.6 (1900), 679–88.

Shepherd's Bush Exhibition Estate, London, *A City for Sale*, London: n.p., 1922.

A Short Description of Burma, Its Inhabitants and Products, Together with an Account of the Burma Pavilion at the British Empire Exhibition of 1924, London, 1924.

Siemens, Werner von, 'Die Berliner Weltausstellung', *National-Zeitung* (12 June 1892).

'Sights of the Paris Exposition of 1900', *Blackwood's Edinburgh Magazine* 168 (1900), 107.

Simmel, Georg, 'Über Kunstausstellungen', *Unsere Zeit* (26 February 1890), 474–80.

——, 'Berliner Gewerbe-Ausstellung', *Die Zeit: Wiener Wochenschrift für Politik, Volkswirtschaft, Wissenschaft und Kunst* 8 (25 July 1896), 59–60 ['Berliner Gewerbe-Ausstellung (25.7.1896)', in *Gesamtausgabe*, vol. 17: *Miszellen, Glossen, Stellungnahmen, Umfrageantworten, Leserbriefe, Diskussionsbeiträge 1889–1918: Anonyme und pseudonyme Veröffentlichungen 1888–1920*, ed. Klaus Christian Köhnke, Cornelia Jaenichen and Erwin Schullerus, Frankfurt am Main: Suhrkamp, 2004, 33–8; reproduced in English trans. 'The Berlin Trade Exhibition', *Theory, Culture and Society* 8.3 (1991), 119–23].

——, *Philosophie des Geldes*, Leipzig: Duncker & Humblot, 1900 [*The Philosophy of Money*, 2nd edn, London: Routledge, 1990].

——, 'Soziologie des Raumes' [1903], in *Schriften zur Soziologie: Eine Auswahl*, Frankfurt am Main: Suhrkamp, 1983, 221–42 ['The Sociology of Space', in *Simmel on Culture: Selected Writings*, ed. David Frisby and Mike Featherstone, London: Sage, 1997, 137–70].

——, 'Die Großstädte und das Geistesleben', in *Die Großstadt: Vorträge und Aufsätze zur Städteausstellung*, ed. Theodor Petermann, Dresden: von Zahn und Faensch, 1903, 185–206 ['The Metropolis and Mental Life', in *Simmel on Culture: Selected Writings*, ed. David Frisby and Mike Featherstone, London: Sage, 1997, 174–86].

——, 'Florenz', in *Zur Philosophie der Kunst*, Potsdam: Kiepenheuer, 1922, 61–6.

Simon, M., 'En visitant l'Exposition coloniale', *Cité moderne* 12 (1931), 6.

Simon, 'Über eine im Jahre 1894 in Berlin zu veranstaltende Allgemeine deutsche Gewerbeausstellung', *Sitzungsberichte des Vereins zur Beförderung des Gewerbefleißes* 70 (6 April 1891), 133–59.

Smith, Swire, 'Should Britain Take Part in International Exhibitions?', *Nineteenth Century* 67 (1910), 983–94.

Snyder, Carl, 'Engineer Ferris and his Wheel', *Review of Reviews* (8 September 1893), 269–76.

Sombart, Werner, 'Die Ausstellung', *Morgen: Wochenschrift für deutsche Kultur* 9 (28 February 1908), 249–56.

——, 'Die Reklame', *Morgen: Wochenschrift für deutsche Kultur* 10 (6 March 1908), 281–6.

——, 'Ihre Majestät die Reklame', *Die Zukunft* 63 (27 June 1908), 475–87.

'Some Impressions from the Paris Exhibition', *Literary Digest* 21.9 (1900), 261–2.

Souvenir of the British Empire Exhibition (1924) including State Opening Ceremony: 50 Views, London: Fleetway, 1924.

Souvenir of the Greater Britain Exhibition: Earl's Court, London, S. W., London: Keliher, 1899.

'Souvenirs des rétrospectives de l'Exposition universelle: Pavillon de la Ville de Paris. Exposition de la Commission municipale du Vieux Paris', *L'Ami des Monuments et des Arts* 14 (1900), 336–49.

Ein Spaziergang von der Kaiser-Wilhelm-Brücke bis zur Weltausstellung: Berliner Briefe vom Jahre 1900, Berlin: Fontane, 1889.

Spielmann, Isidore, *Royal Commission Paris International Exhibition, 1900*, London: Royal Commission, St. Stephen's House, 1900.

——, 'Art at the Franco-British Exhibition', *Burlington Magazine for Connoisseurs* 12 (1907–08), 376–7.

——, *Souvenir of the Fine Arts Section: Franco-British Exhibition 1908*, London: Bemrose, 1909.

Stahl, Fritz, *Paris: Eine Stadt als Kunstwerk*, 17th edn, Berlin: Mosse, 1929.

Ständige Ausstellungskommission für die Deutsche Industrie, ed., *Zusammensetzung, Ziele und Zwecke*, Berlin: Büxenstein, [1914?].

Stangen, Karl, *Carl Stangen's Gesellschaftsreisen nach Paris, Weltausstellung 1900: Ausflüge nach London, Brüssel*, Berlin: Stangen, 1898.

Stanton, Theodore, 'The International Exhibition of 1900', *Century Magazine* 51.2 (1895), 314–17.

Statham, Henry Heathcote, 'The Paris Exhibition', *Fortnightly Review* 68 (1900), 131–42.

Stein, Aurel, 'The International Colonial Exhibition in Paris and the Indian Visitor', *Asiatic Review* 27 (1931), 599–604.

Stevenson, James Lord, 'The British Empire Exhibition', *Landmark/English Speaking World* 6 (1924), 153–8.

——, *British Empire Exhibition: A Lecture Delivered to the Royal Society of Arts (April 16th, 1925)*, London: n.p., 1925 ['The British Empire Exhibition', *Journal of the Royal Society of Arts* 73 (22 May 1925), 609–19].

Stiegler, Georg, *Deutsche Weltausstellung zu Berlin: Ein Beitrag zur Klaerung dieser nationalen Angelegenheit*, Berlin: Steinitz, 1892.

Stinde, Julius, *Hotel Buchholz: Ausstellungs-Erlebnisse der Frau Wilhelmine Buchholz*, Berlin: Freund und Jeckel, 1897.

Stoffers, Gottfried and Arbeits-Ausschuss unter Mitwirkung der Ausstellungsleitung und der Gruppen-Vorsitzenden, eds, *Die Industrie- und Gewerbe-Ausstellung für Rheinland, Westfalen und benachbarte Bezirke, verbunden mit einer deutsch-nationalen Kunst-Ausstellung Düsseldorf 1902*, Düsseldorf: Bagel, 1903.

The Story of the Building of the Greatest Stadium in the World, London: Robert McAlpine, 1923.

Strahan Smith, John, *The Cuckoos: A Narrative of Fact. Showing how the Founder of the British Empire Exhibition was Dispossessed of his Exhibition; and the Means Employed to Accomplish that End*, Westminster: n.p., 1922.

Strauss, Paul, 'L'Exposition de 1900', *Revue Bleue* 32 (15 June 1895), 738–42.

Stroud, Dorothy, *Humphry Repton*, London: Country Life, 1962.

Stüber, Erich, *Das Ausstellungswesen und seine Organisation*, PhD diss., Eberhard-Karls Universität zu Tübingen, 1914/21.

Swann, E. T., 'Britain's "Shop Window"', *British Manufacturer* (1962), 21–3, 35.

Talmeyr, Maurice, 'Notes sur l'Exposition', *Le Correspondant* 165–9 (1899–1900), 177–82, 590–5, 1021–6; 183–8, 589–5, 1000–5; 187–93, 616–20, 1035–9; 197–201, 1051–6, 396–401.

——, 'L'Ecole du Trocadéro', *Revue des Deux Mondes* 70 (1 November 1900), 198–213.

Tanguy, Yves, Georges Sadoul, Louis Aragon, André Breton, André Thirion, Maxime Alexandre, Paul Eluard, Pierre Unik, René Char, Benjamin Péret, René Crevel, Georges Malkine, *Premier Bilan de l'Exposition Coloniale*, Paris: n.p., 1931 [Reprinted *in Tracts surréalistes et déclarations collectives*, ed. José Pierre, vol. 1: *1922–1939*, Paris: Terrain Vague, 1980, 198–200.]

Tarlé, Antoine de, 'A l'Exposition de Wembley', *Revue des Deux Mondes* 94 (1924), 165–82.

Théry, François, 'L'Exposition de l'empire britannique à Wembley', *Etudes* 179 (1924), 513–35, 659–70.

Thiel, Hugo, *Max Eyth zum Gedächtnis: Gedenkrede in der Hauptversammlung der Deutschen Landwirtschafts-Gesellschaft am 15. Februar 1907*, Berlin: Parey, 1907.

Thirion, André, *Révolutionnaires sans révolution*, Paris: Laffont, 1972 [*Revolutionaries Without Revolution*, London: Cassell, 1975].

Thomson, David Croal, *The Paris Exhibition of 1900*, London: Virtue, 1901.

Tony-Dessus, 'Il faut, dès maintenant, assurer le succès de l'Exposition coloniale de 1929', *Revue du Pacifique* 6.1 (15 January 1927), 70–3.

Tranchant, Maurice, *Le Tour du monde en un jour à l'Exposition coloniale*, Paris 1931: Studio du Palmier Nain.

Trillat, Joseph, 'L'Exposition coloniale internationale de 1931: L'Indochine', *Les Conférences et Lectures Populaires: Revue mensuelle de la Société Nationale des Conférence Populaires* 32 (1930), 80–2.

——, *L'Exposition coloniale de Paris*, Paris: Calavas, 1931.

A Trip Through the Paris Exhibition: Underwood's Patent Map System Combined with Sixty Original Stereoscopic Photographs, New York: Underwood & Underwood, 1900.

Twelve Tours to the Paris Exposition of 1900: By the North German Lloyd Steamship Line, New York: Raymond & Whitcomb, [1900?].

'Über Bedeutung und Werth der Ausstellungen', *Glaser's Annalen für Gewerbe und Bauwesen* 5 (1 February 1879), 106–8, 196–8.

'Über die Sonder-Ausstellung von Berolinensien des "Vereins für die Geschichte Berlins"', *Deutscher Reichs-Anzeiger und königlich-preußischer Staats-Anzeiger* 185 (5 August 1896), 3.

'Union of Students of African Descent: Hon. Dr. Jones, M. L. C., on West African Questions', *West Africa* (4 October 1924), 1050.

Vachon, Marius, 'A travers les Expositions françaises de 1798 à 1900', *Nouvelle Revue* 92 (1895), 136–51.

Vaillat, Léandre, 'A l'Exposition coloniale: La Section métropolitaine et la Cité des Informations', *L'Illustration* (30 November 1930), 618–19.

Valona, Louis, 'L'Exposition de 1900: M. Alfred Picard, commissaire général', *Le Magasin Pittoresque* 65 (1897), 179–80.

Varenne, Gaston, 'Le Musée permanent des colonies', *Art et Décoration* 60 (1931), 59–68.

Vatin-Pérignon, E., 'Le Bilan de l'Exposition coloniale', *Revue des Sciences Politiques* 54 (1931), 486–91.

Venice: The Bride of the Sea. A Grand Historic and Romantic Spectacle and Aquatic Pageant, London: Newnes, 1891.

Verein Berliner Kaufleute und Industrieller, eds, *Berlins Aufstieg zur Weltstadt: Ein Gedenkbuch*, Berlin: Hobbing, 1929.

Verhaeren, Emile, 'Chronique de l'Exposition', *Mercure de France* 34.4/6 (1900), 458–65, 743–8, 203–8, 477–82, 170–6, 480–5, 780–5.

Vijayaraghavacharya, Diwan Bahadur T., 'India and the British Empire Exhibition', *Asiatic Review* 19 (1923), 140–5.

——, *The British Empire Exhibition, 1924: Report by the Commissioner for India for the British Empire Exhibition*, Calcutta: Government of India Press, 1925.

'Visite aux chantiers de la reconstitution du "Vieux Paris"', *Bulletin de la Société des Amis des Monuments Parisiens* 12 (1900), 258.

'Visite des Amis des monuments aux chantiers de la reconstitution du "Vieux Paris" par Robida', *L'Ami des Monuments et des Arts* 13 (1899), 211–13.

Vogel, N., 'Bericht, betreffend das Ausstellungswesen', *Sitzungsberichte des Vereins zur Beförderung des Gewerbefleißes* 61 (2 October 1882), 253–72.

Vogüé, Eugène-Melchior de, 'A travers l'exposition: Aux portes – la tour', *Revue des Deux Mondes* 59 (1 July 1889), 186–201.
——, 'La Défunte Exposition', *Revue des Deux Mondes* 70 (15 November 1900), 380–99.
——, 'Au Seuil d'un siècle: Cosmopolitisme et nationalisme', *Revue des Deux Mondes* 71 (1 February 1901), 677–92.
W. G. N., 'Empire', *Architectural Review* 55 (1924), 205.
Wailly, G. de, *A travers l'Exposition de 1900*, Paris: Fayard, 1900.
Walks in Wembley: An Educational Guide. By the Editor of 'The Weekly Bulletin of Empire Study', London: Mills & Boon, 1924.
Wallace, D. Euan, 'Empire Exhibitions and Fairs', *United Empire* 28.4 (1937), 213–16.
Ware, Lewis, *Etude sur la Section Coloniale de l'Exposition Franco-Britannique de Londres en 1908*, Paris: Imprimerie de la Dépêche Coloniale, 1909.
Waters, H. W., *History of Fairs and Expositions: Their Classification, Functions and Values*, London: Reid, 1939.
Watson, John Forbes, 'International Exhibitions', *Times* (28/30 December 1872), 10, 8.
Weaver, Lawrence, 'Agriculture and Horticulture at the British Empire Exhibition', *Journal of the Ministry of Agriculture* 21 (1924), 9–14.
——, 'Exhibition of Modern British Architecture at the British Empire Exhibition: Opening Ceremony', *Journal of the Royal Institute of British Architects* 31 (7 June 1924), 505–8.
——, *Exhibitions and the Arts of Display*, London: Country Life, 1925.
——, *The Place of Advertising in Industry*, London: Baynard, 1928.
Webb, Aston, ed., *London of the Future*, London: Fisher Unwin, 1921.
Weigert, Max, 'Weltausstellungen', *Gewerbliche Einzelvorträge* 5 (1911), 29–55.
Weihe, Carl, *Max Eyth: Ein kurzgefaßtes Lebensbild mit Auszügen aus seinen Schriften. Nebst Neudruck von Wort und Werkzeug von Max von Eyth*, Berlin: Verein deutscher Ingenieure, 1916.
'Die Weltausstellung in Chicago im Jahre 1893', *Das Neue Universum* 15 (1894), 68–86.
'Wembley Park Tower', *Engineer* (8 September 1891), 239–41.
Wendté, Frederika, 'Reading List of Magazine Articles on the Paris Exposition, 1900', *Bulletin of Bibliography* 2.3 (1900), 42.
Wermuth, Adolf, *Ein Beamtenleben: Erinnerungen*, Berlin: Scherl, 1922.
White City Sale: The White City, Shepherd's Bush Exhibition Estate, London, W. 12, to be Sold by Auction on Tuesday, November 7th, 1922, London: n.p., 1922.
Whiteing, Richard, 'Paris in 1900', *Edinburgh Review* 192 (1900), 117–39.
Whittinghill, Dexter G., 'The Milan Exposition', *The World To-Day* 12 (1907), 69–75.
Williams-Ellis, Bertram Clough, *Lawrence Weaver*, London: Geoffrey Bles, 1933.
Wilson, Angus, *No Laughing Matter*, London: Secker & Warburg, 1967.
'With Ships Moving Along Empire Routes: The World in Contour', *Illustrated London News* 164 (24 May 1924), 939.
Witt, Otto N., ed., *Weltausstellung in Paris 1900: Amtlicher Katalog der Ausstellung des Deutschen Reiches*, Berlin: Stargardt, 1900.
——, *Pariser Weltausstellungsbriefe: Mit neunundzwanzig Bildertafeln*, Berlin: Mückenberger, 1900.
——, 'Naturwissenschaftlich-technische Ausstellungen', in *Die Kultur der Gegenwart: Ihre Entwicklung und ihre Ziele*, Teil 1, Abt. 1: *Die Allgemeinen Grundlagen der Kultur der Gegenwart*, ed. Paul Hinneberg, 2nd edn, Berlin: Teubner, 1912, 442–58.
'Wo soll die Weltausstellung hin?', *Der Bär* 18 (1891–92), 393–4.
Wolgast, Eike, 'Ein Mecklenburger auf der Londoner Weltausstellung 1862', *Mecklenburgische Jahrbücher* 108 (1991), 119–27.
The Wonders of Wembley, and Souvenir Guide to London, London: n.p., 1924.
Wood, Henry Trueman, 'Exhibitions', *Nineteenth Century* 20 (1886), 633–47.
——, 'The Paris Exhibition', *Journal of the Society of Arts* 38 (31 December 1889), 45–62.
——, 'International Exhibitions', *Journal of the Society of Arts* 55 (8 November 1907), 1140–6.
——, *A History of the Royal Society of Arts*, London: Murray, 1913.

Woodhead, Howard, 'The First German Municipal Exposition (Dresden, 1903)', *American Journal of Sociology* 9/10 (1904–05), 433–58, 612–30, 812–31, 47–63.

Woodward, B. D., 'The Exposition of 1900', *North American Review* 170.4 (1900), 472–9.

Woolf, Virginia, 'Thunder at Wembley' [1924], in *The Essays of Virginia Woolf*, vol. 3: *1919–1924*, ed. Andrew McNeillie, London: Hogarth, 1988, 410–14.

'Ein Wort über die Gewerbeausstellungen des Zollvereins', *Deutsche Vierteljahrs Schrift* 1 (1845), 255–75.

Wurm, Emanuel, 'Der deutsche Städtetag und die deutsche Städteausstellung', *Die Neue Zeit* 21.2 (1903), 766–72.

Wuttke, Robert, ed., *Die deutschen Städte: Geschildert nach den Ergebnissen der ersten deutschen Städteausstellung zu Dresden 1903*, 2 vols, Leipzig: Brandstetter, 1904.

XX, 'L'Exposition de Berlin', *Revue de Paris* 3 (15 June 1896), 887–902.

Zacher, 'Ausländische Sozialpolitik und Pariser Weltausstellung', *Soziale Praxis: Centralblatt für Sozialpolitik* 7 (24 March 1898), 646–9.

Zopke, Hans, *Professor Franz Reuleaux: A Biographical Sketch*, New York: n.p., 1896.

Zottmann, Alfons, 'Die Jahrhundertfeier in Paris und Rom während des Jahres 1900: Ein Rückblick', *Frankfurter Zeitgemäße Broschüren* 20 (1901), 317–43.

Secondary sources

Abbattista, Guido, 'Torino 1884: Africani in mostra', *Contemporanea* 3 (2004), 369–410.

Abel, Richard, *The Ciné Goes to Town: French Cinema 1890–1914*, Berkeley: University of California Press, 1994.

Adams, Annmarie, 'The Healthy Victorian City: The Old London Street at the International Health Exhibition of 1884', in *Streets: Critical Perspectives on Public Space*, ed. Zeynep Çelik, Diane Favro and Richard Ingersoll, Berkeley: University of California Press, 1994, 203–12.

Ageron, Charles-Robert, 'L'Exposition coloniale de 1931: Mythe républicain ou mythe impérial?', in *Les Lieux de mémoire*, ed. Pierre Nora, vol. 1: *La République*, Paris: Gallimard, 1984, 561–91.

——, 'Les Colonies devant l'opinion publique française (1919–39)', *Revue Française d'Histoire d'Outre-Mer* 77.1 (1990), 31–74.

Agulhon, Maurice, 'Paris: la traversée d'est en ouest', *Les Lieux de mémoire*, ed. Pierre Nora, vol. 3.3: *Les France*, Paris: Gallimard, 1992, 868–909.

Aldrich, Robert, *Greater France: A History of French Overseas Expansion*, Basingstoke: Palgrave Macmillan, 1996.

Allwood, John, *The Great Exhibitions*, London: Studio Vista, 1977.

——, 'International Exhibitions and the Classification of Their Exhibits', *Journal of the Royal Society of Arts* 128 (1980), 450–5.

Altenburg, Jan Philipp, 'Perspektiven der Stadtforschung: Neue Studien zur Stadt um 1900', *Archiv für Sozialgeschichte* 48 (2008), 635–60.

Alter, Peter, ed., *Im Banne der Metropolen: Berlin und London in den zwanziger Jahren*, Göttingen: Vandenhoeck & Ruprecht, 1993.

Altick, Richard Daniel, *The Shows of London*, Cambridge, MA: Harvard University Press, 1978.

Anderson, Norman D., *Ferris Wheels: An Illustrated History*, Bowling Green: Bowling Green State University Popular Press, 1992.

Arbeitsgemeinschaft 'Junge Historiker', *Das Treptower Ehrenmal: Geschichte und Gegenwart des Ehrenmals für die gefallenen sowjetischen Helden in Berlin*, 2nd edn, Berlin: Staatsverlag der Deutschen Demokratischen Republik, 1987.

Armstrong, Meg, '"A Jumble of Foreignness": The Sublime Musayums of Nineteenth-Century Fairs and Expositions', *Cultural Critique* 23 (1992–93), 199–250.

Arnold, Dana, ed., *The Metropolis and its Image: Constructing Identities for London, c. 1750–1950*, Oxford: Basil Blackwell, 1999.

Atmore, Henry, 'Utopia Limited: The Crystal Palace Company and Joint-Stock Politics, 1854–1856', *Journal of Victorian Culture* 9.2 (2004), 189–215.

Auerbach, Jeffrey A., *The Great Exhibition of 1851: A Nation on Display*, New Haven: Yale University Press, 1999.

——, 'The Great Exhibition and Historical Memory', *Journal of Victorian Culture* 6.1 (2001), 89–112.

Auerbach, Jeffrey A. and Peter H. Hoffenberg, eds, *Britain, the Empire, and the World at the Great Exhibition of 1851*, Aldershot: Ashgate, 2008.

Augé, Marc, *Non-Lieux: Introduction à une anthropologie de la surmodernité*, Paris: du Seuil, 1992.

August, Thomas G., 'The Colonial Exhibition in France: Education or Reinforcement?', *Proceedings of the Sixth and Seventh Annual Meetings of the French Colonial Historical Society* (1980–82), 147–54.

——, *The Selling of the Empire: British and French Imperialist Propaganda, 1890–1940*, Westport: Greenwood, 1985.

Ausstellungs- und Messe-Ausschuss der Deutschen Wirtschaft, *AUMA: 75 Jahre im Dienst der Messewirtschaft (1907–1982)*, Cologne: Heider, 1982.

Bacha, Myriam, ed., *Les Expositions universelles à Paris de 1855 à 1937*, Paris: Action Artistique de la Ville de Paris, 2005.

Bachmann-Medick, Doris, *Cultural Turns: Neuorientierungen in den Kulturwissenschaften*, Reinbek: Rowohlt, 2006.

Bakhtin, M. M., *The Dialogic Imagination: Four Essays*, Austin: University of Texas Press, 1981.

Bale, John and Olof Moen, eds, *The Stadium and the City*, Keele: Keele University Press, 1995.

Bancel, Nicolas, Pascal Blanchard, Gilles Boëtsch, Eric Deroo and Sandrine Lemaire, eds, *Zoos humains: XIXe et XXe siècles*, Paris: La Découverte, 2002.

Banham, Mary and Bevis Hillier, eds, *A Tonic to the Nation: The Festival of Britain 1951*, London: Thames & Hudson, 1976.

Baranowski, Shelley, 'An Alternative to Everyday Life? The Politics of Leisure and Tourism', *Contemporary European History* 12.4 (2003), 561–72.

Barclay, Patrick and Ken Powell, *Wembley Stadium: Venue of Legends*, Munich: Prestel, 2007.

Barker, Barbara, 'Imre Kiralfy's Patriotic Spectacles: *Columbus, and the Discovery of America* (1892–1893) and *America* (1893)', *Dance Chronicle* 17.2 (1994), 149–78.

Barker, T. C. and Michael Robbins, *A History of London Transport: Passenger Travel and the Development of the Metropolis*, London: Allen & Unwin, 1974.

Barringer, Tim, 'Re-Presenting the Imperial Archive: South Kensington and its Museums', *Journal of Victorian Culture* 3.2 (1998), 357–73.

——, 'The South Kensington Museum and the Colonial Project', in *Colonialism and the Object: Empire, Material Culture and the Museum*, ed. Tim Barringer and Tom Flynn, London: Routledge, 1998, 11–27.

Barth, Volker, *Mensch versus Welt: Die Pariser Weltausstellung von 1867*, Darmstadt: Wissenschaftliche Buchgesellschaft, 2007.

Barthes, Roland, *Mythologies*, Paris: Seuil, 1957.

——, *The Eiffel Tower and Other Mythologies*, New York: Hill & Wang, 1979 [*La Tour Eiffel*, Paris: Delpire, 1964].

Baumeister, Martin, 'Alteuropäische Städte auf dem Weg in die Moderne: Großausstellungen und metropolitane Identitäten in Turin und Barcelona 1884 bis 1929', *Historische Anthropologie* 10.3 (2002), 449–63.

Beauchamp, Kenneth G., *Exhibiting Electricity*, London: Institute of Electrical Engineers, 1997.

Beckmann, Uwe, *Gewerbeausstellungen in Westeuropa vor 1851: Ausstellungswesen in Frankreich, Belgien und Deutschland. Gemeinsamkeiten und Rezeption der Veranstaltungen*, Frankfurt am Main: Peter Lang, 1991.

Beltran, Alain, 'La "Fée Electricité", reine et servante', *Vingtième Siècle* 16 (1987), 90–5.

Benedict, Burton, 'The Anthropology of World's Fairs', in *The Anthropology of World's Fairs: San Francisco's Panama Pacific International Exposition of 1915*, Berkeley: Lowie Museum of Anthropology, 1983, 1–65.

——, 'International Exhibitions and National Identity', *Anthropology Today* 7.3 (1991), 5–9.

Benjamin, Walter, 'Paris, die Hauptstadt des XIX. Jahrhunderts [1935]', in *Das Passagen-Werk* (*Gesammelte Schriften*, vol. 5.1), Frankfurt am Main: Suhrkamp, 1982, 45–59.

Bennett, Jim, Robert Brain, Simon Schaffer, Heinz Otto Sibum and Richard Staley, *1900: The New Age. A Guide to the Exhibition*, Cambridge: Whipple Museum of the History of Science, 1994.

Bennett, Tony, 'The Exhibitionary Complex', *New Formations* 4 (1988), 73–102.

——, *The Birth of the Museum: History, Theory, Politics*, London: Routledge, 1995.

Bensaude, Bernadette, 'En flânant dans les expos: Images de l'électricité', *Culture technique* 17 (1987), 89–93.

Berenson, Edward, 'Making a Colonial Culture? Empire and the French Public, 1880–1940', *French Politics, Culture and Society* 22.2 (2004), 127–49.

Berghoff, Hartmut, Barbara Korte, Ralf Schneider and Christopher Harvie, eds, *The Making of Modern Tourism: The Cultural History of the British Experience, 1600–2000*, Basingstoke: Palgrave Macmillan, 2002.

Berman, Marshall, *All That Is Solid Melts Into Air: The Experience of Modernity*, London: Verso, 1983.

Betts, Raymond F., 'The Allusion to Rome in British Imperialist Thought of the Late Nineteenth and Early Twentieth Centuries', *Victorian Studies* 15.2 (1971), 149–59.

Bezirksamt Treptow von Berlin and Heimatmuseum Treptow, eds, *Die Berliner Gewerbeausstellung 1896 in Bildern*, Berlin: Berliner Debatte, 1996.

——, *Die verhinderte Weltausstellung: Beiträge zur Berliner Gewerbeausstellung 1896*, Berlin: Berliner Debatte, 1996.

Biggeleben, Christof, 'Kontinuität von Bürgerlichkeit im Berliner Unternehmertum: Der Verein Berliner Kaufleute und Industrieller (1879–1961)', in *Die deutsche Wirtschaftselite im 20. Jahrhundert: Kontinuität und Mentalität*, ed. Volker Berghahn, Stefan Unger and Dieter Ziegler, Essen: Klartext, 2003, 241–74.

——, *Das 'Bollwerk des Bürgertums': Die Berliner Kaufmannschaft 1870–1920*, Munich: C. H. Beck, 2006.

Blackbourn, David, *A Sense of Place: New Directions in German History. The 1998 Annual Lecture of the German Historical Institute*, London: German Historical Institute, 1999.

Blanchard, Pascal and Sandrine Lemaire, eds, *Culture coloniale: La France conquise par son empire, 1871–1931*, Paris: Autrement, 2003.

——, *Culture coloniale en France: De la Révolution française à nos jours*, Paris: Autrement, 2008.

Blanchard, Pascal and Gilles Boetsch, *Marseilles, porte sud, 1905–2005*, Paris: La Découverte, 2005.

Blomeyer, Gerald R. and Barbara Tietze, 'Lunaparkkultur: Kleine Sozialgeschichte des großen Vergnügens', *Bauwelt* 12 (1986), 440–5.

Boberg, Jochen, Tilman Fichter and Eckhart Gillen, eds, *Die Metropole: Industriekultur in Berlin im 20. Jahrhundert*, Munich: C. H. Beck, 1986.

Bogdan, Robert, *Freak Show: Presenting Human Oddities for Amusement and Profit*, Chicago: University of Chicago Press, 1988.

Bohle-Heintzenberg, Sabine, 'Berlin und die Weltausstellung oder: Der Moabiter Ausstellungspark', in *Hülle und Fülle: Festschrift für Tilmann Buddensieg*, ed. Andreas Beyer, Vittorio Lampugnani and Gunter Schweikhart, Alfter: VDG, 1993, 63–81.

Bollenbeck, Georg, 'Industrialisierung und ästhetische Wahrnehmung: Bemerkungen zur Weltausstellung London 1851', in *Fortschrittsglaube und Dekadenzbewußtsein im Europa des 19. Jahrhunderts: Literatur – Kunst – Kulturgeschichte*, ed. Wolfgang Drost, Heidelberg: Winter, 1986, 289–98.

Bonnell, Andrew, '"Cheap and Nasty": German Goods, Socialism, and the 1876 Philadelphia World Fair', *International Review of Social History* 46 (2001), 207–26.

Böröcz, József, 'Travel-Capitalism: The Structure of Europe and the Advent of the Tourist', *Comparative Studies in Society and History* 34.4 (1992), 708–41.

Borges, Jorge Luis, 'On Rigor in Science', in *Dreamtigers*, Austin: University of Texas Press, 1964, 90.

Bosbach, Franz and John R. Davis, eds, *Die Weltausstellung von 1851 und ihre Folgen,* Munich: K. G. Saur, 2002.

Boschke, Friedrich L., 'Gästebuch der Weltausstellung Paris 1900', *Naturwissenschaftliche Rundschau* 38.6 (1985), 237–40.

Bouin, Philippe and Christian-Philippe Chanut, *Histoire française des foires et des expositions universelles*, Paris: Baudouin, 1980.

Bradford, Betty, 'The Brick Palace of 1862', *Architectural Review* 132 (1962), 15–21.

Braibant, Charles Maurice, *Histoire de la Tour Eiffel*, Paris: Plon, 1964.

Brain, Robert, *Going to the Fair: Readings in the Culture of Nineteenth-Century Exhibitions*, Cambridge: Whipple Museum of the History of Science, 1993.

——, 'Going to the Exhibition', in *The Physics of Empire: Public Lectures*, ed. Richard Staley, Cambridge: Whipple Museum of the History of Science, 1994, 113–42.

Braun, Hans-Joachim, 'Franz Reuleaux und der Technologietransfer zwischen Deutschland und Nordamerika am Ausgang des 19. Jahrhunderts', *Technikgeschichte* 48.2 (1981), 112–30.

Breckenridge, Carol A., 'The Aesthetics and Politics of Colonial Collecting: India at World Fairs', *Comparative Studies in Society and History* 31.2 (1989), 195–216.

Brewer, John, *The Pleasures of the Imagination: English Culture in the Eighteenth Century*, London: HarperCollins, 1997.

——, 'Histories, Exhibitions, and Collections: The Invention of National Heritage in Britain, 1770–1820', *Nationalismus vor dem Nationalismus?*, ed. Eckhart Hellmuth and Reinhard Stauber, Hamburg: Meiner, 1998, 11–22.

Brewer, John and Roy Porter, eds, *Consumption and the World of Goods*, London: Routledge, 1993.

Briesen, Detlef, *Berlin – die überschätzte Metropole: Über das System deutscher Hauptstädte von 1850 bis 1940*, Bonn: Bouvier, 1992.

——, *Warenhaus: Massenkonsum und Sozialmoral. Zur Geschichte der Konsumkritik im 20. Jahrhundert*, Frankfurt am Main: Campus, 2001.

Brooke, Michael Z., *Le Play: Engineer and Social Scientist. The Life and Work of Frédéric Le Play*, London: Longman, 1970.

Brown, Robert W., 'Albert Robida's Vieux Paris Exhibit: Art and Historical Re-Creation at the Paris World's Fair of 1900', in *A Yearbook of Interdisciplinary Studies in the Fine Arts*, ed. William E. Grim, vol. 2, Lewiston: Edwin Mellen, 1991, 421–45.

Brown, Julie K., *Contesting Images: Photography and the World's Columbian Exposition*, Tucson: University of Arizona Press, 1994.

——, *Making Culture Visible: The Public Display of Photography at Fairs, Expositions and Exhibitions in the United States, 1847–1900*, Amsterdam: Harwood, 2001.

Brunn, Gerhard and Jürgen Reulecke, eds, *Berlin: Blicke auf die deutsche Metropole*, Essen: Hobbing, 1989.

——, *Metropolis Berlin: Berlin als deutsche Hauptstadt im Vergleich europäischer Hauptstädte 1871–1939*, Bonn: Bouvier, 1992.

Burton, Antoinette, 'Making a Spectacle of Empire: Indian Travellers in Fin-de-Siècle London', *History Workshop Journal* 42 (1996), 127–46.

——, *At the Heart of the Empire: Indians and the Colonial Encounter in Late-Victorian Britain*, Berkeley: University of California Press, 1998.

Burton, Antoinette M., ed., *After the Imperial Turn: Thinking with and through the Nation*, Durham, NC: Duke University Press, 2003.

Buzard, James, *The Beaten Track: European Tourism, Literature, and the Ways to Culture, 1800–1918*, Oxford: Clarendon, 1993.

Cannadine, David, *Ornamentalism: How the British Saw Their Empire*, Harmondsworth: Penguin, 2001.

Carpenter, Kenneth E., 'European Industrial Exhibitions before 1851 and their Publications', *Technology and Culture* 13 (1972), 465–86.

Carré, Patrice A., 'Expositions et modernité: Electricité et communication dans les expositions parisiennes de 1867 à 1900', *Romantisme* 65.3 (1989), 37–48.

Cate, Philip Dennis, ed., *The Eiffel Tower: A Tour de Force. Its Centennial Exhibition*, New York: Grolier Club, 1989.

Çelik, Zeynep, *Displaying the Orient: Architecture of Islam at Nineteenth-Century World's Fairs*, Berkeley: University of California Press, 1992.

Çelik, Zeynep and Leila Kinney, 'Ethnography and Exhibitionism at the *Expositions universelles*', *Assemblage* 13 (1990), 34–59.

Çelik, Zeynep, Diane G. Favro and Richard Ingersoll, eds, *Streets: Critical Perspectives on Public Space*, Berkeley: University of California Press, 1994.

Chafer, Tony and Amanda Sackur, eds, *Promoting the Colonial Idea: Propaganda and Visions of Empire in France*, Basingstoke: Palgrave Macmillan, 2002.

Chakrabarty, Dipesh, *Provincializing Europe: Postcolonial Thought and Historical Difference*, Princeton: Princeton University Press, 2000.

Chalkley, Brian and Stephen Essex, 'Urban Development through Hosting International Events: A History of the Olympic Games', *Planning Perspectives* 14.4 (1999), 369–94.

Charle, Christophe and Daniel Roche, eds, *Capitales culturelles, capitales symboliques: Paris et les expériences européennes XVIIIe-XXe siècles*, Paris: Publications de la Sorbonne, 2002.

Charle, Christophe, *Paris fin de siècle: Culture et politique*, Paris: du Seuil, 1998.

Chartier, Roger, *Cultural History: Between Practices and Representations*, Ithaca, NY: Cornell University Press, 1988.

——, 'Le Monde comme représentation', *Annales ESC* 44.6 (1989), 1505–20.

——, *On the Edge of the Cliff: History, Language, and Practices*, Baltimore: Johns Hopkins University Press, 1997.

Clark, T. J., *The Painting of Modern Life: Paris in the Art of Manet and His Followers*, Princeton: Princeton University Press, 1984.

Clastres, Patrick, ed., *Pierre de Coubertin: La réforme sociale par l'éducation et le sport*, Paris: Archives de la Science sociale, 2003 [*Les Etudes Sociales* 137].

Clendinning, Anne, 'Exhibiting a Nation: Canada at the British Empire Exhibition, 1924–1925', *Histoire sociale/Social History* 39 (2006), 79–108.

Cleve, Ingeborg, *Geschmack, Kunst und Konsum: Kulturpolitik als Wirtschaftspolitik in Frankreich und in Württemberg (1805–1845)*, Göttingen: Vandenhoeck & Ruprecht, 1996.

——, 'Dem Fortschritt entgegen: Ausstellungen und Museen im Modernisierungsprozeß des Königreichs Württemberg (1806–1918)', *Jahrbuch für Wirtschaftsgeschichte* (2000), 149–69.

Cochrane, Allan and Andrew Jonas, 'Reimagining Berlin: World City, National Capital or Ordinary Place?', *European Urban and Regional Studies* 6.2 (1999), 145–64.

Cockx, August and J. Lemmens, *Les Expositions universelles et internationales en Belgique de 1885 à 1958*, Bruxelles: Editorial Office, 1958.

Cohen, Evelyne, *Paris dans l'imaginaire national de l'entre-deux-guerres*, Paris: Publications de la Sorbonne, 1999.

Cohen, Jean-Louis, 'Musée des Arts africains et océaniens', in *Paris: Architecture 1900–2000*, ed. Jean-Louis Cohen and Monique Eleb, Paris: Editions Norma, 2000, 74–81.

Cohen, Scott, 'The Empire from the Street: Virginia Woolf, Wembley, and Imperial Monuments', *Modern Fiction Studies* 50.1 (2004), 85–109.

Colby, Reginald, 'Noble Origins of Earl's Court', *Country Life* 144 (14 November 1968), 1267–73.

Conekin, Becky E., *The Autobiography of a Nation: The 1951 Festival of Britain*, Manchester: Manchester University Press, 2003.

Conklin, Alice L., *A Mission to Civilize: The Republican Idea of Empire in France and West Africa, 1895–1930*, Stanford: Stanford University Press, 1997.

Coombes, Annie E., 'The Franco-British Exhibition: Packaging Empire in Edwardian England', in *The Edwardian Era*, ed. Jan Beckett and Deborah Cherry, Oxford: Phaidon, 1987, 152–66.

——, *Reinventing Africa: Museums, Material Culture and Popular Imagination in Late Victorian and Edwardian England*, New Haven: Yale University Press, 1994.

Corbey, Raymond, 'Ethnographic Showcases, 1870–1930', *Cultural Anthropology* 8.3 (1993), 338–69.

Cornelissen, Christoph, 'Die politische und kulturelle Repräsentation des Deutschen Reiches auf den Weltausstellungen des 19. Jahrhunderts', *Geschichte in Wissenschaft und Unterricht* 52.3 (2001), 148–61.

Cornick, Martyn, '"Putting the Seal on the *Entente*": The Franco-British Exhibition, London, May–October 1908', *Franco-British Studies* 35 (2004), 133–44.

Cornilliet-Watelet, Sylvie, 'Le Musée des Colonies et le Musée de la France d'Outre-Mer (1931–1960)', in *Coloniales 1920–1940*, ed. Emmanuel Bréon and Michèle Lefrançois, Boulogne-Billancourt: Musée Municipal de Boulogne-Billancourt, 1989, 83–94.

Crary, Jonathan, *Techniques of the Observer: On Vision and Modernity in the Nineteenth Century*, Cambridge, MA: MIT Press, 1990.

Crinson, Mark, *Modern Architecture and the End of Empire*, Aldershot: Ashgate, 2003.

Crossick, Geoffrey and Serge Jaumain, eds, *Cathedrals of Consumption: The European Department Store, 1850–1939*, Aldershot: Ashgate, 1999.

Culler, Jonathan, 'Semiotics of Tourism', *American Journal of Semiotics* 1.1/2 (1981), 127–40.

Daeninckx, Didier, *Cannibale*, Lagrasse: Verdier, 1998.

Daniloski, Stan, *The World's Fair and Exposition Information and Reference Guide*: http://www.earthstation9.com/worlds_2.htm (accessed 10 March 2009).

Das Sowjetische Ehrenmal in Berlin-Treptow, Berlin: n.p., 1976.

Dauphiné, Joël, *Canaques de la Nouvelle-Calédonie à Paris en 1931: De la case au zoo*, Paris: L'Harmattan, 1998.

Davis, John R., 'From the Great Exhibition to EXPO 2000: The History of Display', *Bulletin of the German Historical Institute London* 22.2 (2000), 7–19.

De Cauter, Lieven, 'The Panoramic Ecstasy: On World Exhibitions and the Disintegration of Experience', *Theory, Culture and Society* 10.4 (1993), 1–23.

Debord, Guy, *The Society of the Spectacle*, New York: Zone, 1995.

——, *Comments on the Society of the Spectacle*, London: Verso, 1998.

Debusmann, Robert and János Riesz, eds, *Kolonialausstellungen – Begegnungen mit Afrika?* Frankfurt am Main: IKO, 1995.

Dell, Simon, 'The Consumer and the Making of the *Exposition Internationale des Arts Décoratifs et Industriels Modernes*, 1907–1925', *Journal of Design History* 12.4 (1999), 311–25.

Della Coletta, Cristina, *World's Fairs Italian-Style: The Great Expositions in Turin and Their Narratives, 1860–1915*, Toronto: University of Toronto Press, 2006.

Demissie, Fassil, 'Displaying Race and Exhibiting Empires in the 1930s', *Social Identities* 9.17 (2003), 127–38.

Dennis, Richard, *Cities in Modernity: Representations and Productions of Metropolitan Space, 1840–1930*, Cambridge: Cambridge University Press, 2008.

Derex, Jean Michel, *Histoire du Bois de Vincennes: La forêt du roi et le bois du peuple de Paris*, Paris: L'Harmattan, 1997.

Dittrich, Lothar and Annelore Rieke-Müller, *Carl Hagenbeck (1844–1913): Tierhandel und Schaustellungen im Deutschen Kaiserreich*, Frankfurt am Main: Peter Lang, 1998.

Dittrich, Lothar, Dietrich von Engelhardt and Annelore Rieke-Müller, eds, *Die Kulturgeschichte des Zoos*, Berlin: VWB, 2000.

Doctorow, E. L., *World's Fair*, New York: Random House, 1985.

Dörflinger, Johannes, 'Stadtpläne von Wien und Pläne der Wiener Weltausstellung aus dem Jahr 1873', *Studien zur Wiener Geschichte* 47/48 (1991–92), 123–39.

Dreesbach, Anne, *'Gezähmte Wilde': Die Zurschaustellung 'exotischer' Menschen in Deutschland 1870–1940*, Frankfurt am Main: Campus, 2005.

Dresdner Geschichtsverein e.V., ed., *Große Ausstellungen um 1900 und in den zwanziger Jahren*, Dresden: Dresdner Hefte, 2000.

Driver, Felix, 'Geography's Empire: Histories of Geographical Knowledge', *Environment and Planning D: Society and Space* 10/11 (1992), 23–40.

Driver, Felix and David Gilbert, 'Heart of Empire? Landscape, Space and Performance in Imperial London', *Environment and Planning D: Society and Space* 16 (1998), 11–28.

——, eds, *Imperial Cities: Landscape, Display and Identity*, Manchester: Manchester University Press, 1999.

Durosoy, Maurice, *Lyautey: Maréchal de France, 1854–1934*, Paris: Lavauzelle, 1984.

Dyos, H. J. and Michael Wolff, eds, *The Victorian City: Images and Realities*, London: Routledge & Kegan Paul, 1973.

Eade, John, *Placing London: From Imperial Capital to Global City*, Oxford: Berghahn, 2001.

Eco, Umberto, 'A Theory of Expositions', in *Travels in Hyperreality: Essays*, New York: Harcourt Brace Jovanovich, 1986, 291–307.

Eisenberg, Christiane, 'Die kulturelle Moderne – eine Schöpfung der Großstadt? Paris und London in sozialwissenschaftlicher und historischer Perspektive', in *Attraktion Großstadt um 1900: Individuum – Gemeinschaft – Masse*, ed. Ortrud Gutjahr, Berlin: Spitz, 2001, 11–36.

——, 'The Culture of Modernity: London and Paris around 1900', in *Representation of British Cities: The Transformation of Urban Space, 1700–2000*, ed. Andreas Fahrmeir and Elfie Rembold, Berlin: Philo, 2003, 130–48.

Emery, Elizabeth, 'Protecting the Past: Albert Robida and the *Vieux Paris* Exhibit at the 1900 World's Fair', *Journal of European Studies* 35.1 (2005), 65–85.

Escher, Felix, 'Berlin und seine Ausstellungen: Zur Geschichte des Messegeländes unter dem Funkturm', in *Von der Residenz zur City: 275 Jahre Charlottenburg*, ed. Wolfgang Ribbe, Berlin: Colloquium Verlag, 1980, 427–57.

Espuche, A. G., M. Guardia, F. J. Monclús and J. L. Oyón, 'Modernization and Urban Beautification: The 1888 Barcelona World's Fair', *Planning Perspectives* 6.2 (1991), 139–59.

Essex, Stephen and Brian Chalkley, 'Olympic Games: Catalyst of Urban Change', *Leisure Studies* 17.3 (1998), 187–206.

L'Estoile, Benoît de, 'From the Colonial Exhibition to the Museum of Man: An Alternative Genealogy of French Anthropology', *Social Anthropology* 11.3 (2003), 341–61.

Evans, Martin, 'Projecting a Greater France', *History Today* 50.2 (2000), 18–25.

Evans, Martin and Amanda Sackur, eds, *Empire and Culture: The French Experience, 1830–1940*, Basingstoke: Palgrave Macmillan, 2004.

Ezra, Elizabeth, 'The Colonial Look: Exhibiting Empire in the 1930s', *Contemporary French Civilization* 19.1 (1995), 33–49.

——, *The Colonial Unconscious: Race and Culture in Interwar France*, Ithaca, NY: Cornell University Press, 2000.

Fabian, Johannes, *Time and the Other: How Anthropology Makes its Object*, New York: Columbia University Press, 1983.

Felber, Ulrike, Elke Krasny and Christian Rapp, *Smart Exports: Österreich auf den Weltausstellungen 1851–2000*, Vienna: Christian Brandstätter, 2000.

Feldman, David and Gareth Stedman Jones, eds, *Metropolis London: Histories and Representations since 1800*, London: Routledge, 1989.

Ferguson, Eugene S., 'Technical Museums and International Exhibitions', *Technology and Culture* 6.1 (1965), 30–46.

Fesche, Klaus, 'Räumliche Effekte von Weltausstellungen', *Siedlungsforschung* 21 (2003), 145–57.

Findling, John E. and Kimberly D. Pelle, eds, *Encyclopedia of the Modern Olympic Movement*, Westport: Greenwood, 2004.

——, *Encyclopedia of World's Fairs and Expositions*, Jefferson: McFarland, 2008.

Finger, Ch. Ehrhard, *Die Geschichte der Weltausstellungen und die Rolle der Foto- und Kinematografie*, Bitterfeld: Industrie- und Filmmuseum Wolfen e.V., 2000.

Fischer, Claude S., 'Urbanism as a Way of Life: A Review and Agenda', *Sociological Methods and Analysis* 1.2 (1972), 187–242.

Fletcher, F. A. and A. D. Brooks, *British Exhibitions and their Postcards*, 2 vols, London: n.p., 1978–79.

Forgan, Sophie, 'Festivals of Science and the Two Cultures: Science, Design and Display in the Festival of Britain, 1951', *British Journal for the History of Science* 31.2 (1998), 217–40.

Forgey, Elisa, '"Die große Negertrommel der kolonialen Werbung": Die Deutsche Afrika-Schau 1935–1943', *WerkstattGeschichte* 9 (1994), 25–33.

Foucault, Michel, 'Of Other Spaces', *Diacritics* (1986), 22–7.

Fride, Cécile, 'L'Organisation spatiale de trois fêtes nationales révolutionnaires: L'espace et le temps gouvernés', *Revue d'histoire du théâtre* 162.2 (1989), 107–47.

Frisby, David, *Georg Simmel*, Chichester: Ellis Horwood, 1984.

Fritzsche, Peter, *Reading Berlin 1900*, Cambridge, MA: Harvard University Press, 1996.

Fuchs, Eckhardt, ed., *Weltausstellungen im 19. Jahrhundert*, Leipzig: Leipziger Universitätsverlag, 1999 [*Comparativ* 9.5/6].

Furlough, Ellen, 'Making Mass Vacations: Tourism and Consumer Culture in France, 1930s to 1970s', *Comparative Studies in Society and History* 40.2 (1998), 247–86.

——, '*Une Leçon des choses*: Tourism, Empire, and the Nation in Interwar France', *French Historical Studies* 25.3 (2002), 441–73.

Galopin, Marcel, *Les Expositions internationales au XXe siècle et le Bureau International des Expositions*, Paris: L'Harmattan, 1997.

Geppert, Alexander C. T., 'Ausstellungsmüde: Deutsche Großausstellungsprojekte und ihr Scheitern, 1880–1913', *Wolkenkuckucksheim: Internationale Zeitschrift für Theorie und Wissenschaft der Architektur* 5.1 (2000).

——, 'Exponierte Identitäten? Imperiale Ausstellungen, ihre Besucher und das Problem der Wahrnehmung, 1870–1930', in *Nationalismen in Europa: West- und Osteuropa im Vergleich*, ed. Ulrike von Hirschhausen and Jörn Leonhard, Göttingen: Wallstein, 2002, 181–203.

——, 'True Copies: Time and Space Travels at British Imperial Exhibitions, 1880–1930', in *The Making of Modern Tourism: The Cultural History of the British Experience, 1600–2000*, ed. Hartmut Berghoff, Barbara Korte, Ralf Schneider and Christopher Harvie, Basingstoke: Palgrave Macmillan, 2002, 223–48.

——, 'Welttheater: Die Geschichte des europäischen Ausstellungswesens im 19. und 20. Jahrhundert. Ein Forschungsbericht', *Neue Politische Literatur* 47.1 (2002), 10–61.

——, 'Luoghi, città, prospettive: Le esposizioni e l'urbanistica *fin-de-siècle*', *Memoria e Ricerca* 12 (2003), 115–36.

——, 'Città brevi: Storia, storiografia e teoria delle pratiche espositive europee, 1851–2000', *Memoria e Ricerca* 17 (2004), 7–18.

——, 'Weltstadt für einen Sommer: Die Berliner Gewerbeausstellung 1896 im europäischen Kontext', *Mitteilungen des Vereins für die Geschichte Berlins* 103.1 (2007), 434–48.

——, 'Wembley, 1924–1925: British Empire Exhibition', in *Encyclopedia of World's Fairs and Expositions*, ed. John E. Findling and Kimberly D. Pelle, Jefferson: McFarland, 2008, 230–6.

——, 'Die normative Kraft des Flüchtigen: Exponierungen des Globalen in der Welt der Weltausstellungen, 1851–1900', in *Das Planetarische: Kultur – Technik – Medien im post-globalen Zeitalter*, ed. Ulrike Bergermann, Isabell Otto and Gabriele Schabacher, Munich: Fink, 2010, 81–96.

Geppert, Alexander C. T. and Massimo Baioni, eds, *Esposizioni in Europa tra Otto e Novecento: Spazi, organizzazione, rappresentazioni*, Milan: FrancoAngeli, 2004 [*Memoria e Ricerca* 17].

Geppert, Alexander C. T., Jean Coffey and Tammy Lau, *International Exhibitions, Expositions Universelles and World's Fairs, 1851–2005: A Bibliography*, 3rd edn, Berlin/Fresno, 2006: http://www.fresnostate.edu/library/subjectresources/specialcollections/worldfairs/Expo Bibliography3ed.pdf (accessed 22 May 2013).

Geppert, Alexander C. T., Uffa Jensen and Jörn Weinhold, eds, *Ortsgespräche: Raum und Kommunikation im 19. und 20. Jahrhundert*, Bielefeld: transcript, 2005.

Gerbod, Paul, 'Les Touristes français à l'étranger (1870–1914)', *Revue d'Histoire Moderne et Contemporaine* 30 (1983), 283–97.

——, 'Le Tourisme britannique au France au XXième siècle', *L'Information Géographique* 52 (1988), 26–33.

Gernsheim, Helmut and Alison, *L. J. M. Daguerre: The History of the Diorama and the Daguerreotype*, New York: Dover, 1969.

Gessner, Dieter, 'Industrialisierung, staatliche Gewerbepolitik und die Anfänge und Entwicklung des industriellen Ausstellungswesens in Deutschland', *Kunstpolitik und Kunstförderung im Kaiserreich: Kunst im Wandel der Sozial- und Wirtschaftsgeschichte*, ed. Ekkehard Mai, Hans Pohl and Stephan Waetzoldt, Berlin: Mann, 1982, 131–48.

Giedion, Sigfried, 'Sind Ausstellungen noch lebensfähig?', *Schweizerische Bauzeitung* 109.7 (1937), 73–7 ['Can Expositions Survive?', *Architectural Forum* 69 (1938), 7–11].

——, *Space, Time, and Architecture: The Growth of a New Tradition*, 13th edn, Cambridge, MA: Harvard University Press, 1997 [1941].

Gilbert, David, '"London in all its Glory – or How to Enjoy London": Guidebook Representations of Imperial London', *Journal of Historical Geography* 25.3 (1999), 179–97.

——, '*London of the Future*: The Metropolis Reimagined after the Great War', *Journal of British Studies* 43.1 (2004), 91–166.

Gilbert, David and Felix Driver, 'Capital and Empire: Geographies of Imperial London', *GeoJournal* 51 (2001), 23–32.

Gilbert, James, *Perfect Cities: Chicago's Utopias of 1893*, Chicago: University of Chicago Press, 1991.

Girardet, Raoul, 'L'Apothéose de la "plus grande France": L'Idée coloniale devant l'opinion française (1930–1935), *Revue Française de Science Politique* 18.6 (1968), 1085–114.

——, *L'idée coloniale en France de 1871 à 1962*, Paris: La Table Ronde, 1972.

Goerg, Odile, 'Exotisme tricolore et imaginaire alsacien: L'Exposition coloniale, agricole et industrielle de Strasbourg en 1924', *Revue d'Alsace* 120 (1994), 239–68.

Goldmann, Stefan, 'Wilde in Europa: Aspekte und Orte ihrer Zurschaustellung', in *Wir und die Wilden: Einblicke in eine kannibalische Beziehung*, ed. Thomas Theye, Reinbek: Rowohlt, 1985, 243–69.

——, 'Zur Rezeption der Völkerausstellungen um 1900', in *Exotische Welten, Europäische Phantasien*, ed. Hermann Pollig, Stuttgart: Edition Cantz, 1987, 88–93.

Gomaine, Jean-Pierre, 'L'Héritage colonial: Souvenirs d'une exposition', *Etudes* (1981), 745–60.

Gouda, Frances, *Dutch Culture Overseas: Colonial Practice in the Netherlands Indies, 1900–1942*, Amsterdam: Amsterdam University Press, 1995.

Goutalier, Régine, 'Les Etats généraux du féminisme à l'Exposition coloniale, 30–31 mai 1931', *Revue d'Histoire Moderne et Contemporaine* 36 (1989), 266–86.

Grasskamp, Walter, *Museumsgründer und Museumsstürmer: Zur Sozialgeschichte des Kunstmuseums*, Munich: C. H. Beck, 1981.

Greater London Council, ed., *The Museums Area of South Kensington and Westminster*, London: Athlone, 1975 [*Survey of London*, vol. 38].

Green, Abigail, 'Representing Germany? The *Zollverein* at the World Exhibitions, 1851–1862', *Journal of Modern History* 75.4 (2003), 836–63.

Greenhalgh, Paul, 'Art, Politics and Society at the Franco-British Exhibition of 1908', *Art History* 8.4 (1985), 434–52.

——, *Ephemeral Vistas: The Expositions Universelles, Great Exhibitions and World's Fairs, 1851–1939*, Manchester: Manchester University Press, 1988.

——, 'Education, Entertainment and Politics: Lessons from the Great International Exhibitions', in *The New Museology*, ed. Peter Vergo, London: Reaktion, 1989, 74–98.

Gregory, Brendan Edward, *The Spectacle Plays and Exhibitions of Imre Kiralfy, 1887–1914*, PhD diss., University of Manchester, 1988.

Gregory, Derek, *Geographical Imaginations*, Oxford: Basil Blackwell, 1994.

——, 'The Geographical Discourse of Modernity: Hettner Lecture 1997', in *Explorations in Critical Human Geography*, Heidelberg: Geographisches Institut der Universität, 1998, 45–70.

Grewe, Cordula, ed., *Die Schau des Fremden: Ausstellungskonzepte zwischen Kunst, Kommerz und Wissenschaft*, Stuttgart: Steiner, 2006.

Gronberg, Tag, 'Cascades of Light: The 1925 Paris Exhibition as "ville lumière"', *Apollo* 142 (1995), 12–16.

——, *Designs on Modernity: Exhibiting the City in 1920s Paris*, Manchester: Manchester University Press, 1998.

Großbölting, Thomas, 'Die Ordnung der Wirtschaft: Kulturelle Repräsentation in den deutschen Industrie- und Gewerbeausstellungen des 19. Jahrhunderts', in *Wirtschaftsgeschichte als Kulturgeschichte: Dimensionen eines Perspektivenwechsels*, ed. Hartmut Berghoff and Jakob Vogel, Frankfurt am Main: Campus, 2004, 377–403.

——, *'Im Reich der Arbeit': Die Repräsentation gesellschaftlicher Ordnung in den deutschen Industrie- und Gewerbeausstellungen 1790–1914*, Munich: Oldenbourg, 2008.

Gründer, Horst, 'Indianer, Afrikaner und Südseebewohner in Europa: Zur Vorgeschichte der Völkerschauen und Kolonialausstellungen', *Jahrbuch für Europäische Überseegeschichte* 3 (2003), 65–88.

Grunow, Alfred, *Der Kaiser und die Kaiserstadt*, Berlin: Haude & Spener, 1970.

Gugerli, David, 'Technikbewertung zwischen Öffentlichkeit und Expertengemeinschaft: Zur Rolle der Frankfurter elektrotechnischen Ausstellung von 1891 für die Elektrifizierung der Schweiz', in *Kontinuität und Krise: Sozialer Wandel als Lernprozess*, ed. Andreas Ernst, Zurich: Chronos, 1994, 139–60.

Hale, Dana S., *Races on Display: French Representations of Colonized Peoples 1886–1940*, Bloomington: Indiana University Press, 2008.

Hall, Catherine, 'Cities of Empire', *Journal of Urban History* 27.2 (2001), 193–9.

Haltern, Utz, *Die Londoner Weltausstellung von 1851: Ein Beitrag zur Geschichte der bürgerlich-industriellen Gesellschaft im 19. Jahrhundert*, Münster: Aschendorff, 1971.

——, 'Die "Welt als Schaustellung": Zur Funktion und Bedeutung der internationalen Industrieausstellung im 19. und 20. Jahrhundert', *Vierteljahrsschrift für Sozial- und Wirtschaftsgeschichte* 60.1 (1973), 1–40.

Hannerz, Ulf, *Exploring the City: Inquiries Toward an Urban Anthropology*, New York: Columbia University Press, 1980.

Harbsmeier, Michael, 'Schauspiel Europa: Die außereuropäische Entdeckung Europas im 19. Jahrhundert am Beispiel afrikanischer Texte', *Historische Anthropologie* 2.3 (1994), 331–50.

Harbusch, Ute, *Mit Dampf und Phantasie: Max Eyth – Schriftsteller und Ingenieur (1836–1906)*, Kirchheim unter Teck: Städtisches Museum Kirchheim, 2006.

Harris, Joseph, *The Tallest Tower: Eiffel and the Belle Epoque*, Washington, DC: Regnery Gateway, 1975.

Harris, Neil, *Humbug: The Art of P. T. Barnum*, Boston: Little Brown, 1973.

——, *Cultural Excursions: Marketing Appetites and Cultural Tastes in Modern America*, Chicago: University of Chicago Press, 1990.

——, 'Memory and the White City', in *Grand Illusions: Chicago's World Fairs of 1893*, ed. Neil Harris, Wim de Wit, James Gilbert and Robert W. Rydell, Chicago: Chicago Historical Society, 1993, 1–40.

Harvey, David, *The Urban Experience*, Oxford: Basil Blackwell, 1989.

——, *Paris, Capital of Modernity*, London: Routledge, 2003.

Harvey, Penelope, *Hybrids of Modernity: Anthropology, the Nation State and the Universal Exhibition*, New York: Routledge, 1996.

Haupt, Heinz-Gerhard, *Konsum und Handel: Europa im 19. und 20. Jahrhundert*, Göttingen: Vandenhoeck & Ruprecht, 2002.

Häussermann, Hartmut and Walter Siebel, eds, *Festivalisierung der Stadtpolitik: Stadtentwicklung durch große Projekte*, Opladen: Westdeutscher Verlag, 1993.

Henningham, Stephen, '"The Best Specimens in all our Colonial Domain": New Caledonian Melanesians in Europe, 1931–32', *Journal of Pacific History* 29.2 (1994), 172–87.

Herbert, James D., *Paris 1937: Worlds on Exhibition*, Ithaca, NY: Cornell University Press, 1998.

Herzfeld, Hans, 'Berlin als Kaiserstadt und Reichshauptstadt', in *Das Hauptstadtproblem in der Geschichte: Festgabe zum 90. Geburtstag Friedrich Meineckes. Gewidmet vom Friedrich-Meinecke-Institut an der Freien Universität Berlin*, Tübingen: Max Niemeyer, 1952, 141–70.

Hewitt, Martin, 'Why the Notion of Victorian Britain *Does* Make Sense', *Victorian Studies* 48.3 (2006), 395–438.

Hewlett, Geoffrey, ed., *A History of Wembley*, London: Brent Library Service, 1979.

Higonnet, Patrick, *Paris: Capital of the World*, Cambridge, MA: Harvard University Press, 2002.

Hill, Jeff and Francesco Varrasi, 'Creating Wembley: The Construction of a National Monument', *The Sports Historian* 17.2 (1997), 28–43.

Hoage, R. J. and William A. Deiss, eds, *New World, New Animals: From Menagerie to Zoological Park in the Nineteenth Century*, Baltimore: Johns Hopkins University Press, 1996.

Hochreiter, Walter, *Vom Musentempel zum Lernort: Zur Sozialgeschichte deutscher Museen 1800–1914*, Darmstadt: Wissenschaftliche Buchgesellschaft, 1994.

Hodeir, Catherine and Michel Pierre, *L'Exposition coloniale*, Bruxelles: Complexe, 1991.

Hodeir, Catherine, 'Decentering the Gaze at French Colonial Exhibitions', in *Images and Empires: Visuality in Colonial and Postcolonial Africa*, ed. Paul Landau and Deborah D. Kaspin, Berkeley: University of California Press, 2002, 233–52.

Hodgkins, David, *The Second Railway King: The Life and Times of Sir Edward Watkin, 1819–1901*, Whitchurch, Cardiff: Merton Priory Press, 2001.

Hoffenberg, Peter H., *An Empire on Display: English, Indian, and Australian Exhibitions from the Crystal Palace to the Great War*, Berkeley: University of California Press, 2001.

Hoffmann, Andreas, 'Das Ausstellungsgelände am Funkturm', in *Geschichtslandschaft Berlin: Orte und Ereignisse*, ed. Helmut Engel, Stefi Jersch-Wenzel and Wilhelm Treue, vol 1.2: *Charlottenburg: Der neue Westen*, Berlin: Nicolai, 1985, 98–114.

Hofmann, Werner, *Das irdische Paradies: Motive und Ideen des 19. Jahrhunderts*, Munich: Prestel, 1960.

Homo, Roger, 'Lyautey et l'Exposition coloniale internationale de 1931', *Comptes-rendus mensuels des séances de l'Académie des Sciences d'Outre-mer* 21.4 (1961), 185–8.

Honold, Alexander and Klaus R. Scherpe, eds, *Mit Deutschland um die Welt: Eine Kulturgeschichte des Fremden in der Kolonialzeit*, Stuttgart: Metzler, 2004.

Hotta-Lister, Ayako, *The Japan-British Exhibition of 1910: Gateway to the Island Empire of the East*, Richmond, Surrey: Japan Library, 1999.

Hudson, Derek and Kenneth W. Luckhurst, *The Royal Society of Arts*, London: Murray, 1954.

Hughes, Deborah L., 'Kenya, India and the British Empire Exhibition of 1924', *Race and Class* 47.4 (2006), 66–85.

Hundt, Wolfgang J., *Die Wandlung im deutschen Messe- und Ausstellungswesen im 19. Jahrhundert und seine Weiterentwicklung bis zum Jahre 1933 unter besonderer Berücksichtigung der Messen in Frankfurt am Main und Leipzig: Von der Warenmesse zur Mustermesse*, PhD diss., Universität Frankfurt am Main, 1957.

Hütsch, Volker, *Der Münchner Glaspalast 1854–1931: Geschichte und Bedeutung*, Munich: Moos, 1980.

Hyde, Ralph, 'Mr. Wyld's Monster Globe', *History Today* 29 (1970), 118–23.

——, *Printed Maps of Victorian London, 1851–1900*, London: Dawson, 1975.

Jaworski, Rudolf, 'Alte Postkarten als kulturhistorische Quellen', *Geschichte in Wissenschaft und Unterricht* 51.2 (2000), 88–102.

Jay, Robert, 'Taller than Eiffel's Tower: The London and Chicago Tower Projects, 1889–1894', *Journal of the Society of Architectural Historians* 46.2 (1987), 145–56.

Jazbinsek, Dietmar, 'The Metropolis and the Mental Life of Georg Simmel: On the History of an Antipathy', *Journal of Urban History* 30.1 (2003), 102–25.

Jenkins, Frank I., 'Harbingers of Eiffel's Tower', *Journal of the Society of Architectural Historians* 16.4 (1957), 22–8.

Jenkins, Rebecca, *The First London Olympics, 1908*, London: Piatkus, 2008.

Jennings, Eric T., 'Visions and Representations of French Empire', *Journal of Modern History* 77.3 (2005), 701–21.

Johnson, Nichola, 'Briton, Boer and Black in Savage South Africa', in *Museums and the Appropriation of Culture*, ed. Susan Pearce, Athlantic Highlands: Athlone, 1994, 174–97.

Joll, James, 'Die Großstadt – Symbol des Fortschritts oder der Dekadenz?', in *Im Banne der Metropolen: Berlin und London in den zwanziger Jahren*, ed. Peter Alter, Göttingen: Vandenhoeck & Ruprecht, 1993, 23–39.

Jones, Colin, *Paris: Biography of a City*, London: Penguin, 2004.

Jones, Robert W., '"The Sight of Creatures Strange to our Clime": London Zoo and the Consumption of the Exotic', *Journal of Victorian Culture* 2.1 (1997), 1–26.

Jordan, David, *Transforming Paris: The Life and Labors of Baron Haussmann*, New York: Free Press, 1995.

——, 'Haussmann and *Haussmannisation*: The Legacy for Paris', *French Historical Studies* 27.1 (2004), 87–113.

Jungk, Robert, 'Die Weltausstellung als moralische Anstalt: Ein Bericht', *Der Monat* 10 (1958), 3–7.

——, 'Soll man die Weltausstellungen abschaffen?', *Die Zeit* (27 October 1967), 60.

Kaiser, Wolfram, 'Vive la France! Vive la République? The Cultural Construction of French Identity at the World Exhibitions in Paris 1855–1900', *National Identities* 1.3 (1999), 227–44.

——, 'Die Welt im Dorf: Weltausstellungen von London 1851 bis Hannover 2000', *Aus Politik und Zeitgeschichte* B 22/23 (2000), 3–10.

——, 'Cultural Transfer of Free Trade at the World Exhibitions, 1851–1862', *Journal of Modern History* 77.3 (2005), 563–90.

Kalb, Christine, *Weltausstellungen im Wandel der Zeit und ihre infrastrukturellen Auswirkungen auf Stadt und Region*, Frankfurt am Main: Peter Lang, 1994.

Karp, Ivan and Steven D. Lavine, eds, *Exhibiting Cultures: The Poetics and Politics of Museum Display*, Washington, DC: Smithsonian Institution Press, 1991.

Kaschuba, Wolfgang, 'Erkundung der Moderne: Bürgerliches Reisen nach 1900', *Zeitschrift für Volkskunde* 87 (1991), 29–52.

——, *Die Überwindung der Distanz: Zeit und Raum in der europäischen Moderne*, Frankfurt am Main: Fischer, 2004.

Kay, Alison C., 'Villas, Values and the *Crystal Palace Company*, c.1852–1911', *The London Journal* 33.1 (2008), 21–39.

Kearns, Gerry and Chris Philo, eds, *Selling Places: The City as Cultural Capital, Past and Present*, Oxford: Pergamon, 1993.

Kiecol, Daniel, *Selbstbild und Image zweier europäischer Metropolen: Paris und Berlin zwischen 1900 und 1930*, Frankfurt am Main: Peter Lang, 2001.

Kinchin, Perilla and Juliet Kinchin, *Glasgow's Great Exhibitions: 1888, 1901, 1911, 1938, 1988*, Wenlebury, Bicester: White Cockade, 1988.

Kinser, Samuel, 'Chronotopes and Catastrophes: The Cultural History of Mikhail Bakhtin', *Journal of Modern History* 56.2 (1984), 301–10.

Klein, Alexander, *EXPOSITUM: Zum Verhältnis von Ausstellung und Wirklichkeit*, Bielefeld: transcript, 2004.

Knight, Donald R., *The Exhibitions: Great White City, Shepherds Bush, London. 70th Anniversary 1908–1978*, New Barnet: n.p., 1978.

Knight, Donald R. and Alan D. Sabey, *The Lion Roars at Wembley: British Empire Exhibition 60th Anniversary 1924–1925*, London: n.p., 1984.

Koch, Georg Friedrich, *Die Kunstausstellung: Ihre Geschichte von den Anfängen bis zum Ausgang des 18. Jahrhunderts*, Berlin: de Gruyter, 1967.

——, 'Die Bauten der Industrie-, Gewerbe- und Kunst-Ausstellung in Düsseldorf 1902 in der Geschiche der Ausstellungsarchitektur', in *Kunstpolitik und Kunstförderung im Kaiserreich: Kunst im Wandel der Sozial- und Wirtschaftsgeschichte*, ed. Ekkehard Mai, Hans Pohl and Stephan Waetzoldt, Berlin: Mann, 1982, 149–65.

Kohle, Hubertus, 'Der Eiffelturm: Sozialgeschichtliche Aspekte eines Jahrhundert-Bauwerks', *Kunsthistorische Arbeitsblätter* 3 (2001), 5–14.

Korn, Oliver, *Hanseatische Gewerbeausstellungen im 19. Jahrhundert: Republikanische Selbstdarstellung und regionale Wirtschaftsförderung*, Opladen: Leske & Budrich, 1999.

Körner, Hans-Michael and Katharina Weigand, eds, *Hauptstadt: Historische Perspektiven eines deutschen Themas*, Munich: dtv, 1995.

Koshar, Rudy, '"What Ought to be Seen": Tourists' Guidebooks and National Identities in Modern Germany and Europe', *Journal of Contemporary History* 33.3 (1998), 323–40.

——, *German Travel Cultures*, Oxford: Berg, 2000.

Kouwenhoven, John A., 'The Eiffel Tower and the Ferris Wheel', *Arts Magazine* 54.6 (1980), 170–3.

Kowitz, Vera, *La Tour Eiffel: Ein Bauwerk als Symbol und als Motiv in Literatur und Kunst*, Essen: Die Blaue Eule, 1989.

Kretschmer, Winfried, *Geschichte der Weltausstellungen*, Frankfurt am Main: Campus, 1999.

Kriegel, Lara, 'After the Exhibitionary Complex: Museum Histories and the Future of the Victorian Past', *Victorian Studies* 48.4 (2006), 681–704.

——, *Grand Designs: Labor, Empire, and the Museum in Victorian Culture*, Durham, NC: Duke University Press, 2007.

Kroker, Evelyn, 'Publikationen über Weltausstellungen aus dem 19. Jahrhundert als Quelle für die Wirtschafts- und Technikgeschichte', *Technikgeschichte in Einzeldarstellungen* 17 (1969), 131–47.

——, *Die Weltausstellungen im 19. Jahrhundert: Industrieller Leistungsnachweis, Konkurrenzverhalten und Kommunikationsfunktion unter Berücksichtigung der Montanindustrie des Ruhrgebietes zwischen 1851 und 1880*, Göttingen: Vandenhoeck & Ruprecht, 1975.

Kruger, Loren, '"White Cities", "Diamond Zulus", and the "African Contribution to Human Advancement": African Modernities and the World's Fairs', *TDR: The Drama Review* 51.3 (2007), 19–45.

Krutisch, Petra, '"…billig und schlecht!" Das deutsche Kunstgewerbe auf der Weltausstellung in Philadelphia in 1876', in *Renaissance der Renaissance: Ein bürgerlicher Kunststil im 19. Jahrhundert*, ed. G. Ulrich Grossmann, Munich: Deutscher Kunstverlag, 1995, 13–32.

Kuenheim, Haug von, *Carl Hagenbeck*, Hamburg: Ellert & Richter, 2007.

Kundrus, Birthe, ed., *Phantasiereiche: Zur Kulturgeschichte des deutschen Kolonialismus*, Frankfurt am Main: Campus, 2003.

Kuper, Hilda, 'The Language of Sites in the Politics of Space', *American Anthropologist* 74 (1972), 411–25.

Kusamitsu, Toshio, 'Great Exhibitions before 1851', *History Workshop Journal* 9 (1980), 70–89.

Labanca, Nicola, ed., *L'Africa in vetrina: Storie di musei e di esposizioni coloniali in Italia*, Treviso: Pagus, 1992.

Ladd, Brian K., 'Urban Aesthetics and the Discovery of the Urban Fabric in Turn-of-the-Century Germany', *Planning Perspectives* 2.3 (1987), 270–86.

——, *The Ghosts of Berlin: Confronting German History in the Urban Landscape*, Chicago: University of Chicago Press, 1997.

Larson, Erik, *The Devil in the White City: Murder, Magic, and Madness at the Fair that Changed America*, New York: Crown, 2003.

Lebovics, Herman, *True France: The Wars over Cultural Identity, 1900–1945*, Ithaca, NY: Cornell University Press, 1992.

Lees, Andrew, 'Berlin and Modern Urbanity in German Discourse, 1845–1945', *Journal of Urban History* 17 (1991), 153–78.

——, 'Cities, Society, and Culture in Modern Germany: Recent Writings by Americans on the *Großstadt*', *Journal of Urban History* 25.5 (1999), 734–44.

Lefebvre, Henri, *Introduction à la modernité: Préludes*, Paris: Editions de Minuit, 1962.

——, *La Production de l'espace*, Paris: Anthropos, 1974 [*The Production of Space*, Oxford: Basil Blackwell, 1991].

Lemoine, Bertrand, *Gustave Eiffel*, Paris: Fernand Hazan, 1984.

——, *La Tour de Monsieur Eiffel*, Paris: Gallimard, 1996.

Lenger, Friedrich, *Werner Sombart 1863–1941: Eine Biographie*, Munich: C. H. Beck, 1994.

Lenger, Friedrich and Klaus Tenfelde, eds, *Die europäische Stadt im 20. Jahrhundert: Wahrnehmung – Entwicklung – Erosion*, Cologne: Böhlau, 2006.

Leprun, Sylviane, *Le Théâtre des colonies: Scénographie, acteurs et discours de l'imaginaire dans les expositions, 1855–1937*, Paris: L'Harmattan, 1986.

Leventhal, F. M., '"A Tonic to the Nation": The Festival of Britain, 1951', *Albion* 27.3 (1995), 445–53.

Levin, Miriam R., 'The Eiffel Tower Revisited', *The French Review* 62.6 (1989), 1052–64.

Lewis, Arnold, *An Early Encounter with Tomorrow: Europeans, Chicago's Loop and the World's Columbian Exposition*, Urbana: University of Illinois Press, 1997.

Lewis, Russell, 'Everything Under One Roof: World's Fairs and Department Stores in Paris and Chicago', *Chicago History* 12.3 (1983), 28–47.

Ley, David and Kris Olds, 'Landscape as Spectacle: World's Fairs and the Culture of Heroic Consumption', *Environment and Planning D: Society and Space* 6.1 (1988), 191–212.

Lorrain, Jean, *Mes Expositions universelles (1889–1900)*, Paris: Champion, 2002.

Loyrette, Henri, 'Des palais isolés à la ville dans la ville: Paris 1855–1900', in *Le Livre des expositions universelles 1851–1889*, ed. Robert Bordaz, Paris: Union Centrale des Arts Décoratifs, 1983, 219–32.

——, *Gustave Eiffel*, Paris: Payot, 1986.

——, 'La Tour de 300 mètres', *Dix-huit cents-quatre-vingt-quinz* (1989), 220–43.

——, 'La Tour Eiffel', in *Les Lieux de mémoire*, ed. Pierre Nora, vol. 3.3: *Les France*, Paris: Gallimard, 1992, 474–503.

Luckhurst, Kenneth W., *The Story of Exhibitions*, London: Studio, 1951.

Lüdtke, Alf, 'Alltagsgeschichte: Aneignung und Akteure', *WerkstattGeschichte* 17 (1997), 83–91.

Lutchmansingh, Larry D., 'Commodity Exhibitionism at the London Great Exhibition of 1851', *Annals of Scholarship* 7.2 (1990), 203–16.

Lynch, Kevin, *The Image of the City*, Cambridge, MA: Harvard University Press, 1960.

Mabire, Jean-Christophe, ed., *L'Exposition universelle de 1900*, Paris: L'Harmattan, 2000.

MacAloon, John J., *This Great Symbol: Pierre de Coubertin and the Origins of the Modern Olympic Games*, Chicago: University of Chicago Press, 1981.

——, 'Olympic Games and the Theory of Spectacle in Modern Societies', in *Rite, Drama, Festival, Spectacle: Rehearsals Toward a Theory of Cultural Performance*, ed. John MacAloon, Philadelphia: Institute for the Study of Human Issues, 1984, 241–80.

Mace, Rodney, *Trafalgar Square: Emblem of Empire*, London: Lawrence & Wishart, 1976.

MacKenzie, John M., *Propaganda and Empire: The Manipulation of British Public Opinion, 1880–1960*, Manchester: Manchester University Press, 1984.

MacKenzie, John M., ed., *Imperialism and Popular Culture*, Manchester: Manchester University Press, 1986.

Mai, Ekkehard, 'Präsentation und Repräsentativität: Interne Probleme deutscher Kunstausstellungen im Ausland (1900–1930)', *Zeitschrift für Kulturaustausch* 31.1 (1981), 107–23.

——, 'GESOLEI und PRESSA: Zu Programm und Architektur rheinischen Ausstellungswesens in den zwanziger Jahren', in *Zur Geschichte von Wissenschaft, Kunst und Bildung an Rhein und Ruhr*, ed. Kurt Düwell and Wolfgang Köllmann, Wuppertal: Hammer, 1985, 271–87.

——, *Expositionen: Geschichte und Kritik des Ausstellungswesens*, Munich: Deutscher Kunstverlag, 1986.

Mainardi, Patricia, *Art and Politics of the Second Empire: The Universal Expositions of 1855 and 1867*, New Haven: Yale University Press, 1987.

Mandell, Richard D., *Paris 1900: The Great World's Fair*, Toronto: University of Toronto Press, 1967.

Marchand, Bernard, *Paris, histoire d'une ville (XIXe–XXe siècle)*, Paris: du Seuil, 1993.

Marrey, Bernard, *La Vie et l'œuvre extraordinaire de Monsieur Gustave Eiffel*, Paris: Graphite, 1984.

Marschik, Matthias, Rudolf Müllner, Georg Spitaler and Michael Zinganel, eds, *Das Stadion: Geschichte, Architektur, Politik, Ökonomie*, Vienna: Turia & Kant, 2005.

Martayan, Elsa, 'Les Rapports entre l'Etat et la Ville de Paris, au début de la Troisième République: les emplacements des Expositions universelles', *Revue de l'Economie Sociale* 13 (1988), 55–9.

——, 'L'Ephémère dans la ville: Paris et les Expositions universelles', *Revue de l'Economie Sociale* 19 (1990), 39–49.

Massey, Doreen, 'Places and Their Pasts', *History Workshop Journal* 39 (1995), 182–92.

Mathur, Saloni, 'Living Ethnological Exhibits: The Case of 1886', *Cultural Anthropology* 15 (2000), 492–524.

Matthews, George R., 'The Controversial Olympic Games of 1908 as Viewed by the *New York Times* and the *Times* of London', *Journal of Sport History* 7.2 (1980), 40–53.

Mattie, Erik, *World's Fairs*, New York: Princeton Architectural Press, 1998.

Maxwell, Anne, *Colonial Photography and Exhibitions: Representations of the 'Native' and the Making of European Identities*, London: Leicester University Press, 1999.

McArthur, Colin, 'The Dialectic of National Identity: The Glasgow Empire Exhibition of 1938', in *Popular Culture and Social Relations*, ed. Tony Bennett, Colin Mercer and Janet Woollacott, Milton Keynes: Open University Press, 1986, 117–34.

McKean, John, *Crystal Palace: Joseph Paxton and Charles Fox*, London: Phaidon, 1994.

Meller, Helen, *Patrick Geddes: Social Evolutionist and City Planner*, London: Routledge, 1990.

——, 'Philanthropy and Public Enterprise: International Exhibitions and the Modern Town Planning Movement, 1889–1913', *Planning Perspectives* 10.3 (1995), 295–310.

——, *European Cities, 1890–1930s: History, Culture, and the Built Environment*, Chichester: Wiley, 2001.

Mendoza, Eduardo, *La ciudad de los prodigios*, Barcelona: Seix Barral, 1986.

Metcalf, Thomas R., *An Imperial Vision: Indian Architecture and Britain's Raj*, Berkeley: University of California Press, 1989.

——, *Ideologies of the Raj*, Cambridge: Cambridge University Press, 1995.

——, 'Colonial Urbanism in the French and British Empires', *Journal of Urban History* 22.2 (1996), 264–9.

Meusy, Jean-Jacques, 'L'Enigme du Cinéorama de l'Exposition universelle de 1900', *Archives* 37 (1991), 1–16.

Meyer-Künzel, Monika, *Der planbare Nutzen: Stadtentwicklung durch Weltausstellungen und Olympische Spiele*, Hamburg: Dölling und Galitz, 2001.

Mieck, Ilja, *Preußische Gewerbepolitik in Berlin 1806–1844: Staatshilfe und Privatinitiative zwischen Merkantilismus und Liberalismus*, Berlin: de Gruyter, 1965.

——, 'Berlin als deutsches und europäisches Wirtschaftszentrum', in *Berlin im Europa der Neuzeit: Ein Tagungsbericht*, ed. Wolfgang Ribbe and Jürgen Schmädeke, Berlin: de Gruyter, 1990, 121–39.

——, 'Deutschland und die Pariser Weltausstellungen', in *Marianne – Germania: Deutsch-französischer Kulturtransfer im europäischen Kontext/Les Transferts culturels France-Allemagne et leur contexte européen, 1789–1914*, ed. Etienne François, Marie-Claire Hoock-Demarle et al., Leipzig: Leipziger Universitätsverlag, 1998, 31–60.

Miller, Christopher L., 'Hallucinations of France and Africa in the Colonial Exhibition of 1931 and Ousmane Socé's *Mirages de Paris*', *Paragraph* 18.1 (1995), 39–63.

Miller, Donald L., 'The White City: The 1893 World's Columbian Exposition in Chicago', *American Heritage* 44.4 (1993), 70–87.

Misiti, Massimo, 'L'Italia in mostra: Le Esposizioni e la costruzione dello Stato nazionale', *Passato e presente* 37 (1996), 33–54.

Mitchell, Timothy, *Colonising Egypt*, Cambridge: Cambridge University Press, 1988.

——, 'The World as Exhibition', *Comparative Studies in Society and History* 31.2 (1989), 217–36.

Mitchell, W. J. T., 'The Pictorial Turn' [1992], in *Picture Theory: Essays on Verbal and Visual Representation*, Chicago: University of Chicago Press, 1994, 11–34.

Moore, Katharine, 'The 1911 Festival of Empire: A Final Fling?', in *Sport, Culture, Society: International Historical and Sociological Perspectives*, ed. James A. Mangan and Roy B. Small, London: Spon, 1986, 84–90.

Moret, Frédéric, 'Images de Paris dans les guides touristiques en 1900', *Mouvement Social* 160 (1992), 79–98.

Morson, Gary Saul and Caryl Emerson, *Mikhail Bakhtin: Creation of a Prosaics*, Stanford: Stanford University Press, 1990.

Morton, Patricia A., 'National and Colonial: The Musée des Colonies at the Colonial Exposition, Paris, 1931', *The Art Bulletin* 80.2 (1998), 357–77.

——, *Hybrid Modernities: Architecture and Representation at the 1931 Colonial Exposition, Paris*, Cambridge, MA: MIT Press, 2000.

Müller, Hans-Heinrich, 'Eine Parade der Produktion: Die Berliner Gewerbeausstellung von 1896', *Berlinische Monatsschrift* 5.4 (1996), 31–5.

'The Exhibition Building of 1862', in *Survey of London*, ed. Greater London Council, vol. 38: *The Museums Area of South Kensington and Westminster*, London: Athlone, 1975, 137–47.

Nelms, Brenda, *The Third Republic and the Centennial of 1789*, London: Garland, 1987.

Niethammer, Lutz, *Kollektive Identität: Heimliche Quellen einer unheimlichen Konjunktur*, Reinbek: Rowohlt, 2000.

Niquette, Manon and William J. Buxton, 'Meet Me at the Fair: Sociability and Reflexivity in Nineteenth-Century World Expositions', *Canadian Journal of Communication* 22.1 (1997), 81–113.

Nitschke, August, Gerhard A. Ritter, Detlev J. K. Peukert and Rüdiger vom Bruch, eds, *Jahrhundertwende: Der Aufbruch in die Moderne 1880–1930*, 2 vols, Reinbek: Rowohlt, 1990.

Nolte, Paul, '1900: Das Ende des 19. und der Beginn des 20. Jahrhunderts in sozialgeschichtlicher Perspektive', *Geschichte in Wissenschaft und Unterricht* 47.5/6 (1996), 281–300.

——, 'Georg Simmels Historische Anthropologie der Moderne: Rekonstruktion eines Forschungsprogramms', *Geschichte und Gesellschaft* 24.2 (1998), 225–47.

Nora, Pierre, ed., *Les Lieux de mémoire*, 3 vols, Paris: Gallimard, 1984–92.

Nord, Deborah Epstein, 'London and the World', *Journal of British Studies* 41.1 (2002), 131–8.

Norindr, Panivong, 'Representing Indochina: The French Colonial Fantasmatic and the Exposition coloniale de Paris', *French Cultural Studies* 6.1 (1995), 35–60.

——, *Phantasmatic Indochina: French Colonial Ideology in Architecture, Film, and Literature*, Durham, NC: Duke University Press, 1996.

Norton, Paul F., 'World's Fairs in the 1930s', *Journal of the Society of Architectural Historians* 24.1 (1965), 27–30.

Notaro, Anna, 'Exhibiting the New Mussolinian City: Memories of Empire in the World Exhibition of Rome (EUR)', *GeoJournal* 51.1 (2000), 15–22.

Oettermann, Stephan, *Das Panorama: Die Geschichte eines Massenmediums*, Frankfurt am Main: Syndikat, 1980.

Ogata, Amy F., 'Viewing Souvenirs: Peepshows and the International Expositions', *Journal of Design History* 15.2 (2002), 69–82.

Oppenheimer Dean, Andrea, 'Revisiting the White City: The Lasting Influences of the 1893 Chicago World's Columbian Exposition', *Historic Preservation* 45.2 (1993), 42–9, 97–8.

Orsenna, Erik, *L'Exposition coloniale*, Paris: du Seuil, 1988.

Ory, Pascal, *Les Expositions universelles de Paris: Panorama raisonné, avec des aperçus nouveaux et des illustrations par les meilleurs auteurs*, Paris: Ramsay, 1982.

——, 'Le Centenaire de la Révolution française: La preuve par 89', in *Les Lieux de mémoire*, ed. Pierre Nora, vol. 1: *La République*, Paris: Gallimard, 1984, 523–60.

Osterhammel, Jürgen, *Kolonialismus: Geschichte – Formen – Folgen*, Munich: C. H. Beck, 1995.

——, 'Die Wiederkehr des Raumes: Geopolitik, Geohistorie und historische Geographie', *Neue Politische Literatur* 43.3 (1998), 374–97.

——, 'Europamodelle und imperiale Kontexte', *Journal of Modern European History* 2.2 (2004), 157–82.

——, 'Symbolpolitik und imperiale Integration: Das britische Empire im 19. und 20. Jahrhundert', in *Die Wirklichkeit der Symbole: Grundlagen der Kommunikation in historischen und gegenwärtigen Gesellschaften*, ed. Rudolf Schlögl, Bernhard Giesen and Jürgen Osterhammel, Konstanz: UVK, 2004, 395–421.

——, *Die Verwandlung der Welt: Eine Geschichte des 19. Jahrhunderts*, Munich: C. H. Beck, 2009.

Osterhammel, Jürgen and Niels P. Petersson, *Geschichte der Globalisierung: Dimensionen, Prozesse, Epochen*, Munich: C. H. Beck, 2003.

Oudoire, Jean-Marie, 'Le Palais des machines, un palais de la République', *Revue du Nord* 71 (1989), 1031–5.

O'Neill, Morna, 'Rhetorics of Display: Arts and Crafts and Art Nouveau at the Turin Exhibition of 1902', *Journal of Design History* 20.3 (2007), 205–25.

Paulmann, Johannes, *Pomp und Politik: Monarchenbegegnungen in Europa zwischen Ancien Régime und Erstem Weltkrieg*, Paderborn: Schöningh, 2000.

Pelc, Ortwin, 'Hagenbeck auf den Weltausstellungen in Chicago (1893) und St. Louis (1904)', *Zeitschrift des Vereins für hamburgische Geschichte* 86 (2000), 89–113.

Pellegrino, Anna, '"Il gran dimenticato": Lavoro, tecnologia e progresso nelle relazioni degli "operai" fiorentini all'Esposizione di Milano del 1906', in *Esposizioni in Europa tra Otto e Novecento: Spazi, organizzazione, rappresentazioni*, ed. Alexander C. T. Geppert and Massimo Baioni, Milan: FrancoAngeli, 2004 [*Memoria e Ricerca* 17], 165–90.

Pemsel, Jutta, *Die Wiener Weltausstellung von 1873: Das gründerzeitliche Wien am Wendepunkt*, Vienna: Böhlau, 1989.

Perkins, Mike and William E. Tonkin, *Postcards of the British Empire Exhibition Wembley 1924 and 1925*, Chippenham: Rowe, 1994.

Persell, Stuart M., 'The Colonial Career of Jules Charles-Roux', *First Annual Meeting of the Western Society for French History: Proceedings* 1 (1974), 306–22.

Peters, James, 'After the Fair: What Expos Have Done for Their Cities', *Planning* (July/August 1982), 13–19.

Piat, Charles, *Les Expositions internationales relevant du Bureau International des Expositions (B.I.E.)*, Paris: Centre Français du Commerce Extérieur, 1983.

Piggott, J. R., *Palace of the People: The Crystal Palace at Sydenham, 1854–1936*, London: Hurst, 2004.

Pinkney, David, *Napoleon III and the Rebuilding of Paris*, Princeton: Princeton University Press: 1958.

Pinon, Pierre, *Paris: Biographie d'une capitale*, Paris: Hazan, 1999.

Pinot de Villechenon, Florence, *Les Expositions universelles*, Paris: Presses Universitaires de France, 1992.

Plato, Alice von, 'Die "Majestät der Geschichte" vor einem Millionenpublikum: Geschichtsdarstellungen auf den Pariser Weltausstellungen des 19. Jahrhunderts', *WerkstattGeschichte* 8.23 (1999), 39–60.

——, *Präsentierte Geschichte: Ausstellungskultur und Massenpublikum im Frankreich des 19. Jahrhunderts*, Frankfurt am Main: Campus, 2001.

Pohl, Heinz-Alfred, 'Die Weltausstellungen im 19. Jahrhundert und die Nichtbeteiligung Deutschlands in den Jahren 1878 und 1889: Zum Problem der Ideologisierung der außenpolitischen Beziehungen in der 2. Hälfte des 19. Jahrhunderts', *Mitteilungen des Instituts für Österreichische Geschichtsforschung* 97.3/4 (1989), 381–425.

Poirier, René, *Des Foires, des peuples, des expositions*, Paris: Plon, 1958.

Pollard, Sydney, '"Made in Germany": Die Angst vor der deutschen Konkurrenz im spätviktorianischen England', *Technikgeschichte* 53.3 (1987), 183–95.

Porter, Roy, *London: A Social History*, Cambridge, MA: Harvard University Press, 1994.

Potts, Alex, 'Picturing the Modern Metropolis: Images of London in the Nineteenth Century', *History Workshop Journal* 26 (1988), 28–56.

Prochasson, Christophe, *Paris 1900: Essai d'histoire culturelle*, Paris: Calmann-Lévy, 1999.

Przyblyski, Jeannene M., 'Visions of Race and Nation at the Paris Exposition, 1900: A French Context for the American Negro Exhibit', in *National Stereotypes in Perspective: Americans in France, Frenchmen in America*, ed. William L. Chew, Amsterdam: Rodopi, 2001, 209–44.

Purbrick, Louise, ed., *The Great Exhibition of 1851: New Interdisciplinary Essays*, Manchester: Manchester University Press, 2001.

Rabinbach, Anson, *The Human Motor: Energy, Fatigue, and the Origins of Modernity*, Berkeley: University of California Press, 1992.

Rabinow, Paul, *French Modern: Norms and Forms of the Social Environment*, Cambridge, MA: MIT Press, 1989.

Radkau, Joachim, *Technik in Deutschland: Vom 18. Jahrhundert bis zur Gegenwart*, Frankfurt am Main: Suhrkamp, 1989.

Rancière, Jacques and Patrick Vauday, 'Going to the Expo: The Worker, his Wife and Machines', in *Voices of the People: The Social Life of 'La Sociale' at the End of the Second Empire*, ed. Adrian Rifkin and Roger Thomas, London: Routledge, 1988, 23–44.

Rappaport, Erika, 'Art, Commerce, or Empire? The Rebuilding of Regent Street, 1880–1927', *History Workshop Journal* 53 (2002), 94–117.

Rasmussen, Anne, 'Les Congrés internationaux liés aux Expositions universelles de Paris (1867–1900)', *Mil neuf cent* 7 (1989), 23–44.

Rearick, Charles, 'Festivals in Modern France: The Experience of the Third Republic', *Journal of Contemporary History* 12 (1977), 435–60.

——, *Pleasures of the Belle Epoque: Entertainment and Festivity in Turn-of-the-Century France*, New Haven: Yale University Press, 1985.

——, *The French in Love and War: Popular Culture in the Era of the Two World Wars*, New Haven: Yale University Press, 1997.

Rearick, Charles and Rosemary Wakeman, eds, *New Perspectives on Modern Paris*, Durham, NC: Duke University Press, 2004 [*French Historical Studies* 27.1].

Rebérioux, Madeleine, 'Approches de l'histoire des Expositions universelles à Paris du Second Empire à 1900', *Bulletin du Centre d'histoire économique et sociale de la région lyonnaise* 1 (1979), 1–20.

——, 'Au tournant des expos: 1889', *Le Mouvement Social* 149 (1989), 3–13.

Rebérioux, Madeleine, ed., *Mise en scène et vulgarisation: L'Exposition universelle de 1889*, Paris: Editions Ouvrières, 1989 [*Mouvement Social* 149, 3–128].

Reichenbach, Herman, 'Carl Hagenbeck's Tierpark and Modern Zoological Gardens', *Journal of the Society for the Bibliography of Natural History* 9.4 (1980), 573–85.

Reif, Heinz, 'Hauptstadtentwicklung und Elitenbildung: "Tout Berlin" 1871 bis 1918', in *Geschichte und Emanzipation: Festschrift für Reinhard Rürup*, ed. Michael Grüttner, Rüdiger Hachtmann and Heinz-Gerhard Haupt, Frankfurt am Main: Campus, 1999, 679–99.

——, *Metropolen: Geschichte, Begriffe, Methoden*, Berlin: CMS Working Paper, 2006.

Rembold, Elfie, 'Exhibitions and National Identity', *National Identities* 1.3 (1999), 221–5.

Renisch, Franz, *Wilhelm Franz Exner, 1840–1931*, Vienna: Technologisches Gewerbe-Museum, 1999.

Reulecke, Jürgen, 'Kommunikation durch Tourismus? Zur Geschichte des organisierten Reisens im 19. und 20. Jahrhundert', in *Die Bedeutung der Kommunikation für Wirtschaft und Gesellschaft*, ed. Hans Pohl, Stuttgart: Steiner, 1989, 358–78.

Reuter, Elke, 'Die Große Berliner Gewerbeausstellung 1896 im Treptower Park: Berliner Weltausstellungspläne und ihre Realität', *Berlinische Monatsschrift Luisenstadt* 1.5 (1992), 4–10.

Rich, Norman, M. H. Fisher and Werner Frauendienst, eds, *Die Geheimen Papiere Friedrich von Holsteins*, vol. 3: *Briefwechsel (30. Januar 1861 bis 28. Dezember 1896)*, Göttingen: Musterschmidt, 1961.

Richards, Thomas, *The Commodity Culture of Victorian England: Advertising and Spectacle, 1851–1941*, Stanford: Stanford University Press, 1990.

Rieke-Müller, Annelore and Lothar Dittrich, *Der Löwe brüllt nebenan: Die Gründung Zoologischer Gärten im deutschsprachigen Raum, 1833–1869*, Cologne: Böhlau, 1998.

Robinson, Alan, *Imagining London, 1770–1900*, Basingstoke: Palgrave Macmillan, 2004.

Roche, Maurice, *Mega-Events and Modernity: Olympics and Expos in the Growth of Global Culture*, London: Routledge, 2000.

Röhl, John C. G., *Wilhelm II: Der Aufbau der persönlichen Monarchie 1888–1900*, Munich: C. H. Beck, 2001.

Romano, Roberto, 'Le esposizioni industriali italiane: Linee di metodologia interpretativa', *Società e storia* 3.7 (1980), 215–28.

Rorty, Richard, *The Linguistic Turn: Recent Essays in Philosophical Method*, Chicago: University of Chicago Press, 1967.

Ross, Cathy, *Twenties London: A City in the Jazz Age*, London: Wilson, 2003.

Rothfels, Nigel, *Savages and Beasts: The Birth of the Modern Zoo*, Baltimore: Johns Hopkins University Press, 2002.

Rowe, Dorothy, 'Georg Simmel and the Berlin Trade Exhibition of 1896', *Urban History* 22.2 (1995), 216–28.

Rubalcaba-Bermejo, L. and J. R. Cuadrado-Roura, 'Urban Hierarchies and Territorial Competition in Europe: Exploring the Role of Fairs and Exhibitions', *Urban Studies* 32 (1995), 379–400.

Rubey, Norbert and Peter Schoenwald, eds, *Venedig in Wien: Theater- und Vergnügungsstadt der Jahrhundertwende*, Vienna: Ueberreuter, 1996.

Rürup, Reinhard, '"Parvenu Polis" and "Human Workshop": Reflections on the History of the City of Berlin', *German History* 6.3 (1988), 233–49.

Ryan, Deborah S., *The Ideal Home Through the 20th Century*, London: Hazar, 1997.

Ryckelynck, Xavier, 'Les Hommes de l'Exposition universelle de 1889: Le cas Alfred Picard', *Mouvement Social* 149 (1989), 25–42.

Rydell, Robert W., *All the World's a Fair: Visions of Empire at American International Expositions, 1876–1916*, Chicago: University of Chicago Press, 1984.

——, 'The Literature of International Expositions', in *The Books of the Fairs: Materials about World's Fairs, 1834–1916, in the Smithsonian Institution Libraries*, ed. Smithsonian Institution Libraries, Chicago: American Library Association, 1992, 1–62.

——, 'Museums and Cultural History: A Review Article', *Comparative Studies in Society and History* 34.2 (1992), 242–7.

——, *World of Fairs: The Century-of-Progress Expositions*, Chicago: University of Chicago Press, 1993.

——, 'The Complexity of Exhibitionary Complexes', *Cultural Studies* 11.2 (1997), 345–7.

——, 'New Directions for Scholarship about World Expos', in *Seize the Day: Exhibitions, Australia and the World*, ed. Kate Darian-Smith, Richard Gillespie, Caroline Jordan and Elizabeth Willis, Melbourne: Monash University ePress, 2008, 21.1–13.

Rydell, Robert W. and Nancy E. Gwinn, eds, *Fair Representations: World's Fairs and the Modern World*, Amsterdam: VU University Press, 1994.

Rydell, Robert W., John E. Findling and Kimberly D. Pelle, *Fair America: World's Fairs in the United States*, Washington, DC: Smithsonian Institution Press, 2000.

Said, Edward W., *Orientalism*, New York: Vintage Books, 1978.

——, *Culture and Imperialism*, London: Chatto & Windus, 1993.

Sarafian, Nicolas, *Le Bois de Vincennes*, Marseilles: Parenthèses, 1993.

Scherpenberg, Norman van, *Weltausstellungen: Völkerrechtlich geregelte Visionen*, Baden-Baden: Nomos, 2000.

Schivelbusch, Wolfgang, *Geschichte der Eisenbahnreise: Zur Industrialisierung von Raum und Zeit im 19. Jahrhundert*, Frankfurt am Main: Fischer, 1989.

Schlögel, Karl, *Im Raume lesen wir die Zeit: Über Zivilisationsgeschichte und Geopolitik*, Munich: Hanser, 2003.

Schmidt, Willi, 'Die frühen Weltausstellungen und ihre Bedeutung für die Entwicklung der Technik', *Technikgeschichte* 34.2 (1967), 164–78.

Schmoll, Friedemann, 'Der Aussichtsturm: Zur Ritualisierung touristischen Sehens im 19. Jahrhundert', in *Reisebilder: Produktion und Reproduktion touristischer Wahrnehmung*, ed. Christoph Köck, Münster: Waxmann, 2001, 183–97.

Schneer, Jonathan, *London 1900: The Imperial Metropolis*, New Haven: Yale University Press, 1999.

Schneider, William H., 'Colonies at the 1900 World Fair', *History Today* 31 (1981), 31–6.

——, *An Empire for the Masses: The French Popular Image of Africa, 1870–1900*, Westport: Greenwood, 1982.

Schön, Wolf, 'Der Triumph des Industriezeitalters: Paris 1889 und die Weltausstellungen des 19. Jahrhunderts', in *Das Fest: Eine Kulturgeschichte von der Antike bis zur Gegenwart*, ed. Uwe Schultz, Munich: C. H. Beck, 1988, 328–40.

Schor, Naomi, '*Cartes Postales:* Representing Paris 1900', *Critical Inquiry* 18 (1992), 188–244.

Schorske, Carl E., *Fin-de-Siècle Vienna: Politics and Culture*, New York: Knopf, 1980.

Schroeder-Gudehus, Brigitte and Anne Rasmussen, *Les Fastes du progrès: Le guide des expositions universelles, 1851–1992*, Paris: Flammarion, 1992.

Schubert, Dirk and Anthony Sutcliffe, 'The "Haussmannization" of London? The Planning and Construction of Kingsway-Aldwych, 1889–1935', *Planning Perspectives* 11.2 (1996), 115–44.

Schultz, Heiner, 'Angst – Gefühl – Versicherung: Ein Versuch über Folgen der Industrialisierung für das Bewußtsein im 19. Jahrhundert', *Kursbuch* 61 (1980), 95–117.

Schultze, Johannes, 'Warum es in Berlin nicht zu einer Weltausstellung kam', *Mitteilungen des Vereins für die Geschichte Berlins* 67 (1971), 117–18.

Schulz, Marlies, 'Der Treptower Park', in *Topographischer Atlas Berlin*, ed. Senatsverwaltung für Bau und Wohnungswesen, Berlin: Reimer, 1995, 198–9.

Schütte, Wolfgang, *Die Idee der Weltausstellung und ihre bauliche Gestaltung: Eine gebäudekundliche Studie als Material zu einer Baugeschichte des 19. Jahrhunderts*, PhD diss., Technische Hochschule Hannover, Hanover, 1945.

Schwankl, Herbert R., *Das württembergische Ausstellungswesen: Zur Entwicklung der allgemeinen Gewerbe- und Industrieausstellungen im 19. Jahrhundert*, St Katharinen: Scripta Mercaturae, 1988.

Schwartz, Vanessa R., *Spectacular Realities: Early Mass Culture in Fin-de-Siècle Paris*, Berkeley: University of California Press, 1998.

Schwarz, Angela, 'Transfers transatlantici tra le esposizioni universali, 1851–1940', in *Esposizioni in Europa tra Otto e Novecento: Spazi, organizzazione, rappresentazioni*, ed. Alexander C. T. Geppert and Massimo Baioni, Milan: FrancoAngeli, 2004 [*Memoria e Ricerca* 17], 65–93.

Schwarz, Werner Michael, *Anthropologische Spektakel: Zur Schaustellung 'exotischer' Menschen, Wien 1870–1910*, Vienna: Turia & Kant, 2001.

Sheehan, James J., *Geschichte der deutschen Kunstmuseen: Von der fürstlichen Kunstkammer zur modernen Sammlung*, Munich: C. H. Beck, 2002.

Sheppard, Francis, 'London and the Nation in the Nineteenth Century', *Transactions of the Royal Historical Society* 35.5 (1985), 51–74.

Sherman, Daniel J., 'The Arts and Sciences of Colonialism', *French Historical Studies* 23.4 (2000), 707–29.

Sherman, Daniel J. and Irit Rogoff, eds, *MuseumCulture: Histories, Discourses, Spectacles*, London: Routledge, 1994.

Sigel, Paul, *Exponiert: Deutsche Pavillons auf Weltausstellungen*, Berlin: Bauwesen, 2000.

Signat, Colette, *Bibliographie analytique des documents publiés à l'occasion de l'Exposition universelle internationale de 1900 à Paris*, Paris: Conservatoire National des Arts et Métiers, 1959.

Silverman, Debora L., *Art Nouveau in Fin-de-Siècle France: Politics, Psychology, and Style*, Berkeley: University of California Press, 1989.

Simonsen, Kirsten, 'What Kind of Space in What Kind of Social Theory?', *Progress in Human Geography* 20.4 (1996), 494–512.

Singer, Barnett, 'Lyautey: An Interpretation of the Man and French Imperialism', *Journal of Contemporary History* 16.1 (1991), 131–57.

Sloterdijk, Peter, 'Weltmuseum und Weltausstellung: Absolut museal', *Jahresring* 37 (1990), 183–202.

Smalls, James, '"Race" as Spectacle in Late-Nineteenth-Century French Art and Popular Culture', *French Historical Studies* 26.2 (2003), 351–82.

Soja, Edward W., *Postmodern Geographies: The Reassertion of Space in Critical Social Theory*, London: Verso, 1989.

——, *Thirdspace: Journeys to Los Angeles and Other Real-and-Imagined Places*, Cambridge, MA: Blackwell, 1996.

Speich, Daniel, 'Wissenschaftlicher und touristischer Blick: Zur Geschichte der "Aussicht" im 19. Jahrhundert', *Traverse* 6.3 (1999), 83–98.

Spranger, Eduard, *Berliner Geist: Aufsätze, Reden und Aufzeichnungen*, Tübingen: Wunderlich, 1966.

Stamper, John W., 'The Galerie des Machines of the 1889 Paris World's Fair', *Technology and Culture* 30.2 (1989), 330–53.

——, 'The Industry Palace of the 1873 World's Fair: Karl von Hasenauer, John Scott Russell, and New Technology in Nineteenth-Century Vienna', *Architectural History* 47 (2004), 227–50.

Stamper, John W. and Robert Mark, 'Structure of the Galerie des Machines, Paris, 1889', *History and Technology* 10.3 (1993), 127–38.

Stanard, Matthew G., 'Selling the Empire between the Wars: Colonial Expositions in Belgium 1920–1940', *French Colonial History* 6 (2005), 159–78.

Steinle, Holger, 'Das Moabiter Ausstellungsgelände', *Die Bauwelt* 77.6 (1986), 202–5.

Stewart, Lynn, 'Bodies, Visions, and Spatial Politics: A Review Essay on Henri Lefebvre's *The Production of Space*', *Environment and Planning D: Society and Space* 13.5 (1995), 609–18.

Stierle, Karlheinz, *Der Mythos von Paris: Zeichen und Bewußtsein der Stadt*, Munich: Hanser, 1993.

Stovall, Tyler, *The Rise of the Paris Red Belt*, Berkeley: University of California Press, 1990.

——, *Paris Noir: African Americans in the City of Light*, Boston, MA: Houghton Mifflin, 1996.

Stremmel, Ralf, *Modell und Moloch: Berlin in der Wahrnehmung deutscher Politiker vom Ende des 19. Jahrhunderts bis zum Zweiten Weltkrieg*, Bonn: Bouvier, 1992.

——, 'Städtische Selbstdarstellung seit der Jahrhundertwende', *Archiv für Kommunalwissenschaften* 33.2 (1994), 234–64.

Strohmayer, Ulf, 'Pictorial Symbolism in the Age of Innocence: Material Geographies at the Paris World's Fair of 1937', *Ecumene* 3.3 (1996), 282–304.

Sutcliffe, Anthony, *Towards the Planned City: Germany, Britain, the United States and France 1780–1914*, Oxford: Basil Blackwell, 1981.

——, *Paris: An Architectural History*, New Haven: Yale University Press, 1993.

Sweet, Jonathan, 'International Exhibition Postcards: Tangible Reflections of an Ephemeral Past', in *Seize the Day: Exhibitions, Australia and the World*, ed. Kate Darian-Smith, Richard Gillespie, Caroline Jordan and Elizabeth Willis, Melbourne: Monash University ePress, 2008, 8.1–14.

Tartakowsky, Danielle, 'La Construction sociale de l'espace politique: Les usages politiques de la place de la Concorde des années 1880 à nos jours', *French Historical Studies* 27.1 (2004), 145–73.

Thiel, Paul, 'Berlin präsentiert sich der Welt: Die Berliner Gewerbeausstellung 1896 in Treptow', in *Die Metropole: Industriekultur in Berlin im 20. Jahrhundert*, ed. Jochen Boberg, Tilman Fichter and Eckhart Gillen, Munich: C. H. Beck, 1986, 16–27.

Thienel, Ingrid, 'Verstädterung, städtische Infrastruktur und Stadtplanung: Berlin zwischen 1850 und 1914', *Zeitschrift für Stadtgeschichte, Stadtsoziologie und Denkmalpflege* 4.1 (1977), 55–84.

Thies, Ralf, *Ethnograph des dunklen Berlin: Hans Ostwald und die "Großstadt-Dokumente" (1904–1908)*, Cologne: Böhlau, 2006.

Thode-Arora, Hilke, *Für fünfzig Pfennig um die Welt: Die Hagenbeckschen Völkerschauen*, Frankfurt am Main: Campus, 1989.

Thompson, William, '"The Symbol of Paris": Writing the Eiffel Tower', *The French Review* 73.6 (2000), 1130–40.

Thomson, Rosemarie Garland, ed., *Freakery: Cultural Spectacles of the Extraordinary Body*, New York: New York University Press, 1997.

Tilly, Pierre, 'Du 19ème au 20ème siècle: La participation italienne aux expositions internationales en Belgique', *Rassegna Storica del Risorgimento* 89 (2002), 155–70.

Tissot, Laurent, 'How did the British Conquer Switzerland? Guidebooks, Railways, Travel Agencies, 1850–1914', *Journal of Transport History* 16 (1995), 21–54.

Tolini Finamore, Michelle, 'Fashioning the Colonial at the Paris Expositions, 1925 and 1931', *Fashion Theory* 7.3/4 (2003), 345–60.

Toulet, Emmanuelle, 'Le Cinéma à l'Exposition universelle de 1900', *Revue d'Histoire Moderne et Contemporaine* 33 (1986), 179–209.

Towner, John, 'The Grand Tour: A Key Phase in the History of Tourism', *Annals of Tourism Research* 12.3 (1985), 297–333.

Treue, Wilhelm, 'Gewerbeförderung und technische Entwicklung zur Zeit der Frühindustrialisierung in Preußen', *Technikgeschichte* 36 (1969), 68–74.

Trevelyan, George Macaulay, *British History in the Nineteenth Century (1782–1901)*, New York: Longmans, Green, 1922.

Tuan, Yi-Fu, *Space and Place: The Perspective of Experience*, London: Edward Arnold, 1977.

Veit-Brause, Irmline, 'German-Australian Relations at the Time of the Centennial International Exhibition, Melbourne, 1888', *Australian Journal of Politics and History* 32.2 (1986), 201–16.

Verspohl, Franz-Joachim, *Stadionbauten von der Antike bis zur Gegenwart: Regie und Selbsterfahrung der Massen*, Gießen: Anabas, 1976.

Viatte, Germain and Dominique François, eds, *Le Palais des colonies: Histoire du Musée des Arts d'Afrique et d'Océanie*, Paris: Réunion des Musées Nationaux, 2002.

Vigato, Jean-Claude, 'Die Architektur der französischen Kolonialausstellungen/The Architecture of the Colonial Exhibitions in France', *Daidalos* (15 March 1986), 24–37.

Volwahsen, Andreas, *Imperial Delhi: The British Capital of the Indian Empire*, Munich: Prestel, 2002.

Wagner, Monika, 'Vom Ewigen und Flüchtigen zum ewig Flüchtigen: Die erste Londoner Weltausstellung als Wahrnehmungsproblem', in *Nachmärz: Der Ursprung der ästhetischen Moderne in einer nachrevolutionären Konstellation*, ed. Thomas Koebner and Sigrid Weigel, Opladen: Westdeutscher Verlag, 1996, 209–29.

——, *Das Material der Kunst: Eine andere Geschichte der Moderne,* Munich: C. H. Beck, 2001.

Wainwright, Clive and Charlotte Gere, 'The Making of the South Kensington Museum. I: The Government Schools of Design and Founding Collection, 1837–51. II: Collecting Modern Manufactures: 1851 and the Great Exhibition. III: Relationships with the Trade: Webb and Bardini', *Journal of the History of Collections* 14.1 (2002), 3–23, 25–43, 45–61, 63–78.

Wakeman, Rosemary, 'Paris and London in the Nineteenth Century', *Journal of Urban History* 27.2 (2001), 200–5.

Walkowitz, Judith R., *City of Dreadful Delight: Narratives of Sexual Danger in Late Victorian London*, Chicago: Chicago University Press, 1992.

——, 'The "Vision of Salome": Cosmopolitanism and Erotic Dancing in Central London, 1908–1918', *American Historical Review* 108.2 (2003), 337–76.

Walter, Rolf, 'Märkte, Börsen, Messen, Ausstellungen und Konferenzen im 19. und 20. Jahrhundert', in *Die Bedeutung der Kommunikation für Wirtschaft und Gesellschaft*, ed. Hans Pohl, Stuttgart: Steiner, 1989, 379–440.

Walthew, Kenneth, 'The British Empire Exhibition of 1924', *History Today* 31 (1981), 34–9.

Watt, Tom and Kevin Palmer, *Wembley: The Greatest Stage. The Official History of 75 Years at Wembley Stadium*, London: Simon & Schuster, 1998.

Weaver, Lawrence Trevelyan, *Lawrence Weaver, 1876–1930: An Annotated Bibliography*, York: Inch's Books, 1989.

Webb, David, 'For Inns a Hint, for Routes a Chart: The Nineteenth-Century London Guidebook', *The London Journal* 6.2 (1980), 207–14.

Weber, E., 'Pierre de Coubertin and the Introduction of Organized Sport in France', *Journal of Contemporary History* 5.2 (1970), 3–26.

Weidenhaupt, Hugo, 'Die Gewerbe- und Kunst-Ausstellung zu Düsseldorf 1880', *Düsseldorfer Jahrbuch* 57/58 (1980), 412–30.

Weigel, Sigrid, 'Zum "topographical turn": Kartographie, Topographie und Raumkonzepte in den Kulturwissenschaften', *KulturPoetik: Zeitschrift für kulturgeschichtliche Literaturwissenschaft* 2.2 (2002), 151–65.

Weinert, Hermann, 'Die Weltausstellungen als Zeugen der Weltgesellschaft unserer Zeit', *Universitas* 26 (1971), 1081–8.

Weisbrod, Bernd, 'Der englische "Sonderweg" in der neueren Geschichte', *Geschichte und Gesellschaft* 16.2 (1990), 233–52.

——, 'Medien als symbolische Form der Massengesellschaft: Die medialen Bedingungen von Öffentlichkeit im 20. Jahrhundert', *Historische Anthropologie* 9.2 (2001), 270–83.

Welter, Volker M., 'Stages of an Exhibition: The *Cities and Town Planning Exhibition* of Patrick Geddes', *Planning History* 20.1 (1998), 25–35.

——, *Biopolis: Patrick Geddes and the City of Life*, Cambridge, MA: MIT Press, 2002.

Wembley History Society, *The British Empire Exhibition Wembley 1924: Fiftieth Anniversary*, Wembley: n.p., 1974.

Wesemael, Pieter van, *Architecture of Instruction and Delight: A Socio-Historical Analysis of World Exhibitions as a Didactic Phenomenon (1798–1851–1970)*, Rotterdam: Uitgeverij 010, 2001.

White, Jerry, *London in the Twentieth Century: A City and Its People*, London: Penguin, 2001.

Wilder, Gary, 'Framing Greater France Between the Wars', *Journal of Historical Sociology* 14.2 (2001), 198–25.

Wildman, Stephen, 'Great, Greater? Greatest?? Anglo-French Rivalry at the Great Exhibitions of 1851, 1855 and 1862', *Journal of the Royal Society of Arts* 137 (1989), 660–4.

Williams, Rosalind H., *Dream Worlds: Mass Consumption in Late Nineteenth Century France*, Berkeley: University of California Press, 1982.

Willms, Johannes, *Paris: Hauptstadt Europas 1789–1914*, 2nd edn, Munich: C. H. Beck, 1999.

Wilson, Brian and John R. Day, 'A London Rival to the Eiffel Tower', *Country Life* (19 May 1955), 1298.

Wilson, Michael, 'Consuming History: The Nation, the Past, and the Commodity at *l'Exposition Universelle de 1900*', *American Journal of Semiotics* 8.4 (1991), 131–53.

Winckler, Lutz, 'Die weiße Stadt: Die Weltausstellung von 1937 und der Mythos der "ville lumière"', in *Nachmärz: Der Ursprung der ästhetischen Moderne in einer nachrevolutionären Konstellation*, ed. Thomas Koebner and Sigrid Weigel, Opladen: Westdeutscher Verlag, 1996, 230–44.

Wirth, Louis, 'Urbanism as a Way of Life', *American Journal of Sociology* 44.1 (1938), 1–24.

Wohl, R. Richard and Anselm L. Strauss, 'Symbolic Representation and the Urban Milieu', *American Journal of Sociology* 63.5 (1958), 523–32.

Woodham, Jonathan, 'Images of Africa and Design at the British Empire Exhibitions between the Wars', *Journal of Design History* 2.1 (1989), 15–33.

Wörner, Martin, *Vergnügung und Belehrung: Volkskultur auf den Weltausstellungen 1851–1900*, Münster: Waxmann, 1998.

Wright, Gwendolyn, 'Tradition in the Service of Modernity: Architecture and Urbanism in French Colonial Policy, 1900–1930', *Journal of Modern History* 59 (1987), 291–316.

——, *The Politics of Design in French Colonial Urbanism*, Chicago: University of Chicago Press, 1991.

Wright, Paul, 'The Festival of Britain: Some Memories', *Journal of the Royal Society of Arts* 143 (1995), 52–5.

Yack, Bernard, *The Fetishism of Modernities: Epochal Self-Consciousness in Contemporary Social and Political Thought*, Notre Dame: University of Notre Dame Press, 1997.

Yengoyan, Aram A., 'Universalism and Utopianism', *Comparative Studies in Society and History* 39.4 (1997), 785–98.

——, 'Simmel, Modernity, and Germanisms', *Comparative Studies in Society and History* 44.3 (2002), 620–5.

Young, Paul, *Globalization and the Great Exhibition: The Victorian New World Order*, Basingstoke: Palgrave Macmillan, 2009.

Zanten, David van, *Building Paris: Architectural Institutions and the Transformation of the French Capital, 1830–1870*, Cambridge: Cambridge University Press, 1994.

Zeldin, Theodore, *Histoire des passions françaises (1848–1945)*, vol. 3: *Goût et corruption*, Paris: Payot et Rivages, 1995.

Zelljadt, Katja, 'Presenting and Consuming the Past: Old Berlin at the Industrial Exhibition of 1896', *Journal of Urban History* 31.3 (2005), 306–33.

Zerbini, Laurick, 'L'Outre-mer à Lyon: Mémoire et musées coloniaux', *Cahiers d'Histoire* 40.3–4 (1995), 271–85.

Zimmermann, Clemens, *Die Zeit der Metropolen: Urbanisierung und Großstadtentwicklung*, Frankfurt am Main: Fischer, 1996.

Zimmermann, Clemens, ed., *Zentralität und Raumgefüge der Grossstädte im 20. Jahrhundert*, Stuttgart: Steiner, 2006.

Zimmermann, Clemens and Jürgen Reulecke, eds, *Die Stadt als Moloch? Das Land als Kraftquell? Wahrnehmungen und Wirkungen der Großstädte um 1900*, Basel: Birkhäuser, 1999.

Zippelius, Adelhart, 'Der Mensch als lebendes Exponat', in *Volkskultur in der Moderne: Probleme und Perspektiven empirischer Kulturforschung*, ed. Utz Jeggle, Gottfried Korff, Martin Scharfe and Bernd Jürgen Warneken, Reinbek: Rowohlt, 1986, 410–29.

Zubaida, Sami, 'Exhibitions of Power', *Economy and Society* 19.3 (1990), 359–75.

Index

Page numbers appearing in **bold** refer to illustrations; page numbers in *italics* refer to biographical sketches in the Appendix. 'n.' after a page reference indicates a note number on that page. Expositions are listed individually by their respective names.

Printed and bound by CPI Group (UK) Ltd, Croydon, CR0 4YY